RALPH WALDO EMERSON

RALPH WALDO EMERSON

SELECTED JOURNALS
1820–1842

Lawrence Rosenwald, editor

THE LIBRARY OF AMERICA

Distributed to the trade in the United States
by Penguin Group (USA) Inc.
and in Canada by Penguin Books Canada Ltd.

Library of Congress Control Number: 2009935638
ISBN 978–1–59853–067–4

First Printing
The Library of America—201

Manufactured in the United States of America

Ralph Waldo Emerson: Selected Journals
is published with support from

THE GOULD FAMILY FOUNDATION

and is kept in print by a gift from

THE BERKLEY FOUNDATION

to the Guardians of American Letters Fund,
established by The Library of America
to ensure that every volume in the series
will be permanently available.

—

The Library of America wishes to thank the editors of
The Journals and Miscellaneous Notebooks of Ralph Waldo
Emerson (Harvard University Press, 1960–1982): Linda Allardt,
Ruth H. Bennett, Ronald A. Bosco, George P. Clark, Merrell R.
Davis, Alfred R. Ferguson, William H. Gilman, Harrison
Hayford, David W. Hill, Glen M. Johnson, Ralph H.
Orth, J. E. Parsons, A. W. Plumstead, Merton M.
Sealts, Jr., and Susan Sutton Smith. The present
edition is greatly indebted to their scholarship.

Contents

from *Wide World 1* (1820) 1

from *Wide World 2* (1820–1821) 17

from *Wide World 3* (1822) 27

from *Wide World 4* (1822) 32

from *Wide World 6* (1822) 38

from *Wide World 7* (1822) 50

from *Wide World 8* (1822) 54

from *Wide World 9* (1822–1823) 64

from *Wide World 10* (1823) 70

from *Wide World 11* (1823) 75

from *Walk to the Connecticut* (1823) 83

from *Wide World 12* (1823–1824) 91

from *Wide World XIII* (1824) 100

from *No. XV* (1824–1826) 117

from *Journal 1826* 131

from *Journal 1826–1828* (1824–1828) 139

from *Memo St. Augustine* (1827) 150

from *Sermons and Journal* (1828–1829) 154

from *Blotting Book Υ* (1829–1830) 162

from *Blotting Book Psi* (1830–1831, 1832) 169

from *Blotting Book III* (1831–1832) 175

from *Q* (1832–1833) 191

from *Sicily* (1833) 217

from *Italy* (1833) 239

from *Italy and France* (1833) 259

from *Scotland and England* (1833) 281

from *Sea* 289

from *A* (1833–1834) 293

from *Maine* (1834) 387

from *France and England* (1833) 389
from *B* (1835–1836) 392
from *C* (1837–1838) 501
from *D* (1838–1839) 604
from *E* (1839–1842) 702
from *F2* (1840–1841) 793

Editor's Afterword 813
Chronology 816
Note on the Texts 825
Note on the Illustrations 828
Notes 831
Biographical Notes 869
Index 888

from
Wide World 1
1820

Jan. 25, 1820. Mixing with the thousand pursuits & passions & objects of the world as personified by Imagination is profitable & entertaining. These pages are intended at this their commencement to contain a record of new thoughts (when they occur); for a receptacle of all the old ideas that partial but peculiar peepings at antiquity can furnish or furbish; for tablet to save the wear & tear of weak Memory & in short for all the various purposes & utility real or imaginary which are usually comprehended under that comprehensive title *Common Place book*. O ye witches assist me! enliven or horrify some midnight lucubration or dream (whichever may be found most convenient) to supply this reservoir when other resources fail. Pardon me Fairy Land! rich region of fancy & gnomery, elvery, sylphery, & Queen Mab! pardon me for presenting my first petition to your enemies but there is probably one in the chamber who maliciously influenced me to what is irrevocable; pardon & favour me!—& finally Spirits of Earth, Air, Fire, Water, wherever ye glow, whatsoever you patronize, whoever you inspire, hallow, hallow, this devoted paper.— Dedicated & Signed Jan 25, 1820, Junio.—

Jan. 26. After such a dedication what so proper to begin with as reflections on or from Edward Search? It is a fine idea which he either intends to convey or else the form of expression unintentionally did (pray let us believe the latter for the credit of Originality) that those parts of the world which man cannot or does not inhabit are the abodes of other orders of sentient being invisible or unpercieved by him. To amplify— Perhaps the centre of the earth, the bottomless depths & the upper paths of Ocean, the lands circumjacent to the poles, the high rock & clefts of the rock are peopled by higher beings than ourselves;—animals cast in more refined mould; not subject to the inconveniencies, woes &c of our species to whom as to us this world appears made only for them & among whom our very honest & honourable species are classed only as the highest order of brutes—perhaps called of the *bee* kind.—When Imagination has formed this class of beings & given them the name of Supromines it will be perfectly convenient to rise again to an order higher than these last, holding our self complacent friends the Supromines in as utter contempt as they, us, or as we the beasts, & then she may rise to another & another till for aught I know she may make this world one of the Mansions of heaven & in parts of it though in & around yet thoroughly unknown to us the seraphim & cherubim may live & enjoy. I have now already fallen into an errour which may be a very common one, to hunt an idea down when obtained, in such a remorseless manner as to render dull & flat an idea originally plump, round, & shining.—But before I proceed further, I do hereby nominate & appoint "Imagination" the generallissimo & chief marshal of all the luckless raggamuffin Ideas which may be collected & imprisoned hereafter in these pages (signed) Junio.—Jan 26th

It enlarges the mind & certainly gratifies it to hold large contemplations regarding the material Universe. Perhaps our system and all the planets & stars we can discover, nay, the whole interminable Universe is moving on as has been supposed in one grand circle round the centre of light & since the world began it has never completed a single revolution. It is an improvement on the grandeur of this supposition to suppose there is a source of light before us & the whole vast machinery has been forever & is now sweeping forward in a direct line through the interminable fields—extensions of space.—It is a singular fact that we cannot present to the imagination a longer space than just so much of the world as is bounded by the visible horizon; so that even in this stretching of thought to comprehend the broad path lengthening itself & widening to recieve the rolling Universe stern necessity bounds us to a little extent of a few miles only. But what matters it? We can talk & write & think it out. We can imagine the shadow of the incomprehensibly large, glorious mass blackening the infinity behind it; we can send Conjecture forth to ride on the wings that are bearing the worlds forward & sit & explore & discover what is to occur when the wheels shall stop & the wings fall in the immediate presence of the source of light to which for ages past & ages to come they have been & will be advancing. Conjecture weary & overwhelmed only exclaims Time shall be no more.—Everett's "Man standing on the confines of that other world where Goodness & Happiness those stranger sisters shall meet together & know each other, & seeing creation on creation sweeping by to their doom, then he shall learn to pity little Man piling up his monuments of marble & calling it fame"—is very very fine. Chateaubriand's "the universe is the imagination of the deity made manifest" is worthy him.—Personification of moral attributes or things is a fine employment. Grandeur would make a fine personage in poem. Represent him sitting in pomp of silence on the high places of the world holding a creative wand & the unborn glories & minds & powers of monarchs & men strewed round him in embryo. Let him bestow on the bold Genius of ancient Rome all splendour & majesty; but Destiny is abroad & his magnificent chariot must roll on. It set forth in its career before the systems of existence were compacted, it has long been upon the earth & its heavy wheels are now hastening from the north. Hark the lumbering of its wheels is already sounding in the ears of Rome! it came,—it passed over her— Grandeur flung away his withered wand & his crown fell, the wide world was yielding before the coming of Destiny but Nature & the powers of the universe interposed, averted the course of his steeds & smoothed away his frown. New nations arose from beneath the ruins of Rome like Milton's angels from the superincumbent mountains & Grandeur resumed his crown & wand.—

"Mount on thy own path to Fame nor swerve for man or more than man" says Caswallon (in Samor) & it will be a fine motto by striking out the last four words. It were a sublime spirit that implicitly followed the rule. I may admire, I fear I cannot obey, & there is an apology which every man makes for himself when his independence is put to the test that by nature we are social beings & it is utterly against the order of things for a single man to presume to encounter all the prejudices & violence & power & war of the world, invidious & alone. With this plausible answer he stands his ground, worms himself into good opinion & patronage of men & secures himself present peace by the sacrifice of his high honour. But there are on earth great men who disdainful alike of the multitude's scorn & the multitude's applause elevate themselves by their own exertion to heights of human exaltation where the storm of varying opinion cannot hurt them & the levin-bolts of furious envy & disappointed passion will not reach or harm them. Every man of talents & application has it in his power to be one of these.—

—

Feb. 6th. The immediate presence of God is a fine topic of sublimity. In charging a minister for instance "above all remember the omniscience of God—His allseeing eye is upon you now, it will always be upon you—& in his immediate presence we now charge you fear him, obey him." His throne is founded far above the stars.—Descend ye Nine—

Feb. 7. Mr K. a lawyer of Boston gave a fine character of a distinguished, individual in private conversation which in part I shall set down. "Webster is (Feb 7th) a rather large man, about 5 feet, 7, or 9, in height & 39 or 40 years old—he has a long head, very large black eyes, bushy eyebrows, a commanding expression,—& his hair is coal black & coarse as a crow's nest. His voice is sepulchral.—There is not the least variety or the least harmony of tone—it commands, it fills, it echoes, but is harsh & discordant.—He possesses an admirable readiness, a fine memory and a faculty of perfect abstraction, an unparallelled impudence & a tremendous power of concentration—he brings all that he has ever heard, read, or seen to bear on the case in question. He growls along the bar to see who will run & if nobody runs he *will* fight. He knows his strength, has a perfect confidence in his own powers & is distinguished by a Spirit of fixed determination; he marks his path out & will cut off fifty heads rather than turn out of it; but is generous & free from malice & will never move a step to make a severe remark. His genius is such that if he descends to be pathetic he becomes ridiculous. He has no wit & never laughs though he is very shrewd & sarcastic & sometimes sets the whole court in a roar by the singularity or pointedness of a remark. His imagination is what the light of a furnace is to its heat, a necessary attendant—nothing sparkling or agreeable but dreadful & gloomy." This is the finest character I have ever heard pourtrayd & very truly drawn with little or no exaggeration. With respect to the cause of a town's condition of bad society he said well "there is stuff to make good society but they are discordant atoms" & regarding the contrasting & comparing the worthy and great dead—"you may not tell a man 'your neighbour's house is higher than yours' but you may measure gravestones & see which is the tallest."—

Cambridge March 11th 1820

Thus long I have been in Cambridge this term (three or four weeks) & have not before this moment paid my devoirs to the Gnomes to whom I dedicated this quaint & heterogeneous manuscript. Is it because matter has been wanting—no—I have written much elsewhere in prose, poetry, & miscellany—let me put the most favourable construction on the case & say that I have been better employed. Beside considerable attention however unsuccessful to college studies I have finished Bisset's Life of Burke as well as Burke's regicide Peace together with considerable variety of desultory reading generally speaking highly entertaining & instructive. The Pythologian Poem does not proceed very rapidly though I have experienced some poetic moments. Could I seat myself in the alcove of one of those public libraries which human pride & literary rivalship have made costly, splendid, & magnificent it would indeed be an enviable situation. I would plunge into the classic lore of chivalrous story & of the fairy-land bards & unclosing the ponderous volumes of the firmest believers in magic & in the potency of consecrated crosier or elfin ring I would let my soul sail away delighted in to their wildest phantasies. Pendragon is rising before my fancy & has given me permission to wander in his walks of Fairy-land & to present myself at the bower of Gloriana. I stand in the fair assembly of the chosen; the brave & the beautiful; honour & virtue, courage & delicacy are mingling in magnificent joy. Unstained knighthood is sheathing the successful blade in the presence of unstained chastity. And the festal jubilee of Fairy land is announced by the tinkling of its silver bells. The halls are full of gorgeous splendour & the groves are joyous with light & beauty. The birds partake & magnify the happiness of the green-wood shades. & the music of the harp comes swelling on the gay breezes. Or other views more real, scarcely less beautiful should attract, enchain me. All the stores of Grecian & Roman literature may, be unlocked & fully displayed—or with the Indian enchanters send my soul up to wander among the stars till "the twilight of the gods."

April 2d. Spring has returned & has begun to unfold her beautiful array, to throw herself on wild flower couches, to walk abroad on the hills & summon her songsters to do her sweet homage. The Muses have issued from the library & costly winter dwelling of their votaries & are gone up to build their bowers on Parnassus, & to melt their ice-bound fountains. Castalia is flowing rapturously & lifting her foam on high. The hunter & the shepherd are abroad on the rock & the vallies echoe to the merry merry horn. The Poet of course is wandering while Nature's thousand melodies are warbling to him. This soft bewitching luxury of vernal gales & accompanying beauty overwhelms.—It produces a lassitude which is full of mental enjoyment & which we would not exchange for more vigorous pleasure. Although so long as the spell endures little or nothing is accomplished, nevertheless, I believe it operates to divest the mind of old & worn-out contemplations & bestows new freshness upon life & leaves behind it imaginations of enchantment for the mind to mould into splendid forms & gorgeous fancies which shall long continue to fascinate, after the physical phenomena which woke them have ceased to create delight. Perhaps we have dwelt too long on the beautiful & fanciful of thought & forgot or perhaps avoided too sedulously what is darksome & grand. But we hope in time to devote pages to this department of the moral world. At all events we will now prosecute the chase for the lovely & beautifying. The Naiads are bathing in their streams, the Dryads & Fauns are threading the wild-wood—the eagle is mounting aloft—"mewing his mighty youth & kindling his undazzled eyes at the full mid-day beam"—the cattle are lowing on a thousand hills & the far voice of joy resounds in the solitary place. Who can wonder that at such an hour we forsake the abodes of solemn sorrow or reject the discordant voice that summons us to mourn & plunge deeply into pure & boundless happiness? The unimproved hour may refuse to return.

April 4th 1820. Judging from opportunity enjoyed I ought to have this evening a flow of thought rich, abundant, & deep; after having heard Mr Everett deliver his Introductory Lecture, in length 1 & ½ hour, having read much & profitably in the Quarterly Review and lastly having heard Dr Warren's introductory lecture to Anatomy,—all in the compass of a day— & the mind possessing a temperament well adapted to recieve with calm attention what was offered. Shall endeavour to record promiscuously received ideas. Though the literature of Greece give us sufficient information with regard to later periods of their commonwealth, as we go back before the light of tradition comes in the veil drops. "All tends to the mysterious east." From the time of the first dispersion of the human family to the time of Grecian rise every thing in the history of man is obscure & we think ourselves sufficiently fortunate "if we can write in broad lines the fate of a dynasty" tho we know nothing of the individuals who composed it. The cause is the inefficiency & uncertainty of tradition in those early & ignorant times when the whole history of a tribe was lodged in the head of its patriarch & in his death their history was lost. But even after the invention of letters much, very much, has never reached us. This we need not regret. What was worth knowing was transmitted to posterity, the rest buried in deserved forgetfulness. Every thing was handed down which ought to be handed down. The Phenicians gave the Greeks their *Alphabet* yet not a line of all which they wrote has come down while their pupils have built themselves an imperishable monument of fame. The Greeks have left us a literature the most complete in all its parts which the world has ever shown. The long controversy which has made so much stir in the world with regard to the comparative merit of ancient & modern literature is senseless. We do not judge of the literature of Greece considering its age but considering its merit. The moderns' best efforts have only imitated them, & the mod. composed theirs with them for models but they theirs without. Some

history of the controversy will be useful. It commenced long
ago for Quinctilian speaks of it & holds up the Grecian models
to admiration—Horace also recommends them, & Cicero, but
mention the dispute then commenced regarding superiour
merit of ancient or mod. It was inherited through a succession of lines by France in 15 & 1600, the subject then
warmly agitated. Boileau, Fontenelle, Racine on the side of the
ancients.

—

Fontenelle having in youth espoused the cause applied four
times for a place in French Academy & "4 times Demosthenes,
Plato, Theocritus pleaded against him." Undoubtedly many
sensible people thought correctly of the dispute & engaged on
neither side but it is immaterial to know. From France the
quarrel passed over to England & Sir William Temple wrote
for the moderns & was answered by Wattle whose work is superiour, for he seconds his arguments with the illustrious
"names of Bacon, Bentley, Boyle, Locke, Milton, Shakspeare,
& weak must be the cause or powerful the advocate which is
not assisted by these auxiliaries." Swift joined the controversy
by writing The battle of the books, a work which has not even
the uncertain merit of originality as a French work had previously been published in France, Le combat des livres. Swift's
wit is wholly that which Locke has defined wit, unexpected association of ideas. Addison's posthumous works contained
some reflections on this question. Since then it has slumbered.

(The above is a very concise abstract of Prof. E's lecture as
far as the Eulogy—not more—)

Greece is the land of contrast. A principle of contrast runs
through all that we know of it. Drama, Manners, Climate,
Houses, Women—every thing—*Destiny* presided in their
Tragedy very sublimely.—They passed the temples of the
Furies without daring to behold them.

Apr. 10. I here make a resolution to make myself acquainted
with the Greek language & antiquities & history with long &
serious attention & study, (always with the assistance of circumstances.) To which end I hereby dedicate & devote to the
down-putting of sentences quoted or original which regard

Greece—historical, poetical, & c.ial, page 47 of this time honoured register. By the way, I devote page 44 to the notation of
Inquirenda & of books to be sought signed Apr. 10th Junio.
There is a fascination which the elegance & genius of the ancients has thrown over their productions here stenography
begins & wh rndrs mdrn lbrs cntmptbll .n cmprsn. I mst rd
Hrdts & Arstphns & ll Grk trgdns snr or ltr. Wld tht sm rlcks
of Egptn ltrtr rmnd I wld prse thm wth .rdr & strnge .ntrst! Bt
nthng .s lft .s bt . fw prd smbls .f dprtd grndr. It ws rmrkd in th
Qrtrl Rvw tht .s you g. wst sprsttn grws mr fntckl & inhmn;
i.e. Hndstn .s mr crl .n hr crmns & pnhts thn Egpt, & Egpt
thn Erp. But .t .ll .vnts ths stngrphy .s msrble.—

Apr 30th. Have malignant demons possessed themselves of
my mind & my pen & my tongue & my book? It is rarely that
I sit myself down to this common place book which was intended to restore the sinking soul, to keep alive the fire of enthusiasm in literature, & literary things, to be the register of
desultory but valuable contemplations. Etherial beings to whom
I dedicated the pages of my "Wide World" do not I entreat
you neglect it; when I sleep waken me; when I weary animate!
Wander after moon-beams, fairies! but bring them home here.
Indeed you cannot imagine how it would gratify me to wake
up from an accursed Enfield lesson & find a page written in
characters of light by a moon-beam of Queen Mab! I will give
you a subject—a thousand if you wish;—for instance 'Pendragon,' your own Pendragon; record his life & his glories.—
'Prince Arthur' if it is not too trite; or 'the Universe' or a
'broom stick'; either or all of these or 50 thousand more. "In
the Capuchin Church at Vienna sixty six emperours are
sleeping;—none of your mock emperours; none of your mushroom kings but &c" *Mr Everett*—

Sabbath Evening. Would not Pestilence be a good personage in poetry for description? Wrapt in the long white robes of
sickness, entering the town in her awful chariot & her slow approach heard afar off by the anxious fearful listeners—it
comes—it rolls over the distant pavement—it draws near—the
haggard terrifick form is presented to their view & in vain they
fly; she stretches forth her hand & withereth & polluteth &

destroyeth—in vain they strive & struggle to avoid her grasp:
her arm stretches out, her form enlarges to a supernatural size,
like the magnified limb in a distorted mirrour, as they retreat;
& she goes on unchecked, unrelenting, diffusing mad desolation & dismay.—Every where the roaring voices of Joy are still,
& the mourners go about the streets. But Health dwelleth in
his tabernacle on the mountain & is waking the woods at
dawn with the shout & noise of industry & the joyous peal
of the hunter's merry merry horn—he is climbing the cliff &
swimming the flood & labouring in the field.—The mountains
& the grove are his dominions & Pestilence may not come
near them.

May 27 Thou changest his countenance & sendest him
away!—

May 28th I am now sitting before the *Pedagogue's* Map of
Europe & startled almost to behold the immense region which
Alexander governs. The ample domains of the emperour of
Russia are nearly equal to the rest of Europe. One man is insignificant in the extremest degree set down in this mighty
land; yet all the millions of population planted in this stretching territory & seemingly bound by no ties but the eternal
bands of their common earth bow to the despotism of an individual like themselves. One would think his mind would dilate,
"expand with strong conception" to meet the grandeur of circumstances with which God has surrounded him & accomodate himself to his vast commission. The bell rings.

—

June 7th—A very singular chance led me to derive very sensible answers to the two questions I proposed to Virgil. For
the first I opened to the line

O crudelis Alexi, nihil mea carmina curas.

for the other I opened to a line, Dryden's translation of which is

Go let the gods & temples claim thy care.

—Have been of late reading patches of Barrow & Ben Jonson; & what the object—not curiosity? no—nor expectation of
edification intellectual or moral—but merely because they are
authors where vigorous phrases & quaint, peculiar words &
expressions may be sought & found, the better "to rattle out

the battles of my thoughts." I shall now set myself to give a
good sentence of Barrow's (the whole beauty of which he has
impaired by a blundering collocation) in purer & more fashionable English. Obvious manifestations may be sometimes
seen of the ruling government of God: Sometimes in the career of triumphant guilt when things have come to such a pass
that iniquity & outrage do exceedingly prevail so that the life
of the offender becomes intolerably grievous a change comes
upon the state of things however stable & enduring in appearance, a revolution in a manner sudden & strange & flowing from
causes mean & unworthy which overturneth the towering fabric of fortune & reduces its gigantic dimensions, and no strug-
glings of might, no fetches of policy, no circumspection or
industry of man availing to uphold it; there is outstretched an
invisible hand checking all such force & crossing all such
devices—a stone cut out of the mountain without hands &
breaking in peices the iron & the brass & the clay & silver &
the gold.—In looking over the sentence however though the
grand outline of the whole was originally Rev Isaac Barrow's
yet we very self complacently confess that great alterations have
rendered it editorially Mr Ralph Emerson's & I intend to make
use of it hereafter after another new modelling for it is still very
susceptible of improvement. People prate of the dignity of
human nature. Look over the whole history of its degradation
& find what odious vice, what sottish & debasing enormity the
degenerate naughtiness of man has never crouched unto &
adored? to things animate & things inanimate, to the ghosts of
dead men whose lives were bloody & cruel, lewd & foul.—to
beasts & grovelling reptiles, dogs, serpents & crocodiles—they
have bowed down & adored—nay with a brutal folly more revolting than this they have prostituted their obedience & worship, they have sacrificed their dearest pledges of life &
fortune, fawning in abominable adulation they have abandoned their interests & welfare to the cursed fiends of hell. Ingenuity has been exercised to drag forth new unimagined
objects such as these on whose altars mankind might offer
their devotion, pay their respect, & repose their confidence.
But it is a joyful change to see human nature unshackling herself & asserting her divine origin;—employed in encountering
prejudices & detecting frauds; checking & chastising profane

abuse; subjecting to legitimate controul those fiery passions which corrode & fret the soul; & woe to those whose malignity would fright her from her pursuit. Let these men vilify their own nature, & disparage themselves as they please, we will acknowledge & avow that "Mentem e coelesti demissam traximus arce," that the soul hath appetites & capacities by which when well guided she soars & climbs continually towards perfection & is backed by omnipotence in her magnificent career. The whole complication of good affections & actions pushing forward this object should spur on conscientious endeavour despite the torment of unprosperous envy & baffled malice, in whose destruction providence seems to exceed or contravene the ordinary course of nature; their estates without visible means do moulder & decay, a secret moth devouring them.—

June 19th. When those magnificent masses of vapour which load our horizon are breaking away disclosing fields of blue atmospher there is an exhilaration awakened in the system of a susceptible man which so invigorates the energies of mind & displays to himself such manifold power & joy superiour to other existences that he will triumph & exult that he is a man. I love the picturesque glitter of a summer morning's landscape; it kindles this burning admiration of nature & enthusiasm of mind.

We feel at these times that eternal analogy which subsists between the external changes of nature & scenes of good & ill that chequer human life. Joy cometh but is speedily supplanted by grief & we look at the approach of transient adversities like the mists of the morning fearful & many but the fairies are in them & *White Ladies* beckoning.——For better recollection of the meridian of papal power—mark this. In A.D. 1077 Henry IV emperour of Germany waited barefooted & bareheaded for three days at the outer gate of the fortress of Canosa in the depth of winter—expecting the pardon & forgiveness of Gregory VII.—

————

July 25. If power could make man happy the ancient great Roman citizens ought to have been the happiest of subjects. It was a strange state of Society. Pompy or Ceaesar or Milo though private citizens from their own revenues builded edifices & exhibited shows which would ruin a king of modern Europe. This immense flowing in of national treasuries to the coffers of private citizens throws a splendour & magnificence around eminent Romans which we feel for no other human beings. But we are told that their lives were an unceasing struggle with embarassments, enmities, & terrors; that they were harassed by petulant Tribunes or awed by rival nobles— oh it was worth their factions & their fears to live in that agony of high excitement, those tremendous strivings for power, enjoying the more than mortal grandeur of Roman glory! Since those mighty times there has been no man of whom it might be said that he stood forth like a Consul of Rome as proud as all earth's crowded honours could render a man!—

Aug 8th. Have been reading the Novum Organum. Lord Bacon is indeed a wonderful writer; he condenses an unrivalled degree of matter in one paragraph. He never suffers himself "to swerve from the direct forthright" or to babble or speak unguardedly on his proper topic, & withal writes with more melody & rich cadence than any writer (I had almost said, of England.) on a similar subject. Although I have quoted in my "Universe" of composition, (by which presumptuous term I beg leave to remind myself that nothing was meant but to express—wideness & variety of range) yet I will add here a fine little sentence from the 30th section of the 2d Vol of the Novum Organum. Speaking of bodies composed of two different species of things he says; "but these instances may be reckoned of the singular heteroclite kind as being rare & extraordinary in the universe; yet for their dignity they ought to be separately placed & treated. For they excellently indicate the composition & structure of things; & suggest the causes of the number of the ordinary species in the universe; & lead the understanding from that which is, to that which may be."

There is nothing in this sentence which should cause it to be quoted more than another. It does not stand out from the rest; but it struck me accidentally as a very different sentence from those similarly constructed in ordinary writers. For instance in the last three clauses (beginning "For they excellently") it is common to see an author construct a fine sentence in this

way with idle repetitions of the same idea, embellished a little
for the sake of shrouding the deception. In this, they all convey ideas determinate but widely different & all beautiful &
intelligent.—But says Sterne, "the Cant of Criticism is the
most provoking."

—There is a strange face in the Freshman class whom I
should like to know very much. He has a great deal of character in his features & should be a fast friend or a bitter enemy.
His name is Gay. I shall endeavour to become acquainted with
him & wish if possible that I might be able to recall at a future
period the singular sensations which his presence produced at
this.—
                                                        —

A strange idea or two may find place here to relieve this
metaphysical prolixity. Imprimis. In Lapland the intense cold
freezes the words of men as they come out in breath & they
are heard not until the sun thaws them! Item. When Astrology
was much in vogue, a mighty man of gramarye repaired to
Gregory VII to give the science a patron saint. The pontiff—
well pleased directed him to make his choice from the Pantheon. Accordingly the conjurer was hood-winked & marched
into the building and took hold first of the statue of the *Devil*
as combating with the Archangel Michael! Item. Lord Bacon
notices a singular fact that the opposite shores of S. America &
Africa correspond—bay to cape—gulf to coast &c "which
could not be without a cause." Vide Map.
                                    —

Aug 21st. In the H. C. Athenaeum I enjoyed a very pleasant
hour reading the life of Marlborough in the Quarterly Review.
I was a little troubled there by vexatious trains of thought; but
once found myself stopping entirely from my reading & occupied in throwing guesses into futurity while I was asking myself if, when ten or a dozen years hence, I am gone far on the
bitter perplexing roads of life, when I shall then recollect these
moments now thought so miserable shall I not fervently wish
the possibility of their return & to find myself again thrown
awkwardly on the tilted chair in the Atheneum study with my
book in my hand; the snuffers & lamps & shelves around; &
Motte coughing over his newspaper near me & ready myself to

saunter out into gaiety & Commons when that variously-meaning *bell* shall lift up his *tongue*.

"Sed fugit interea, fugit irreparabile tempus."

Aug 23d 1820. Tomorrow finishes the Junior year. As it is time to close our accounts we will conclude likewise this book which has been formed from the meditations & fancies which have sprinkled the miscellany-corner of my mind for two terms past. (It was begun in the winter vacation.) I think it has been an improving employment decidedly. It has not encroached upon other occupations & has afforded seasonable aid at various times to enlarge or enliven scanty themes &c. Nor has it monopolized the energies of composition for literary exercises. Whilst I have written in it I have begun & completed my Pythologian Poem of 260 lines—& my Dissertation on the character of Socrates. It has prevented the ennui of many an idle moment & has perhaps enriched my stock of language for future exertions. Much of it has been written with a view to their preservation as hints for a peculiar pursuit at the distance of years. Little or none of it was elaborate—its office was to be a hasty sketchy composition containing at times elements of graver order.

So fare ye well gay Powers & Princedoms! To you the sheets were inscribed. Light thanks for your tutelary smiles. Grim witches from Valhalla, & courteous dames from Faery-lond, whose protection was implored, & whose dreams were invoked to furnish forth the scroll—adieu to you all;—you have the laughing poet's benison & malison, his wish & his forgetfulness. Abandoning your allegiance he throws you to the winds, recklessly defying your malice & fun. Pinch the red nose; lead him astray after will-o'-the-wisp over wilderness & fen; fright him with ghastly hobgoblins—wreak your vengeance as you will— He gives you free leave on this sole condition,—if you can.——

Junio. August 24. 1820.

October 1820.

I have determined to grant a new charter to my pen, having finished my common-place book which I commenced in January & with as much success as I was ambitious of—whose whole aim was the small utility of being the exchequer to the accumulating store of organized verbs, nouns, & substantives, to wit, sentences. It has been a source of entertainment & accomplished its end & on this account has induced me to repeat or rather continue the experiment. Wherefore On!—

Oct. 3, 1820. To forget for a season the world & its concerns, & to separate the soul for sublime contemplation till it has lost the sense of circumstances & is decking itself in plumage drawn out from the gay wardrobe of Fancy is a recreation & a rapture of which few men can avail themselves. But this privilege in common with other great gifts of nature is attainable if not inborn. It is denied altogether to three classes at least of mankind, viz. the *queer*, the downright, & the ungainly. This is by no means a careless or fanciful classification although rather a restricted sense belongs to these epithets. By "the queer" I understand those animals of oddity whose disgusting eccentricity flows from a conceited character & the lack of common-sense. I characterize "the downright" only as people who do *jobs*. And "the ungainly" points exclusively at some gaunt lantern countenances who have at one time and another shocked my nerves & nauseated my taste by their hideous aspects. With cautious explanation we advance from these degraded stages of intellect, this doleful frontispeice of creation to prouder orders of mind. Ordinary men claim the intermittent exercise of this power of beautiful abstraction; but to the souls only of the mightiest is it given to command the disappearance of land & sea, & mankind & things, & they

16

vanish.—Then comes the Enchanter illuminating the glorious visions with hues from heaven, granting thoughts of other worlds gilded with lustre of ravishment & delight, till the Hours teeming with loveliness & Joy roll by uncounted. Exulting in the exercise of this prerogative the poet, truly called so, has entreated the reluctant permission

"And forever shalt thou dwell
In the spirit of this spell."

Oct. 3, 1820

Instruction by *Dictation* is a mode of teaching older than the art of printing. Owing to the scarcity of books, the professor possessed himself of a classic, perhaps the only copy in the community & dictated a sentence from it to the students. This they immediately copied off—each for himself—& the Professor proceeded to make his remarks on the sentence which also it was the duty of the scholars to note down. Slavish as was this custom it survived the Invention of printing & is practised to this day in the Dutch Universities. It is done with exact minuteness; when the professor comes to a stop he exclaims "Comma," when to a period "punctum," & when he begins a paragraph—"nova linea." The lectures are universally Latin. (The above was related to the class by Prof. Everett.) A good illustration of Dr. Blair's observation that in imperfect languages the most important word in the sentence comes first—is the Indian beggary in Alibama as related by JUA. "Sugar—little bit—give me some."

Oct 6th 1820

I thought I percieved the fit coming—the humour of inspiration & straightway seized the pen. I fear it was a false alarm. I have listened this evening to an eloquent lecture of the elegant Professor of French & Spanish Literature.

On the subject of the extent of the language, a subject which bears on the face of it dulness & dread—every soul present warmly acknowledged the force of delineation when the great deluge of the French language sweeping down all the feeble barriers of ephemeral dialects carried captive the languages & literature of all Europe while in the commotions of politics the German thrones were dashed to peices against each other on this great & wide sea.

> When bounding Fancy leaves the clods of earth
> To riot in the regions of her birth
> Where robed in light the Genii of the Stars
> Launch in refulgent space their diamond cars
> Or in pavilions of celestial pride
> Serene above all influence beside
> Vent the bold joy which swells the glorious soul
> Rich with the rapture of secure controul
> Onward, around their golden visions stray
> Till only Glory can their range delay.

Well I began with prose & have mustered up 10 lines of poetry which will answer rarely to lighten the labour of the next theme. It is half past 10—& time to put away the Wide World & its concerns & consign my indolent limbs to comfortable repose. Ergo cease, my pen,

> "To witch the world with noble *pen*-manship."

Oct. 15th 1820

Different mortals improve resources of happiness which are entirely different. This I find more apparent in the familiar instances obvious at college recitations. My more fortunate neighbours exult in the display of mathematical study, while I after feeling the humiliating sense of dependance & inferiority which like the goading soul-sickening sense of extreme poverty, palsies effort, esteem myself abundantly compensated, if with my pen, I can marshal whole catalogues of nouns & verbs, to express to the life the imbecility I felt.

Mr Everett says—The shout of admiration is lost ere it reaches the arches of heaven but there is an allseeing eye which looks deep down into the recesses of the obscurest heart. It is a small matter to abstain from vice to which there is no temptation or to perform a Virtue which is standing by you with crowns for your head; but it is the obscure struggling & unsuccessful virtue which meets with reward.——

*

Oct 20.

The supreme Pontiff sent a confessor to Rabelais on his deathbed charging him to recieve absolution. Rabelais dismissed the messenger & bid him tell the Pontiff He was now going to visit the great *Perhaps*.

Oct 24

Exhibition night. This tumultuous day is done. The character of its thought-weather is always extremely singular. Fuller than any other day of great thoughts—& poets' dreams, of hope & joy & pride & then closed with merriment & wine evincing or eliciting gay fraternal feeling enough, but brutalized & defiled with excess of physical enjoyment; leaving the mind distracted & unfit for pursuits of soberness. Barnwell's Oration contained sublime images.—One was of great power —a terrible description of the fire tempest which overshadowed Sodom & Gomorrha.—Another description of the waterspout of the Pacifick was noble. A great struggle of ambition is going on between Barnwell & Upham. Thundering & lightning are faint & tame descriptions of the course of astonishing eloquence. You double the force of painting if you describe it as it is. The flashing eye, that fills up the chasms of language; the living brow, throwing meaning & intellect into every furrow & every frown; the stamping foot, the labouring limbs, the desperate gesture, these must all be seen in their strong exercise, before the vivid conception of their effect can be adequately felt.—And then a man must separate & discipline & intoxicate his mind before he can enjoy the glory of the orator, when mighty thoughts come crowding on the soul; he must learn to harrow up unwelcome recollections & concentrate woe & horror & disgust till his own heart sickens; he must stretch forth his arm & array the bright ideas which have settled around him till they gather to forceful & appalling sublimity.

Oct. 24th

I begin to believe in the Indian doctrine of eye-fascination. The cold blue eye of   has so intimately connected him with my thoughts & visions that a dozen times a day & as often by night I find myself wholly wrapped up in conjectures of his character & inclinations. We have had already two or three long profound stares at each other. Be it wise or weak or superstitious I must know him.

Oct. 25

I find myself often idle, vagrant, stupid, & hollow. This is somewhat appalling & if I do not discipline myself with diligent care I shall suffer severely from remorse & the sense of inferiority hereafter. All around me are industrious & will be great, I am indolent & shall be insignificant. Avert it heaven! avert it virtue! I need excitement.

"Delivery from Sun-burning & Moonblasting."

Nov. 1.

My opinion of ⑭ was strangely lowered by hearing that he was "proverbially idle." This was redeemed by learning that he was a "superior man." This week, a little eventful in college, has brought a share of its accidents to him.

—

I wish I might be so witched with study, so enamoured of glory for a little time, that it were possible to forget self & professions & tasks & the dismal crowd of ordinary circumstances in a still & rapid & comprehensive course of improvement. How immensely would a scholar enlarge his power could he abstract himself wholly, body & mind from the dinning throng of casual recollections that summon him away, from his useful toil to endless, thankless, reveries; informing him for instance, for a whole rueful half hour of what he has done, is doing, & will do today, all which he knew at six o'clock in the morning & is condemned to learn anew twenty times in the course of the day. Perhaps this ugly disorder is peculiar to myself & I must envy that man's uninterrupted progress, who is not obliged by his oath to nature to answer this idle call. If this is to continue it will weaken the grasp with which I would cling,—with which every young man would cling, to "visions of glory." My talents, (according to the judgement of friends or to the whispered suggestions of vanity,) are popular, are fitted to enable me to claim a place in the inclinations & sympathy of men. But if I would excel & outshine the circle of my peers those talents must be put to the utmost stretch of exertion, must be taught the confidence of their own power; and lassitude & these desultory habits of thinking with their melancholy pleasure must be grappled with & conquered. These soliloquies are certainly sweeter than Chemistry!

—

Nov 10
A Recipe!!!
Young Waldo, when in your thick-coming whims, you feel an itching to *engrave*, take a piece of glass & cover it with a thin film of wax or isinglass & trace the proposed figure with a steel point. Place this over a vessel containing a mixture of powdered fluor spar & sulphuric acid gently heated. The acid gas coming into contact with the uncovered parts of the glass combines with & removes the silex, as well probably as the alkali with which it is united & lines more or less deep are thus formed—according to Gorham's Chemistry—(Article—Silicon—) page 265—Vol. I.

Item. On a Grave Stone in Framingham is a poetical Epitaph concluding with these words.—

    —"Killed by lightning sent from heaven
    In———1777."———

Nov 15th

De La Fontaine was an easy lazy sort of a gentleman from whom also Scott derived some of his notions of Dominie Sampson particularly the manner of furnishing him with new clothes. He was a child of genius whom every body protected & when one of his patronesses died, who had said that she had dismissed everything except her three domestic animals—her dog, her parrot, & De La Fontaine—the old man then at the age of 70 was taken up as one who had not yet arrived at years of discretion merely from the delight which was awakened by his simple, childlike & original genius. Madame de   said to him, that he should dedicate his tale to the king;—So I think said De la Fontaine & did it, but with an ignorant simplicity, which loved to defeat its own purposes, informed the king in the dedication that he did so by the orders of Madame de   . He informs us that he spent half his time in sleeping & the other half in doing nothing: & that he holds money to be a thing not necessary. So much for Jean de la Fontaine & Mr Ticknor.

Observe this. Mr Everett notices that a temperate climate has always been found necessary to a high national character. Also Mr. Waldo if you would like to find the sublimest attainable sayings on the destruction of Nations.—Vide 4th book of the Sybilline Collections.

Nov 18th

I shall subjoin some recipes for the cure of the horrible void which ruins ever & anon the mind's peace, & is otherwise called Unhappiness.

1. Take Scott's Novels & read carefully the mottoes of the chapters; or if you prefer reading a novel itself take the Bride of Lammermoor.

2. Sometimes (seldom) the finest parts of Cowper's Task will answer the purpose. I refer to the home-scenes.

3. For the same reason that I would take Scott's Mottoes I would also take an old tragedy such as Ben Jonson's, Otway's, Congreve's, in short, any thing of that kind which leads as far as possible from the usual trains of thought.

4. Make recipes to add to this list.

Dec 5th

It appears to me that it is a secret of the art of eloquence to know that a powerful aid would be derived from the use of forms of language which were generally known to Men in their infancy & which now under another and unknown garb but forcibly reminding them of early impressions are likely to be mistaken for opinions whose beginning they cannot recollect & therefore suppose them innate. At least if by such operation they cannot convince the mind they may serve to win attention by this awakening but ambiguous charm. By these forms of language I mean a paraphrase of some sentence in a *Primer* or other Child's book common to the country.—The spell would be more perfect perhaps if instead of such a paraphrase the words of a sentence should be modulated to the cadence of the aforesaid infant literature. I dare not subjoin an example.

Dec

The human soul, the world, the universe are labouring on to their magnificent consummation. We are not fashioned thus marvellously for nought. The straining conceptions of man, the monuments of his reason & the whole furniture of his faculties is adapted to mightier views of things than the mightiest he has yet beheld. Roll on then thou stupendous Universe in sublime incomprehensible solitude, in an unbeheld but sure path. The finger of God is pointing out your way. And when ages shall have elapsed & time is no more, while the stars shall fall from heaven & the Sun become darkness & the Moon blood, human intellect purified & sublimed shall mount from perfection to perfection of unmeasured & ineffable enjoyment of knowledge & glory.—Man shall come to the presence of Jehovah. (In the manner of Chateaubriand.)

Attended Mr Ticknor's Lecture on Voltaire.—Wonderful homage accorded to him on his appearance at Paris after 27 years absence. The greatest triumph which literary history can boast.—Various fortune of Voltaire's Adelaide de Guesclin— first representation was hissed throughout. Voltaire only said "Saturday I witnessed the burial of Adelaide & I was glad to see so respectable a procession." The next time a little altered it was decently received. The third time it was tumultuously applauded & those parts most clamorously praised which before were the most hissed. Voltaire says, "I can only say with the Venetian advocate to his judges 'Last week your Excellencies judged thus—today your Excellencies have judged exactly the reverse—and in both cases your Excellencies have judged admirably well.'"

———

Jan 9th 1821. How frequently I am led to consider the distinguished advantages which this generation enjoy above our fathers. Have heard today another consecrated display of genius—of the insinuating & overwhelming effect of eloquent manners & style when made sacred & impregnable by the subject which they are to enforce. Mr Everett's sermon before the Howard Benevolent Society. He told a very affecting anecdote. "I have known a woman in this town go out to work with her own hands to pay for the wooden coffin which was to enclose the dust of her only child. I prayed with her when there was none to stand by her but he who was to bear that dust to the tomb."

There was a vast congregation, but while he spoke, as silent as death. Unluckily, in the pauses, however they shook the house with their hideous convulsions; for when he raised his handkerchief to his face after a pause in the sermon it seemed almost a concerted signal for the Old South to cough.

> Let those now cough who never coughed before
> And those who always cough cough now the more.

Feb 7th

The religion of my Aunt is the purest & most sublime of any I can conceive. It appears to be based on broad & deep & remote principles of expediency & adequateness to an end—principles which few can comprehend & fewer feel. It labours to reconcile the apparent insignificance of the field to the surpassing grandeur of the Operator & founds the benignity & Mercy of the Scheme on adventurous but probable comparisons of the Condition of other orders of being. Although it is an intellectual offspring of beauty & splendour, if that were all, it breathes a practical spirit of rigid & austere devotion. It is independent of forms & ceremonies & its ethereal nature gives a glow of soul to her whole life. She is the Weird-woman of her religion & conceives herself always bound to walk in narrow but exalted paths which lead onward to interminable regions of rapturous & sublime glory.

Feb 1821—Martial in one of his Epigrams complains that Livy takes up his whole library & he has room for no more. Such was the clumsy length of a great work in the miserable copying system which prevailed in those days. I must give Mr Channing a theme on the influence of weather & skies on mind; I have tried poetry but do not succeed as well as might be wished. Plan—The poor inhabitants of Indostan are distressed & degraded by the horrors of a flimsy & cruel Superstition. The iron hath entered into their souls, & their situation is in all respects abominable. Why is it their misery is thus darkened & deepened far different from the lot of the rejoicing nations of Europe & America? It is because a flaming sky boils their blood & blackens their skin & maddens their nature enervating the mind while it renders it fiercer & more brutal. It is just so in other climes an Indian day fires the spirits, a dull day depresses them, & a glorious one exhilarates, & Man vainly endeavours to oppose the order of nature & contend with superiour ordinations. Discurse a little & done with the same.

—

Cambridge April 1

It is Sabbath again & I am for the most part recovered. Is it a wise dispensation that we can never know what influence our own prayers have in restoring the health we have prayed God to restore? It had been thought by Some that in these immediate effects they have no influence in general, that their good is prospective, & that the world is governed by Providence through the instrumentality of general laws which are only broken on the great occasions of the world or other portions of the Creator's works. But what have I wandered from I think that it infinitely removes heavenly dispensations from earthly ones—this manner of giving gifts without expressing the reason for which they are bestowed & leaving it to the heart to make the application & to discover the Giver is worthy of a supreme, ineffable Intelligence.

Well, I am sorry to have learned that my friend is dissolute; or rather the anecdote which I accidentally heard of him shews him more like his neighbours than I should wish him to be. I shall have to throw him up, after all, as a cheat of fancy. Before I ever saw him, I wished my *friend* to be different from any individual I had seen. I invested him with a solemn cast of mind, full of poetic feeling, & an idolater of friendship, & possessing a vein of rich sober thought. When I saw   's pale but expressive face & large eye, I instantly invested him with the complete character which fancy had formed and though entirely uuacquainted with him was pleased to observe the notice which he appeared to take of me. For a year I have entertained towards him the same feelings & should be sorry to lose him altogether before we have ever exchanged above a dozen words.

NB By the way this book is of an inferiour character & contains so much doubtful matter that I believe I shall have to burn the second number of the Wide World immediately upon its completion.

———

I am more puzzled than ever with   's conduct. He came out to meet me yesterday and I observing him, just before we met turned another corner and most strangely avoided him. This morning I went out to meet him in a different direction and stopped to speak with a lounger in order to be directly in   's way, but   turned into the first gate and went towards Stoughton. All this baby play persists without any apparent design, and as soberly as if both were intent on some tremendous affair. With a most serious expectation of burning this book I am committing to it more of what I may by and by think childish sentiment than I should care to venture on vagabond sheets which Somebody else may light upon. (Mr Somebody, will it please your impertinence to be conscience-struck!)

from
Wide World 3
1822

Boston Jan 12, 1822.

After a considerable interval I am still willing to think that these commonplace books are very useful and harmless things, —at least sufficiently so, to warrant another trial. Besides every one writes differently when he composes for the eyes of others, and when his pen scampers away over mote and rut for the solitary edification of its lord and master. The peculiar cause why this moment should be distinguished above others by the commencement of my third creation is that I am ambitious to say some fine things about Contrast, while, at the same time, the scattered undefined connection of my ideas leads me to mistrust my ability to shine upon this topic in theme, *poem*, or *review*.—What therefore is left, but for me to confide in the silent sheets of my book which cannot insult and will not betray?

Contrast is a law which seems to exist not only in the human mind with regard to the objects of imagination as an associating principle but also to obtain in the course of providence & the laws which regulate the World. When the day grows very bright and the atmosphere burns with unusual splendour, the mind reverts to the storm which will cloud, or the night which will speedily blacken it. Before the time of Mahomet and the comparative civilization of the deserts the merciless Arab celebrated a feast of peace annually of seven days in which the deadliest enemy & the longest feud were forgotten & reconciled in a religious harmony & joy until the Close of the period.—And were the Arab tenfold more keen & terrible in his vengeance and his selfishness more sordid & savage than it is now, we feel sure, that the feast should be longer & the friendship closer. The principle of Contrast which we find engraven within proves that such a state of things would follow. For how came it there, whence did we derive it? Either the

Deity has written it as one of his laws upon the human mind or
we have derived it from an observation of the invariable course
of human affairs—and either of these suppositions proves the
truth of the inference. For we could not have learned ourselves
to range from one present object over all the immense circuit
of intermediate objects to that one, most remote of all, from
our present contemplation.

In this principle is lodged the safety of human institutions
and human life. For suppose ambition excite against the peace
of the World one of those incarnate fiends which have at different periods arisen to destroy the peace & good order of one
community after another & of nation after nation. Gradually
the lust of excess engendered by sudden prosperity de-
bauches every virtue and steals away the Moral sense. The in-
solence of power tramples upon the laws of God and the rights
of man. The thirst of fame arrays millions in the field which the
sword reaps down crying blood, blood! Which no vengeance
can satisfy, no agony avert. Justice pleads in vain to the destroyer; Patriotism plots wisely, but her stern efforts are frus-
trated and she dies by the knife which was whetted for the
tyrant. But the victor rides onward in his car of conquest ex-
terminating the race which are made in the image of God until "Men said openly that Jesus and his Saints were asleep."
Policy watches all night to contrive their destruction. The
Statesman's aching brow, the winning hand of the Merchant,
the art of the Engineer are joined for their persecution. Here,
when the day of triumph burns with consuming splendour—
here, the mind of itself pauses to anticipate change near at
hand. The victor must cease. Else would the very stones cry
out—Day and Night contend against him; the Elements which
he wielded rebel and crush him; the clouds nurse their
thunders to blast him; he is lifted up on rebellious spears
between heaven and earth unworthy and abhorred of both, to
perish.

—

Every being is judged by his own law. Besides, these laws
may never jar, may never come into comparison. They are as
entirely unlike as the ideas of *reason* and a *daisy* and have no
analogous points except perhaps the common analogies prevailing throughout the universe of a common creation by one

Mind. They may severally be productions of several thoughts of the divine Mind. One system may be the representation, the Shadowing out of the *divine Imagination*; a second—of the *reason*; a third—of some other faculty incomprehensible to us. All this may take place just as the human sciences and arts are severally the embodyings of a faculty;—poetry, of the *imagination*; Mathematics of the reason; painting of sight; Music of the hearing &c &c. Each may be as different from the rest as one sense from another and yet when all are learned (as may take place when we are freed from the restraint of this one world) all may form a beautiful harmony, which shall be the perfection of knowledge.

Will the disputes upon the Nature of God, upon Trinitarianism & Unitarianism, never yield to a purer pursuit and to practical inquiry? It is possible, for all we know to the contrary that God may exist in a threefold Unity; but if it were so, since it is inconceivable to us, he would never have revealed to us such an existence which we cannot describe or comprehend. Infinite Wisdom established the foundations of knowledge in the Mind so that twice two could never make any thing else than four. As soon as this can be otherwise, our faith is loosened and science abolished.—Three may be one, and one—three.

———

The Arts are mostly the production of some tendency in the human mind.

There are few things which the wellwishers of American literature have more at heart than our national poetry. For every thing else, for science, and morals, and art they are willing to wait the gradual progress but they are in haste to pluck the blossoms from the fair tree which grows fast by the hill of Parnassus. For when a nation has found time for the luxury and refinement of poetry it takes off the reproach of a sluggish genius and of ignorant indifference. Moreover, although the learned nations of the east and west acquired by their arts and learning a claim to renown yet it was the Muse which inscribed that title upon the temple of fame and it would be a kind of fraud perhaps not unparalleled should we forestal our merit by writing the name before we deserved the record.

Poetical expression serves to embellish dull thoughts but we love better to follow the poet when the muse is so ethereal and the thought so sublime that language sinks beneath it.

When the heart is satisfied and the pulse beats high with health man is apt to exclaim "Soul, thou hast much goods laid up for many years, eat drink and be merry; Life is long and time is pleasant,—I rejoice that my maker has clothed me with strength and poured this buoyant blood into the vessels of life; I will go to the banquet and the dance, I will go to the fields to play."—I would remind him that far off stand the ruins of Palmyra and Persepolis; the hands that builded them are unknown,—the gods that were worshipped there have perished also and for ages they have served as a memento of death and ruin—I would remind him of the vast cemetery of the dead which is peopled with countless nations and outnumbers a thousand fold the population of the earth.

———

I was the pampered child of the East. I was born where the soft western gale breathed upon me the fragrance of cinnamon groves and through the seventy windows of my hall the eye fell on the Arabian harvest. An hundred elephants apparelled in cloth of gold carried my train to war and the smile of the Great King beamed upon Omar. But now—the broad Indian moon looks through the broken arches of my tower, and the wing of Desolation fans me with poisonous airs; the spider's threads are the tapestry which adorns my walls and the rain of the night is heard in my halls for the music of the daughters of Cashmere. Wail, wail for me, ye who put on honour as gay drapery!

———

Η γαρ φυσις βεβαιος, οθ τα χρηματα
Soph. Electra, 937 l.

The Greek long ago reasoned upon the folly of the rich man's hope. "Is it well, he said, to value thy self on a pile of gold? for what is it, but to have seen riches familiarly for a little time; nature is stable, but not wealth; for Nature remaining forever, corrects her own faults, but wealth, when it is unjustly acquired, or partaken with fools, having *displayed* * *its plumage* a little while, flies out of the house." He described it well when

———

*The word is ανθησας (q. v.), and therefore the figure inconsistent.

he said that *wealth* was only "*to see riches familiarly*," not to feel and enjoy them. To acquire riches, and to be rich, is to hope and to be disappointed, for Care & Pain keep so close to the chariot of Wealth, that they are not seen by those panting after it, until they have reached the wheel, and then the appetite of pursuit is overpaid by the chagrin of success.—Fortune is fleeting, and riches take to themselves wings, but is the second part of his proposition true, is Nature eternal? Is the rose on the cheek of youth perennial? Will the locks remain on the brow of manhood? All flesh is grass &c. Nothing of nature is firm but the eternal mountains and the naked rocks. But are these unchanged? The Winter has stripped them, the earthquake has rent their foundations. And can the whole earth and the centres of nature show a fairer claim to permanence? I fear not. There are the Fire, the Wind, the Waters, Earthquakes and lightning buried within it to tear it asunder. Without, there is an Order of the Universe—broken, if the Arm which sustains it be withdrawn; and the forerunner of this dissolution, the Angel of Prophecy has already published the day.— Watch, for the Time is at hand—when the heavens shall be rolled together as a scroll and the elements shall melt with fervent heat. What then is Nature?—it is the transitory pleasure of the Divine Mind.

———

The circle of the sciences is no more firmly bound together than the circle of the virtues; but in the first a man cannot hope to be thoroughly acquainted with all, for they are in some degree incompatible; whereas in the last, his character will be defective if it do not combine the whole & form that harmony which results from all.

from
Wide World 4
1822

Boston Feb 22 1822

DEDICATION.

I have invoked successively the Muse, the fairies, the witches, and Wisdom, to preside over my creations; I have summoned Imagination from within, and Nature from without; I have called on Time, and assembled about the slight work the Hours of his train.—But the Powers were unpropitious, fate was averse. Some other spell must be chaunted, some other melody sung. I will devote it to the dead. The mind shall anticipate a few fleeting hours, and borrow its tone from what all that have been are, and all that are, will shortly be. All that adorns this world are the gifts which they left in their passage through it. To these monuments which they bequeathed, and to their shades which watch in the universe, I apply for excitement, and I dedicate my short-lived flowers.

———

The novelist must fasten the skirts of his tale to scenes or traditions so well known as to make it impossible to disbelieve and so obscure as not to obtrude repugnant facts upon the finished deception he weaves.

Tuesday, Evg. Feb. 26

A ghost may not appear because *no* one answers the question—why should he appear. As soon as the cause is adequate, there is every reason in nature to expect such an appearance.

Somebody says that it makes no difference how many believe in a recieved opinion, but that it does weaken the presumption in its favour—how many dissent from it. If this be true, the vast number of voices who consent to be orthodox, and which seems at first the chief argument in its favour fall away at once from the purpose and the minority of cool-

33

judging, prudent men who secede do greatly prejudice the cause.

I have not much cause, I sometimes think, to wish my Alma Mater well, personally; I was not often highly flattered by success, and was every day mortified by my own ill fate or ill conduct. Still, when I went today to the ground where I had had the brightest thoughts of my little life and filled up the little measure of my knowledge and had felt sentimental for a time, and poetical for a time, and had seen many fine faces, and traversed many fine walks, and enjoyed much pleasant, learned, or friendly society,—I felt a crowd of pleasant thoughts—as I went posting about from place to place, and room to chapel. I met   .

Feb. 28, 1822. Few of my pages have been filled so little to my own satisfaction as these—and why?—because the air has been so fine, and my visits so pleasant, and myself so full of pleasant social feelings—for a day or two past that the mind has not possessed sufficiently the cold frigid tone which is indispensable to become so *oracular* as it hath been of late. Etsi mearum cogitationum laus et honor non tam magna quam antea fuit, tamen gaudium voluptatemque majorem accipit, quoniam sentire principia amoris me credebam. Vidi amicum, etsi veterem, ignotum; alteram vidi notam et noscendam; ambo, forsitan, si placet Deo, partem vitae, partem mei facient. Poenitet mei res magnas narrare cum verbis qualibus tyro uti solet.

Such is the contrary condition of things that pride subjects a man oftenest to humiliation; for its nature being to render the possessor ever mindful of himself, that very mindfulness is exhibited in the features of the face, and serves only to provoke the frown, anger, and contempt of others. Every slight, while it irritates the pride, darkens the brow, and repels the more, the more fretful it becomes. Be content then to jostle with the multitude, to bow your head and let the world wag.

"Hark rascal!"
    At mid day, in the crowd of care,
    The unbidden thought will come,
    And force the obedient blush prepare

Reluctant welcome home;
And in the corners of the heart,
And in the Passions' cell,
It bids my thoughts to battle start,
Which fain would peaceful dwell.
Peace, Pleasure, Pride, and Joy, and Grief
Awake the chaos wild,—
But worse and cursed the relief
Which sense & strife beguiled. (to wit Indifference.)

So much poetry for peculiar sources of pride old and inveterate and perhaps hereafter unintelligible. Still one's feelings are well worth speculation and I am desirous of remembering a date. (as that of the last page)

—scripsi nomen, supra.

A beautiful thought struck me suddenly, without any connection, which I could trace, with my previous trains of thought and feeling. It had no analogy to any notion I ever remembered to have formed; it surpassed all others in the energy and purity in which it clothed itself; it put by all others by the novelty it bore, and the grasp it laid upon every fibre; for the time, it absorbed all other thoughts;—all the faculties—each in his cell, bowed down and worshipped before this new Star.—Ye who roam among the living and the dead, over flowers or among the cherubims, in real or ideal universes, do not whisper my thought!

—

Animi ardor de quo supra dixi non extinctus est, sed mihi videtur non esse tam potens tam clarus tam magnus quam antea. Timeo ne caderet. Spero ut viveret.

March 4. A breathless solitude in a cottage in the woods beneath the magnificent splendour of this moonlight and with this autumnal coolness might drive one mad with excitement. Precipitous and shadowy mountains, thick forests and far-winding rivers should sleep under the light, and add their charm to the fascination. The silence broken only by the far cry of the night bird; or disturbed by the distant shout of the peasant, or, at intervals, by those melancholy moanings of the wind, which speak so expressively to the ear,—who would not admire? Let the Hours roll by uncounted, let the universe sleep on in this grand repose, but be the spell unbroken by aught of this world, by vulgar and disquieting cares; by a regret or a thought which might remind us of aught but Nature. Here is her Paradise, here is her throne. The stars in their courses roll silently; the oaks rock in their forests to the voice of the sighing breeze; the wall-flower on the top of the cliff nods over its giddy edge, and the worshipping enthusiast stands at the door of his tent mute and happy, while the leaves rustle down from the topmost boughs and cover his feet. A cry in the wilderness! the shriek and sudden sound of desolation! howl for him that comes riding on darkness through the midnight; that puts his hand forth to darken the moon, and quenches all the stars. Lo! where the awful pageantry rolleth now to the corners of the heaven; the fiery form shrouds his terrible brow behind the fragment of a stormy cloud, and the eyes of Creation gaze after the rushing chariot. Lo! he stands up in the Universe and with his hands he parts the firmament asunder from side to side. And as he trode upon the dragons I saw the name which burned underneath—Wake, oh wake, ye who keep watch in the Universe! Time, Space, Eternity, ye Energies that live, for his name is DESTRUCTION!—who keep the *Sceptre* of its eternal order, for He hath reached unto your treasuries, & he feeleth after your Sceptre to break it in pieces. Another cry went up like the crash of broken spheres, the voice of dying worlds. It is night.—An exceeding noisy vision!—

—

This book in ordinary is peculiarly devoted to original ideas but I cannot resist the pleasure of setting down, in black & white, verses which I have repeated so often. It is a charm in one of Ben Jonson's Masques.

> "The faery beam upon you,
>   The stars to glister on you,
>   A moon of light,
>   In the noon of night,
>   Till the fire-drake hath o'er-gone you.
>   The wheel of fortune guide you,
>   The boy with the bow beside you,

> Run aye in the way,
> Till the bird of day,
> And the luckier lot, betide you."

March 7

———

Thus have I fulfilled enough of my design in this book to authorise my dedication on the first page. This shall not prevent me from resuming the topics upon the slightest indications of my Noömeter.

———

The origin of Fiction is buried in the darkness of the remotest ages. If it were a question of any importance, perhaps its secret springs are not yet beyond the reach of the inquirer. To paint what is not, should naturally seem less agreeable to the mind than to describe what is. "Nothing," (said the author of the Essay on the human Understanding) "is so beautiful to the eye, as truth to the mind." But if we look again, I apprehend we shall find that the source of fable, is *human misery*; that to relieve one hour of life, by exciting the sympathies to a tale even of imaginary joy, was accounted a praiseworthy accomplishment; and honour & gold were due to him, whose rare talent took away, for the moment, the memory of care and grief. Fancy, which is ever a kind of contradiction to life & truth, set off in a path remote as possible from all human scenes & circumstances; and hence the, first legends dealt altogether in monstrous scenes, and peopled the old mythology and the nursery lore, with magicians, griffins, and metamorphoses which offend the ear of taste, and could only win away the credulity of a savage race, and the simplicity of a child. Reason soon taught the bard that the deception was infinitely improved by being reduced within the compass of probability; and the second fictions introduced imaginary persons into the manners & dwellings of real life.

———

Sabbath Evening, March 10

We complain of change and vicissitude. Say rather, there pursues us always an eternal sameness, an unchanging identity. Did not Caesar and the men of Rome see the same stars, suffer from the same storms, feel the same infirmities? Were they not chilled, wet, and warmed, by the same variations of weather, were they not hungry, athirst, ragged & unfortunate, like the men of this month? Our common conversation but translates theirs, just as we apply to ourselves their addresses to the elements or to the feelings. The world, the universe is just the same; only, each man's mind undergoes a perpetual change, and the vainglorious dreamer attributes to Nature and Fortune the alteration which transpires within himself alone. The Ocean heaves up his stormy pride alike against all through each age of empire;—the Assyrian, the Jewish, the Grecian, the Roman, the Vandal, the Turkish, the British, the American;

> "Time writes no wrinkle on thine azure brow;
>   Such as Creation's dawn beheld, thou rollest now."

How is it that we preserve so accurately the knowledge of events and minds coeval with the Pyramids? How know we the history of the causes of private ambition or public outrage? It is because every man bears within him a record of other men's motives; inasmuch as there is engraven upon his soul passion & perception of outward things—which tend every where to the same effects, so he can form fair & probable judgements of the manner in which—comfort, plenty, power, all which are comprehended in the possession of a Crown would act upon him. The Egyptian priestess who had washed her sacred robe, the crafty Greek at Delphi who had succeeded indifferently well in his oracular riddle, the Corinthian merchant who added in his books another talent as his future dues from the extravagant proconsul—all felt in their repose the same kind of satisfaction which pleases me in closing another book.

"Maximus partus temporis," quoth giggling Vanity. "Burn the trash," saith Fear.

> "There the Northern light reposes
>   With ruddy flames in circles bright
> Like a wreath of ruby roses
>   On the dusky brow of Night"

Boston, April 14, 1822.
(DEDICATION.)

In aforetime, while to the inhabitants of Europe, the existence of America was yet a secret in the heart of time, there dwelled a Giant upon the South Mountain Chimborazo, who extended a beneficent dominion over hills and clouds and continents, and sustained a communication with his mother— Nature. He lived two hundred years in that rich land, causing peace and justice, and he battled with the Mammoths, and slew them. Upon the summit of the mountain, amid the snows of all the winters, was the mouth of a cave which was lined with golden ore. This cavity, termed "The Golden Lips" admitted downwards into the centre of the mountain which was a vast and spacious temple, and all its walls and ceilings glowing with pure gold. Man had never polluted it with his tools of art. Nature fashioned the mighty tenement, for the bower of her son. At midday, the vertical sun was perpendicular to the cavity, and poured its full effulgence upon the mirror floor; and its reflected beams blazed on all sides from the fretted roof, with a lustre which eclipsed the elder glory of the temple of Solomon. In the centre of this gorgeous palace, bareheaded and alone, the Giant Californ performed the incommunicable rite, and studied the lines of destiny. When the sun arrived at the meridian, a line of light traced this inscription upon the wall—"A thousand years, A thousand years, and the Hand shall come, and shall tear the Veil for all." Two thousand years have passed, and the mighty progress of improvement & civilization have been forming the force which shall reveal Nature to Man. To roll about the outskirts of this Mystery and ascertain and describe its pleasing wonders—be this the journey of my Wideworld. The *Hand* shall come;—I traced its outline in the mists of the morning.

—

Tuesday Evg Apr 16

It is strange that a world should be so dear which speculatively and seriously we acknowledge to be so unsatisfying and so dark. Not all its most glorious array when Nature is apparelled in her best, and when Art toils to gratify,—not the bright sun itself, and the blazing firmament wherein he stands as chief —can prevent a man, at certain moments, from saying to his soul—"It is vanity." No wild guesses, no elaborate reasoning can surmount this testimony to the familiar truth, that the human spirit hath a higher origin than matter, a higher home than the earth; that it is too capacious to be always cheated with trifles, and too long-lived, to amalgamate with mortality. But this is more strange and unaccountable; that in a bad world at which all are content to rail, the mind should rarely look up, of its own accord to seek the consolation of a better hope; that true and rational pleasure should never dictate an early fondness to anticipate and weigh these expectations; while on the contrary it is *now* left to *pain,* to physical or mental *distress,* to drive us reluctantly upon this *hard formidable* prospect of our happiness & perfection. No honest and noble aspirations to fulfil the duties of our highest sphere, to meet with the Divinity, find place within us;—but contemptible bodily pain which we have not the courage to encounter, or the force of mind to despise, sets upon idle wishing for a better world, from so mean a motive as to escape a transitory pang of this. It plainly shews that though there be a spirit, it is narrowly crowded & mingled with coarse & sordid *clay* which can be tickled with the straws & baubles of a dazzling world and easily moulded to its vain purposes. It was found by philosophy

that luminous matter wastes itself ever; it is true without a
metaphor of this shining world which goes on decaying and
still attracting by its false lustre.

—

"Jesuits are a people who lengthen the creed and shorten
the decalogue." Abbé Boileau

—

April 1822

In the eternal & enchanting variety of sky & season, amid
the softness of the first vernal airs, there is yet a melancholy
voice which makes itself heard, teaching the vanity of joy, the
neighbourhood of remorse; saying that Nature acts the part of
a deciever, when in this scene of human danger & fate, she
wears so gay & gorgeous apparel. Upon a field as beautiful as
the plains of Eden, painted & perfumed with flowers, and
bright with morning dews, two armed hosts of men array their
lines to murder each other. This is a mockery of God's beautiful creation; but this is an emblem of the whole world. In the
spicy gardens and beneath the orange groves of the Indies the
abused captive sighs & toils. The intoxicating gales which
please the sense with odours as you sail upon the waters of
Arabia & Africa waft in the same course the chained slave to
the land of his captivity. This wide vegetable creation whose
bud & bloom and fruit delight the heart with beauty, & support the life of man, does also nurse in its expanding leaves the
seeds of corruption; and man shall find as he lifteth up his eyes
to enjoy his wide dominion that there lurks amidst this abundant Paradise an infant pestilence growing up to be a Minister
of Vengeance and the enemy of the nations.

—Now here again is another detached morsel intended to
be merely the first lines of a long treatise upon fate & life, &c,
but it is cropped in the bud by the fiend Caprice; and I must
gallop away to some new topic which my fantastic Genius may
suggest.

Something Silly.

There died an old man at St. Mary's the Pier
And his body was buried from a beautiful bier
But his wife the next night was assailed by his ghost
Which she saw in the doorway, but did not accost.

That evening the lamps in the street were all lit
And though the rain poured, they did not intermit;
While the wide dusky puddles, by reflection, that shone,
Still blushed to *reflect*—that it was not their own.

That light dimly poured through the glass window-pane
Dust-coated by time, but new-washed by the rain.
And the crooked rays fell on the lady's new cap
And her features portending some dismal mishap

The ghost of her spouse in the corner did stand
Gently holding the ghost of his hat in his hand
He made a low bow; she stared at the ghost
And he suddenly turned himself into a post!

—

Dum a dum, now, but the book *does* grow better.

The Ancients' idea of Fate is thus expressed by Seneca. "Ille ipse omnium conditor et rector scripsit quidem fata sed sequitur. Semper paret, semel jussit."

—

May 7, Tuesday Evg. Amid my diseases & aches & qualms I will write to see if my brains are gone. For a day or two past we have had a wind precisely *annual*; which I discover by *this*, that I have a return of the identical thoughts & temperament which I had a year ago. But this Sun shines upon & these ill winds blow over—a changed person in condition, in hope. I was then delighted with my recent honours, traversing my chamber (Hollis 9) flushed & proud of a poet's fancies, & the day when they were to be exhibited; pleased with ambitious prospects & Careless because ignorant of the future. But now I'm a hopeless Schoolmaster just entering upon years of trade to which no distinct limit is placed; toiling through this miserable employment even without the poor satisfaction of discharging it well, for the good suspect me, & the geese dislike me. Then again look at this: there was pride in being a collegian, & a poet, & somewhat romantic in my queer acquaintance with Gay; and poverty presented nothing mortifying in the meeting of two young men whom their common relation & character as scholars equalised. But when one becomes a droning schoolmaster, and the other is advancing his footing in good company & fashionable friends, the cast of countenance on meeting is somewhat altered. Hope, it is true, still hangs out, though at further distance, her gay banners; but I have found her a cheat once, twice, many times, and shall I trust the deciever again? And what am I the better for two, four, six years delay? Nine months are gone, and except some rags of Wideworlds, half a dozen general notions &c I am precisely the same World's humble servant that left the University in August. Good people will tell me that it is a Judgement & lesson for my character, to make me fitter for the office whereto I aspire; but if I come out a dispirited, mature, broken hearted miscreant,—how will Man or myself be bettered? Now I have not thought all this time that I was complaining at Fate although I suppose it amounts to the same; these are the suggestions only of a disappointed spirit brooding over the fall of castles in the air. My fate is enviable contrasted with that of others; I have only to blame myself who had no right to build them. Waldo E.

"And there is a great difference whether the tortoise gathers himself within his shell hurt or unhurt."

I shall bless Cadmus, or Chod, or Hermes, for inventing letters & written language—You, my dear little wideworld, deducing your pedigree from that pretty event.

Mowna Roa, mountain in Sandwich Isles was seen by Marchand at the distance of 53 leagues ie. 159 miles—Greatest distance at which a terrestrial object hath been seen from the level of the sea.

Trust not the Passions; they are blind guides. They act, by the confessed experience of all the world, by the observation within reach of a child's attention, contrary to Reason. It were madness & manifest perdition for a man who beheld from the shore a stormy & ranging ocean darkened by clouds & broken by rocks—to cast himself into a boat upon it without oar or helm to be tossed to savage shores perhaps, perhaps to famine, perhaps to the wild wilderness of waves, inevitably to death for no other purpose but to gratify a moment's caprice. But this is the strict history of one who trusts himself to the government of passion. He voluntarily puts away from him that godlike prerogative which distinguishes him from the beasts, and which determines & fortifies his actions and throws himself into the wild tempest of temptation & vice, into the direct commission of those crimes which human & divine laws have fenced round & forbidden. He has become another being, and under this strange metamorphosis he dares & delights in enormities at which his calm mind but now shuddered. He has made himself accountable & perchance execrable for high handed wickedness from which a moment's firmness would have extricated him entirely; he had made himself liable to new temptation, and fatally easy to the triumphs of Sin.

We take our impressions of the world from the *average* results of our own limited experiments. These form our general notions from which we reason in cold moments. But we always derive a transient & partial prejudice from the last contact which we had with it. We feel a low & miserable humiliation when we have been in company with beings of that worst sort—like John of Cappadocia in "Decline & Fall," or Glossin in Guy Mannering or Clodius at Rome. This is by far the most tremendous character, (in species), which can be found. Another portrait of it is Richardson's Lovelace. It is a worse being than Byron's personifications; the pirate Cleaveland is of Byron's kind, with the laughing devil in his sneer, but is hardly so dreadful in many respects as these; because the character of which I speak exactly comes up to the best limit of human nature at the same time that it appertains more to the fiend: Byron's have redeeming gentle affections;—these exhibit the gentle affections only to laugh at them, and shock you by butchering human beings & divine things in a *genteel* way,—in becoming popular in proportion as they become outrageous. The frequent acquaintance with these pictures hath a dreadful tendency in roughly wearing off the moral delicacy by such a familiarity with profanity & abomination. To my imagination, the analogy always presents itself between the history of these & that remark of Buchanan at the temple of Juggernaut "that the vultures were shockingly tame." But I am tired of this doleful delineation. I turn gratefully to the opposite circumstances. I saw a toll-taker recieve his debt from two men who had walked a mile on purpose to pay the owed fees, has an agreeable impression of the honesty of all passengers which extends itself to trust the next petitioner with ease & confidence. A frank avowal of fault in one who hath injured you, puts you in humour with the world, and a fine moonlight specimen of nature makes you loth to lose her beauty. Hence it follows that our conclusions upon human nature are transitory & prejudiced, and often contradictory and that only we can speak with authority when in philosophical coldness & abstraction, we weigh well the opposing interests & determine upon Man as an universal idea of which few & cautious things must be said to be said safely.—The day labourer is easily seduced by a high reward & liberal treatment, to think well of the rich, by a festive impulse, to imagine himself patriotic.

(All this might be as well continued as not.)

May 12. I have a nasty appetite which I will not gratify.

May 13. In twelve days I shall be nineteen years old; which I count a miserable thing. Has any other educated person lived so many years and lost so many days? I do not say acquired so little for by an ease of thought & certain looseness of mind I have perhaps been the subject of as many ideas as many of mine age. But mine approaching maturity is attended with a goading sense of emptiness & wasted capacity; with the conviction that vanity has been content to admire the little circle of natural accomplishments, and has travelled again & again the narrow round, instead of adding sedulously the gems of knowledge to their number. Too tired and too indolent to travel up the mountain path which leads to good learning, to wisdom & to fame, I must be satisfied with beholding with an envious eye the laborious journey & final success of my fellows, remaining stationary myself, until my inferiors & juniors have reached & outgone me. And how long is this to last? How long shall I hold the little acclivity which four or six years ago I flattered myself was enviable, but which has become contemptible now? It is a child's place & if I hold it longer I may quite as well resume the bauble & rattle, grow old with a baby's red jocky on my grey head & a picturebook in my hand, instead of Plato and Newton. Well, and I am he who nourished brilliant visions of future grandeur which may well appear presumptuous & foolish now. My infant imagination was idolatrous of glory, & thought itself no mean pretender to the honours of those who stood highest in the community, and dared even to contend for fame with those who are hallowed by time & the approbation of ages.—It was a little merit to concieve such animating hopes, and afforded some poor prospect of the possibility of their fulfilment. This hope was fed & fanned by the occasional lofty communications which were vouchsafed to me with the Muses' Heaven and which have at intervals made me the organ of remarkable sentiments & feelings which were far above my ordinary train. And with this lingering earnest of better hope (I refer to this fine exhilaration which now & then quickens my clay) shall I resign every aspiration to belong to that family of giant minds which live on earth many ages & rule the world when their bones are slumbering, no matter, whether under a pyramid or a primrose? No I will yet a little while entertain the Angel.

Look next from the history of my intellect to the history of my heart. A blank, my lord. I have not the kind affections of a pigeon. Ungenerous & selfish, cautious & cold, I yet wish to be romantic. Have not sufficient feeling to speak a natural hearty welcome to a friend or stranger and yet send abroad wishes & fancies of a friendship with a man I never knew. There is not in the whole wide Universe of God (my relations to Himself I do not understand) one being to whom I am attached with warm & entire devotion,—not a being to whom I have joined fate for weal or wo, not one whose interests I have nearly & dearly at heart;—and this I say at the most susceptible age of man.

Perhaps at the distance of a score of years, if I then inhabit this world, or still more, if I do not, these will appear frightful confessions; they may or may not; it is a true picture of a barren & desolate soul.

*

(Be it remembered that it was last evening that I heard that prodigious display of Eloquence in Faneuil Hall, by Mr Otis—which astonished & delighted me above any thing of the kind I ever witnessed.)

I love my Wideworlds.

May 14. Two things may be noticed here which are anecdotes of Italian manners at the date 1412. "Squarcia Giramo, ranger to Jean Marie Visconti, (of his father Jean Galeaz Visconti, I intend to speak again,) who had nourished his dogs with human flesh was his principal favourite. When victims failed, he declared that he would avenge the death of his mother to which he had contributed more than any one & he gave up to be torn to pieces by his hounds John de Posterla, Antoine Visconti, his brother Francis, & a great number of Gibelin gentlemen. He delivered up to them also the son of John Posterla aged only twelve, but when the boy cast himself on his knees to ask pardon, the dogs stood still & would not touch him. Squarcia, with his knife stabbed the child & the dogs refused still to taste of his blood & his entrails."—

"The Emperour Sigismond & the Pope John 23d visited Cremona & the emperour pardoned Gabrino Fondolo, tyrant of this city. When they were both ascended to the top of the steeple of Cremona, where almost all Lombardy & the majestic course of the Po opened to their view, Gabrino Fondolo, who had already obtained by a black perfidy the sovereignty which he enjoyed, concieved for an instant the thought of precipitating the emperor & the pope from the top of the tower to occasion in Christendom an unexpected revolution, from which he might profit. This same tyrant being beheaded at Milan 11 years after by order of Philippe Marie declared dying that his only remorse was for having weakly renounced that thought." (1414) Sismondi is very diligent in collecting anecdotes; it is singular that in narrating the death of John Huss, 1415, which he does at some length, he should make no mention of that remarkable prophecy, "Post centum annos" &c. Such an omission leads you to suspect that an author has not read all. (See a better story of this in "Bennett's Memorial.")

*

My body weighs 144 pounds.——In a fortnight I intend, Deo volente, to make a journey on foot. A month hence I will answer the question whether the pleasure was only in the *hope*.

——

And now it is Friday at even, and I am come to take leave of my pleasant Wideworld, for a little time, & commence my journey tomorrow. I look to many pleasures in my fortnight's absence, but neither is my temperament so volatile & gay, nor my zeal so strong as to make my expectations set aside the possibility of disappointment. I am so young an adventurer, that I am alive to regret & sentiment upon so little an occasion as this parting; though one would judge from my late whispered execrations of the school that a short suspension of its mortefications would be exceedingly delightful. I may also observe here that I had never suspected myself of so much feeling as rose within me at taking leave of Mrs E. at the water side and seeing so delicate a lady getting into a boat from those steep wharf stairs among sailors & labourers; and leaving her native shore for Louisiana without a single friend or relation attending her to the shore, and seeing her depart.—For myself I was introduced to her upon the wharf. Her husband behaved very well. God speed them!*

——

It is difficult to assign the causes of difference in the attainments of two nations. For although the character of the species does obey the grand natural distinctions of the earth, and is found, savage at the poles, & civilized in the temperate zone, yet of nations in the same latitude, one shall be found no whit advanced in knowledge or greatness, & the other shall have arrayed itself with such splendour as to fill an hundred urns with the lustre of its beams. Why is England renowned for arts and arms while an equally high latitude in Russia, and while Norway and the fine climates of North America have languished in barbarism? What imparted that impulse to Greece which may be said to have created literature which has been communicated through Rome to the world? It is a curious spectacle to a

*She is dead & her husband also, a thousand miles away from their kindred. 1824.

contemplative man to observe a little population of twelve or
twenty thousand men for a couple of generations setting their
minds at work more diligently than men were accustomed and
effecting something altogether new & strange; to see them lie
quietly down again in darkness, while all the nations of the
world rise up to do them a vain reverence; and all the wisest
among them exhausting their powers to make a faint imitation
of some one excellence of Greece in her age of glory; to see
this admiration continued & augmented as the world grows
older, and with all the advantages of an experience of 6000
years to find those departed artists never paralleled. It certainly
is the most manly literature in the world, being composed of
histories, orations, poems, & dramatic pieces, in which no sign
of accomodation is discovered to the whims of fashion or patronage. Simplicity is a remarkable characteristic of the productions of all the ancient masters. Upon their most admirable
statue they were content to engrave "Apollodorus the Ephesian made it"; and we respect the republican brevity which, in
the place of a studied eulogium upon a drama which had been
represented with unbounded applause, simply wrote, "Placuit"
(it pleased.)

This last effort of the pen seems to have been tortured out
for the mere purpose of ending the book, and I really regret
that the sixth wideworld which boasts of several swelling
paragraphs, should close its page with so heartless an oration.
Giant Californ would contemn the gift, whose outside, shews
so poor. It should meet an honourable fate to consume by the
sun-light on his golden altar.

Boston July 10, 1822.

> "Let us plait the garland & weave the chi,
>   While the wild waves dash on our iron strand;
>   Tomorrow, these waves may wash our graves,
>   And the moon look down on a ruined land."

The islanders who sung this melancholy song, presaging the
evil fates which waited for them—have passed away. No gir-
dled chieftain sits upon their grim rocks to watch the dance of
his tribe beneath the yellow lustre of the Moon; the moan of
the waves is the only voice in their silent land; the moan of the

waves is the only requiem of the brave who are buried on the seashore or in the main. But their memory has not failed from among men; the mournful notes which foreboded their fall have given it immortality. For there is a charm in Poetry, which binds the world, and finds its effect in the East and in the West.

"Let me not, like a worm, go by the way." Chaucer.

FINIS.

from

Wide World 7

1822

"Ζητῶ γαρ την αλεθειαν, ὑφ' ἡς ὀυδεις πωποτε εβλαβη."
MARC. ANTONINUS
Boston, July 11, 1822.

Dedication.

I dedicate my book to the Spirit of America. I dedicate it to that living soul, which *doth* exist somewhere beyond the Fancy, to whom the Divinity hath assigned the care of this bright corner of the Universe. I bring my little offering, in this month, which covers the continent with matchless beauty, to the shrine, which distant generations shall load with sacrifice, and distant ages shall admire afar off. With a spark of prophetic devotion, I hasten to hail the Genius, who yet counts the tardy years of childhood, but who is increasing unawares in the twilight, and swelling into strength, until the hour, when he shall break the cloud, to shew his colossal youth, and cover the firmament with the shadow of his wings.

Evening.

It is a slow patriotism which forgets to love till all the world have set the example. If the nations of Europe can find anything to idolize in their ruinous & enslaved institutions, we are content, though we are astonished at their satisfaction. But let them not ignorantly mock at the pride of an American, as if it were misplaced or unfounded, when that freeman is giving an imperfect expression to his sense of his condition. He rejoices in the birthright of a country where the freedom of opinion & action is so perfect that every man enjoys exactly that consideration to which he is entitled, and each mind, as in the bosom of a family, institutes & settles a comparison of its powers with those of its fellow, & quietly takes that stand which nature intended for it. He points to his native land as the only one where freedom has not degenerated to licentiousness; . . in

whose well ordered districts education & intelligence dwell
with good morals; whose rich estates peacefully descend from
sire to son, without the shadow of an interference from private
violence or public tyranny; whose offices of trust and seats of
science are filled by minds of republican strength & elegant accomplishments.* Xenophon and Thucydides would have
thought it a theme, better worthy of their powers, than Persia
or Greece; and her Revolution would furnish Plutarch with a
list of heroes. If the Constitution of the United States outlives
a century, it will be matter of deep congratulation to the
human race; for the Utopian dreams which visionaries have
pursued and sages exploded, will find their beautiful theories
rivalled & outdone by the reality, which it has pleased God to
bestow upon United America.

—

"Judgement is like a clock or watch where the most
ordinary machine is sufficient to tell the hours; but the
most elaborate alone can point out the minutes & seconds and distinguish the smallest differences of time."
Fontenelle.

—

When I was a lad—said the bearded islander—we had commonly a kind of vast musical apparatus in the Pacific islands
which must appear as fabulous to you as it proved fatal to us.
On the banks of the rivers there were abundance of Siphar
Trees which consist of vast trunks perforated by a multitude of
natural tubes without having any external verdure. When the
roots of these were connected with the waters of the river the
water was instantly sucked up by some of the tubes and discharged again by others and when properly echoed the operation attended by the most beautiful musical sounds in the
world. My countrymen built their churches to the Great Zoa
upon the margin of the water and enclosed a suitable number
of these trees, hoping to entertain the ears of the god with this
sweet harmony. Finding however by experience that the more
water the pipes drew the more rich and various were the
sounds of the Organ, they constructed a very large temple

*Such an one died yesterday—Professor Frisbie will hardly be supplied by
any man in the community.

with high walls of clay and stone to make the echoes very
complete, and enclosed a hundred Siphars. When the edifice
was complete six thousand people assembled to hear the long
expected song. After they had waited a long time and the
waters of the river were beginning to rise, the Instrument suddenly began to emit the finest notes imaginable. Through
some of the broader pipes the water rushed with the voice of
thunder, and through others with the sweetness of one of your
lutes. In a short time the effect of the music was such that it
seemed to have made all the hearers mad. They laughed and
wept alternately and began to dance and such was their delight
that they did not percieve the disaster which had befallen their
Organ. Owing to the unusual swell of the River and to some
unaccountable irregularity in the ducts the pipes began to discharge their contents within the chapel. In a short time the evil
became but too apparent, for the water rose in spouts from the
top of the larger ducts and fell upon the multitudes within.
Meantime the Music swelled louder and louder, and every
note was more ravishing than the last. The inconvenience of
the falling water which drenched them, was entirely forgotten
until finally the whole host of pipes discharged every one a volume of water upon the charmed congregation. The faster
poured the water the sweeter grew the music and the floor
being covered with the torrent the people began to float upon
it with intolerable extacies. Finally the whole Multitude swam
about in this deluge holding up their heads with open mouths
and ears as if to swallow the melody whereby they swallowed
much water. Many hundreds were immediately drowned and
the enormous pipes as they emptied the river swelled their harmony to such perfection that the ear could no longer bear it
and they who escaped the drowning died of the exquisite music.
Thenceforward there was no more use of the Siphar trees in
the Pacific islands.

Thursday Evg.

—

Saturday Evening, Nov. 2, 1822.
My adventurous and superficial pen has not hesitated to advance thus far upon these old but sublime foundations of our
faith; and thus without adding a straw to the weight of evidence
or making the smallest discovery, it has still served to elevate

somewhat my own notions by bringing me within prospect of
the labours of the sages. After the primitive apostles, I apprehend that Christianity is indebted to those who have established
the grounds upon which it rests; to Clarke, Butler, and Paley;
to Sherlock, and to the incomparable Newton. And when it
shall please my wayward imagination to suffer me to go drink
of these chrystal fountains; or when my better judgement shall
have at last triumphed over the daemon Imagination, and shall
itself conduct me thither,—I shall be proud and glad of the
privilege. For the present, I must be content to make myself
wiser as I may, by the same loose speculations upon divine
themes.

———

I have come to the close of the sheets which I dedicated to
the Genius of America, and notice that I have devoted nothing
in my book to any peculiar topics which concern my country.
But is not every effort that her sons make to advance the intellectual interests of the world, and every new thought which is
struck out from the mines of religion & morality—a forward
step in the path of her greatness? Peace be with her pro-
gressing greatness,—and prosperity crown her giant minds. A
victory is achieved today for one,* whose name perchance is
written highest in the volume of futurity.
Boston, November 4th, 1822.

CONCLUSION

*Webster was chosen representative to Congress by a majority of 1078 votes
this morning.

from
Wide World 8
1822

Boston, November 6, 1822.

DEDICATION.

To glory which is departed, to majesty which hath ceased, to intellect which is quenched—I bring no homage,—no, not a grain of gold. For why seek to contradict the voice of Nature and of God, which saith over them, "It is finished," by wasting our imaginations upon the deaf ear of the dead? Turn rather to the mighty multitude, the thunder of whose footsteps shakes now the earth; whose faces are flushed by the blood of life; whose eye is enlightened by a living soul. Is there none in this countless assembly who hath a claim on the reverence of the sons of Minerva?

I have chosen one from the throng. Upon his brow have the Muses hung no garland. His name hath never been named in the halls of Fashion, or the palaces of State; but I saw Prophecy drop the knee before him, and I hastened to pay the tribute of a page.

In my dreams, I departed to distant climes and to different periods and my fancy presented before me many extraordinary societies, and many old and curious institutions. I sat on the margin of the river of Golden Sands when the thirsty leopard came thither to drink. It was just dawn, and the shades were chased rapidly from the Eastern firmament by the golden magnificence of day. As I contemplated the brilliant spectacle of an African morning I thought on those sages of this storied land who instructed the infancy of the world. Meanwhile the sun arose and cast a full light over a vast and remarkable landscape. About the river, the country was green and its bed reflected the sunbeams from pebbles and gold. Far around was an ample plain with a soil of yellow sand, glittering everywhere with dew and interspersed with portions of forest, which extended into

54

the plain, from the mountains which surrounded this wide Amphitheatre. The distant roar of lions ceased to be heard, and I saw the leopard bathing his spotted limbs and swimming towards the woods which skirted the water. But his course was stopped; an arrow from the wood pierced his head, and he floated lifeless ashore. I looked then to see whence the slayer should have come, and beheld not far off a little village of huts built of canes. Presently I saw a band of families come out from their habitations; and these naked men, women, and children sung a hymn to the sun and came merrily down to the river with nets in their hands to fish. And a crimson bird with a yellow crest flew over their heads as they went, and lighted on a rock in the midst of the river and sung pleasantly to the savages while he brushed his feathers in the stream. The boys plunged into the river and swam toward the rock. But upon a sudden I saw many men dressed in foreign garb run out from the wood where the leopard had been killed; and these surrounded the fishers, and bound them with cords, and hastily carried them to their boats, which lay concealed behind the trees. So they sailed down the stream, talking aloud and laughing as they went; but they that were bound, gnashed their teeth and uttered so piteous a howl that I thought it were a mercy if the river had swallowed them.

In my dream, I launched my skiff to follow the boats and redeem the captives. They went in ships to other lands and I could never reach them albeit I came near enough to hear the piercing cry of the chained victims, which was louder than the noise of the Ocean. In the nations to which they were brought they were sold for a price and compelled to labour all the day long and scourged with whips until they fell dead in the fields, and found rest in the grave.

Canst thou ponder the vision, and shew why Providence suffers the land of its richest productions to be thus defiled? Do human bodies lodge immortal souls,—and is this tortured life of bondage and tears a fit education for the bright ages of heaven and the commerce of angels? Is man the Image of his Maker,—and shall this fettered & broken frame, this marred and brutalized soul become perfect as He is perfect? This slave hath eat the bread of captivity and drank the waters of bitterness and cursed the light of the Sun as it dawned on his bed of straw, and worked hard and suffered long while never an idea of God hath kindled in his mind from the hour of his birth to the hour of his death; and yet thou sayest that a merciful Lord made man in his benevolence to live and enjoy; to take pleasure in His works and worship him forever. Confess that there are secrets in that Providence, which no human eye can penetrate, which darken the prospect of Faith, and teach us the weakness of our Philosophy.

Nov. 8.

At least we may look farther than to the simple fact and perhaps aid our faith by freer speculation. I believe that nobody now regards the maxim 'that all men are born equal,' as any thing more than a convenient hypothesis or an extravagant declamation. For the reverse is true,—that all men are born unequal in personal powers and in those essential circumstances, of time, parentage, country, fortune. The least knowledge of the natural history of man adds another important particular to these; namely, what class of men he belongs to— European, Moor, Tartar, African? Because Nature has plainly assigned different degrees of intellect to these different races, and the barriers between are insurmountable.

This inequality is an indication of the design of Providence that some should lead, and some should serve. For when an effect invariably takes place from causes which Heaven established, we surely say with safety, that Providence designed that result.

Throughout Society there is therefore not only the direct and acknowledged relation of king & subject, master & servant, but a secret dependence quite as universal, of one man upon another, which sways habits, opinions, conduct. This prevails to an infinite extent and however humbling the analogy, it is nevertheless true, that the same pleasure and confidence which the dog and horse feel when they rely upon the superior intelligence of man is felt by the lower parts of our own species with reference to the higher.

Now with these concessions the question comes to this: whether this known and admitted assumption of power by one part of mankind over the other, can ever be pushed to the extent of total possession, and that, without the will of the slave?

It can hardly be said that the whole difference of *the will*, divides the *natural* servitude of which we have spoken from the forced servitude of 'Slavery.' For it is not voluntary, on my part, that I am born a subject; contrariwise, if my opinion had been consulted, it is ten to one I should have been the Great Mogul. The circumstances in which every man finds himself he owes to fortune and not to himself. And those men who happen to be born in the lowest caste in India, suffer much more perhaps than the kidnapped African with no other difference in their lot than this, that God made the one wretched and man, the other. Except that there is a dignity in suffering from the ordinances of Supreme power, which is not at all common to the other class—one lot is as little enviable as the other.

When all this is admitted, the question may still remain entirely independent and untouched—apart from the consideration of slavery as agreeable or contradictory to the analogies of nature—whether any individual has a right to deprive any other individual of freedom without his consent; or whether he may continue to withold the freedom which another hath taken away?

Upon the first question 'whether one man may forcibly take away the freedom of another,' the weakness and incapacity of Africans would seem to have no bearing; though it may affect the second. Still it may be advanced that the beasts of the field are all evidently subjected to the dominion of man, and, with the single restriction of the laws of humanity, are left entirely at his will. And why are they, and how do we acquire this declaration of heaven? Manifestly from a view of the perfect adaptation of these animals to the necessities of man and of the advantage which many of them find in leaving the forest for the barnyard. If they had *reason*, their strength would be so far superior to ours, that, besides our inability to use them, it would be inconsistent with nature. So that these three circumstances are the foundation of our dominion; viz. their want of reason; their adaptation to our wants; and their own advantage, (when domesticated.) But these three circumstances may very well apply to the condition of the Blacks and it may be hard to tell exactly where the difference lies. Is it in *Reason*? If we speak in general of the two classes Man and Beast, we say that they are separated by the distinction of Reason, and the want of it; and the line of this distinction is very broad. But if we abandon this generalization, and compare the classes of one with the classes of the other we shall find our boundary line growing narrower and narrower and individuals of one species approaching individuals of the other, until the limits become finally lost in the mingling of the classes.

It can hardly be true I think that the difference lies in the attribute of Reason; I saw ten, twenty, a hundred large lipped, lowbrowed black men in the streets who, except in the mere matter of language, did not exceed the sagacity of the elephant. Now is it true that these were created superior to this wise animal, and designed to controul it? And in comparison with the highest orders of men, the Africans will stand so low as to make the difference which subsists between themselves & the sagacious beasts inconsiderable. It follows from this, that this is a distinction which cannot be much insisted on.

And if not this, what is the preeminence? Is it in the upright form, and countenance raised to heaven,—fitted for command? But in this respect also the African fails. The Monkey resembles Man, and the African degenerates to a likeness of the beast. And here likewise I apprehend we shall find as much difference between the head of Plato & the head of the lowest African, as between this last and the highest species of Ape.

If therefore the distinction between the beasts and the Africans is found neither in Reason nor in figure i.e. neither in mind or body—where then is the ground of that distinction? is it not rather a mere name & prejudice and are not they an upper order of inferior animals?

Moreover if we pursue a revolting subject to its greatest lengths we should find that in all those three circumstances which are the foundations of our dominion over the beasts, very much may be said to apply them to the African species; even in the last, viz. the advantage which they derive from our care; for the slaveholders violently assert, that their slaves are happier than the freedmen of their class; and the slaves refuse oftentimes the offer of their freedom. Nor is this owing merely to the barbarity which has placed them out of the power of attaining a competence by themselves. For it is true that many a slave under the warm roof of a humane master with easy labours and regular subsistence enjoys more happiness than his naked brethren parched with thirst on a burning sand or endangered in the crying wildernesses of their native land.

This is all that is offered *in behalf* of slavery; we shall next attempt to knock down the hydra. Nov. 14.

———

Saturday Evening, Nov. 23d.

The hours of social intercourse, of gratified hope, of the festive board, have just now yielded to quieter pleasures of the closet and the pen. This tender flesh is warmly clad, the blood leaps in the vessels of life, Health and Hope write their results on the passing moment,—and these things make the *pleasure* of a mortal bodily mental being. There are in the world at this moment an hundred million men whose history today may match with mine, not counting the numberless ones whose day was happier; there are also in existence here a countless crowd of inferior animals who have had their lesser cup filled full with pleasure. The sunny lakes reflect the noonday beams from the glittering tribes which cover its bottom, rapid as thought in their buoyant motions, leaping with the elasticity and gladness of life. The boundless Ocean supports in its noisy waves its own great population,—the beautiful dolphin, the enormous whale and huge sea-monsters of a thousand families and a thousand uncouth gambols dash through its mighty domain in the fulness of sensual enjoyment. The air is fanned by innumerable wings, the green woods are vocal with the song, of the insect and the bird; the beasts of the field fill all the lands untenanted by man, and beneath the sod the mole and the worm take their pleasure. All this vast mass of animated matter is moving and basking under the broad orb of the Sun,—is drinking in the sweetness of the air, is feeding on the fruits of nature,—is pleased with life, and loth to lose it. All this pleasure flows from a source. That source is the Benevolence of God.

This is the first superficial glance at the economy of the world and necessarily leaves out a thousand circumstances. Let us take a closer view, and begin with the human mind. I find within me a motley array of feelings that have no connection with my clayey frame and I call them my *mind*. Every day of my life, this mind draws a thousand curious conclusions from the different things which it beholds. With a wanton variety which tires of sameness it throws all its thoughts into innumerable lights and changes the fantastic scene by varying its own operations upon it; by combining & separating, by comparing and judging, by remembering and inventing all things. Every one of these little changes within, produces a pleasure; the pleasure of power or of sight. But besides the mere fact that the mind acts, there is a most rich variety in thought, and I grossly undervalue the gift I possess if I limit its capacity to the puny round of every day's sensations. It is a ticket of admission to another world of ineffable grandeur—to unknown orders of things which are as *real* as they are stupendous. As soon as it has advanced a little in life it opens its eye to thoughts which tax its whole power, and delight it by their greatness and novelty. These suggest kindred conceptions which give birth to others and thus draw the mind on in a path which it percieves is interminable, and is of interminable joy. To this high favoured intellect is added an intuition that it can never end and that with its choice it can go forward to take the boon of immortal Happiness. These are causes and states of pleasure which no reason can deny. But this is the true history of all the individuals of the mighty nations that breathe today. These point also to a Source—which is the Benevolence of God.

But a groan of the dying, a cry of torture from the diseased, the sob of the mourner, answer to this thanksgiving of human nature and produce a discord in our Anthem of praise. If God is good, why are any of his creatures unhappy?

———

To establish by whatever specious argumentation the perfect expediency of the worst institution on earth is *prima facie* an assault upon Reason and Common sense. No ingenious sophistry can ever reconcile the unperverted mind to the pardon of *Slavery*, nothing but tremendous familiarity, and the bias of private *interest*. Under the influence of better arguments than can be offered in support of Slavery, we should sustain our tranquillity by the confidence that no surrender of our opinion is ever demanded and that we are only required to discover the lurking fallacy which the disputant acknowledges to exist. It is an old dispute which is not now and never will be totally at rest, whether the human mind be or be not a free agent. And the assertor of either side must be scandalized by the bare naming of the theory that man may impose servitude on his brother. For if he is himself free, and it offends the attributes of God to have him otherwise, it is manifestly a bold stroke of impiety to wrest the same liberty from his fellow. And if he is not free, then this inhuman barbarity ascends to derive its origin from the author of all necessity.

A creature who is bound by his hopes of salvation to imitate the benevolence of better beings, and to do all the kindness in his power, fastens manacles on his fellow with an ill grace.

A creature who holds a little lease of life upon the arbitrary tenure of God's good pleasure improves his moment strangely by abusing God's best works, his own peers.

—

The ardour of my college friendship for Gay is nearly extinct, and it is with difficulty that I can now recall those sensations of vivid pleasure which his presence was wont to waken spontaneously, for a period of more than two years. To be so agreeably excited by the features of an individual personally unknown to me, and for so long a time, was surely a curious incident in the history of so cold a being, and well worth a second thought. At the very beginning of our singular acquaintance, I noticed the circumstance in my Wideworld, with an expression of curiosity with regard to the effect which time would have upon those feelings. To this day, our glance at meeting, is not that of indifferent persons, and were he not so thoroughly buried in his martial cares, I might still entertain the hope of departed hours. Probably the abatement of my solitary enthusiasm is owing to the discouraging reports which I have gathered of his pursuits and character, so entirely inconsistent with the indications of his face. But it were much better that our connexion should stop, and pass off, as it now will, than to have had it formed, and then broken by the late discovery of insurmountable barriers to friendship. From the first, I preferred to preserve the terms which kept alive so much sentiment rather than a more familiar intercourse which I feared would end in indifference. Nov. 29th, 1822.

Pish

—

Dec. 21.

There is everything in America's favour, to one who puts faith in those proverbial prophecies of the Westward progress of the Car of Empire. Though there may be no more barbarians left to overrun Europe & extinguish forever the memory of its greatness yet its rotten states like Spain may come to their decline by the festering & inveteracy of the faults of government. Aloof from the contagion during the long progress of their decline America hath ample interval to lay deep & solid foundations for the greatness of the New World. And along the shores of the South Continent, to which the dregs & corruption of European society had been unfortunately transplanted, the fierceness of the present conflict for independence, will, no doubt, act, as a powerful remedy to the disease, by stirring up the slumbering spirits of those indolent zones to a consciousness of their power & destiny. Here then, new Romes are growing, & the Genius of man is brooding over the wide boundaries of infant empires, where yet is to be drunk the intoxicating draughts of honour & renown; here are to be played over again the bloody games of human ambition, bigotry, & revenge and the stupendous Drama of the passions to be repeated. Other Cleopatras shall seduce, Alexanders fight, and Caesars die. The pillars of social strength which we occupy ourselves in founding thus firmly to endure to future ages as the monuments of the wisdom of this, are to be shaken on their foundations with convulsions proportioned to their adamantine strength. The time is come, the hour is struck; already the actors in this immense & tremendous scene have begun to assemble. The doors of life in our mountain-land are opened, and the vast swarm of population is crowding in, bearing in their hands the burden of Sorrow & Sin, of glory & science, which are to be mingled in their future fates. In the events & interests of these empires, the old tales of history & the fortunes of departed nations shall be thoroughly forgotten & the name of Rome or Britain fall seldom on the ear.

In that event, when the glory of Plato of Greece, of Cicero of R., & of Shakspeare of E. shall have died, who are they that are to write their names where all time shall read them, & their words be the oracle of millions? Let those who would pluck the lot of Immortality from Fate's Urn, look well to the future prospects of America.

Friday Evg., Dec. 21, 1822.

Whilst the fat fool prates nonsense to the pack
Filled with the folly echo blabs it back.

Wide World 9

Christmas, Dec. 25. ⸺

If, (as saith Voltaire) all that is related of Alfred the Great be true, I know not the man that ever lived, more worthy of the gratitude of posterity. I hope the reservation means nothing. There is not one incredible assertion made either of his abilities, his character, or his actions. Besides it was not an age, nor were Saxon monks the men, to invent and adorn another Cyropaedia. Sharon Turner, an ambitious flashing writer, & elsewhere a loon, hath done well by Alfred. His praise rests not upon monkish eulogy or vague tradition, but upon *facts*. Critics may quarrel upon the reputed foundation of Oxford; it is not at all necessary to his fame. In the first place he had the smartest man of his age for his enemy, with whom he repeatedly, constantly, & vigorously fought until he finally drove him utterly from the kingdom. *Hastings*, in despair, retired to France, & obtained some little settlement from the king, where he obscurely died. The fact, that after his entire loss of every acre of England & every man of his armies he should be able to reproduce *ab initio* his cause & kingdom, equals the Return of Bonaparte. The skilful policy of domesticating the conquered Danes and thus lulling the opposition of those myriads which swarmed in Northumbria, and at the same time creating upon his shores a formidable bulwark to the future invasions of the sea-kings, by giving their brothers a stake in the commonwealth to defend;—this policy was not unworthy of the profound art of Augustus Caesar. The admirable military genius discovered in his position between the two divisions of Hastings' Northmen so as to menace at the same time both armies & to separate both from the East Anglians, (too ready to join the aggressions of their countrymen,) the vigilance of his patrolling bands & the strict adherence to measures of *defence* alone,—indicate his masterly generalship. An instance is like-

wise recorded of military skill which discovers an active invention. When Hastings went up with his ships the River Lea, Alfred dug three new channels below, & thus drew off so much
water as to leave the ships aground. He built a castle on either
bank to protect his works & the Northmen were obliged to
abandon their ships and escape as they best might from their
strongholds in Essex. His enthusiastic attachment to learning
(the more laudable as it was solitary,) his care of courts & ministers of justice, his zealous & useful piety, all these combined
in so extraordinary a manner with his warlike talents, are the
foundation of his surpassing fame, of his title to the surname
of Great. I am anxious to understand fully the merits & honesty of the records in which he is transmitted to us. Asser, his
friend & instructer, is the chief source. Turner says nothing
about his authenticity.

There is a book which Alfred translates containing one of
the most singular funeral ceremonies I ever met with. The
book is the narration of the voyage of Wulfstan towards the
east of the Baltic. The custom among those of "the Eastland"
is that when a man dieth his body is preserved one, two, or
even six months according to the wealth of the deceased, un-
burnt. For the Eastmen have a mode of producing cold so as
to prevent the body from becoming foul. All the time that the
body lieth within, the wealth of the deceased furnishes the rev-
elry of his kinsmen without. "Then the same day that they
chuse to bear them to the pile his property that remains after
this drink & play is divided into five or six parts, sometimes
more as the proportion of his wealth admits. They lay these
along a mile apart; the greatest portion *from* the town, then
another, then a third till it be all laid at one mile asunder; and
the least part shall be nearest to the town where the dead man
lieth. Then shall be collected all the men that have the swiftest
horses in the land for the way of 5 miles or 6, from the property. Then run they all together to the property. Then cometh
the man that hath the swiftest horse to the first portion & to
the greatest & so on, one after another, till it be all taken away;
he taketh the least who is nearest the town & runs to it: then
each rides away with his prize and may have it all. And because
of this the swift horse is inconceivably dear." This is Turner's
translation from Alfred.—

Dec. 26th, 1822.

I have heard this evening & shall elsewhere record Prof. Everett's lecture upon Eleusinian mysteries, Dodona, & St Sophia's temple. The modes of response in the Dodonean Groves were full of poetical beauty; by bells, by fountains, by the wind in the oaks, & by doves; to interpret these signs was the peculiar faculty & prerogative of the priests. For two thousand years the celebrity of the Mysteries continued, originating in a natural & simple harvest home & proceeding to august ceremonies in which sound moral truths were no doubt always inculcated & the best views though imperfect which antiquity entertained of God & his providence. Just in proportion as Christianity advanced, the Eleusinian Mysteries declined in splendour & importance, until they were finally suppressed by Theodosius in 404 A.D. Though the Lecture contained nothing original, & no very remarkable views, yet it was an account of antiquities bearing everywhere that "fine Roman hand" & presented in the inimitable style of *our Cicero.* "Bigotry & Philosophy are the opposite poles of the judgement & the scepticism of Hume, & Gibbon is as different as the superstition of the Catholic from the freedom of the Protestant." Pr. E.

—

Saturday Ev.g., January 11th.

My bosom's lord sits lightly on his throne; I cannot distinctly discern the cause; tomorrow he will sit heavily there; and after a few days more, he shall cease to be. The connexions which he nursed with earthly society shall be broken off, and the memory of his individual influence shall be obliterated from human hearts. It may chance that he will resume his thought elsewhere; that while the place from whence he passed forgets him, he shall nourish the fires of a pure ambition in some freer sanctuary than this world holds. It is possible that the infinity of another world may so crowd his conception, as to divest him of that cumberous sense of *self* that weighs him down,— until he lose his individual existence in his efforts for the Universe.

—

"If 20,000 naked Americans were not able to resist the assaults of but 20 well armed Spaniards, I see little possibility for one honest man to defend himself against 20,000 knaves who are all furnished with the defensive arms of worldly prudence & the offensive too of craft & malice." Cowley Essays p. 104. Dangers of company. There is nothing in fable so dark & dreadful but had its first model in the houses & palaces of men. Iniquity, malice, & rage find many homes with the lords of the creation & Devils were not *invented* for our poetry, but were copied from originals among ourselves.

The history of America since the Revolution is meagre because it has been all that time under better government, better circumstances of religious, moral, political, commercial prosperity than any nation ever was before. History will continually grow less interesting as the world grows better. Professor Playfair of Edinburgh, the greatest or one of the greatest men of his time died without a biography for there was no incident in the life of a great & good man worth recording. Nelson & Buonaparte, men of abilities without principle, found four or five biographers apiece.

The true epochs of history should be those successive triumphs which age after age the communities of men have achieved, such as the Reformation, the Revival of letters, the progressive Abolition of the Slave-trade.

Falstaff saith—"It is certain that either wise bearing or ignorant carriage is caught as men take diseases one of another."

All our researches into antiquity look to this ultimate end— of ascertaining the private life of our fellow beings who have occupied the different parts of the globe before us. But these domestic manners are fleeting & leave no trace where they are not themselves transmitted. If we had a series of faithful portraits of private life in Egypt, Assyria, Greece, & Rome we might relinquish without a sigh their national annals. The great passions which move a whole nation, and are made up, it should be remembered, of the passion & action of the individuals & the common sense of mankind are alike everywhere, and these determine the foreign relations & the political counsels of men. But private life hath more delicate varieties, which differ in unlike circumstances; and the barbarian in his tent by the Rhine, the Tartar burrowing in the ground, the Spartan in the humble house of the Republic, the Roman in the luxurious palace of the Emperors, the Chinese in his floating house, & the Englishman in his comfortable tenement fill up the hours of the day with very different thoughts & different actions: and he who enables us to form just estimates & comparisons of all, unfolds an instructive page which we can never hope to see. Exactly to appreciate the weight of influence which these several situations cast upon the love of action & the love of pleasure (Gibbon's two ultimate principles) would be to get well that most useful of all lessons—the knowledge of human nature. Our vague & pompous outlines of history serve but to define in geographical & chronological limits the faint vestiges we possess of former nations. But of what mighty moment is it that we know the precise scene of a Virtue or a Vice? Give us the bare narrative of the *moral* beings engaged, the *moral* feelings concerned & the result—and you have answered all our purpose, all the ultimate design which leads the mind to explore the past. (That is of a speculative mind—apart from all purposes of government and policy*). For the history of nations is but the history of private Virtues & Vices collected in a more splendid field, a wider sky. It would be to little purpose you would show the curious philosopher a mighty forest extending at a distance its thousand majestic trees; a single branch, a stem, a leaf in his hand is of more value to him for all the purposes of science. Even the Eternal Geometer, in the fancy of Leibnitz deduces the past & present condition of the Universe from the examination of the single atom.

———

Tush, he said, thoughts & imaginations! I tell thee, man, that I who have got my bread & fame by informing the world, can write in twenty lines, all the *thoughts* that ever I had; while the imaginations, would fill a thousand fair pages.

*For the purposes of another world, rather than for this.

March 6, 1823.

My brother Edward asks me Whether I have a right to make use of animals? I answer "Yes," and shall attempt to give my reasons. A poor native of Lapland found himself in mid winter destitute of food, of clothing and light, and without even a bow to defend himself from the beasts. In this perplexity he met with a reindeer which he killed & conveyed to his hut. He now found himself supplied with oil to light his lamp, with a warm covering for his body & with wholesome & strengthening food, and with bowstrings withal, whereby he could again procure a similar supply. Does any mind question the innocence of this starving wretch in thus giving life & comfort to a desolate family in that polar corner of the world?—Now there is a whole *nation* of men precisely in this condition, all reduced to the alternative of killing the beasts, or perishing themselves. Let the tender hearted advocate of the brute creation go there, & choose whether he will make the beasts *his* food, or be himself, *theirs.*

Just such a picture may be made of the Arabian & his camel; and of the Northern Islanders & their Whales; in all these instances, the positive law of Necessity asserts our right. But the use of the sheep for clothing, the ox, the horse, & the ass, for beasts of burden is parallel to these, and their necessity though less seen is equally strong. "Increase & Multiply" said the Creator to Man; and caused all the brute creation to pass before him & recieve their names in token of subjection. The use of these enables man to *increase & multiply* a thousand fold more rapidly, than would be practicable if he abstained from their use. Their universal application to our purposes & especially that remarkable adaptation that is observed in many instances of the Animal to the wants of the country in which he is found constitute the grand Argument on this side. (Besides Camel, Whale &c, that were mentioned, I believe the Mule, surest footed animal which walks, is found in the mountains to transverse whose precipices man wants his steady step.)

But it will be said they have rights

—

from

Wide World 10

1823

Boston, March 18, 1823

DEDICATION

When God had made the beasts, & prepared to set over them an intelligent lord, He considered what external faculty he should add to his frame, to be the seal of his superiority. Then He gave him an articulate voice. He gave him an organ exquisitely endowed, which was independent of his grosser parts,—but the minister of his mind & the interpreter of its thoughts. It was designed moreover as a Sceptre of irresistible command, by whose force, the great & wise should still the tumult of the vulgar million, & direct their blind energies to a right operation. The will of Heaven was done, & the morning & evening gales wafted to the Highest, the harmonious accents of Man. But the generations of men lived & died, while yet their expanding powers were constrained by the iron necessities of infant civilization, & they had never, with, perchance, a few solitary exceptions, ascertained the richness of this divine gift. Suddenly, in a corner of Europe, the ripe seeds of Greatness burst into life, & covered the hills & valleys of Greece with the golden harvest. The new capacities & desires which burned in the human breast, demanded a correspondent perfection in *speech*,—to body them forth. Then a voice was heard in the assemblies of men, which sounded like the language of the gods; it rolled like music on the ear, and filled the mind with undefinable longings; it was peremptory as the word of Kings; or mournful as a widow's wailing or enkindling as the martial clarion. That voice men called Eloquence, and he that had it, unlocked their hearts, or turned their actions whithersoever he would. Like sea waves to the shore, like mountain sheep to their shepherd, so men crowded around this commander of their hearts to drink in his accents, & to mould their passions to his will. The contagion of new desires & improvements went abroad,—and tribe after tribe of barbarians uplifted the banner of Refinement. This spirit stirring art was propagated also and although its light sunk often in the socket, it was never put out. Time rolled, & successive ages rapidly developed the mixed & mighty drama of human society, and among the instruments employed therein, this splendid art was often & actively used. And who that has witnessed its strength, and opened every chamber of his soul to the matchless enchanter, does not venerate it as the noblest agent that God works with, in human hearts? My Muse, it is the idol of thy homage and deserves the dedication of thine outpourings.

After two moons I shall have fulfilled twenty years. Amid the fleeting generations of the human race and in the abyss of years I lift my solitary voice unheeded & unknown & complain unto inexorable Time. 'Stop, Destroyer, Overwhelmer, stop one brief moment this uncontrollable career. Ravisher of the creation, suffer me a little space, that I may pluck some spoils, as I pass onward, to be the fruits & monuments of the scenes, through which I have travelled.'—Fool! you implore the deaf torrent to relax the speed of its cataract,

at ille

Labitur et labetur in omne volubilis aevum.

—

Sunday Evg., March 23d, 1823.

A man is made great by a concentration of motive. Bacon might have lived & died a courtier, disgraced & forgotten, but for a fixed resolution at eighteen years old—to reform Science. Milton should have slumbered but for that inspiration to write an epic; Luther, but for his obstinate hatred of Papacy; Newton, but for his perseverance, thro' all obstacles, to identify the fall of his apple & of the moon; (Shakespeare is an outlaw from all systems and would be great in despite of all.) So of inferior men; Peter the Hermit sent men to die in Crusades; Modern Mr Lancaster, a stupid man, fills the world with his schools; only from a concentrated attention to one design. Human power is here of indefinite extent; no one can prescribe the bound beyond which human exertions cannot go with effect. But *times* must be observed, and in great things a man always acts with more effect when the evil is far gone, than when it is nascent. Thus if Luther had preached one or two centuries earlier it might have been vain. For it is with nations as with individuals. A man altogether in the wrong may more easily be convinced than one half right; for when the error is pointed out he is obliged to give up the whole, at once; whereas, the other, is so much the more tenacious of his opinion as he percieves it to be partly right. And a nation may be more violently roused to a reform when the mischief is great & indisputable than when it is concealed & may be denied. In like manner a man with the arts of civilization would be recieved by a nation of savages with admiration & gratitude, while a small positive improvement arising among them would obtain very slowly.— Compare also the fate of Socrates, Galileo, Roger Bacon, who made vast discoveries, with that of Hermit Peter, or the silly Schoolmen lauded to the skies—which may perchance force me to reverse the last sentence about savages.—

—

I have rambled far away from my original thought, still there is a loose unity which binds these reflections together and which leads me back to the dubious theme—myself. One youth among the multitudes of mankind, one grain of sand on the seashore, unknown in the midst of my contemporaries, I am hastening to put on the manly robe. From childhood the names of the great have ever resounded in my ear. And it is impossible that I should be indifferent to the rank which I must take in the innumerable assembly of men, or that I should shut my eyes upon the huge interval which separates me from the minds which I am wont to venerate. Every young man is prone to be misled by the suggestions of his own ill founded ambition which he mistakes for the promptings of a secret Genius, and thence dreams of an unrivalled greatness. More intercourse with the world and closer acquaintance with his own faults wipes out from his fancy every trace of this majestic dream. Time, who is the rough master of the feast, comes to this concieted & highly-placed guest, and saith, 'Friend come down to this lower seat, for thy neighbour is worthier than thou.' Nevertheless it is not Time nor Fate nor the World that is half so much his foe as the demon Indolence within him. A man's enemies are those of his own household. Men sometimes carelessly & sometimes profanely cast off the blame of their insignificance in society, upon God their maker, or upon Circumstance, the god (as they term him) of this world. It is a skilful masquerade which they have vamped up to tickle the sense & to lull them to repose. They thus contrive to lay quietly an oppressive burden upon the Atlantean shoulders of fate. But if a man shall diligently consider what it is which most forcibly impedes the natural greatness of his mind, he will assuredly find that slothful sensual indulgence is the real unbroken barrier, and that when he has overleaped this, God has set no bounds to his progress. The maxim is true to an indefinite extent—"Faber quisque fortunae suae." We boast of our free agency. What is this but to say God has put into our hands the elements of our character, the iron & the brass, the silver & the gold, to choose & to fashion them as we will. But we are afraid of the toil, we bury them in a napkin instead of moulding them into rich & enduring vessels.

This view is by far the most animating to exertion. It speaks life & courage to the soul. Mistrust no more your ability, the rivalry of others, or the final event. Make speed to plan, to execute, to fulfil; forfeit not one moment more in the dalliance of sloth; for the work is vast, the time is short, and Opportunity is a headlong thing which tarries for no man's necessities. Habits of labour are paths to Heaven.—It commands no outward austerities. Do not put ashes on your head, nor sackcloth on your loins nor a belt of iron for your girdle.—But Mortify *the mind*, put on humility & temperance, for ashes, and bind about the soul as with iron. The soul is a fertile soil which will grow rank & to waste if left to itself. If you wish therefore to see it bud out abundantly & bring an harvest richer an hundred, and a thousandfold, bind it, bind it with the restraint of Cultivation. (March 26) It is overgrown with tares & poisons. Suffer no longer this noisome barrenness. Harrow it up with thoughts. Fill it with the joys & wholesome apprehensions of a reasonable being, instead of the indifference of a brute. There are a million loiterers in the moral ways, laughing as they stop to pick flowers of sin or pleasure in the fields;—but their gaiety hangs ill upon a haggard countenance, and they are covered with rags.—Far before them I see a chosen few, clad in shining garments, and pressing eagerly forward with honourable industry. *Make Haste*. Cast off your burden of apologies &

compliances which retard your steps, and flee after them lest they reach their Lord & enter in before you and the door be shut.——

These are the clamours with which conscience pursues & upbraids me—happy if they were undeserved—happiest could they accomplish their end! But the inscrutable future, comes down in darkness and finds us in the thrall of the same old enemies, with all our hopes & fullblown intentions thick on our heads.—For your life, then, for your life! crawl on a few steps farther in the next twelvemonth!

——

June 11.——   Epilogue.

When Memory rakes up her treasures, her ingots of thought, I fear she will seldom recur to the Muse's tenth son; and yet it should have been able to gather & condense something from the wealth of fancy which Nature supplies in the beautiful summer. I have played the Enthusiast with my book in the greenwood, the huntsman with my gun; have sat upon rocks, & mused o'er flood & fell, have indulged the richest indolence of a Poet & am therefore a creditor to Nature for some brilliant & unusual inspiration. But the Goddess is slow of payment—or has forgotten an old bantling. If she was partial once, she is morose now; for Familiarity, (if awful Nature will permit me to use so bold a word,) breeds disgust; & Vinegar is the son of Wine; peradventure I may yet be admitted to the contemplation of her inner magnificence, & her favour may find me, no shrine indeed, but some snug niche, in the temple of Time. 'Tut,' says Fortune—'and if you fail,—it shall never be from lack of vanity.'

Canterbury Sept., 1823.

I have often found cause to complain that my thoughts have an ebb & flow. Whether any laws fix them & what the laws are I cannot ascertain. I have quoted a thousand times the memory of Milton & tried to bind my thinking season to one part of the year or to one sort of weather; to the sweet influence of the Pleiades, or to the summer reign of Lyra. The worst is, that the ebb is certain, long & frequent, while the flow comes transiently & seldom. Once when *vanity* was full fed, it sufficed to keep me at work & to produce some creditable scraps; but alas! it has long been dying of a galloping starvation & the Muse, I fear me, will die too. The dreams of my childhood are all fading away & giving place to some very sober & very disgusting views of a quiet mediocrity of talents & condition— nor does it appear to me that any application of which I am capable, any efforts, any sacrifices could at this moment restore any reasonableness to the familiar expectations of my earlier youth. But who is he that repines? Let him read the song about the linter-goose.

Melons & plums & peaches, eating & drinking & the bugle, all the day long. These are the glorious occupations which engross a proud & thinking being, running his race of preparation for the eternal world. Man is a foolish slave who is busy in forging his own fetters. Sometimes he lifts up his eyes for a moment, admires freedom, & then hammers the rivets of his chain. Who does not believe life to be an illusion when he sees the daily, yearly, livelong inconsistency that men indulge, in thinking so well & doing so ill. Young men, who from time to time, take pleasure in ascertaining their own rights & claims on the universe, who measure with laudable eagerness what portion of good, life is heir to, of the esteem of mankind they may fairly expect to reward their future powers &

virtues—though they resolve fervently & ponder much on the goodness of their intentions, though for sometime their hearts are wrapt & their faces glow with magnanimous hopes & fancied selfdevotion to the cause of God & Man—yet these—when by & bye, the flush has gone from the countenance, & the ordinary temptations of indolence, of sensual gratification, return upon them—are accustomed to forget the noble promises they just now plighted to heaven & their own souls, & the lavish good dispositions of their excited hours. They forget for a long & weary interval that to eat, & to drink, & to lie down in sleep is not the life of man but the life of swine;—that meats & wines & dress are not the real ends of existence, but *thought*, *affection*, & *virtue*, that God is not honoured nor man served by misspent or vacant time. To sit day after day, nay month after month amid the sufferings & cries of barren ignorance & rank depravity—to hear on every side the frightful burden of human lamentation, curses, & fears rising on the winds to heaven, to read by our warm & idle firesides the miserable report of all evil that is done under the sun; & this without a solitary effort of charity, without stirring hand or foot to rescue & save because we are given up to a mean sloth which is accursed of God & good men—is the sort of approbation which we deem fittest to secure our future happiness. We bury in an undefined procrastination, all our obligations. We should be shocked at any formal resignation in words of our hopes of activity in life, while our abominable listlessness amounts to the same. You call the squandered hour—a reverie.—It is, say you, a casual relaxation which nature requires but the real objects of existence will grow dim & dimmer in your sight, until your eyes are shut fast, & you will sleep out life in this desperate reverie—the purposes for which you live unsought, unfound.

—

Sunday, Oct.   I heard Dr Channing deliver a discourse upon Revelation as standing in comparison with Nature. I have heard no sermon approaching in excellence to this, since the Dudleian Lecture. The language was a transparent medium, conveying with the utmost distinctness, the pictures in his mind, to the minds of the hearers. He considered God's word to be the only expounder of his works, & that Nature had always been found insufficient to teach men the great doctrines which Revelation inculcated. Astronomy had in one or two ways an unhappy tendency. An universe of matter in which Deity would display his power & greatness must be of infinite extent & complicate relations and of course too vast to be measured by the eye & understanding of man. Hence errors. Astron. reveals to us infinite number of worlds like our own accommodated for the residence of such beings as we of gross matter. But to kindle our piety & urge our faith, we do not want such a world as this but a purer, a world of morals & of spirits. La Place has written in the mountain album of Switzerland his avowal of Atheism. Newton had a better master than Suns & Stars.—He learned of heaven ere he philosophized. & after travelling through mazes of the universe he returned to bow his laurelled head at the feet of Jesus of Nazareth. Dr C. regarded Revelation as much a part of the order of things as any other event. It would have been wise to have made an abstract of the Discourse immediately.

O keep the current of thy spirits even;
If it be ruffled by too full a flood,—
'Tis turbid; or, if drained, goes dry. The mind,
In either case, obeys the animal pulse,
And weeps the loss of unreturning time.

Mr Hume's Essay upon Necessary Connexion proves that Events are conjoined, and not connected; that, we have no knowledge but from Experience. We have no Experience of a Creator & therefore know of none. The constant appeal is to our feelings from the glozed lies of the deciever but one would feel safer & prouder to see the victorious answer to these calumnies upon our nature set down in impregnable propositions.

Pride carves rich emblems on its seals
And slights the throng that dogs its heels
Fair vanity hath bells on cap & shoes
And eyes his moving shadow as he goes.

We put up with time & chance because it costs too great an effort to subdue them to our wills, and minds that feel an embryo greatness stirring within them let it die for want of nourishment. Plans that only want maturity, ideas that only need

expansion to lead the thinker on to a far nobler being than
now he dreams of; good resolutions whose dawning was like
the birth of Gods in their benevolent promise, sudden throbs
of charity & impulses to goodness that spake most auspicious
omens to humanity are suffered to languish & blight in hopeless barreness. And is it supposed, is it to be suggested that this
is a vague & groundless alarm? I would to God it were! I
would to God that none of the good purposes of his children
upon earth failed of their accomplishment; that every humane
design; every heart bleeding for the sorrows of men; every liberal feeling which would pardon their faults or relieve their
woes—might go on to the fine ultimate issues which it contemplated. The melancholy truth is that there are ten thousand abortive to one successful accomplishment. Who does
not know, who has not felt that unnumbered good purposes
spring up in the clean & strong soil of the youthful breast, until Sloth gives a relaxing fatness to the ground, which kills the
growth. I call every man to witness whatever be his lot, be he
the minion of fortune or the child of sorrow, Pagan or Christian, bond or free, that if he be sinful his hands have not always
ministered to his designs, that virtue is not a name unknown
to his ears or overlooked in his thoughts. No there is an impulse to do good continually urging us, an eternal illumination
upon virtuous deeds that attracts the beholder. His heart ap-
plauds; it is his hands that fail. It strikes my mind as a beautiful
& adorable truth that the good spirit who made all things is
daily working in this lower sphere by presenting to ten thousand thousand minds images & occasions of goodness, striving
as he can, without infringing their freedom to bind them to
the right interest, inviting them with benignant importunity
to thought & duty, & imparting a bias which if obeyed will
make the heart burn with gratitude. The more we magnify this
benevolence the more depraved & besotted is man's negligence or frowardness. He averts his sullen eye from all the
riches to which his nature made him heir.——

It will not be a very wide digression from the somewhat
desultory train of thoughts which I have strung together, if I
here consider a notorious fact which is strange as it is common. I mean the coldness & poverty of our views of *heaven* &,

what is the result of this, the meagreness & hollow declamation of all uninspired descriptions of the same.

It is not a characteristic of our joys that the hope of them
should be languid, & the consequent desires of them, cold.
Nature has not iced our passions & affections in their prospect
of gratification. In the perfectly confident hope of future indulgence, the labourer toils. The hope of the lover is not apathy. Political & literary ambition are not apathy. Hope is so
strong that on it is founded the uninterrupted sedulous labour
of many years. Imagine it removed from the human breast &
see how Society will sink, how the strong bands of order & improvement will be relaxed, & what a deathlike stillness would
come over the restless energies that now move the world. The
scholar will extinguish his midnight lamp, the merchant will
furl his white sails & bid them seek the deep no more. The
anxious patriot who stood out for his country to the last, &
devised in the last beleaguered citadel, profound schemes of
deliverance & aggrandizement, will sheath his sword & blot
his fame. Remove hope, & the world becomes a blank &
rotteness. Human breasts lose their indestructible impulse to
improve that now triumphs over time & disappointment &
altered fortunes: the human eye loses its fire; the voice its eloquent tones of joy & animation; the hand its cunning, & the
heart its feeling. Kill this bright lord of the bosom's throne
& man's imagination will leave going forward with him &
decking the future with gay colours, & will go out instead into
the melancholy past, into the forlorn history of old time, to
walk among comfortless graves, into the infamous scenes of
human guilt, into fields whose grass is crimsoned with blood.
Distempered fancy will give a ghastly life to darkness & curdle
the blood with the apparition of a thousand fell spectres. If the
past were presented to our hearts in all its dark reality relieved
by no contrasted Hope for the future, men would rebel in
spirit against the Providence which placed them here & had
darkened their lot with such deep & damning shades. Why
does omnipotence, they would murmur, send the poor slaves
of its power into this wide prisonhouse to run the selfsame
round of madness & sorrow that the long train of generations have run already; to bear the same burden of curses &

infirmities: to be disfigured by the same angry passions; to be crushed by the same unrelenting course of events; to be thrown & abandoned without friend or strength upon the same tremendous theatre amidst the play of human passions, a lamb before the lions, a prey to the fighting Kings & Nimrods of the earth, to be eaten up by their rage, or tortured by their Caprice? — Indeed the most benevolent philanthropist when in sober thought he reverts his eye to the solemn annals of departed Time must sometimes shudder at the suspicion that if the delusions of Hope were dispelled Futurity might be modelled on this pattern. He sees how a wretch's extravagant ambition in one hour strowed in ashes cities that had struggled up into civilization & magnificence by the tardy & toilsome efforts of many hundred years; how nations are swallowed in one day; how vice mounts the throne & virtue retires to dungeons: how mind falls before barbarism; how God is forgotten whilst men pass thro' fire to Baal.

If Hope be the beautifier that out of such darkness creates such light; it must needs have potent energy. Now why does it limit its action to earth? If it brightens all the years of life as they rise in dim futurity, why cannot its rays reach over the abyss & illuminate the country beyond? Why does Youth bound with rapture in the prospect of the emancipation & strength of manhood; and why does the youth of the Soul not rejoice in the hope of *her* deliverance from this mortal coil, & the shackles of a fleshly appetite? Is there anything intrinsically disagreeable in those circumstances which divines describe as taking place at death in the man who has done well & worthily here? Can it be a distressing summons, which calls us to strip off what we call vile incumbrances? to get rid of the clods that shut in the soul & bar it from better society; that substitute the dim & obscure language of sensations, for the acquaintance with real beings; that subject it to the pollution of gross passions; to the poor temptations of Sense, & the uncomfortable agitations of little affairs? Or is it that we are to part with life, that is, with the trivial succession of wants, inconveniences, & petty actions that occur every day; with the wretched & unceasing care of the body? for it is these drawbacks upon life & not life itself we are to lose. It can hardly be, that men are so loath to lose things of which they complain so strenuously &

so often. And yet it must be *here*, that the fear rankles; there must needs be some deprivation of body the dread of which freezes in their spring the affections that should flow towards heaven. For I cannot bring myself to imagine that they are afraid of hurt from the other parts of that glorified state. The other parts are a nearer connexion with Deity; an unlimited & increasing capacity of knowledge; pure & fervent affections; & the rich gratification of all our desires. A wise man who does not confine his attention to the words in which these promises are enumerated but recalls incessantly these thoughts, as things having a *real existence*, to his mind, will soon learn to give them a preference so decided as to go nigh to banish all other thoughts. All men, indeed, who could be induced to give these hopes their just weight (which is infinite,) would find the tone of all their associations rapidly changed. The difficulty is to rouse them from resting in the terms to an intense attention to the things, & this, though marvellous easy in its distant appearance is the hardest labour appointed to the human mind. Men's lives have been devoted sedulously to this attempt. Writing & preaching & example have been exhausted in the cause. The most mighty, the almost supernatural impulses of the intellect have been applied to it. The blood of martyrdom has been spilled in its behalf. And all this—to make men pass over words to things. But the invincible repugnance which the mind has shewn is that one element which neutralizes the good qualities & quenches the heaven directed ardour of all the rest. There is a Vis inertiae of mind as well as of matter, an inherent almost uneradicable indolence in human nature which pauses at the threshold & is immoveably passive, where it is of the last importance that it should go on, & where delay is tremendous peril. The dull ear hears that Eternity is a solemn name & that vast meaning is wrapped up in it; & it is feared that the developement will cost much thought & action, possibly much pain, & is therefore most unfriendly to that darling repose which is to be soothed at every hazard. So the dream is indulged, these obscure notions of heaven are repeated with plausible terms of respect, (as an apology to the world & to the inward monitor,) & the barrier which separates their awful import from the understanding & the heart is never overleaped.

Dec. 13, 1823. Edinburgh Rev has a fine eulogy of Newton &
Dr Black &c in the first article of the 3d Vol. No. XXXVI contains a review of Mrs. Grant on Highlanders, and, in it, good
thoughts upon the progress of *manners*. 'A gentleman's character is a compound of obligingness & self esteem.' The same
volume reviews Alison & gives an excellent condensed view of
his theory. The charm of all these discussions is only a fine luxury, producing scarce any good, unless that of substituting a
pure pleasure for impure. Occasionally this reading helps one's
conversation; but seldom. The reason & whole mind is not
forwarded by it, as by *history*. The good in life that seems to be
most *real*, is not found in reading, but in those successive triumphs a man achieves over habits of moral or intellectual indolence, or over an ungenerous spirit and mean propensities.

There is danger of a *poetical* religion from the tendencies of
the age. There is a celebrated passage in the prose works of the
great Christian bard, which is precious to the admirers of Milton. I refer to the II Book of Reason of Ch. Government, &c.
There is probably no young man who could read that eloquent chapter, without feeling his heart warm to the love of
virtue & greatness & without making fervent resolutions that
his age should be made better, because he had lived. Yet these
resolutions, unless diligently nourished by prayer & expanded
into action by intense study will be presently lost in the host of
worldly cares. But they leave one fruit, that may be poisonous;
they leave a self complacency arising from having thought so
nobly for a moment, which leads the self deciever to believe
himself better than other men.

from
Walk to the Connecticut
1823

Framingham, Aug. 22d, 1823.
Friday Noon
Warren's Hotel—

After a delightful walk of 20 miles I reached this inn before Noon, and in the near recollection of my promenade through Roxbury, Newton, Needham, Natick, do recommend the same, particularly as far as the Lower Falls in Newton, to my friends who are fond of fine scenery.

To this stage of mine errantry no adventure has befallen me; no, not the meeting with a mouse. I both thought & talked a little with myself on the way, and gathered up & watered such sprigs of poetry as I feared had wilted in my memory. I thought how History has a twofold effect, viz intellectual pleasure & moral pain. And in the midst of a beautiful country I thought how monotonous & uniform is Nature; but I found now as ever that maugre all the flights of the sacred Muse, the profane solicitudes of the flesh, elevated the Tavern to a high rank among my pleasures.

Worcester Evening 8 o'clock

I reached Worcester ½ an hour ago having walked 40 miles without difficulty. Every time I traverse a turnpike I find it harder to concieve how they are supported; I met but 3 or four travellers between Roxbury & W. The scenery, all the way was fine, and the turnpike, a road of inflexible principle, swerving neither to the right hand nor the left, stretched on before me, always in sight. A traveller who has nothing particular to think about is apt to make a very lively personification of his Road & so make the better companion of it. The Kraken, thought I, or the Sea-Worm, is *three English* miles long; but this *land-worm* of mine is some forty, & those of the hugest.

Saturday, Rice's Hotel, Brookfield.

After passing through Leicester, Spencer & North Brookf. I am comfortably seated in South B. 60 miles from home. In Leicester, I met with Stephen Elliot in the Bar room of the inn, on his way, it appeared, to Stafford Springs. He guessed with me a few minutes concerning the design & use of a huge white building opposite the house & could not decide whether it were Courthouse or whether it were Church. But the stageman called, & he went on his way. The building I found to be an Academy containing ordinarily 80 students— boys & girls. "Not so many girls now," added the bar-keeper, "because there is no female instructer, & they like a woman to teach them the higher things."—Ye stars! thought I, if the Metropolis get this notion, the Mogul & I must lack bread. At Spencer I sympathized with a Coachman who complained, that, 'ride as far or as fast as he would, the milestones were all alike, & told the same number.' Mr Stevens of N. Brookfield is an innholder after my heart—corpulent & comfortable, honest to a cent, with high opinions of the clergy. And yet he told me there was a mournful rise of schisms since he was a boy,— Unitarians & Universalists—which, he said, he believed were all one, and he never heard their names till lately. I asked him the cause of all this frightful heterodoxy? The old Serpent, he said, was at work decieving men. He could not but think people *behaved* about as well now as their fathers did; but then Mr Bisby (the Universalist minister of B.) is a cunning fox. & by & bye he & his hosts will show what & how bad they really are. My good landlord's philanthropic conclusion was, that there was a monitor within and if we minded that, no matter how we speculated.

Sunday Evg., Aug. 24.

I rested this Sabbath day on the banks of the Quebog. Mr Stone, a worthy Calvinist, who had been already recommended to my respect, by the hearty praises of my last-named landlord, preached all day, and reminded me forcibly of one of my idols, Dr. N. of Portland. My lord Bacon, my trusty counsellor all the week, has six or seven choice essays for holy time. The aforesaid lord knew passing well what was in man, woman, & child, what was in books, & what in palaces. This possessor of transcendant intellect was a mean slave to courts and a conniver at bribery. And now perchance if mental distinctions give place to moral ones at the end of life—now this intellectual giant who has been the instructor of the world and must continue to be a teacher of mankind till the end of time—has been forced to relinquish his preeminence and in another world to crawl in the dust at the feet of those to whom his mounting spirit was once a sacred guide. One instant succeeding dissolution will perhaps satisfy us, that there is no inconsistency in this. Till then I should be loth to ascribe any thing less than celestial state to the Prince of philosophers.

> Belchertown, Clapp's Hotel
> Monday Afternoon.

After noticing the name of M. Rice upon the Hatstore, upon the Blacksmith's shop, & upon the Inn of S. Brookfield, I made inquiries of my landlord, and learned that this omnitrader was he himself, who, moreover, owned two lines of stages! This morning, Phoebus and I set out together upon our respective journies; and I believe we shall finish them together, since this village is ten miles from Amherst. The morning walk was delightful; and the Sun amused himself & me by making rainbows on the thick mist which darkened the country. After passing through W. Brookfield I breakfasted among some right worshipful waggoners at the pleasant town of Western, and then passed through a part of Palmer (I believe) & Ware to this place. I count that road pleasant & that air good, which forces me to smile from mere animal pleasure, albeit I may be a smiling man; so I am free to commend the road from Cutler's Tavern in Western, as far as Babcock's in *Ware*, to any youthful traveller, who walks upon a cloudless August Morning. Let me not forget to record here, the benevolent landlady of Ware who offered me her liquors & crackers upon the precarious credit of my return, rather than exchange my bills.

> Monday Evg.
> Bartlett's, Amherst.

I sit here 90 miles from home, & 3 from the Institution, and have the pleasure & eke the honour, to waft, on the winged steeds of a wish, my best regards to the lords & ladye who sit at home; to the majesty of Tartary,—chiefest of men calling the young satraps to order from the elbow chair & secretly meditating golden schemes in an iron age; then to the young lion of the tribe, (to change the metaphor) now resting & musing on his honourable *Oars; next to my loudvoiced & sparebuilt friend, loving duty better, oh abundantly better than pudding; last to the medalled youth, the anxious Driver & Director of the whole establishment; Peace to his Bones.

My worthy landlord wishes blessings to the Amherst Institution, which, saith he, howbeit it may have had a muddy foundation, yet the Lord hath blessed.

Thursday, August
Tuesday Morning I engaged Mr Bartlett to bring me to Mrs Shepard's and I think the worthy man returned with some complacent recollections of the instructions & remarks he had dropped on the way for the stranger's edification. Our wagon ride was somewhat uneasy from below but its ups & downs were amply compensated by the richness & grandeur visible above & around. Hampshire County rides in wagons. In this pleasant land I found a house-full of friends, a noble house— very good friends. In the afternoon I went to the College. The infant college is an Infant Hercules. Never was so much striving, outstretching, & advancing in a literary cause as is exhibited here. The students all feel a personal responsibility in the support & defence of their young Alma Mater against all antagonists, and as long as this battle abroad shall continue, the Government, unlike all other Governments, will not be compelled to fight with its students within. The opposition of other towns & counties produces moreover a correspondent friendship & kindness from the people in Amherst, and there is a daily exhibition of affectionate feeling between the inhabitants & the scholars, which is the more pleasant as it is so uncommon. They attended the Declamation & Commencement with the interest which parents usually shew at the exhibitions of schools where their own children are engaged. I believe the affair was first moved, about three years ago, by the Trustees of

*A word which I take to be an abbreviation.

the Academy. When the corner stone of the South College was laid, the Institution did not own a dollar. A cartload of stones was brought by a farmer in Pelham, to begin the foundation; and now they have two large brick edifices, a President's house, & considerable funds. Dr Moore has left them six or seven thousand dollars. A poor one-legged man died last week in Pelham, who was not known to have any property, & left them 4000 dollars to be appropriated to the building of a Chapel, over whose door is to be inscribed his name, Adams Johnson. Wm Phillips gave a thousand & Wm Eustis a hundred dollars and great expectations are entertained from some rich men, friends to the Seminary who will die without children.

They have wisely systematized this spirit of opposition which they have found so lucrative, & the students are all divided into thriving opposition societies which gather libraries, laboratories, mineral cabinets, &c, with an indefatigable spirit, which nothing but rivalry could inspire. Upon this impulse, they write, speak, & study in a sort of fury, which, I think, promises a harvest of attainments. The Commencement was plainly that of a young college, but had strength and eloquence mixed with the apparent 'vestigia ruris.' And the scholar who gained the prize for declamation the evening before, would have a first prize at any Cambridge competition. The College is supposed to be worth net 8500 dollars.

After spending three days very pleasantly at Mrs Shepard's, among orators, botanists, mineralogists, & above all, Ministers, I set off on Friday Morning with Thos Greenough & another little cousin in a chaise to visit Mount Holyoke. How high the hill may be, I know not; for, different accounts make it 8, 12, & 16 hundred feet from the river. The prospect repays the ascent and although the day was hot & hazy so as to preclude a distant prospect, yet all the broad meadows in the immediate vicinity of the mountain through which the Connecticutt winds, make a beautiful picture seldom rivalled. After adding our names in the books to the long list of strangers whom curiosity has attracted to this hill we descended in safety without encountering rattlesnake or viper that have given so bad fame to the place. We were informed that about 40 people ascend the mountain every fair day during the summer. After passing through Hadley meadows, I took leave of my companions at Northampton bridge, and crossed for the first time the far famed Yankee river.

From the Hotel in Northampton I visited Mr. Theodore Strong, where I have been spending a couple of days of great pleasure. His five beautiful daughters & son make one of the finest families I ever saw. In the afternoon, I went on horse back (oh Hercules!) with Allen Strong to Round Hill, the beautiful site of the Gymnasium, & to Shepherd's Factory about 4 miles from the centre of the town. Saturday Morning we went in a chaise in pursuit of a lead mine said to lie about five miles off which we found after great & indefatigable search. We tied our horse & descended, by direction, into a somewhat steep glen at the bottom of which we found the covered entrance of a little canal about 5 ft. wide. Into this artificial cavern we fired a gun to call out the miner from within. The report was long & loudly echoed & after a weary interval we discerned a boat with lamps lighted in its sides issuing from this dreary abode. We welcomed the Miner to the light of the Sun and leaving our hats without, & binding our heads we lay down in the boat and were immediately introduced to a cave varying in height from 4 to 6 & 8 feet, hollowed in a pretty soft sandstone through which the water continually drops. When we lost the light of the entrance & saw only this gloomy passage by the light of lamps it required no effort of imagination to believe we were leaving the world, & our smutty ferryman was a true Charon. After sailing a few hundred feet the vault grew higher & wider overhead & there was a considerable trickling of water on our left; this was the ventilator of the mine & reaches up to the surface of the earth. We continued to advance in this manner for 900 feet & then got out of the boat & walked on planks a little way to the end of this excavation. Here we expected to find the lead vein, & the operations of the subterranean man, but were sadly disappointed. He had been digging through this stone for 12 years, & has not yet discovered any lead at all. Indications of lead at the surface led some Boston gentleman to set this man at work in the expectation that after cutting his dark canal for 1000 feet, he would reach the vein, & the canal would then draw off the water which prevented them from digging from above. As yet, he has found no lead but, as he gravely observed 'has reached some *excellent granite.*' In this part of the work he has 40 dollars for every foot he advances and it occupies him ten days to earn this. He has advanced 975 feet & spends his days, winter & summer, alone in this damp & silent tomb. He says the place is excellent for meditation, & that he sees no goblins. Many visiters come to his dark residence, & pay him a shilling apiece for the sight. A young man, he said, came the day before us, who after going in a little way was taken with terrors & said he felt faint, & returned. Said Miner is a brawny personage & discreet withal; has a wife, & lives near the hole. All his excavations are performed by successive blastings.

In the afternoon I set out on my way to Greenfield intending to pass the Sabbath with George Ripley. Mr Strong insisted on carrying me to Hatfield, & thence I passed chiefly on foot through Whately & Deerfield over sands & pinebarrens, & across Green River to Greenfield, and did not arrive there till after ten o'clock & found both taverns shut up. I should have staid in Deerfield if Mr S. had not ridiculed the idea of getting to Greenfield that night. In the morning I called at Mr Ripley's, & was sorely disappointed to learn that his son was at Cambridge. The family were exceedingly hospitable, and I listened with no great pleasure to a sermon from Rev. Mr Perkins of Amherst in the morng & in the afternoon rode over to the other parish with Mr R. to hear Rev Lincoln Ripley. After service Mr L. R returned with us, and in the evening we heard another sermon from Mr Perkins which pleased me abundantly better than his matins. He is a loudvoiced scripture-read divine, & his compositions have the elements of a potent eloquence, but he lacks taste. By the light of the Evening star, I walked with my reverend uncle, a man, who well sustains the character of an aged missionary. It is a new thing to him, he said, to *correspond* with his wife, and he attends the mail regularly every Monday morng. to send or recieve a letter.

After a dreamless night, & a most hospitable entertainment I parted from Greenfield & through an unusually fine country, crossed the Connecticut (shrunk to a rivulet in this place somewhere in Montagu). My solitary way grew somewhat more dreary, as I drew nearer Wendell and the only relief to hot sandy roads & a barren monotonous region was one fine forest with many straight clean pinetrees upwards of a hundred feet high 'fit for the mast of some great Admiral.' All that day was a thoughtless heavy pilgrimage and Fortune deemed that such a crowded week of pleasure demanded a reaction of pain. At night I was quartered in the meanest caravansera which has contained my person since the tour began. Traveller! weary & jaded, who regardest the repose of thine earthly tenement; Traveller, hungry & athirst whose heart warms to the hope of animal gratification; Traveller of seven or seventy years beware, beware, I beseech you of Mr Haven's Inn in New Salem. Already he is laying a snare for your kindness or credulity in fencing in a mineral spring for your infirmities. Beware——

From Mr Haven's garret bed I sallied forth Tuesday morng towards Hubbardston, but my cramped limbs made little speed. After dining in Hubbardston I walked seven miles farther to Princeton designing to ascend Wachusett with my tall cousin Thomas Greenough if I should find him there, & then set out for home in the next day's stage. But when morning came, & the stage was brought, and the mountain was a mile & a half away,—I learned again an old lesson, that, the beldam Disappointment sits at Hope's door. I jumped into the stage & rode away, Wachusett untrod. At Sterling I learned that Oliver Blood studies physic in Worcester; at Bolton I saw Nat Wood on his way to Amherst N. H. to study law, his pedagogical career being terminated—O fortunate nimium!

Close cooped in a stage coach with a score of happy dusty rustics the pilgrim continued his ride to Waltham, and alighting there, spent an agreeable evening at Rev. Mr Ripley's. Home he came from thence the next morning, right glad to sit down once more in a quiet wellfed family—at Canterbury.

from
Wide World 12
1823–1824

He wondered how he could be created for so ignoble a life. His mind that should be so quick with thought was a barren blank. His heart, which should be so full of warm affections reaching out to all beings, languished in a dearth of all sympathies. Such a being is man, then, now, & ever.

> Alas our young affections run to waste
> Or water but the desert

The chimney of the
volcano

December 21. Who is he that shall controul me? Why may not I act & speak & write & think with entire freedom? What am I to the Universe, or, the Universe, what is it to me? Who hath forged the chains of Wrong & Right, of Opinion & Custom? And must I wear them? Is Society my anointed King? Or is there any mightier community or any man or more than man, whose slave I am? I am solitary in the vast society of beings; I consort with no species; I indulge no sympathies. I see the world, human, brute & inanimate nature; I am in the midst of them, but not *of* them; I hear the song of the storm, —the Winds & warring Elements sweep by me—but they mix not with my being. I see cities & nations & witness passions,— the roar of their laughter,—but I partake it not;—the yell of their grief,—it touches no chord in me; their fellowships & fashions, lusts & virtues, the words & deeds they call glory & shame,—I disclaim them all. I say to the Universe, Mighty one! thou art not my mother; Return to chaos, if thou wilt, I shall still exist. I live. If I owe my being, it is to a destiny greater than thine. Star by Star, world by world, system by system shall be crushed,—but I shall live.

'Animasque in vulnere ponunt.'

Virgil

—

I see no reason why I should bow my head to man or cringe in my demeanour. When the soul is disembodied, he that has nothing else but a towering independence has one claim to respect; whilst genius & learning may provoke our contempt for their supple knees. When I consider my poverty & ignorance, & the positive superiority of talents, virtues, & manners, which I must acknowledge in many men, I am prone to merge my dignity in a most uncomfortable sense of unworthiness. But when I reflect that I am an immortal being, born to a destiny immeasurably high, deriving my moral & intellectual attributes directly from Almighty God, & that my existence & condition as his child, must be forever independent of the controul or will of my fellow children,—I am elevated in my own eyes to a higher ground in life & a better self esteem. But, alas! few men hold with a strong grasp the sceptre of self-government & can summon into exercise, at will, whatever set of feeling suits their judgement best. One is apt, when in society to be tormented with this odious abasement, to wonder reluctantly with a foolish face of praise, & to consent, with bitter inward reproaches, to things & thoughts he cannot combat; and, in solitude, only, to be uplifted by this manly but useless independence. A vigorous resolution is not enough to conquer this abominable habit. A humble Christian would not wallow in his humility. His reverence for the Creator precludes an extravagant deference to the Creature.

—

A nation like a tree does not thrive till it is engraffed with a foreign stock.

The tendencies of literature in different ages observable. In France & England has sometimes run strongly towards drama, as in the rude Mysteries; in England in the last Century was historical—Hume, Gibbon, Robertson. In this day runs to Periodical writing, to newspaper, magazine, encyclopedia, & review. Causes & uses. Newspapers not known in Greece or

Rome; (the first was published in England, in Elizabeth's time) 1538 their help & harm pretty evenly balanced. Inasmuch as it is good the peasant in his humble cot should be acquainted with his government, the actions, interests, characters, of his rulers & distinguished fellow citizens; that he should have a rational & exciting amusement; that he should not be liable to be misled by rumours, parents of national evils—in so much, a newspaper is good. In a nation large as the United States, without prints, to what unruly extravagance false reports about men & events would grow before they could be corrected, is easily concieved. For a report cannot be *denied*, but a *printed* rumour can. But as vehicles of slander, & virulent party spirit they are fatally convenient. Dr Channing thought them eminently useful in enlarging the sphere of human sympathy; confederating us with distant Greece, enabling a nation to unite in one feeling & hence in one effort. ——But Crusades without prints excited intenser sympathy. This example will go in favour of newspapers, for, as was said above, they were, for want of rapidly circulating information, ignorant, foolish, uncorrected, excitements.—Newspapers, are the proper literature of America, which affects to be so practical & unromantic a land.

The Indian Pantheon is of prodigious size; 330 million Gods have in it each their heaven, or rather each their parlour, in this immense "goddery." "In quantity & absurdity their superstition has nothing to match it, that is or ever was in the world." (See two articles on Hindu Mathematics; & Mythology in the 29 Vol. of the Edin Review.)   IND.

The theory of Mr Alison assigning the beauty of the object to the mind of the beholder, is natural & plausible. This want of uniformity is useful. It prevents us all from falling in love with the same face & as the associations are accidental enables them to hope & to succeed to whose form & feature partial Nature has been niggard of her ornaments. A homely verse of blessed truth in human history saith

> "There lives no goose so gray, but soon or late
> She finds some honest gander for her mate."—

—

1824.—A merry new year to the Wideworld

—

"A friend should bear a friend's infirmities." This does not chime perfectly with my fancies. Friends should not have infirmities; that is, discordant infirmities; Friendship will melt like snow if there be anything likely to disgust, between parties. I may be the friend of a passionate man perhaps but not of an ill-humoured one & bear his ill humour nor of a proser, & bear his long stories; nor of a plebeian, & tolerate his vulgarities. Hearts must be of a mould to match. I have heard of instances indeed where contrary inclinations have agreed well, the projections of one character happening to adjust themselves, as it seemed to the cavities of the other. But I believe this was a companionship & no nearer love. For there must be no hollowness or artifice in the sympathy that would be permanent. As there necessarily must be where one cannot relish or concieve the pleasures of the other.

It is curious how deceptive history when most authentic, is. Fifty, twenty, or ten men, sometimes one man become in it the representatives of a nation & what is worse for truth do not speak for the nation but only for themselves. In very unquiet times the number augments, but is always comparatively insignificant, & in this case compensates the better number by a worse character. We gravely write or read as the history of France the account of a miscreant mob who in pursuit of pillage & rapine acted out their own horrible will for a series of months without any settled design, and who no further dreamd of revolution than as far as it would gratify their own appetite for bacchanalian disorder. A great deal, perhaps the greater proportion, was done at random & afterwards taken advantage of from time to time by the bolder sort of men of influence who found themselves thrown by circumstances into power. Their views also, were not premeditated; but opened as events opened wider & wilder changes. The only connexion in these events was mere succession. But when the fray is over, comes the sage annalist, with wise political saws, affecting to give order to the Chaos, & ascends for remote causes two or three reigns to the profligate splendour of an elder King. Whilst nobody doubts that with as imbecile a monarch & ill-advised a ministry Lord George Gordon's mob or Jack Cade's mob or Mr Cobbett's mobs might effect as bloody wonders in free & enlightened London. That the famine & despotism of France made the difference between their Revolution & ours cannot be doubted. But nevertheless the history is much farce.

Jan. 10, 1824.—I apprehend every thinking man's experience attests the accordance to Nature of the Baconian maxim, of not building our theories except upon the slow & patient accumulation of a sufficiency of experiments. Youth says I will be famed—I will write. But wheresoever Youth turns his eyes for the subject of his vast meditation, he is met by the barrenness of facts, & forced to go labour in the chronicles for the substance he pants to adorn.

—

Aristocracy is a good sign. Aristocracy has been the hue & cry in every community where there has been anything good, any society worth associating with, since men met in cities. It must be every where. 'Twere the greatest calamity to have it abolished. It went nearest to its death in the French Revolution, of all time. And if, tonight, an earthquake should sink every patrician house in the city, tomorrow there would be as distinct an aristocracy as now. The only change would be that the second sort would have become first but they would be as unmingling, as much separated from the lower class as ever the rich men of today were from them. No man would consent to live in society if he was obliged to admit every body to his house that chose to come. Robinson Crusoe's island would be better than a city if men were obliged to mix together indiscriminately heads & points with all the world. Envy is the tax which all distinction must pay.

—

Men pay a price for admission to the civilization of society. Some pay 20, 30, 40, or 50 hundred dollars a year to be permitted to take certain high & higher seats therein. My mother & I might subsist on 200 but we are willing to buy with twelve or thirteen times as much a more convenient & reputable place in the world. Every man who values this bargain which he drives so zealously must give the whole weight of his support to the public, civil, religious, literary institutions which make it worth his toil. Keep the moral fountains pure. Open Schools. Guard the Sabbath, if you be a member or lover of Civil Society, as you would not tremble at the report of its earthquake convulsions, & be shocked at the noise of its fall.

It is excellent advice both in writing & in action to avoid a too great elevation at first. Let one's beginnings be temperate & unpretending & the more elevated parts will rise from these with a just & full effect. We were not made to breath oxygen or to talk poetry, or to be always wise. We are sorry habitants of an imperfect world. And it will not do for *such* beings to take admiration by storm. One who would take his friend captive by eloquent discourse must forego the vulgar vanity of a great outset, which cannot last, but dwindles down to flatness & disgust. He must lull the suspicion of art asleep by the unambitious use of familiar commonplaces. He must be willing to say 'How do you do?' and "What's the news?" He must not disdain to be interested in the weather or the time of day. And when the talk has gradually got into those channels where he wished to lead it, knowledge that is in place & fervour that is well-timed will have their reward.

Forms are not unimportant in society. It is supremely necessary that you regulate men's conduct, whether you can affect their principles or no. For the thoughts of the mass of men are ever in a crude, ungrown, unready state. But their actions regular & ready. They *must act*; but there is no compulsion to *think*. Therefore when the understanding is sluggish & indicates no course of conduct, they are forced to obey Example, & surrender the whole ordering of life to the judgements of other men. Thus a whole community go to church; acquiesce in the existence of a certain law, or in the government of a certain ruler while, if their hearts were all read, it might appear that these institutions had but a few strong favourers, & that, for the rest, each man leaned on his neighbor; nay, a critical in-

quiry should make it plain that the majority of opinions re-
belled in secret against the custom complied with, but that
doubts were too shadowy & unformed to venture to challenge
an old established mode.

Men in fact so openly borrow their common modes of
thinking, i.e. those outside modes on which their actions depend (for when they act in a certain way they commonly go
armed with some obvious reason whether they believe it or
no) that it is surprising how small an amount of originality of
mind is required to circulate all the thought in a community.
The common conversation that has place in a city for a year
does not embrace more intelligence than one vigorous thinker
might originate; & one who carefully considers the flow &
progress of opinion from man to man & rank to rank thro'
Society, will soon discover that three or four masters present
the people with all that moderate stock of conclusions upon
politics, religion, commerce, & sentiment which goes current.
The kingdom of thought is a proud aristocracy.

1790   England had three great names in her parliament,
Burke, Fox, & Pitt. The two latter interest us by the engaging
shew of youthful might. They seem to be beardless boys, abandoning their college with youthful impatience to mix with
men; they come among the grayhaired statesmen who are
aghast at the storm which gathers around, & fearlessly grasp &
hurl the thunderbolts of power with graceful majesty. Fox took
his seat in parliament at 19 years of age. Pitt was prime minister
of England at 24. Burke, who lacked the aristocratical interest
to back him, which Fox who descended from Henry IV of
Navarre, & Pitt who was son of Chatham, could muster—was
somewhat later. The two former were friends; true hearted &
noble friends, so matched as the world hath seldom seen & so
parted, as we would hardly have had it otherwise. They were
two large & philosophical understandings both lit with the fire
of eloquence. Fox, with tears in his eyes lamented in parliament that an uninterrupted friendship of twenty three years
should be invaded by the intemperance of a debate, & that his
friend should have applied such violent & angry epithets to his
name. Burke said he did not recollect any epithets. The reply

of Fox was in the spirit of a gentleman. "My honourable friend
has forgotten the epithets, they are out of his mind, and they
are out of mine forever."

Burke's *principle* was dearer to him even than his friend, & he
broke with a stoic's heart, his ancient attachment. Burke said
afterwards of Fox 'he was a man made to be loved.' & Goldsmith said of B.

"born for the universe narrowed his mind
And to *party* gave up, what was meant for mankind."

It is not easy, for a common mind perhaps it is not possible to
appreciate this magnanimous sacrifice (of his friendship.) No
man perhaps was ever fitter to enjoy fully this best & purest of
pleasures. F. & B agreed upon the American & their foresight
triumphed over their adversaries who laughed at the "vagrant
congress, one Hancock, one Adams & their crew," who
spurned them when they "might have been led," as Franklin
told them, "by a thread" until they broke chains & scattered
armaments like flaxen strings. In the dark tempest of the
French Revolution, *Pitt* was "the pilot that weathered the
storm." Fox, in Westminster Abbey lies 18 inches from Pitt &
close by Chatham. Pitt, Fox, Burke,—since one was in office,
one in favour, & one in neither, perhaps it is just to say Pitt was
a practical statesman; Fox, a theoretical statesman; & Burke, a
philosophic statesman.

Franklin was political economist, a natural philosopher, a
moral philosopher, & a statesman. Invents & dismisses subtle
theories (e.g. of the Earth) with extraordinary ease. Unconscious of any mental effort in detailing the profoundest solu-
tions of phenomena & therefore makes no parade. He writes
to a friend when aet. 80 "I feel as if I was intruding among
posterity when I ought to be abed & asleep. I look upon death
to be as necessary to the Constitution as Sleep. We shall rise refreshed in the morning."

"Many," said he, "forgive injuries, but none ever forgave contempt."—See Edin. Rev.

That age abounded in greatness: Carnot, Moreau, Bonaparte, &c, Johnson, Gibbon, &c, Washington, &c.

Institutions are a sort of home. A man may wander long with profit, if he come home at last but a perpetual Vagrant is not honoured. Men may alter & improve their laws so they fix them at last.

"Humanity does not consist in a squeamish ear." Fox.

Men in this age do not produce new works but admire old ones; Are content to leave the fresh pastures awhile, & to chew the cud of thought in the shade.

"A Great empire like a great cake is most easily diminished at the edges." Franklin.

———

Does *Marriage* produce good-Order in Society or the desire & necessity of good order give rise to marriage. Yea or Nay?

Perhaps the question is reducible to this. Is man infinitely improvable, or only to such extent & in such direction?

"La nature," says Pascal, "confond les pyrrhoniens et la raison confond les dogmatistes." & Sir J. Mackintosh calls the sentence the sublimest of human composition. It is fortunate & happy but a sublimity not difficult to gain, as it did not occur to Pascal when first he revolved the subject, but is the last generalization at which he arrives. And it is easier to build up one subject into a cone with broad base of examples narrowing up into a formula expressing a general truth, than to detach subtle facts from subjects partially known.

"Montesquieu's Lettres Persanes sold like bread."
Vie.

'Please to praise me,' is the ill disguised request of almost all literary men. All men are cheered by applause & vexed by censure

——Nihil est quod credere de se
Non possit. Juv.

but literary men alone cannot do without it. The reason is obvious,—other men toil for gold & get gold for their toil but scholars cannot get gold & appetite in them craves another food. They are no more insatiable for their proper reward, than are the pursuers of Mammon for theirs. But why are the askers of praise ridiculous & not the askers of silver? (Minor negatur) Idle beggars of praise or of money alike are treated with contempt but one who laboriously seeks for reputation as one who laboriously seeks wealth, in their proper fields & by just means will find both reputation & wealth. Both must be earned; neither will be given on bare demand. As for Fortune, she will coquette with both.

The vice of wealth & of fame is an outward pomp. But as cautious rich men are not forward to publish the amount of their property for fear of the tax gatherer, so men of merit must beware how they vaunt their wares lest detraction which is distinction's tax make them repent their vanity.

See No 104 Rambler.

In education it seems to be safer to praise than to censure abundantly. For myself I have ever been elated to an active mind by flattery & depressed by dispraise. Perhaps a Muse that soared on a stronger wing would scorn to be so slightly disheartened. I like the lines

> "Praise is the salt that seasons right in man
> And whets the appetite of moral good." Young

It is noticeable how much a man is judged of by the praise he gives. It is best not to be too inflammable, not to be lavish of your praise on light occasions for it will be remembered long after your fervent admiration has cooled into disgust. Milton was very frugal of his praise. A man is not more known by the company he keeps. Dat veniam corvis, vexat censura columbas—is a decisive index of perverted character.

'Somebody conquered somebody—the amount of Caesar's fame,' says Wollaston.

> ——uxorem, Posthume, ducis?
> Dic quâ Tisiphone, quibus exagitare colubris?

Beauty is but skin-deep. In some instances that I have known that in matrimony have sought neither beauty or wealth have not found wisdom but folly. Choice has been the fruit of weakness of mind or body; it were too appalling to affirm that this is always or generally the case.

Pliny's uncle had a slave read while he eat. In the progress of Watt & Perkin's philosophy the day may come when the scholar shall be provided with a Reading Steam Engine; when he shall say Presto—& it shall discourse eloquent history—& Stop Sesame & it shall hush to let him think. He shall put in a pin, & hear poetry; & two pins, & hear a song. That age will discover Laputa.   Feb. 17.

———

Boethius was great & good—from 470 to 524 A. D.

In the beginning, which I spake of a few lines above, there
was some good. Would it not have been well to have lived in
Nineveh or to have been the mighty hunter or to have floated
on the Deluge or have been dead before? Hope at least would
have been a Contemporary. Now she has long been dead or
doating—as good as dead. Moreover men's thoughts were
their own then. Noah was not dinned to death with Aristotle
& Bacon & Greece & Rome. The patriarchs were never puzzled with libraries of names, dates, with First ages & dark ages;
& Revivals & upper empires & lower empires; with the balance of power & the balance of trade; with fighting chronolo-
gies & dagger-drawing creeds. Life is wasted in the necessary
preparation of finding which is the true way, & we die just as
we enter it. An antedeluvian had the advantage—an advantage
that has been growing rare as the world has grown older of
forming his own opinion & indulging his own hope without
danger of contradiction from Time that never had elapsed or
observation that never had been made. Unknown troubles
perplex the lot of the scholar whose inexpressible unhappiness it is to be born at this day. He is born in a time of *war*. A
thousand religions are in arms. Systems of Education are
contesting. Literature, Politics, Morals, & Physics, are each engaged in loud civil broil. A chaos of doubts besets him from
his outset. Shall he read or shall he think? Ask the wise. The
wise have not determined. Shall he nourish his faculties in solitude or in active life? No man can answer. He turns to books—
the vast amount of recorded wisdom but it is useless from its
amount. He cannot *read all; no, not in Methuselah's multiplied days;—but now to choose—hoc opus est. Must he read
History & neglect Morals; or learn what *ought* to be, in ignorance of what *has been*? Or must he slight both in the pursuit of
(physical) science, or all, for practical knowledge & a profession? Must he, in a last alternative abandon all the rest to be
profoundly skilled in a single branch of art, or understanding
none smatter superficially in all?
  A question of equal moment to each new Citizen of the

*One had need read as Pliny elder to accomplish anything.

world is this; shall I subdue my mind by discipline, or obey its native inclination? govern my imagination with rules or cherish its originality? Shall I cultivate Reason or Fancy? educate one power with concentrated diligence or reduce all to the same level?

These & similar questions (which I challenge all the wisdom now collected in the world to set at rest & I should be glad at heart to be answered) are a real & recurring calamity. I do not know that it were extravagant to say that half of the time of most scholars is dissipated in fruitless & vexatious attempts to solve one or another of them in succession. It is a an evil oftener felt than stated. It is an evil that demands a remedy. It requires that what master minds have done for some of the sciences, should be done for Education. Teach no more arts but how those which are already, should be learned. Feb. 17. How few appreciate what they praise!

———

A. D. 820 Michael II ascended the Greek throne from the prison in which he was about to be executed, & a smith not being nigh he wore the irons on his legs some hours after his accession.

Dr Franklin

If any apology be demanded for the seeming neglect in classical journals of a name so much the ornament of America as Franklin's, there is but one answer. It is not because we do not appreciate the manifold merits of this distinguished person or would ungratefully cancel the debt we owe to his philosophy or political wisdom; but because his fame has a wider circulation than our page & his character has that sort of commanding excellence which is as undisputed as it is unrivalled, it was not worth while to beat the air in vindicating the justice of his claims to the veneration of mankind. It is never too early or too late to hold up moral & intellectual worth to respect & imitation. The reputation of living heroes is almost always clouded by envy, distrust, & ignorance & the tardy compensation which posterity can make must on no account be withheld. For, if the pitiful ingratitude which shortened the lives of Socrates, Columbus, Galileo, were not in some measure

retrieved in the eye of their distant admirers by the regret &
honours of another generation, the appetite of fame which has
in all ages wrought so much good would altogether cease in
despair of gratification. Franklin's lot was happier than these;
yet certainly we need no apology for adorning a page with his
name.

———

The theological notions of a Chinese are anomalous I trust
in besotted perversity. The godhead that infests his thoughts is
a certain cleverness & skill that implies no merit in the divinity
but of which the yellow man may avail himself as he would of
the swiftness of a horse or the fecundity of the earth. So he
prays to his God for an event; if his prayer be answered he puts
a copper or two on his shrine; if not, he curses & kicks him;
the day, it may be, is not distant when the huge & sluggard
wave of oriental population shall be stirred & purified by the
conflict of counter currents, when the Resurrection of the East
shall cast off the incubus that has so long ridden its torpid
mind.

Metaphysicians are mortified to find how entirely the whole
materials of understanding are derived from sense. No man is
understood who speculates on mind or character until he bor-
rows the emphatic imagery of Sense. A mourner will try in
vain to explain the extent of his bereavement better than to
say a *chasm* is opened in society. I fear the progress of Meta-
physi. philosophy may be found to consist in nothing else than
the progressive introduction of apposite metaphors. Thus the
Platonists congratulated themselves for ages upon their knowing that Mind was a dark chamber whereon ideas like shadows
were painted. Men derided this as infantile when they
afterwards learned that the Mind was a sheet of white paper
whereon any & all characters might be written. Almost every
thing in language is bound up in your memory is of this significant sort. Sleep, the cessation of toil, the loss of volition, &c.,
what is that? but 'sleep that knits up the ravelled sleave of
care,' is felt. Life is nothing, but the *lamp* of life that blazes,
flutters, & goes out, the *hill* of life which is climbed & tottered
down, the *race* of life which is run with a thousand Competi-

tors & for a prize proposed, these are distinctly understood. We love tellers of good tidings is faint but 'how beautiful upon the mountains are their feet' is excellent. 'The world is the scaffold of Divine Justice,' said Saurin.

How do you do sir? Very well sir. You have a keen air among your rocks & hills. Yes sir. I never saw a country which more delighted me. A man might travel many hundred miles & not find so fine woodland as abound in this neighbourhood. But the good people who live in them do not esteem them. It is people born in town who are intoxicated with being in the country. It certainly is a good deal like being drunk, the feelings of a cit in the hills. In Cambridge there is some wild land called Sweet Auburn upwards of a mile from the Colleges & yet the students will go in bands over a flat sandy road & in summer evenings the woods are full of them. They are so happy they do not know what to do. They will scatter far & wide too among some insignificant whortleberry bushes, pricked with thorns & stung by musquetoes for hours for the sake of picking a pint of berries; occasionally chewing a bug of indescribable bad relish. You count it nothing more to go among green bushes than on the roads, but those who have been educated in dusty streets enjoy as much from sauntering here as you would in the Orange groves & Cinnamon gardens of the East Indies. They say there is a tune which is forbidden to be played in the European Armies because it makes the Swiss desert since it reminds them so forcibly of their hills at home. I have heard many *Swiss tunes* played in college. Balancing between getting & not getting a hard lesson, a breath of fragrant air from the fields coming in at the window would serve as a Swiss tune & make me *desert* to the glens from which it came. Nor is that vagabond inclination wholly gone yet. And many a sultry afternoon last summer I left my Latin & my English to go with my gun & see the rabbits & squirrels & robins in the woods. Good bye, Sir. Stop a moment. I have heard a clergyman of Maine say that in his Parish are the Penobscot Indians & that when any one of them in summer has been absent for some weeks a hunting he comes back among them a different person & altogether unlike any of the rest, with an eagle's eye, a wild look, & commanding carriage & gesture; but after a few weeks it wears off again into the indolent drone like apathy which all exhibit. Good day Sir.

I notice that Words areas much governed by Fashion as dress, both in written & spoken style. A negro said of another today 'That's a *curious genius.*'

Such a change as Hume remarks to have taken place in men's minds about the reign of James I may be found also perhaps in a careful observation of the early & later books of this country. The race who fought the revolution out were obviously, not of the same temper & manners as the first comers to the wilderness. They had dropped so much of the puritanism of their sires, that they would hardly have been acknowledged by them as sound members of their rigorous society. This nation is now honourably distinguished above all others for greater moral purity. But the constant intercourse with Europe constantly lessens the distinction; & liberality of religious & political sentiment gain ground rapidly. The great men of our first age were Bradford, Standish, Cotton, Winthrop, Phipps, & Underwood, of our second the Mathers, John Elliot, Witherspoon, & Prest Edwards, and of the third Otis, Adams, Washington, Franklin. Smith of Virginia would not have been admitted to the Plymouth doors unless perchance on account of the slaughter of the three Saracens. Liberality of religion & of politics do not always go hand in hand. For the same puritans who framed the Eng Constitution, persecuted the quakers & hanged the witches. The adventurous spirit which distinguished the settlers was begotten by the fanaticism of the Reformation—a spirit which confides in its own strength for the accomplishment of its ends & disdains to calculate the chance of failure. It is gratifying to see how faithfully the feelings of one generation may propagated to another amid the adverse action of all outward circumstances, poverty, riches, revolution. From the close of Elizabeth's reign the intolerance & bigotry of the Puritans continued & multiplied until its outbreak in England in 1640 (?) & in the branch of the stock in America in the eccles. tyranny. After that effervescence men corrected the faults of inexperience & the following genera-

tion here were more marked by *Good Sense*. Of which Gibbon
sd 'twas as rare as genius.

This huge continent shrink to an islet.

All human pleasures have their dregs & even Friendship itself hath the bitter lees. Who is he that thought he might clasp
his friend in embraces so tight, in daily intercourse so familiar
that they two should be one? They met in equal conversation.
I saw their eyes kindle with the common hope that they should
climb life's hill together & totter down hand in hand. But the
violent flame of youthful affection rapidly wasted itself. They
foolishly trusted to each other the last secret of their bosoms,
their weakness. Every man has his failing, & these no more than
others. But Men prudently cloak up the sore side, & shun to
disgust the eye of the multitude. These erred in fancying that
friendship would pardon infirmities & that a just confidence
demanded that the last door of the heart should be unclosed,
and even its secret sensuality revealed. They fell in each other's
respect; they slighted, disliked, & ridiculed each other & regret & fear remained at last of the consequences of the implicit
confidence of their violent love. Men must have great souls &
impregnable integrity of mind, to run no risks from the indiscreet ardor of their attachments. Heroes can be friends. Belisarius might love Narses; Aristides, Themistocles; Fox, Burke;
& Jefferson, Adams, in their old age; true the warmest connexions subsist in humbler life & groom loves groom, & fat
citizen, fat citizen; with as faithful an affection, (tho' destitute
of romance, because it grew moderately up in humble acquaintance) as ever united in its hoop of gold the finest minds.
The history of these sympathies is very curious; one cannot
conjure up this violent fondness for a long known & highly
valued acquaintance, but it is a stranger, of whom Nothing is
known, & nothing will come, whose eye, hair, or coat takes
the fancy. So James I's propensity to favourites, who successively disgusted him. Misery to himself & seed grew out of his
intemperate fondness for Robert Carre, & George Villiers.
. . . March 1.

If divine Providence shall always mix the fates of man, if
good & evil must ever encamp side by side then Europe must

decline as Asia rises & Civilization will not be propagated but only *transferred*. Travellers, those missionaries of science & scholars of Observation, have in the case of China rather added to the marvel than otherwise; a case unusual. The romance which they refuted only gave place to another of a less brilliant but more original & extravagant sort, and of whose incidents the worst feature is that they are true. Our forefathers believed that in the East was a great empire whose simple political institutions had a recorded antiquity at least triple the fabled period of any other; that this nation augmented its territory with its age, incorporating all it took by the inherent virtues of its policy; that by reason of its perfect adaptation to human wants the paternal yoke of the government embraced the densest population in the world; that this population had for ages enjoyed all the great inventions that had recently been imparted to Europe as the Compass, the Press, & Gunpowder, that it was possessed of science unknown in Europe & that the peasants of this sunny land lived in greater luxury than the priveleged orders in the Western nations. This plausible tale is true in the particular but false on the whole. The Celestial Empire,—hang the Celestial Empire! I hate Pekin. I will not drink of the waters of the Yellow Sea. Exorciso *tea*, celestissime, even *tea*. One is apt to mix up an idea of the production of a nation in our opinion of the producers, & Tea the insignificant sop of an herb, wholly a luxury in the West, the frivolous employment of millions in the making & tens of millions in the drinking is a fit representative of China. It is useful to know the state of man in circumstances widely dissimilar. It is a help to an inference concerning our progress. 'Tis like getting two angles to compute a third. But I hate China. 'Tis a tawdry vase. Out upon China. Words! Words.—

Myself.   Sunday, Apr. 18, 1824.

"Nil fuit unquam sic dispar sibi." Hor.

I am beginning my professional studies. In a month I shall be *legally* a man. And I deliberately dedicate my time, my talents, & my hopes to the Church. Man is an animal that looks before & after; and I should be loth to reflect at a remote period that I took so solemn a step in my existence without some careful examination of my past & present life. Since I cannot alter I would not repent the resolution I have made & this page must be witness to the latest year of my life whether I have good grounds to warrant my determination.

I cannot dissemble that my abilities are below my ambition. And I find that I judged by a false criterion when I measured my powers by my ability to understand & to criticise the intellectual character of another. For men graduate their respect not by the secret wealth but by the outward use; not by the power to understand, but by the power to act. I have or had a strong imagination & consequently a keen relish for the beauties of poetry. The exercise which the practice of composition gives to this faculty is the cause of my immoderate fondness for writing, which has swelled these pages to a voluminous extent. My reasoning faculty is proportionately weak, nor can I ever hope to write a Butler's Analogy or an Essay of Hume. Nor is it strange that with this confession I should choose theology, which is from everlasting to everlasting 'debateable Ground.' For, the highest species of reasoning upon divine subjects is rather the fruit of a sort of moral imagination, than of the 'Reasoning Machines' such as Locke & Clarke & David Hume. Dr Channing's Dudleian Lecture is the model of what I mean, and the faculty which produced this is akin to the higher flights of the fancy. I may add that the preaching most in vogue at the present day depends chiefly on imagination for its success, and asks those accomplishments which I believe are most within my grasp. I have set down little which can gratify my vanity, and I must further say that every comparison of myself with my mates that six or seven, perhaps sixteen or seventeen, years have made has convinced me that there exists a signal defect of character which neutralizes in great part the just influence my talents ought to have. Whether that defect be in the *address*, in the fault of good forms, which Queen Isabella said, were like perpetual letters commendatory, or deeper seated in an absence of common *sympathies*, or even in a levity of the understanding, I cannot tell. But its bitter fruits are a sore uneasiness in the company of most men & women, a frigid fear of offending & jealousy of disrespect, an inability to lead & an unwillingness to follow the current conversation, which contrive to make me second with all those among whom chiefly I wish to be first.

Hence my bearing in the world is the direct opposite of that good humoured independence & self esteem which should mark the gentleman. Be it here remembered that there is a decent pride which is conspicuous in the perfect model of a Christian man. I am unfortunate also, as was Rienzi, in a propensity to laugh or rather snicker. I am ill at ease therefore among men. I criticize with hardness; I lavishly applaud; I weakly argue; and I wonder with a foolish face of praise.

Now the profession of Law demands a good deal of personal address, an impregnable confidence in one's own powers, upon all occasions expected & unexpected, & a logical mode of thinking & speaking—which I do not possess, & may not reasonably hope to obtain. Medicine also makes large demands on the practitioner for a seducing Mannerism. And I have no taste for the pestle & mortar, for Bell on the bones or Hunter or Celsus.

But in Divinity I hope to thrive. I inherit from my sire a formality of manner & speech, but I derive from him or his patriotic parent a passionate love for the strains of eloquence. I burn after the 'aliquid immensum infinitumque' which Cicero desired. What we ardently love we learn to imitate. My understanding venerates & my heart loves that Cause which is dear to God & man—the laws of Morals, the Revelations which sanction, & the blood of martyrs & triumphant suffering of the saints which seal them. In my better hours, I am the believer (if not the dupe) of brilliant promises, and can respect myself as the possessor of those powers which command the reason & passions of the multitude. The office of a clergyman is twofold; public preaching & private influence. Entire success in the first is the lot of few, but this I am encouraged to expect. If however the individual himself lack that moral worth which is to secure the last, his studies upon the first are idly spent. The most prodigious genius, a seraph's eloquence will shamefully defeat its own end, if it has not first won the heart of the defender to the cause he defends; but the coolest reason cannot censure my choice when I oblige myself *professionally* to a life which all wise men freely & advisedly adopt. I put no great restraint on myself & can therefore claim little merit in a manner of life which chimes with inclination & habit. But I would learn to love Virtue for her own sake, I would have my pen so guided as was Milton's when a deep & enthusiastic love of goodness & of God dictated the Comus to the bard, or that prose rhapsody in the 3rd Book of Prelaty. I would sacrifice inclination to the interest of mind & soul. I would remember that "Spare Fast oft with Gods doth diet," that Justinian devoted but one out of twenty four hours to sleep & this week (for instance) I will remember to curtail my dinner & supper sensibly & rise from table each day with an appetite; & so see if* it be fact that I can understand more clearly.

I have mentioned a defect of character; perhaps it is not one, but many. Every wise man aims at an entire conquest of himself. We applaud as possessed of extraordinary good sense, one who never makes the slightest mistake in speech or action; one in whom not only every important step of life, but every passage of conversation, every duty of the day, even every movement of every muscle——hands, feet, & tongue, are measured & dictated by deliberate reason. I am not assuredly that excellent creature. A score of words & deeds issue from me daily, of which I am not the master. They are begotten of weakness & born of shame. I cannot assume the elevation I ought,—but lose the influence I should exert among those of meaner or younger understanding, for want of sufficient *bottom* in my nature, for want of that confidence of manner which springs from an erect mind which is without fear & without reproach. In my frequent humiliation, even before women & children I am compelled to remember the poor boy who cried, "I told you, Father, they would find me out." Even those feelings which are counted noble & generous, take in me the taint of frailty. For my strong propensity to friendship, instead of working out its manly ends, degenerates to a fondness for particular casts of feature perchance not unlike the doting of old King James. Stateliness & silence hang very like Mokannah's suspicious silver veil, only concealing what is best not shewn. What is called a warm heart, I have not.

The stern accuser Conscience cries that the Catalogue of Confessions is not yet full. I am a lover of indolence, & of the

*N.B. Till Tuesday Evg next

belly. And the good have a right to ask the Neophyte who wears his garment of scarlet sin, why he comes where all are apparelled in white? Dares he hope that some patches of pure & generous feeling, some bright fragments of lofty thought, it may be of divine poesy shall charm the eye away from all the particoloured shades of his Character? And when he is clothed in the vestments of the priest, & has inscribed on his forehead 'Holiness to the Lord', & wears on his breast the breastplate of the tribes, then can the Ethiopian change his skin & the unclean be pure? Or how shall I strenuously enforce on men the duties & habits to which I am a stranger? Physician, heal thyself. I need not go far for an answer to so natural a question. I am young in my everlasting existence. I already discern the deep dye of elementary errors, which threaten to colour its infinity of duration. And I judge that if I devote my nights & days *in form*, to the service of God & the War against Sin,—I shall soon be prepared to do the same *in substance.*

I cannot accurately estimate my chances of success, in my profession, & in life. Were it just to judge the future from the past, they would be very low. In my case I think it is not. I have never expected success in my present employment. My scholars are carefully instructed, my money is faithfully earned, but the instructor is little wiser. & the duties were never congenial with my disposition. Thus far the dupe of hope I have trudged on with my bundle at my back, and my eye fixed on the distant hill where my burden would fall. It may be I shall write *dupe* a long time to come & the end of life shall intervene betwixt me & the release. My trust is that my profession shall be my re-generation of mind, manners, inward & outward estate; or rather my starting point, for I have hoped to put on eloquence as a robe, and by goodness and zeal and the awfulness of virtue to press & prevail over the false judgments, the rebel passions & corrupt habits of men. We blame the past, we magnify & gild the future and are not wiser for the multitude of days. Spin on, Ye of the adamantine spindle, spin on, my fragile thread.

———

Intervals of mentality are faint & few & the intent of exis-tence by no means clearly made out. Seemingly obedient to the intimations of nature society has yet arrived at an artificial, tame & pigmy result. It puzzles & mortifies the bounding spirit to be brought so soon to a goal. A choice of three professions, in either of which but a small portion of time is professedly devoted to the analysis of those high relations which unite us to God & those inexplicably curious cords that fasten us to matter. Men's creeds can never, at least in youth, set the heart entirely at ease. They strike the eye ever & anon as fine spun textures through which rebellious doubt is impatient, sometimes desperate, to plunge. There is a dreaminess about my mode of life (which may be a depravity,) which loosens the tenacity of what should be most tenacious—this my grasp on heaven & earth. I am the servant more than the master of my fates. They seem to lead me into many a slough where I do no better than despond. And as to the life I lead & the Works & the days, I should blush to recite the unprofitable account. But prophets & philosophers assure me that I am immortal and sometimes my own imagination goes into a fever with its hopes & conceptions. Tell me, my soul, if this be true; if these indolent days & frivolous nights, these insignificant accomplishments, this handful of thought, this pittance of virtues are to form my trust & claim on an existence as imperishable as my Maker's. There is no such thing accorded to the universal prayer of man, as satisfactory knowledge. Metaphysics teach me admirably well what I knew before; setting out in order particular after particular, bone after bone, the anatomy of the mind. My knowledge is thus arranged, not augmented. Morals, too, the proud science which departs at once from the lower creation about which most of man's philosophy is conversant, & professes to deal with his sublimest connexions & separate destiny, morals are chiefly occupied in discriminating between what is general & what is partial, or in tying rules together by a thread which is called a system or a principle. But neither metaphysics nor ethics are more than outside sciences. They give me no insight into the nature & design of my being & the profoundest scholar in them both is as far from any clue to the Being & the work behind the scenes, as the Scythian or the Mohawk. For, Morals & Metaph Cudworth & Locke may both be true, and every system of religion yet offered to man wholly false. To glowing hope moreover 'tis alarming to see the full & regular series of animals from mites & worms up to man; yet he who has the same organization & a little more mind pretends to an insulated & extraordinary destiny to which his fellows of the stall & field are in no part admitted, nay are disdainfully excluded. x x x x But for myself wo is me! these poor & barren thoughts are the best in my brain.

───'the glow
That in my spirit dwelt, is fluttering faint & low'───

I am ambitious not to live in a corner, or, which is tenfold perdition, to be contemptible in a corner. Meantime my prospect is no better; my soul is dark or is dead. I will hope. 'She is not dead, but sleepeth.'   May 2.───

───

It is wrong to say generally that the suicide is a hero or that he is a coward. The Chinese, the most timid people in the world, die as often in that as in another manner. The old Romans & Greeks as Cato & Themistocles, who killed themselves, were brave men, far braver than the mass of their countrymen who survived to the sufferings which they avoided. The merit of the action must obviously depend in all cases upon the particular condition of the individual. It may be in one the effect of despair, in one of madness, in one of fear, in one of magnanimity, in one of ardent curiosity to know the wonders of the other world. 'If the smoke be troublesome,' said the Stoic, 'I leave it; The door is open.'

───

The multitude of books is the great good & evil of the present day & when our times of whose reputation we are so tender come under the rude comparison of posterity to be grouped a will with Augustan or Middle Ages the extraordinary fecundity of our press may by dint of overdoing have damned us to oblivion or have nursed up a learning that will record us. These books naturally divide themselves into several classes, some of great use & some worse than vain. Apart from the vast mess of transitory volumes which occasional politics or a thousand ephemeral magnalia elicit, books for the most part record the progress of science or exhibit only successive forms of taste in Poetry, letters & fiction. But there is another sort of book which appears now & then in the world once in two or three Centuries perhaps and which soon or late gets a foothold in popular esteem. I allude to those books which collect & embody the wisdom of their times & so mark the stages of human improvement. Such are the Proverbs of Solomon, the Essays of Montaigne, & eminently the Essays of Bacon. Such also (though in my judgment in far less degree) is the proper merit of Mr. Pope's judicious poems, the Moral Essays & Essay on Man which without originality seize upon all the popular speculations floating among sensible men & give them in a compact & graceful form to the following age. I should like to add another volume to this valuable work. I am not so foolhardy as to write Sequel to Bacon on my title page, and there are some reasons that induce me to suppose that the undertaking of this enterprise does not imply any censurable arrogance. Although it is perhaps a generalization which the mind but tardily makes to speak of the character of a *Nation* or *Age*, it is yet a manner of thinking which has a foundation in fact. There is frequently, perhaps invariably, a spirit & tone of thought according to which a multitude's habits of feeling may be guided without any one reaching all its results or viewing more than a few subjects in that light. (Thus in a *practical* day or day of small things, like the present, those who have heard the word & known its influence will be so wedded severally to their own prejudices that each man will spare out of the censure he bestows his own particular extravagance from the censure he casts upon useless & fanciful plans. And no one man shall be found to have weighted & applied all the popular maxims.) It may be made clear that there may be the Wisdom of an age indepent of & above the Wisdom of any individual whose life is numbered in its years. And the diligence rather than the genius of one mind may compile the prudential maxims, domestic & public maxims, current in the world and which may be made to surpass the single stores of any writer . . . as the richest private funds are quickly exceeded by a public purse. Compound Interest V.

——

Philip never saw a gate shut so tight that he could not edge in a mule laden with a bag of gold.

Misery acquaints a man with strange bedfellows. Most poor matters point to rich ends; grind their joints with dry convulsions, shorten up their sinews with aged cramps.

Why has my motley diary no jokes? Because it is a soliloquy & every man is grave alone. I. There is no royal road to Learning. II Let not your virtue be of the written or spoken sort but of the practised. III The two chief differences among men (touching talents) consist 1. in the different degrees of *attention* they are able to command; 2. in the unlikely expression they give to the same ideas. IV There is time enough for every business men are really resolved to do. V Obsta principiis. Take heed of getting cloyed with that honeycomb which Flattery tempts with. 'Tis apt to blunt the edge of appetite for many wholesome viands & rob you of many days of health. X. Let no man flatter himself with the hope of true good or solid enjoyment from the *study* of Shakspeare or Scott. Enjoy them as recreation. You cannot please yourself by going to stare at the moon; 'tis beautiful when in your *course* it comes.

Martial, 3d Epigram (l. IX) asserts that if the emperor should call in his debts Jupiter himself tho' he should make a general auction of Olympus would be unable to pay 2 shillings in the pound.

———

Dec. 1.—I may digress, where all is digression to utter a wish not altogether fruitless that there might be an Order introduced into the mass of reading that occupies or impends over me. It was a reasonable advice that a scholar gave me to *build* in the studies of a day; to begin with solid labour as Hebrew & Greek—Moral Philosophy & laborious writing should succeed; then history; then elegant letters—that species of books which is at once the most elevated amusement & the most productive suggester of thought of which the instant specimens are the bulk of Johnson's works as Lives of Poets, Rambler, &c, Pope's Moral Essays, & conspicuously Montaigne's Essays. Thus much for the day. But what arrangement in priority of subjects? When shall I read Greek, when Roman, when Austrian, when Ecclesiastical, when American history? Whilst we deliberate, time escapes. A poor plan is better than none; as a poor law. I propose therefore every morning before breakfast to read a chapter in Greek Test. with its Commentary. Afterwards, if time serve Le Clerc; or my reading & writing for dissertations; then Mitford (all history is Ecclesiastical, and all reasonings go back to Greece,) & the day end with Milton, Shakspeare, Cicero or Everett, Burke, Mackintosh, Playfair, Stewart, Scott. Pope, Dryden.

———

Dec. 10, 1824.

I confess I am a little cynical on some topics & when a whole nation is roaring Patriotism at the top of its voice I am fain to explore the cleanness of its hands & purity of its heart. I have generally found the gravest & most useful citizens are not the easiest provoked to swell the noise tho' they may be punctual at polls. And I have sometimes thought the election an individual makes between right & wrong more important than his choice between rival statesman & that the loss of a novel train of thought was ill paid by a considerable pecuniary gain. It is pleasant to know what is doing in the world & why should a world go on if it does no good. The man whom your vote supports is to govern some millions—and it would be laughable not to know the issue of the naval battle. In ten years this great competition will be very stale & a few words will inform you the result which cost you so many columns of the newsprints, so many anxious conjectures. Your soul will last longer than the ship; & will value its just & philosophical associations long after the memory has spurned all obtrusive & burdensome contents. Merriment to relieve care, occupation to amuse sorrow, may be gathered in a thousand corners at a less expense than men usually incur. There has lately been shewn to the world an economist of time who by rigid attention to his course of reading acquired more knowledge than others from the same number of pages. This is plainly a laudable & practicable triumph over common obstacles. Such is the admirable abridgement of which knowledge is made capable (by the exquisite skill of the Artificer of mind) that it is found that the human understanding can digest & command a sum of ideas which is altogether prodigious & that it contrives to become acquainted with the history of all empires in all ages with a facility which could scarce be anticipated in first periods of time. It recieves & contains without embarassment that inundation of facts & deductions which bursts in an age of inquiry from a thousand fountains. Instead of being oppressed & buried under the mass of its acquisitions the strength & excellence of its capacity is fed thereby. Master of all its treasures it administers all, sans inconvenience, & swells its power to a diviner nature by their use. A metaphysician would exhibit a work of magic who should describe all the means in which knowledge is mastered, arranged, & abridged. The arrival at general laws, the connexion of associated principles, the enlargement of meaning in words which permits the grand discovery that hundreds of laborious minds promoted, to be conveyed in a bare epithet,—would be a picture to astonish & delight. It would also instruct by suggesting the method of using time to most advantage in accumulating wisdom.

> "To be no more; sad cure; for who would lose
> Tho' full of pain this intellectual being
> Those tho'ts that wander thro' eternity?"

———

Roxbury, Jan. 4th, 1825.

I have closed my school. I have begun a new year. I have begun my studies. And this day a moment of indolence engendered in me phantasms & feelings that struggled to find vent in rhyme. I thought of the passage of my years, of their even & eventless tenor and of the crisis which is but a little way before when a month will determine the dark or bright dye they must assume forever. I turn now to my lamp & my tomes. I have nothing to do with society. My unpleasing boyhood is past, my youth wanes into the age of man and what is the unsuppressed glee, the cheering games, the golden hair & shining eyes of youth unto me? I withdraw myself from their spell. A solemn voice commands me to retire. And if in those scenes my blood & brow have been cold, if my tongue has stammered where fashion & gaiety were voluble & I have had no grace amid the influences of beauty & the festivities of Grandeur I shall not hastily conclude my soul ignobly born & its horoscope fully cast. I will not yet believe that because it has lain so tranquil, great argument could not make it stir. I will not believe because I cannot unite dignity, as many can to Folly that I am not born to fill the eye of great expectation, to speak when the people listens nor to cast my mite into the great treasury of morals & intellect. I will not quite despair nor quench my flambeau in the dust of Easy live & quiet die.

Those men to whom the muse has vouchsafed her inspirations, fail, when they fail, by their own fault. They have an instrument in their hands that discourses music by which the multitude cannot choose but be moved. Yet the player has sometimes so many freaks or such indolence as to waste his life. If you have found any defect in your sympathies that puts a bar between you and others go & study to find those views & feelings in which you come nearest to other men. Go &

school your pride & thaw your icy benevolence & nurse somewhere in your soul a spark of pure & heroic enthusiasm. Ambition & curiosity—they will prompt you to prove by experiments the affections & faculties you possess. You will bind yourself in friendship; you will obey the strong necessity of Nature and knit yourself to woman in love.* & the exercise of these affections will open your apprehension to a more common feeling & closer kindred with men. You will explore your connexion with the world of spirits & happy will you be if the flame of ardent piety towards the Infinite Spirit shall be taught to glow in your breast.

—

(Pray in your multifarious reading look out for an instance to disprove Bacon's & the common opinion that the armed nation is the prosperous one. Can ye not find in the extent of time one people, one hour, when a conquered unambitious community surpassed the Victor in comfort, in intelligence, in real enjoyment? It concerns the weal of mankind that the position be denied. Dies delet commenta opiniorum, etc.) Whoever was the author of the pleasant biography of John Horner must have had in his eye the insipid lives & language of thousands of mankind

> "Little Jack Homer
>   Sat in a corner
>   Eating his Christmas pie
>   He put in his thumb
>   He pulled out a plum
>   Says What a great man am I!"

When some fifty pages back my communicative mood was on me & I was fain to take captive in print not as before, one or two compassionate eyes whom accident brought to my page but the whole world of hearts I attempted to bespeak some kindness for my fortunes by promising to make the reader acquainted with my friends, my habits & my worldly lot. I frankly told him that I spurned the vanity of external greatness & had no sympathy with the effeminate soul that was cheated by the unmeaning names of Grace & majesty. For me, I had as

---

*No thought infirm altered his cheek

lief be the Simple Cobler of Agawam as the lineal Bourbon of the house of Capet; and a thousand times rather recieve my immortal life from Sophroniscus the stone-cutter & his plain spouse the midwife so that I should be to future times the godlike mind, the Liberator of the Understanding who sprung from them,—than be any Porphyrogenet of them all. I shall have future occasion to give a reason of my dissent from the universal prejudice to which no man can succumb & be wise. I return to my purpose of describing my connexions. . . .

It is my own humor to despise pedigree. I was educated to prize it. The kind Aunt whose cares instructed my youth (& whom may God reward) told me oft the virtues of her & mine ancestors. They have been clergymen for many generations & the piety of all & the eloquence of many is yet praised in the Churches. But the dead sleep in their moonless night; my business is with the living. The Genius that keeps me, to correct the inequalities of my understanding did not make me brother to clods of the same shape & texture as myself but to my Contraries. Thus one of my house is a person of squared & methodical conduct. Another on whose virtues I shall chiefly insist is an accomplished gentleman of a restless worldly ambition who will not let me dream out my fine spun reveries but ever and anon jogs me and laughs aloud at my metaphysical sloth. In the acquaintance I propose to form with my readers I shall insist on my brother's opinions as often as my own and without knowing or caring whence spring the differences in character between equals in education or whence falls the seed of virtues & abilities into the child which were not seen in the sire. I shall yet try to clothe him to the reader's eye in those attractions & dignities wherein he appears to my own. The day is gone by with me,—such are the connexions into which Providence has thrown me,—the day has gone by, when the useless & the frivolous should command my respect. I know very well that the great brotherhood of folly in the world, the idlers, the maniacs, & the fools in society exercise an influence over the daily course of events as vast and intimate as that of men of study & soul. Since it is not truth but bread that men seek; & when bread is procured, the exercise of their faculties delights them not so much as love & pride it follows that very different agents enter into the offices of life from those of which wise men would compose their ideal commonwealths. A fair skin, a bank note, a fashionable dress, a tapestried parlor, a granite house, cause more steps and acts each day & keep more eyelids open by night than all the theories of the French Academy or all the lofty images of Paradise lost. If one of those silly angels that writers sometimes feign, to help them out of their difficulties, should be stationed at the corner of Court Street to inquire of every passenger the business he was upon, no doubt he would marvel much for what ends this world was made. For, not one in a thousand could inform him of any mental or moral concern he had in hand. Every one, whatever bait attract him, whatsoever associates accompany him, picks out his own course, forgets in his own engrossing occupations the infinite multitude that bustles round him. It slips his memory that there are six hundred times ten hundred thousand persons on the planet; and set aside the score of people with whom he has habits of familiar connexion & the one or two hundred more with whom he has occasional intercourse & the rest are of as little consequence to his life & his death as if they were the tenants of another globe. No information transmitted from one man to another can be more interesting than the accurate description of this little world in which he lies. & I shall deserve the thanks of every knowing reader, if I shall shew him the colour, orbit, & composition of my particular star.

Jack Cade was not more inclined to proscribe grammar from his domains than I method from mine. I had a freak three days ago to describe Tom, Dick, & Harry but my freak is clean gone by. I have been at an Ordination hearing maxims on eloquence till I burned to speak. I have been reading Everett's rich strains at Plymouth,—gazing at the Sun till my eyes are blurred. This consenting declamation from every quarter on the auspicious promise of the times; this anxious and affectionate watching of the elder brothers over the painful birth of new nations in South America, Asia, Africa, (this "transfusion of youthful blood into aged veins" in Greece) is an authentic testimony to the reality of the good, or at least to a degree of it. It is infinitely better than that ill omened cry of warning & fear that in the Middle age bemoaned an enormous present degeneracy and the destruction of the world drawing nigh.

Men congregated together in processions, fasts, penances, miseracordias impelled by the sympathies of fear. The tremblers saw nothing in nature but symptoms of decay; nothing in the heavens but the torches that should light the conflagration. Nation shouted to nation the melancholy elegy which was the natural language of depraved manners, deformed institutions, raging vice in public & in private, when their bitter fruit was apparent in the world & the eye of conscience was suddenly turned to the hideous ruin. It is better to go to the house of feasting than to such a house of mourning as that.

He that searches analogies arts & life will discern something akin to what in painting is called *keeping*, in many corners where 'tis unlooked for. For tho' mine ear is untaught by nature or art in the mysteries of music yet I have found my guess that such performance was good or bad, on more than one occasion borne out by competent hearers when my only means of forming a judgment was the observation that there were abrupt transitions from loud to soft sounds without the just degrees which might be termed the *keeping* of music. A skilful critic will readily see the justice of the application of this figure to any composition also whether in verse or prose. (Tho' I admit the propriety of certain exceptions in all the applications of the rule; as when in Haydn's "Creation," an explosion of sound announces the change from darkness to light; or in Dryden's Ode on St Cecilia's day violent transition of subject and manner is permitted.)

The Parnassian nag I rode I percieve has thrown me, and I have been bestriding a hobby. It was my design & must be the topic of a true discussion of this nature to commend Study, meditation, the preference of moral & intellectual things to appetites for outward things; and as far as Solitude can be a generalization of these things it may be admitted as the cardinal topic. But in this light, 'twere foolish to admit Newton, Bacon, & Shakspear as counter instances or at all as exceptions. For all that made them great, is my very argument, the very stuff I praise; and all that subtracted from their respective worth is the very object of my invective, sarcasm, admonition, rebuke, irony, satire, derision, assault. O ye words, I have no breath to utter 'em. The philanthropist will perchance throw in the teeth of the anchorite the verse of Milton

> The Mind is its own place & in itself
> Can make a Heaven of hell a hell of heaven
> What matter where if I be still the same?

I only propose to let that mind be unswaddled, unchained and there is no danger of any excess in the practice of this doctrine "so forcible within our hearts we feel The bond of nature draw us to our own." Nature vindicates her rights & society is more delicious to the occasional absentee. Besides tho' I recommend the wilderness I only enforce the doctrine of stated or frequent and habitual closetings.

Men may be read as well as books too much.

Old in sin, every honest and natural virtue being festered and eaten out, you keep a fair outside & go down reputably to the dust. Your eyes are decently closed by your kindred. "They Maintain a mourning ostentation, And on your family's old monument, Hang mournful epitaphs, and do all rites That appertain unto a burial." But here the curtain falls, & hides from the eyes of mortals the unutterable history of the following hour.

~~Jan~~ Feb not Jan for he is gone over the flood.

February 6. And if Henry Clay is dead, another great spirit has gone like Byron's over the unvoyageable gulf, another contemner of moral distinctions to the award of the Divinity who set those distinctions, and not the less created the genius which defied them. Man feels a property in the eloquence as in the poetry of his fellows or rather owes allegiance to those who exercise lordship over his noblest & dearest capacities & so the public loss is mourned as when a sovereign dies. But it is a paradox that is again & again forced on our wonder how those who act a part so important in its influences on the world should be permitted to give their genius to the worst passions, to cast the children's bread before the dogs. That ancient doctrine that a human soul is but a larger or less emanation from the Infinite Soul is so agreeable to our imagination that something like this has always been a cherished part of popular belief. He who brings home to his daily convictions the events of life as the functions of Providence and men tho' scornful & proud as limitary beings,—in each extraordinary effort of human intelligence reverently sees a new bestowment of high & gorgeous revelations of an unutterable agency he sees that what the true poet miscalls his Muse is the secret suggestion of an illimitable mind; that the torrent of eloquence which prostrates the understanding of a multitude; the thought, the exclamation, that strikes with sudden ghastliness an armed throng & casts down with invincible persuasion the sword & lance is the inspiration of the dread Spirit who *made* the *clay creatures on whom he acts.* Man is but the poor organ thro' which the breath of Him is blown. A pipe on which stops are sounded of strange music. A torch not lighted for itself. Yet these, such is the mystery of Free Will, turn on the hand that feeds them, dishonour the energy that inspires them, blaspheme the spirit that in them blasphemes. Byron, who partook richest of Divinity, foully ridicules the virtues practised to obey Him. *Clay* scorns the laws which bind all God's creatures.

Feb. 8. He is not dead. The story of the duel was false. Alas! for mine ejaculations.——

—

(Roxbury)

February 8, 1825. It is the evening of February eighth, which was never renowned that I know. But be that as it may 'tis the last evening I spend in Canterbury. I go to my College Chamber tomorrow a little changed for better or worse since I left it in 1821. I have learned a few more names & dates, additional facility of expression, the gage of my own ignorance, its sounding places, & bottomless depths. I have inverted my inquiries two or three times on myself, and have learned what a sinner & a saint I am. My cardinal vice of intellectual dissipation—sinful strolling from book to book, from care to idleness, is my cardinal vice still; is a malady that belongs to the Chapter of Incurables. I have written two or three hundred pages that will be of use to me. I have earned two or three thousand dollars which have paid my debts & obligated my neighbours so that I thank Heaven I can say none of my house is the worse for me. In short, I have grown older and have seen something of the vanity & something of the value of existence, have seen what shallow things men are & how independent of external circumstances may be the states of mind called good & ill.

Cambridge, Feb. 1825. Today I went to Quincy to see its Patriarch. The old President sat in a large stuffed arm chair, dressed in a blue coat, black small-clothes, white stockings. And a cotton cap covered his bald head. When we were introduced he held out his hand & welcomed us. We told him he must let us come & join our Congratulations to those of the nation on the happiness of his house. He thanked us & said "I am rejoiced because the nation is happy. The time of gratulations & congratulations is nearly over with me. I am astonished that I have lived to see & know of this event. I have lived now nearly a century (He will be ninety next October) a long harrassed & distracted life." I said, the world thinks a good deal of joy has been mixed with it. "The world does not know" he said "how much toil anxiety & sorrow I have suffered." I asked if Mr Adams' letter of acceptance had been read to him. Yes, he said, and then added, My son has more political prudence than any man that I know who has existed in my time. He never was put off his guard. And I hope he will continue so. But what effect age may work in diminishing the power of his mind, I do not know; it has been very much on the stretch ever since he was born. He has always been laborious child & man from infancy. When Mr J. Q. Adams' age was mentioned he said he was 58, or would be in July, and mentioned that all the Presidents were of the same age. Gen Washington was about 58, and I was about 58, & Mr Jefferson & Mr Madison, & Mr Monroe. We asked him when he expected to see Mr Adams, he said, "never; Mr Adams will not come to Quincy but to my funeral. It would be a great satisfaction to me to see him but I don't wish him to come on my account." He spoke of Mr Lechmere whom he well remembered "to come down daily at great age to walk in the old townhouse, and I wish I could walk as well as he. He was collector of the customs for many years under the royal government." Edward said, "I suppose, Sir, you wouldn't have taken his place even to walk as well as he." "No," he said, "*that* was not what I wanted." He talked of Whitfield and remembered when he was Freshman in College to have come in to the Old South (I think) to hear him, but could not get in; he however saw him thro' a window & distinctly heard all. "He had a voice such as I never heard before or since. He *cast* it out so that you might hear it at the meeting hs (pointing towards Quincy Meeting house) and had the grace of a dancing master, of an actor of plays. His voice & his manner helped him more than his sermons. I went with Jonathan Sewall." And you were pleased with him, Sir? "Pleased, I was delighted beyond measure." We asked if at Whitfield's return the same popularity continued, "Not the same fury, he said, "not the same wild enthusiasm, as before but a greater esteem as he became more known. He did not terrify, but was admired."

We spent about an hour in his room. He talks very distinctly for so old a man—enters bravely into long sentences which are interrupted by want of breath but carries them invariably to a conclusion without ever correcting a word. He spoke of the new novels of Cooper, & Peep at the Pilgrims & Saratoga with approbation & named with accuracy the characters in them. He likes to have a person always reading to him or company talking in his chamber, and is better the next day we were told after having visitors in his chamber from morning till night. He received a premature report of his son's election on Sunday afternoon without any excitement and calmly told the reporter he had been hoaxed for it was not yet time for any news to arrive. The informer however something damped in his heart insisted on repairing to the Meetinghouse & the Congregation in the midst of service were so overjoyed that they rose in their seats & cheered thrice. Mr. Whitney dismissed them immediately. We were told that his son Judge Adams can at any time excite him in a moment to great indignation. He mentioned to us that he had spoken to the President of the late Plymouth oration & said Mr Everett had ambition enough to publish it doubtless. The old gentleman exclaimed with great vehemence "I would to God there were more ambition in the country, ambition of that laudable kind to excel."

Cambridge, Feb. 1825.

I have a mind to try if my muse hath not lost a whit of her nimbleness; if the damps of this new region, its prescribed & formal study haven't chilled a little her prurient & prolific heat. I would boldly take down a topic and enter the lists were there not reason to remember & fear the old orthodoxy concerning fortune (& I think I have heard it whispered of fairies too & of Wit even) that when the humoursome jealous Coquet is presumed on she withdraweth straight her smiles & leaves the audacious votary to curse his selfconceit in the dark. Nevertheless I am fain to solicit of the Muse some revelations on the matter of Solitude on which heretofore we held some sweet counsel together. I am anxious to gage the doctrine that was propounded, doubtless, o Muse! with oracular darkness. And I would gladly know how far the same should be accounted grave doctrine & how far fanciful. It is submitted whether a matter like this intimately concerning the education & daily habits of men be visionary & unfit for discussion & whether a decision on the expediency of seclusion, *that is*, by no means absolute & perpetual but habitual & stated seclusion, a decision fortified by the precept & the practice of the wisest men, strongly confirmed by the observations we can make on the present condition of society & impugned by the uniform immemorial habits of the majority of men—whether this decision be unsubsantial & false.

I propose to sketch a sermon soon or late on the daily habits, the outward observances of life, on the moral of manners. I will praise temperance in meats & drinks, early rising, cautious conversation, the hour perhaps & the frequency of prayer, etc. It is hard to preserve bold & true conceptions of this life as altogether a relative condition, as a mere school, entry, introduction to the Enlarged life. But assuredly things of such hourly recurrence & things woven by their nature into the texture of moral condition, deserve exact consideration. I insert here that there seems to me a fine moral in the passage of the ancient hist. who says the Lacedemonians were in the habit of rising up very early to pray, that so they might be beforehand of their enemies & preoccupy the ear of the Gods.

Yes but the world will be sadly changed to you when these novelties have grown old & dull & disgusting to you. When there are no more praises to be earned, no more offices for you to discharge, no more books for you to read; when your eyes are quenched & the Eye of your understanding is dim; when your heart has become cold & the hearts of your friends are grown cold toward *you*, when the obstruction & decay that attend your spirit down to the dust scare men with the suggestion that no morning of resurrection will awaken it again, will that dismal season be cheered by the memory of a brilliant & voluptuous imagination, of profuse leisure dedicated to amusement &c.? Alas I fear these accusing recollections will cleave unto you living, will cleave unto you dying, will not be left behind with the carcass they pampered in its hour of bloom.

—

Jan. 8, 1826.

I come with mended eyes to my ancient friend & consoler. Has the interval of silence made the writer wiser? Does his mind teem with well weighed judgments? The moral & intellectual universe has not halted because the eye of the observer was closed. Compensation has been woven to want, loss to gain, good to evil, & good to good, with the same industry, & the same concealment of an intelligent Cause. And in my joy to write & read again I will not pester my imagination with what is done unseen, with the burden that is put in the contrary scale, with the sowing of the death-seed in the place of the nettle that was rooted up. I am a more cheerful philosopher and am rather anxious to thank Oromasdes than to fear Ahriman.

Since I wrote before, I know something more of the grounds of hope & fear for what is to come. But if my knowledge is greater so is my courage. I know that I *know* next to nothing but I know too that the amount of probabilities is vast, both in mind & in morals. It is not certain that God exists but that he does not is a most bewildering & improbable chimera.

I rejoice that I live when the world is so old. There is the same difference between living with Adam & living with me as in going into a new house unfinished damp & empty, & going into a long occupied house where the time & taste of its inhabitants has accumulated a thousand useful contrivances, has furnished the chambers, stocked the cellars and filled the library. In the new house every comer must do all for himself. In the old mansion there are butlers, cooks, grooms, & valets. In the new house all must work & work with the hands. In the old one there are poets who sing, actors who play & ladies who dress & smile. O ye lovers of the past, judge between my houses. I would not be elsewhere than I am.

—

Simonides was asked why wise men followed the rich & not the rich the wise. Because said he the former know their interest & the latter do not.

To stop the slave traffic the nations should league themselves in indissoluble bands, should link the thunderbolts of national power to demolish this debtor to all Justice human & divine.

———

Mar. 14. I hate this vasty notion of poetry that is going the rounds nowadays thro' the whole circle of pulpits, criticism, & poets. This "aliquid immensum &c" is best left to each man's youthful & private meditations. This straining to say what is unutterable & vain retching, with the imbecile uses of great words is nauseous to sound sense & good taste. 'Tis a forgotten maxim that 'accuracy is essential to beauty.'

I know something may be well said for what I impugn. There is a philosophy in expectation & wonder; & this account of mind, beneath which language sinks, is bottomed on the fine verse

"Est deus in nobis, agitante calescimus illo."

It should be noted as one of the particulars in which the difference & superiority of our times appears the space that is occupied in society by men of letters. Court pageantry has lost some of its lustre. Names have kept their places but power has changed its proprietors. Who are the real sovereigns of Britain & France? Not surely the simple gentlemen that are kept in the palaces & produced on state occasions with gaudy frocks & baubles on their heads & in their hands & saluted with the smooth old title of King. Surely these are not they who act most powerfully on the fortunes & the minds of the British & the French. But Scott & Mackintosh & Jeffery & Laplace, these are the true de facto sovereigns who rule in those countries. They never affect the airs nor assume the trappings of vulgar majesty but they recieve the secret & open homage of all classes, they command feelings, determinations, & actions.

Mar. 16. My external condition may to many seem comfortable, to some enviable but I think that few men ever suffered *more genuine misery than I have suffered. And the same confession I doubt not candor would extort from many men of prouder fortunes. Hence I willingly hear an oft unwelcome doctrine, harsh & unwelcome in the ear of poverty & complaint that God has administered a real not apparent equality in the fortunes of men, has mixed pleasure & pain, tho' in differing shapes & unlike circumstances, yet in exact proportions has enabled the wretch to be proud & the prosperous to repine.

('Tis an obstacle to the prevalence of this opinion that what causes us no happiness, if it be notwithstanding associated with the idea of happiness in the understanding of other men, we are vain of exhibiting & find a foolish pleasure in enumerating what to others appear the advantages of our condition, tho' to us they have ceased to appear in that light.)

Pulchrum est laudari a laudato viro. Newton said of Cotes, "If he had lived we should have known something."

I am pleased with every token however slight in nature, in institutions, in arts, of progressive adaptation to wants—. The men of Switzerland cover their houses with shingles of the Larch tree which in a little time give out their pitch to the sun & fill up every joint so that the roof is impervious to rain.

It is the order of Providence that great objects must be purchased by great sacrifices; the best thing in the world, the New Testament, rests its genuineness (by a sort of appeal to this very principle) on the flood of the purest human blood which was shed to seal its authenticity. The next best thing in human possession is the American Constitution which hundreds & thousands of valiant patriots perished to obtain. And it seems to be out of a sort of obedience & acknowledgement of this

*in degree not in amount.

high & melancholy necessity that America has yielded up her vast indigenous family tribe after tribe to the haughty Genius of Civilization who cannot found his noble structure on her shores but at this stern forfeiture of a national existence. Many died at Marathon, at Salamis & Plataea, many at Mycale, many & the immortal 300 at Thermopylae to win the independence of Greece. The Reformation was not effected but by the death of the reformers & the death, imprisonment, or political disqualification of the protestants. The sword of Simon de Montfort attests the price paid by the poor Albigenses. America could not be discovered but the bold benefactor who gave that munificent present to men, must languish in Spanish dungeons. The ground gained by the patriots in France has cost a dearer price. So has the freedom of England.

The Wind who is the great poet of the world sings softer measures on summer eve in groves & gardens, & hoarser & sublimer music in mountains & on the desolate sea.

—

March 27, 1826.

My years are passing away. Infirmities are already stealing on me that may be the deadly enemies that are to dissolve me to dirt and little is yet done to establish my consideration among my contemporaries & less to get a memory when I am gone. I confess the foolish ambition to be valued, with qualification. I do not want to be known by them that know me not but where my name is mentioned I would have it respected. My recollections of early life are not very pleasant. I find or imagine in it a meanness, a character of unfounded pride cleaving to certain passages which might come to many ears that death has not yet shut. I would have the echoes of a good name come to the same ears to remove such imputation. I do fully disclaim the vulgar hunger to be known, to have one's name hawked in great capitals in the street like a Murdered Man's dismal renown or a naval victor or Erostratus the Ephesian incendiary. Mine is a refined appetite pleased with a calm & limited glory, satisfied with the respect of *one Plato* like a certain Athenian lecturer of whom I have heard so that absolutely nothing is known by the rest. Now for this I claim of myself the praise of great moderation for even Demosthenes with his athletic understanding & uncompromising philosophy confessed that it *was* to him a gratification to hear the Oyster woman whose stall he daily passed on his way to the Agora say 'This is that Demosthenes.'

Montaigne is right when he saith the applause of consenting thousands is mere dirt, for no wise man will value that in the bulk which he despises in the particular. And yet I suppose that this shouting of stinking breath & tossing of greasy caps make one of the most delicious pleasures whereto man has access. Of such impurities is our mold composed. Phocion when the people applauded turned to his friends & said 'What have I said amiss?'

———

Cambridge May 28, 1826.

Friendship is something very delicious to my understanding. Yet the friends that occupy my thoughts are not men but certain phantoms clothed in the form & face & apparel of men by whom they were suggested & to whom they bear a resemblance. The gods gave life to Prometheus' ivory statue and the revolution of events may one day give me the men for the prototypes.

You love your friend for your sake, not for his own, might say Hobbists & wolves, for you would not have that good fortune befal him that should raise him above your reach of your society. I please myself that I can dimly see how it would gratify me to promote that very good fortune of my friend. In God's name what is in this topic? It encourages, exhilarates, inspires me. I feel that the affections of the soul are sublimer than the faculties of the intellect. I *feel* immortal. And the evidence of immortality comes better from consciousness than from reason.

In the order of recorded History, Chaos is the parent of things, then came paradise & now is the degenerate world; before us, the contingences of Heaven & Hell. I represent to myself—the Opinion of men ever calling all the past, Chaos, at present walking through Hell to a retreating Paradise "the unreached Paradise of our despair."

What is worth remembering is remembered. The memory of the wicked shall rot. A value has been imputed to History as presenting occasions of sympathy & moral emotion. The

newspaper of a judicious editor, the romance of a good novelist would serve this purpose quite as well.

I please myself with contemplating & nourishing my own
independence—the invincibility of thought; with imagining a
firmness of purpose, or if that be not philosophically tenable, a
fixedness of opinion which opinion is the growth of the Deity's laws indeed but over which even Omnipotence has no
controul. The conspiring universe cannot make me feel wrong
to be right without altering the Constitution of my nature.
Tho' I am prone to love & second this independence there are
many things in mere speculation I dare not say and the last
page affords an instance of the limits thus set by mind to its
daring. This seems to me an evidence from my instincts of
God's existence. Sublimity of character must proceed from
sublimity of motive. Nature never gave a propensity to action
like the tendencies & attractions inherent to matter except as
the result of reason.

Happiness is that butterfly which fluttered so gaily before
the eyes of a boy that he set himself with all his might to catch
it but when he clutched it, he crushed blood & dirt betwixt his
fingers.

A bad despot is not a prophet but a magician who can turn
water to blood but cannot turn blood to water.

A man's *style* is his intellectual Voice only in part under his
controul. It has its own proper tone & manner which when he
is not thinking of it, it will always assume. He can mimic the
voices of others, he can modulate it with the occasion & the
passion, but it has its own individual nature.

———

Ballads, bon mots, anecdotes, give us better insight into the
depths of past centuries than grave & voluminous chronicles.
"A straw" says Selden "thrown up into the air will show how
the wind sits which cannot be learned by casting up a stone."

———

Cambridge Aug. 3d, 1826.

Yesterday I attended the funeral solemnities in Fanueil Hall
in honor of John Adams & Thomas Jefferson. The Oration of
Mr Webster was worthy of his fame & what is much more was

worthy of the august occasion. Never I think were the awful charms of person, manners, & voice outdone. For tho' in the beginning unpromising & in other parts imperfect in what was truly grand he fully realized the boldest conception of eloquence.

———

Of French Anarchy it may be said as Milton of the fight of angels—

> — —"War seemed a civil game
> To this uproar."——

"The Translator," says Butler, "is a small Factor that imports Books of the growth of one language into another but it seldom turns to account, for the commodity is perishable & the finer it is the worse it endures transportation as the most delicate of Indian fruits are by no art to be brought over."

Notes on Poetry.

A fault that strikes the readers of Mr Wordsworth is the direct pragmatical analysis of objects, in their nature *poetic*, but which all other poets touch incidentally. He mauls the moon & the waters & the bulrushes as his main business. Milton & Shakespeare touch them gently as illustration or ornament. Beds of flowers send up a most grateful scent to the passenger who hastens by them but let him pitch his tent among them & he will find himself grown insensible to their fragrance. And it must have occurred frequently to our reader that brilliant moonlight will not bear acquaintance. Nothing is more glorious than the full moon to those who ride or walk under its beams. But whoso goes out of doors expressly to see it returns disappointed. Mr W. is a poet with the same error that wasted the genius of the alchemists & astrologers of the Middle Age. These attempted to extort by direct means the principle of life, the secret & substance of matter from material things; & those to extract intelligence from remoter nature, instead of observing that science is ever approximating to truth by dint of application to present wants & not by the search after general & recondite Truth. Mr W. is trying to distill the essence of poetry from poetic things instead of being satisfied to adorn common scenes with such lights from these sources of poetry as nature will always furnish to her true lovers. We feel the same sort of regret that is occasioned when Aristotle forsakes the Laws of the Intellect & the Prin. of Ethics for researches into the nature of mind.

> "The world's all face the man who shows his heart
> Is hooted for his nudities & scorned."

There's a great difference between good poetry & everlasting poetry.

Shakespare alludes to himself nowhere in his drama. The sonnets. Homer keeps out of sight except in two places. A grand trait. It is like Providence. Vide Herder. Mem. Pope's acct. of his own resemblance to Providence in my blotting-book.—— A different age. In antiquity nature towered above all man had done: it sunk the personal importance of man. The bard taught as the Minister preaches & felt an impertinence in introducing self. Now Man has grown bigger, a commercial, political, canalling, writing animal. Philosophy inverts itself & poetry grows egotistical.

Shakspeare immortalizes his characters. They live to every age & as we say of Christianity have a prospective adaptation. Ben Jonson's are all dead. Read Alchemist & the rest. They are all in brocade. We feel that they are a past generation, our great grandfathers & mothers & so their motives & manners are in brocade not vital to us; as the Euphuism of one. But universal man appreciates Shakspeare—boys, rabble, every man of strong sense tho' uncultivated as Seth Robinson. Exceptions rare. Gibbon but he had no acumen for poetry: that ear was deaf. Witness his poetical opinions in notes. So Dr Priestley I guess had no ear; he calls Mrs Barbauld one of the best poets England can boast of (see his Life p. 49). Milton does not get this general suffrage.—

I find today one of Shakspeare's quibbles. Miranda tells Ferdinand who carries wood to the pile—"When this burns, t'will weep for having wearied you."

Feb. 1828. A very unaccountable poem that "Pelican island." A mixture of greatness with defects that don't appear to be slovenliness like the slovenly greatness of Dryden so much as want of delicate poetic perception but all along at intervals glitter lines that might decorate Paradise Lost. And there's a general grandeur of conception. But in the minor poems he is decidedly an ordinary genius again. It is the singular merit of the P. I. that 'tis original both in the design which perhaps makes all its greatness & in the execution. It is a poem worth ten "Excursions" being generally a complete contrast to Wordsworth's verses. These abounding in fact & Wordsworth wanting. These seizing coarse & tangible features for description or allusion & W. the metaphysical & evanescent. This treating body, & W. soul. This using a very large encyclopedical diction & W. affecting that which may be proper to the passions in common life. It seems to me that who could write this could write ten times as well. Milton would write it off in unpremeditated manuscript & lay it up as a block to be hewn & carved & polished. But Milton would as soon have hanged himself as published it as it stands. Had it been found & printed by Montgomery's executors instead of Montgomery it would not surprize. The puzzle is that there's quite a large portion of the poem that is mere extemporaneous blank verse only fit for the Fount of a Newspaper.

from
Journal 1826–1828

Sept. 10, 1826.

The days blow me onward into the desarts of Eternity; I live a few strong moments in the course perhaps of each day; I observe a little the ways of man and in them accumulated, the ways of God. I act a little. I shape my fortunes, as it seems to me, not at all. For in all my life I obey a strong necessity and all that sacrifice of time and inclination which certain of my fond friends regard as virtue, I see and confess to be only a passive deference to the course of events. For in reference to those passages of my life which please their moral sense I could not have done otherwise without doing violence to my own or my neighbour's feelings. There was in those instances, in the very likely supposition that I had disliked to play the martyr, no nook, no pretence such as commonly falls to other people under cover of which I might plausibly decline the assured alternative of inconvenience & loss. It is melancholy to suffer on account of others without any appeal to our own self devotion as the cause. It is low & ridiculous to be the football of vulgar circumstances and never by force of character to have surmounted them. And yet inasmuch as the course of events in the world appears to consent to virtue these regretted evils may be ennobled by being a portion of the sublime necessity which links all agents and events together under an omnipotent jurisdiction. Be the theories as they may, it suits my humour to sit and speculate, a civil philosopher mild and composed in the presence of little & of majestic minds; without contempt of reptiles, and, as the Stoics say, without being afraid of Gods.

Our American press does not often issue such productions as Sampson Reed's observations on the Growth of the mind, a book of such a character as I am conscious betrays some pretension even to praise. It has to my mind the aspect of a revelation, such is the wealth & such is the novelty of the truth unfolded in it. It is remarkable for the unity into which it has resolved the various powers, feelings & vocations of men, suggesting to the mind that harmony which it has always a propensity to seek of action & design in the order of Providence in the world.

———

Poison, poison, poison. The poison of vanity, the poison of fear, the poison of testimony. 'Poison expels poison, and vices are expelled by pride.'

"The aenigma of ourselves swallows up like the sphinx thousands of systems which pretend to the glory of having guessed its meaning." De Stael

———

I have heard Shakespeare's Blow winds & crack your cheeks, &c. & the rest, accused of false taste & bombast. I do not find this fault. And tho' I might not allow it in another, even in his mad king, yet I am not offended by this passage in Lear. For as the Romans were so idolatrous of Cato's virtue that when he had drunk wine they would rather believe that intemperance was virtue than that Cato was guilty of a vice, so I am afraid to circumscribe within rhetorical rules, the circuits of such a towering & majestic mind, and a taste the most exquisite that God ever informed among men.——
We seem to recognize a truth the first time we hear it. Fontenelle.

Cambridge, Nov.
1826
I would write something worthily on the most affecting of topics, upon the personal character & influence & upon the death of Jesus Christ, a being whose nature has divided the opinions of men more than did ever any question; who was so great as to leave foundation for the idea that he was a portion of the Deity, and, in the opinions least reverent, that he was first of men; a being who would be called renowned, did not fame & what men call glory sink before his majesty into things offensive & ridiculous, a human being whose influence on

the fortunes of human society taking out of account all super-natural influence has been far the most powerful foreign influence that ever acted thereon, a being whose character was so pure & whose death was so sublime as if no consequences had followed would for himself have attracted the greatest admiration.

Language is the great study of man; and the degree of its perfection in every nation is I suppose an unerring index of the degree of civilization. Mathematics are said to be an unerring measure of human advancement. Music is one language, Algebra another.

I find in Burke almost the same thought I had entertained as an original remark three years ago that nothing but the moral quality of actions can penetrate thro' vast intervals of time.

—

At Sea; Sunday, Dec. 3, 1826.

'Tis a ninedays' wonder to me, this voyage of mine. Here I have been rolling thro' the weary leagues of salt water, musing much on myself and on man with some new but incoherent thinking. I revolved a thought I had somewhere found that dangers were companions of illustrious minds; and applying it to society which may like individuals by its education & fortune emerge from obscurity & grow illustrious, I perceived that in its progress it would overtake dangers not known to its infancy. It would embrace dangers and ennoble itself by its company. The men of this age work & play between steam engines of tremendous force, amid the roaring wheels of manufactories, brave the incalculable forces of the storm here in the seat of its sovereignty and fulfil in these perilous crises all the minute offices of life, as calm & unawed as they would compose themselves to sleep in the shade of a forest. Such facts assert a sovereignty in the mind that is very dear to the philanthropist.

After a day or two I found I could live as comfortably in this tent tossed on the ocean, as if it were pitched on the mountains ashore. But it is the irresistible sentiment of the first day whilst your philosophy is sea sick to fancy man is violating the order of nature in coming out here where he assuredly has no business & that in virtue of this trespass on his part the wind has a right to his canvass & the shark to his body. Whilst his philosophy is distempered, so is his imagination. The whole music of the sea is desolate & monitory. The wave & the cloud & the wind suggest power more than beauty to the ear & eye. But the recovery is rapid & the terrible soon subsides into the sublime.

—

It has been remarked that notwithstanding the prodigious impression which theological controversies respecting the nature of Jesus Christ have made on human history, & the passions they daily excite in men's minds, the real difference between the sentiments of the disputants when rigidly analyzed is very subtle & inconsiderable. For the Trinitarian whilst he names the name of God is very careful to separate the idea of God from his account of the life of Jesus Christ but considers him only in his human nature, considers him as a man. Hence it happens well that to whatever party names, education or inclination has attached us we sympathize all in the same affecting views of the life & passion of our Lord.

Manners seem to be more closely under the influence of climate. They belong more to the body than the soul, & so come under the influence of the sun. They are accomodations of the motions of the body to moods of the mind. In Lapland men are savage; in Norway they are plain spoken and use no ceremony; in England some; in France much; in Spain more. In like manner no man has travelled in the United States from the North to the South without observing the change & amelioration of manners. In this city, it is most observable, the use of the conventions of address among the lowest classes which are coarsely neglected by the labouring classes at the North. Two negroes recognize each other in the street tho' both in rags & both it may be balancing a burden on their heads with the same graduated advances of salutation, that well bred men who are strangers to each other would use in Boston. They do not part before they have shaken hands & bid Goodbye with an inclination of the head. There is a grace & perfection too about these courtesies which could not be imitated by a northern labourer where he designed to be extremely civil. Indeed I have never seen an awkward Carolinian.

January 4, 1827.

Charleston S. C.

A new year has opened its bitter cold eye upon me, here where I sought warm weather. A new year has opened on me & found my best hopes set aside, my projects all suspended. A new year has found me perchance no more fit to live & no more fit to die than the last. But the eye of the mind has at least grown richer in its hoard of observations. It has detected some more of the darkling lines that connect past events to the present, and the present to the future; that run unheeded, un-commented in a thousand mazes wherever society subsists and are the moral cords of men by which the Deity is manifested to the vigilant or more truly to the illuminated observer. It does not always—this gifted observation—it does not always pre-suppose, a regulated soul. A man may be a shrewd judge of the finest shades of character, whose own conscience is contami-nated with habitual guilt. But such a man is not blind to the discrepancy betwixt his morals & his mind. He perceives the discord & cannot perceive it without alarm. For he has an in-stinctive dread of the tendencies to harmony in the Universe which he has often observed, & which betoken some future vi-olence to root out this disorder. If the string cannot be made to accord, it must be broken.

—

If an ingenious man lived long enough, he mt. learn to talk by system, in a manner out of all comparison better than men now use. Suppose him to keep a book of commonplaces & as his knowledge grew to put down on the page of each the the-ories that occurred. It is clear that in process of time it would embrace all the ordinary subjects of hum. discourse. He wouldn't talk so well as those who have the natural talent. Na-ture has fetches which art cannot reach; bewitching felicities, affecting pauses that the mere practice of a moderate genius wouldn't attain. But something would doubtless be accom-plished that would put to shame the cheap extemporaneous draggletail dialogue that takes place in our evening companies even among men of letters & ambition from candlelight till the bell strikes nine & breaks up the company.

—

Peculiarities of the present Age.

1. Instead of the systematic pursuit of science men cultivate the knowledge of anecdotes.
2. It is said to be the age of the first person singular
3. The reform of the Reformation
4. Transcendentalism. Metaphysics & ethics look inwards—and France produces Mad. de Stael; England, Wordsworth; America, Sampson Reed; as well as Germany, Swedenborg.—
5) The immense extent of the English language & influence. The Eng. tongue is spreading over all N. America except Mexico, over Demerary &c, Jamaica &c, Indostan, New Holland & the Australian islands.
6) The paper currency.
   Joint stock companies
7) The disposition among men of *associating* themselves to promote any purpose. (Millions of societies.)

—

St. Augustine, Feb. 2, 1827.—
With a little thinking, passive almost amidst our sensations, & rounding our lives with a little sleep, we count off our days with a prodigal hand. The months depart & soon I shall measure back my way to my own people. But I feel how scanty is the addition I have made to my knowledge or my virtue. Day by day I associate with men to whom my society yields no noticeable amount of advantage or pleasure. I have heard of heights of virtue & lives of philanthropy. I am cold & solitary & lead a life comfortable to myself & useless to others. Yet I believe myself to be a moral agent of an indestructible nature & designed to stand in sublime relations to God & to my fellow men; to contribute in my proper enjoyments to the general welfare. What then, young pilot, who by chart & compass point out to others the shoals they must shun & the haven they must seek—art not thyself a castaway? Will you say you have no call to more austere virtue than you daily exhibit? Have you computed the moral influences of this quiescence, this waking torpor of the soul & found them adequate to what may in equity be demanded of you? Young pilot! you dare not say Aye.——

—

You go to the house of God without the love of God. Alas my brethren, Ye know not what ye do. Is it possible you would bandy compliments with the Deity?

March 11, 1827. To believe too much is dangerous because it is the near neighbour of unbelief. Pantheism leads to Atheism.
St. Augustine E. F. 1827.
11 March.

25 March weighed 152 lb.

Charleston, April 6, 1827.
A new event is added to the quiet history of my life. I have connected myself by friendship to a man who with as ardent a love of truth as that which animates me, with a mind sur-passing mine in the variety of its research, & sharpened & strengthened to an energy for *action*, to which I have no pre-tension by advantages of birth & practical connexion with mankind beyond almost all men in the world,—is, yet, that which I had ever supposed a creature only of the imagination —a consistent Atheist, and a disbeliever in the existence, &, of course, in the immortality of the soul. My faith in these points is strong & I trust, as I live, indestructible. Meantime I love & honour this intrepid doubter. His soul is noble, & his virtue as the virtue of a Sadducee must always be, is sublime.

—

Charleston S. C. April 17, 1827.
Let the glory of the world go where it will, the mind has its own glory. What it doth, endures. No man can serve many masters. And often the choice is not given you between great-ness in the world & greatness of soul which you will choose, but both advantages are not compatible. The night is fine; the stars shed down their severe influences upon me and I feel a joy in my solitude that the merriment of vulgar society can never communicate. There is a pleasure in the thought that the particular tone of my mind at this moment may be new in the Universe; that the emotions of this hour may be peculiar & unexampled in the whole eternity of moral being. I lead a new life. I occupy new ground in the world of spirits, untenanted before. I commence a career of thought & action which is

expanding before me into a distant & dazzling infinity. Strange thoughts start up like angels in my way & beckon me onward. I doubt not I tread on the highway that leads to the Divinity. And why shall I not be content with these thoughts & this being which give a majesty to my nature & forego the ambition to shine in the frivolous assemblies of men where the genuine objects of my ambition are not revered or known? Yet my friend is at home in both these jarring empires and whilst he taxes my powers in his philosophic speculations can excel the coxcombs, & that, *con amore*, in the fluency of nonsense. Nevertheless I cannot but remember that God is in the heavens, God is here, and the eye of my friend is dull & blind and cannot percieve Him. But what matter if this Being be acknowledged or denied, if the faith cannot impose any more effective restraint on vice & passion, than morals unsupported by this foundation?——

Alexandria, May 5, 1827.——

My days run onward like the weaver's beam. They have no honour among men, they have no grandeur in the view of the invisible world. It is as if a net of meanness were drawn around aspiring men thro' which their eyes are kept on mighty objects but the subtile fence is forever interposed. "They also serve who only stand & wait." Aye but they must wait in a certain temper & in a certain equipment. They must wait as the knight on the van of the embattled line standing in the stirrups, his spear in rest, his steed foaming, ready for the career with the speed of a whirlwind. Am I the accomplished cavalier?

In the view of Compensations nothing is given. There is always a price. Purity is the price at which impurity may be sold. If I sell my cruelty I shall become merciful of necessity. No man ever had pride but he suffered from it or parted with it for meekness without feeling the advantage of the blessed change.

——

Alexandria May 19, 1827.

Mr Adams went out aswimming the other day into the Potomac and went near to a boat which was coming down the river. Some rude blackguards were in it who not knowing the character of the swimmer amused themselves with laughing at his bald head as it poppled up & down in the water & as they drew nearer threatened to crack open his round pate if he came nigh them. The President of the United States was I believe compelled to wave the point of honour & seek a more retired bathing place.—

—

I have seen a skilful experimenter lay a magnet among filings of steel & the force of that subtle fluid entering into each fragment arranged them all in mathematical lines & each metallic atom became in its turn a magnet communicating all the force it received of the loadstone.
                                            —

Aunt Mary used her thimble twice as a seal to once for her needle & I have heard my mother remark that her own was too much worn ever to make the indented impression on wax that Aunt Mary's did.——

—

I ought to apprise the reader that I am a bachelor & to the best of my belief have never been in love.

Robinson Crusoe when in any perplexity was wont to retire to a part of his cave which he called his thinking corner. Devout men have found a stated spot so favorable to a habit of religious feeling that they have worn the solid rock of the oratory with their knees. I have found my ideas very refractory to the usual bye laws of Association. In the graveyard my muscles were twitched by some ludicrous recollections and I am apt to be solemn at a ball. But whilst places are alike to me I make great distinction between states of mind. My days are made up of the irregular succession of a very few different tones of feeling. These are my feasts & fasts. Each has his harbinger, some subtle sign by which I know when to prepare for its coming. Among these some are favorites, and some are to me as the Eumenides. But one of them is the sweet asylum where my greatest happiness is laid up, which I keep in sight whenever disasters befal me & in which it is like the life of angels to live.

It is said public opinion will not bear it. Really? Public opinion, I am sorry to say, will bear a great deal of nonsense. There is scarce any absurdity so gross whether in religion, politics,

science, or manners, which it will not bear. It will bear the
amazing Conference of New Lebanon. It will bear Andrew
Jackson for President. It will bear the convicted ignorance of
Capt. Symmes. It will bear the obscenities of the Boston The-
atre. Lord Bacon never spoke truer word than when he said
There's more of the fool in the world than the wise.

January 8, 1828. I have once or twice been apprehensive that I
was reading in vain, that the cultivation of my mind did not turn
to any good account in my intercourse with men. I am now
satisfied of the contrary. I have every inch of my merits. More is
conceded to me than I have a just title to. I am oftener compelled to deplore my ignorance than to be pleased with my
knowledge. I have no knowledge that I do not want.

In Concord, N.H. I visited the prison & went into the cells.
At this season, they shut up the convicts in these little granite
chambers at about 4 o'clock P.M. & let them out, about
7 o'clock A.M.—15 dreadful hours.

—

January 16. The main difficulty of life is to strike the balance
betwixt contending claims. I am embarrassed by doubts in all
my purposes, & in all my opinions. The best & surest advantages in the world are thought by large numbers of people &
on very plausible grounds to be evils. The freedom of thought
& action in this country often appears tending to the worst &
most malignant results, chaos come again. The expediency of
publishing truth is daily denied. The best manner of em-
ploying the mind whether in study or in invention who will
determine even for himself?

For me I fear I lose days in determining how hours should
be spent. A scholar is perplexed by the necessity of choosing
between many books & many studies and a shade of sorrow
thrown over his meditation by the comparison between the
magnitude of the work to be done & the shortness of life. I regard them all, these doubts of ours, as hints God has inter-
woven in our condition to remind us of the temper that
becomes us; that diffidence & candor suit us better than arrogance & dogmatism & to quicken our curiosity (a curiosity
always respectable) to know the secrets of the other world.

Montaigne says he is sorry Brutus' treatise on Virtue is lost because he would hear one who so well understood the practice discuss the theory of Virtue. 'Tis well said. It is always dangerous when an appeal is made from the sermon to the Preacher, when the bold reason of the hearer quotes his life against his doctrine.

Demades told the Athenians that he had observed that they never treated of peace except in black clothes; so says Plutarch men never reduce their diet except amidst cataplasms, clysters, & medicines. So also men do not turn for enjoyment to another world till their hopes in this have failed them.—

"Age gives good advice when it is no longer able to give a bad example"

—

There was a wise citizen of Athens, the wisest certainly of all the pagans that preceded Christ—I mean Socrates—who taught his countrymen that he was always attended by an invisible Genius which governed his actions. This daemon, as he said, never urged him to the performance of any action but if at any time he proposed to do anything wrong gave him a customary signal to forbear. He said he was accustomed to obey these signals as if they were the voice of God. This man was hunted by an atrocious conspiracy in his native city* & most unjustly doomed to die. In pleading his cause he told his judges that they bid him be silent but God bid him teach. &c When his friends bribed the jailer & furnished him with means of escape he refused to fly for the Daemon he said forbade him. The last hours of his life he spent in explaining to his friends his own grounds for believing that the soul was immortal & when his hour was come drank the poison with cheerful determination.

I suppose that by this Daemon, Socrates designed to describe by a lively image the same judgment which we term conscience. We are all attended by this daemon. We are acquainted with that signal which is as the voice of God.

*The motives of their ill will it is not easy, with all the lights of history, to fathom.

from
Memo St. Augustine
1827

Jan 16. 1827.

The colonies observe the customs of the parent country however ill they may be adapted to the new territory. The Dutch cut canals in Batavia, because they cut canals in Holland, but the fierce sun of the E. Indies stagnated the water & slew the Dutch. In like manner the Spaniards & the Yankees dig cellars here because there are cellars in Madrid & Boston; but the water fills the cellars & makes them useless & the house unhealthy. Yet still they dig cellars. Why? Because there are cellars in Madrid & Boston.

Over the gate of the Fort is an inscription which being in Spanish & in an abbreviated character I was unable to read. After many inquiries in town I could not find an individual who had ever read it or knew anything about it. Mr Gay the public interpreter took the card on which I had written what letters were not defaced of the inscription & succeeded in decyphering the following record.

Regnando en Espana el Senor Don Fernando Gobernador y Capitan General de esta plaza de San Agostino de la Florida y su provincia el Mariscal de Campo Don Alonzo Fernandes d'heredia se concluio este castillo el año de 1756 dirigiendo las obras el Capitan ynceniero Don Pedro de Brozas y Garay. which runs in English thus.

"Don Ferdinand VI being king of Spain, and the Field Marshal Don Alonzo Fernandez d'Heredia being Governor & Captain General of this place of St Augustine of Florida, & of its province, this fort was finished in the year 1756. The works were directed by the Captain engineer Don Pedro de Brozas y Garay."

It is commonly said here that the fort is more than a century old. It seems there was an old one of much earlier date standing on the same site which was the foundation of the present erection.

There are two graveyards in St. A., one of the Catholics, another of the Protestants. Of the latter the whole fence is gone having been purloined by these idle people for firewood. Of the former the fence has been blown down by some gale, but not a stick or board has been removed,—and they rot undisturbed such is the superstition of the thieves. I saw two Spaniards entering this enclosure, and observed that they both took off their hats in reverence to what is holy ground. In the Protestant yard among other specimens of the Sepulchral Muse, the following epitaph is written over the body of Mr Happoldt "a native of Germany"

> Rest in this tomb raised at thy children's cost
> Here sadly summoned what they had & lost
> For kind & true a treasure each alone
> A father, brother, & a friend in one;
> O happy soul if thou canst see from high
> Thy large & orphan family.

—

March 1. I found here a gentleman from N. Carolina who gave me some account of the monstrous absurdities of the Methodists at their Camp Meetings in that state. He related an instance of several of these fanatics jumping about on all fours, imitating the barking of dogs & surrounding a tree in which they pretended they had "*treed Jesus!*"

The Minorcans are very much afraid of the Indians. All the old houses have very strong walls & doors, with apertures thro' which a musket can be discharged. They are delighted to find that under the American flag the Indians are afraid of the whites. Some of them however do not like to venture far out of the town at this day. "But what are you afraid of? Don't you know Gen Jackson conquered all the Indians?" "Yes, but Gen Jackens no here now." "But his son is, for, you know the Indians call col. Gadsden his son." "Ay, Ay. but then they Indians, for all that."

I saw by the city gates two iron frames in the shape of a

mummy with iron rings on the head. They were
cases in which the Spanish governor had hung
criminals upon a gibbet. There is a little iron
loop on one side by the breast in which a loaf of
bread & a vessel of water were contained. Thus
provided the wretch was hung up by suspending the ring over
his head to a tree & left to starve to death. They were lately
dug up full of bones.

The worthy father of the Catholic church here by whose
conversation I was not a little scandalized has lately been arrested for debt & imprisoned in St. Marks. This exemplary divine on the evening of his arrest said to Mr Crosby, "If you can
change ten dollars for me I will pay you the four which I owe
you." Crosby gave him six which the father put in his waistcoat
pocket, &, being presently questioned, stoutly denied that he
had any thing from him. But Crosby was the biggest & compelled him to restore the money. I went yesterday to the
Cathedral, full of great coarse toys, & heard this priest say
mass, for his creditors have been indulgent & released him for
the present.

I met some Indians in the street selling venison. I asked the
man where he lived? "Yonder." Where? "In the big swamp."
He sold his haunch for 5 bits. The purchaser offered him one
bit & a bill worth half a dollar & counted on his fingers this,
one, & this *four*. "You lie," said the Indian—which I found was
his only word for *no*. I gave him a half bit for "piccaniny." Indian notions about the creation   & three pairs & three
boxes. Col. Humphreys Ind. agent.

Feb. 27.

A fortnight since I attended a meeting of the Bible Society.
The Treasurer of this institution is Marshal of the district & by
a somewhat unfortunate arrangement had appointed a special
meeting of the Society & a Slave Auction at the same time &
place, one being in the Government house & the other in the
adjoining yard. One ear therefore heard the glad tidings of
great joy whilst the other was regaled with "Going gentlemen,
Going!" And almost without changing our position we might
aid in sending the scriptures into Africa or bid for "four children without the mother who had been kidnapped there-

from." It was singular enough that at the annual meeting of this society one week after, the business should have been interrupted by an unexpected quarrel of two gentlemen present, both, I believe, members of the society, who with language not very appropriate to the occasion collared each other—& were not without difficulty separated by the interference of some members.——There is something wonderfully *piquant* in the manners of the place, theological or civil. A Mr Jerry, a Methodist minister, preached here two Sundays ago, who confined himself in the afternoon to some pretty intelligible strictures upon the character of a President of the Bible Soc. who swears. The gentleman alluded to was present. And it really exceeded all power of face to be grave during the divine's very plain analysis of the motives which probably actuated the individual in seeking the office which he holds. It fairly beat the "Quousque Catilina."

Feb. 25.

I attended mass in the Catholic Church. The mass is in Latin & the sermon in English & the audience who are Spaniards understand neither. The services have been recently interrupted by the imprisonment of the worthy father for debt in the Castle of St Marks.

The people call the place Botany Bay & say that whenever Presidents or Bishops or Presbyteries have danglers on their hands fit for no offices they send them to Florida.

Sermons and Journal

Aug. 11

Inter se convenit ursis
Juvenal
The world has people of all sorts. Locke

Whereby a clause, an epithet becomes a comprehensive litany of whole annals, of events, & discoveries.

A single house will shew whatever is done or suffered in the world. Juv.

I Seid Abn Haer built this pyramid in six years. Let him that cometh after me & says he is equal to me pull down the pyramid in thirty. And yet it is easier to pluck down than to build up. I Abn Seid covered this pyramid with satin; let him that cometh after me cover it with mats.

In few words, mysteries are due to secrecy. Besides, to say truth, nakedness is uncomely as well in mind as in body and it addeth no small reverence to men's manners & actions if they be not altogether open. Bacon

———

A text is the hat of a sermon. Who buys a hat before a head is made?—

———

The gospel has gone out through all the earth. It is read in every language. That simple tale addressed to the heart by him who made the heart is now familiar to all. No matter what barbarous tongue he speaks, no matter what swarthy tint an Indian sun may have burnt on his face his heart shall answer to this simple strain. The same Creator made him. Courage & indignation & charity are of no sect or colour. He understands them as well as you. See as this simple anecdote that had its origin in a paltry Jewish hamlet so many ages ago is made known now to this idle savage in his native speech, see how he recognizes what his maker made him to love, see how his heart beats & his eye glistens with pleasure rising from the perception of a moral beauty which centuries do not exhale, for it is everlasting. I talk of the Samaritan parable. The ships on every sea are freighted with this beneficent message. A thousand presses are labouring in the multiplication of its copies. A thousand excellent heads are night & day exhausting their powers on its illustration or its defence. & I firmly trust in God who has made nothing & permitted nothing in vain that all this profuse exertion shall be made to cooperate to an irresistible effect.

April 15, 1828. It is natural to be selfish you may say. I own I have seen very good men in a quarrel very selfish. But when a young man after the explosion of the quarrel with me when I am reproaching myself with the harsh things I said & am lamenting the regrets I conceive him to feel—when I perceive that at this moment he is calculating for himself upon my self-reproaches I am disheartened. It seems to me something black & malignant.

—

That time enters as largely into the account of life which we spend in waiting for an appointment as the time occupied by the appointments. I am as great a man whilst I sit alone scanning the soot on my chimney back as when in the duties of my profession I fix the eyes of a thousand men on me or invoke as their organ the name of the Deity. I have as just views of my nature & of the secrets of metaphysics when I am blacking my boots. I think as coolly and am therefore as respectable in the eye of angels, as in an extacy of devotion or the hour of death. He that in a mud cottage measures time by the sun & stars & judges of domestic contingences not by the follies of the place but by the everlasting laws of moral & physical being; who sees the glory of goodness thro' the disguise of coarse clothes & begrimed hands.

—

Divinity Hall 10 July.

I am always made uneasy when the conversation turns in my presence upon popular ignorance & the duty of adapting our public harangues & writings to the minds of the people. 'Tis all pedantry & ignorance. The people know as much & reason as well as we do. None so quick as they to discern brilliant genius or solid parts. And I observe that all those who use this cant most, are such as do not rise above mediocrity of understanding.

I am not so enamoured of liberty as to love to be idle. But the only evil I find in idleness is unhappiness. I love to be my own master when my spirits are prompt, when my brain is vegete & apt for thought. If I were richer I should lead a better life than I do; that is, better divided & more able. I should ride on horseback a good deal; I should bowl, & create an appetite for my studies by intermixing some heat & labour in affairs. The chief advantage I should propose myself in wealth would be the independence of manner & conversation it would bestow & which I eagerly covet & seldom quite attain, & in some companies never.

It is a peculiarity (I find by observation upon others) of humour in me, my strong propensity for strolling. I deliberately shut up my books in a cloudy July noon, put on my old clothes & old hat & slink away to the whortleberry bushes & slip with the greatest satisfaction into a little cowpath where I am sure I can defy observation. This point gained, I solace myself for hours with picking blue berries & other trash of the woods far from fame behind the birch trees. I seldom enjoy hours as I do these. I remember them in winter; I expect them in spring. I do not know a creature that I think has the same humour or would think it respectable. Yet the friend, the Anteros, whom I seek through the world, now in cities—now in wildernesses—now at sea—will know the delight of sauntering with the melancholy Jaques.

When I consider the constitutional calamity of my family which in its falling upon Edward has buried at once so many towering hopes—— with whatever reason I have little apprehension of my own liability to the same evil. I have so much mixture of *silliness* in my intellectual frame that I think Providence has tempered me against this. My brother lived & acted & spoke with preternatural energy. My own manner is slug-gish; my speech sometimes flippant, sometimes embarrassed & ragged; my actions (if I may say so) are of a passive kind. Ed-ward had always great power of face. I have none. I laugh; I blush; I look ill tempered; against my will & against my inter-est. But all this imperfection as it appears to me is a caput mor-tuum, is a ballast—as things go—is a defence.

My practice conforms more to the Epicurean, than to the Stoic rule:

> "I will be flesh & blood;
> For there was never yet philosopher,
> That could endure the tooth ache patiently,
> However they have writ the style of gods
> And made a pish at chance & sufferance."

Wo is me my brother for you! Please God to rescue & re-store him!

I like to have a man's knowledge comprehend more than one class of topics, one row of shelves. I like a man who likes to see a fine barn as well as a good tragedy.

—

Est deus in nobis, &c. & when outraged this deus becomes di-abolus, a spectre that no exorcism will bind.

Divinity Hall 18 August 1828.

Keep a thing by you seven years, & you shall find use for it. You will never have waste knowledge. I like the sentence of Locke: "that young men in their warm blood are often for-ward to think they have in vain learned to fence if they never show their skill in a duel."

One of the great defects of the world is this that it is not enough that an objection has been fully answered. In my sim-plicity I should have thought Richardson's engaging novel of Sir Chas. Grandison a settlement of the subject of duelling: that all the common prejudices on that question were manifestly shown to be paltry. But no it must be hammered into the head of society as Latin nouns into the head of a blockhead at school.

—

'Tis a striking proof of the power of *situation* to drop a penknife or a glove upon the ground & see how they look there.

—

Dec., 1828.

It is strange when the Spirit of Contradiction in the mind becomes a principle of action so uniform that you may calculate with great precision upon its opinions by always reversing the opinions of those minds next to it. J'attends toujours le temps quand mon ami levera l'étendard pour Jackson.

"The face of persuasion is prevalent" ap. Plut.

The echo of Plutarch is philosophy —ap. C. Mather. Essays.

I read things in Montaigne, Caius, that you cannot; much as he said himself. I will give you Scougal & you shall not find any thing in it valuable to you. It sounds to the intelligent. The lapidary will let you choose a stone from a handful of chrystals knowing that your eye is not skilful enough to detect the unpolished diamond.

—

Is it not true what we so reluctantly hear that men are but the mouthpieces of a great progressive destiny in as much as regards literature. I had rather asked is not the age gone by of the great splendour of English poetry, & will it not be impossible for any age soon to vie with the pervading etherial poesy of Herbert, Shakspeare, Marvell, Herrick, Milton, Ben Jonson, at least to represent any thing like their peculiar form of ravishing verse? It is the head of human poetry. Homer & Virgil & Dante & Tasso & Byron & Wordsworth have powerful genius whose amplest claims I cheerfully acknowledge.—But 'tis a pale ineffectual fire when theirs shines. They would lie on my shelf in undisturbed honour for years, if these Saxon lays stole on my ear. I have for them an affectionate admiration I have for nothing else. They set me on speculations. They move my wonder at myself. They suggest the great endowments of the spiritual man. They open glimpses of the heaven that is in the intellect. When I am caught by a magic word & drop the book to explore the infinite charm—to run along the line of that ray—I feel the longevity of the mind; I admit the evidence of the immortality of the soul. Well, as I said, I am afraid the season of this rare fruit is irrecoverably past; that the earth has made such a mutation of its nodes, that the heat will never reach again that Hesperian garden in which alone these apricots & pomegranates grew.

Concord N. H. Dec. 21, 1828. I have now been four days engaged to Ellen Louisa Tucker. Will my Father in Heaven regard us with kindness, and as he hath, as we trust, made us for each other, will he be pleased to strengthen & purify & prosper & eternize our affection! Sunday Morning.

January 17, 1829. She has the purity & confiding religion of an angel. Are the words common? the words are true. Will God forgive me my sins & aid me to deserve this gift of his mercy.

Divinity Hall 30 Dec., 1828.

"Forgive our Sins." Were it not desireable that we should have a guardian angel that should go on our errands between heaven & earth, that should tell us how God receives our actions; when he smiles & when he frowns; what petitions he hears with favour, & what he rejects? Well we have such a report rendered back to us. Consider this prayer, Forgive our Sins. I believe every man may answer to himself when he utters this ejaculation, the precise degree of consideration it has received from the Almighty mind. That consideration depends wholly upon the sentiment which accompanied the prayer. If when I say, Forgive my Sins, I am in a frame of mind that sorrowfully repents of all my perversity, if I am struck with a deep & contrite sense of the enormity of sin; if I feel the evil of guilt & the virtue to sin no more, then God hears me, then

Cambridge, 17 January, 1829.

My history has had its important days within a brief period. Whilst I enjoy the luxury of an unmeasured affection for an object so deserving of it all & who requites it all,—I am called by an ancient & respectable church to become its pastor. I recognize in these events, accompanied as they are by so many additional occasions of joy in the condition of my family, I recognize, with acute sensibility, the hand of my heavenly Father. This happiness awakens in me a certain awe: I know my imperfections: I know my ill-deserts; & the bounty of God makes me feel my own sinfulness the more. I throw myself with humble gratitude upon his goodness. I feel my total dependance. O God direct & guard & bless me, & those, & especially *her*, in whom I am blessed.——

———

Truth is irresistible. They that fight against it are like the devils in Pandaemon who were forced to hiss when they meant to shout applause at their evil Captain. And I have seen in the controversies of the day many instances of this. Whilst the word of contradiction is on their tongues they find themselves forced to affirm the very truth which they opened their mouths to deny.

Chardon St July 21, 1829.

The passion for novels is natural. Every child asks his Grandpapa to tell him a story. Cinderella & Red Ridinghood are the novels of the two shoeses, & Walter Scott is the grandpa of the grown up children.

There appeared in the world as Civilization advanced a marked character which was its creature—A fashionist.—He never laughs, he never weeps, is never surprized, never moved. He is completely selfish. By his selfcommand he aspires to an influence over society which owes nothing to rank, wealth, office, talents, or learning—the command of fashion. He derides & is cool & so reigns. This person has been shown to the public under several names, Vivian Grey, Lord Etherington, Mr Brummel, Ld. Dalgarno, Pelham. But 'tis all one rascal with all his aliases. Now the question arises whether these novels of fashionable life—whether these representations of this scoundrel have a good or bad effect. It is an impertinent question. As long as the original exists the copies will be multiplied. If the moral is bad, as it is, get rid of the character & the pictures will no more be made. Therefore let every man cultivate benevolence in himself.

———

Oh Ellen, I do dearly love you—

———

Sept., 1829.—
Let a man look round upon his acquaintances; if he remembers any with dislike it is because he has not behaved well to that one.—

July 3, 1829. My weight is 144 lb.

Owls & birds of defective Vision have a knack at finding, darting into crannies & dark places in tower.

November 1. The power of the individual depends upon the power of society. If we lived in the world—each man emperor of himself & his acre of ground & without any social league—Mr Touchstone & Mr Zany's opinion would be worth a brass farthing & so would Mr Webster's & Mr Canning's. But now by dint of the social system a person of genius like Mr Canning is able to touch with his long fingers India & America, & if a private person in Wales is robbed or insulted he can avail himself of enginery that shall search under the line or in the forests of Labrador or the jungles of Bengal to find out wherever in the civilized world skulks the aggressor.

—

January, 1830. I read in Plutarch's Political Precepts, that when Leo Bizantinus went to Athens to appease the Dissensions in that city—when he arose to speak he perceived that they laughed on account of the littleness of his stature. "What would you do," he exclaimed "if you saw my wife who scarce reaches to my knees?" And they laughing the more he said "yet as little as we are, when we fall out, the city of Byzantium is not big enough to hold us."—

—

There were two vultures; One of them was taken with so strong a fit of vomiting that he said I believe I shall cast up my very bowels. His companion answered "What's the harm? for thou wilt not throw up thine own entrails but those of a deceased person which we devoured the other day." Plutarch. Usury.

—

It is strange that the greatest men of the time only *say* what is just trembling on the lips of all thinking men.

Jan. 4.—
Knowledge even, God's own attribute & delight & mean, I
fear it is but the cock's pearl when it is in a spirit which is not
united to the great Spirit. Quantum sumus scimus.

Jan. 4.—
If will not do for us to dogmatize. Nothing is more untrue
to nature. The meanest scholar in Christian practice may often
instruct the greatest doctor both in faith & practice. I have no
shame in saying I lean to this opinion but am not sure—I do
not affect or pretend to instruct—oh no—it is God working in
you that instructs both you & me. I only tell how I have
striven & climbed, & what I have seen, that you may compare
it with your own observations of the same Object. It is important to have some *formal* observer, whether a keen sighted one
or not, in order to furnish some πον στω, some *other point* to
measure thoughts by.—

That man will always speak with authority who speaks his
own convictions—not the knowledge of his ear or eye—i.e.
superstitions got in conversation, or errors or truths remembered from his reading—but that which true or false he hath
perceived with his inward eye—which therefore is true to him
—true even as he tells it, & absolutely true in some element
though distorted & discoloured by some disease in the soul.

Omnia exeunt in mysterium
—

It is the praise of most critics that they have never failed
because they have attempted nothing. It is generous in a
youthful hero who bears an unspotted shield to adventure his
fame in that difficult field of Metaphysics—where from the intrinsic inaccessibilities of the positions the strongest & the
weakest assailants are brought nearly to a level & where much
may be gained by the losses of the individual. He will console
himself when he comes out smeared & baffled with the saying
of Wotton that "Critics are brushers of noblemen's clothes."
— — "The Eternal hath fixed his canon 'gainst self slaughter"
shall be my answer to the Pyrrhonist.

The system of Aristotle, the labour of a thousand years which had become the religion of the intellect of Europe comes to be called an *experiment*; some happy genius epitomizes it in a word & that becomes its history—the algebraic x by which it is to be designated now that its value has been evolved, & that it cannot be spared more room in the opulence of human knowlege——repositories where 'tis huddled away.——

—

February. 26. Whether, saith Ellen, the Spirits in heaven look onward to their immortality as we on earth, or are absorbed in the present moment?

—

March 3. Read with admiration & delight Mr Webster's noble speech in answer to Hayne. What consciousness of political rectitude & what confidence in his intellectual treasures must he have to enable him to take this master's tone! Mr Channing said he had 'great Self Subsistence.' The beauty & dignity of the spectacle he exhibits should teach men the beauty & dignity of *principles*. This is one that is not blown about by every wind of opinion, but has mind great enough to see the majesty of moral nature & to apply himself in all his length & breadth to it & magnanimously trust thereto.

Wednesday Night. The power that we originate outlives us, takes imposing & stable forms & Caesar becomes a dynasty; & Luther & Calvin each a church; & Mahomet *re*-presents himself in a third of the human race.

April 24 Noah Ripley, the good deacon, is himself an affecting argument for the immortality of the soul.

Johnson says that Pope left Addison "to be punished by what has been considered as the most painful of all reflections, the remembrance of a crime perpetrated in vain."

I know not which is best, to justify a good reputation by one's performance or to surpass a poor expectation: to be Webster always or to write a Life of Lafayette as T.

"Every man's strength," says Edin. Reviewer of Godwin, "is his weakness, & turns in some way or other against himself."

———

May 12. It was said of Jesus that "he taught as one having authority"—a distinction most palpable. There are a few men in every age I suppose who teach thus. Stubler the Quaker whom I saw on board the boat in Delaware Bay was one. If Sampson Reed were a talker, he were another. There is nevertheless a foolish belief among teachers that the multitude are not wise enough to discern between good manner & good matter. And that voice & rhetorick will stand instead of truth. They can tell well enough whether they have been convinced or no. The multitude suppose often that great talents are necessary to produce the elaborate harangues which they hear without emotion or consequence. & so they say what a fine speaker, what a good discourse but they will not leave any agreeable employment to go again & never will do a single thing in consequence of having heard the discourse. But let them hear one of these Godtaught teachers & they surrender to him. They leave their work to come again. They go home & think & talk and act as he said. Men know truth as quick as they see it.

It is remarkable how this mastery shows itself in the tone that is taken as much as in the facts that are presented. A tone of authority cannot be taken without truths of authority. It is impossible to mimick it. There is no favoritism in the public; Buckminster had it; Greenwood has it in some measure. F.m has not a particle. It proceeds directly from the perception of Principles.—Dr Johnson was one.

———

July 30. Immense significance of the precept *Know Thyself*. In view of this, how ridiculous is Alexander, & Buonaparte wandering from one extreme of civilization to the other to conquer men, himself the while yet unconquered, unexplored, unknown, to himself. Yet Europe & Asia are not so broad & deep, have nothing so splendid, so durable as the possessions of this Empire. How ridiculous the gladiators on our republican arena, greedy of a little showy power over their fellow citizens' property & rights & foregoing the sceptre of spiritual might that belongs to the self comprehender. He that knows himself must always be felt as the superior of him that does not, let the last rule the globe if he will.

But I am disposed to think that our habits of thought are so different & so civilized that few Americans could covet with any eagerness the empire of Bonaparte. It would be a great bore. We had rather be rich or good Orators, as a nation.

Brookline 3 August 1830. My weight is 157 lb.

I have learned this day a fact I might have known long ago that men give unconscious testimony to their inborn opinion that happiness always results from virtue in this fact, that they always desire to be thought happy. It shows how long we may know the data before we draw the conclusion. I found this in Stewart.—

Aug. 18. In the resurrection they neither marry nor are given in marriage. That is to say there is no sex, in thought, in knowledge, in virtue; & the kingdom of heaven is the kingdom of these.

We never ask the reason of what is good. The sun shines & warms & lights us & we have no curiosity to know why this is so; but we ask the reason of all evil, of pain, & hunger, & musquitoes, & silly people. —

Here is a man whom a melon & a glass of wine will make happy. Here is one of another temper,—a fantastic book will serve his turn. Here is one whom power will make happy. And here is one who has got hold of his bible, & must have the Universe, & God himself to satisfy him.

9 September. 1830.

There are some kingdoms of Europe whose whole population for ages does not possess an equal interest in history with some single minds. The history of John Locke or of Isaac Newton is a far more important part of the stock of knowledge we carry out of the world, than the whole history of Poland or Hungary.

Well, what of this? You accuse yourself perhaps. Before God Poland is a greater affair than Locke.

Mr Stewart's works are like Dr Clarke's description of the entrance of Moscow—All splendour & promise till you enter the gate, & then you look before & behind but only cottages & shops.

Judge Howe advised his pupils to make study their business & business their amusement.

Sept. 10. It is my purpose to methodize my days. I wish to study the scriptures, in a part of every day, that I may be able to explain them to others & that their light may flow into my life. I wish not to be strait laced in my own rules but to wear them easily & to make wisdom master of them. It is a resolving world, but God grant me persistency enough, so soon as I leave Brookline & come to my books, to do as I intend.

27 Sept. Brookline. I would have a man trust himself, believe that he has all the endowments necessary to balance each other in a perfect character; if only he will allow them all fair play. I have sometimes wished I had not some acuteness or minuteness of observation that seemed inconsistent with dignity of character; but thus to wish seems to me now to be false to oneself, to give up a tower in my castle to the enemy which was given me as a bulwark of defence. It is a wondrous structure this soul in me infinitely beyond my art to puzzle out its principles. I admire a flower & see that each lily & aster is perfect in its kind, though different in its proportions & arrangement of petals from every other aster in the field, & shall I not beleive as much of every mind? that it has its own beauty & character, & was never meant to resemble any other one. Every man has his own voice, manner, eloquence, & just as much his own sort of love & grief & imagination & action. Let him scorn to imitate any being, let him scorn to be a secondary man, let him fully trust his own share of God's goodness, that correctly used it will lead him on to perfection which has no type yet in the Universe save only in the Divine Mind.

A man who forsakes his first impressions of a book or a

character & adopts new ones from complaisance is likely to be compelled to receive his own again with the mortification of being overcome by his own weapons.

Then it seems to be true that the more exclusively idiosyncratic a man is, the more general & infinite he is, which though it may not be a very intelligible expression means I hope something intelligible. In listening more intently to our own reason, we are not becoming in the ordinary sense more selfish, but are departing more from what is small, & falling back on truth itself & God. For it is when a man does not listen to himself but to others, that he is depraved & misled. The great men of the world, the teachers of the race, moralists, Socrates, Bacon, Newton, Butler, & the like, were those who did not take their opinions on trust, but explored themselves and that is the way ethics & religion were got out.

29 Sept. 1830. A man is invincible, be his cause great or small, an abstract principle or a petty fact whenever he expresses the simple truth. This makes the cogency of the talk of common people in common affairs. They perfectly understand that a commodity sold for so much or that a stage runs on such a road or the numbers arrayed on either side a contested vote or any other chance topic of matters of fact. No ingenuity, no sophism of learned or eloquent men is any match for such persons in such a matter. It would seem ridiculous. They are become mere organs thro' which these very facts speak. Now if a man would always as entirely consult his own thoughts in all things as these men do in these things he would always speak with the same force, a force which would be felt to be far greater than belonged to him or any mortal but was proper to the immortal truth. But men think what is proper to say, what is expected to be said, what have others said, what is safest to be said until they lose in such habits the instinctive habit—of speaking their convictions.

It ought to be considered that the meanest human soul contains a model of action greater than is realized by the greatest man. Nobody can read the life of Newton or Franklin or Washington without detecting imperfections in those astonishing instances of the conduct of life.

Population of U S A 12,821,181. souls
slaves 2,000,000.

———

To the matter of patriotism remember the saying of Anaxagoras when blamed for neglecting his country. "Wrong me not; my greatest care is my country," pointing to heaven.

November 19. 'Tis a good definition Coleridge gives in the "Friend," of Talent, that it pursues by original & peculiar means vulgar conventional ends. 'Tis dexterity intellectual applied to the purpose of getting power & wealth. Genius on the contrary is its end in the means. It concerns our peace to learn this distinction as quick as we can.

———

The speech that a man repeats which is not his own but was borrowed from another with the hope to pass for original is like a flower held in the hand or a dead feather in the cap manifestly cut off from all life & can deceive none but a child into the belief that it is a part of himself.

———

Ellen Tucker Emerson died 8th February. Tuesday morning 9 o'clock.

Chardon St, Feb. 13, 1831—

Five days are wasted since Ellen went to heaven to see, to know, to worship, to love, to intercede. God be merciful to me a sinner & repair this miserable debility in which her death has left my soul. Two nights since, I have again heard her breathing, seen her dying. O willingly, my wife, I would lie down in your tomb. But I have no deserts like yours, no such purity, or singleness of heart. Pray for me Ellen & raise the friend you so truly loved, to be what you thought him. When your friends or mine cross me, I comfort myself by saying, you would not have done so. Dear Ellen (for that is your name in heaven) shall we not be united even now more & more, as I more steadfastly persist in the love of truth & virtue which you loved? Spirits are not deceived & now you know the sins & selfishness which the husband would fain have concealed from the confiding wife—help me to be rid of them; suggest good thoughts as you promised me, & show me truth. Not for the world, would I have left you here alone; stay by me & lead me upward. Reunite us, o thou Father of our Spirits.

There is that which passes away & never returns. This miserable apathy, I know, may wear off. I almost fear when it will. Old duties will present themselves with no more repulsive face. I shall go again among my friends with a tranquil countenance. Again I shall be amused, I shall stoop again to little hopes & little fears & forget the graveyard. But will the dead be restored to me? Will the eye that was closed on Tuesday ever beam again in the fulness of love on me? Shall I ever again be able to connect the face of outward nature, the mists of the morn, the star of eve, the flowers, & all poetry, with the heart & life of an enchanting friend? No. There is one birth & one baptism & one first love and the affections cannot keep their youth any more than men.

Her end was blessed & a fit termination to such a career. She prayed that God would speedily release her from her body & that she might not make this prayer to be rid of her pains "but because thy favor is better than life." "Take me o God to thyself" was frequently on her lips. Never any one spake with greater simplicity or cheerfulness of dying. She said, 'I pray for sincerity & that I may not talk, but may realize what I say.' She did not think she had a wish to get well, & told me "she should do me more good by going than by staying; she should go first & explore the way, & comfort me." She prayed earnestly & suitably for me.

A little after 2 o'clock on Tuesday morn, she said she felt that she was going soon & having asked if Mother, Margaret, & Paulina were all present she wished them to be still & she would pray with them. And truly & sweetly did she pray for herself & for us & infused such comfort into my soul as never entered it before & I trust will never escape out of it. After this she kissed all, & bid her nurses, 'love God;' & then sunk very fast, occasionally recovering her wandering mind. One of the last things she said after much rambling & inarticulate expression was 'I have not forgot the peace & joy.' And at nine o'clock she died. Farewell blessed Spirit who hast made me happy in thy life & in thy death make me yet happy in thy disembodied state.

She frequently requested me that I would be with her when she died.

Heu! quantominus est cum reliquis versari, quam tui meminisse!

15 Feb.

> Dost thou not hear me Ellen
> Is thy ear deaf to me
> Is thy radiant eye
> Dark that it cannot see
>
> In yonder ground thy limbs are laid
> Under the snow
> And earth has no spot so dear above
> As that below
>
> And there I know the heart is still
> And the eye is shut & the ear is dull
>
> But the spirit that dwelt in mine
> The spirit wherein mine dwelt
> The soul of Ellen the thought divine
> From God, that came—for all that felt
>
> Does it not know me now
> Does it not share my thought
> Is it prisoned from Waldo's prayer
> Is its glowing love forgot
> —

1 April 1831.

The spring is wearing into summer & life is wearing into death; our friends are forsaking us, our hopes are declining; our riches are wasting; our mortifications are increasing and is the question settled in our minds, what objects we pursue with undivided aim? Have we fixed ourselves by principles? Have we planted our stakes?

———

Dear Ellen do you despise knowledge, or through holier organs does the soul fill her thirst & add to her appetite? Do you despise goodness? Oh no never here did you underrate a miser's mite, & not there, not there, my love. O suggest, coming from God's throne, suggest to this lone heart some hint of him. O forget me not, think with me, pray with me.

———

It is a luxury to be understood.

Boston, 4 April, 1831.

The days go by, griefs, & simpers, & sloth, & disappointments. The dead do not return, & sometimes we are negligent of their image. Not of yours Ellen—I know too well who is gone from me. And here come on the formal duties which are to be formally discharged, and in our sluggish minds no sentiment rises to quicken them, they seem——

———

Apr. 9.   The Bride of Lammermoor.

Pleasure taken in Ravenswood's grand feudal character great. And why? because the contemplation of somebody that we could depend upon, & should without risk admire & love if we should converse with him, is pleasing. The soul believes in its own immortality & whilst this character floats before it, is already anticipating intercourse with such in other states of being. Is it not too, that by the law of sympathy the soul sees in every great character only a mirror in which its own pinched features are expanded to true dimensions, "the shows of things to the desires of the mind."

And does it not find a lesson herein, the suggestion that a mind raised above circumstances may fight this heroic battle day by day; that Sir William Ashton is only another name for a vulgar temptation; that Ravenswood castle is only another name for proud poverty & the 'foreign mission of state' only a Bunyan disguise for honest industry; that we may all shoot a wild bull that would toss the good & beautiful by fighting down the unjust & sensual; that Lucy is another word for fidelity which is always beautiful & always liable to great suffering in this world but which is true to itself & trusts God for success in the abysses of his designs.

—

15 June 1831.

After a fortnight's wandering to the Green Mountains & Lake Champlain yet finding you dear Ellen nowhere & yet everywhere I come again to my own place, & would willingly transfer some of the pictures that the eyes saw, in living language to my page; yea translate the fair & magnificent symbols into their own sentiments. But this were to antedate knowledge. It grows into us, say rather, we *grow wise* & not take wisdom; and only in God's own order & by my concurrent effort can I get the abstract sense of which mountains, sunshine, thunder, night, birds, & flowers are the sublime alphabet.

—

"High over the full toned Sea."

The days pass over me
And I am still the same
The aroma of my life is gone
Like the flower with which it came

June 25, 1831. No love without sympathy. Minds must be alike. All love a seeking in another what is like self. Difference of opinion separates, common thought ties us. If we find a person esteems excellence that we have loved we love him. No bond of kindness to me that A is a keen hunter or B fond of horses or C a great driver of business but if D is fond of flowers or of books, of poems, of De Stael, of Platonism, then I find a tie nearer & nearer as his tastes approach or unite with mine. And the higher is the principle on which we sympathize the more the love. The fact that we both drink hyson tea or both walk before breakfast—or delight in swimming are low points of union that do not create any permanent kindness but that we are both admirers of a great & good man is a very strong bond. If we both love God we shall be wholly alike & wholly love each other.

Wherever goes a man, there goes a great soul. I never more fully possess myself than in slovenly or disagreeable circumstances. When I stamp thro' the mud in dirty boots, I hug myself with the feeling of my immortality. I then reflect complacently on whatever of delicacy is in my taste, of amplitude in my memory. In a university I draw in my horns. On nothing does wise man plume himself so much as on independance of circumst. that in a kitchen, or dirty street or sweltering stage coach, he can separate himself from impure contact & embosom himself in the sublime society of his recollections, of his hopes, & of his affections. Ambassador carries his country with him. So does the Mind.—

—

Boston, 26 Jan., 1832.

Heard Dr Channing last evg at the Peace Society. Very good views. Freedom unfits for War. Unchains industry & so makes property; then men are unwilling to put it at stake improves men & gives them individuality do not follow leaders. Only two men have ever controuled public opinion in this country Washington & Jefferson. Efforts of this country in the last war paralyzed by the minority. Then Freedom unfits men for Soldiers. Soldier is a slave.

Great extent of territory. Federal principle beneficent. Rise of public opinion in Europe. False predictions of politicians a year or two ago at the Three days of July. All expected War. But no War. Why? Predominance of peace party; of men of property; fears of the Sovereigns who see a liberal party in their subjects & in their armies reverse in a war with France would have been revolution at home. He was not the prophet of peace; he saw the two parties of improvement & antiquity, of freedom & legitimacy arrayed against each other, but hoped.

Sorry to see the soldier adorned. "If I should see the executioner decked out in gay trappings when he conducted the criminal to the gallows he should think it in bad taste. But the soldier has as solemn a work to do as the executioner. If it is necessity, it is a melancholy necessity. He should go in mourning. These ornaments have come down from an earlier age when every class in society had its own costume—badge profusion of ornaments the badges of its vocation, but they have all been disused in the advance of refinement. The soldier is the only harlequin that has come down to us from the middle ages."

Blotting Book III

1831–1832

5 July.—It is remarkable that we cannot be willing to say, *I do not know*. I am ashamed of my ignorance of history, of science, of languages, daily. "All Error," Dr Johnson said, "is mean." And by this powerful shame doth God wonderfully indicate to us his intention that we should study & learn without end.

6 July, 1831. President Monroe died on the fourth of July,— a respectable man, I believe.

———

8 July.
No man can write well who thinks there is any choice of words for him. The laws of composition are as strict as those of sculpture & architecture. There is always one line that ought to be drawn or one proportion that should be kept & every other line or proportion is wrong, & so far wrong as it deviates from this. So in writing, there is always a right word, & every other than that is wrong. There is no beauty in words except in their collocation. The effect of a fanciful word misplaced, is like that of a horn of exquisite polish growing on a human head.

Oct. 27. To the same purpose I find at this date in Guesses at Truth—"In good prose, (says Schlegel) every word should be underlined." "no italics in Plato."—In good writing every word means something. In good writing words become one with things. I take up a poem; if I find that there is not a single line there nor word but expresses something that is true for me as well as for him then

Oct. 28, 1831. I may safely apply the words beautiful, grand, sweet, for whatever is true of thought is true of the poem. It is adamant. Its reputation will be slow but sure from every caprice of taste. No critic can hurt it; he will only hurt himself by tilting against it. This is the confidence we feel concerning Shakspeare. We know Charles says, that his record is true. And this is the ordeal which the new aspirant Wordsworth must undergo. He has writ lines that are like outward nature—so fresh, so simple, so durable. But whether all or half his texture is as firm I doubt, tho' last evg (27 Oct.) I read with high delight his Sonnets to Liberty.

A rule given in Guesses at Truth, was,—When you sit down to write the main thing is to say what you have to say.

9 July, 1831. Kingdom of heaven is like a little leaven which a householder took, & put in meal till it leavened the whole lump. Progress of religious character. It is leaven. It is essentially active. It is the liveliest thing in the Universe, for it is life itself.

10 July. Old English writers are the standards not because they are old but simply because they wrote well. They deviated every day from other people but never from truth & so we follow them. If we write as well we may deviate from them & our deviations shall be classical.

'He invents who proves.' Every man says a hundred things every day that are capable of much more meaning than he attaches to them. The Declaration of Independence as Webster intimates deserves its fame tho' every sentence had been somewhere said before. That gave it *flesh* & power. Not that man is the Abolisher of Slavery or Intemperance who calls them evils but he whose discerning eye separates between the existence of society & these evils & sees that these may peel off & perish & the institutions remain whole.

14 July. One of the arguments with which nature furnishes us for the Immortality of the Soul is, it always seemed to me, the awful solitude in which here a Soul lives. Few men communicate their highest thoughts to any person. To many they cannot, for they are unfit receivers. Perhaps they cannot to any. Yet are these thoughts as much made for communication as a

sex. Ellen wondered why dearest friends, even husband & wife did so little impart their religious thoughts. And how rarely do such friends meet. Here I sit alone from month to month filled with a deep desire to exchange thoughts with a friend who does not appear—yet shall I find or refind that friend? Sampson goes about yet never speaks what his soul is full of. Barnes also, Mrs Lee; Motte; S.A.R. They cannot discharge this subtle electricity for defect of medium or of receiver.

But was this glorious fabric made for nothing? Will not its day & means & Object come? Will not Heaven's Matches be made or restored?

—

July 21, 1831. God cannot be intellectually discerned.

The feast is pleasant, but its joys have no afterlife, & seem to be a subtraction from our mortal workday of so much. Why not follow out the great idolatry, no, the great penchant of the human mind for friendship? Is it not beautiful this yearning after its mate—its mate I mean by spiritual affinities & not by sex? I never hear of a person of noble feelings but I have the emotion of the *moral sublime* such as is caused by reading Young's line

"Forgive his crimes—forgive his virtues too
    Those minor faults—half converts to the right"

or Shakespear's "*The More Angel She,*" which Coleridge quotes, or Bacon's sentence "Animus qui generosos fines semel optaverit—non virtutes solum sed et numina circumstant." & Εις οιωνος αριστος &c I put together these with pleasure as two or three specimens of that peculiar & beautiful class of thoughts which set you aglow—"non verba sed tonitrua audio." Well just such a feeling I have in hearing of C.G.L.'s or J. A.'s or any body else's noble sentiments. Now if surely I knew there was a mind somewhere thinking & willing that is a repository of these sentiments, a hive of chosen knowledge, a knower & lover of the golden laws of the intellect & the heart; and that in future I am to meet this mind in connexions of most cheerful & close fellowship should not I be glad? Yes indeed: the rainbow, the evening star, day, night, storm, sorrow, death, they would seem preparations, they would seem subjects for this delicious conversation. I am preparing for this conversation. When I think of you sweet friend, wife, angel, Ellen on whom the spirit of knowledge & the spirit of hope were poured in equal fulness—when I think of you I am sure we have not said everlasting farewells.

The impulses of a heart of faultless sentiments would be as much an object of exact calculation as the effects of caloric or azote.

How very thin are the disguises of action! These men that came today to ΦΒΚ, came with their purposes writ as legibly on every proposition as if they had said—'I wish an audience when I hold forth'; another, 'I hate Everett'; another, 'I am an Antimason'; another, 'I love young men'; another, 'Truth'.

—

July 26. There happened to me yesterday morning a little incident very pleasing & singular. I started from sleep thinking that a bedbug was creeping on my breast & at the moment I thought I saw the insect. But on opening my eyes fully & thoroughly examining my clothes & the bed I found there was none. I looked at my watch & found it wanted 20 minutes of five o'clock. It immediately occurred to me that the night before as I sat on the front doorstep Charles had expressed his wish to get up early to go & swim, & if possible to set out by 5 o'ck. I told him "well, I will give it in commission to one of the red rovers to wake me" as I had been complaning an hour before that I had found such inmates. The moment I remembered this conversation I ceased to look for a carnal bug & rose & dressed me. It was 30 minutes earlier than my usual waking time.

July 26.
Dined with President Adams yesterday at Dr Parkman's.
Mr —— said to a woman doubting—'Do you not fear God—? does not the feeling that your whole future destinies for happiness or misery are in his hands terrify you?' She said 'no, she wished it did.' The question was false theology. It does not recognize an immutable God. It was for the woman to become happy or miserable, not for God to make her so.

—

There is an engine at Waltham to watch the watchmen of the factory. Every hour they must put a ring on to the wheel or if they fall asleep & do not, the machine will show their neglect & which hour they slept. Such a machine is every man's Reputation.

Aug. 26.—Yesterday I heard John Quincy Adams deliver an Eulogy upon President Monroe. But he held his notes so close to his mouth that he could be ill heard. There was nothing heroic in the subject, & not much in the feelings of the orator, so it proved rather a spectacle than a speech.

—

Sept. 15. *Rhetoric*
I often make the criticism on my friend Herbert's diction that his thought has that heat as actually to fuse the words so that language is wholly flexible in his hands & his rhyme never stops the progress of the sense. And, in general, according to the elevation of the soul will the power over language always be, & lively thoughts will break out into spritely verse. No measure so difficult but will be tractable so that you only get up the temperature of the thought. To this point I quote gladly my old gossip Montaigne "For my part I hold, & Socrates is positive in it, That whoever has in his mind a spritely & clear imagination, he will express it well enough in one kind or another, & tho' he were dumb, by signs."

'Verbaque praevisam rem non invita sequentur.'
(Horace)
& again Seneca "Cum Res animum occupavere verba ambiunt" & Cicero "ipsae res verba rapiunt." See p. 261 Vol. I.
—I am glad to have these learned Thebans confirm my very thought.

—

19 September.
>   She never comes to me
>   She promised me a thousand times
>   That she would dearly dearly love me
>   That in sickness & in health
>   Others present others absent
>   Whilst air was round & heaven above me

She would be present as my life
My holy gentle tender wife

She promised in my secret ear
When none but God & I could hear
That she would cleave to me forever
There was one will between us
There was one heart within us
And God upon his children smiled
As we the hours with love beguiled

And now I am alone
Unheard I moan
She never comes to me
Sits never by my side
I never hear her voice
She comes not even to my dreams
O Ellen

And comes she not
Ask thy heart, Waldo.
Doth she break her word
Doth not her love embrace thee yet
Even from the Spirits' land?

———

3 October. I wish the Christian principle, the *ultra* principle
of nonresistance & returning good for ill might be tried fairly.
William Penn made one trial. The world was not ripe & yet it
did well. An angel stands a poor chance among wild beasts; a
better chance among men; but among angels best of all. And
so I admit of this system that it is like the Free Trade, fit for
one nation only on condition that all adopt it. Still a man may
try it in his own person & even his sufferings by reason of it
shall be its triumphs. "The more falls it gets, moves faster on."
Love is the adamantean shield that makes blows ridiculous. If
Edward Everett were a sanguine philanthropist not a shade
would attach to his name from the insults of Platt. But he is
thought a selfish man so by his own law must he be judged.
The Mussulman by the Koran. The Jew by the Pentateuch.

One thing more; it is said that it strips the good man bare & leaves him to the whip & license of pirates & butchers.

———

Oct. 27—I read Shakspeare last ev.g & admired with all the fine minds his singular power, singular among men. Charles & I agreed that he is distinguished from other poets as Webster is among our speakers by always speaking to the thing itself i.e. after truth, & by always advancing. His poetry never halts, but has what Coleridge defines Method, viz. progressive arrangement.

Another thing strikes me in the sonnets, which in their way seem as wonderful as the plays & perhaps are even more valuable to the analysis of the genius of Shakspear and that is the assimilating power of passion that turns all things to its own nature.

———

27 October. What we love that shall we seek. What cares the lover sick with his passion how long is the way to his mistress or how poor is her house? What cares the ardent philosopher how fast it rains or what brilliant party he loses when he posts away to the conversation of a wise man? What cares the merchant on what wharves the goods he would monopolize are to be sought? What cares the fervent Methodist how obscure the place or how humble the attendants on his class? The heart is the sole world, the universe, & if its wants are satisfied there is no defect perceived. But how little love is at the bottom of these great religious shows;—congregations and temples & sermons—how much sham! Love built them, be sure. Yea they were the heart's work; but the fervent generation that built them passed away, things went downward & the forms remain but the soul is well nigh gone. Calvinism stands, fear I, by pride & ignorance & Unitarianism as a sect, stands by the opposition of Calvinism. It is cold & cheerless, the mere creature of the understanding, until controversy makes it warm with fire got from below. But is there no difference in the objects which the heart loves? Is there no truth? Yes. And is there no power in truth to commend itself? Yes. It alone can satisfy the heart. Are we asking you to love God as if there was any arbitrary burdensome duty imposed? As if we said, apart from your

usual loves come & cultivate this. It is sour but it must be done for such is the hard law—No; God forbid; we call you to that which all things call you unto with softest persuasion, to that which your whole Reason enjoins with absolute sovereignty. We call you to that which all the future shall teach, far more forcibly & simply than we now. These things are true & real & grand & lovely & good.

—

3 November, 1831. Have been at the Examination of Derry Academy, & had some sad, some pleasant thoughts.

Is it not true that every man has before him in his mind room in one direction to which there is no bound but in every other direction he runs against a wall in a short time? One course of thought, affection, action is for him—that is his *use*, as the new men say. Let me embark in polit. economy, in repartee, in fiction, in verse, in practical counsels, (as here in the Derry case) & I am soon run aground; but let my bark head its own way toward the law of laws, toward the Compensation or action & reaction of the Moral Universe & I sweep serenely over God's depths in an infinite sea.

In an unknown wood the traveller gives the reins to his horse & seeks his safety in the instincts of the animal. Trust something to your instincts far more trustworthy.

As there is always a subject for life so there is always a subject for each hour, if only a man has wit enough to find what that is. I sit Friday night & note the first thought that rises. Presently another, presently five or six—of all these I take the *mean*, as the subject for Saturday's sermon.

—

So excellent also is the piece called the Happy Warrior. Come up William Wordsworth, almost I can say Coleridge's compliment "Quem quoties lego non verba mihi videor audire sed tonitrua."

His noble distinction is that he seeks the truth & shuns with brave self-denial every image and word that is from the purpose —means to stick close to his own thought & give it in naked simplicity & so make it God's affair not his own whether it shall succeed. But he fails of executing this purpose fifty times for the sorry purpose of making a rhyme in which he has no skill, or from imbecillity of mind losing sight of his thought, or from self surrender to custom in poetic diction. (e.g. the inconsistency with his own principles in the two lines about the Cestus & Thunderer's eye &c Vol 3. p. 27)

He calls his brother "a *silent* poet."

And almost every moral line in his book might be framed like a picture, or graven on a temple porch & would gain instead of losing by being pondered.

Dec. 19. I apologized for his baby pieces to my mother by saying that he was Agesilaus who rode on a cane with his children. She said that *Agesilaus did not ride out of doors.*

———

May I not value my griefs, & store them up. I am imprisoned in the forms & uses of every day, & cannot surrender myself to the sweet bitterness of lamenting my beauty, my glory, the life of my life.

———

2 December 1831.

The day is sad, the night is careful, the heart is weighed down with leads, what shall he do who would belong to the Universe, "& live with living nature a pure rejoicing thing?" O friend, that said these words, are you conscious of this thought & this writer? I would not ask any other consolation than to be assured by one sign that the heart never plays false to itself when in its scope it requires by a necessity the permanence of the soul.

———

Dec. 10. Write upon the coincidence of first & third thoughts. And apply it to affairs; and to religion & skepticism. I should like to know if any one ever went up on a mountain so high as that he overlooked right & wrong & saw them confounded, saw their streams mix—that justice did not mean anything to his mind.

———

Unevenness of characters. Every man is one half of a man, either benevolent & weak or firm & unbenevolent, either a speaker & no doer, or a doer & no speaker, either contemplative or practical, & excellence in any one kind seems to speak defect in the others. This wisely ordered for the *social* state; &

the individual expectation & effort seems to promise completeness of character in the whole future. Our very defects are
the shadows of our virtues.

Opposition of first thoughts & common opinion. God has
the first word. The devil has the Second but God has the last
word. We distrust the first thought because we can't give the
reason for it. Abide by it, there is a reason, & by & by long
hence perhaps it will appear.

How we came out of silence into this sounding world is the
wonder of wonders. All other marvels are less.

Charles has gone away to Porto Rico. God preserve & restore him. When you confer a favor be very careful how you do
it. It must be done with the remembrance of your own
squirming when you have received one and feel that the whole
difficulty lies in receiving not in giving.

—

December 19. When I talk with the sick they sometimes
think I treat death with unbecoming indifference and do not
make the case my own, or, if I do, err in my judgment. I do
not fear death. I believe those who fear it have borrowed the
terrors thro' which they see it from vulgar opinion, & not
from their own minds. My own mind is the direct revelation
which I have from God & far least liable to mistake in telling
his will of any revelation. Following my own thoughts, especially as sometimes they have moved me in the country, (as in
the Gulf-Road in Vermont,) I should lie down in the lap of
earth as trustingly as ever on my bed.

—

Boston Dec. 28, 1831. The year hastens to its close. What is it
to me? What I am that is all that affects me. That I am 28 or 8
or 58 years old is as nothing. Should I mourn that the spring
flowers are gone, that the summer fruit has ripened, that the
harvest is reaped, that the snow has fallen? Should I mourn
because so much addition has been made to the capital of
human comfort?

*

In my study my faith is perfect. It breaks, scatters, becomes confounded in converse with men. Hume doubted in his study & believed in the world.—

Mr Robert Haskins quoted a significant proverb That a woman could throw out with a spoon faster than a man could throw in with a shovel.

"Always be sticking a tree, Jock,—it will be growing when ye're sleeping," was the thrifty Scotchman's dying advice. Always be setting a good action to grow—is the advice of a divine thrift. It is bearing you fruit all the time—knitting you to men's hearts, & to men's good, & to God, & beyond this it is benefitting others by remembrance, by emulation, by love. The progress of moral nature is geometrical. Celestial economy!

Boston, 4 January 1832.

More is understood than is expressed in the most diffuse discourse. It is the unsaid part of every lecture that does the most good. If my poor Tuesday evening lectures (horresco referens) were to any auditor the total of his exposition of Christianity what a beggarly faith were it!

—

Shall I not write a book on topics such as follow
    Chap. 1 That the mind is its own place
    Chap. 2. That exact justice is done
    Chap. 3. That good motives are at the bottom of many bad
                actions. e.g. 'Business before friends'
    Chap. 4. That the Soul is immortal
    Chap. 5. On prayers
    Chap. 6 That the best is the true.
    Chap. 7 That the Mind discerns all things.
    Chap 8. That the Mind seeks itself in all things
    Chap. 9 That truth is its own warrant.

—

Jan. 7.

There is a process in the mind very analogous to crystallization in the mineral kingdom. I think of a particular fact of singular beauty & interest. In thinking of it I am led to many more thoughts which show themselves first partially and afterwards more fully. But in the multitude of them I see no order. When I would present them to others they have no beginning. There is no method. Leave them now, & return to them again. Domesticate them in your mind, do not force them into arrangement too hastily & presently you shall find they will take their own order. And the order they assume is divine. It is God's architecture.

9 Jan. I cannot help quoting from Mendelsohn's Phedo the following rule, "All that which, being admitted as true, would procure the human race a real advantage or a feeble consolation, acquires by that alone a high degree of probability."——— "When the Skeptics," says his Socrates, "object against the belief in God & virtue that it is a simple political invention imagined for the good of society, I reply 'O imagine a doctrine as indispensable to man & I will pledge myself upon its truth.'"

This is a true account of our instinctive faith. Why do I believe in a perfect system of compensations, that exact justice is done? Certainly not upon a narrow experience of a score or a hundred instances. For I boldly affirm & believe the universality of the law. But simply that it is better in the view of the mind than any other way, therefore must be the true way. Whatever is better must be the truer way.

"Little matters it to the simple lover of truth to whom he owes such or such a reasoning." Mendelsohn.

Hideous dreams last night and queried today whether they were any more than exaggerations of the sins of the day. We see our own evil affections embodied in frightful physiognomies. The account of Flaxman quoted in N. Jerusalem Mag. No. 52 fell in with this. I have read that on the Alps or Andes the traveller sometimes sees a singular phenomenon, his own shadow upon the mist magnified to a giant so that every gesture of his hand is terrific. So it seems to me does every man see himself, in colossal, in the world without knowing that it is himself he sees. The good that he sees compared to the evil that he sees is as his own good to his own evil. Every quality of his mind is represented *in magnifico* in some one acquaintance & every emotion of his heart in some one. He is like a quincunx which counts 5 east, west, north, or south. Or an initial, medial, & terminal acrostic. The way of this correspondence is seen by considering that his peculiar character leads him to increase his acquaintance with one person & neglect that of another according to their likeness or unlikeness to himself so that he is truly seeking himself in his fellow men, & moreover in his trade & habits & gestures & meats & drinks & comes finally to be represented faithfully by any view you take of his circumstances.

———

"Regard not dreams since they are but the images of our hopes & fears." *Cato*, apud Fielding's Proverbs.

10 Jan.

It is the best part of the man, I sometimes think, that revolts most against his being the minister. His good revolts from official goodness. If he never spoke or acted but with the full consent of his understanding, if the whole man acted always, how powerful would be every act & every word. Well then or ill then how much power he sacrifices by conforming himself to say & do in other folks' time instead of in his own! The difficulty is that we do not make a world of our own but fall into institutions already made & have to accomodate ourselves to them to be useful at all. & this accommodation is, I say, a loss of so much integrity & of course of so much power.

But how shall the droning world get on if all its *beaux esprits* recalcitrate upon its approved forms & accepted institutions & quit them all in order to be single minded? The double refiners would produce at the other end the double damned.

11 Jan. People sometimes wonder that persons wholly uneducated to write yet eminent in some other ability should be able to use language with so much purity & force. But it is not wonderful. The manner of using language is surely the most decisive test of intellectual power & he who has intellectual force of any kind will be sure to show it there. For that is the

first & simplest vehicle of mind, is of all things next to the mind, & the vigorous Saxon that uses it well is of the same block as the vigorous Saxon that formed it & works after the same manner.—

———

21 Jan. Write on personal independance. There are men whose language is strong & defying enough, yet their eyes & their actions ask leave of other men to live. A man considers the fashion of his better neighbor's coat & hat, & then condemns his own. The only way to improve the fashion of his own coat & hat is to forget his neighbor, & work out his own results; to eat less dinner; to rise earlier; to work harder; do more benefits, & more strictly adhere in his acts to the decisions of his own judgment. So to do will make his own coat & hat very respectable in the eyes of all men. Lord Falkland—

"Say not then, 'This with that lace will do well;'
But 'This with my discretion will be brave.'" Herbert

What is the fault of Hotspur's avowal? It seems just.

I'll give thrice so much land
To any well deserving friend
But in the way of bargain, mark ye me,
I'll cavil on the ninth part of a hair.

Be as beneficent as the sun or the sea but if your rights as a rational being are trenched on die on the first inch of your territory. It requires circumspection. Else he will be surprized by his good nature into acquiescence in false sentiments uttered by others. Be a Cato, & it will be easier to keep out of sin & shame than in the ease & social habit of Maecenas.

———

18 Feb. 1832. What can we see, read, acquire, but ourselves? Cousin is a thousand books to a thousand persons. Take the book, my friend, & read your eyes out; you will never find there what I find. If I would have a monopoly of the delight or the wisdom I get, I am as secure now the book is Englished as if it were imprisoned in Syriack. Judge of the use different persons can make of this book by the use you are able to make of it at different times; sometimes very imperfectly

apprehending the author & very little interested; again delighting in a sentence or an argument; another time ascending to the comprehension of the whole reasoning but implicitly following him as a disciple; at another not only understanding his reasoning but understanding his mind, able not only to discern but to predict his path & its relation to other paths, to discern his truth & his error. Feb. 20. Due to J. P. for RBE 25.09

To introduce a man to a good book is like introducing him to fine company. It is nothing if he is nothing. The company is perfectly safe & he is not one of them though he is there. Let him come out & brag of his company, a well bred person who was not there will discover presently what place he occupied.

19 Feb. Was not all truth always in the world? Even the Lord's Prayer Grotius represents as a compilation of Jewish petitions. & the German commentators trace almost all the precepts of Xt to Hebrew proverbs. And I learn today that the Copernican system, it is gathered from the writings of Aristotle, was *maintained* by some *philosophers before his* (A.'s) *time*. [Lib. Usef. Knowl. Life of Galileo.] And the new light, bran new, of the Swedenborgians even, is old as thought. I match every saying of theirs with some Greek or Latin proverb. e.g. 'the wise man lifting his finger.'

Feb. 20, 1832. One is tempted to write a lecture on the right use of the senses from having attention called to the fact that Galileo lost his sight in 1636. "The noblest eye is darkened" said Castelli, "which nature ever made. An eye so privileged & gifted with such rare qualities, that it may with truth be said to have seen more than all of those who are gone, & to have opened the eyes of all who are to come." See also the expressions of Galileo himself, quoted p. 75 Life of G. in Lib. Usef. Knowl. Galileo died 1642 aet 78.
So the eye of Milton.

It is idle in us to wonder at the bigotry & violence of the persecution of Galileo. Every man may read the history of it in himself when he is contradicted & silenced in argument by a person whom he had always reckoned his inferior.

I wrote one day after being puzzled by a mechanical Alderman that the first questions remain to be asked. 'Tis even so; and many a profound genius, I suppose, who fills the world with fame of his exploding renowned errors, is yet every day posed by trivial questions at his own suppertable.

from

Q

1832–1833

28 March my food per diem weighed 14¼ oz
29 ——   ——   —— 13 oz
2 April   12½

What ails you gentlemen said Jupiter—What ails you my wobegone friend? Speak, what are you?—'Bilious'—And you? 'A slave'. And You? 'Hypp'd' And you?—'Poor.' And you? 'Lame.' And you? 'A Jew'

—

29 March. I visited Ellen's tomb & opened the coffin.

—

May 3. Sir J. Mackintosh said well, that every picture, statue, and poem was an experiment upon the human mind. I hunt in Charles's dish of shells each new form of beauty & new tint, & seem, as Fontenelle said, "to recognize the thing the first time I see it." Every knot of every cockle has *expression*, that is, is the material symbol of some cast of thought.

To analyze a foolish sermon may require much wisdom. Strange that so learned & gifted a man as my friend should please himself with drawing for an hour such gingerbread distinctions.

May 7. Charles says that Porto Rico is a place where one is never pestered with cold feet & never needs a pocket-handker-chief, and never is unwilling to get out of bed in the morning.

Mutato nomine de te fabula narratur. To be at perfect agree-ment with a man of most opposite conclusions you have only to translate your language into his. The same thought which you call *God* in his nomenclature is called *Christ*. In the lan-guage of William Penn moral sentiment is called *Christ*.

191

—

"Truth never is, always is a-being." Does not that word signify that state in which a man ever finds himself, conscious of knowing nothing but being just now ready to begin to know? He feels like one just born. He is ready to ask the first questions.

Strange how abysmal is our ignorance. Every man who writes a book or pursues a science seems to conceal ambitiously his universal ignorance under this fluency in a particular.

The higher the subjects are, which occupy your thoughts, the more they tax yourself; and the same thoughts have least to do with your individuality, but have equal interest for all men. Things moreover are permanent in proportion to their inwardness in your nature.

16 May, 1832. Shakspear's creations indicate no sort of anxiety to be understood. There is the Cleopatra, an irregular, unfinished, glorious, sinful character, sink or swim—there she is—& not one in the thousand of his readers apprehends the noble dimensions of the heroine. Then Ariel, Hamlet, & all—all done in sport with the free daring pencil of a Master of the World. He leaves his children with God.

It is a good sign in human nature the unmixed delight with which we contemplate the genius of Shakspear & if it were ten times more should be glad.

17 May,—King James liked old friends best, as he said his old shoes were easiest to his feet. We are benefitted by coming to an understanding, as it is called, with our fellow men, and with any fellow man. It empties all the ill blood; it ventilates, purifies the whole constitution. And we always feel easiest in the company of a person to whom the whole nature has been so made known. No matter what, but how well known.

The moment you present a man with a new idea, he immediately throws its light back upon the mass of his thoughts, to see what new relation it will discover. And thus all our knowledge is a perpetually living capital, whose use cannot be exhausted, as it revives with every new fact. There is proof for noblest truths in what we already know but we have not yet drawn the distinction which shall methodize our experience in a particular combination.

———

"You send out to the Sandwich islands one missionary & twenty five refutations in the crew of the vessel" said Mr Sturgis.——

———

Indeed is truth stranger than fiction. For what has imagination created to compare with the science of Astronomy? What is there in Paradise Lost to elevate & astonish like Herschel or Somerville? The contrast between the magnitude & duration of the things observed & the animalcule observer. It seems a mere eye sailing about space in an eggshell & for him to undertake to weigh the formidable masses, to measure the secular periods & settle the theory of things so vast & long, & out of the little cock-boat of a planet to aim an impertinent telescope at every nebula & pry into the plan and state of every white spec that shines in the inconceivable depths. Not a white spot but is a lump of Suns, the roe, the milt of light & life.
Who can be a Calvinist or who an Atheist?—
God has opened this knowledge to us to correct our theology & educate the mind.

———

June 2, 1832. Cold cold. Thermometer Says Temperate. Yet a week of moral excitement.

It is years & nations that guide my pen.

I have sometimes thought that in order to be a good minister it was necessary to leave the ministry. The profession is antiquated. In an altered age, we worship in the dead forms of our forefathers. Were not a Socratic paganism better than an effete superannuated Christianity?

Does not every shade of thought have its own tone so that wooden voices denote wooden minds?

Whatever there is of Authority in religion is that which the mind does not animate.
Conway, N.H. 6 July. Here among the mountains the

pinions of thought should be strong and one should see the errors of men from a calmer height of love & wisdom. What is the message that is given me to communicate next Sunday? Religion in the mind is not credulity & in the practice is not form. It is a life. It is the order & soundness of a man. It is not something else *to be got*, to be *added*, but is a new life of those faculties you have. It is to do right. It is to love, it is to serve, it is to think, it is to be humble,

Ethan Allen Crawford's. White Mountains, 14 July 1832.

There is nothing to be said. Why take the pencil? I believe something will occur. A slight momentum would send the planet to roll forever. And the laws of thought are not unlike. A thought I said is a country wide enough for an active mind. It unrolls, it unfolds, it shows unlimited sense within itself. A few pains, a few pleasures, how easily we are amused, how easily scared. A too benevolent man is at the mercy of every fop he meets & every householder. His willingness to please withdraws him from himself. Sure he ought to please but not please at the expense of his own view by accomodation of   .

——

The good of going into the mountains is that life is reconsidered; it is far from the slavery of your own modes of living and you have opportunity of viewing the town at such a distance as may afford you a just view nor can you have any such mistaken apprehension as might be expected from the place you occupy & the round of customs you run at home.

He who believes in inspiration will come here to seek it. He who believes in the woodloving muses must woo them here. And he who believes in the reality of his soul will therein find inspiration & muses & God & will come out here to undress himself of pedantry & judge righteous judgment & worship the First Cause.

The reason why we like simplicity of character, the reason why grown men listen with untiring interest to a lively child is the same, viz it is something more than man, above man, & we hearken with a curiosity that has something of awe. We should so listen to every man if his soul spake, but it does not; his fears speak, his senses speak, & he himself seldom.

July 15, 1832, White Mountains. A few low mountains, a great many clouds always covering the great peaks, a circle of woods to the horizon, a peacock on the fence or in the yard, & two travellers no better contented than myself in the plain parlor of this house make up the whole picture of this unsabbatized Sunday. But the hours pass on—creep or fly—& bear me and my fellows to the decision of questions of duty; to the crises of our fate; and to the solution of this mortal problem. Welcome & farewell to them, fair come, fair go. God is, & we in him.

The hour of decision. It seems not worth while for them who charge others with exalting forms above the moon to fear forms themselves with extravagant dislike. I am so placed that my aliquid ingenii may be brought into useful action. Let me not bury my talent in the earth in my indignation at this windmill. But though the thing may be useless & even pernicious, do not destroy what is good & useful in a high degree rather than comply with what is hurtful in a small degree. The Communicant celebrates on a foundation either of authority or of tradition an ordinance which has been the occasion to thousands,—I hope to thousands of thousands—of contrition, of gratitude, of prayer, of faith, of love, & of holy living. Far be it from any of my friends,—God forbid it be in my heart—to interrupt any occasion thus blessed of God's influences upon the human mind. I will not, because we may not all think alike of the means, fight so strenuously against the means, as to miss of the end which we all value alike. I think Jesus did not mean to institute a perpetual celebration, but that a commemoration of him would be useful. Others think that Jesus did establish this one. We are agreed that one is useful, & we are agreed I hope in the way in which it must be made useful. viz; by each one's making it an original Commemoration.

I know very well that it is a bad sign in a man to be too conscientious, & stick at gnats. The most desperate scoundrels have been the over refiners. Without accomodation society is impracticable. But this ordinance is esteemed the most sacred of religious institutions & I cannot go habitually to an institution which they esteem holiest with indifference & dislike.

—

August 11.—A stomach ache will make a man as contemptible as a palsy. Under the diarrhoea have I suffered now one fortnight & weak am as a reed. Still the truth is not injured, not touched though thousands of them that love it fall by the way. Serene, adorable, eternal it lives, though Goethe, Mackintosh, Cuvier, Bentham, Hegel die in their places which no living men can fill.

———

August 12. The British Plutarch & the modern Plutarch is yet to be written. They that have writ the lives of great men have not written them from love & from seeing the beauty that was to be desired in them. But what would operate such gracious motions upon the spirit as the death of Lord Cobham & of Sir Thomas More & a censure of Bacon & a picture of George Fox & Hampden, & the chivalrous integrity of Walter Scott & a true portrait of Sir Harry Vane, & Falkland, & Andrew Marvell? I would draw characters, not write lives. I would evoke the spirit of each and their relics might rot. Luther, Milton, Newton, Shakspear. Alfred a light of the world. Adams. I would walk among the dry bones & wherever on the face of the earth I found a living man I would say here is life & life is communicable. Jesus Christ truly said my flesh is meat indeed. I am the bread. For of his life or character have the nations of the earth been nourished. Socrates I should like well if I dared to take him. I should repeat Montaigne though. I wouldn't.

> "Eyes that the beam celestial view
> Which evermore makes all things new."

These I claim sole qualification, ewe lamb. I would make Milton shine. I would mourn for Bacon. I would fly in the face of every cockered prejudice, feudal or vulgar, & speak as Christ of their good & evil.

> "There are very few examples of life full & pure, & we wrong our instruction every day to propose to ourselves those that are weak & imperfect, scarce good for any one service, that pull us back, & that are rather Corrupters than Correctors of Manners." Montaigne Vol 3. p. 548

When we look at the world of past men, we say, What a host of heroes but when we come to particularize, it is like counting the stars which we thought innumerable, but which prove few & rare. Bacon, Shakspear, Caesar, Scipio, Cicero, Burke, Chatham, Franklin, none of them will bear examination or furnish the type of a *Man*.

—

18 Aug.

To be genuine. Goethe they say was wholly so. The difficulty increases with the gifts of the individual. A ploughboy can be, but a minister, an orator, an ingenious thinker, how hardly! George Fox was. "What I am in words," he said, "I am the same in life." Swedenborg was. "My writings will be found," he said, "another self." George Washington was; 'the irreproachable Washington.' Whoever is genuine, his ambition is exactly proportioned to his powers. The height of the pinnacle determines the breadth of the base.

—

October 1. I am cheered & instructed by this paper on Corn Law Rhymes in the Edinburgh by my Germanick new-light writer whoever he be. He gives us confidence in our principles. He assures the truthlover everywhere of sympathy. Blessed art that makes books & so joins me to that stranger by this perfect railroad.

Has the doctrine ever been fairly preached of man's moral nature? The whole world holds on to formal Christianity, & nobody teaches the essential truth, the heart of Christianity for fear of shocking &c. Every teacher when once he finds himself insisting with all his might upon a great truth turns up the ends of it at last with a cautious showing *how* it is agreeable to the life & teaching of Jesus—as if that was any recommendation. As if the blessedness of Jesus' life & teaching were not because they were agreeable to the truth. Well this cripples his teaching. It bereaves the truth he inculcates of more than half its force by representing it as something secondary that can't stand alone. The truth of truth consists in this, that it is selfevident, selfsubsistent. It is light. You don't get a candle to see the sun rise. Instead of making Christianity a vehicle of truth you make truth only a horse for Christianity. It is a very operose way of making people good. You must be humble because Christ says, 'Be humble'. 'But why must I obey Christ?' 'Because God sent him.' But how do I know God sent him? 'Because your own heart teaches the same thing he taught.' Why then shall I not go to my own heart at first?

2 Oct.

It well deserves attention what is said in N.J.M. concerning External Restraint. It is awful to look into the mind of man & see how free we are—to what frightful excesses our vices may run under the whited wall of a respectable reputation. Outside, among your fellows, among strangers, you must preserve appearances,—a hundred things you cannot do; but inside,— the terrible freedom!

True freedom is his only who has learned to live within as he would appear without.

There are men—are there not?—who are more afraid of their opinions than their will, who are more afraid to express their own opinions than to trust themselves to this inland sea. Good it is to grow familiar with your own thoughts & not shun to speak them.

9 October

'I teach by degrees,' says Landor's Epicurus. It is not the will but the necessity of the wise. None are wise enow to teach otherwise. All this pedantry about the peoples not bearing the whole truth,—what else does it mean than that the teacher has not yet arrived at the safe, that is, the *true* statement of the particular doctrine which he would oppose to the ruling error. He knows in general there is an error; he has not yet found its boundary lines.

How do we attain just views? In conversation somebody says something about God or heaven which makes us feel uneasy. It is so specious we cannot contradict it. It is so false we cannot assent to it & we get off the best we may. Take that remark for your thesis, & work upon it till you detect the fallacy.

The true statement concerning retribution, is, that human nature is self retributive. Every moment is a judgment day, because, every act puts the agent in a new condition.

"The mighty tread
   Brings from the dust the sound of liberty."

"Wisdom & goodness to the vile seem vile
   Filths savour but themselves"

"The true Philosophy is the only true prophet" rose colour

All our art is how to use the good God provides us. There is water enough; we are only so to shape aqueducts as to bring it to our door. There is air enough; we must only so build as that it shall ventilate our house. So with man's education. There is truth enough; only open the mind's door, & straighten the passages. There are men enough; only so place yourself to them in true position (en rapport) i.e. by amity, as to suck the sweetness of society. There is power & happiness enough.

I will not live out of me
I will not see with others' eyes
My good is good, my evil ill
I would be free—I cannot be
While I take things as others please to rate them
I dare attempt to lay out my own road
That which myself delights in shall be Good
That which I do not want,—indifferent,
That which I hate is Bad. That's flat
Henceforth, please God, forever I forego
The yoke of men's opinions. I will be
Lighthearted as a bird & live with God.
I find him in the bottom of my heart
I hear continually his Voice therein
And books, & priests, & worlds, I less esteem
Who says the heart's a blind guide? It is not.
My heart did never counsel me to sin
I wonder where it got its wisdom
For in the darkest maze amid the sweetest baits
Or Amid horrid dangers never once
Did that gentle Angel fail of his oracle
The little needle always knows the north

The little bird remembereth his note
And this wise Seer never errs
I never taught it what it teaches me
I only follow when I act aright.
Whence then did this Omniscient Spirit come?
From God it came. It is the Deity.

13 Oct. "If thou lovest true glory, thou must trust her truth."
Landor

'She followeth him who doth not turn & gaze after her.'

"Our national feelings are healthy & strong by the closeness of their intexture. What touches one class is felt by another: it sounds on the rim of the glass, the hall rings with it, & it is well if the drum & the trumpet do not catch it."

Landor.

"The true philosophy is the only true prophet." He that hath insight into principles alone hath commanding prospect of remotest results.

"No men are so facetious as those whose minds are somewhat perverted. Truth enjoys good air & clear light, but no playground."

"Since all transcendent, all true & genuine greatness must be of a man's own raising & only on the foundations that the hand of God has laid, do not let any touch it; keep them off civilly, but keep them off."

Landor

"Abstinence from low pleasures is the only means of meriting or of obtaining the higher.

Kindness in us is the honey that blunts the sting of unkindness in another."

Landor's Epicurus.

"I found that the principal" (means of gratifying the universal desire of happiness) "lay in the avoidance of those very things which had hitherto been taken up as the instruments of enjoyment & content, such as military commands, political offices, clients, adventures in commerce, & extensive landed property."

L's Epicurus

"The heart in itself is free from evil but very capable of receiving & too tenacious of holding it."

13 October. Exhortations & examples are better than psalms & sermons.

We have thoughts but we don't know what to do with them, materials, that we can't manage or dispose. We cannot get high enough above them to see their order in reason. We cannot get warm enough to have them exert their natural affinities & throw themselves into crystal. We see a new Sect devoted to certain ideas & we go to individuals of it to have them explained. Vain expectation! They are possessed with the ideas but do not possess them.

—

My aunt had an eye that went through & through you like a needle. 'She was endowed,' she said, 'with the *fatal* gift of penetration.' She disgusted every body because she knew them too well.

To live in a field of pumpkins yet eat no pie.

Oct. 27. "Luther's words were half battles." At Worms to the Diet he said "Till such time as either by proofs from Holy Scripture or by fair reason & argument I have been confuted & convicted I cannot & will not recant. It is neither safe nor prudent to do aught against conscience. Here stand I, I cannot otherwise. God assist me. Amen!"

V. Fraser's Mag. Vol 2 p 743

—

We want lives. We want characters of worthy men, not their books nor their relics. As the cultivation of an individual advances he thinks less of condition, less of offices & property & more keenly hunts for characters. Was it Henry who loved *a man*? So do men who would not have admitted him to their presence but for charity. There are very few finished men in the history of the world. To be sure the very expression is a solecism against faith. But there are none finished as far as they go.—

I propose to myself to read Schiller of whom I hear much. What shall I read? His Robbers? oh no, for that was the crude fruit of his immature mind. He thought little of it himself. What then: his Aesthetics? oh no, that is only his struggle with Kantean metaphysics.
His poetry? oh no, for he was a poet only by study. His histories? & so with all his productions, they were the fermentations by which his mind was working itself clear, they were the experiments by which he got his skill & the fruit, the bright pure gold of all was—Schiller himself.

—

Saturday, 11 h. A.M. 24 November, 1832. Died my sister Margaret Tucker. Farewell to thee for a little time my kind & sympathizing sister. Go rejoice with Ellen, so lately lost, in God's free & glorious universe. Tell her if she needs to be told how dearly she is remembered, how dearly valued. Rejoice together that you are free of your painful corporeal imprisonment. I may well mourn your loss, for in many sour days I had realized the delicacy & sweetness of a sister's feeling. I had rejoiced too, as always, in the gifts of a true lady in whom was never any thing little or mean seen or suspected, who was all gentleness, purity, & sense with a rare elevation of sentiments. God comfort the bitter lonely hours which the sorrowing mother must spend here. Twice a mother has she been to all but Paulina.

—

Winter less interesting here than in the north or in the south, but beautiful.

Farewell dear girl. I have a very narrow acquaintance & of it you have been a large part. We anchor upon a few. & you have had the character & dignity that promised every thing to the esteem & affection of years. Think kindly of me. I know you will, but perchance the disembodied can do much more—can

elevate this sinking spirit & purify & urge it to generous purposes, teach me to make trifles, trifles, & work with consistency & in earnest to my true ends. The only sister I ever
had—pass on, pure soul! to the opening heaven.

———

Dec. 1. I never read Wordsworth without chagrin.—A man
of such great powers & ambition, so near to the Dii majores to
fail so meanly in every attempt. A genius that hath epilepsy, a
deranged archangel. The Ode to Duty conceived & expressed
in a certain high severe style does yet miss of greatness & of all
effect by such falsities or falses as

"And the most Ancient heavens thro thee are fresh & strong"

which is throwing dust in your eyes because they have no more
to do with duty than a dung cart has. So that fine promising
passage about "the mountain winds being free to blow upon
thee" &c flats out into "*me & my benedictions.*" If he had cut
in his Dictionary for words he could hardly have got worse.

———

18 Oct. It occurred last night with much force that we are all
guarded often from our worst enemies by what we think our
greatest weaknesses. Aesop's stag who praised his horns & despised his feet aptly paints the truth. The stammering tongue
& awkward formal manners which hinder your success in
social circles keep you true to the mark which is your own—to
that particular power which God has given you for your own
& others' benefit.

———

Harbor of Malta, Marsa Muscetto 3 February, 1833. Here in
the precincts of St John, the isle of old fame under the high
battlements once of the Knights & now of England I spend
my Sunday, which shines with but little Sabbath light. 'Tout
commence', as Pere Bossuet says. It is hardly truer of me at
this point of time when I am setting foot on the old world &
learning two languages than it is of every day of mine so rude
& unready am I sent into this world. Glad very glad to find the
company of a person quite the reverse of myself in all these
particulars in which I fail most, who has all his knowledge &
it is much & various, at his sudden command. I seem on all

trivial emergences, to be oppressed with an universal ignorance. If I rightly consider that for this point of time which we
call a Life, tout commence, I shall rejoice in the omen of a
boundless future & not be chagrined, oh heavens, no. It is
however a substantial satisfaction to benefit your companions
with your knowledge, a pleasure denied me. 'Time' said friend
Carlyle, 'brings Roses.' A capital mot putting a little rouge on
the old skeleton's cheeks.

February 10. Perhaps it is a pernicious mistake yet rightly
seen I believe it is sound philosophy, that wherever we go,
whatever we do, self is the sole subject we study & learn. Montaigne said, himself was all he knew. Myself is much more than
I know, & yet I know nothing else. The chemist experiments
upon his new salt by trying its affinity to all the various sub-
stances he can command arbitrarily selected & thereby discloses the most wonderful properties in his subject & I bring
myself to sea, to Malta, to Italy, to find new affinities between
me & my fellowmen, to observe narrowly the affections, weaknesses, surprises, hopes, doubts, which new sides of the panorama shall call forth in me. Mean sneakingly mean would be
this philosophy, a reptile unworthy of the name, if *self* be used
in the low sense, but as self means Devil so it means God. I
speak of the Universal Man to whose colossal dimensions each
particular bubble can by its birthright expand. Is it the hard
condition upon which the love of highest truth is given, such
extreme incapacity for action & common conversation as to
provoke the contempt of the bystander, even of kindred &
debtors? Or is it that we will put off upon our nature the bad
consequence of our faults? Hang out your temperance, my
friend, as your amulet, your benevolence as your shield, your
industry as your advocate and perhaps you will not have so
much reason as you think to complain of your reception
among men. I am a full believer in the doctrine that we always
make our own welcome.

———

1833, February.
    Malta. I am now pleased abundantly with St John's Church
in Valetta. Welcome these new joys. Let my American eye be a
child's again to these glorious picture books. The chaunting

friars, the carved ceilings, the Madonnas & Saints, they are lively oracles, quotidiana et perpetua.

Silver gates

—

Naples, 13 March. When I was at home & felt vaunty I pestered the good folks with insisting on discarding every motive but the highest. I said you need never act for example's sake; never give pledges; &c. But I think now that we need all the advantages we can get, that our virtue wants all the crutches; that we must avail ourselves of our strength & weakness & want of appetite & press of affairs & of calculation & of fear as well as of the just & sublime considerations of the love of God & of self respect. Not that any others will bear comparison with these but because the temptations are so manifold & so subtle & assail archangels as well as coarser clay that it will not do to spare any strength.

The remembrance of the affectionate anxious expectation with which others are intent upon your contest with temptation is a wonderful provocative to virtue. So is it when in a vast city of corrupt men you ask who are the elegant & great men, to reflect that in all & by all you may be making yourself the elegant, the great, the good man, day by day.—

—

Rome
21 April. I went this morn to the Church of Trinita di Monte to see some nuns take the veil. Can any ceremony be more pathetic than to see youth, beauty, rank thus self devoted to mistaken duty?

—

Florence
7 May. To-day I heard by Charles's letter of the death of Ellen's mother. Fast fast the bonds dissolve that I was so glad to wear. She has been a most kind & exemplary mother, & how painfully disappointed. Happy now. And oh what events & thoughts in which I should have deepest sympathy does this thin partition of flesh entirely hide. Does the heart in that world forget the heart that did beat with it in this? Do jealousies, do fears, does the observation of faults intervene? Dearest friends, I would be loved by all of you: dearest friend! we shall meet again.

May 11. How little is *expressed* or can be! In the least action
what an infinity is *understood*! I heard La Straniera performed
last night. Moreover cannot a lesson of wisdom & glory be got
even from the hapless prima donna of an Italian opera? At least
one is informed of the extent of female powers & warned not
to be too easily satisfied with the accomplishments of vulgar
pretty women.

I have heard that the old king George was so impatient of
his state that he delighted to dress himself plainly & escape in
a morning from Windsor to the market or the lanes & mix in a
crowd. Well I have seen a man, the lord of quite another sort
of principality, forced to pay the same price for all his knowledge & to unking himself & take knocks from such "parma-
ceti" gentlemen in order to have a peep at men.

May 18. I told Landor I thought it an argument of weak
understanding in Lord Chesterfield, his slippery morality. It is
inexcusable in any man who pretends to greatness to confound
moral distinctions. True genius, whatever faults of action it
may have, never does. Shakespear never does, though a loose
liver. But such fry as Beaumont & Fletcher & Massinger do
continually. And Chesterfield did. Well for him if he had often
thought & spoken as when he said—"I judge by every man's
truth of his degree of understanding."

I think it was of Socrates that Landor dared to say, so far can
a humoursome man indulge a whim, "he was a vulgar sophist
& he could not forgive vulgarity in any body; if he saw it in a
wise man he regretted it the more."

"un tale le cui mani giugnevano spesso dove non arri-
vava la vista degli altri." I Promessi Sposi Vol. 2. p. 121.

I like the sayers of No better than the sayers of Yes.

On bravely thro' the sunshine or the showers
Time hath his work to do & we have ours.

"Il tempo il suo mestiere, ed io il mio" I promessi sposi

"Dorremmo pensare piu a far bene che a star bene."

Uomo di studio, egli non amava nè di comandare ne di obbedire.

25 May. Is not Santa Croce a grand church! Nobody knows how grand who only sees it once. Its tombs! Its tombs! And then the mighty windows of stained glass which a man sees at noon & thinks he knows what they are worth & comes back after sunset & finds to his delight (I did) a wholly novel & far more beautiful effect. They should be seen just about the hour of candlelight.——We come out to Europe to learn what man can,——what is the uttermost which social man has yet done. And perhaps the most satisfactory & most valuable impressions are those which come to each individual casually & in moments when he is not on the hunt for wonders. To make any sincere good use, I mean what I say, of what he sees, he needs to put a double & treble guard upon the independency of his judgments. The veriest Luther might well suspect his own opinion upon the Venus or the Apollo.

Venice. 2 June, 1833. The ancient metropolis of the merchants. In coming into it, it seemed a great oddity but not at all attractive. Under the full moon, later in the evening St Mark's piazza showed like a world's wonder, but still I pity the people, who are not beavers, & yet are compelled to live here. But what matter where & how, as long as all of us are estranged from truth & love, from Him who is truth & love? Sometimes I would hide myself in the dens of the hills, in the thickets of an obscure country town, I am so vexed & chagrined with myself,—with my weakness, with my guilt. Then I have no skill to live with men, that is, with such men as the world is made of, & such as I delight in, I seldom find. It seems to me, no boy makes so many blunders or says such awkward, contrary, disagreeable speeches as I do. In the attempt to oblige a person I wound & disgust him. I pity the hapless folks that have to do with me. But would it not be cowardly to flee out of society & live in the woods? I comfort myself with a reference to the great & eternal revolution which, under God, bears the good of us all,—thine & mine—& that of each by the instrumentality of the other, on the wings of these dull hours & months & years.

I collect nothing that can be touched or tasted or smelled, neither cameo, painting, nor medallion; nothing in my trunk but old clothes, but I value much the growing picture which the ages have painted & which I reverently survey. It is wonderful how much we see in five months, in how short a time we learn what it has taken so many ages to teach.

Milan, 10 June.

Architecture,—shall I speak what I think,—seems to me ever an imitation. Accustomed to look at our American churches as imitative I cannot get it out of my head that these which I now see are only more splendid & successful imitations also. I am perplexed with my inveterate littleness. I must & will see the things in detail & analyze all, every noble sentiment to the contrary notwithstanding. It seems to me nothing is truly great, nothing impresses us, nothing overawes, nothing crowds upon us, & kills calculation. We always call in the effect of imagination, coax the imagination to hide this & enlarge that & even St Peter's, nor this frostwork cathedral at Milan with its 5000 marble people all over its towers can charm down the little Imp.

It is in the soul that architecture exists & Santa Croce & this Duomo are poor far-behind imitations. I would rather know the metaphysics of architecture as of shells & flowers than anything else in the matter—But one act of benevolence is better than a cathedral, so do you duty, yours. Architecture, said the lady, is frozen music. And Iarno says in Wilhelm that he who does the best in each one thing he does, does all. For he sees the connexion between all good things.

—

July 11. Does any man render written account to himself of himself? I think not. Those who have anything worth repeating, ah! the sad confession! Those who are innocent have been employed in tape & pins. When will good work be found for great spirits? When shall we be able without a blush & without harm to utter to the world our inmost thought?

Thus shall I write memoirs? A man who was no courtier but loved men went to Rome & there lived with boys. He came to France & in Paris lives alone & in Paris seldom speaks. If he do not see Carlyle in Edinburgh he may go to America with out saying anything in earnest except to Cranch & to Landor.

The errors of traditional Christianity as it now exists, the popular faith of many millions, need to be removed to let men see the divine beauty of moral truth. I feel myself pledged if health & opportunity be granted me to demonstrate that all necessary truth is its own evidence; that no doctrine of God need appeal to a book; that Christianity is wrongly received by all such as take it for a system of doctrines,—its stress being upon moral truth; it is a rule of life not a rule of faith.

———

London, July 24. Here in the great capital it needs to say some thing of the creature immortal that swarms on this spot. Coming to Boulogne, I thought of the singular position of the American traveller in Italy. It is like that of a being of another planet who invisibly visits the earth. He is a protected witness. He sees what is that boasted liberty of manners—free of all puritan starch—& sees what it is worth—how surely it pays its tax. He comes a freeman among slaves. He learns that old saws are true which is a great thing. He is not now to be answered any longer in his earnest assertions of moral truth by the condescending explanation that these are his prejudices of country & education. He has seen how they hold true through all the most violent contrasts of condition & character.

28 July. Attended divine service at Westminster Abbey. The bishop of Gloucester preached. It is better than any church I have seen except St Peter's.

Happy the man who never puts on a face but receives every visiter with that countenance he has on.

Liverpool, 1 September, 1833. I thank the great God who has led me through this European scene, this last schoolroom in which he has pleased to instruct me from Malta's isle, thro'

Sicily, thro' Italy, thro' Switzerland, thro' France, thro' England, thro' Scotland, in safety & pleasure & has now brought me to the shore & the ship that steers westward. He has shown me the men I wished to see—Landor, Coleridge, Carlyle, Wordsworth—he has thereby comforted & confirmed me in my convictions. Many things I owe to the sight of these men. I shall judge more justly, less timidly, of wise men forevermore. To be sure not one of these is a mind of the very first class, but what the intercourse with each of these suggests is true of intercourse with better men, that they never *fill the ear*—fill the mind—no, it is an *idealized* portrait which always we draw of them. Upon an intelligent man, wholly a stranger to their names, they would make in conversation no deep impression —none of a world-filling fame—they would be remembered as sensible well read earnest men—not more. Especially are they all deficient all these four—in different degrees but all deficient —in insight into religious truth. They have no idea of that species of moral truth which I call the first philosophy. (Peter Hunt is as wise a talker as either of these men. Don't laugh.)

The comfort of meeting men of genius such as these is that they talk sincerely. They feel themselves to be so rich that they are above the meanness of pretending to knowledge which they have not & they frankly tell you what puzzles them. But Carlyle. Carlyle is so amiable that I love him. But I am very glad my travelling is done. A man not old feels himself too old to be a vagabond. The people at their work, the people whose avocations I interrupt by my letters of introduction accuse me by their looks for leaving my business to hinder theirs.

These men make you feel that fame is a conventional thing & that man is a sadly 'limitary' spirit. You speak to them as to children or persons of inferior capacity whom it is necessary to humor; adapting our tone & remarks to their known prejudices & not to our knowledge of the truth.

I believe in my heart it is better to admire too rashly, as I do, than to be admired too rashly as the great men of this day are. They miss by their premature canonization a great deal of necessary knowledge, & one of these days must begin the world again (as to their surprize they will find needful) poor. I speak now in general & not of these individuals. God save a great man from a little circle of flatterers. I know it is sweet, very sweet, rats bane.

—

Liverpool, 2 September, 1833.
No sailing today, so you may know what I have seen & heard in the four days I have been here. Really nothing external, so I must spin my thread from my bowels. It must be said this is the least agreeable city to the traveller in all England—a good packet office—no more. Glad I bid adieu to England, the old, the rich, the strong nation, full of arts & men & memories; nor can I feel any regret in the presence of the best of its sons that I was not born here. I am thankful that I am an American as I am thankful that I am a man. It is its best merit to my eye that it is the most resembling country to America which the world contains.——The famous burden of English taxation is bearable. Men live & multiply under it, though I have heard a father in the higher rank of life speak with regret of the increase of his family.

That is all I can say. I am at a dead stand. I can neither write nor read more. If the vessel do sail they say we shall be drowned on the lee shore; if she do not sail I perish waiting. What's the odds? I have plainly said my last word; it is the prodigality of ink, the wanton destruction of paper to add another syllable & withal a singular exhibition of what fatuity a man is capable who reckons himself sometimes an educated & thinking man. Yet must I write still. Why—these lines are the expectants of the dinner; it is cold & I cannot go out—Why should I? I have bid goodbye to all the people. Shall I make them repeat their tears & benedictions? There are no books in the house. I have digested the newspaper. I have no companion. Even Mr P. when at home has finished his communications, & we have got to theology at last. If it won't rain after the soles & cutlets I will brave one family whom I have parted from. Ah me Mr Thomas Carlyle I would give a gold pound for your wise company this gloomy eve. Ah we would speed the hour. Ah I would rise above myself. What self complacent glances casts the soul about in the moment of fine conversation esteeming itself the author of the fine things it utters & the master of the riches the memory produces & how scornfully looks it back upon the plain person it was yesterday without a thought. It occurs forcibly, yea some what pathetically, that he who visits a man of genius out of admiration for his parts should treat him tenderly. 'Tis odds but he will be disappointed. That is not the man of genius's fault. He was honest & human but the fault of his own ignorance of the limits of human excellence. Let him feel then that his visit was unwelcome & that he is indebted to the tolerance & good nature of his idol & so spare him the abuse of his own reacting feelings, the backstroke.

—

At sea. Sunday, 8 September, 1833. I wrote above my conviction that the great men of England are singularly ignorant of religion. They should read Norton's Preface to his new book who has stated that fact well. Carlyle almost grudges the poor peasant his Calvinism. Must I not admit in the same moment that I have practical difficulties myself? I see or believe in the wholesomeness of Calvinism for thousands & thousands. I would encourage or rather I would not discourage their scrupulous religious observances. I dare not speak lightly of usages which I omit. And so with this hollow obeisance to things I do not myself value I go on not pestering others with what I do believe & so I am open to the name of a very loose speculator, a faint heartless supporter of a frigid & empty theism, a man of no rigor of manners, of no vigor of benevolence. Ah me! what hope of reform, what hope of communicating religious light to benighted Europe if they who have what they call the Light are so selfish & timid & cold & their faith so unpractical & in their judgment so unsuitable for the middling classes. I know not, I have no call to expound, but this is my charge plain & clear to act faithfully upon my own faith, to live by it myself, & see what a hearty obedience to it will do.

(Carlyle deprecated the state of a man living in rebellion as he termed it with no worship, no reverence for any body. Himself he said would worship any one who showed him more truth. And Unitarians he thought were a tame limitary people who were satisfied with their sciolistic system & never made great attainments—incapable of depth of sentiment.)

Back again to myself. I believe that the error of religionists lies in this, that they do not know the extent or the harmony or the depth of their moral nature, that they are clinging to little, positive, verbal, formal versions of the moral law & very imperfect versions too, while the infinite laws, the laws of the Law, the great circling truths whose only adequate symbol is the material laws, the astronomy, &c, are all unobserved, & sneered at when spoken of, as frigid & insufficient. I call Calvinism such an imperfect version of the moral law. Unitarianism is another, & every form of Christian and of Pagan faith in the hands of incapable teachers is such a version. On the contrary in the hands of a true Teacher, the falsehoods, the pitifulnesses, the sectarianisms of each are dropped & the sublimity & the depth of the Original is penetrated & exhibited to men. I say also that all that recommends each of these established systems of opinion to men is so much of this Moral Truth as is in them, & by the instinctive selection of the preacher is made to shine forth when the system is assailed.

And because of this One bottom it is that the eminent men of each church, Socrates, A Kempis, Fenelon, Butler, Penn, Swedenborg, Channing think & say the same thing.

But the men of Europe will say, Expound; let us hear. What is it that is to convince the faithful & at the same time the philosopher? Let us hear this new thing. It is very old. It is the old revelation that perfect beauty is perfect goodness; it is the development of the wonderful congruities of the moral law of human nature. Let me enumerate a few of the remarkable properties of that nature. A man contains all that is needful to his government within himself. He is made a law unto himself. All real good or evil that can befal him must be from himself. He only can do himself any good or any harm. Nothing can be given to him or taken from him but always there is a compensation. There is a correspondence between the human soul & everything that exists in the world,—more properly, everything that is known to man. Instead of studying things without the principles of them, all may be penetrated unto within him. Every act puts the agent in a new condition. The purpose of life seems to be to acquaint a man with himself. He is not to live to the future as described to him but to live to the real future by living to the real present. The highest revelation is that God is in every man.

—

Loud winds last night but the ship swam like a waterfowl betwixt the mountains of sea. The wise man in the storm prays God not for safety from danger but for deliverance from fear. It is the storm within which endangers him, not the storm without. But it is a queer place to make one's bed in, the hollows of this immense Atlantic; Mazeppalike we are tied to the side of these wild horses of the Northwest. But this rough breath of Heaven will blow me home at last, as once it blew me to Gibraltar. The powerful trumpet of the blast finds a response to all its stops in the bottom of the heart of the men in the cabin.

At sea. 17 September. Yesterday I was asked what I mean by Morals. I reply that I cannot define & care not to define. It is man's business to observe & the definition of Moral Nature must be the slow result of years, of lives, of states perhaps of being. Yet in the morning watch on my berth I thought that Morals is the science of the laws of human action as respects right & wrong. Then I shall be asked—And what is Right? Right is a conformity to the laws of nature as far as they are known to the human mind.—These for the occasion but I propound definitions with more than the reserve of the feeling abovenamed—with more because my own conceptions are so dim & vague. But nevertheless nothing darkens, nothing shakes, nothing diminishes my constant conviction of the eternal concord of those laws which are perfect music & of which every high sentiment & every great action is only a new statement & therefore & insomuch speaks aloud to the whole race of man. I conceive of them by no types but the apparent hollow sphere of the whole firmament wherein this ball of the earth swims. Not easy are they to be enumerated but he has some idea of them who considers such propositions as St. Bernard's, Nobody can harm me but myself, or who developes the doctrine in his own experience that nothing can be given or taken without an equivalent.

Milton describes himself in his letter to Diodati as enamoured of moral perfection. He did not love it more than I. That which I cannot yet declare has been my angel from childhood until now. It has separated me from men. It has watered my pillow; it has driven sleep from my bed. It has tortured me for my guilt. It has inspired me with hope. It cannot be defeated by my defeats. It cannot be questioned though all the martyrs apostatize. It is always the glory that shall be revealed; it is the 'open secret' of the universe; & it is only the feebleness & dust of the observer that makes it future, the whole *is* now potentially in the bottom of his heart. It is the soul of religion. Keeping my eye on this I understand all heroism, the history of loyalty & of martyrdom & of bigotry, the heat of the methodist, the nonconformity of the dissenter, the patience of the Quaker. But what shall the hour say for distinctions such as these—this hour of southwest gales & rain dripping cabin? As the law of light is fits of easy transmission & reflexion such is also the soul's law. She is only superior at intervals to pain, to fear, to temptation, only in raptures unites herself to God and Wordsworth truly said

> Tis the most difficult of tasks to keep
> Heights which the soul is competent to gain.

What is this they say about wanting mathematical certainty for moral truths? I have always affirmed they had it. Yet they ask me whether I know the soul immortal. No. But do I not know the now to be eternal?

—

Is it not singular & not at all unpleasing the fact that almost all great men have been so yoked together by the accidents of their lives & few or none stand alone but all in genial constellation? John Evelyn gave a pension to Jeremy Taylor. Jeremy Taylor & John Milton both did homage to the same lady Countess of Carbery one in his Dedication, the other in his Comus. Milton & Galileo. Clarke, Butler, & Hume. Cervantes & Shakespear. Sir Henry Wotton was a hoop of gold to what a company! Dante died at Ravenna, 1321. Fifty one years after, Boccacio was made professor at Florence to lecture upon the Divine Comedy & in 1351 Boccacio was sent by the Florentines to Padua to intreat Petrarch to return & end his days in his native city. These are God's mnemonics. Newton was born the year Galileo died. Cuvier, Scott, & Mackintosh were born & died in the same years.

—

Newtown, 20 October. A Sabbath in the country but not so odoriferous as I have imagined. Mr. Bates a plain, serious Calvinist not winning but not repelling: one of the useful police which God makes out of the ignorance & superstition of the youth of the world. I dare not & wish not speak disrespectfully of these good, abstemious, laborious men. Yet I could not help asking myself how long is the society to be taught in this dramatic or allegorical style? When is religious truth to be distinctly uttered—what it is, not what it resembles? Thus every Sunday ever since they were born this congregation have heard tell of *Salvation*, and of going to the door of heaven & knocking, & being answered from Within, "Depart, I Never Knew You" & of being sent away to eternal ruin. What hinders that instead of this parable the naked fact be stated to them? Namely that as long as they offend against their conscience they will seek to be happy but they shall not be able, they shall not come to any true knowledge of God, they shall be avoided by good & by wise men, they shall become worse & worse.

from
Sicily
1833

At Sea. Jan. 2, 1833. Sailed from Boston for Malta Dec. 25, 1832 in Brig Jasper, Capt Ellis, 236 tons laden with logwood, mahogany, tobacco, sugar, coffee, beeswax, cheese, &c.

A long storm from the second morn of our departure consigned all the five passengers to the irremediable chagrins of the stateroom, to wit, nausea, darkness, unrest, uncleanness, harpy appetite & harpy feeding, the ugly sound of water in mine ears, anticipations of going to the bottom, & the treasures of the memory. I remembered up nearly the whole of Lycidas, clause by clause, here a verse & there a word, as Isis in the fable the broken body of Osiris.—

Out occasionally crawled we from our several holes, but hope & fair weather would not, so there was nothing for it but to wriggle again into the crooks of the transom. Then it seemed strange that the first man who came to sea did not turn round & go straight back again. Strange that because one of my neighbors had some trumpery logs & notions which would sell for a few cents more here than there he should thrust forth this company of his poor countrymen to the tender mercies of the northwest wind.

We study the sailor, the man of his hands, man of all work; all eye, all finger, muscle, skill, & endurance; a tailor, a carpenter, cooper, stevedore, & clerk & astronomer besides. He is a great saver, and a great quiddle by the necessity of his situation.

The Captain believes in the superiority of the American to every other countryman. "You will see, he says, when you get out here how they manage in Europe; they do everything by main strength & ignorance. Four truckmen & four stevedores at Long Wharf will load my brig quicker than 100 men at any port in the Mediterranean." It seems the Sicilians have tried once or twice to bring their fruit to America in their own bottoms, & made the passage, he says, in 120 days.

P.M. A crop of meditations in the berth. Thought again of the sailor & how superficial the differences—How shallow to make much of mere coat & hat distinctions. You can't get away from the radical, uniform, interior experiences which peep out of the new faces identical with those of the old. New tongues repeat the old proverbs, primeval truths. The thought occurred, full of consolation, that if he would deal towards himself with severest truth, man must acknowledge the Deity. So far from being a conventional idea, built on reason of State, it is in strict soliloquy, in absolute solitude when the soul makes itself a hermit in the creation, that this thought naturally arises. This unavoidable acknowledgment of God, this valid prayer puts the soul in equilibrium. In this state the question whether your boat shall float in safety or go to the bottom is no more important than the flight of a snowflake.

3 Jan. I rose at sunrise & under the lee of the spencer sheet had a solitary thoughtful hour. All right thought is devout. 'The clouds were touched & in their silent faces might be read unutterable love.' They shone with light that shines on Europe, Afric, & the Nile, & I opened my spirit's ear to their most ancient hymn. What, they said to me, goest thou so far to seek——painted canvass, carved marble, renowned towns? But fresh from us, new evermore, is the creative efflux from whence these works spring. You now feel in gazing at our fleecy arch of light the motions that express themselves in Arts. You get no nearer to the principle in Europe. It animates man. It is the America of America. It spans the ocean like a handbreadth. It smiles at Time & Space. Yet welcome young man! the Universe is hospitable. The great God who is Love hath made you aware of the forms & breeding of his wide house. We greet you well to the place of History as you please to style it; to the mighty Lilliput or ant hill of your genealogy, if, instructed as you have been, you must still be the dupe of shows, & count it much, the three or four bubbles of foam that preceded your own on the Sea of Time. This strong-winged sea gull & striped sheer-water that you have watched as they skimmed the waves under our vault—they are works of art

better worth your enthusiasm, masterpieces of Eternal power strictly eternal because now active & ye need not go so far to seek what ye would not seek at all if it were not within you. Yet welcome & hail! So sang in my ear the silver grey mists & the winds & the sea said Amen.

Thursday 3 Jan. N. lat 37.53. Dr Johnson rightly defends conversation upon the weather. With more reason we at sea beat that topic thin. We are pensioners of the wind. The weather cock is the wisest man. All our prosperity, enterprize, temper come & go with the fickle air. If the wind should forget to blow we must eat our masts. Sea farmers must make hay when the sun shines. The gale collects plenty of work for the calm. Now are we all awaiting a smoother sea to stand at our toilette. A headwind makes grinning Esaus of us. Happy that there is a time for all things under the moon, so that no man need give a dinner party in a brig's cabin, nor shave himself by the gulf lightning.

Sat. Eve. 5 Jan. I like the latitude of 37° better than my bitter native 42°. We have sauntered all this calm day at one or two knots the hour & nobody on board well pleased but I. And why should I be pleased? I have nothing to record. I have read little. I have done nothing. What then? Need we be such barren scoundrels that the whole beauty of heaven, the main, & man cannot entertain us unless we too must needs hold a candle & daub God's world with a smutch of our own insignificance? Not I, for one. I will be pleased though I do not deserve it. I will act in all up to my conceit of last week when I exulted in the power & art with which we rode tilting over this January ocean, albeit to speak truth, our individual valours lay very sick the while, lodged each in the waistcoat pocket of the brave brig's transom. So that each passenger's particular share in the glory was much the same as the sutler's or grocer's who turns his penny in the army of Leonidas or Washington. The southing latitude does not yet make early mornings. The steward's lanthorn & trumpery matutinal preparations are to me for the rosy ray, the silver cloud, or chaunt of earliest bird. But days will come.

Poor book this Scelta di Goldoni. He is puffed in the Preface and also by Sismondi as the Restorer or Reformer of the Italian stage. &c &c not a just sentiment or a well contrived scene in the book. His highest merit is that of a good phrase book. Perrin might as well knit his conversations into a dialogue & call it a Drama.

Sunday 6 Jan. lat 37 23. long. 39 59 w. Last ev'g fair wind & full moon suddenly lost in squall & rain. There are no attractions in the sailor's life. Its best things are only alleviations. "A prison with the chance of being drowned." It is even so and yet they do not run blind into unmeasured danger as seems to the landsman; those chances are all counted & weighed & experience has begotten this confidence in the proportioned strength of spars & rigging to the ordinary forces of wind & water which by being habitual constitutes the essence of a sailor's fearlessness. Suppose a student confined to a ship, I see not why he might not trim his lamp to as good purpose as in college attic. Why should he be less efficient in his vocation than the poor steward who ingloriously deals ever in pork & beans, let the quadrant or the chart or the monsoon say what they will? The caboose is his Rome.

It occurred forcibly this morning whether suggested by Goldoni or Bigelow or some falsetto of my own that the thing set down in words is not affirmed. It must affirm itself or no forms of grammar & no verisimilitude can give it evidence. This is a maxim which holds to the core of the world.

Storm, storm; ah we! the sea to us is but a lasting storm. We have had no fine weather to last an hour. Yet I must thank the sea & rough weather for a truckman's health & stomach,— how connected with celestial gifts!

The wind is the sole performer in these parts of nature & the royal Aeolus understands his work well, &, to give him his due, shifts the scene & varies the accompaniment as featly & as often as the audience can desire. Certainly he rings his few chimes with wondrous skill of permutation. Sometimes we his pets are cross & say 'tis nought but salt & squalls & sometimes we are ourselves & admit that it is divine Architecture.

7 Jan. w long. 36.11. n. lat. 37.4. Sailors are the best dressed of mankind. Convenience is studied from head to heel, & they have a change for every emergency. It seems to me they get more work out of the sailor than out of any other craftsman. His obedience is prompt as a soldier's & willing as a child's, & reconciles me to some dim remembrances of authority I wondered at. Thin skins do not believe in thick. Jack never looks an inch beyond his orders. "Brace the yards," quoth the master; "Ay Ay, sir," answers Jack, and never looks over the side at the squall or the sea that cometh as if it were no more to him than to the capstan.

But though I do not find much attraction in the seaman yet I can discern that the naval hero is a hero. It takes all the thousand thousand European voyages that have been made to stablish our faith in the practicability of this our hodiurnal voyage. But to be Columbus, to steer WEST steadily day after day, week after week, for the first time, and wholly alone in his opinion, shows a mind as solitary & self-subsistent as any that ever lived.

I am learning the use of the quadrant. Another voyage would make an astronomer of me. How delicately come out these stars at sea. The constellations show smaller & a ship though with the disadvantage of motion is a fine observatory. But I am ashamed of myself for a dull scholar. Every day I display a more astounding ignorance. The whole world is a mill stone to me. The experiment of the philosopher is but a separation to bring within his optics the comprehension of a fact which is done masterly & in harmony in God's laboratory of the world.

Wednesday 9 Jan. w. long 28 58. Still we sail well & feed full & hope tomorrow to make St Mary's, the southernmost of the Azores. When the Abbey grew rich the fat monk cut up all his quills for toothpicks. So do we.

Thursday Eve at 9 o'clock passed St Mary's, a dim black hummock of land. Our dead reckoning agreed with its longitude in the bearings to a mile.

13 Jan. We have but 14 degrees of longitude to make to reach the rock of Gibraltar but the fickle wind may make these fourteen longer measure than all we have meted. A gale day before yesterday; yesterday a heavy sea & a cold head wind to-day. Yet still we hope & drift along. In the Ocean the vessel gains a large commission on every mile sailed even with a wind dead ahead. In a narrow sea much less. A sea voyage at the best is yet such a bundle of perils & inconveniences that no person as much a lover of the present moment as I am would be swift to pay that price for any commodity which any thing else would buy. Yet if our horses are somewhat wild & the road un-even & lonely & without inns yet experience shows us that the coward eye magnifies the dangers.

14 Jan. W. long. 14° 14′
Well blithe traveller what cheer?
What have the sea & the stars & the moaning winds & your discontented thoughts sung in your attentive ears? Peeps up old Europe yet out of his eastern main? hospitably ho! Nay the slumberous old giant cannot bestir himself in these his chair days to loom up for the pastime of his upstart grandchildren as now they come shoal after shoal to salute their old Progenitor, the old Adam of all. Sleep on, old Sire, there is muscle & nerve & enterprise enow in us your poor spawn who have sucked the air & ripened in the sunshine of the cold West to steer our ships to your very ports & thrust our inquisitive American eyes into your towns & towers & keeping-rooms. Here we come & mean to be welcome. So be good now, clever old gentleman.

I comfort the mate by assuring him that the sea life is excel-lent preparation for life ashore. No man well knows how many fingers he has got nor what are the faculties of a knife & a needle or the capabilities of a pine board until he has seen the expedients, & the ambidexterous invincibility of Jack Tar. Then he may buy an orchard or retreat to his paternal acres with a stock of thrifty science that will make him independent of all the village carpenters, masons, & wheelwrights & add withal an enchanting beauty to the waving of his yellow corn

& sweetness to his shagbarks in his chimney corner. No squally Twelve o'clock Call the Watch shall break his dreams.

Tuesday. 15 Jan. W. Long 13°. 27. Calm, clear, warm, idle day; holiday to the senses, rest to the sailor, vexation to the captain, dubiously borne by the passenger. Yesterday or day before saw three sail, one Englishman. Today one French brig & saluted them both by exchanging the sight of our colours. John Bull, they say is very sulky at sea as assuredly sometimes very rude. But how comes my speculative pencil down to so near a level with the horizon of life, which commonly proses above?

I learn in the sunshine to get an altitude & the latitude but am a dull scholar as ever in real figures. Seldom I suppose was a more inapt learner of arithmetic, astronomy, geography, political economy than I am as I daily find to my cost. It were to brag much if I should there end the catalogue of my defects. My memory of history—put me to the pinch of a precise question—is as bad; my comprehension of a question in technical metaphysics very slow, & in all arts practick, in driving a bargain, or hiding emotion, or carrying myself in company as a man for an hour, I have no skill. What under the sun canst thou do then, pale face! Truly not much, but I can hope. "In a good hope," said Bias, "the wise differ from the unwise." I am content to belong to the great *all*, & look on & see what better men can do, & by my admiration realize a property in their worth. I did not put me here, yet God forbid I should therefore decline the responsibility into which I am born. Space & Time & venerable Nature & beautiful Stars & all ye various fellow beings, I greet ye well, & will not despond but even out of my acre God shall yet rear himself some tardy fruit. If not still is it not sublime unprofitably to pray & praise?

Wednesday, 16 Jan. W. long. 11.30 North latitude 30
16 Jan. I rose betimes & saw every fold of the banner of the morning unrolled from starlight to full day. We are as poor as we are rich. We brag of our memory but in the lonely night watch it will not always befriend us but leaves the scholar's brain as barren as the steward's. But that I sat in the confessional last night I should parade my rags again. The good Captain

rejoices much in my ignorance. He confounded me the other day about the book in the Bible where God was not mentioned & last night upon St Paul's shipwreck. Yet I comforted myself at midnight with Lycidas. What marble beauty in that classic Pastoral. I should like well to see an analysis of the pleasure it gives. That were criticism for the gods.

The inconvenience of living in a cabin is that people become all eye. 'Tis a great part of wellbeing to ignorize a good deal of your fellowman's history & not count his warts nor expect the hour when he shall wash his teeth.

17 Jan. n. lat 36 29 w long 9.48 Another day as beautiful as ever shines on the monotonous sea but a wind so soft will not fill our sails & we lie like a log so near our haven too. Ατρυγετη θαλασση—the sea is a blank & all the minstrelsy of nature rings but a few changes on the instrument. The more it should send us to the inner Music; but that is a capricious shell which sometimes vibrates wildly with multitudinous impulses & sometimes is mute as wood. The inner shell is like its marine archetype which murmurs only where there is already noise.

Friday 18 Jan. lat 36 36 long 8 20 w.

Well thou navigating Muse of mine 'tis now the hour of Chinese inspiration, the post-tea-cup-time, the epical creative moment to all thinking heads of the modern world & what print have the ethereal footsteps of Night & Morn left upon your tablets? Another day, another profusion of the divine munificence yet taken & spent by us as by the oysters. The boar feeds under the tree & never looks up to see who shakes down the mast & I glide in leisure & safety & health & fulness over this liquid Sahara & the Invisible Leader so venerable is seldom worshipped & much a stranger in the bosom of his child. We feel sometimes as if the sweet & awful melodies we have once heard would never return. As if we were deaf and fear we shall not again aspire to the glory of a moral life, of a will as punctual as the little needle in the binnacle over my head. The sea tosses on the horns of its waves the framework of habits so slight & epicurean as mine & I make the voyage one long holiday which like all holidays is dull.

Sat. 19 Jan. Mem. No trust to be put in a seaman's eye. He can see land wherever he wishes to see it & always has a cloud & "the stuff" ready to cover up a mistake. No word suits the sea but I hope. Every sign fails.

20 Jan. Straits of Gibraltar. Last evening they saw land from the mast-head & this morng broke over the bold & pictur-esque mountains of Africa behind Cape Spartel & Tangiers. On the left was Cape Trafalgar & Spain. The passengers greeted each other & mused each in his own way on this ani-mating vision. But now as Tarifa light opened upon us we have encountered an adverse current, a thing unknown in the books or to the sailors in these waters where they say the current always sets from the Ocean into the Mediterranean. Meantime all the other craft great & small are flying by us & we seem an-chored in the middle of the stream. What is this to me beyond my fellowfeeling for the master? Shall not I be content to look at the near coast of Andalusia & Morocco? I have seen this morn the smokes of Moorish fishers or mountaineers on one side & of Spanish on the other. We could not quite open Tangier Bay enow to see that Mauritanian town, but the watch towers & the cultivated enclosures & the farm houses of the Spaniard are very discernible. Not many weeks ago I should scarce have been convinced that I should so soon look on these objects, yet what is their poetry or what is it not? Is not a hut in Amer-ica a point that concentrates as much life & sentiment as a hut in Europe or on the ragged side of Mount Atlas? Ah! it is all in the Anointed eye. Yet will not I refine overmuch on the love of the remote & the renowned, nor affirm them both to be only a mixture of colors upon the retina of the eye, nor say of a man he is mammiferous & of beauty it is but gelatine & oxygen.

—

25 Jan. N. Lat. 37° 31 E. long. 1° 20′ Head winds are sore vexa-tions & the more passengers the sorer. Yesterday the Captain killed a porpoise & I witnessed the cutting up of my mammif-erous fellow creature.

When men & women sit mum by the hour & week, shall I doubt the doctrine that every natural character is interesting? By no means; there is always sweet music in the pipe but it needs a skilful player to draw it out, else month by month we may be packed in the same closet, & shall be all only so much ash & ebony.

If the sea teaches any lesson it thunders this through the throat of all its winds "That there is no knowledge that is not valuable." How I envied the fellow passenger who yesterday had knowledge & nerve enough to prescribe for the sailor's sore throat & this morning to bleed him. In this little balloon of ours, so far from the human family and their sages & colleges & manufactories every accomplishment, every natural or acquired talent, every piece of information is some time in request. And a short voyage will show the difference between the man & the apprentice as surely as it will show the superior value of beef & bread to lemons & sugarplums. Honour evermore aboard ship to the man of action,—to the brain in the hand. Here is our stout master worth a thousand philosophers —a man who can strike a porpoise, & make oil out of his blubber, & steak out of his meat; who can thump a mutineer into obedience in two minutes; who can bleed his sick sailor, & mend the box of his pump; who can ride out the roughest storm on the American coast, &, more than all, with the sun & a three cornered bit of wood, & a chart, can find his way from Boston across 3000 miles of stormy water into a little gut of inland sea 9 miles wide with as much precision as if led by a clue.

2 Feb. Made St Elmo's light at 1 o'clock this morng; lay to in a gale till daylight & then sailed into St Paul's bay. The pilot boat was quickly followed by a procession of boats who after a short loud wrangling with the unflinching captain came into his terms & took the rope & brought us in. So here we are in Malta, in the renowned harbor of Marsa Muscette the Quarantine roads for a fortnight, imprisoned for poor dear Europe's health lest it should suffer prejudice from the unclean sands & mountains of America. The truth is it is all pro forma on the part of the English government, this quarantine being enforced in accordance with the rules of Naples & Trieste merely that vessels quarantined here may be admitted to full pratique in those ports.

We were presently visited by the Harbor-master, then by the

boats of the grocer & ship chandler presenting their cards at the end of a pole to us leprous men, then the clamorous *Spenditori* to offer their services, then by the merchant signor Paul Eynaud.

This P.M. I visited the Parlatorio where those in quarantine converse with those out across barriers. It looked to me like the wildest masquerade. There jabbered Turks, Moors, Sicilians, Germans, Greeks, English, Maltese, with friars & guards & maimed & beggars. And such grotesque faces! It resembled more some brave antique picture than a congregation of flesh & blood. The human family can seldom see their own differences of color & form so sharply contrasted as in this house. I noticed however that all the curiosity manifested was on our part. Our cousins of Asia & Europe did not pay us the compliment of a second glance.

In Quarantine, our acquaintance has been confined chiefly to the Maltese boatmen, a great multitude of poor, swarthy, goodnatured people, who speak their own tongue, not much differing from the Arabic, & most of them know very few words of Italian & less of English.

16 February, La Valetta. Yesterday we took pratique & found lodgings once more on dry ground with great joy. All day with my fellow travellers I perambulated this little town of stone. It is from end to end a box of curiosities. & though it is very green & juvenile to express wonder, I could not hinder my eyes from rolling continually in their sockets nor my tongue from uttering my pleasure & surprize. It is an advantage to enter Europe at the little end so we shall admire by just degrees from the Maltese architecture up to St Peter's. I went to St John's Church & a noble house it is to worship God in; full of marble & mosaic & pictures & gilding; the walls are eloquent with texts & the floor covered with epitaphs. The Verger led me down into a dim vault full of solemn sculpture & showed me the tomb of L'Isle Adam, the Grand Master of the Knights of St John, to whom Charles V gave the island of Malta when he & his knights had been driven by the Turks from Rhodes. Next to him, rests the body of La Valetta who so bravely defended the island against the Sultan   in

*

But I shall have more to say about this fine temple when I have paid another visit. Every where as I went, the wretched beggars would steal up beside me, with, "Grazia, Signore, sono miserabile, uno grano per carita." Look hard at a Maltese, said my friend, Mr H. & he instinctively holds out his hand. I went to the churches of St Popilius & St Thomas. The first is no other than 'Publius, the chief man of the island' in Acts XXVIII & much honor hath he in Malta at least on the walls of his church.

In all these churches there were many worshippers continually coming in, saying their prayers, & going their way. I yielded me joyfully to the religious impression of holy texts & fine paintings this soothfast faith though of women & children. How beautiful to have the church always open, so that every tired wayfaring man may come in & be soothed by all that art can suggest of a better world when he is weary with this.

I hope they will carve & paint & inscribe the walls of our churches in New England before this century, which will probably see many grand granite piles erected there, is closed. To be sure there is plenty of superstition. Every where indulgence is offered, and on one convent on our way home I read this inscription over the gate, "Indulgentia plenaria, quotidiana, perpetua, pro vivis et defunctis." This is almost too frank, may it please your holiness.

———

A few beautiful faces in the dancing crowd, & a beautiful face is always worth going far to see. That which is finest in beauty is *moral*. The most piquant attraction of a long descended maiden is the imputation of an immaculate innocence, a sort of wild virtue (if I may so term it) wild & fragrant as the violets. And the imagination is surprised & gratified with the strong contrast—meeting the Divinity amidst flowers & trifles.

———

Syracuse 23 Feb.

Shall I count it like the Berber at Rome the greatest wonder of all to find myself here? I have this day drank the waters of the fountain Arethusa & washed my hands in it. I ate the very fragrant Hyblaean honey with my breakfast. I have been into

the old temple of Minerva praised for its beauty by Cicero &
now preserved & concealed by having its pillars half buried in
the walls of the Cathedral. A modern facade conceals the front
but the severe beauty of a Parthenon peeps from the sides in
projecting flutes & triglyphs. It was 7 in the morning, & I
found the priests saying mass in the oratories of the church.
The American Consul called upon our party in the forenoon
& we rode with him into the country. We stopped at a crumbled arch reputed as the spot where Cicero found the globe &
cylinder, the tomb of Archimedes. Did I hold my breath for
awe? Then went we to the Catacombs—old enough—nothing
else—mere excavations in the living rock for cemeteries, but
the air was soft & the trees in bloom & the fields covered with
beautiful wild flowers to me unknown and amidst ruins of
ruins Nature still was fair. Close by we found the Aqueduct,
which once supplied the magnificent city of Hiero, now turning
a small grist mill. Then we went to Dionysius' Ear; a huge excavation into the hard rock which I am not going to describe.
Poor people were making twine in it & my ear was caught on
approaching it by the loud noise made by their petty wheels in
the vault. A little beyond the entrance the floor was covered
with a pool of water. We found a twine maker who very readily
took us, one after another on his shoulders into the recess 250
ft, & planted us on dry land at the bottom of the cave. We
shouted & shouted & the cave bellowed & bellowed; the
twine maker tore a bit of paper in the middle of the cave, &
very loud it sounded; then they fired a pistol at the entrance &
we had our fill of thunder.

I inquired for the tyrant's chamber in the wall, the focus of
sound where he was wont to hear the whispers of his prisoners,
—but in this unvisited country it is inaccessible. High up the
rock, seventy or eighty feet, they pointed to a little inlet to
which once there was a stair, but not now. If we had time &
spirit would we not go up thither in baskets, as sundry English
have done? I affirm not. A little way off, along the same quarry
of rock we found another great excavation in which they were
making saltpetre. It was the place from which the great pillars
of the Temple of Minerva, it is said, were taken. Then we
visited the Theatre or rather the rows of stone benches which
are all of it that remains. From this spot we looked down upon

the city & its noble harbour and a beautiful sad sight it was. The town stands now wholly within the little peninsula, the ancient Ortygia (not a third of the size of the peninsula of Boston, I judge) and the three great suburbs or parts, Neapoli, Tycha, & Acradina, have almost no house or church where they stood. And Syracuse is very old & shabby, with narrow streets & few people & many, many beggars. Once 800000 people dwelt together in this town. Its walls were according to historical measurements twenty two English miles in circuit. Of its two ports, the northern was called the Marmoreus because surrounded with marble edifices. The southern is 5 miles round, & is the best harbor in the Mediterranean Sea.

In the old time every Sicilian carried honey & wheat & flowers out of the port & threw them into the sea as soon as he lost sight of the statue of Minerva aloft on her temple. Once Dion, once Timoleon, once Archimedes dwelt here & Cicero dutifully visited their graves.

———

What is a passenger? He is a much enduring man who bends under the load of his leisure. He fawns upon the Captain, reveres the mate, but his eye follows the Steward; scans accurately as symptomatic, all the motions of that respectable officer.

The species is contemplative, given to imitation, viciously inquisitive, immensely capable of sleep, large eaters, swift digesters, their thoughts ever running on men & things ashore & their eye usually squinting over the bulwark, to estimate the speed of the bubbles.

———

I lodge in the Strada Amalfitania. In a Caffé in our street, they have had the good taste to paint the walls in very tolerable frescoes with Archimedes drawing the famous galley by means of a windlass. A sign over our Locanda contains this sentence of Cicero's 4th Oration in Verrem "Urbem Syracusas elegerat."

Was it grand or mournful that I should hear mass in this Temple of Minerva this morn? Though in different forms, is it not venerable that the same walls should be devoted to divine worship for more than 2500 years? Is it not good witness to the ineradicableness of the religious principle? With the strange practice that in these regions every where confounds pagan & Christian Antiquity & half preserves both, they call this cathedral the Church of 'our Lady of the pillar.'

Abundance of examples here of great things turned to vile uses. The fountain Arethuse, to be sure, gives name to the street Via Aretusa in which it is found: but an obscure dark nook it is & we walked up & down & looked in this & that court yard in vain for some time. Then we asked a soldier on guard Where it was? He only knew that "Questa e la batteria," —nothing more. At last an old woman guided us to the spot and I grieve—I abhor to tell—the fountain was bubbling up in its world renowned waters within four black walls serving as one great washing tub to fifty or sixty women who were polluting it with all the filthy clothes of the city.

It is remarkable now as of old for its quantity of water springing up out of the earth at once as large as a river. Its waters are sweet & pure & of the colour of Lake George.

All day from the balcony, Mount Etna is in sight, covered with snow. From the parlor window I look down on the broad marshes where the Carthaginian army that came to rescue Syracuse from the Romans, perished.

They say in this country you have but to scratch the soil & you shall find medals, cameos, statues, temples.

February 24. Visited the Latomié of the Gardens of the Capuchins—a strange place—. It is a large & beautiful garden full of oranges & lemons & pomegranates in a deep pit, say 120 feet below the surrounding grounds. All this is a vast excavation in the solid rock, & we first came upon it from above & peeped down the precipice into this fragrant cellar far below us. "Opus est ingens magnificum regum ac tyrannorum. Totum est ex saxo in mirandam altitudinem depresso, &c" *Cicero*. All this excavation is manifestly the work of art— Cyclopean all. After circumambulating the brink above we went to the Convent & got admission to the garden below. A handsome & courteous monk conducted us, & showed us one huge arch wherein he said the Athenian prisoners recited the verses of Euripides for their ransom. Wild & grand effect. All Syracuse must have been built out of this enormous quarry. Traces of works on a vast scale in oldest time.

Went into the Convent & the Fathers set before us bread, olives, & wine. Our conductor then showed us the dormitories (over each of which was a latin inscription from the bible or the Fathers,) the Chapel, &c. of the House. There is no better spot in the neighborhood of Syracuse than the one they have chosen. The air, the view, the long gallery of the chambers, the peace of the place quite took me & I told the Padre that I would stay there always if he would give me a chamber. He said, 'I should have his,' which he opened—a little neat room, with a few books, "Theologia Thomae ex Charmes," & some others. My friend's whipcords hung by the bed side. There are only 22 or 23 persons in this fine old house. We saw but 4 or 5. I am half resolved to spend a week or fortnight there. They will give me board, I am informed, on easy terms. How good & pleasant to stop & recollect myself in this worn out nook of the human race, to turn over its history & my own. But, ah me!

Hence we went to the Campo Santo where several Americans have been buried; & thence to other Latomie, the gardens of the Marquis di Casal. Similar to those we had left but the rich soil is now filled with flowers in wildest profusion of scent & color. The bergamot lemon, the orange, the citron, we plucked & ate; & lavender & rosemary & roses & hyacinths & jasmine & thyme, which were running wild all over the grounds we filled our hands & hats with.

Here we found the Marchesino or son of the Marchese, who was very polite to us, & Mr Baker, the English consul, & his family, whom we greeted warmly for the love of the fatherland & language. Well pleased we came back to the Locanda where we received the American Consul Signor Nicosia & his friend Signor Giuseppe Ricciardi to dine.

February 25. Still, melancholy, old metropolis! under the moon, last eve, how wan & grey it looked. Took a boat this morning & crossed the Porto Maggiore & sailed up the mouth of the river Anapus; full of canes & bulrushes & snails & a very little, narrow, mean puddle to be famed in song. We did not go up so far as the fountain Cyane, but disembarked about 3 miles lower, where the stream was an oar's length wide. It was a pretty fable of Pluto's metamorphosis of Cyane & if we had more time should have stamped on the very ground where "gloomy Dis" stamped, & the rather that our 'plan' afterwards showed us this was the spot of the Athenian Encampment. No wonder Proserpine gathered flowers; they grow everywhere of prettiest forms & liveliest colors now in February, & I stopped ever & anon to pick them.

On the banks of the Anapus grows the Papyrus—the immortal plant.—It is a sightly, clean, green, triangular stem 20 feet high surmounted by a bunch of threads which the people call parroca (perriwig). We cut down a good many, & then crossed the fields to the columns of the Temple of Olympian Jove.

Here stand two broken shafts, the sole remains of the temple which Gelo enriched with the spoils of the Carthaginians 2500 years ago. The site is a commanding one, facing the centre of the mouth of the Great Harbor. Seven of these fluted columns were standing in the last century, but Earthquakes are added to Time here in the work of destruction.

We crossed the bridge of the Anapus & went home by way of the Catacombs. We sat down on the benches of the Theatre which was entire in the days of Nero. We asked a goatherd who smoked his pipe on the same bench what they were for? "per il mulino", mulino. We could not easily get him by our questions beyond the Mill; at last he said, "antichita!" On the lowest circuit of benches we read the inscriptions ΒΑΣΙΛΙΣΣΑΣ ΦΙΛΙΣΤΙΔΟΣ and ΒΑΣΙΛΙΣΣΑΣ ΝΕΡΗΙΔΟΣ. There are medals with the first inscription, supposed to denote the daughter of Philistus, wife of the elder Dionysius.

In the afternoon, I went to the Museum & saw the Venus Kallipyge, dug up here in 1810, a headless beauty.

February 27. At dinner, a Frate dei Padri Capuccini was announced who brought olives & lemons in his hand, & would accompany us to the Latomié of the Church of St John. Thither we went, and descended into subterranean caverns cut regularly in the living rock. Two Fathers & two boys attended with torches. On each side of the main passages were catacombs, some larger, some less. Occasionally the ceiling was vaulted up to admit light & air. I asked how far these long passages extended; the friar said, he knew not how far, but the air was bad, & no one went further than we. Cicero visited them before us.

Then went to the Church—very old, small, & poor; but by stone stairs descended into one far older, which they say is St John's Church, & coeval with the planting of Christianity in Sicily. The bold carving of the granite all around made me think it of Greek age & afterwards converted to this use.

Signor Ricciardi, a friend of the Consul Nicolini's, was very civil to us & spoke good English. At parting he gave each of us a handful of sugar plums.

Catania, 1 March. Fine strange ride & walk yesterday coming by mules from Syracuse hither, 42 miles, thirteen hours. Our party (3 gentlemen 2 ladies) were accomodated with seven beasts, 2 for the Lettiga containing the ladies, 2 for the baggage, one for each saddle. The morning road led us by catacombs without number. What are they but evidences of an immense ancient population that every rock should be cut into sepulchres. The road, a mere mule-path through very stony soil, was yet not so rough but that I preferred walking to riding, & for an hour or two kept up easily with the caravan. Fine air, clear sun, Mount Aetna right before us, green fields— laborers ploughing in them, many flowers, all the houses of stone. Passed the trophy of Marcellus, a pile of broken masonry and yet it answers its purpose as well as Marcellus could have hoped. Did he think that Mr Emerson would be reminded of his existence & victory this fine spring day 2047 years to come? Saw the town of Mellili. Dined from our own knapsack at the strangest tavern; hills of olive trees all around, an oil mill or press adjoining, & a dozen big Morgiana jars thereby; what seemed the remains of some most ancient church or temple with the stumps of pillars still standing, in the rear and the hostelry itself a most filthy house of stone, more stable than house, the common dwelling of men, women, beasts, & vermin. "Siamo pronti, Signore," then said the muleteer, which he of our party to whom it was said, misapprehending to be a call for *brandy*, we waited yet a little.

The afternoon ride was pleasanter much—flowers abounding, the road smooth and Aetna glorious to behold with his cap of smoke, & the Mountainettes like warts all over his huge sides. Then wound the road down by the seaside and for many miles we traversed a beach like that of Lynn paved with pretty shells. We crossed the Simaethus in a ferry & going a little inland we tramped through miles of prickly pears gigantic, but though Catanea had been in sight much of the time since twelve o'clock nothing could be ruder than this mule path from Syracuse to a city of 70000 souls. Had I opened my eyes from sleep here almost under the shadows of the town I might have thought myself near Timbuctoo. Yet has Nature done all it could for this drowsy nation. I suppose the bay of Naples cannot be so beautiful as the spacious bay, round the shore of which we straggled & stumbled with tinkling mules, & sighing & shouting drivers. Tzar, Tzar, gia, hm, and many an odd, nondescript, despairing sound they utter to that deliberate animal. As the day went down the mules began to tire, & one slipt into the mud, & was with difficulty got out. Another fell down with the lettiga. The sun set, the moon rose, & still we did not reach the town so near at noon till eight o clock.

———

Town of lava of earthquakes. The mountain is at once a monument & a warning. Houses are built, streets paved with lava; it is polished in the altars of the churches. Huge black rocks of it line the shore, & the white surf breaks over them. A great town full of fine old buildings, long regular streets thronged with people, a striking contrast to the sad solitude of Syracuse. Cathedral church of St Agatha. What exhilaration does the mere height of these prodigious Churches produce! We feel so little & so elated upon the floor. All the interior & exterior of this edifice is costly & the cost of ages. The ancient Roman Amphitheatre was robbed for the columns & bas reliefs of its porch & much of its walls. Its niches & altars shine with many colored marbles & round the whole ample square whereon the church stands runs a large marble fence.

But what is even this church to that of the Benedictines? Indeed, my holy Fathers, your vows of poverty & humility have cost you little. Signor Ricciardi of Syracuse gave me a letter to Padre Anselmo Adorno, the Celleraio of this monastery & this morn I waited upon his reverence in his cell, & the kings of France & England, I think, do not live in a better house. The Padre with great courtesy showed us the church & its paintings, & its organ, here reputed the finest in Europe. It imitates sackbut, harp, psaltery, & all kinds of music. The Monk Donatus who built it, begged that he might be buried under it, & there he lies. To my ignorance, however, the organ neither appeared very large nor very richly toned. But the Church shall be St Peter's to me till I behold a fairer shrine. Have the men of America never entered these European churches that they build such mean edifices at home? Contini was the Architect but Father Anselm only knew that it was more than a hundred years old. But O the marbles! & oh the pictures & oh the noble proportions of the pile! A less inter- esting exhibition was the Treasury of the Convent, some sil- ver richly wrought, seats & stools embroidered & gilt, & a wardrobe, —drawers full of copes & things of cloth-of-gold & silver. Then the long lofty cloisters, galleries of chambers, then gardens, too artificially laid out. About 50 monks are laid up in clover & magnificence here. They give bread twice in a week, one roll to every comer. I saw hundreds of women & children in the yard each receiving her loaf & passing on into a court, that none should come twice to the basket.

Visited the Museum of the Prince of Biscari, one of the best collections of the remains of ancient art. Bronzes, marbles, mosaics, coins, utensils dug up all over Sicily of Greek & Roman manufacture are disposed with taste & science.

A head of Scipio took my fancy. & some more heads. The Prince of Biscari is a venerable name here. He was the Roscoe, the Petrarch of the town. Everywhere his beneficent hand is shown in restoring the old & saving the new.

I have been under the Cathedral into the ancient baths: and into the subterranean ruins of the ancient theatre, & now I will leave this primeval city, said to have been built by the Siculi 85 years before the destruction of Troy! & engage with the Vetturo for a visit to Messina.

I have been to the Opera, & thought three taris, the price of a ticket, rather too much for the whistle. It is doubtless a vice to turn one's eyes inward too much, but I am my own comedy & tragedy. Did ye ever hear of a magnet who thought he had lost his virtue because he had fallen into a heap of shavings? Our manners are sometimes so mean, our blunders & improprieties so many and mulish that it becomes a comfort to think that people are too much occupied with themselves to remember even their neighbor's defects very long.

Messina. March 5. From Catania my ride to this city was charming. The distance is but 60 miles but that is two days' journey here. Mount Etna was the grand spectacle of the first day & a fine sight it is. This monarch of mountains they say supports a population of 115000 souls, & is 180 miles in circuit. And its ample sides are belted with villages & towers up almost to the snow. As the wind blew fresh I *smelt* the snowbanks. Village of Giarre; old country; catholic all over; scarce a house or a fence but hath a shrine or cross or inscription. "Basta a chi non ha. Basta a chi morra." Another, "Viva la Divina Providenza," & a thousand more. It is a poor philosophy that dislikes these sermons in stones. But what green fields, & trees in bloom, & thick villages the turns in the road showed; & my Sicilian companions would break out "O che bella veduta!"

These companions were four, a priest of the Church of St Iago in Messina, named Itellario, his two nephews Lorenzo Gaetano, & Francesco Nicolosi, a tailor. I name them all because they were very kind to me. They speedily found I was a stranger & took great pleasure in hearing my bad Italian & in giving me the names of things & places. They brought their viveri with them & at Giardini, where we spent the night, they made me dine with them & paid all reckonings in the morng. It was amusing enough first, to see how a Sicilian dines. Then their intercourse with me was all a comedy. (their pronunciation & dialect are very different from Tuscan) When I could not understand they would raise their voices, & then all say the same thing, & then the worthy priest after a consultation among them inquired if I could understand Latin, & I declaring that I could, he essayed to communicate in that tongue, but his Sicilian accent made his Latin equally unintelligible to me. All the household collected gradually around us. At last I hit upon the sense of what they would say, & much acclamation & mutual congratulation there was. Coachey came in too, & he told them I was a *Sacerdote*, a *preté*, in my own country, a fact he had picked up in Catania. This was wonders more. Then at every sentence which I forged & uttered was profound silence followed by acclamations "che bravo Signore!" so modulated as only Italians can.

The little dark Locanda was on the beach of cape   & the roar of the sea lulled me to sleep. Next morning I awoke right early & found myself in the most picturesque of places. High overhead was Taormina, so high & steep that it seemed inaccessible, & if men could get there, not safe to live on the edge of a rock. Presently we set forth & every step of the road showed new beauty & strangeness. The ruins of the amphitheatre at Taormina in very good preservation, I saw. & much I doubt if the world contains more picturesque country in the same extent than in the thirty miles betwixt Giardini & Messina.

At the Viceroy's Palace, I saw nothing but a small chapel which they vaunted much. I went to the Capuchin Convent. That pleased me better. I like these Capuchins, who are the most esteemed of the Catholic clergy. Their profession is beggary but they distribute large alms to the poor. You approach their houses thro' a regiment of beggars. The Fathers were at dinner so I took a turn in their sober garden. Then came a monk & led me down into their Cemetery. A strange spectacle enough. Long aisles the walls of which on either side are filled with niches & in every niche the standing skeleton of a dead Capuchin; the skull & the hands appearing, the rest of the anatomy wrapped in cearments. Hundreds & hundreds of these grinning mortalities were ranged along the walls, here an abbot, there a General of the Convent. Every one had his label with his name, when in the body, hanging at his breast. One was near 300 years old. On some the beard remained, on some the hair. I asked the monk how many there were? He said, since 300 years half a million; and he himself would stand there with his brothers in his turn.

My cicerone conducted me next to the Spedale dei Pazzi. I did not know where I was going or should not have visited it. I could not help them & have seen enough of their sad malady without coming to Sicily. Then to the pleasant gardens of the Prince di Buttera. At the tavola rotonda of the Giacheri perhaps 8 persons dined. I believe no one but I, spoke English. So I sat mute. The same gentlemen spoke alternately French, Spanish, & Italian. A traveller should speak all the four & his pocket should be a wellspring of taris & bajochhi.

———

Mr Gardner the American Consul lives in a fine house. Mrs G. has a rich collection of shells & fossils. She tells me, all her society is English; none native. If you ask a Sicilian to your house, he will bring twenty more. They will always accept your invitations, but never ask you in return to visit them but at their box at the opera. Their pride is in an equipage to ride on the Marina. Even shoemakers & hairdressers will go hungry to keep a carriage.

No learned or intelligent men or next to none. Abate Ferrara is. The daughters are sent to a convent for their education, & learn to make preserves & needlework. The English here, & now some Sicilians, send their sons to Switzerland, to excellent schools.

The steamboat must stay another day & I must use philosophy. So I have been to the Monte Reale on foot & I suppose the world has not many more beautiful landscapes than the plain & the port of Palermo as seen therefrom. Olive & orange & lemon groves wide around. After visiting St Simon's Church & the Benedictine Convent, I followed my vivacious little guide Raimondo to his house & he set before me wine & olives & oranges & bread.

At the tavola rotonda with eight persons we had five languages. At the opera in the evening I had a thought or two that must wait a more convenient page. I do not know whether I can recommend my domestique de place Michele Beleo to the patronage of my friends, but I promised to remember his name. And now for Naples.

At sea in the steamboat Re Ferdinando II March. I tried last night in my berth to recal what had occurred at the opera. Ποιημα. What is really good is ever a new creation. I could not help pitying the performers in their fillets & shields & togas, & saw their strained & unsuccessful exertions & thought on their long toilette & personal mortification at making such a figure. There they are—the same poor Johns & Antonios they were this morning, for all their gilt & pasteboard. But the moment the Prima donna utters one tone or makes a gesture of natural passion, it puts life into the dead scene. I pity them no more. It is not a ghost of departed things, not an old Greece & Rome but a Greece & Rome of this moment. It is living merit which takes ground with all other merit of whatever kind,— with beauty, nobility, genius, & power. O trust to Nature, whosoever thou art, even though a strutting tragedy-prince. Trust your simple self & you shall stand before genuine princes. The play was tedious, & so are the criticisms.

Two pleasant young Englishmen, who had just ascended Etna, on board the boat. One named Barclay, the other, Hussey, fond of geology. Kind domestic manners are more elegant than too civil ones. "This is the most capital place of all—" was better than twenty Sirs & scrupulosities.

Naples, 12 March. And what if it is Naples, it is only the same world of cake & ale—of man & truth & folly. I won't be imposed upon by a name. It is so easy, almost so inevitable to be overawed by names that on entering this bay it is hard to keep one's judgment upright, & be pleased only after your own way. Baiae & Misenum & Vesuvius, Procida & Pausilippo & Villa Reale sound so big that we are ready to surrender at discretion & not stickle for our private opinion against what seems the human race. Who cares? Here's for the plain old Adam, the simple genuine Self against the whole world. Need is, that you assert yourself or you will find yourself overborne by the most paltry things. A young man is dazzled by the stately arrangements of the hotel & jostled out of his course of thought & study of men by such trumpery considerations. The immense regard paid to clean shoes & a smooth hat impedes him, & the staring of a few dozens of idlers in the street hinders him from looking about him with his own eyes; & the attention which he came so far to give to foreign wonders, is concentrated instead, on these contemptible particulars. Therefore it behooves the traveller to insist first of all upon his simple human rights of seeing & of judging here in Italy as he would in his own farm or sitting room at home.

March 15. A nation of little men, I fear. No original art remains. I have been to the Academia & seen the works of Raffaelle, Titian, Guido, Correggio. A good many artists were making indifferent copies of the best. I hear nothing of living painters, but perhaps there are. A rich collection of marble & bronze & frescoes, &c from Herculaneum, Pompeii, & the Baths of Caracalla.—Many fine statues, Cicero, Aristides,

Seneca, and Dianas, Apollos, &c without end. Nothing is more striking than the contrast of the purity, the severity expressed in these fine old heads, with the frivolity & sensuality of the mob that exhibits & the mob that gazes at them. These are the countenances of the first born, the face of man in the morning of the world & they surprize you with a moral admonition as they speak of nothing around you but remind you of the fragrant thoughts & the purest resolutions of your Youth.

16 March. Last night stayed at home at my black lodgings in the Croce di Malta & read Goethe. This morn, sallied out alone & traversed I believe for the seventh time that superb mile of the Villa Reale; then to the tomb of Virgil. But here the effect of every Antiquity is spoiled by the contrast of ridiculous or pitiful circumstances. The boy who guided me was assailed by men, women, & children with all manner of opprobrium. A gang of boys & girls followed me, crying, "Signore, C'e un mariolo." Yea the venerable silence of the poet's sepulchre must be disturbed with the altercation of these Lilliputians. The tomb is well enough for so great a name, but its rich ashes are long ago scattered. It has an aperture which looks down into the entrance of the Grotto of Posilippo. Then descending, I passed through this Cyclopean excavation to the bright & beautiful country of vineyards & olive groves beyond with the fine ridges of Camaldoli.

Presently I met a company of muleteers who set up a shout of "ladre" & "mariolo" when they saw my cicerone; so I hasted to get rid of my suspicious companion, & engaged another to conduct me to the Grotto del Cane. Through lanes of plenty he led me to the beautiful Lake of Agnana & the Grotto where they expose a dog to the sulphurous vapor & the animal in a short time loses all signs of life, but is restored by being brought out. They offered the poor dog for the experiment if I would pay six carlines; & I told them I would not; so the dog was saved his fainting. A pleasant place is this little lake.

Thence I followed my guide for two or three miles to the Solfatura of Pozzuoli & saw these volcanic springs of ever boiling sulphur. The soil was hot under my feet & the mountain smoked above at different openings. We always look at volcanoes with great respect. Thence to Pozzuoli & the well preserved remains of the Coliseum or Amphitheatre. Here underground I could have a lively recollection of that great nation for whose amusement these fabrics were reared, but above ground in Pozzuoli, it is impossible to connect the little dirty suburb full of beggars, & beggar-boatmen, & beggar-coacheys with the most ancient city which the Cumaeans founded, the old Dicearchia, & long after the Puteoli of Cicero, his 'little Rome', as he affectionately called this garden of palaces.

Alas! no! here by the temple of Serapis one stout fellow tried to pick my pocket of my torn handkerchief & here too my guide warned me with demanding three or four times as much as his due and a swarm of boys settled on me with 'antiquities' to sell, old coins & fragments of brass & copper. & beggars as usual a regiment. Ah sirs of Naples! you pay a high price for your delicious country & famed neighborhood in this swarming, faithless, robber population that surrounds & fills your city today. I was very glad to see no more antiquities, but to get home as fast as I could. I dined with Mr Rogers and found some pleasant gentlemen at his hospitable house.

One must be thoroughly reinforced with the spirit of antiquity to preserve his enthusiasm through all the annoyances that await the visitor of these ruins. Long ago when I dreamed at home of these things, I thought I should come suddenly in the midst of an open country upon broken columns & fallen friezes, & their solitude would be solemn & eloquent. Instead of this, they are carefully fenced round like orchards and the moment the unhappy traveller approaches one of them, this vermin of ciceroni & padroni fasten upon him, a class of people whose looks & manners are more like those of Mac Guffog & the duke of Alsatia than the vain & flippant character I had imagined as the exhibitor *con amore*. What with these truculent fellows, & the boys & the beggars & the coachmen all sentiment is killed in the bud, & most men clap both hands on their pockets & run.

March 17. This morning under the kind guidance of Mr Durante I have visited six or seven churches the finest in the city. They are truly splendid & compare with the best I have seen. The Cathedral is a suite of churches & there the blood of St

Januarius is annually liquefied. Its wealth must be immense. They showed me thirty busts of saints, large as life, composed of solid silver, & lamps, & angels, & candelabra, many more. Huge gates of brass richly carved admitted us to this chapel. It was thronged with worshippers, so was the nave of the cathedral.

Then the private chapel of the family of the Severini, in the Strada St Severino, contains the famous veiled statues, which are wonders in their way.

Then Santa Clara, Santo Geronimo, St Laurentio, Gesu Nuovo, St Gaetano.

All which, I trust, I shall find again, for they were superb structures & of their ornaments was there no end. Such churches can only be finished in ages. They were all well attended this Sabbath morn. Who can imagine the effect of a true & worthy form of worship in these godly piles? It would ravish us. I do not mean the common protestant service, but what it should be if all were actual worshippers. It would have something of this Catholic ceremony too & yet not show a priest hither & thither, & buzzing now on this side then on that.

These mighty dwelling houses rise to 5 & 6 tall stories & every floor is occupied by a different family. Opposite my window at the Crocelle, on the 4th story, a family lived with poultry cackling around them all day, 40 feet from the ground; & today I observe a turkey in the chamber across the street stepping about the 2d story. A goat comes up stairs every day to be milked. But the woes of this great city are many & conspicuous. Goethe says 'he shall never again be wholly unhappy, for he has seen Naples.' If he had said '*happy*,' there would have been equal reason. You cannot go five yards in any direction without seeing saddest objects & hearing the most piteous wailings. Instead of the gayest of cities, you seem to walk in the wards of a hospital. Even Charity herself is glad to take a walk in the Villa Reale, & extricate herself from beggars for half an hour. Whilst you eat your dinner at a Trattoria, a beggar stands at the window, watching every mouthful.

March 18. Left my watch this morning with Signor Tavassi, Largo di Gesa Nuovo, to be repaired.

March 19. It rains almost every day in showers, to the great discomfiture of all the inhabitants of a town where people live out of doors. The streets are full of tables & stands of all sorts of small tradesmen. When the shower comes, the merchant takes out his pocket handkerchiefs & covers up his table-full of goods. Then rises the cry of "La Carozza! la Carozza" from the thousands of hackney coachmen that infest every street & square.

It takes one 'Grand tour' to learn how to travel.

March 20. And today to the Lake Avernus, to the Lucrine Lake, to Baiae, the Arco Felice or gate of Cuma; and at Baiae to the Temple of Venus, the Temple of Mercury, & many many nameless ruins. A day of ruins. The soil of Baiae is crumbled marble & brick. Dig anywhere, & they come to chambers & arches & ruins. What a subterranean taste those Roman builders had. On each side I saw structures peeping out of the ground that must have been originally built into the side of the hill. Here & there could be traced for some distance in the hill-side the remains of a floor composed of small pieces of white marble. I broke some out. It is a most impressive spot. Before you is this ever beautiful bay, & Capri (always more like a picture than a real island) & Vesuvius with his smoke; and about you are the great remains of this pleasure-ground of the Roman Senators, their magnificent Nahant not only broken by time but by earthquakes & covered even with new soil by the volcanic action which has raised Monte Nuovo, a large hill within a fourth of mile from this spot. Then to what base uses turned. The temple of Venus which is almost all standing, & even some delicate bas-reliefs remain upon the ceiling, is now a cooper's shop, & asses bray in it. They turn the chambers of the Roman ladies into little stables for the goats & all Baiae & Pozzuoli swarm with the gang of ciceroni & beggars. I saw the lake of Avernus, a beautiful little sheet of water—but what gave it its evil classic name, it is not easy to see. Nor did the Acherontian Marsh at all suggest the images of the sheeted dead & the Judges of Hell. As to the Lucrine lake, it is not above three times the size of Frog Pond, nor quite three times as pretty.

March 21. Well I have been to Herculaneum & Pompeii.
Herculaneum is nothing but a specimen of the mode of destruction, a monument of the terrors of the volcano. Nothing
is excavated but a path or tunnel through the stone around
the Theatre, for besides the immense cost & labor of excavation through hard stone, all Portici & Resina are built overhead & the habitations of the existing generation must not be
endangered to explore those of the past. But at Pompeii one
quarter part of a town three miles in circumference, is opened
to the sun, 1700 years after it had been hid under a mountain
of ashes. Here is the resurrection of a Roman town. I walked
in the shops, the bake-houses, the mills, the baths, the dining
halls, the bed chambers, the theatre, the court of justice, the
prison, the temples of this ancient people, & read the inscriptions, & scribblings on the walls, & examined the frescoes, as
if in houses not twenty years vacant. In the temple of Venus I
climbed a ruin which commanded a view of almost the whole
excavation. The whole world has no such other view; for half a
mile around me on every side were rows of columns, & streets
of roofless houses. The houses are all built much in the same
way, & only of one story. The frescoes are very pretty & in
almost every house. Yellow & red are the prevailing colours.
The marble baths in some private houses were very rich & the
mosaic painting, on the floor of one chamber, of Alexander &
Darius, of the highest beauty. The statues & utensils have all
been carried away to the Museums of Naples & Sicily. Pity
they could not be left here,—'twould make so impressive a
spectacle.

The theatre is very perfect & the view from its top made me
wish to sit down & spend the day. Far around is this green &
fertile land sprinkled plentifully with white villages & palaces,
washed by the sea adorned with islands, & close at hand on the
other side the solemn mountain, author of all this ruin, & now
black with recent streams of lava, without a green shrub, or so
much as a blade of grass upon its side and a little smoke stealing out of the summit as if to say—The fire that once & again
has ravaged this garden, is not quenched.

About a quarter of a mile from this building by a road
leading through well cultivated fields where corn & wine grow

above the buried city, we came to the Amphitheatre in almost perfect preservation. All the intermediate space remains to be explored, as the Amphitheatre is on the edge of the town. Here we were reminded of a new distinction in property. This land is Signor Aquila's to plant cauliflowers & brocoli, but as fast as it is excavated, & the work goes on every day, it is the king's. Signor Aquila may have the surface, but all underneath, the king owns, to the centre.

We drank wine that grew here and gave our guide a piastre & returned home.

March 23. Tired am I with a visit to Vesuvius. But it is well paid fatigue. I left the coach at Resina & was accommodated with a braying ass who but for his noise was a good beast & thus ascended about a mile above the Hermitage. Thence we climbed with good staves straight up thro' the loose soil wholly composed of lava & cinders. The guide showed us the limits of the different eruptions down to that of December 1832. Presently we came to the top of the old crater. Out of this has risen a new mass which is fast filling up & will soon probably obliterate the old crater. The soil was warm & smoking all around & above us. The ascent from this point to the summit looked dangerous & was not easy. The wind blows the smoke & fumes in your face almost to suffocation & the smoke hides all your party much of the time from your sight. We got to the top & looked down into the red & yellow pits, the navel of this volcano. I had supposed there was a chasm opening downward to unknown depths, but it was all closed up; only this hollow of salt & sulphur smoking furiously beneath us. We put paper between the stones & it kindled & blazed immediately. We found many parties going up & down the mountain & ladies are carried in chairs to the top.

—

March 28. We came hither Tuesday a little after noon. But that day I saw nothing but a passing view of the Coliseum as we entered the city & afterwards the yellow Tiber. Yesterday morn at 9 I set forth with a young Englishman Mr Kingston & crossed the Tiber & visited St Peter's. Another time I will say what I think about this temple. From St Peter's to the Chambers of Raffaelle & saw the pictures of the great master. It was a poor way of using so great a genius to set him to paint the walls of rooms that have no beauty &, as far as I see, no purpose. Then we threaded our way through narrow streets to the Temple of Vesta & the house of Rienzi, 'last of Romans', then to the FORUM & the Coliseum. Here we spent some hours in identifying ruins & fixing in mind the great points of the old topography.

March 28. I went to the Capitoline hill then to its Museum & saw the Dying Gladiator, The Antinous, the Venus.——to the Gallery. then to the Tarpeian Rock. then to the vast & splendid museum of the Vatican. A wilderness of marble. After traversing many a shining chamber & gallery I came to the Apollo & soon after to the Laocoon. 'Tis false to say that the casts give no idea of the originals. I found I knew these fine statues already by heart & had admired the casts long since, much more than I ever can the originals.

Here too was the Torso Hercules, as familiar to the eyes as some old revolutionary cripple. On we went from chamber to chamber through galleries of statues & vases & sarcophagi & bas reliefs & busts & candelabra—through all forms of beauty & richest materials—till the eye was dazzled & glutted with this triumph of the arts. Go & see it, whoever you are. It is the wealth of the civilized world. It is a contribution from all ages & nations of what is most rich & rare. He who has not seen it does not know what beautiful stones there are in the planet, & much less what exquisite art has accomplished on their hard sides for Greek & Roman luxury.

In one apartment there were three statues of Canova, the Perseus, & two fighting gladiators. Then lions & horses & fauns & cupids & cars. Then the sitting philosophers & such Scipios & Caesars. It is vain to refuse to admire. You must in spite of yourself. It is magnificent.

Even all this unrivalled show could not satisfy us. We knew there was more. Much will have more. We knew that the first picture in the world was in the same house & we left all this pomp to go & see the Transfiguration by Raphael.

A calm benignant beauty shines over all this picture and goes directly to the heart. It seems almost to call you by name. How the father of the poor mad boy looks at the apostles! And the sister. And the sweet & sublime face of Jesus above, is beyond praise, & ranks the artist with the noble poets & heroes of his species—the first born of the Earth. I had thought in my young days that this picture & one or two more were to surprize me with a blaze of beauty, that I was to be delighted by I know not what bright combination of colours & forms, but this familiar simple home-speaking countenance I did not expect.

After the pictures St Peter's again.

March 29. I have seen St John Lateran, & the Pantheon & the Baptistery of Constantine & the sad remnants of the Palace of the Caesars. & many many ruins more. Glad I was amidst all these old stumps of the past ages to see Lewis Stackpole as fresh & beautiful as a young palm tree in the desert. Rome is very pleasant to me, as Naples was not, if only from one circumstance, that here I have pleasant companions to eat my bread with & there I had none.

March 30. This morng went with young Warren & Grant to Thorwaldsen's Studio & saw his fine statue of Byron. 'Tis good as a history. I saw three or four rooms of stone things but nothing else to look at. Then to the Barberini Palace & saw the Beatrice Cenci of Guido & the Fornarina of Raffaelle.

Thence to the Borghese Palace & saw Raffaelle's portrait of Caesar Borgia & many fine things but nothing that pleased me more than a Madonna by Andrea del Sarto. Whoso loves a beautiful face, look at this.

Then to the Colonna palace, a proud old mansion of this ancient family—the finest suite of apartments I have ever seen & hung around with master pictures & many of them portraits of the heroes & the beauties of their own line. Two fine portraits of Luther & Calvin by Titian & the Martyrdom of St Sebastian by Guido. But I liked the whole show—the hall itself, better than any part of it. William Pratt very kindly acted the part of cicerone & introduced me to his relatives.

Then I found under the Capitoline hill the famous Mamertine Prison, the scene of the death of Cethegus & Lentulus & of the captivity of St Peter & St Paul, & the reputed dungeon of the 'Roman daughter.'

This P.M. I went to the palace of Cardinal Wield, where Bishop England delivered a discourse in explanation of the ceremonies of the Catholic church tomorrow (Palm Sunday) to the English & American residents. I was led in the evening, so easy is it to be led, to a violin concert. I was glad however to learn the power of a fiddle. It wailed like a bugle & reminded me of much better things & much happier hours.

Sunday, March 31. I have been to the Sistine Chapel to see the Pope bless the palms & hear his choir chaunt the Passion. The Cardinals came in one after another, each wearing a purple robe, an ermine cape, & a small red cap to cover the tonsure. A priest attended each one to adjust the robes of their Eminences. As each Cardinal entered the chapel, the rest rose. One or two were fine persons. Then came the Pope in scarlet robes & a bishop's mitre. After he was seated the cardinals went in turn to the throne & kneeled & kissed his hand. After this ceremony the attendants divested the cardinals of their robes & put on them a gorgeous cope of cloth of gold. When this was arranged a sort of ornamental baton made of the dried palm leaf was brought to his holiness & blessed and each of the cardinals went again to the throne & received one of these from the hands of the pope. They were supplied from a large pile at the side of the papal chair. After the Cardinals, came other dignitaries, bishops, deans, canons, I know them not— but there was much etiquette, some kissing the hand only, & some the foot also of the pope. Some received Olive branches. Lastly several officers performed the same ceremony. When this long procession of respect was over and all the robed multitude had received their festal palms & olives his Holiness was attended to a chair of state & being seated was lifted up by bearers & preceded by the long official array & by his chaunting choir he rode out of the chapel.

It was hard to recognize in this ceremony the gentle Son of Man who sat upon an ass amidst the rejoicings of his fickle countrymen. Whether from age or from custom, I know not, but the pope's eyes were shut or nearly shut as he rode. After a few minutes he reentered the chapel in like state. And soon after retired & left the Sacred College of Cardinals to hear the Passion chaunted by themselves. The chapel is that whose walls Michel Angelo adorned with his 'Last Judgment.' But today I have not seen the picture well.

All this pomp is conventional. It is imposing to those who know the customs of courts & of what wealth & of what rank these particular forms are the symbols. But to the eye of an Indian I am afraid it would be ridiculous. There is no true majesty in all this millinery & imbecility. Why not devise ceremonies that shall be in as good & manly taste as their churches & pictures & music?

I counted twenty one cardinals present. Music at St Peter's in the afternoon & better still at Chiesa Nuova in the evg. Those mutilated wretches sing so well it is painful to hear them.

Monday. April 1. Today at the Grotto of Egeria whence came the laws of Rome, then to tomb of Cecilia Metella 'the wealthiest Roman's wife'. A mighty tomb; the wall is 30 feet thick. Then to the tomb of Scipio, then to the Spada Palace, & saw the statue of Pompey, at whose base great Caesar fell. Then to the Palace Farnesina, to see Raffaelle's frescoes. Here Raffaelle painted whilst Michel Angelo locked himself up in the Sistine Chapel. Then to the Vatican. And at night to an American Soirée.

Tuesday, 2 Apr. What is more pathetic than the Studio of a young Artist? Not rags & disease in the street move you to sadness like the lonely chamber littered round with sketches & canvass & colourbags. There is something so gay in the art itself that these rough & poor commencements contrast more painfully with it. Here another enthusiast feeds himself with hope & rejoices in dreams & smarts with mortifications. The melancholy artist told me that if the end of painting was to please the eye, he would throw away his pallet. And yet how many of them not only fail to reach the soul with their conceptions, but fail to please the eye.

These beggarly Italians! If you accept any hospitality at an Italian house a servant calls upon you the next day & receives a fee, & in this manner, the expense of your entertainment is defrayed. In like manner, if you are presented to the Pope, it costs you five dollars.

Plain good manners & sensible people—how refreshing they are. A bashful man is cramped among the fine people who have polished manners but dull brains; but he is relieved & recreated by a better influence & regains his natural shape & air & powers.

Today I have seen the fine church of Sta Maria Maggiore, the third best in Rome. Then the Doria Palace. There was Nicholas Machiavel by Titian & landscapes of Claude Lorraine.

3 Apr. Wednesday. The famous Miserere was sung this afternoon in the Sistine Chapel. The saying at Rome, is, that it cannot be imitated not only by any other choir but in any other chapel in the world. The Emperor of Austria sent Mozart to Rome on purpose to have it sung at Vienna with like effect, but it failed.

Surely it is sweet music & sounds more like the Eolian harp than any thing else. The pathetic lessons of the day relate the treachery of Judas & apply select passages from the prophets & psalms to the circumstances of Jesus. Then whilst the choir chaunt the words "Traditor autem dedit eis signum, dicens, Quem osculatus fuero, ipse est, tenete eum," all the candles in the chapel are extinguished but one. During the repetition of this verse, the last candle is taken down & hidden under the altar. Then out of the silence & the darkness rises this most plaintive & melodious strain, (the whole congregation kneeling) "Miserere mei, Deus, &c." The sight & the sound are very touching.

Every thing here is in good taste. The choir are concealed by the high fence which rises above their heads. We were in a Michel Angelo's chapel which is full of noblest scriptural forms & faces.

Thursday. April 4. These forms strike me more than I expected, & yet how do they fall short of what they should be. Today I saw the Pope wash the feet of thirteen pilgrims, one from each nation of Christendom. One was from Kentucky. After the ceremony he served them at dinner; this I did not see. But Gregory XVI is a learned & able man; he was a monk & is reputed of pure life. Why should he not leave one moment this formal service of fifty generations & speak out of his own heart, the Father of the Church to his Children, though it were but a single sentence or a single word? One earnest word or act to this sympathetic audience would overcome them. It would take all hearts by storm.

To night I heard the Miserere sung in St Peter's & with less effect than yesterday. But what a temple! When night was settling down upon it & a long religious procession moved through a part of the Church, I got an idea of its immensity such as I had not before. You walk about on its ample marble pavement as you would on a common, so free are you of your neighbors; & throngs of people are lost upon it. And what beautiful lights & shades on its mighty gilded arches & vaults & far windows & brave columns, & its rich clad priests, that look as if they were the pictures come down from the walls & walking. Thence we came out (I was walking with two painters Cranch & Alexander) under the moon & saw the planet shine upon the finest fountain in the world. & upon all the stone saints on the piazza & the great church itself. This was a spectacle which only Rome can boast—how faery beautiful! An Arabian night's tale—

Good Friday. April 5. The Mystery of the Tre Ore is said & shewn in all the churches, in some with scenic representations; I have seen nothing affecting tho' it is sometimes, I am told, very much so. Many religious processions in the streets muffled in black with staves surmounted by death's-heads.
This night I saw with Cranch the great Coliseum by moonlight. It is full of dread.

Saturday. April 6. I did not go to the baptism of the Jew today. Usually it is a weary farce. 'Tis said they buy the Jews at 150 scudes the head, to be sprinkled. This man was respectable. This P.M. I heard the Greek Mass. The chaunts are in Armenian.

Sunday. April 7. This morng the Pope said Mass at St Peter's. Rich dresses, great throngs, lines of troops, but not much to be said for the service. It is Easter & the curtains are withdrawn from the pictures & statues to my great joy & the Pope wears his triple crown instead of a mitre.

At twelve o clock the benediction was given. A canopy was hung over the great window that is above the principal door of St Peter's & there sat the Pope. The troops were all under arms & in uniform in the piazza below, & all Rome & much of England & Germany & France & America was gathered there also. The great bell of the Church tolled, drums beat, & trumpets sounded over the vast congregation.

Presently, at a signal, there was silence and a book was brought to the Pope, out of which he read a moment & then rose & spread out his hands & blessed the people. All knelt as one man. He repeated his action (for no words could be heard,) stretching his arms gracefully to the north & south & east & west—pronouncing a benediction on the whole world. It was a sublime spectacle. Then sounded drums & trumpets, then rose the people, & every one went his way.

This evening I have seen the illumination of the Church. When it was dark, I took the wellknown way and on reaching the Bridge of St Angelo found the church already hung with lights from turret to foundation. But this was only partial. At the moment when the bell in the tower tolled 8 o'clock out flashed innumerable torches in the air & the whole edifice blazed with fires which cast the first lamps into shade & lit up every face in the multitude on the piazza as with daylight. But it is very melancholy to see an illumination in this declining church & impoverished country.

Alas the young men that come here & walk in Rome without one Roman thought! they unlearn their English & their morals, & violate the sad solitude of the mother of the nations.

They think the Coliseum is a very *nice* place.

I love St Peter's Church. It grieves me that after a few days I shall see it no more. It has a peculiar smell from the quantity of incense burned in it. The music that is heard in it is always good & the eye is always charmed. It is an ornament of the earth. It is not grand, it is so rich & pleasing; it should rather be called the sublime of the beautiful.

—

10 Apr. Walked alone in the spacious grounds & fine groves of the Villa Borghese, whilst the birds sang to me. I thought it would be good to spend an hour there by myself every day. ποιημα πραξεως.

April 11. How have all nations & ages contributed to the magnificence of the Vatican. If we could only know the history of each marble there, when, & by whom, & for whom it was carved; of what luxurious villa it formed an ornament, it would open to us the story of the whole world. Each has figured in splendid scenes & served the pleasure of the lords of mankind.

Then again most gladly would I know the place of all these works in the history of art, how this vase & that statue were designed, what the sculptor & what his patron thought of them & the marks of the eras of progress & decline. But now they amaze me & beget a vague curiosity which they cannot satisfy, nor can any living man.

I went up to the top of St Peter's & climbed into the copper ball. It is necessary to go up into the dome in order to estimate the prodigious dimensions of the edifice. It takes one's breath away, to look down into the church from the Giro within the cupola, & at first the temptation is terrible to throw yourself down, though the walk is wide, & the railing is high. With some pauses & some conversation I succeeded in getting round the dizzy promenade; but like many things in Rome, it is a quite unimaginable spot. The view from the exterior of the cupola, of the Campagna di Roma is delicious, from the Appenines on one side to the Sea on the other, & Tiber flowing through his marble wilderness below.

April 13. Rome fashions my dreams. All night I wander amidst statues & fountains, and last night was introduced to Lord Byron! It is a graceful termination to so much glory that Rome now in her fallen state should be the metropolis of the arts. Art is here a greater interest than any where else. The

Caffés are filled with English, French, & German artists, both sculptors & painters. The number of Mosaicistas & print shops is surprizing. Rinaldi has just finished a Mosaic picture of Paestum which is valued at a thousand louis d'ors.

———

April 15. Few pictures please me more than the Vision of St Romoaldo by Andrea Sacchi in the Vatican. What a majestic form is the last Carmelite in the train who ascends the steps. One is greater for knowing that such forms can be. What a cant of the head has this same figure! Look at him.

I shall I think remember few sculptures better when I get back into my Chimney Corner than the beautiful head of the Justice who sits with Prudence on the monument of Paulus III on the left of the Tribuna in St Peter's. It was designed by Michel Angelo, executed by William de la Porta, but where in the Universe is the Archetype from which the Artist drew this sweetness & grace? There is a heaven.

I have been to see the library of the Vatican. I think they told me the hall was a quarter of a mile long. Afterwards, the Elgin marble-casts. What heads & forms!

In Rome all is ruinous. In the garden before my window the flowerpots stand upon blocks made of the capitals of old columns, turned upside down. Everywhere you may see in the walls & the foundations of houses fragments of carved & fluted stone now cemented in with rough stones, but once the ornament of the Luculli or Scauri or even of Vesta or Jove.

———

April 17. I have been to the Church of St Onofrio to see the tomb of Tasso. Then in the convent the courteous fathers showed us his bust in wax. He died in the convent & this head was taken at the time from the corpse. A noble head it is, full of independence & genius. It resembles strongly the prints I have seen of his head, but is better, I should think than any. I shall always like him the better for having seen this face. I have never yet learned to feel any strong interest in a poet so imitative, but since God marked him I will attend to him.

———

In Rome at the best Trattoria you may get a good dinner for 15 bajocchi. Thus today & yesterday I have dined at the Lepri on this fashion; 'Maccaroni a la Napolitana' 3; 'Mongana con spinnagio' 5; 'Crema in piatta', 5; & two rolls of bread to eat with it, 2; = 15 cents for a good dinner in the best house. Add one or two for waiter. My breakfast at the most expensive Caffé in Rome costs 16 cents. Coffee in the evg 5 & my chambers at the Gran Bretagna 50 cents.

Rome, April 20, 1833.

Yesterday I went with Cranch & Smith & Wall to Tivoli. I cannot describe the beauty of the Cascade nor the terror of the Grotto nor the charm of the iris that arched the torrent. The Temple of Vesta is one of the most beautiful of ruins & in a chosen place. The whole circuit of about four miles which we make with the Cicerone, showed everywhere a glorious landscape. All was bright with a warm sun. The ground was sprinkled with gay flowers, & among others that pink thing with a spicy smell we used to call 'Rabbit's ears.' Then there was the great aloes with its formidable fleshy spine growing about, & (which is a rare sight,) one of these plants was in bloom. We found the remains of the villa of Catullus, then the reputed site of the house of Horace, & hard by, the arched ruins of the Villa of Q. Varus. Here too, they say, Maecenas lived; & no wonder that poet & patron should have come to this fair specular mount escaping from the dust of the Capitol. The Campagna lies far & wide below like a sea. Then we went to the Villa d'Este whose beauty in my eyes outshone the beauty of the cascade. Such trees, such walks, such fountains, such grottoes, such adornments, the long long house—all its empty halls painted in fresco; the piazza with its vast prospect, the silver river, the sun that shone, & the air that blew—I would fain keep them in my memory the fairest image of Italy. The Villa belongs to the Duke of Modena who never saw it & it is occupied only by a custode.

I have paid a last visit to the Capitoline Museum & Gallery. One visit is not enough, no, nor two to learn the lesson. The dying Gladiator is a most expressive statue but it will always be indebted to the muse of Byron for fixing upon it forever his pathetic thought. Indeed Italy is Byron's debtor, and I think no one knows how fine a poet he is who has not seen the subjects of his verse, & so learned to appreciate the justness of his thoughts & at the same time their great superiority to other men's. I know well the great defects of Childe Harold.

In the Gallery I coveted nothing so much as Michel Angelo's Portrait by himself.

April 21. I went this afternoon to see Michel Angelo's statue of Moses at the Church of San Pietro in Vinculo, and it is grand. It seems he sought to embody the Law in a man. Directly under the statue, at the side where the whole face is seen, the expression is terrible. I could wish away those emblematic horns. "Alzati, parla!" said the enthusiastic sculptor.

———

And how do you like Florence? Why, well. It is pleasant to see how affectionately all the artists who have resided here a little while speak of getting home to Florence. And I found at once that we live here with much more comfort than in Rome or Naples. Good streets, industrious population, spacious well furnished lodgings, elegant & cheap Caffés, the cathedral & the Campanile, the splendid galleries and no beggars—make this city the favorite of strangers.

How like an archangel's tent is this great Cathedral of many-coloured marble set down in the midst of the city and by its side its wondrous campanile! I took a hasty glance at the gates of the Baptistery which Angelo said ought to be the gates of Paradise "degne chiudere il Paradiso" and then of his own David & hasted to the Tribune & to the Pitti Palace. I saw the statue that enchants the world. And truly the Venus deserves to be visited from far. It is not adequately represented by the plaster casts as the Apollo & the Laocoon are. I must go again & see this statue. Then I went round this cabinet & gallery & galleries till I was well nigh "dazzled & drunk with beauty." I think no man has an idea of the powers of painting until he has come hither. Why should painters study at Rome? Here, here.

I have been this day to Santa Croce which is to Florence what Westminster Abbey is to England. I passed with consideration the tomb of Nicholas Machiavelli but stopped long before that of Galileus Galileo, for I love & honor that man, except in the recantation, with my whole heart. But when I came to Michel Angelo Buonaroti my flesh crept as I read the inscription. I had strange emotions, I suppose because Italy is so full of his fame. I have lately continually heard of his name & works & opinions; I see his face in every shop window, & now I stood over his dust.

Then I came to the empty tomb of Dante who lies buried at Ravenna. Then to that of Alfieri.

2 May. I revisited the Tribune this morning to see the Venus & the Fornarina and the rest of that attractive company. I reserve my admiration as much as I can; I make a continual effort not to be pleased except by that which ought to please *me*. And I walked coolly round & round the marble lady but when I planted myself at the iron gate which leads into the chamber of Dutch paintings & looked at the statue, I saw & felt that mankind have had good reason for their preference of this excellent work, & I gladly gave one testimony more to the surpassing genius of the artist.

—

How bare & poor are these Florentine churches after the sumptuous temples of Naples & Rome. Ah! ah! for St Peter's, which I can never more behold. Close by my door is the Church of Santa Maria Novella which Michel Angelo called his *bride*; my eye has not yet learned why; it still looks naked & unfinished to me. The Church of St John's in Malta, he might well have distinguished by such a name.

Evg. Beautiful days, beautiful nights. It is today one of the hundred festas of this holiday people; so was yesterday; so is tomorrow. The charming Cascina, & the banks of the Arno are thronged, but moonshine or sunshine are indispensable to a festa; as they say in France, "there will be no revolution today, for it rains."

—

May 10. Visited Professor Amici & saw his optical instruments. He is reputed the maker of the best microscopes in Europe. He has also made a telescope for Herschel in London. He has a microscope whose magnifying power is 6000 diameters, or 36,000,000 superficies. To instruments of this enormous power he applies the camera lucida & then draws the outline of the object with pencil. His experiments upon polarised light are beautiful.

The price of his best instruments is 800 francs. He has just made one for Dr Jarvis for 45 dollars.

Speak out, my boy, speak plain, non capisco. "Ed io anche non intendo lei," said the beggar.

May 11. Last night I went to the Pergola, and to my eyes, unused to theatres, it was a glorious show. The prima donna, Signora Delsere, is a noble Greek beauty, full of dignity, & energy of action & when she sang the despair of Agnes, she was all voice. She had moreover so striking a resemblance to a valued friend in America, that I longed to know who & what Signora Delsere was, much more than the issue of the play. But nobody knew. The whole scenery & the dresses of the performers were in admirable taste, everything good but the strutting of the actors. Is it penal for an actor to *walk*? Before the play was done, my eyes were so dazzled with the splendor of light & colors that I was obliged to rest them & look at my shoes for half an hour, that I might keep them for the last act.

For my seat in the pit, where ladies sit also, I paid three pauls, 30 cts.

I ought not to forget the ballet between the acts. Goethe laughs at those who force every work of art into the narrow circle of their own prejudices & cannot admire a picture as a picture & a tune as a tune. So I was willing to look at this as a ballet, & to see that it was admirable, but I could not help feeling the while that it were better for mankind if there were no such dancers. I have since learned God's decision on the same, in the fact that all the *ballerine* are nearly ideotic.

May 12. I dined today with Mr Askew at his villa seven miles out of Florence and all the road was through a garden. We rode on our return through a *shower* of flies, all the way.

I gladly hear much good of the order of Misericordia. I see these philanthropists now with quite new feeling, when they carry by the dead with their hasty chaunt. This order is composed of men of all professions & ages & ranks who for a penance or for love enter into it for a longer or shorter period. They devote themselves to all works of mercy especially to the care of the sick. They watch & attend them but never speak, & their faces are never seen being always covered with a silken hood. They are not known to each other. Cardinals & princes sometimes take the dress of this order for a time. The last Grand duke was once a member. Miss Anna Bridgen tells me that she saw in Rome a coachman driving a splendid coach with chasseurs attendant, who attempted to pass directly through a funeral procession, when one of the Misericordes ran forward & laid a powerful arm upon the rein of the horse & lifted his veil to the coachman who instantly drew up his horses & waited with the utmost respect for the train to pass.

They have taken down the old marble bench on which Dante used to sit & look at the beautiful Campanella, & set it into the pavement with the inscription "Sasso di Dante." Well he might sit and admire that charming tower which is a sort of poem in architecture. One might dream of such a thing, but it seems strange that it should have been executed in lasting stone. Giotto built it, that old Gothic Painter.

May 13. At the Arena di Goldoni this afternoon I saw a Hercules of a man lie on his back & raise his feet upon which two men stood, upon the men two boys climbed; two women then stood, one upon each of his hands, & he held them all up in the air. Afterwards he lifted a weight of 1500 lbs.

May 15. Today I dined with Mr Landor at his villa at San Domenica di Fiesole. He lives in a beautiful spot in a fine house full of pictures & with a family most engaging. He has a wife & four children. He said good & pleasant things & preferred Washington to all modern great men. He is very decided, as I might have expected, in all his opinions, & very much a connoisseur in paintings. He was not very well today & I go to breakfast with him next Friday. He thinks that no great man ever had a great son, if Philip & Alexander be not an exception, & Philip he calls the greater man. Montaigne he likes very much, & praised Charron. He thought Degerando indebted to Lucas on Happiness! & Lucas on Holiness! Sir James Mackintosh he would not praise, nor my Carlyle. He pestered me with Southey; what is Southey? And the Greek histories he thought the only good, & after them Voltaire's. In art he loves the Greeks & in sculpture them only. He prefers the Venus to every thing else, & after that the head of Alexander in the gallery here. He prefers John of Bologna to Michel Angelo. In painting, Raffaelle & Perugino & Giotto. Mr Hare was present, the author of 'Guesses at Truth'; & Mr Worsley.

May 16. This day is the festival of the Ascension which is a great annual holiday of the Florentines & pours them all out under the trees & along the lawns of the beautiful Cascina. There they keep a sort of rural Saturnalia. The Grand duke came up towards evening & took a turn round the Square in his coach & bowed gracefully to the bowing multitude. His little children were with him in the coach.

In the evening the grounds were light as day with countless lamps hung in the trees & in the centre of all an obelisk of flambeaux. Then played the band, & all the people danced. I believe this rude ball was continued all night. I left them in full activity about 10 o'clock.

May 18. Visited Mr Landor again yesterday. He talked with spirit & learning & quoted some half a dozen hexameters of Caesar, from Donatus. He glorified Lord Chesterfield more than was necessary. And Burke he undervalues. But far worse, he undervalues Socrates. He spoke of three of the greatest men as Washington, Phocion, & Timoleon, & remarked the similar termination of their names.* "A great man should make great sacrifices," he said, "he should kill his hundred oxen without knowing whether they would be eaten, or whether the flies would eat them." He spoke contemptuously of entomology, yet said that 'the sublime was in a grain of dust.' & the second thought should have condemned the first. He spoke of Wordsworth, Byron, Massinger, Beaumont & Fletcher, & Davy. Herschel he knew nothing about, not even his name.

—

Mr L. has a fine cabinet of pictures & as Greenough remarked, he, in common with all collectors, imagines that his

*He might have added Bacon, Newton, &   .

are the only masterpieces. "Ne sutor"—and I remembered the story of Voltaire & Congreve. Mr Hare told me that Mr L. has not more than twelve books in his library.

Noon. I went to the Museum of Natural History & to the representation in wax of the *Plague* of *Florence*, & saw how man is made & how he is destroyed. This museum contains an accurate copy in wax from nature of every organ & process in the human frame, & is beautiful & terrible. For in life nature never intends that these things should be uncovered.

I have looked into Santa Croce this afternoon & if I spoke ill of it before I will unsay it all. It is a grand building, and its windows of stained glass charm me. It is lined & floored with tombs, & there are two or three richly furnished Chapels. In one is a fine painting of the Last Supper by Vasari. While we were walking up & down the church the organ was played & I have never heard a more pleasing one. I saw the bust of Michel Angelo & his eight wrinkles.

When I walk up the piazza of Santa Croce I feel as if it were not a Florentine no nor an European church but a church built by & for the human race. I feel equally at home within its walls as the Grand duke, so *hospitably* sound to me the names of its mighty dead. Buonaroti & Galileo lived for us all. As Don Ferrante says of Aristotle, "non è nè antico nè moderno; è il filosofo, senza piu."

I met the fair Erminia today. These meetings always cost me a crazie & it is fit that she should not be slighted in the journal. Erminia is a flower-girl who comes to the Caffé every morning & if you will not buy her flowers she gives them to you & with such a superb air. She has a fine expression of face & never lets her customers pass her in the street without a greeting. Every coach too in Florence that ventures to stop near the Piazza di Trinita is a tributary of Erminia's. I defy them to escape from her nosegays. She has a rich pearl necklace worth I know not how much, which she wears on festas. Mr Wall wishes to paint her portrait but she says she is not handsome enough. "E brutto il mio ritratto."

Went again to the Opera to see a piece called Ivanhoe. What a miserable abuse to put a woman of dignity & talent into men's clothes to play the part of Wilfrid. The Signora Delsere who delighted me so much the other night was strutting about ineffectually with sword & helmet. They had spoiled a fine woman to make a bad knight. I came home disgusted.

The Italians use the Superlative too much. Mr Landor calls them the nation of the *issimi*. A man to tell me that this was the same thing I had before, said "E l'istessissima cosa;" and at the trattoria, when I asked if the cream was good, the waiter answered, "Stupendo." They use three negatives; it is good Italian to say, 'Non dite nulla a nessuno'.

May 19. Hot weather steadily for three weeks past & Florence is a degree of latitude farther north than Boston. Six or seven blazing hours every day, when, as the Florentines say, 'there's nobody but dogs & Englishmen in the streets.' Then the pleasant evening walk from 6 to 7 or 8 o'clock upon the Cascina, or the banks of the little sylvan Mugnone, or in the Boboli gardens. And wherever I go, I am surrounded by beautiful objects; the fine old towers of the city; the elegant curve of the Ponte Trinità; the rich purple line of the Appenines; broken by the bolder summits of the marble mountains of Carrara. And all all is Italian; not a house, not a shed, not a field that the eye can for a moment imagine to be American.

Miss Anna Bridgen said very wittily, "that so inveterate were her Dutch instincts, that she sees almost no work of art in Italy, but she wants to give it a good scrubbing; the Duomo, the Campanella, & the statues."

May 21. Rose early this morng. & went to the Bello Sguardo out of the Roman gate. It was a fine picture this Tuscan morning and all the towers of Florence rose richly out of the smoky light on the broad green plain. I passed the Michelozzi Villa, where Guicciardini wrote his history. Returning I saw the famous fresco painting on the wall within the city, directly opposite the Roman gate, the work of Giovanni da S. Giovanni; executed, they say, to show the skill of Tuscan art. A story is told that some Roman painter having been sent for to execute a public work in Florence, the Florentine Artists painted this wall that he might see it on his entrance into the city. When he came & saw this painting he inquired whose work it was; & being informed it was done by Florentines, he returned immediately to Rome, saying that they had no occasion for foreign artists.

"Birbo, sì ma profondo,"* says Manzoni of Machiavelli. I have finished the "Promessi Sposi", and I rejoice that a man exists in Italy who can write such a book. I hear from day to day such hideous anecdotes of the depravity of manners, that it is an unexpected delight to meet this elevated & eloquent moralist.

Renzo, & Lucia, Fra Cristoforo, & Federigo Borromeo—all are excellent &, which is the highest praise, all excite the reader to virtue.

May 25. It is the Festa of San Zenobio once bishop of Florence. And at the churches, the priests bless the roses & other flowers which the people bring them, & they are then esteemed good for the cure of head ache & are laid by for that purpose. Last night in the Duomo I saw a priest carrying a silver bust of San Zenobio which he put upon the head of each person in turn who came up the barrier. This ceremony also protects him from the head ache for a year. But, asked I of my landlady, do you believe that the bust or the roses do really cure the head ache of any person? "Secondo alla fede di ciascuno," she replied.
It is my Festa also.

I wrote to G. A. S. yesterday what I have found true, that it is necessary for the traveller in order to see what is worth seeing & especially *who* is worth seeing in each city, to go into society a little. Now no man can have society upon his own terms. If he seek it, he must serve it too. He immediately & inevitably contracts debts to it which he must pay at a great expense often of inclination & of time & of duty.

*

*"diceva don Ferrante"

"Comanda niente Signore?"—Niente.—"Felice notte, Signore."—Felice notte. Such is the dialogue which passes every evening betwixt Giga & me when the worthy woman lights my lamp, & leaves me to Goethe & Sismondi, to pleasant study hours, & to sound sleep.

I have been to the Academia delle belle Arti, & there saw an unfinished work of Michel Angelo's. His opinion was asked concerning a block of marble, whether it were large enough to make a statue of? "Yes," he said, "a Colossus." And the inquirers doubting, he went to work, & cutting a little here & a little there, rudely sketched a figure of gigantic dimensions & left it so, a sort of sculptor's puzzle.

—

Arrived at Mestre the place of embarcation for Venice 5 miles off. Here we took a boat & sailed for the famous city. It looked for some time like nothing but New York. We entered the Grand Canal & passed under the Rialto & presently stepped out of the boat into the front entry of the Grande Bretagna. The front entry of the Grande Bretagna opens also upon a little bridge which connects by a narrow alley with the Piazza of St Mark so out we went under the full moon to see the same. It was all glorious to behold. In moonlight this arabesque square is all enchantment—so rich & strange & visionary. June 2. Again I have been to St Mark's & seen his horses & his winged lion, the bridge of sighs, the doge's palace, the piazza, the canals. We took a gondola—three of us—(that is, one too many for the perfect enjoyment of that cunning vehicle) & proceeded to the Churches & the Academy. There is Titian's picture of the Assumption of the Madonna—so glorified by the painters. The young men whom I converse with prefer it to Raphael. There also is another of Titian's, the Presentation of the Virgin yet a child to the High priest, a very large picture, and I thought I might call it the *handsomest* picture I have seen but certainly not the best. It lacks the expression of Raffaelle. It will not do to compare any thing, in my opinion, with his Transfiguration. A great man will find a great subject or which is the same thing make any subject great & what tenderness & holiness beams from the face of the Christ in that Work. What emotion! I have never yet seen the face copied in all the soi disant copies of that picture.

In the Academy is a cast of the Hercules of Canova. The original is in the Torlonia Palace at Rome. It is a tremendous action. Here too are casts of his best works. The chair in which he has seated Mme Buonaparte is the same beautiful form I admired in the Caffe at Padua. Grand pictures here of Paul Veronese, Tintoretto, & Titian.

These churches of Venice surpass all the churches in Florence in splendor. The Chiesa dei Carmeliti has eight chapels built at the expense of eight families & they are superb. The Chiesa dei Gesuiti is a most costly imitation in marble of tapestry hangings throughout the interior. Hiram & Solomon could not beat it.

In the Chiesa della Salute is a monument of Canova built from Canova's design of a tomb for Titian. Canova's design, however, if that little model I saw in the Academy be it, is more impressive than this gorgeous marble *execution* of the same in the Salute. These churches are all rich with monuments on many of which is figured the horned bonnet worn by the Doges of Venice. From these we came to the Ducal Palace up the Giant Stair Case.

At the side of the door we were shown the 'Lion's Mouth,' a hole in the wall into which anciently were thrown the anonymous accusations of any citizen for the eye of the Council of State. Thence we were conducted to the Library, then to the Hall—a grand chamber whose whole walls & ceiling are adorned by the best pictures of great size by Paul Veronese & his son and Tintoretto & Palma Vecchio & Palma Giovane & Bonifacio. All the paintings are historical. This hall & the adjoining chambers contain in this splendid way a chronicle of the republic. The portraits of 116 doges hang around on high, among which is the black board where should be the head of Marino Faliero. On the ceiling, most of the pieces are allegorical—(which is as bad in painting as it is in poetry). And at one extremity of the Hall a Paradise by Tintoretto a picture of amazing size. From this hall to the Audience Chamber where the Doge & his Council received foreign ambassadors —then to the Council Chamber of the 300, with its rostrum & other realities. After seeing these noble apartments we were

conducted to the prisons below and all the hideous economy & arrangement of them explained. I saw the little blackened chamber from whose walls Lord Byron had those sad inscriptions copied and passed the dreaded door opening on the bridge of Sighs down to the third noisome story of the subterranean dungeon. It is a sickening place, & 'tis enough to make one dance & sing that this horrid tyranny is broken in pieces. To be sure the Austrians are here but their rule is merciful to that whose story is written here in stone & iron & mire. The policy of the Venetian government kept even the existence of their state prison a secret & on the approach of the French in 1796, they hastily built up the secret passages. The French acted with good sense in opening these damnable holes to the day & exposing them to the public in order to make their own invasion popular.

—

I am speedily satisfied with Venice. It is a great oddity—a city for beavers—but to my thought a most disagreeable residence. You feel always in prison, & solitary. Two persons may live months in adjoining streets & never meet, for you go about in gondolas and all the gondolas are precisely alike & the persons within commonly concealed; then there are no Newsrooms; except St Mark's piazza, no place of public resort. —It is as if you were always at sea. And though, for a short time, it is very luxurious to lie on the eider down cushions of your gondola & read or talk or smoke, drawing to now the cloth lined shutter, now the venetian blind, now the glass window, as you please, yet there is always a slight smell of bilgewater about the thing, & houses in the water remind me of a freshet & of desolation—any thing but comfort. I soon had enough of it.

—

Then to Brescia. All the Italian towns are different & all picturesque, the well paved Brescia. The Church of the Madonna dei Miracoli—how daintily it is carved without to the very nerves of the strawberry & vine leaf! Italy is the country of beauty but I think specially in the northern part. Every thing is ornamented. A peasant wears a scarlet cloak. If he has no other ornament he ties on a red garter or knee band. They wear flowers in the hat or the buttonhole. A very shabby boy will

have the eye of a peacock's feather in his hat. In general the great coats & jackets of the common people are embroidered. And the other day I saw a cripple leaning on a crutch very finely carved. Every fountain, every pump, every post is sculptured, and not the commonest tavern room but its ceiling is painted. Red is a favorite color and on a rainy morning at Messina the streets blazed with red umbrellas.

—

I visited the Church of San Domenico to see the famous fresco painting of the Last Supper by Leonardo da Vinci. It is sadly spoiled by time & damp. The face of Christ is still very remarkable.

Milan is a wellbuilt town with broad streets and a little railroad of stone for the wheels to run upon in the middle of the street. It looks too modern to be so conspicuous in European history as it has been, for Lombardy was the theatre of every war.

There is an advantage which these old cities have over our new ones that forcibly strikes an American. Namely that the poorest inhabitants live in good houses. In process of time a city is filled with palaces, the rich ever deserting old ones for new, until beggars come to live in what were costly & well accommodated dwellings. Thus all the trattorias, even of little pretension, have their carved work & fresco painting, as this of the Marino where I dine with my companions.

Left Milan Tuesday, June 11, in the diligence, with Wall & Stewardson & the Misses Bridgen. Before sunset, we arrived on the beautiful banks of the Lago Maggiore, & crossed the Adda which is there an arm of the lake, at Sesto Calendo, & stopped at Arona to dine. Though we passed directly below the famous colossal statue of San Carlo Borromeo, after leaving Arona, it was so dark that I could not see it, which I regretted much. We rode all night and reached Domo d'Ossola next morn to breakfast, the town at the foot of the Alps. The maitre d'hotel here spoke English, & we were much cheated, two facts which are said to be concomitant. The whole of the day, 12 June, was spent in crossing the mountain by the celebrated road, of the Simplon, cut & built by Buonaparte. Let it be a glory to his name, him, the great Hand of our age. Truly it is a

stupendous work passing thro' every variation of ragged mountain scenery, now thro' the earth or solid rock in the form of a tunnel, now in successive easy inclined planes called galleries climbing the sides of a precipice, now crossing some rift in the mountain on a firm bridge, & so working its way up from the hot plain of Lombardy to cold waterfalls & huge snowbanks & up & upward to the bleak hamlet of Sempione which almost crowns the top. Here we see our own breath, & are very glad to get into the house & avoid the cold air. Over wild mountain cascade & within a gallery cut thro' the rock Buonaparte has had the honesty to write "Italo Aere, Nap. Imp. MDCCCV." Céard was his principle engineer.

And these, I thought, are the mountains of freedom. This queer ridge of matter is of such proved moral efficiency. Let their Spartan hymn ascend. I saw a good many of the Swiss peasantry on the hill sides: how different from the Italians on one side, or the French on the other, but exactly resembling the faces & dresses of their countrymen who emigrate to the United States. It is marvellous to see their houses on such narrow lodgments, half way up a mural precipice, as was said of Cortona, "like a picture hanging on a wall." What can they do with their children?

—

We are getting towards France. In the café where we breakfasted we found a printed circular inviting those whom it concerned to a rifle-match, to the intent, as the paper stated, "of increasing their skill in that valuable accomplishment, & of drawing more closely the bonds of that regard with which we are, &c." After breakfast I inquired my way to Gibbon's house & was easily admitted to the garden. The summerhouse is removed but the floor of it is still there, where the History was written & finished. I stood upon it & looked forth upon the noble landscape of which he speaks so proudly. I plucked a leaf of the limetree he planted, & of the acacia—successors of those under which he walked. I have seen however many landscapes as pleasant & more striking.

At 10 o'clock we took the steamboat for Geneva & sailed up lake Leman. The passage was very long—seven hours—for the wind was ahead, & the engine not very powerful. We touched at Coppet. The lake is most beautiful near Geneva. It was not clear enough to see Mont Blanc or else it was not visible. Mount Varens & Monte Rosa were seen.

Geneva, 16 June. Here am I in the stern old town, the resort of such various minds—of Calvin, of Rousseau, of Gibbon, of Voltaire, of De Stael, of Byron—on the blue Rhone by the placid Lake Leman. Mont Blanc towers above the Alps on the east sublimely with his three summits; Jura on the west is marking the line of France, & the lake lies in beauty before me. Every body is polite.

Yesterday to oblige my companions & protesting all the way upon the unworthiness of his memory I went to Ferney to the chateau, the saloon, the bed chamber, the gardens of Voltaire, the king of the scorners. His rooms were modest & pleasing & hung with portraits of his friends. Franklin & Washington were there. The view of the lake & mountains commanded by the lawn behind the chateau is superior to that of Gibbon's garden at Lausanne. The old porter showed us some pictures belonging to his old master & told a story that did full justice to his bad name. Yet it would be a sin against faith & philosophy to exclude Voltaire from toleration. He did his work as the bustard & tarantula do theirs.

We had a fine ride home, so royally towers up Mont Blanc with his white triple top. On the way we passed the stone which marks the boundary of France which made Dr S crow like chanticleer,—and the grass he thought greener.

Visited the music box manufactory & the watch-maker's. The music man offered to make a box with two airs of Beethoven for 50 francs, to be received by me in Paris.

Prices of the best watches that they can make are 500 francs. Of the second class without a compensation but esteemed as good for all ordinary purposes, 300 francs. S. bought one for 275 the difference of value being in the weight of the case. They speak of smuggling with perfect simplicity & offer to send you the watch to Paris (via smuggler, that is) for a few francs.

Through the Misses Bridgens' acquaintance in Mr Wolf's family I was carried away to hear M. Gissot a very worthy Calvinist who has been ejected from the National Church. His exercise was a catechism & exhortation of a large class of children. Then I was introduced to Mr Cordis & others of their brethren, very worthy men they seemed. I spent the day at the house of Mr Wolf. The daughter told me that "if I was, as I said, a seeker, she thought I ought to make it a point of duty to stop longer at Geneva," & offered in very pretty broken English "to intrude me to the minister who bégun the exercise." She had learned English because her house was destined to receive boarders, &c, &c.

—

France France. It is not only a change of name—the cities, the language, the faces, the manners have undergone a wonderful change in three or four days. The running fight we have kept up so long with the fierté of postillions & padroni in Italy is over & all men are complaisant. The face of the country is remarkable, not quite a plain but a vast undulating champaign without a hill, and all planted like the Connecticutt intervales. No fences, the fields full of working women. We rode in the Coupée of a Diligence by night & by day, through   for three days & a half & arrived in Paris at noon Thursday.

Paris, 20 June. My companions who have been in the belle ville before, & wished it to strike me as it ought, are scarce content with my qualified admiration. Certainly the eye is satisfied on entering the city with the unquestionable tokens of a vast, rich, old capital.

We crossed the Seine by the Pont Neuf & I was glad to see my old acquaintance Henry IV very respectably mounted in bronze on his own bridge but the saucy faction of the day has thrust a tricolor flag into his bronze hand as into a doll's & in spite of decency the stout old monarch is thus obliged to take his part in the whirligig politics of his city. Fie! Louis Philippe.

We were presently lodged in the Hotel Montmorenci on the Boulevard Mont Martre. I have wandered round the city but I am not well pleased. I have seen so much in five months that the magnificence of Paris will not take my eye today. The gardens of the Louvre looked pinched & the wind blew dust in my eyes and before I got into the Champs Elysees I turned about & flatly refused to go farther. I was sorry to find that in leaving Italy I had left forever that air of antiquity & history which her towns possess & in coming hither had come to a loud modern New York of a place.

I am very glad to find here my cousin Ralph Emerson who received me most cordially & has aided me much in making my temporary establishment. It were very ungrateful in a stranger to be discontented with Paris, for it is the most hospitable of cities. The foreigner has only to present his passport at any public institution & the doors are thrown wide to him. I have been to the Sorbonne where the first scientific men in France lecture at stated hours every day & the doors are open to all. I have heard Jouffroy, Thenard, Gay Lussac.

Then the College Royale de France is a similar institution on the same liberal foundation. So with the College du Droit & the Amphitheatre of the Garden of Plants.

I have been to the Louvre where are certainly some firstrate pictures. Leonardo da Vinci has more pictures here than in any other gallery & I like them well despite of the identity of the features which peep out of men & women. I have seen the same face in his pictures I think six or seven times. Murillo I see almost for the first time with great pleasure.

July. It is a pleasant thing to walk along the Boulevards & see how men live in Paris. One man has live snakes crawling about him & sells soap & essences. Another sells books which lie upon the ground. Another under my window all day offers a gold chain. Half a dozen walk up & down with some dozen walking sticks under the arm. A little further, one sells cane tassels at 5 sous. Here sits Boots brandishing his brush at every dirty shoe. Then you pass several tubs of gold fish. Then a man sitting at his table cleaning gold & silver spoons with emery & haranguing the passengers on its virtues. Then a person who cuts profiles with scissors "Shall be happy to take yours, Sir." Then a table of card puppets which are made to crawl. Then a hand organ. Then a wooden figure called   which can put an apple in its mouth whenever a child buys a plum. Then a flower merchant. Then a bird-shop with 20 parrots, 4 swans, hawks, & nightingales. Then the show of the boy with four legs &c &c without end. All these are the mere boutiques on the sidewalk, moved about from place to place as the sun or rain or the crowd may lead them.

4 July. Dined today at Lointier's with Gen Lafayette & nearly one hundred Americans. I sought an opportunity of paying my respects to the hero, & inquiring after his health. His speech was as happy as usual. A certain Lieut. Levi   did what he could to mar the day.

13 July. I carried my ticket from Mr Warden to the Cabinet of Natural History in the Garden of Plants. How much finer things are in composition than alone. 'Tis wise in man to make Cabinets. When I was come into the Ornithological Chambers, I wished I had come only there. The fancy-coloured vests of these elegant beings make me as pensive as the hues & forms of a cabinet of shells, formerly. It is a beautiful collection & makes the visiter as calm & genial as a bridegroom. The limits of the possible are enlarged, & the real is stranger than the imaginary. Some of the birds have a fabulous beauty. One parrot of a fellow, called *Psittacus erythropterus* from New Holland, deserves as special mention as a picture of Raphael in a Gallery. He is the beau of all birds. Then the hummingbirds little & gay. Least of all is the Trochilus Niger. I have seen beetles larger. The *Trochilus pella* hath such a neck of gold & silver & fire! Trochilus Delalandi from Brazil is a glorious little tot— la mouche magnifique.

Among the birds of Paradise I remarked the Manucode or P. regia from New Guinea, the Paradisaea Apoda, & P. rubra. Forget not the Veuve à epaulettes or Emberiza longicauda, black with fine shoulder knots; nor the Ampelis cotinga nor the Phasianus Argus a peacock looking pheasant; nor the Trogon pavoninus called also Couroncou pavonin.

I saw black swans & white peacocks, the ibis the sacred & the rosy; the flamingo, with a neck like a snake, the Toucan rightly called *rhinoceros*; & a vulture whom to meet in the wilderness would make your flesh quiver, so like an executioner he looked.

In the other rooms I saw amber containing perfect musquitoes, grand blocks of quartz, native gold in all its forms of crystallization, threads, plates, crystals, dust; & silver black as from fire. Ah said I this is philanthropy, wisdom, taste—to form a Cabinet of natural history. Many students were there with grammar & note book & a class of boys with their tutor from some school. Here we are impressed with the inexhaustible riches of nature. The Universe is a more amazing puzzle than ever as you glance along this bewildering series of animated forms,—the hazy butterflies, the carved shells, the birds, beasts, fishes, insects, snakes,—& the upheaving principle of life everywhere incipient in the very rock aping organized forms. Not a form so grotesque, so savage, nor so beautiful but is an expression of some property inherent in man the observer,—an occult relation between the very scorpions and man. I feel the centipede in me—cayman, carp, eagle, & fox. I am moved by strange sympathies, I say continually "I will be a naturalist."

There's a good collection of skulls in the Comparative anatomy chambers. The best skull seemed to be English. The skeleton of the Balena looks like the frame of a schooner turned upside down.

The Garden itself is admirably arranged. They have attempted to classify all the plants *in the ground*, to put together, that is, as nearly as may be the conspicuous plants of each class on Jussieu's system.

Walk down the alleys of this flower garden & you come to the enclosures of the animals where almost all that Adam named or Noah preserved are represented. Here are several lions, two great elephants walking out in open day, a camelopard 17 feet high, the bison, the rhinoceros, & so forth—all manner of four footed things in air & sunshine, in the shades of a pleasant garden, where all people French & English may come & see without money. By the way, there is a caricature in the printshops representing the arrival of the giraffe in Paris, exclaiming to the mob "Messieurs, il n'y a qu'un bete de plus." It is very pleasant to walk in this garden.

As I went out, I noticed a placard posted on the gates giving notice that M. Jussieu would next Sunday give a public herborisation, that is, make a botanical excursion into the country & inviting all & sundry to accompany him.

15 July. I have just returned from Pere le Chaise. It well deserves a visit & does honour to the French. But they are a vain nation. The tombstones have a beseeching importunate vanity and remind you of advertisements. But many are affecting. One which was of dark slate stone had only this inscription, 'Mon Pere.' I prefer the "Ci git" to the "Ici repose" as the beginning of the inscriptions but take the cemetery through I thought the classics rather carried the day. One epitaph was so singular, or so singular to be read by *me*, that I wrote it off.

"Ici repose Auguste Charles Collignon mort plein de confiance dans la bonte de Dieu à l'age de 68 ans et 4 mois le 15 Avril 1830. Il aima et chercha à faire du bien et mena une vie douce et heureuse, en suivant autant qu'il put, la morale et les lecons des essais de Montaigne et des Fables de la Fontaine." —I notice that, universally, the French write as in the above, "*Here lies Augustus, &c.*" & we write, "*Here lies the body of, &c*" a more important distinction than *roi de France* & *roi des Francais*.

I live at *pension* with Professor Heari at the corner of Rue Neuve Vivienne directly over the entrance of the Passage aux Panorames. If I had companions in the City it would be something better to live in the Café & Restaurant. These public rooms are splendidly prepared for travellers & full of company & of newspapers.

This Passage aux Panorames was the first Arcade built in Paris & was built by an American Mr Thayer. There are now probably fifty of these passages in the city. And few things give more the character of magnificence to the city than the suite of these passages about the Palais Royal.

Notre Dame is a fine church outside but the interior quite naked & beggarly. In general, the churches are very mean inside.

I went into the Morgue where they expose for 24 hours the bodies of persons who have been drowned or died in the streets, that they may be claimed by their friends. There were three corpses thus exposed, & every day there are some.

Young men are very fond of Paris, partly, no doubt, because of the perfect freedom—freedom from observation as well as interference,—in which each one walks after the sight of his own eyes; & partly because the extent & variety of objects offers an unceasing entertainment. So long as a man has francs in his pocket he needs consult neither time nor place nor other men's convenience; wherever in the vast city he is, he is within a stone's throw of a patissier, a cafe, a restaurant, a public garden, a theatre & may enter when he will. If he wish to go to the Thuilleries, perhaps two miles off, let him stop a few minutes at the window of a printshop or a bookstall, of which there are hundreds & thousands, and an Omnibus is sure to pass in the direction in which he would go, & for six sous he rides two or three miles. Then the streets swarm with Cabinets de Lecture where you find all the journals & all the new books. I spend many hours at Galignani's & lately at the English Reading Room in the Rue Neuve Augustine where they advertise that they receive 400 journals in all languages & have moreover a very large library.

Lastly the evening need never hang heavy on the stranger's hands, such ample provision is made here for what the newspapers call "nos besoins recreatifs." More than twenty theatres are blazing with light & echoing with fine music every night from the Academie Royale de la Musique, which is the French Opera, down to the Children's Drama; not to mention concerts, gardens, & shows innumerable.

The Theatre is the passion of the French & the taste & splendour of their dramatic exhibitions can hardly be exceeded. The Journal in speaking of the opera last night, declares that "Mme D. was received by the dilettanti of Paris with not less joy than the lost soul by the angels in heaven." I saw the Opera Gustave performed the other night & have seen nothing anywhere that could compare with the brilliancy of their scenic decoration. The moonlight scene resembled nothing but Nature's; and as for the masked ball, I think there never was a real fancy-ball that equalled the effect of this.

At the Theatre Francais where Talma played & Madame Mars plays I heard Delavigne's new piece Enfans d'Edouard excellently performed; for although Madame Mars speaks French beautifully & has the manners of a princess yet she scarcely excels the acting of the less famous performers who support her. Each was perfect in his part.

Paris is an expensive place. Rents are very high. All Frenchmen in all quarters of their dispersion never lose the hope of coming hither to spend their earnings, and all the men of pleasure in all the nations come hither, which fact explains the existence of so many dazzling shops full of most costly articles of luxury. Indeed it is very hard for a stranger to walk with eyes forward ten yards in any part of the city.

I have been to the Faubourg St. Martin to hear the Abbe Chatel, the founder of the Eglise Catholique Francaise. It is a singular institution which he calls his church with newly invented dresses for the priests & martial music performed by a large orchestra, relieved by interludes of a piano with vocal music. His discourse was far better than I could expect from these preliminaries.

Sometimes he is eloquent. He is a Unitarian but more radical than any body in America who takes that name.

I was interested in his enterprize for there is always something pathetic in a new church struggling for sympathy & support. He takes upon himself the whole pecuniary responsibilities of the undertaking, & for his Chapel in the Rue St Honoré pays an annual rent of 40,000 francs. He gave notice of a grand funeral fête which is to be solemnized on the anniversary of the Three Days at that Chapel.

In the printshops they have a figure of the Abbe Chatel on the same picture with Pere Enfant, & Le Templier.

I went this evening into Frascati's, long the most noted of the gambling houses or hells of Paris, & which a gentleman had promised to show me. This establishment is in a very handsome house on the Rue Richelieu.

Several servants in livery were waiting in the hall who took our hats on entering, & we passed at once into a suite of rooms in all of which play was going on. The most perfect decorum & civility prevailed; the table was covered with little piles of Napoleons which seemed to change masters very rapidly but scarce a word was spoken. Servants carry about lemonade, &c but no heating liquor. The house, I was told, is always one party in the game. Several women were present, but many of the company seemed to be mere spectators like ourselves. After walking round the tables, we returned to the hall, gave the servant a franc for our hats, & departed. Frascati has grown very rich.

—

At Boulogne on Saturday Morn 19th took the steam-boat for London. After a rough passage of 20 hours we arrived at London & landed at the Tower Stairs.

We know London so well in books & pictures & maps & traditions that I saw nothing surprizing in this passage up the Thames. A noble navigable stream lined on each side by a highly cultivated country, full of all manner of good buildings. Then Greenwich & Deptford, hospital, docks, arsenals, fleets of shipping, & then the mighty metropolis itself, old, vast, & still. Scarce any body was in the streets. It was about 7 o'clock Sunday Morning & we met few persons until we reached St Paul's. A porter carried our baggage, & we walked through Cheapside, Newgate St., High Holborn, and found lodgings (according to the direction of my friend in Paris) at Mrs Fowler's No 63 Russell Square. It was an extreme pleasure to hear English spoken in the streets; to understand all the words of Children at play, & to find that we must not any longer express aloud our opinion of every person we met, as in France & Italy we had been wont to do.

Scotland and England

1833

8 Oct. 1833.

My God who dost animate & uphold us always on the sea &
on land, in the fields, in cities & in lonely places, in our homes
& among strangers, I thank thee that thou hast enlightened &
comforted & protected me to this hour. Continue to me thy
guard & blessing. May I resist the evil that is without by the
good that is within. May I rejoice evermore in the consciousness that it is by Thee I live. May I rejoice in the Divine Power
& be humble. O that I might show forth thy gift to me by
purity, by love, by unshrinking industry & unsinking hope &
by unconquerable courage. May I be more thine, & so more
truly myself every day I live.—

—

Glasgow, 23 Aug. 1833.

May I send you an account of my romancing from Edinburgh to the Highlands? I was told it was so easy at an expense
of two days to see that famous country of Ben Lomond, Loch
Katrine, & the rest. So up the Forth sailed I, in the steamboat,
for Stirling. Cold rainy wind in our teeth, all the way; we past
Alloa & Falkirk, yes close by Bannockburn I quietly reading
my book in the cabin. At Sterling, I saw the ruin of the Abbey
of Cambus Kenneth & the view from Sterling Castle.

At night, in a car, being too late for the coach, I rode
through the rain ten miles to Doune & Callender. Of the
scenery I saw little more than my horse's head. At Callendar I
slept hard from 10 till 5, & was then waked to hasten to the
Trosachs Inn. This passage was made in a uncovered car again
& the rain wet me thro' my own coat & my landlord's over
that, & tho' we passed Loch Vennachar, & then Loch Achray,
yet the scenery of a shower bath must be always much the
same & perpendicular rather than horizontal. Once when the
flood intermitted, I peeped out from under the umbrella, & it

was a pretty place. We dried & breakfasted at the Trosachs. I walked with a party a mile & a half to the head of Loch Kater-ine. It had cleared up tho' the wind blew stoutly and I had the satisfaction of the Trosachs. The ornament of Scottish scenery is the heather, which colours the country to the hue of a rose. In two boats with four oars each we pushed into the lake and got as far as Helen's Island, the Isle of the Lady of the Lake. Ben Venue & Ben An rise on either side. The lake was rough, the wind was strong, our party were spattered, & the rowers made such little way that it seemed impracticable to attempt to go thro' the lake which is nine miles long. They put into the first cove the shore afforded, part of the company returned to the Trosachs, & a part who were bent on reaching that night Glasgow, had nothing for it but to walk to the end of the lake, which following the windings of the shore, is fourteen miles. There was no better road than a sheep track thro' every variety of soil, now sand, now morass, now fern, & brake, now stones. But the day was fine & on we fared, one of the boat men acting as guide. We embarked in the boat at 9 o'clock. Five out of fifteen reached the little hut at the end of the lake at 12 ½. Here we dried our shoes, & drank (I drank) whiskey, & eat oat cake. It was five miles to Inversnaid, where we must take the steam boat on Loch Lomond. There was no conveyance but our legs, which served us again. A country as bare almost as a paved street—mountains mountains but I don't remember that I saw a sheep. At Inversnaid a hut full of Highlandmen & women talking Gaelic. No chimney & the peat smoke escaped as it could. Behind the house was a roaring cataract. The steamboat came (& through much fear & tribulation on the rough waves) we were transported in a little boat & embarked therein. And so on we fared thro' this lake about 15 miles to Balloch. The wind blew my cap off which had travelled with me from Malta where it was made & it fell into Loch Lomond. My hat was with the baggage all at Glasgow, & the loss not to be repaired so I shivered & sweltered when need was in the rain & wind with a handkerchif on my head. We landed at Bal-loch & took coach 5 miles farther to Dumbarton. At Dumbar-ton we were carried to the steam boat on the Clyde & went up to Glasgow where we arrived about 10 o'clock at night. My own appearance was no doubt resolute arriving at an inn (where my trunk had not) in the old surtout without a hat & without a rag of baggage.

They put me in a little room aloft. I was in no condition to dictate & crept to bed. This morn came the trunk & armed with razors & clean shirt I recovered courage. I visited the Cathedral of 1123 spared by Knox, & now a Presbyterian church. In the vaulted cellar of the same is laid the scene of part of Rob Roy. Then to the Saltmarket & to the Hunterian Museum & to the walks behind the College. A little girl named Jeanie was my guide to the tower of the Church. Broad Scotch she spake but she said her name was not Deans.

Carlisle in Cumberland. Aug. 26.

I am just arrived in merry Carlisle from Dumfries. A white day in my years. I found the youth I sought in Scotland & good & wise & pleasant he seems to me. Thomas Carlyle lives in the parish of Dunscore 16 miles from Dumfries amid wild & desolate heathery hills & without a single companion in this region out of his own house. There he has his wife a most accomplished & agreeable woman. Truth & peace & faith dwell with them & beautify them. I never saw more amiableness than is in his countenance. He speaks broad Scotch with evident relish. "in London yonder," "I liked well," "aboot it," Ay Ay, &c &c. Nothing can be better than his stories—the philosophic phrase —the duchess of Queensbury was appointed to possess this estate—by God Almighty added the lady—Wordsworth. The Earl of Lonsdale, the town of Whitehaven, the Liverpool duelist—.

—

London. Heart of the world. Wonderful only from the mass of human beings. Muffins. Every event affects all the future, e.g. Christ died on the tree, that built Dunscore Church yonder & always affects us two. The merely relative existence of Time & hence his faith in his immortality.

Books, puffing Coulburn & Bentley. £10000 per annum pd. for puffing. Hence it came to be that no newspaper is trusted & now no books are bought & the booksellers are on the eve of bankruptcy. Pauperism crowded country; government should direct poor men what to do. Poor Irishmen come wandering over these moors; my dame makes it a rule to give to every son of Adam bread to eat & supply his wants to the next house but here are thousands of acres which might give them all meat & nobody to bid these poor Irish go to the moor & till it. They burned the stacks & so found a way to force the rich people to attend to them.

Liverpool man that fought a duel.

Splendid bridge from the new world to the old built by Gibbon.

Domestic animals. Man the most plastic little fellow on the planet. Nero's death 'qualis artifex perio'.

T.C. had made up his mind to pay his taxes to William & Adelaide Guelph with great cheerfulness as long as William is able to compel the payment & he shall cease to do so the moment he ceases to compel them.

Landor's principle is mere rebellion & he fears that is the American principle also. Himself worships the man that will manifest any truth to him.

Mrs C. told of the disappointment when they had determined to go to Weimar & the letter arrived from the bookseller to say the book did not sell & they could not go.

The first thing Goethe sent was the chain she wore round her neck, & how she capered when it came! but since that time he had sent many things.

Mrs. C. said when I mentioned the Burns piece that it always had happened to him upon those papers to hear of each two or three years after.

T.C. prefers London to any other place to live in. John S. Mill the best mind he knows, more purity, more force—has worked himself clear of Benthamism.

The best thing T.C. thought in Stuart's book was the story of the bootblack—that a man can have meat for his labor.

Ambleside, 28 August, 1833.

This morng. I went to Rydal Mt & called upon Mr Wordsworth. His daughters called in their father, a plain looking elderly man in goggles & he sat down & talked with great simplicity. A great deal to say about America, the more so that it gave occasion for talk upon his favorite topic, which is this, that Society is being enlightened by a superficial tuition out of all proportion to its being restrained by moral Culture.

Schools do no good. Tuition is not education. He thinks far more of the education of circumstances than of tuition. It is not whether there are offences of which the law takes cognisance but whether there are offences of which the law does not take cognisance. Sin, sin, is what he fears. & how society is to escape without greatest mischiefs from this source he cannot see.

He has even said what seemed a paradox, that they needed a civil war in America to teach them the necessity of knitting the social ties stronger.

There may be in America some vulgarity of manner but that's nothing important; it comes out of the pioneer state of things; but, 1. I fear they are too much given to making of money & secondly to politics; that they make political distinction the end & not the means. And I fear they lack a class of men of leisure—in short of gentlemen to give a tone of honor to the community. I am told that things are boasted of in the second class of society there that in England (God knows are done in England every day) but never would be spoken of here.

Carlyle he thinks insane sometimes. (I stoutly defended Carlyle.)

Goethe's Wilhelm Meister he abused with might & main—all manner of fornication. It was like flies crossing each other in the air. He had never got further than the first book, so disgusted was he. I spoke *for* the better parts of the book & he promised to look at it again.

Carlyle he said wrote the most obscurely. Allowed he was clever & deep but that he defied the sympathies of everybody. Even Mr Coleridge wrote more clearly though he always wished Coleridge would write more to be understood.

He carried me out into his garden & showed me the walk in which thousands of his lines were writ. His eyes are inflamed —no loss except for reading because he never writes prose & poetry he always carries even hundreds of lines in his memory before writing it. He told me he had just been to Staffa & within a few days had made three sonnets upon Fingal's Cave & was making a fourth when he was called in to see me. He repeated the three to me with great spirit. I thought the second & third more *beautiful* than any of his printed poems. The third is addressed to the flowers which, he said, especially the ox-eye daisy, are very abundant above it. The second alludes to the name of the Cave which is Cave of Music; the first to the circumstances of its being visited by the promiscuous company of the steamboat.

———

I hoped he would publish his promised poems. He said he never was in haste to publish, partly because he altered his poetry much & every alteration is ungraciously received but what he wrote would be printed whether he lived or died. I said Tintern Abbey was the favorite poem but that the more contemplative sort preferred the Excursion & the sonnets. He said yes they were better to him. He preferred himself those of his poems which touched the affections to any others, for what was more didactic, what was to theories of society & so on might perish fast but the others were a κτημαεϛαε—what was good today was good forever. He preferred the Sonnet on the feelings of a high minded Spaniard to any other (I so understood him) & the "two Voices" & quoted with great pleasure some verses addressed to the skylark.

He spoke of the Newtonian theory as if it might be superseded & forgotten & of Dalton's atomic theory.

The object of his talking upon political aspects of society was to impress it upon me & all good Americans to cultivate the moral, the conservative &c &c & never to call into action the physical strength of the people as lately in the Reform — — &c, a thing prophesied by De Lolme.   making a fortune.

He had broken a tooth lately walking with two lawyers & said he was glad it did not happen 40 years ago whereupon they praised his philosophy. Lucretius's poem far better than any other poem in Latin, far more a poet than Virgil—his system nothing, but his illustrations.—

Faith he said was necessary & to explain anything, to reconcile the foreknowledge of God with human evil.—
Cousin he knew nothing about but the name.
In America he wished to know not how any churches or schools but what *newspapers*? He had been told by a friend of his at the bottom of the hill who was a year in America that the newspapers were atrocious, & openly accused members of the

Legislature of stealing silver spoons, &c. He was against taking off the tax upon newspapers in England which the Reformers represented as a tax upon knowledge for this reason; they would be inundated with base prints.

Then to show me what a common person in England could do, he carried me into the inclosure of his clerk, a young man whom he had given this slip of ground which was laid out, or its natural capabilities shown, with great taste.

He then walked near a mile with me talking and ever & anon stopping short to impress the word or the verse & finally parted from me with great kindness & returned across the fields.

His hair is white, but there is nothing very striking about his appearance.

The poet is always young and this old man took the same attitudes that he probably had at 17—whilst he recollected the sonnet he would recite.

His egotism was not at all displeasing—obtrusive—as I had heard. To be sure it met no rock. I spoke as I felt with great respect of his genius.

He spoke very kindly of Dr Channing, who, he said, sat a long time in this very chair, laying his hand upon an armchair.

He mentioned Burns's sons.

—

29 Aug. From Kendal this morng to Lancaster; thence to Manchester & there was deposited with my luggage in the coach on the railway to Liverpool. We parted at 11 minutes after six, & came to the 21st milestone at 11 minutes after seven. Strange it was to meet the return cars; to see a load of timber, six or seven masts, dart by you like a trout. Every body shrinks back when the engine hisses by him like a squib. The fire that was dropped on the road under us all along by our engine looked as we rushed over it as a coal swung by the hand in circles not distinct but a continuous glare. Strange proof how men become accustomed to oddest things: the laborers did not lift their umbrellas to look as we flew by them on their return at the side of the track. It took about 1 ½ hours to make the journey, 32 miles. It has been performed in less than the hour.

—

Always day & night
Day before me
Night behind me

This I penned
Sitting on two stakes
Under the apple tree
Down in the swamp
To guard a friend

First questions always to be asked. Even Goethe, Newton, Gibbon seem to me nothing more than expert spinners of an extended superficies to hide the Universe of our ignorance. Poems, Histories with some are expedients to get bread & with others to conceal their bottomless & boundless ignorance. So that scarce can I blame the man who frankly affects to philosophize on the matter as some sensualists do, & says my fun is profound calculation.

Deep sense of Socrates' famous saying. It is the recantation of Man.

Friday September 6. Fair fine wind, still in the Channel—off the coast of Ireland but not in sight of land. This morning 37 sail in sight.

I like my book about nature & wish I knew where & how I ought to live. God will show me. I am glad to be on my way home yet not so glad as others & my way to the bottom I could find perchance with less regret for I think it would not hurt me, that is the ducking or drowning.

—

Astronomy, I thank Herschel, promises every thing. It refers me to a higher state than I now occupy. I please myself rather with contemplating the penumbra of the thing than the thing itself. But no moralities now, the good the holy day.

Sept. 9. Monday. The road from Liverpool to New York as they who have travelled it well know is very long, crooked, rough, & eminently disagreeable. Good company even, Heaven's best gift, will scarce make it tolerable. Four meals a day is the usual expedient (& the wretchedness of the expedient will show the extremity of the case) & much wine & porter—these are the amusements of wise men in this sad place. The purest wit may have a scurvy stomach.

The letterbag is our captain's best passenger. It neither eats nor drinks & yet pays at least Liverpool a passenger's fare. Capt. H. tells me that he usually carries between 4 & 5,000 letters each way. At the N.Y Post Office they count his letters & pay him two cents for every one. At Liverpool two pence. The last time he received in Liverpool £ 39. for them.

—

Sept 13. Friday. The sea to us is but a lasting storm. How it blows, how it rocks. My sides are sore with rolling in my berth; the coverlet is not wide enough that a man should wrap himself in it. It is only strange that with such a sea & wind & rain, such wild distressful noisy nights, no harm should befal us. We have torn a sail & lost a hencoop & its inmates but the bulwarks are firm, & I often hear of the sea breaking the bulwark of ships.

———

What a machine is a ship changing so fast from the state of a butterfly all wing to the shape of a log—all spar.

Poor Ireland! they told a story of an Irish boy at school asking a holiday to go to the market town. "What to go for?" "To see Uncle hanged."

Monday, September 16th. Gale & calm—pitch & rock—merrily swim we, the sun shines bright. The mate says they took up about where we are now a year ago the crew of Leonidas, a Portland vessel loaded with salt which sprang a leak. The Capt would not leave the ship after putting quadrant & compass & his own things in the boat, & saw the boat leave the ship.

One of this line of packets struck an island of ice, & the whole company with 35 passengers escaped in the boat.

Dull stormday yesterday. I kept Sunday with Milton & a Presbyterian magazine. Milton says, "if ever any was ravished with moral beauty, he is the man."

It occurred with sad force how much we are bound to be true to ourselves—(the old string)—because we are always judged by others as *ourselves* & not as those whose example we would plead. A reads in a book the praise of a wise man who could unbend & make merry & so he tosses off his glass whilst round him are malicious eyes watching his guzzling & fat eating, &   . The truth is, you can't find any example that will suit you, nor could, if the whole family of Adam should pass in procession before you, for you are a new work of God.

———

In this world, if a man sits down to think, he is immediately asked if he has the headache.

Sunday, 22 September. Gales & headwinds producing all the variety of discomfort & ennui in the Cabin. We try in vain to keep bright faces & pleasant occupation below, heedless of the roar of the tempest above. We are too nearly interested in every rope that snaps & every spar that cracks overhead to hear the ruin with philosophy. We may keep our eyes on the Cicero or Addison in our hands but that noise touches our life. I would I were in the bushes at Canterbury, for my part. Yesterday was too fine a day to lose at sea. Calm shining after the wild storm of two preceding days. This time I have not drawn the golden lot of company. And yet far better than the last voyage. But that little one to Charleston from St. Augustine with Murat was worth all the rest. Yet thanks to the good God who leads & protects me for the measure of comfort & intellectual occupation that is possible in the valleys of the sea by means of this wonderful chef d'oeuvre of human Art the ship. Sad for the steerage passengers, old women & children sitting up all night or lying in wet berths. The poor cow refuses to get up & be milked, & four dogs on board shiver & totter about all day, & bark when we ship a sea.

—

Beautiful songs B. J. can write, & his vocabulary is so rich & when he pleases so smooth that he seems to be prosing with a design to relieve & display better the bright parts of the piece. Then he shows himself master of the higher, the moral taste & enriches himself occasionally with those unquestionable gems which none but the sons of God possess. Strange that among his actors, & not the first is Will Shakspeare. He never was dull to relieve his brilliant parts. He is all light—sometimes terrestrial, sometimes celestial—but all light.

—

Friday, 4 October. Long. 67, je crois.
Our month expires today, & therefore 'tis time to look for land. The poor Malay saith to the wind in his petulance "Blow, me do tell you blow" but not of that mind are we, but contrariwise, very glad of this fine weather. Capt's merry account

of his capture by pirates in S. America in 1822 when they cut up his sails for trowzers & ripped off the copper sheathing of the vessel for French horns & appointed him fifer. He played in that capacity the dead march of two priests, whom the worthy lieut. gen. shot for smuggling.

"Chap from Wiggin, Manchester man, & a gentleman from Liverpool" said Coachey.—Sea of all colours. Today indigo, yesterday grass green, & day before grey.

from

A

1833–1834

Ch' apporta mane, e lascia sera.

Not of men neither by man.

—

May I "consult the auguries of time
And through the human heart explore my way
And look & listen"

This Book is my Savings Bank. I grow richer because I have somewhere to deposit my earnings; and fractions are worth more to me because corresponding fractions are waiting here that shall be made integers by their addition.

—

Boston, 11 December, 1833.
The call of our calling is the loudest call. There are so many worthless lives, apparently, that to advance a good cause by telling one anecdote or doing one great act seems a worthy reason for living.——When a poor man thanked Richard Reynolds for his goodness, he said, "Do you thank the clouds for rain?" The elder Scipio said, "he had given his enemies as much cause to speak well of him as his friends." Fontenelle said "I am a Frenchman. I am sixty years old, & I never have treated the smallest virtue with the smallest ridicule."

——Took possession of my chamber at Mr Pelletier's, Tuesday 10 Dec.

Alexander gave away the conquered provinces,—"And what have you left for yourself?" "Hope"; replied the hero.—"How do the wise differ from the unwise?" was the question put to Bias. He replied, "In a good hope." It is the true heroism & the true wisdom. Hope. The wise are always cheerful. The

293

reason is, (& it is a blessed reason,) that the eye sees that the ultimate issues of all things are good. There is always a presumption in favor of a cheerful view.

14 Dec. I please myself with contemplating the felicity of my present situation. May it last. It seems to me singularly free & it invites me to every virtue & to great improvement.

The plough displaces the spade, the bridge the watermen, the press the scrivener.

The Siphon. Reaumur's angles of bee-cells. Smeaton built Eddystone lighthouse on the model of an oaktree as being the form in nature designed to resist best a constant assailing force. Dollond (?) formed his achromatic telescope on the model of the human eye. The Caraibs in Guiana use the sheaths of their palm tree to evaporate seawater for its salt, drawing the hint from Nature. Du Hamel built a bridge by letting in a piece of stronger timber for the middle of the under surface, getting a hint from the shin bone. See Bell on the Hand.

December 19. The moral of your piece should be cuneiform & not polygonal. Judge of the success of the piece by the exclusive prominence it gives to the subject in the minds of all the audience.

2 January, 1834. The year, the year, but I have no thoughts for time. It occurs that a selection of natural laws might be easily made from botany, hydraulics, natural philosophy, &c. which should at once express also an ethical sense. Thus, 'Water confined in pipes will always rise as high as its source'. 'A hair line of water is a balance for the ocean if its fount be as high'. "Durable trees make roots first," C. reads. A cripple in the right road beats a racer in the wrong road. "Fractures well cured make us more strong." Action & reaction are equal. Concentrated nourishment is unhealthy; there must be mixture of excrement.

January 3. To Goethe there was no trifle. Glauber picked up what every body else threw away. Cuvier made much of humblest facts. The lower tone you take the more flexible your voice is. The whole landscape is beautiful though the particulars are not. "You never are tired whilst you can see far."

There is no weakness no exposure for which we cannot find consolation in the thought—Well 'tis a part of my constitution, part of my relation & office to my fellow creature. I like to see the immense resources of the creature.—5 January. "Newton", says Fourrier, "knew not yet the perfections of the Universe." "What La Place called great, was really great." I read in Herbert a beautiful verse, a high example of what the rhetorician calls the moral sublime.

"Ah, my dear God! though I am clean forgot,
Let me not love thee, if I love thee not."

12 January. I was well pleased with Dr Bradford's view of judgment the other day. Particular men are designated as persons of good judgment. It is merely that they are persons of experience in such affairs as interest most men. Their opinion on any question where they have not experience is worthless. Men of good sense act in certain conjunctures in a most imbecile manner. It is because it is their first trial. Others act with decision & success. It is because they have made many trials before & of course got through their failures. Then some men reserve their opinion & so never speak foolishly. Others publish every opinion they hold, & so though the first thoughts of all were equally ineffectual & foolish yet the abstemious have the credit of forming sound opinions the first time & the prompt speakers, if of active & advancing minds, are always uttering absurdities.

January 19. What is it that interests us in biography? Is there not always a silent comparison between the intellectual & moral endowments portrayed & those of which we are conscious? The reason why the Luther, the Newton, the Bonaparte concerning whom we read, was made the subject of panegyric, is, that in the writer's opinion, in some one respect this particular man represented the idea of Man. And as far as we accord with his judgment, we take the picture for a standard Man, and so let every line accuse or approve our own ways of thinking & living by comparison.—At least I thought thus in reading Jeffery's fine sketch of Playfair the other evening.

January 21. Is not the use of society to educate the Will which never would acquire force in solitude? We mean Will, when we say that a person has a good deal of character. Women generally have weak wills, sharply expressed perhaps, but capricious unstable. When the will is strong we inevitably respect it, in man or woman. I have thought that the perfection of female character seldom existed in poverty, at least where poverty was reckoned low. Is not this because the rich are accustomed to be obeyed promptly & so the will acquires strength & yet is calm & graceful? I think that involuntary respect which the rich inspire in very independent & virtuous minds, arises from the same circumstance, the irresistible empire of a strong will. There is not nor ever can be any competition between a will of words & a real will. Webster, Adams, Clay, Calhoun, Chatham, and every statesman who was ever formidable are wilful men. But Everett & Stanley & the Ciceros are not; want this backbone. Meantime a great many men in society speak strong but have no oak, are all willow. And only a virtuous will is omnipotent.

January 21. I add that in a former age the men of might were men of will, now the men of wealth.

January 22. Luther & Napoleon are better treatises on the Will than Edwards's. Will does not know if it be cold or hot or dangerous; he only goes on to his mark & leaves to mathematicians to calculate whether a body can come to its place without passing through all the intermediates. "Men have more heart than mind."
Buy land by the acre & sell it by the foot.

Different faces things wear to different persons. Whole process of human generation how bifronted! To one it is bawdy, to another wholly pure. In the mother's heart every sensation from the nuptial embrace through the uncertain symptoms of the quickening to the birth of her child is watched with an interest more chaste & wistful than the contemplations of the nun in her cloister. Yet the low minded visiter of a woman in such circumstances has the ignorant impertinence to look down & feel a sort of shame.

"The Emperor Nicholas lately delivered a speech to the Council of Administration of Warsaw assembled at Modlin in which the following remarkable words occurred; "Gentlemen, you must persevere in your course; and as to myself, as long as I live, I will oppose a will of iron to the progress of liberal opinions. The present generation is lost, but we must labor with zeal & earnestness to improve the spirit of that to come. It may perhaps require a hundred years. I am not unreasonable. I give you a whole age; but you must work without relaxation." "Boston Merc. Jour." Jan. 21.

Akin to the pathetic sublime of the two lines of Herbert on the last leaf, are the lines in the last Canto of Il Paradiso, thus translated;

> "O virgin mother, daughter of thy Son!
> Created beings all in lowliness
> Surpassing, as in height above them all."

23 Jan. I cannot read of the jubilee of Goethe, & of such a velvet life without a sense of incongruity. Genius is out of place when it reposes fifty years on chairs of state & inhales a continual incense of adulation. Its proper ornaments & relief are poverty & reproach & danger. & if the grand-duke had cut Goethe's head off, it would have been much better for his fame than his retiring to his rooms after dismissing the obsequious crowds to arrange tastefully & contemplate their gifts & honorary inscriptions.

New Bedford. 29 Jan. Michel Angelo's life in the Lib. Usef. Knowl. & his poetry by Signor Radici in the Retrospective Review Vol 13. These elevate my respect for the artist. His life, they say too, was a poem. Beautiful is his Platonic passion, before that word had been perverted by affectation & hypocrisy. Heroic is his treaty with the pope on assuming the charge of the building of St Peter's. No fee & no interference. Like my admirable Persian who would neither serve nor command; or like (is it not) Don Ferrante 'Uomo di studio, non amava ni comandare ni ubbedire.' Towards his end seems to have grown in him an invincible appetite of dying, for he knew that his spirit could only enjoy contentment after death. "Bel fin fa, Che vien amando more," said Petrarch. So vehement was this desire that 'his soul could no longer be appeased by the wonted seductions of painting & sculpture.' He blames his nephew for celebrating the birth of a son with pomp, saying "That a man ought not to smile when all those around him weep, & that we ought not to show that joy when a child is born which ought to be reserved for the death of one who has lived well." He nothing vulgar did or mean. He had a deep contempt of the vulgar, not of "the simple inhabitants of lowly streets or humble cottages, but of that abject & sordid crowd of all classes & all places, who *obscure*, as much as in them lies, *every beam of beauty in the Universe.*" He had intense love of solitude & the country & rejoices in the remembrance of his residence with the hermits in the mountains of Spoleti so much that, he says, he is only half in Rome; 'since, truly, peace is only to be found in the woods.' Berni said of him, "*Ei dice cose*, e voi dite parole." He sought to penetrate by just degrees to the centre of that eternal radiance in which is hidden "l'amor che move il sole e l'altre stelle."

Are not his struggles & mortifications a more beautiful wreath than the milliners made for Goethe?

In reference to this appetite for death, shall I say it is sometimes permissible? that the object of life is answered when the uses of time are discovered; when the soul has so far discovered its relation to external truth, that time can never more be a burden, & nothing but the evils inseparable from human condition prevent it from being a heaven?—

1 Feb. In viewing the greatness of men of the first ages, Homer & Alfred equal to Goethe & Washington, does it not seem a little additional force of Will in the individual is equivalent to ages-ful of the improvements we call civilization? But

these Anakim do yet yield to the sad observer of his race real & great consolation (I am thinking now of Michel Angelo & his Platonism) for they seem to him himself without his faults & in favorable circumstances he recognizes their lofty aspirations as the thoughts of his own childhood; he looks at these heroes as nothing peculiar & monstrous but as only more truly men, & he perceives that a heaven of truth & virtue is still possible. Some thoughts always find us young, and keep us so. Such a thought is the love of the universal & eternal beauty. Every man leaves that contemplation with the feeling that it rather belongs to ages than to mortal life.

2 Feb. How often our nature is conscious of & labors with its own limits. In the very act of pretension it is oppressed with secret humiliation.

February 3. I have read Corinne with as much emotion as a book can excite in me. A true representation of the tragedy of woman which yet (thanks to the mysterious compensation which nature has provided) they rarely feel. The tragedy of genius also. The story labors with the fault of an extravagant I may say ridiculous filial passion in Oswald which no man of such intelligence can carry so far & then with the second impossibility of his rapid marriage. No matter; though the circumstances are untrue the position & the feelings of Corinne are possible, &, as Plato would say, more true than history.

New Bedford. 7 Feb. I have been to Plymouth & stood on the Rock & felt that it was grown more important by the growth of this nation in the minutes that I stood there. But Barnabas Hedge ought not—no man ought—to own the rock of Plymouth.

Mr Bond said he had learned that men can never learn by experience. In the last depression of trade he had resolved never to be caught again; and now amid his perplexities resolves again. At sea we always judge by the present weather the probable length of the voyage.

10 Feb. The Newspapers say they might as well publish a thunderstorm as a report of Webster's speech in answer to Wright. His tones were like those of a commander in a battle. Times of eloquence are times of terror. I wrote to C. last night that the obstinate retention of simple & high sentiments in obscurest duties is hardening the character to that temper that will work with honor, if need be, in the tumult, or on the scaffold. Yet perhaps the courage of heroes in revolutions is extemporary and what seems superhuman fortitude is the effect of an ecstasy of sorrow. Evil times have the effect of making men think. I suppose in the last few weeks men have thrown more searching glances at the structure & interdependence of society than in years of prosperous times. They begin to trace the path of an ear of corn from its stalk to their table.

G.A.S. confirms the views (21 Jan.) of the education of the Will, by saying, that in his experience a very great change is produced in men by the possession of property, a great addition of force, which would remain to them if their property were taken away. It is not the possession of luxuries but the exercise of power which belongs to wealth that has wrought this effect. The possession of Office has the same effect. What a pepper corn man is B.S. if he had been poor. By this education of things & persons he is now a person of decision & influence.

How imbecile is often a young person of superior intellectual powers for want of acquaintance with his powers; bashful, timid, he shrinks, retreats, before every confident person & is disconcerted by arguments & pretensions he would be ashamed to put forward himself. Let him work as many merchants do with the forces of millions of property for months & years upon the wills of hundreds of persons & you shall see him transformed into an adroit fluent masterful gentleman, fit to take & keep his place in any society of men. This is the account to be given of the fine manners of the young Southerners brought up amidst slaves, & of the concession that young Northerners make to them, yes, & old Northerners to old Southerners. The story of Caesar among the Corsairs who took him prisoner—rehearsing his speeches to them, abusing them if they did not admire, & threatening to crucify them one day, *which he did*,—is a good illustration of the natural empire of a strong Will. They had caught a Tartar.

This part of education is conducted in the nursery & the playground, in fights, in frolics, in business, in politics. My manners & history would have been very different, if my parents had been rich, when I was a boy at school. Herein is good ground for our expectation of the high bearing of the English nobleman.

B.R. called his friend the naval architect, a perfect ship. Mr Hillman

New Bedford, 12 February, 1834. The days & months & years flit by, each with his own black riband, his own sad reminiscence. Yet I looked at the Almanack affectionately as a book of Promise. These last three years of my life are not a chasm— I could almost wish they were—so brilliantly sometimes the vision of Ellen's beauty & love & life come out of the darkness. Pleasantly mingled with my sad thoughts the sublime religion of Miss Rotch yesterday. She was much disciplined, she said, in the years of Quaker dissension and driven inward, driven home, to find an anchor, until she learned to have *no choice*, to acquiesce without understanding the reason when she found an obstruction to any particular course of acting. She objected to having this spiritual direction called an impression, or an intimation, or an oracle. It was none of them. It was so simple it could hardly be spoken of. It was long, long, before she could attain to anything satisfactory. She was in a state of great dreariness, but she had a friend, a woman, now deceased, who used to advise her to dwell patiently with this dreariness & absence, in the confidence that it was necessary to the sweeping away of all her dependence upon traditions, and that she would finally attain to something better. And when she attained a better state of mind, its beginnings were very, very small. And now it is not any thing to speak of. She designed to go to England with Mr & Mrs Farrar, & the plan was very pleasant and she was making her preparations & the time was fixed, when she conceived a reluctance to go for which she could not see any reason, but which continued; and she therefore suspended her purpose, and suffered them to depart without her. She said she had seen reason to think it was best for her to have staid at home. But in obeying it, she never felt it of any importance that she should know now or at any time what the reasons were. But she should feel that it was presumption to press through this reluctance & choose for herself. I said it was not so much any particular power, as, a *healthful state of the mind*, to which she assented cordially. I said, it must produce a sublime tranquillity in view of the future—this assurance of higher direction; and she assented.

Can you believe, Waldo Emerson, that you may relieve yourself of this perpetual perplexity of choosing? & by putting your ear close to the soul, learn always the true way. I cannot but remark how perfectly this agrees with the Daimon of Socrates, even in that story which I once thought anomalous, of the direction as to the choice of two roads. And with the grand Unalterableness of Fichte's morality. Hold up this lamp & look back at the best passages of your life. Once there was *choice* in the mode, but *obedience* in the thing. In general there has been pretty quiet obedience *in the main*, but much recusancy *in the particular*.

———

Boston, Feb. 19. A seaman in the coach told the story of an old sperm whale which he called a white whale which was known for many years by the whalemen as Old Tom & who rushed upon the boats which attacked him & crushed the boats to small chips in his jaws, the men generally escaping by jumping overboard & being picked up. A vessel was fitted out at New Bedford, he said, to take him. And he was finally taken somewhere off Payta head by the Winslow or the Essex. He gave a fine account of a storm which I heard imperfectly. Only 'the whole ocean was all feather white.' A whale sometimes runs off three rolls of cord, three hundred fathom in length each one.

———

February 21. The true reasons for actions are not given. G.P.B. says that he is so well understood at Plymouth that he can act naturally without being reckoned absurd. That is a valid reason for going there. But how many would not understand it & how many understanding it would hoot at it? They think a cheaper board is a good reason for going to one house or the prospect of making acquaintance that give parties, or the like; but such a reason as this which affects happiness & character seems unworthy attention. As George says, it is agreed in society to consider realities as fictions & fictions realities.

February 22. It were well to live purely, to make your word worth something. Deny yourself cake & ale to make your testimony irresistible. Be a pure reason to your contemporaries for God & truth. What is good in itself can be bad to nobody. As I went to Church I thought how seldom the present hour is seized upon as a new moment. To a soul alive to God every moment is a new world. A new audience, a new Sabbath affords an opportunity of communicating thought & moral excitement that shall surpass all previous experience, that shall constitute an epoch a revolution in the minds on whom you act & in your own. The awakened soul, the man of genius makes every day such a day, by looking forward only but the professional mob look back only to custom & their past selves.

February 25th. "The day is immeasureably long to him who knows how to value & to use it." said Goethe.

2 March. It is very seldom that a man is truly alone. He needs to retire as much from his solitude as he does from society into very loneliness. While I am reading & writing in my chamber I am not alone though there is nobody there. There is one means of procuring solitude which to me & I apprehend to all men is effectual, & that is to go to the window & look at the stars. If they do not startle you & call you off from vulgar matters I know not what will. I sometimes think that the atmosphere was made transparent with this design to give man in the heavenly bodies a perpetual admonition of God & superior destiny. Seen in the streets of cities, how great they are! When I spoke of this to G.A.S. he said, that he had sought in his chamber a place for prayer & could not find one till he cast his eye upon the stars.—

New Bedford, 15 March. I have been again to Plymouth and the families & the faces are almost as tranquil as their pines. The blue ocean reminded me of Goethe's fine observation that "Nature has told every thing once;"—one illustration of it is

Playfair's bough of a tree which was perfect wood at one end, and passed through imperceptible gradations to perfect mineral coal at the other. Another illustration of it was to me this noble line of sea by which Nature is pleased to reveal to the asking eye the dimensions of the globe by showing the true outline of the world. Fine objects in Plymouth from men & women down to vegetables, & saw & relished all even to the epigaea & the byssus or pulvis simplicissimus, ground pine, sabbatia, & empetrum.

"I will cast about for the causes of my disposition to take this view."

Mary Rotch

"I found though the sympathy of friends was most pleasant, yet the little faith I had, tho' but a grain of mustard seed, nothing could shake, and I found that nothing could confirm it."

"Nature tells every thing once." Yes our microscopes are not necessary. They are a mechanical advantage for chamber philosophers; she has magnified every thing somewhere. Each process, each function, each organ is disproportionately developed in some one individual. Go study it there, instead of wearing your eyes out in your 6 million magnifier.

I count no man much because he cows or silences me. Any fool can do that. But if his conversation enriches or rejoices me, I must reckon him wise. Being & Seeming.

New Bedford, 21 March. I have been much interested lately in the Mss Record of the debates in the Quakers' Monthly Meetings here in 1823, when Elizabeth Rodman & Mary Rotch were proposed to be removed from the place of Elders for uniting in the prayers of Mary Newhall. I must quote a sentence or two from two of these speakers. Feb. 1823, "M.N. rose in the meeting & began with As the stream does not rise higher than the fountain, &c spoke of the Mosaic dispensation in which the performance of certain rituals constituted the required religion, the more spiritual dispensation of our Saviour, of the advent of Christ & the yet more inward spiritual dispensation of the present day. These dispensations she compared to the progressive stages of the human heart in the work of religion, from loving our neighbor as ourselves to loving our enemies & lastly arriving at that state of humility when self would be totally abandoned & we could only say Lord be merciful to me a sinner."

New Bedford. My Swedenborgian friend Dr Stebbins tells me that "he esteems himself measureably excused for not preaching whilst I remain here, as I am giving as much New Jerusalem doctrine as the people will bear."—

Fine thought in the old verse by Barbour describing Bruce's soldiers crowding around him as with new unsated curiosity after a battle.

> "Sic wordis spak they of their king;
> And for his hie undertaking
> Ferleyit & yernit him for to see,
> That with him ay was wont to be."

22 March. The subject that needs most to be presented is the principle of Self reliance, what it is, what is not it, what it requires, how it teaches us to regard our friends. It is true that there is a faith wholly a man's own, the solitary inmate of his own breast, which the faiths of all mankind cannot shake, & which they cannot confirm. But at the same time how useful, how indispensable has been the ministry of our friends to us, our teachers,—the living & the dead.

I ask advice. It is not that I wish my companion to dictate to me the course I should take. Before God, No. It were to unman, to un-god myself. It is that I wish him to give me information about the facts, not a law as to the duty. It is that he may stimulate me by his thoughts to unfold my own, so that I may become *master of the facts* still. My own bosom will supply, as surely as God liveth, the direction of my course.

This truth constitutes the objection to *pledges.* They are advocated on the principle that men are not to be trusted. They are to be trusted. They can never attain to any good, until they are trusted with the whole direction themselves & therefore it is pernicious, it is postponing their virtue & happiness whenever you substitute a false principle for the true in a mind capable of acting from a right motive.

March 23. It occurs that the distinction should be drawn in treating of Friendship between the *aid of commodity*, which our friends yield us, as in hospitality, gifts, sacrifices, &c. & which, as in the old story about the poor man's will in Montaigne, are evidently esteemed by the natural mind (to use such a cant word) the highest manifestations of love; and, secondly, the spiritual aid—far more precious & leaving the other at infinite distance,—which our friends afford us, of confession, of appeal, of social stimulus, mirroring ourselves. March 26. As the flower precedes the fruit, & the bud the flower, so long before the knowledge, comes the opinion, long before the opinion, comes the instinct, that a particular act is unfriendly, unsuitable, wrong. We are wonderfully protected. Much wisdom is in the fable of the stag who scorned his feet & praised his horns.

March 27. We learn to esteem our own censure above any other from the consideration that we shall always dwell with ourselves, & may abide with one another only a short time. There are two purposes with which we may seek each other's society—for finite good as when we desire protection, aid in poverty, furtherance in our plans, even political societies & philanthropical. All have relation to present well being. But there is a desire of friends for the sake of no finite mercenary good small or great. There is a seeking of friends that thoughts may be exchanged, sympathies indulged, & a purity of intercourse established that would be as fit for heaven as it is for earth. The object of this intercourse is, that a man may be made known to himself to an extent that in solitude is not practicable. Our faculties are not called out except by means of the affections.

But we do not seek friends for conversation. We act for, with, upon each other. Our duty our necessity is continually forcing us into active relations with others. Very well. This serves the same purpose to make you master of your own powers. The service you render to others may be accomplished in another manner, but only by it can your own faculties & virtues be trained.

March 28. Wherever the truth is injured, defend it. You are there on that spot within hearing of that word, within sight of that action as a Witness, to the end that you should speak for it.

March 29. In the Am. Quarterly Review in an article on Parisian society occurs the remark, "The French have unquestionably carried society to as high a degree of perfection as it can well be brought."!!!

> "My Heritage how long & wide
> Time is my heritage my field is Time."

Boston, 10 April. Is it possible that in the solitude I seek I shall have the resolution the force to work as I ought to work—as I project in highest most farsighted hours? Well, & what do you project? Nothing less than to look at every object in its relation to Myself.

———

11 April. Went yesterday to Cambridge & spent most of the day at Mount Auburn, got my luncheon at Fresh Pond, & went back again to the woods. After much wandering & seeing many things, four snakes gliding up & down a hollow for no purpose that I could see—not to eat, not for love, but only gliding; then a whole bed of Hepatica triloba, cousins of the Anemone all blue & beautiful but constrained by niggard Nature to wear their last year's faded jacket of leaves; then a black capped titmouse who came upon a tree & when I would know his name, sang *chick a dee dee*; then a far off tree full of clamorous birds, I know not what, but you might hear them half a mile. I forsook the tombs & found a sunny hollow where the east wind could not blow & lay down against the side of a tree to most happy beholdings. At least I opened my eyes & let what would pass through them into the soul. I saw no more my relation how near & petty to Cambridge or Boston, I heeded no more what minute or hour our Massachusetts clocks might indicate—I saw only the noble earth on which I

was born, with the great Star which warms & enlightens it. I
saw the clouds that hang their significant drapery over us.—It
was Day, that was all Heaven said. The pines glittered with
their innumerable green needles in the light & seemed to challenge me to read their riddle. The drab-oak leaves of the last
year turned their little somersets & lay still again. And the
wind bustled high overhead in the forest top. This gay &
grand architecture from the vault to the moss & lichen on
which I lay, who shall explain to me the laws of its proportions
& adornments?

See the perpetual generation of good sense:

Nothing wholly false, fantastic, can take possession of men
who to live & move must plough the ground, sail the sea, have
orchards, hear the robin sing, & see the swallow fly.

Today I found in Roxbury the Saxifraga Vernalis.

12 April. Glad to read in my old gossip Montaigne some robust rules of rhetoric: I will have a chapter thereon in my
book. I would Thomas Carlyle should read them. "In good
prose (said Schlegel(?)) every word should be underscored."
Its place in the sentence should make its emphasis. Write solid
sentences & you can even spare punctuation. The passages in
Montaigne are in Vol. 3. pp. 144–6.

We are always on the brink of an ocean of thought into
which we do not yet swim. We are poor lords—have immense
powers which we are hindered from using. I am kept out of
my heritage. I talk of these powers of perceiving & communicating truth, as my powers. I look for respect as the possessor
of them. & yet, after exercising them for short & irregular
periods, I move about without them—quite under their sphere
—quite unclothed. "'Tis the most difficult of tasks to keep
Heights—which the soul is competent to gain." A prophet
waiting for the word of the Lord. Is it the prophet's fault that
he waits in vain? Yet how mysterious & painful these laws.
Always in the precincts—never admitted; always preparing,—
vast machinery—plans of life—travelling—studies—the country—solitude—and suddenly in any place, in the street, in the
chamber will the heaven open & the regions of boundless
knowledge be revealed; as if to show you how thin the veil,
how null the circumstances. The hours of true thought in a

lifetime how few! And writing they say makes the feet cold &
the head hot. And yet are we not ever postponing great actions
& ineffable wisdom? We are ever coming up with a group of
angels still in sight before us, which we refer to when we say
'the Truth' & the Wise Man, & the corrections these shall
make in human society.

All the mistakes I make arise from forsaking my own station
& trying to see the object from another person's point of view.
I read so resolute a self-thinker as Carlyle & am convinced of
the riches of wisdom that ever belong to the man who utters
his own thought with a divine confidence that it must be true
if he heard it there.

We live, animals in the basement story, & when Shakspeare
or Milton or even my fantastical Scotchman who fools his humour to the top of his bent—calls us up into the high region,
we feel & say 'this is my region, they only show me my own
property—I am in my element, I thank them for it.' Presently
we go about our business into the basement again, cumbered
with serving & assured of our right to the halls above, we
never go thither.

I had observed long since that to give the thought a just &
full expression, I must not prematurely utter it. Better not talk
of the matter you are writing out. It was as if you had let the
spring snap too soon. I was glad to find Goethe say to the
same point, 'that he who seeks a hidden treasure must not
speak.'

April 13. Sabbath. There are some duties above courtesy. And
were it not lawful for the discontented unfed spirit sometimes
to cry out 'Husks, Husks, Ye feed the people with words,' even
in their solemn assembly? They distress me by their prayers,
and all the discourse was an impertinence. There sat too, the
gifted man, and if he unlawfully withheld his word, this wearisome prose was his just punishment.

Elsewhere, certainly not there, but from M.M.E., from Carlyle, or from this delicious day, or whatever celestial fingers
touched the divine harp,—I woke to a strain of highest
melody. I saw that it was not for me to complain of obscurity,
of being misunderstood; it was not for me even in the filthy
rags of my unrighteousness to despond of what I might do

& learn. Can you not do better than clear your action to the highest of these puppets or these potentates around you, by clearing it to your Creator? by being justified to yourself?

Absolve yourself to the universe, &, as God liveth, you shall ray out light & heat,—absolute good.

Were it not noble gratitude since we are the fruit of Time & owe all to the immeasureable past—its nations & ages guide our pen—to live for the world; to inspect the present &, in the present, report of the future for the benefit of the existing race; & having once seen that Virtue was beautiful, count that, portion enough without higgling for our particular commodity to boot? Down with that fop of a Brutus. Peace to the angel of Innocency for evermore.

It occurs how much friction is in the machinery of society. The materiel is so much that the spirituel is overlaid & lost. A man meditates in solitude upon a truth which seems to him so weighty that he proposes to impart it to his fellowmen. Immediately a society must be collected & books consulted & much paper blotted in preparation of his discourse. Alien considerations come in, personal considerations—& finally when he delivers his discourse, 'tis quite possible it does not contain the original message so that it was no superfluous rule he gave who said, When you write do not omit the thing you meant to say. The material integuments have quite overlaid & killed the spiritual child. Not otherwise it falls out in Education. A young man is to be educated & schools are built & masters brought together & gymnasium erected & scientific toys & Monitorial Systems & a College endowed with many professorships & the apparatus is so enormous & unmanageable that the e-ducation or *calling out of his faculties* is never accomplished, he graduates a dunce. See how the French Mathematics at Cambridge have quite destroyed the slender chance a boy had before of learning Trigonometry.

Is it otherwise in our philanthropic enterprizes? They wish to heal the sick, or emancipate the African, or convert the Hindoo, and immediately agents are appointed, & an office established, & Annual Reports printed, and the least streamlet of the Vast contributions of the public trickles down to the healing of the original evil. The Charity becomes a job.

Well now is it otherwise with life itself? We are always getting ready to live, but never living. We have many years of technical education; then, many years of earning a livelihood, & we get sick, & take journeys for our health, & compass land & sea for improvement by travelling, but the work of self-improvement—always under their nose,—nearer than the nearest, is seldom seldom engaged in. A few few hours in the longest life.

Set out to study a particular truth. Read upon it. Walk to think upon it. Talk of it. Write about it. The thing itself will not much manifest itself, at least not much in accommodation to your studying arrangements. The gleams you do get, out they will flash, as likely at dinner, or in the roar of Faneuil Hall, as in your painfullest abstraction.

Very little life in a lifetime.

M.M.E. writes, that "the world is full of children, & what in our hearts we take no merit in—blush that it is no more generous—we expose to the weak as justification."

April 15. The least change in our point of vision gives the whole world a pictorial air, shall I say, dramatizes it. Thus get into a stage coach & ride through Boston and what a ludicrous pathetic tragical picture will the streets present. The men, the women, those that talk earnestly, the hammering mechanic, the lounger, the beggar, the boys, the dogs are unrealized at once, or at least wholly detached from all relation to the observer & seen as phenomenal not actual beings. Get into the railroad car & the Ideal Philosophy takes place at once.—

20 April. A good Inaugural Sermon from Mr Stearns at Old South this morning; & from Mr Frothingham this P.M. a good unfolding of the Parting of Elijah & Elisha. Elijah said "Ask What thou wilt." Who could have stood this test? To whom would it not have been a snare? But Elisha said, "Let a double portion of thy spirit be on me". The preacher should have added, I think, that the blessing descended in the asking, the prayer answered itself, as all real prayers do.

Awake, arm of the Lord! Awake thou God-like that sleepest! dear God, that sleepest in Man I have served my apprenticeship of bows & blushes, of fears & references, of excessive admiration. The young man is guided as much by opinion of society as if he came to you & me, & said, what shall I read? what shall I wear? what shall I say?

The whole secret of the teacher's force lies in the conviction that men are convertible. And they are. They want awakening. Get the soul out of bed, out of her deep habitual sleep, out into God's universe, to a perception of its beauty & hearing of its Call and your vulgar man, your prosy selfish sensualist awakes a God & is conscious of force to shake the world. It seemed to me tonight as if it were no bad topic for the preacher to urge the talent of hearing good sermons upon their congregations. I can hear a good sermon where Surd shall hear none, & Absurd shall hear worse than none. Spend the Sunday morning well & the hours shall shine with immortal light, shall epitomize history, shall sing heavenly psalms. Your way to church shall be short as the way to the playground is to a child, and something holy & wise shall sit upon all the countenances there & shall inspire the preacher's words with a wisdom not their own. Spend the Sunday morning ill, & you will hardly hear a good sermon anywhere.

Could it be made apparent what is really true that the whole future is in the bottom of the heart, that, in proportion as your life is spent within,—in that measure are you invulnerable. In proportion as you penetrate facts for the law, & events for the cause, in that measure is your knowledge real, your condition gradually conformed to a stable idea, & the future foreseen. I have laid my egg, but 'tis either old or empty. It was nobly said by Goethe that he endeavored to show his gratitude to all his great contemporaries, Humboldt, Cuvier, Byron, Scott, or whosoever by meeting them half way in their various efforts by the activity & performances of his own mind. It is like the worthy man whom I once took up in my chaise as I rode, & who, on parting, told me he should thank me by rendering the same service to some future traveller.

April 22. The most original sermon is adopted by each hearer's selflove as his old orthodox or unitarian or quaker preaching.—

There are people who read Shakspear for his obscenity as the glaucous gull is said to follow the walrus for his excrement. I would be as great a geographer as an eagle—& every winter like a bird or member of congress go south.

23d April. In desert lands the bird alights on the barrel of the hunter's gun, and many other facts are there, but that which I would say is that every teacher acquires a cumulative inertia; the more forcible the more eloquent have been his innovating doctrines, the more eagerly his school have crowded around him, so much the more difficult is it for him to forfeit their love, to compromise his influence by advancing farther in the same track. Therefore the wise man must be wary of attaching followers. He must feel & teach that the best of wisdom cannot be communicated; must be acquired by every soul for itself. And the prudent world cannot wish that the gifted Channing should advance one step, lest it be left without the confidence in its Conductor.

April 26, Newton. The muses love the woods & I have come hither to court the awful Powers in this sober solitude. Whatsoever is highest, wisest, best, favor me! I will listen & then speak.

—

Good is promoted by the worst. Don't despise even the Kneelands & Andrew Jacksons. In the great cycle they find their place & like the insect that fertilizes the soil with worm casts or the scavenger bustard that removes carrion they perform a beneficence they know not of, & cannot hinder if they would.

I saw a hawk today wheeling up to heaven in a spiral flight & every circle becoming less to the eye till he vanished into the atmosphere. What could be more in unison with all pure & brilliant images? Yet is the creature an unclean greedy eater & all his geography from that grand observatory was a watching of barn yards, or an inspection of moles & field mice. So with the pelican crane & the tribes of sea-fowl—disgusting gluttons all. Yet observe how finely in nature all these disagreeable individuals integrate themselves into a cleanly & pleasing whole.

April 26.
Here is a Mytilus Margaritiferus as large as a moon & of the same color, & a Tellina radiata which reminds the beholder of the rising sun. I think they should call one of these shells,

Moon; & the other, Morn. Today I found also the Andromeda Calyculata, Houstonia, Potentilla sarmentosa. This empetrum & smilax & kalmia & privet I have wondered oft to what end they grew. How ridiculous! Ask wrens & crows & bluebirds. As soon as you have done wondering & have left the plant, the bird & the insect return to it as to their daily table. And so it renews its race, for a thousand thousand summers.

Nat. Hist gives *body* to our knowledge.

No man can spare a fact he knows. The knowledge of nature is *most permanent*, clouds & grass are older antiquities than pyramids or Athens, then they are *most perfect*. Goethe's plant a genuine creation. Then they bear strange but well established affinities to us. Nobody can look on a cistus or a brentus without sighing at his ignorance. It is an unknown America. Linnaeus is already read as the Plato who described Atlantis. A classification is nothing but a Cabinet. The whole remains to be done thereafter.

The boy & the W.

A religion of forms is not for me. I honor the Methodists who find like St John all Christianity in one word, Love. To the parishes in my neighborhood Milton would seem a free thinker when he says "they (the Jews) thought it too much license to follow the charming pipe of him who sounded & proclaimed liberty & relief to all distresses."

Roger Rain
Come Again!

28 April. Vaccinium Tenellum, Pyrus Ovalis, Anemone nemorosa, Fragaria Virginiana. The day is as good for these as for oaks & corn. The air vibrates with equal facility to the thunder & to the squeak of a mouse, invites man with provoking indifference to total indolence & to immortal actions. You may even shun the occasions of excitement by withdrawing from a profession & from society & then the Vast Eternity of capacity of freedom, opens before you but without a single impulse. A day is a rich abyss of means yet mute & void. It demands something godlike in him who has cast off the common yokes & motives of humanity & has ventured to trust

himself for a taskmaster. High be his heart, faithful his will, vast his contemplations, that he may truly be a world, society, law to himself, that a simple purpose may be to him as strong as iron necessity is to others. It is a faithful saying worthy of all acceptation that a reasoning Man conscious of his powers & duties annihilates all distinction of circumstances. What is Rome, what is royalty, what is wealth? His place is the true place & superior therefore in dignity to all other places. Linnaeus at Copenhagen, Oberlin on the high Alps, White at Selborne, Roger Bacon at Oxford, Rammohun Roy in India & Heber at Bombay, Washington in the Jerseys.—These are the Romes, the Empires, the Wealth of these men. The place which I have not sought but in which my duty places me is a sort of royal palace. If I am faithful in it I move in it with a pleasing awe at the immensity of the chain of which I hold the last link in my hand & am led by it. I perceive my commission to be coeval with the antiquity of the eldest causes.

—

April 29. Fontenelle said, if men should see the principles of Nature laid bare they would cry 'What! is this all?' How simple are they. How is the Wonder perpetually lessened by showing the disproportionate effect upon the eye of simple combination. The shell is a marvel until we see that it was not one effort but each knot & spine has been in turn the lip of the structure. Shakspeare how inconceivable until we have heard what Italian Novels & Plutarch's Lives & old English Dramas he had, also what contemporary fund of poetic diction. A Webster's Speech is a marvel until we have learned that a part of it he has carried in his head for years, & a part of it was collected for him by young lawyers & that Mr Appleton furnished the facts, & a letter from Mr Swain turned the paragraph. St Peter's did not leap fullgrown out of the head of the Architect. The part that was builded instructed the eye of the next generation how to build the rest. Mirabeau has his Dumont. The tree did not come from the acorn but is an annual deposit of vegetation in a form determined by the existing disposition of the parts. Every leaf contains the eyes which are sufficient to originate a forest. The magnet is a marvel when we simply see it spontaneously wheel to the north & cling to iron like one alive. The wonder diminishes when it is shown to be only one

instance of a general law that affects all bodies & all phenomena: light, heat, electricity, animal life. A ship, a locomotive, a
cotton factory is a wonder until we see how these Romes were
not built in a day but part suggested part & complexity became simplicity. The poem, the oration, the book are superhuman, but the wonder is out when you see the manuscript.
Homer how wonderful until the German erudition discovered
a cyclus of homeric poems. It is all one; a trick of cards, a jug-
gler's sleight, an astronomical result, an algebraic formula,
amazing when we see only the result, cheap when we are
shown the means. This it is to conceive of acts & works, to
throw myself into the object so that its history shall naturally
evolve itself before me. Well so does the Universe, Time, History, evolve itself, so simply, so unmiraculously from the All
Perceiving Mind.

G.P.B. tells a ridiculous story about the boy learning his alphabet. That letter is A; says the teacher. A—drawls the boy.
"That is B," says the teacher. "B," drawls the boy, & so
on, "That letter is W," says the teacher. "The Devil! Is that
W?" enquires the pupil.—Now I say that this story hath an
alarming sound. It is the essence of Radicalism. It is Jack Cade
himself. Or is it not exquisite ridicule upon our learned Lin-
naean Classifications? What shell is this? "It is a strombus."
"The devil! is that a strombus?" would be the appropriate reply.

—

April 30. There are more purposes in Education than to keep
the man at Work. Self-questioning is one; a very important
end. The disturbance the self-discord which young men feel is
a most important crisis indispensable to a free improvable race.
Give me the eye to see a navy in an acorn.

If I could write like the wonderful bard whose sonnets I
read this afternoon I would leave all & sing songs to the
human race. Poetry with him is no verbal affair; the thought
is poetical & Nature is put under contribution to give analogies & semblances that she has never yielded before. Whether
the same or an equal tone of natural Verse is now possible?
Whether we are not two ages too late? But how remarkable
every way are Shakspear's sonnets! Those addressed to a beautiful young man seem to show some singular friendship

amounting almost to a passion which probably excited his youthful imagination. They are invaluable for the hints they contain respecting his Unknown Self. He knew his powers; he loved Spenser; he deplored his own way of living &c &c. What said C.C.E. the other day touching a common impression left by Jesus of Nazareth & this poet? . . .

The war of the telescope & the Microscope, the mass & the particular. Science ever subdivides. It separates one star into two, a nebula into a constellation, a class into genera, a genus into species & ever the most interesting facts arise from ascertaining habits of an individual. We should find the individual traits of a robin or a bee probably far more interesting than their generic habits when once we arrive to know them, as much as the traits of one dog affect us more than, though interesting, the canine character. Newton & Webster charm us more than accounts of the character of the Saxon Race.

It occurred also in the forest that there is no need to fear that the immense accumulation of scientific facts should ever incumber us since as fast as they multiply they resolve themselves into a formula which carries the world in a phial. Every common place we utter is a formula in which is packed up an uncounted list of particular observations. And every man's mind at this moment is a formula condensing the result of all his conclusions.

1 May: In this still Newton we have seven Sabbaths in a week. The day is as calm as Eternity—quite a Chaldean time.

The philosophy of the Wave. The wave moves onward but the Water of which it is composed does not. The same particle does not rise from the valley to the ridge. Its unity is only phenomenal. So is it with men. There is a revolution in this country now, is there? Well I am glad of it. But it don't convert nor punish the Jackson men nor reward the others. The Jackson men have made their fortunes; grow old; die. It is the new comers who form this Undulation. The party we wish to convince loses its identity. Elect Webster President,——& find the Jackson party if you can. All gone, dead, scattered, Webstermen, Southerners, Masons, any & every thing. Judicial or even moral sentence seems no longer capable of being inflicted.

France we say suffered & learned; but the red Revolutionists did not. France today is a new-born race that had no more to do with that regicide France than the Sandwich islanders.

3 May. The Idea according to which the Universe is made is wholly wanting to us; is it not? Yet it may or will be found to be constructed on as harmonious & perfect a thought, self explaining, as a problem in geometry. The Classification of all Nat. Science is arbitrary I believe, no Method philosophical in any one. And yet in all the permutations & combinations supposable, might not a Cabinet of shells or a Flora be thrown into one which should flash on us the very thought? We take them out of composition & so lose their greatest beauty. The moon is an unsatisfactory sight if the eye be exclusively directed to it & a shell retains but a small part of its beauty when examined separately. All our classifications are introductory & very convenient but must be looked on as temporary & the eye always watching for the glimmering of that pure plastic Idea. If Swammerdam forgets that he is a man, &, when you make any speculative suggestion as to the habits or origin or relation of insects, rebukes you with civil submission that you may think what you please he is only concerned for the facts, he loses all that for which his science is of any worth. He is a mere insect hunter, & no whit more respectable than the nuthatch or titmouse who are peeping & darting about after the same prey.

This was what Goethe sought in his Metamorphosis of plants. The Pythagorean doctrine of transmigration is an Idea; the Swedenborgian of Affections Clothed, is one also. Let the Mind of the student be in a natural, healthful, & progressive state; let him in the midst of his most minute dissection, not lose sight of the place & relations of the subject. Shun giving it a disproportionate importance but speedily adjust himself & study to see the thing though with added acquaintance of its intimate structure under the sun & in the landscape as he did before. Let it be a point as before. Integrate the particulars.

We have no Theory of animated Nature. When we have, it will be itself the true Classification. Perhaps a study of the cattle on the mountainside as they graze, is more suggestive of truth than the inspection of their parts in the dissection-room.

The way they classify is by counting stamens or filaments or teeth & hoofs & shells. A true argument, what we call the unfolding an idea, as is continually done in Plato's Dialogues, in Carlyle's Characteristics, or in a thousand acknowledged applications of familiar ethical truths, these are natural classifications containing their own reason in themselves, & making known facts continually. They are themselves the formula, the largest generalization of the facts, & if thousands on thousands more should be discovered this idea hath predicted already their place & fate. When shall such a classification be obtained in botany? This is evidently what Goethe aimed to do, in seeking the Arch plant, which, being known, would give not only all actual but all possible vegetable forms. Thus to study would be to hold the bottle under water instead of filling it drop by drop. I wrote once before that the true philosophy of man should give a theory of Beasts & Dreams. A German dispatched them both by saying that Beasts are dreams, or "the nocturnal side of Nature."

5 May. Monday—The parliamentary people say, we must not blink the question. There is an intellectual duty as imperative & as burdensome as that moral one. I come e.g. to the present subject of Classification. At the centre it is a black spot—no line, no handle, no character; I am tempted to stray to the accessible lanes on the left hand & right, which lead round it— all outside of it. Intellectual courage, intellectual duty says we must not blink the question, we must march up to it & sit down before it & watch there incessantly getting as close as we can to the black wall, and watch & watch, until slowly lines & handles & characters shall appear on its surface & we shall learn to open the gate & enter the fortress, unroof it & lay bare its ground-plan to the day.

Mr Coleridge has written well on this matter of Theory in his Friend. A lecture may be given upon insects or plants, that, when it is closed irresistibly suggests the question, 'Well what of that?' An enumeration of facts without method. A true method has no more need of firstly, secondly, &c. than a perfect sentence has of punctuation. It tells its own story, makes its own feet, creates its own form. It is its own apology. The best argument of the lawyer is a skilful telling of the story. The true Classification will not present itself to us in a catalogue of a hundred classes, but as an idea of which the flying wasp & the grazing ox are developments. Natural History is to be studied not with any pretention that its theory is attained, that its classification is permanent, but merely as full of tendency.

6 May. Well, my friend, are you not yet convinced that you should study plants & animals? To be sure the reasons are not very mighty; but words. To it again. Say then that I will study Natural history to provide me a resource when business, friends, & my country fail me, that I may never lose my temper nor be without soothing uplifting occupation. It will yet cheer me in solitude or I think in madness, that the mellow voice of the robin is not a stranger to me, that the flowers are reflections to me of earlier, happier, & yet thoughtful hours.

Or again say that I am ever haunted by the conviction that I have an interest in all that goes on around me, that I would overhear the powers what they say.—No knowledge can be spared, or any advantage we can give ourselves. And this is the knowledge of the laws by which I live. But finally say frankly, that all the reasons seem to me to fall far short of my faith upon the subject, therefore—boldly press the cause as its own evidence; say that you love nature, & would know her mysteries, & that you believe in your power by patient contemplation & docile experiment to learn them.

—

May 16. I remember when I was a boy going upon the beach & being charmed with the colors & forms of the shells. I picked up many & put them in my pocket. When I got home I could find nothing that I gathered—nothing but some dry ugly mussel & snail shells. Thence I learned that Composition was more important than the beauty of individual forms to effect. On the shore they lay wet & social by the sea & under the sky.

The sun illuminates the eye of the man but the eye & the heart of the child. His heart is in the right place.

Many eyes go through the meadow, but few see the flowers in it.

*

21 May. I will thank God of myself & for that I have. I will not manufacture remorse of the pattern of others, nor feign their joys. I am born tranquil, not a stern economist of Time but never a keen sufferer. I will not affect to suffer. Be my life then a long gratitude. I will trust my instincts. For always a reason halts after an instinct, & when I have deviated from the instinct, comes somebody with a profound theory teaching that I ought to have followed it. Some Goethe, Swedenborg, or Carlyle. I stick at scolding the boy, yet conformably to rule, I scold him. By & by the reprimand is a proven error. "Our first & third thought coincide." I was the true philosopher in college, & Mr Farrar & Mr Hedge & Dr Ware the false. Yet what seemed then to me less probable?

—

May 29. Dr Darwin's work has lost all its consequence in the literary world. Why? not from Currie nor from Brown. No. A dim venerable public decides upon every work. When it offers itself, a sort of perplexity, an uneasy waiting for judgment appears in the living literary judges, but the work presently takes its true place by no effort friendly or hostile, but by the real importance of its principles to the Constant Mind of Man. And this in a way that no individual can much affect, by blame or praise. It is the specific gravity of the atom.

An aspiring young man readily distinguishes in the first circles those who are there by sufferance & those who constitute them first circles, & attaches himself to the fountains of honor not to the conduits. The true aspirant goes one step further & discerns in himself the Fountain of these fountainlets & so becomes the giver of all fine & high influences. In him is the source of all the romance, the lustre, the dignity, that fascinates him in some saloons with an inexpressible charm; for, truth, honor, learning, perseverance are the Jove & Apollo who bewitched him.

30 May. Languages as discipline, much reading as an additional atmosphere or two, to gird the loins & make the muscles more tense. It seems time lost for a grown man to be turning the leaves of a dictionary like a boy to learn German, but I believe he will gain tension & creative power by so doing.

Good books have always a prolific atmosphere about them &
brood upon the spirit.

———

2 June. The life of women is unfortunately so much for exhibition that every trait pleases which is wholly natural, even
to a girl's crying because it thundered, et ce que disent les
femmes l'une de l'autre.   What more sensible than what
they say of Mr Cushing that he sells his splendid Chinese
house & goes to live at Watertown because he cannot make a
bow & pleasantly entertain the crowd of company that visit
him. C C E says he should build a large room.

Preached at Waltham yesterday. Expect every day when
some trenchant Iarno will come across me & read me such a
lesson. Is the preacher one to make a fool of himself for the entertainment of other people? would he say. When there is any
difference of level felt in the foot board of the pulpit & the
floor of the parlor, you have not said that which you should
say. The best sermon would be a quiet conversational analysis
of these felt difficulties, discords: to show the chain under the
leather; to show the true within the supposed advantage of
Christian institutions. There are several worthy people making
themselves less because they would act the police officer, &
keep the factory people at church. I say Be genuine. They answer, If we should, our society which has no real virtue, would
go to pot. And so the yoke it is confessed, is only borne out of
fear. Suppose they should let the societies go down, and form
new & genuine ones? Let such as felt the advantage of a sermon & social worship meet voluntarily & compel nobody.

3 June. The lower tone you take the more flexible your
voice is.

5 June. What perpetual working & counterworking in us so
that many good actions spring from bad motives & many bad
actions from good motives. Verily. Then how slovenly & despite ourselves we are continually jostled into knowledge of
truth. D.P. commends peace to the boys, the boys debate the
matter & give such cogent reasons to the contrary, that D.P. in
anger & fear to be put down, wades out beyond his depth in
the other direction, & gets unawares a knowledge of the infi-

nite reason of love. Highest praise & happiness is it to go forward one step of our own seeing & find ourselves in a position
whose advantages we foresaw.

Fatal tendency to hang on to the letter & let the spirit go.
We will debate the precept about 'turning the cheek to the
smiter,' the 'coat & cloke,' the 'not taking thought what ye
shall speak,' &c & question whether it is now practicable, & is
now obligatory. Yet every one of us has had his hours of illumination by the same spirit when he fully understood those
commands & saw that he did not need them. He had the
Commander; giving fresh precepts fit for the Moment & the
Act. Yet it is well that Christ's are recorded; they show how
high the waters flowed when the Spirit brooded upon them &
are a measure of our deficiency. The wonder that is felt at these
precepts is a measure of our Unreason.

There are persons both of superior character & intellect
whose superiority quite disappears when they are put together.
They neutralize, anticipate, puzzle, & belittle each other.

8 June. The solitary bird that sung in the pine tree reminded
me of one talker who has nothing to say alone, but when friends
come in, & the conversation grows loud, is forthwith set into
intense activity mechanically echoing & strengthening every
thing that is said, without any regard to the subject or to truth.
The soul has its diurnal, annual, & secular periodic motions
like the needle. You may doubt for a day but you will believe
before the week's end; you may abandon your friendships &
your designs as you think on good advice for these months,
but by & by it will come back as with thunder from all heaven,
that God crowns him who persists in his purposes—no fair
weather friend—that the very armory of heroes & sages is in
obscurity, conflict, high heart which sustained itself Alone.
You are there in that place to testify. There was a man in Sais
who was very good to all people but he could not be trusted
alone. When he was left alone all the devils associated themselves to him, & he robbed, murdered, committed adultery,
blasphemed, lied, cringed.

10 June. One has dim foresight of hitherto uncomputed mechanical advantages who rides on the rail-road and moreover a

practical confirmation of the ideal philosophy that Matter is phenomenal whilst men & trees & barns whiz by you as fast as the leaves of a dictionary. As our teakettle hissed along through a field of mayflowers, we could judge of the sensations of a swallow who skims by trees & bushes with about the same speed. The very permanence of matter seems compromised & oaks, fields, hills, hitherto esteemed symbols of stability do absolutely dance by you. The countryman called it 'Hell in harness.'

What habits of observation has my friend, what keen senses. It would seem as if nothing though under your nose was permitted to be visible to you until he had seen it. Thereafter, all the world may see it, & it never leaves your eyes.

Washington wanted a fit public. Aristides, Phocion, Regulus, Hampden had worthy observers. But there is yet a dearth of American genius.

I went to the Menagerie Tuesday & saw 14 pelicans, a sacred ibis, a gazelle, zebras, a capibra, ichneumon, hyena, &c. It seems to me like 'visiting the spirits in prison.' Yet not to '*preach*.' There was the mystery. No *Word* could pass from me to them. Animals have been called by some German 'the dreams of Nature.' I think we go to our own dreams for a conception of their consciousness. In a dream I have the same instinctive obedience, the same torpidity of the highest power, the same un-surprised assent to the Monstrous as these metamorphosed Men exhibit. The pelicans remind one of Nick Bottom. One has a kind of compassionate fear lest they should have a glimpse of their forlorn condition. What horrible calamity would be to them one moment's endowment of reason.

Yet sometimes the negro excites the same feeling & sometimes the sharpwitted prosperous white man. You think if he could overlook his own condition he could not be kept from suicide. But to the contemplations of the Reason is there never penitence.

———

The scholar seeks the ingenuous boy to apprize him of the treasures within his reach, to show him poetry, religion, philosophy, & congratulate him on being born into the Universe. The boy's parents immediately call to thank him for his interest in their Son & ask him to procure him a Schoolmaster's situation. 18 June. Every thing teaches, even dilettantism. The dilettante does not, to be sure, learn anything of botany by playing with his microscope & with the terminology of plants but he learns what dilettantism is; he distinguishes between what he knows & what he affects to know & through some pain & self accusation he is attaining to things themselves.

Webster's speeches seem to be the utmost that the unpoetic West has accomplished or can. We all lean on England, scarce a verse, a page, a newspaper but is writ in imitation of English forms, our very manners & conversation are traditional & sometimes the life seems dying out of all literature & this enormous paper currency of Words is accepted instead. I suppose the evil may be cured by this rank rabble party, the Jacksonism of the country, heedless of English & of all literature—a stone cut out of the ground without hands—they may root out the hollow dilettantism of our cultivation in the coarsest way & the new-born may begin again to frame their own world with greater advantage. Meantime Webster is no imitator but a true genius for his work if that is not the highest. But every true man stands on the top of the world. He has a majestic understanding, which is in its right place the servant of the reason, & employed ever to bridge over the gulf between the revelations of his Reason, his Vision, & the facts within in the microscopic optics of the calculators that surround him. Long may he live.

It is singular that every natural object how wearisome soever in daily observation is always agreeable in description & doubly so in illustration.

20 June. What a charm does 'Wilhelm Meister' spread over society which we were just getting to think odious. And yet as I read the book today & thought of Goethe as the Tag und Jahres Hefte describes him, he seemed to me—all-sided, gifted, indefatigable student as he is,—to be only another poor monad after the fashion of his little race bestirring himself immensely to hide his nothingness, spinning his surface directly before the eye to conceal the Universe of his ignorance. The finest poems of the world have been expedients to get bread or

else expedients to keep the writer from the madhouse & amuse him & his fellowmen with the illusion that he knew; but the greatest passages they have writ, the infinite conclusions to which they owe their fame are only confessions. Throughout Goethe prevails the undersong of confession & amazement; the apophthegm of Socrates; the recantation of Man. The first questions are always to be asked, & we fend them off by much speaking & many books. So that scarcely can I blame the man who affects to philosophize as some sensualists do, & says his fun is profound calculation. And yet it is best in the poorest view to keep the powers healthy & supple by appropriate action. All things, complained the philosopher, hasten back to Unity.

The bells in America toll because Lafayette has died in France. The bells in all the earth, in church, monastery, castle, & pagoda might well toll for the departure of so pure, faithful, heroic, secular a Spirit out of the earth to which it has been salt & spikenard. Go in, great heart! to the Invisible, to the Kingdom of love & faith. He has

> "Lingered among the last of those bright clouds
> Which on the steady breeze of Honor sail
> In long procession calm & beautiful."

It occurred that the gestures of the Reason are graceful & majestic, those of the Understanding quick & mean. The uplifted eye of Memory, the solemn pace, perfect repose & simple attitudes of Meditation inspire respect, but the moment the senses call us back, & the Understanding directs us, we run, start, look askance, or turn & look behind us, we skulk, fumble, exceed in manner & voice, & suffer. Live by Reason, & you will not make the foul mouths, nor utter the foul breath, nor drag disgracefully sleepy days that convince Alexander that he is mortal. When Minerva, they say, saw her distorted face in a brook she threw away her hautboy.

June 26. If friendship were perfect there would be no false prayers. But what could Wilhelm have done at the Crab's house?

The rare women that charm us are those happily constituted persons who take possession of society wherever they go & give it its form, its tone. If they sit as we sit to wait for what shall be said we shall have no Olympus. To their genius elegance is essential. It is enough that we men stammer & mince words & play the clown & pedant alternately. They must speak as cleanly & simply as a song. I say all this is a happiness not a merit, & few there be that find it. Society cannot give it, nor the want of society withhold it. Aunt Mary & S.A.R. never wait for the condescending influences of society, but seek it out, scrutinize it, amuse themselves with the little, sympathize with & venerate the great. And Ellen in a life of solitude was incapable of an inelegance.

Yesterday the attentions of the poor girl with flowers made me think how elegant is kindness. Kindness is never vulgar. Genius & strong Will may be only phenomena in the chain of causes & most men & women may grow up to be what they are as the cows & horses grow in the pastures but Kindness from a perfect stranger—a sudden will to benefit me & every body is a salient spring, it is a hint of the presence of the living God. The condition of young women even the most favored excites sometimes a profound pity. 'When a daughter is born,' said the Sheking 'she sleeps on the ground, she is clothed with a wrapper, she plays with a tile, she is incapable either of evil or of good.' But kindness, native courtesy redeems them at once out of your pity; they are happy & the objects of your joy & your respect.

> "Happy, happier far than thou,
>   With the laurel on thy brow,
>   She who makes the humblest hearth
>   Lovely but to one on earth"

Next door to us lives a young man who is learning to drum. He studies hard at his science every night. I should like to reward his music with a wreath of smilax peduncularis.

Goethe & Carlyle & perhaps Novalis have an undisguised dislike or contempt for common virtue standing on common principles. Meantime they are dear lovers, steadfast maintainers of the pure ideal Morality. But they worship it as the highest beauty; their love is artistic. Praise Socrates to them, or Fenelon, much more any inferior contemporary good man & they freeze at once into silence. It is to them sheer prose.

The *Tag und Jahres Hefte* is a book unparalleled in America, an account of all events, persons, studies, taken from one point of view. The problem to be solved, is, How shall this soul called *Goethe* be educated? And whatever he does or whatever befals him is viewed solely in relation to its effect upon the development of his mind. Even in the arms of his mistress at Rome he says he studied sculpture & poetry.

To husband our admiration is an intellectual temperance indispensable to health. But Goethe was a person who hated words that did not stand for things, & had a sympathy with every thing that existed, & therefore never writes without saying something. He will be Artist, & look at God & Man, & the Future, & the infinite, as a self-possessed spectator, who believed that what he saw he could delineate. Herder wisely questioned whether a man had a right thus to affect the god instead of working with all his heart in his place. Self-cultivation is yet the moral of all that G. has writ, & in indolence, intolerance, & perversion, I think we can spare an olive & a laurel for him.

No man has drawn his materials of fiction from so wide a circuit. Very properly he introduces into the machinery of his romance whatever feeling or impulse the most rapt enthusiast has trusted in. Coincidences, dreams, omens, spiritual impressions, & a habitual religious faith—all these are the materials which as a wise Artist he avails himself of.

Nevertheless there is a difference between thought & thought, & it is as real a defect in a man not to perceive the right of his moral sentiments to his allegiance, as it is not to be conscious of moral sentiments. Yet Goethe with all his fine things about *Entsagen* can write & print too like Rochester & Beranger.

As to Carlyle, he is an exemplification of Novalis's maxim concerning the union of Poetry & Philosophy. He has married them, & both are the gainers. Who has done so before as truly & as well? Sartor Resartus is a philosophical Poem.

Nov. 30.

Goethe is praised as μυριονους or all-sided. And if I under-stand it this is the apology that is made for his epicurean life compared with his religious perceptions. To praise a man for such quality is like praising an observatory for being very low & massive & a very good fort. It is not more the office of man to receive all impressions, than it is to distinguish sharply between them. He that has once pronounced intelligently the word "Self-renouncement," "Invisible Leader," "Powers of Sorrow", & the like, is forever bound to the service of the Superhuman.

We are wonderfully protected. We have scarce a misfortune, a hindrance, an infirmity, an enemy, but it is somehow produc-tive of singular advantage to us. After groaning thro' years of poverty & hard labor the mind perceives that really it has come the shortest road to a valuable position, that though the rough climate was not good for leaves & flowers, it was good for tim-ber. It has been saved from what associations. It has been in-troduced to what thoughts & feelings. 'He knows you not ye mighty Powers! who knows not sorrow.' God brings us by ways we know not & like not into Paradise.

12 July. *On War. Chap I.* Assacombuit a sagamore of the Anasagunticook tribe was remarkable for his turpitude & fe-rocity. He was above all other known Indians inhuman & cruel. In 1705 Vaudreuil sent him to France, & he was intro-duced to the king. When he appeared at court, he lifted up his hand, & said, "This hand has slain 150 of your Majesty's ene-mies within the territories of New England." This so pleased the king that he forthwith knighted him, & ordered a pension of eight livres a day to be paid him during life. On his return home, he undertook to exercise a despotic sway over his brethren in which he murdered one & stabbed another, & thus exasperated their relations to such a degree, that they sought to take his life, & would have killed him, had he not fled his country. See Williamson, Hist. of Maine, Vol 2. p. 69.

On War Chap. II. At the close of the ten years' war in 1713 (after the treaty of Utrecht,) there was now in Maine "scarcely remaining a vestige of the fur trade, the lumber-business, or the fisheries. What we call enterprize excited no emulation. The virtues of the people in these times were of another & higher order;—courage, fortitude, & brotherly kindness. These appeared in nameless exploits & in thousands of occurrences every year." See Williamson, p. 68. Vol 2.

"Lincoln bell flings o'er the fen
His far renowned alarum."

I read this & straight regret that I did not visit Lincoln Cathedral & hear the far renowned alarum; such superstitious preference do we give to other men's senses. Undoubtedly something in my own sphere or spherule takes the place to me of that particular gratification. I have some 'Lincoln bell'— heard with joy in my ordinary movements. Yet I long to hear this other, simply out of deference to my fellows in England who have exalted it by their love. Better believe in the perfection of thine own lot. Retreat upon your own spontaneous emotions. Mark the occasions of them, & cheerfully believe that what has excited true & deep pleasure in one man is fitted to excite the same emotions in all men. So will I find my Lincolnshire in the next pasture & the 'bell' in the first thrush that sings. Napoleon sat back on his horse in the midst of the march to catch the fine tone of a bell. With myself I shall always dwell, but Lincoln & Niagara & Cairo are less accessible. And yet and yet can aught approach the effect of the Sabbath Morn in quietest retreats? And yet is its sacredness derivative & alien. Some thoughts are superficial,—others have their root in your being. Always discriminate when you would write, between them & never chuse the first for a topic. Diogenes moved his tub in winter into the sun, & in summer into the shade, & compared himself to the Persian King who spent the one season at Susa & the other at Ecbatana.

"As many languages as a man knows, said Charles V., so many times is he a man." Our eagerness to possess this gift of foreign speech rather hinders than helps us to it. I stand in a company where circulates how much wit & information, yet not one thought can pass from them to me,—I do not understand their speech. My countryman enters who understands it & the communication between them & him, is perfect. Stung with desire I devote myself to the task of learning the language but this perpetual poetic vision before me which is quite foreign from their experience, & which I shall lose as soon as I master the speech, affords me so much entertainment as to embarrass every particular effort at dialogue & dispirits me & unfits me for simple effort to know the thing said to me, & to convey my thought in return, which is the best instructer. Ralph Emerson said to me in Paris, that the Americans think there is some magic in speaking & writing French. He who has mastered the tongue sees nothing behind him but simple addition of particulars, & this new knowledge blends harmoniously with all his experience; and, moreover, it has lost all its anticipated value.

When the wrong handle is grasped of comparative anatomy the tresses of beauty remind us of a mane. How much is an assembly of men restrained! It seems often like a collection of angels, & a collection of demons in disguise.

> Come dal fuoco il caldo, esser diviso
> Non puo'l bel dall' eterno. *M. Angelo B*

The great Spirit has given every tribe of Indians a goodly river with fine salmon. The Indian has rights & loves good as well as the Englishman. We have a sense too of what is kind & great. When you first came from the morning waters, we took you into our open arms. We thought you children of the sun. We fed you with our best meat. Never went white man cold & starving from an Indian wigwam.

We are now told that the country spreading far from the sea is passed away to you forever—perhaps for nothing,—because of the names & seals of our sagamores. Such deeds be far from them! They never turned their children from their homes to suffer: their souls were too great. The English law-makers took our lands when they had given us rum.

*

It was an Indian maxim 'That the first blow is the best part of the battle.' They said of Sir William Pepperell "that whatever he willed came to pass." Williamson Hist. of Maine.

—

Noble strain of the revolutionary papers. See Williamson Vol 2 pp 408, 9, 10, 11. And when the port of Boston had been closed (in June 1774) 16 days they tolled the bells in the town of Falmouth all day, & addressed an affectionate letter to the inhabitants of Boston. "We look upon you," they say, "as sufferers for the common cause of American liberty. We highly appreciate your courage to endure privation & distress —sensibly aware that the season puts to severest trial, the virtues of magnanimity, patience, & fortitude, which your example will honorably exemplify. We beg leave to tender you all the encouragements which the considerations of friendship & respect can inspire, & all the assurances of succor which full hearts & feeble abilities can render."

July 18. The abomination of desolation is not a burned town nor a country wasted by war but the discovery that the man who has moved you, is an enthusiast upon calculation.

"Indeed all that class of the severe & restrictive virtues are at a market almost too high for humanity." May be so. That gives them their worth. It is that we ourselves the observers have been imposed upon & led to condemn the actor before, & the farsighted heroism of the sufferer has felt the condemnation & yet persisted in his own judgment & kept up his courage—it is that conviction that adds eagerness to our commendation now.

What is there of the divine in a load of bricks? What is there of the divine in a barber's shop or a privy? Much. All. Yesterday at the installation they seemed like woodsawyers dressed up. It would not out of my imagination. By & by a true priest spoke.

George A. Sampson died Wednesday evening 23 July, 1834.

Newton 9 August. Carlyle says, Society is extinct. Be it so. Society existed in a clan; existed in Alaric & Attila's time, in the Crusades, in the Puritan Conventicles. Very well. I had rather be solitary as now, than social as then. Society exists now where there is love & faithful fellow working. Only the persons composing it are fewer—societies of two or three, instead of nations. Societies, parties are only incipient stages, tadpole states of man as caterpillars are social but the butterfly not. The true & finished man is ever alone. Men cannot satisfy him; he needs God, & his intercourse with his brother is ever condescending, & in a degree hypocritical.

He charged them that they should tell no man. "Hold thy tongue for one day; tomorrow thy purpose will be clearer." Why yea, & it would be good if the minister put off his black clothes & so affirmed the reality of spiritual distinctions. When I was at the ordination at Bangor the other day the men in the pulpit seemed woodsawyers dressed up, as they stood up & spoke in succession. It would not out of my head. By & by a true priest spoke. x x x Renounce. Work hard. In the great heats why should you leave your labor for a little sweat, since the haymaker does not? He *cannot*; therefore, if you are noble, you will not. Renounce. When I was in the pasture & stopped to eat, the familiar cried, Eat not. Tut, replied I, does Nemesis care for a whortleberry? I looked at the world, & it replied, Yea. But the clock struck two & the table was covered with fishes & fowls & confections. They are very good & my appetite is keen, & I could not see any good in refusing the pleasure of a hearty meal that was as great as the pleasure. Look back, cried the familiar, at years of good meat in Boston. Do you miss any thing that you forbore to eat? Nothing, replied I.

First thoughts are from God; but not the numerically first; allow what space you may, for the mind to grasp the facts, then the thoughts that are first in place are divine & the second earthly.

Sunday, 10 Aug. At Mr Grafton's church this P.M. and heard the eloquent old man preach his Jewish sermon dryeyed. Indeed I felt as a much worse spirit might feel among worshippers—as if the last link was severed that bound him to their traditions & he ought to go out hence. Strange that such fatuity as Calvinism is now, should be able to stand yet—mere shell as it is—in the face of day. At every close of a paragraph it almost seemed as if this devout old man looked intelligence &

questioned the whole thing. What a revival if St Paul should come & replace these threadbare rags with the inexhaustible resources of sound Ethics. Yet they are so befooled as to call this sucked eggshell hightoned orthodoxy, & to talk of anything true as *mere morality*. Is it not time to present this matter of Christianity exactly as it is, to take away all false reverence from Jesus, & not mistake the stream for the source? 'It is no more according to Plato than according to me.' God is in every man. God is in Jesus but let us not magnify any of the vehicles as we magnify the Infinite Law itself. We have defrauded him of his claim of love on all noble hearts by our superstitious mouth honor. We love Socrates but give Jesus the Unitarian Association—.

See two sincere men conversing together. They deport themselves as if self-existent. Are they not for the time two Gods? For every true man is as if he should say, I speak for the Universe; I am here to maintain the truth against all comers; I am in this place to testify.

August 11. Is not man in our day described by the very attributes which once he gave his God? Is not the sea his minister; the clouds his chariot; the flame his wheels; & the winds his wings?

August 13. Blessed is the child; the Unconscious is ever the act of God himself. Nobody can reflect upon his *unconscious* period or any particular word or act in it, with regret or contempt. Bard or Hero cannot look down upon the word or gesture of a child; it is as great as they. Little Albert Sampson asks when his father will come home, & insists that *his father can't die*.

August 14. We look up sometimes with surprize to see that the tree, the hill, the schoolhouse are still there, & have not vanished in our mood of pyrrhonism. If there were many philosophers, the world would go to pieces presently, all sand, no lime. Quam parva sapientia. All society & government seems to be *making believe* when we see such hollow boys with a grave countenance taking their places as legislators, Presidents, & so forth. It could not be but that at intervals throughout society there are real men intermixed whose natural basis is broad enough to sustain these paper men in common times, as the carpenter puts one iron bar in his banister to five or six wooden ones.

Yet when at other times I consider the capacities of man & see how near alike they all are & that always seem to be on the edge of all that is great & yet invisibly retained in inactivity & unacquaintance with our powers, it seems as if men were like the neuters of the hive every one of which is capable of transformation into the Queenbee, which is done with some one as soon as the sovereign is removed. The fourth chapter of my Meditation is the observation that the soul or the day is a turning wheel which brings every one of its manifold faces for a brief season to the top. Now this dunghill quality of animal courage, indomitable pluck, seems to be the supreme virtue; anon, patience; then elegance; then learning; then wit; then eloquence; then wealth; then piety; then beauty; each seems in turn the one desireable quality & thus every dog has his day.

It occurred furthermore that the fine verse of "Honorable age" &c in Wisd. of Solomon is quite Greek in its genius, not Jewish.

For the Lecture on Nat. Hist.

August 15. Natural history by itself has no value; it is like a single sex. But marry it to human history, & it is poetry. Whole Floras, all Linnaeus' & Buffon's volumes contain not one line of poetry, but the meanest natural fact, the habit of a plant, the organs, or work, or noise of an insect applied to the interpretation of or even associated with a fact in human nature is beauty, is poetry, is truth at once.

August 16, Saturday Eve. King Lear & Ant. & Cleopatra still fill me with wonder. Every scene is as spirited as if writ by a fresh hand of the first class and there is never straining; sentiments of the highest elevation are as simply expressed as the stage directions. They praise Scott for taking kings & nobles off their stilts & giving them simple dignity but Scott's grandees are all turgid compared with Shakspear's. There is more true elevation of character in Prince Hal's sentence about the pleached doublet than in any king in the romances.

Another mastership of Shakspear is the immortality of the style; the speeches of passion are writ for the most part in a style as fresh now as it was when the play was published. The remarkable sentences of Lear, Hamlet, Othello, Macbeth, might as naturally have been composed in 1834 as in 1600.

> "I tax not you ye elements with unkindness
> I never gave you kingdoms, called you daughters
> You owe me no subscription &c"

August 17. Freedom. A very small part of a man's voluntary acts are such as agree perfectly with his conviction & it is only at rare intervals that he is apprized of this incongruity—"so difficult is it to read our own consciousness without mistakes." Whose act is this churchgoing? Whose this praying? The man might as well be gone so he leave a Maelzel machine in his place.

On the wisdom of ignorance.

Evg. Milton was too learned, though I hate to say it. It wrecked his originality. He was more indebted to the Hebrew than even to the Greek. Wordsworth is a more original poet than he. That seems the poet's garland. He speaks by that right that he has somewhat yet unsaid to say. Scott & Coleridge & such like are not poets, only professors of the art. Homer's is the only Epic. He is original yet he separates before the German telescopes into two, ten, or twenty stars. Shakspeare by singular similarity of fortune undeniably an original & unapproached bard—first of men,—is yet infolded in the same darkness as an individual Writer. His best works are of doubted authenticity and what was his, & what his novelist's, & what the players', seems yet disputed. A sharp illustration of that relentless disregard of the individual in regard for the race which runs through history. It is not an individual but the general mind of man that speaks from time to time quite careless & quite forgetful of what mouth or mouths it makes use. Go to the bard or orator that has spoken & ask him if what he said were his own? No. He got it he knows not where, but it is none of his. For example; Edward Emerson whence had you those thunderous sentences in your 'Master's Oration'? There is nothing in Wordsworth so vicious in sentiment as Milton's account of God's chariots, &c. standing harnassed for great days. We republicans cannot relish Watts' or Milton's royal imagery.

Is it not true that contemplation belongs to us & therefore outward worship *because* our reason is at discord with our understanding? And that whenever we live rightly thought will express itself in ordinary action so fully as to make a special action, that is, a religious form impertinent? Is not Solomon's temple built because Solomon is not a temple, but a brothel & a change house? Is not the meeting-house dedicated because men are not? Is not the Church opened & filled on Sunday because the commandments are not kept by the worshippers on Monday? But when he who worships there, speaks the truth, follows the truth, is the truth's; when he awakes by actual Communion to the faith that God is in him, will he need any temple, any prayer? The very fact of worship declares that God is not at one with himself, that there are two gods. Now does this sound like high treason & go to lay flat all religion? It does threaten our forms but does not that very word 'form' already sound hollow? It threatens our forms but it does not touch injuriously Religion. Would there be danger if there were real religion? If the doctrine that God is in man were faithfully taught & received, if I lived to speak the truth & enact it, if I pursued every generous sentiment as one enamoured, if the majesty of goodness were reverenced: would not such a principle serve me by way of police at least as well as a Connecticutt Sunday?

But the people, the people. You hold up your pasteboard religion for the people who are unfit for a true. So you say. But presently there will arise a race of preachers who will take such hold of the omnipotence of truth that they will blow the old falsehood to shreds with the breath of their mouth. There is no material show so splendid, no poem so musical as the great law of Compensation in our moral nature. When an ardent mind once gets a glimpse of that perfect beauty & sees how it envelopes him & determines all his being, will he easily slide back to a periodic shouting about 'atoning blood'? I apprehend that the religious history of society is to show a pretty rapid abandonment of forms of worship & the renovation & exaltation of preaching into real anxious instruction.

18 Aug. The Mussulman is right by virtue of the law of Compensations in supposing the scraps of paper he saves will be a carpet under his feet over the bridge of Purgatory. He has learned the lesson of reverence to the name of Allah.

19 Aug. Never assume. Be genuine. So wrote I for my own guidance months & years ago but how vainly! Show me in the world the sincere man. Even the wit the sentiment that seasons the dinner is a sort of hypocrisy to hide the coarseness of appetite. The child is sincere, and the man when he is alone, if he be not a writer, but on the entrance of the second person hypocrisy begins.

What mischief is in this art of Writing. An unlettered man considers a fact to learn what it means; the lettered man does not sooner see it than it occurs to him how it can be told. And this fact of looking at it as an artist blinds him to the better half of the fact. Unhappily he is conscious of the misfortune which rather makes it worse. As cultivated flowers turn their stamina to petals so does he turn the practick part to idle show. He has a morbid growth of eyes; he sees with his feet. What an unlucky creature is Dr Channing. Let him into a room; would not all the company feel that simple as he looked, the cat was not more vigilant, that he had the delirium tremens & its insomnolency, that he heard what dropped from any as if he read it in print?

We sit down with intent to write truly & end with making a book that contains no thought of ours but merely the tune of the time. Here am I writing a ΦBK poem free to say what I choose & it looks to me now as if it would scarce express thought of mine but be a sort of fata Morgana reflecting the images of Byron, Shakspear, & the newspapers.

We do what we can, & then make a theory to prove our performance the best.

21 Aug. How much alike are all sorts of excellence: Mr Webster's arguments like Shakspear's plays. One wakes up occasionally with a desire to unfold the simplest facts; to announce for example to the world the delight that is to be found in

reading; & to commend to their especial attention Shakspear's
Antony & Cleopatra.

August 22. The greatest men have been most thoughtful for
the humblest. Socrates, of whom see the fine story told in
Plutarch on Tranquillity, Alfred, Franklin, Jesus Christ, & all
the Pauls & Fenelons he has made. It requires no ordinary elevation to go by the social distinctions & feel that interest in
humanity itself which is implied in attentions to the obscure.
Wordsworth is a philanthropist; Fox; Wilberforce; Howard;
Montaigne. And, so keep me heaven, I will love the race in
general if I cannot in any particular. Washington introduced
the ass into America.

  30 August. Were it not a heroic adventure in me to insist on
being a popular speaker & run full tilt against the Fortune who
with such beautiful consistency shows evermore her back?
Charles's naïf censure last night provoked me to show him a
fact apparently wholly new to him that my entire success, such
as it is, is composed wholly of particular failures,—every public
work of mine of the least importance, having been (probably
without exception) noted at the time as a failure. The only success (agreeably to common ideas) has been in the country &
there founded on the false notion that here was a Boston
preacher. I will take Miss Barbauld's line for my motto "And
the more falls I get, move faster on."

  I never was on a coach which went fast enough for me.

  It is extremely disagreeable, nay, a little fiendish to laugh
amid dreams. In bed I would keep my countenance, if you
please.

  A poem is made up of thoughts each of which filled the
whole sky of the poet in its turn.

  Newton, Sept. 13. There are some things which we should
do if we considered only our own capacity & safety, which we
stick at doing when we think of the estimates & prejudices of

other people. For the freest man society still holds some bribe.
He wants of it a living, or a friend, or a wife, or a fit employment, or a reputation correspondent to his self esteem. Is it
not possible to draw in his importunate beggar hands & ask
nothing but what he can himself satisfy? In some respects certainly. In this matter of reputation—is it not possible to settle
it in one's mind immoveably that merit of the first class cannot
in the nature of things be readily appreciated; that immortal
deeds over which centuries are to pass as days, are not brought
to light & wholly comprehended & decided upon in a few
hours? The wise man is to settle it immoveably in his mind,
that he only is fit to decide on his best action; he only is fit to
praise it; his verdict is praise enough, and as to society, 'their
hiss is thine applause.' It is an ordinary enhancement of our
admiration of noble thinking & acting that it was done in wilful defiance of present censure out of a clear foresight of the
eternal praise of the just. Let others be born to castles & manners & influence. Be thou a noble man. Be a man to whom
meanness & duplicity are impossible. Overlook from thy judgment seat IN ETERNITY the titled & the untitled rabble, &
in thy heart call them all rabble whilst they judge externally,
though their names be Scott & Canning & Brougham & Webster & England & America. Next, as to thoughts of the first
class. Do not cease to utter them & make them as pure of all
dross as if thou wert to speak to sages & demigods and be no
whit ashamed if not one, yea, not one in the assembly should
give sign of intelligence. Make it not worthy of the beggar to
receive but of the emperor to give. Is it not pleasant to you,
unexpected wisdom? depth of sentiment in middle life? Iarnos
& Abbés that in the thick of the crowd are true kings & gentlemen without the harness & the envy of the throne? Is it not
conceivable that a man or a woman in coarse clothes may have
unspeakable comfort in being the only human being privy to a
virtuous action which he or she is in the act of consummating?

But the young gentlemen & ladies of the present day care
not for the worth of the action, so it *shines*, nor for the nobleness of reputation, so the name be well-aired.

Perhaps you cannot carry too far the doctrine of self respect.
The story that strikes me; the joke that makes me laugh often;
the face that bewitches me; the flower, the picture, the building,

that, left to myself, I prefer—these I ought to remember, love, & praise. For there is nothing casual or capricious in the impression they make (Provided always that I act naturally,) but they make this strong impression because I am fit for them & they are fit for me. But if I forsake my peculiar tastes overawed by the popular voice or deferring to Mr Everett's or Mr Wordsworth's or Baron Swedenborg's tastes I am straightway dwarfed of my natural dimensions for want of fit nourishment & fit exercise. It is as if you should fill the stomach of a horse with the food of a fish. Lean without fear on your own tastes. Is there danger in the doctrine as if it permitted self indulgence? Fool! Every man hath his own Conscience as well as his own Genius & if he is faithful to himself he will yield that Law implicit obedience. All these doctrines contained in the proposition Thou art sufficient unto thyself (Nec te quaesiveris extra) are perfectly harmless on the supposition that they are heard as well as spoken in faith. There is no danger in them to him who is really in earnest to know the truth but like every thing else may be a mere hypocrite's cloak to such as seek offence. Or to such as talk for talk's sake.

Lean without fear on your own tastes. But the young gentlemen of the day choose their profession by what they call public opinion; & marry for the eyes of others; & dwell in town though they prefer the country & postpone what they love to what is popular.

Sunday, Sept. 14

What is the doctrine of *infallible guidance* if *one will abdicate choice*, but striving to act unconsciously, to resume the simplicity of childhood? It is to act on the last impression derived from a knowledge of all the facts & not wilfully to secure a particular advantage. The single minded actor insists on the tranquillity of his own mind.

———

Nec te quaesiveris extra. I would insist so far on my own tastes as to read those books I fancy & postpone reading those which offer me no attraction. If Dr Lindberg would have me study Swedenborg because I have respect for his doctrines, I shall hold it sufficient answer that the aura of those books is not agreeable to my intellectual state. See p. 368 I will not so far do violence to myself as to read them against my inclination, believing that those books which at any time I crave are the books fittest at that time for me. This is Carlyle's justification for giving such humorous prominence to such incidents as George Fox's leather suit of clothes. If I obey my passion instead of my reason that is another affair. The appeal is always open from Philip drunk to Philip sober.

Sept. 15. Heard Mr Blagden preach yesterday with much interest. What an orator would some extraordinary discipline of events make of him. Could some Socrates win him to the love of the True & the Beautiful; or extreme sorrows arouse the mighty interior reactions; or revolutionary violence call into life the best ambition; could any event acquaint him with himself, he would with his rare oratorical talents absolutely command us. His manner is the best I know of, and seems to me unexceptionable. As to his preaching that was good too in the main. The skeleton of his sermon, or, as Charles called it, the frame of his kite, was fallacious, illogical after the most ordinary fashion of the Wisners & Beechers but his strong genius led him continually to penetrate this husk & leaning simply on himself speak the truth out of this unnecessary mask. The conflict of the tradition & of his own genius is visible throughout. He gets his hands & eyes up in describing Jehovah exalted as in Calvinistic state, & then saves the whole by ending with— "in the heart's affections." I listen without impatience because though the whole is literally false, it is really true; only he speaks Parables which I translate as he goes. Thus, he says, 'the carnal mind hates God continually': & I say, 'It is the instinct of the understanding to contradict the reason.' One phrase translates the other.

The charm of Italy is the charm of its names. I have seen as fine days from my own window. Then what Boswellism it is to travel! Illustrate, eternize your own woodhouse. It is much cheaper & quite possible to any resolute thinker. What matters it I said to myself on my journey as the persons in the coach disputed as to the name of the town, whether this bunch of barberry bushes & birches visible from the coach window be called Bridgewater or Taunton. So, what matter whether this hill & yon green field be called Garofalo, Terni or Ipswich & Cape Cod. Let the soul once be fully awake & its thought is so much that the place becomes nothing. Remember the Sunday morning in Naples when I said 'This moment is the truest vision, the best spectacle I have seen amid all the wonders & this moment, this vision, I might have had in my own closet in Boston.' Hence learn that it is an unworthy superstition for seers to go to Italy or France & come home & describe houses & things. Let them see men & magnify the passages of common life. Let them be so Man-wise that they can see through the coat, the rank, the language & sympathize promptly with that other self that under these thin disguises wholly corresponds to their own. See what I wrote, p. 330, on Lincoln bell.

You do not know any Socrates. Very likely. The philosopher whom you have admired in discourse makes a different impression in private life. Very likely. Most men do: their aims are not distinct enough. As his aim becomes more distinct it will insensibly pervade & characterize his private action, his manners, his table-talk.

A brilliant young man easily becomes a satellite to some rich or powerful or eloquent man or set of men but as soon as he reflects, he is transformed from a Satellite into a central orb, & rich & great & kings & idols revolve around him.

A man in the New Bedford coach told me a story of a lady who took an egg in her hand & the warmth of her body hatching it the little serpents came out & ran all over her hand.

The whole matter of Riches & Poverty is reversed by the act of reflexion, whenever it begins. The intellect at once takes possession of another's wealth & habits & performances as if it were its own. Who is rich in the room where Socrates sits but he? Whilst Webster speaks to the Senate who is formidable but he? The Intellect fairly excited overleaps all bounds with equal ease & is as easily master of millions as master of one. With each divine impulse it rends the thin rinds of the visible & finite & comes out into Eternity, inspires & expires its air. It converses with truths that have always been spoken in the world & becomes conscious of a closer sympathy with Phocion & Epictetus than with the persons in the house.

P.M.

No art càn exceed the mellow beauty of one square rood of ground in the woods this afternoon. The noise of the locust, the bee, & the pine, the light, the insect forms, butterflies, cankerworms hanging, balloon spiders swinging, devil's-needles cruising, chirping grasshoppers; the tints & forms of the leaves & trees. Not a flower but its form seems a type, not a capsule but is an elegant seed box. Then the myriad asters, polygalas, and golden rods & through the bush the far pines, & overhead the eternal sky. All the pleasing forms of art are imitations of these, & yet before the beauty of a right action all this beauty is cold & unaffecting.

———

Young men struck with particular observations begin to make collections of related truths & please themselves as Burton did with thinking the wheel, an arc of whose curve they discern, will, by their careful addition of arc to arc as they descry them, by & by come full circle, & be contained in the field of their vision. By & by they learn that the addition of particular facts brings them no nearer to the completion of an infinite orbit.

Shall I say that the use of Natural Science seems merely ancillary to Moral? I would learn the law of the diffraction of a ray because when I understand it, it will illustrate, perhaps suggest, a new truth in ethics.

He knew what was in man.

16 Sept.

How despicable are the starts, sidelong glances, & lookings back of suspicious men. Go forward & look straight ahead though you die for it. Abernethy says in his Hunter book, that the eye-sockets are so formed in the gods & heroes of Greek Sculpture that it would be impossible for such eyes to squint & take furtive glances on this side & that. You have looked behind you at the passenger & caught his eye looking behind

also. What dastards you both are for that moment! The unconscious forever which turns the whole head or nothing!

17 Sept. Make a very slight change in the point of view, &
the most familiar objects are the most interesting. We read our
own advertisement in the newspaper. In a camera obscura the
butcher's cart & the figure of one's own barber or washer-
woman delight us. Turn the head upside down by looking at
the landscape through your own legs & how charming is the
picture though of your own woodhouse & barnyard.

How truly has poetry represented the difficulty of reflexion
in the story of Proteus or Silenus is it? & in that of Odin's
Prophetess. Any evasion, any digression, any thing but sitting
down before the gates with immoveable determination that
they must open. One of the forms the Proteus takes is that of
civil self depreciation. 'You quite mistake, sir; I am not that
you took me for. A poor evanescent topic really not worth
your consideration; it was my resemblance to a relation that
deceived you. Had you not better seek that?'

September 21. The poet writes for readers he little thinks of.
Persons whom he could not bear, & who could not bear him,
yet find passages in his works which are to them as their own
thoughts.

———

There is in some men as it were a preexistent harmony stab-
lished between them & the course of events so that they *will* at
the precise moment that which God *does*. They are pitched to
the tune of the time. Or shall I say they are like the fly in the
coach.

22 Sept. One is daunted by every one of a multitude of rules
which we read in books of criticism but when we speak or
write *unconsciously* we are carried through them all safely without offending or perceiving one.

October 6. In September the roads & woods were full of
crickets & as fast as one falls by the way the rest eat him up.

Wind & seed. Every thing may be painted, every thing sung. But to be poetized

The high prize of eloquence may be mine, the joy of uttering what no other can utter & what all must receive.

I thought how much not how little accomplishment in manners, speech, practick address an open eye discovers in each passenger. If an equal vitality is dealt out to each man how strange if diverging by all that force from your line your neighbor had not attained a degree of mastery in one sort admirable to you. Insist on yourself. Never imitate. For your own talent you can present every moment with all the force of a lifetime's cultivation but of the adopted stolen talent of anybody else you have only a frigid brief extempore half possession. Adhere to your own & produce it with the meek courage that intimates This possession is my all; is my inheritance from Almighty God & must have value.

To be poetized any object must be lifted from off its feet.

Disgusting to have genius treated as a medical fact, an inflammation of the brain, & thought & poetry as evacuations.

"One first question I ask of every man; Has he an aim which with undivided soul he follows & advances towards? Whether his aim is a right one or a wrong one forms but my second question."

14 Oct. Every involuntary repulsion that arises in your mind give heed unto. It is the surface of a central truth. Madame de Stael's Works & Plutarch & Bacon & Coleridge were a library to retire with.

18 Oct. New York. Received the tidings of the death of my dear brother Edward on the first day of this month at St John's, Porto Rico. So falls one pile more of hope for this life. I see I am bereaved of a part of myself.

> "Whatever fortunes wait my future life
> The beautiful is vanished & returns not."

In Boston, at Second Church, George Sampson told me after I preached my sermon on Habit, that Mr Washburn said to him, that "he wished he was in the habit of hearing such sermons as that;" which speech I found to be good praise & good blame.

27 October. "Let them rave!" said Tennyson's Dirge. Thou art quiet in thy grave. Even so, how oft saith the spirit, that happier is the lot of the dead than of the living that are yet alive. Who that sees the Spirit of the Beast uppermost in the politics & the movements of the time, but inly congratulates Washington that he is long already wrapped in his shroud & forever safe, that he was laid sweet in his grave the Hope of humanity not yet subjugated in him. And Edward's fervid heart is also forever still, no more to suffer from the tumults of the Natural World. And they who survive & love men have reason to apprehend that short as their own time may be they may yet outlive the honor, the religion, yea the liberty of the country. Yet yet is
"Hope the paramount duty which Heaven lays
   For its own honor, on man's suffering heart."
Otherwise one would be oppressed with melancholy & pray to die whenever he heard of the orgies of the Julien Hall or of the outrages of a mob.

The best sign which I can discover in the dark times is the increasing earnestness of the cry which swells from every quarter that a systematic Moral Education is needed. Channing, Coleridge, Wordsworth, Owen, Degerando, Spurzheim, Bentham. Even Saul is among the Prophets. The gentleman will by & by be found to mean the man of Conscience. Carlyle also. Pestalozzi.

"Where every man may take liberties there is little Liberty for any man."

All around us in vulgar daylight are hid (yes hid in daylight) sublimest laws. De Stael saw them. Ours have not yet been seen. Do not multiply your facts but seek the meaning of those you have.

This eternal superiority belongs to the contemplative man over his more forcible & more honored neighbor styled the practical man, that the former moves in a real world the latter in a phenomenal, that though the seasons of the former's activity may be rare & with intermissions of deepest gloom yet when he works it is life properly so called whilst the latter's endless activity & boundless pretension reminds him too often of the laborer at the poor-house who worked all winter shovelling a ton of coal from the yard to the cellar & then from the cellar to the yard. Euler's truth against all experience.

It is losing time to inquire anxiously respecting the opinions of another speculator. The way his opinions have attained any value is by his forbearing to inquire & merely observing.

Man is great not in his goals but in his transition from state to state. Great in act but instantly dwarfed by self-indulgence.

Not Universal Education but the Penny Magazine has failed. Brougham may have failed but Pestalozzi has not. Leibnitz said; "I have faith that man may be reformed, when I see how much Education may be reformed." Why not a moral Education as well as a discovery of America?

The education of the mind consists in a continual substitution of facts for words, as in petrifaction a particle of stone replaces a particle of wood. But observe that what are called facts are commonly words as regards the fact-man.

It is rather humiliating to attend a public meeting such as this New York Caucus last evening & see what words are best received & what a low animal hope & fear patriotism is. There is however great unity in the Audience. What pleases the Audience *very much*, pleases every individual in it. What tires me, tires all.

Greatest care is taken instinctively on both sides to represent their own cause as the winning one. The word "Why then do we despond?" was manifestly a mistake in Mr Hone's speech. This party-lie aims to secure the votes of that numerous class (whose veto *weighed* would kick the beam) of indifferent, effeminate, stupid persons who in the absence of all internal strength obey whatever seems the voice of their street, their ward, their town, or whatever domineering strength will be at the trouble of civilly dictating to them. But their votes count like real votes.

Transcribe from Quarterly Review the sentences on the progressive influence of the man of genius.

—If you kill them I will write a hymn to their memory that shall sing itself, might Luther say.

29 October.—Michel Angelo Buonaroti: John Milton: Martin Luther: George Fox: Lafayette: Falkland: Hampden. Are not these names seeds? "Men akin unto the universe." The sentiment which like Milton's comes down to new generations is that which was no sham or half-sentiment to Milton himself but the utterance of his inmost self.

> "——plainest taught & easiest learnt
>   What makes a nation happy & keeps it so."

Thanks for my sins, my defects as the stag should have thanked for his feet. As no man thoroughly understands a truth until he has first contended against it so no man has a thorough acquaintance with the hindrances or the talents of men until he has suffered from the one & seen the triumph of the other over his own want of the same. I should not be a bard of common life, wants, individualities, in the pulpit, were I not the foolish parlor & table companion that I am.

Dr Gerard ascended on Himmaleh 20000 feet; Humboldt on Andes 19374. Gay Lussac in a balloon 23000 ft. "Galen is not medicine nor Herodotus history but Euclid is geometry."

We always idealize. Hard to find in Paul, Luther, Adams, Lafayette anything so fine as to bear out our praises. For said not Aristotle Action is less near to vital truth than description? We tinge them with the glories of that Idea in whose light they are seen.

We should hold to the usage until we are clear it is wrong.

How different is one man in two hours! Whilst he sits alone in his studies & opens not his mouth he is God manifest in flesh. Put him in a parlor with unfit company and he shall talk like a fool.

October 31. It is not to be doubted that the subjectivity (to use the Germanic phrase) of man clothes itself with a different objectivity in every age. Satan who plays so prominent a part in the theology of the last age is a hollow word now but the evil principles which the word designated are no whit abated in virulence. I am bound by all my tastes to a reverence for Luther yet can I by no means find any but a subjective that is essential correspondence in me to his mind. I cannot reanimate & appropriate his difficulties & speculations. Socrates. Bacon. How then Jesus & the apostles? Sometimes it seems nations, ages were the body of shades of thought. Wrote Mother of Edward what is true of all, that No words but his *name* can describe the peculiarities of any remarkable person.

But what shall be the action of society? How superficial are our fears & hopes! We meet with a single individual or read a single newspaper expressing malignant sentiments & we despond for the republic. By one declaimer of an opposite character our confidence is renewed that all will go well. In these times a ragged coat looks sinister & revolutionary.

"Who injures one threatens all."

Luther says "Pull not by force any one person from the *mass*. Reflect on my conduct in the affair of the indulgences. I had the whole body of the papists to oppose. I preached, I wrote, I pressed on men's consciences with the greatest earnestness the positive declarations of the Word of God, but I used not a particle of force or constraint. What has been the consequence? This same Word of God has while I was asleep in my bed, given such a blow to papal despotism as not one of the German princes not even the Emperor himself could have done. It is not I, it is the divine Word that has done all."

Sublimely is it said in Nat. Hist Fanaticism, of angry persons "Night does not part the combatants."

At least let the good side of these truths be applied to the true Word which the Poet has uttered whilst he is asleep in his bed, & when he is asleep in the grave it never halts or faints but prospers in the work whereto it is sent.

I believe in the existence of the material world as the expression of the spiritual or real, & so look with a quite comic & condescending interest upon the show of Broadway with the air of an old gentleman when he says "Sir I knew your father." Is it not forever the aim & endeavor of the real to embody itself in the phenomenal? Broadway is Trade & Vanity made flesh. Therein should the philosophers walk as the impersonations of states as if Massachusetts, Carolina, Ohio, should go out to take an airing.

1 November.

The Union of extreme sensitiveness & a defiance of opinion is not very uncommon. Every man is bipolar; never a circle: somewhere therefore in each one of never so many million you shall find the contrariety, inconsistency of his nature. And as language translates language, verb verb, & noun noun so could their surfaces be adjusted to each other, might we find one age corresponding to another age in every minute peculiarity and every one man to every other man. This makes the interest of biography. I have heard men say they were afraid to read the accounts of suicides in the newspapers last year so remarkable for that crime.

Humboldt's scientific imagination will make the mnemonics of science. I read yesterday his designations of the sudden & violent disturbance of the magnetic equilibrium as "magnetic storms." So before of "Volcanic paps."

The speculations of one age do not fit another. The great man of one age is a showing how the great man of this time would have acted in that. Now & then comes a crisis when the contemporaries of one opinion become contemporaries of another & then the great man becomes the man of two ages as was Burke. Fault of our mortality we cannot act in a past age: we compensate ourselves by choosing out of that generation its most human individual & say 'Lo how man acted.'

Some men stand on the solid globe; others have no basis but some one stands by & puts a shovel under their feet at any moment.

Euler having demonstrated certain properties of Arches, adds, "All Experience is in contradiction to this; but this is no reason for doubting its truth."

Nov. 5. The elections. Whilst it is notorious that the Jackson party is the *Bad* party in the cities & in general in the country except in secluded districts where a single Newspaper has deceived a well disposed community, still, on all the banners equally of tory & whig good professions are inscribed. The Jackson flags say "Down with corruption!" "We ask for nothing but our Right." "The Constitution, the Laws," "the Laboring Classes," "Free trade," &c &c. So that they have not yet come to the depravity that says, "Evil be thou my good." Should the Whig party fail, which God avert! the patriot will still have some confidence in the redeeming force of the latent i.e. deceived virtue that is contained within the tory party; and yet more in the remedial regenerative Nature of Man which ever reproduces a healthful moral sense even out of stupidity & corruption. Thus the children of the Convicts at Botany Bay are found to have sound moral sentiments. Mr H. says the Tories deserve to succeed, for they turn every stone with an Irishman under & pick him up.

Surprizing tendency of man *in action* to believe in his continuance. If these stormy partisans doubted their immortality in these hours as in others it would calm their Zeal.

> "The moral & intelligent instrumentality from which the Sovereign Grace refuses to sever itself, is nothing else than the Vital force which animates each single believer." *Fanaticism* p. 8

Noisy Election; flags, boy processions, placards, badges, medals, bannered coaches—everything to get the hurrah on our side. That is the main end. Great anxiety, pale faces are become florid. They count that 1600 minutes are all the time allowed in all three days. Indisposition to business & great promptness to spend.

The philosophy of the erect position: God made man upright.

The sublime of the Ship is that in the pathless sea it carries its own direction in the chart & compass. See Herrick's verses.

'Tis as hard to blow a flageolet—it takes so little breath—as to blow a flute which costs so much, so in writing poetry to speak simply enough in the abundance of thoughts & images is not easier than to be profound enough in their superficiality.

There is a way of making the biography of Luther as practical & pertinent today as the last paragraph from Liverpool upon the price of cotton.

The children of this world are wiser than the children of light. The good cause is always on the defensive, the evil assailant. Because the unscrupulous can not only avail themselves of innocent means to their ends but all evil ones likewise. The Whigs can put in their own votes. But the Tories can do this & put them in again in another ward or bring a gang of forsworn gallows birds to boot, to elect the officers that are to hunt, try, imprison, & execute them.

Let the worst come to the worst & the Whig cause be crushed for a season & the Constitution be grossly violated, then you should see the weak Whig become irresistible. They would then acquire the gloom & the might of fanaticism & redeem America as they once redeemed England & once aforetime planted & emancipated America.

—

It is a great step from the thought to the expression of the thought in action. Without horror I contemplate the envy, hatred, & lust that occupy the hearts of smiling well dressed men & women but the simplest most natural expressions of the same thoughts in action astonish & dishearten me. If the wishes of the lowest class that suffer in these long streets should execute themselves, who can doubt that the city would topple in ruins. Do not trust man, great God!, with more power until he has learned to use his little power better. Does not our power increase exactly in the measure that we learn how to use it?

Concord, 15 November, 1834. Hail to the quiet fields of my fathers! Not wholly unattended by supernatural friendship & favor let me come hither. Bless my purposes as they are simple & virtuous. Coleridge's fine letter (in London Lit. Gazette Sept. 13, 1834.) comes in aid of the very thoughts I was revolving. And be it so. Henceforth I design not to utter any speech, poem, or book that is not entirely & peculiarly my work. I will say at Public Lectures & the like, those things which I have meditated for their own sake & not for the first time with a view to that occasion. If otherwise you select a new subject & labor to make a good appearance on the appointed day, it is so much lost time to you & lost time to your hearer. It is a parenthesis in your genuine life. You are your own dupe. & for the sake of conciliating your audience you have failed to edify them & winning their ear you have really lost their love & gratitude.

Respect a man! assuredly, but in general only as the potential God & therefore richly deserving of your pity, your tears. Now he is only a scrap, an ort, an end & in his actual being no more worthy of your veneration than the poor lunatic. But the simplest person who in his integrity worships God becomes God: at least no optics of human mind can detect the line where man the effect ceases, & God the Cause begins.

Unhappy divorce of Religion & Philosophy

Nov. 16. Our instincts, Sampson Reed thinks, would command & Reason would gladly serve, "as the preceptor of a prince," if we were restored to primitive health.

As soon as I read a wise sentence anywhere I feel at once the desire of appropriation. How shall I use it? If I possessed the power of excluding all other readers from that sentence I should be conscious of some temptation to do it. At the same time I know the lower & the higher objections to this meanness. 1. That striking as the thought is to you at this moment yet to judge from your past experience it is more likely that you will forget it than that another will anticipate you in using it. 2 That though you should write the passage in light upon the firmament, yet would no other man or very few other men be able to read in it what you read. 3. That however profound this thought may appear, it is really but a superficial statement of a truth whose depths are only to be sounded by unceasing & manifold consideration. 4 Every thought, every subject is capable of being presented with the same exclusive prominence that this now possesses and all that is known is nothing in comparison with what you are assured may be known.

I suppose the materials may now exist for a Portraiture of Man which should be at once history & prophecy. Does it not seem as if a perfect parallelism existed between every great & fully developed man & every other? Take a man of strong nature upon whom events have powerfully acted—Luther or Socrates or Sam Johnson—& I suppose you shall find no trait in him, no fear, no love, no talent, no dream in one that did not translate a similar love, fear, talent, dream, in the other. Luther's Pope, & Turk, & Devil, & Grace, & Justification, & Catherine de Bore, shall reappear under far other names in George Fox, in John Milton, in George Washington, in Goethe, or, long before, in Zeno & Socrates. Their circles, to use the language of geometry, would coincide. Here & there, to be sure, are anomalous unpaired creatures, who are but partially developed, wizzeled apples, as if you should seek to match monsters, one of whom has a leg, another an arm, another two heads.

If one should seek to trace the genealogy of thoughts he would find Goethe's "Open Secret" fathered in Aristotle's answer to Alexander "that these books were published & not published." And Mme. De Stael's "Architecture is frozen music," borrowed from Goethe's "Arche. is dumb music," borrowed from Vitruvius, who said, 'the Architect must not only understand drawing but also Music'.* And Wordsworth's "plan that pleased his childish thought" got from Schiller's "Reverence the dreams of his youth," got from Bacon's Primae cogitationes et consilia juventutis plus Divinitatis habent.

19 Nov. The aged grandsire came out of his chamber last evening into our parlor for the first time since his sickness in cloak & velvet cap and attended prayers. In things within his experience he has the most robust erect common sense, is as youthful vigorous in his understanding as a man of thirty. In things without his circle often puerile. He behaved & spoke

---

*"——if those great Doctors truly said That th' Ark to Man's proportion was made."

                                                                    Donne.

last evening as Jefferson or Franklin might. His prayer as usual
with the happiest pertinence. "We have been variously disciplined; bereaved, but not destitute; sick, but thou hast healed,
in degree, our diseases; and when there was but a step between
us & death, thou hast said, Live." He ever reminds one both
in his wisdom & in the faults of his intellect of an Indian Sagamore, a sage within the limits of his own observation, a child
beyond. His discourse & manners so far fittest, noblest, simplest. The grace & dignity of a child. What could be better
than his speech to me after Grandmother's death? "Well, the
bond that united us, is broken, but I hope you & your
brothers will not cease to come to this house. You will not like
to be excluded, and I shall not like to be neglected." And his
conversation with the Miles family after the death of their
father I admired. The son was supposed to be intemperate in
his habits. The family & friends were all collected for the funeral when we went in. "Madam, I condole with you; Sir, I
condole with you; & with you all. I remember, Sir, when I
came to this town Your Grandfather was living on this farm
and a most respectable citizen. His father lived here before
him. Your father has stood in their place & lived a useful & respected life. Now, Sir, the name & respectability of your family
rests on you. Sir if you fail—Ichabod—the glory is departed.
And I hope you will not."——

History teaches what man can do & not less what man can
suffer & what he can believe. The slowness with which the
stirps generosa seu historica in Europe opened their eyes to the
monstrous lie of Popery might startle us as to the possible
depth of our own degradation through the sleep of Reason, &
prompt a hope of what height we may yet attain.

There are ever & anon in history expressions uttered that
seem to be fourfold-visaged & look with significant smile to all
the quarters of time. Thus when Luther & Carolstadt had disputed publicly upon the new doctrines at Leipsic, the Duke
George put an end to the controversy by declaring "Be his
right divine, or be it human, he is still Pope of Rome." Yet
doubt not the same universality of application might be detected by a discerning eye in every homeliest utterance. This
Duke George seems the Tory of the World.

Is it not an instructive fact in literary history that of Luther's sending from Wittemberg to Spalatin for the Elector's collection of gems to assist him in translating the 21 Chap. Revelations? They were sent & after a careful examination returned. (V. Seckendorf p. 204)

And here is another eulogy, a true eulogy of that great man. King Christian of Denmark passing through Saxony sent for Luther. He afterwards declared "Never have I heard the gospel so well explained as by Luther. So long as I continue to live I shall hold his discourse in remembrance, and shall submit with greater patience to whatever I am destined to endure." Longinus could not improve the sentence, and the last clause should be writ in the diary of every preacher.

———

Luther was a great man & as Coleridge says, acted poems. And his words, if they will, they may characterize as half-battles. But the sublime of them, critically considered, is the material sublime not the moral. "If the heavens should pour down Duke Georges for nine days" &c. "If I don't burn them 'tis because I can't find fire"—"I'll go if all the devils are in the way" &c. It is like Mahomet's description of the Angel whom he saw in heaven, 'It was nine days' journey from one of his eyes to the other.' Mere sublimity of magnitude & number, but Landor says well, "where the heart is not moved, the gods stride & thunder in vain. The pathetic is the true sublime." I speak of course of the homely monk's sayings as sentences.

———

November 21, 1834. Ah how shone the moon & her little sparklers last eve. There was the light in the selfsame vessels which contained it a million years ago.

I perceived in myself this day with a certain degree of terror the prompting to retire. What! is this lone parsonage in this thin village so populous as to crowd you & overtask your benevolence? They who urge you to retire hence would be too many for you in the centre of the desert or on the top of a pillar. How dear how soothing to man arises the Idea of God peopling the lonely place, effacing the scars of our mistakes & disappointments. When we have lost our God of tradition & ceased from our God of rhetoric then may God fire the heart with his presence.

23 Nov. The root & seed of democracy is the doctrine Judge for yourself. Reverence thyself. It is the inevitable effect of that doctrine where it has any effect (which is rare) to insulate the partizan, to make each man a state. At the same time it replaces the dead with a living check in a true delicate reverence for superior congenial minds. "How is the king greater than I, if he is not more just?"

How does every institution, every man, every thought embody, clothe itself externally with dress, houses, newspapers, societies. As I sat in the Orthodox Church this day I thought how brick & laths & lime flew obedient to the master idea that reigns in the minds of many persons be that idea what it may, Jackson, Antimasonry, Diffusion of Knowledge, Farm School, or Calvinism. Why then should the Swedenborgian doctrine be obnoxious that in the Spritual world the affections clothe themselves with appropriate garments, dwellings, & other circumstances? Very philosophical was their tale that in the other world certain spirits tried to pronounce a word representing somewhat which they did not believe. They twisted their lips into all manner of folds even to indignation but could not utter the word.

What concerns me more than Orthodoxy, Antimasonry, Temperance, Workingmen's party, & the other Ideas of the time?

Is the question of Temperance pledges a question whether we will in a pestilence go into quarantine?

C. knew all law from the Constitution of his country to the usage of the next cider-mill.

———

26 Nov. Goethe says of Lavater, that, "it was fearful to live near a man to whom every boundary within which Nature has seen fit to circumscribe us was clear."

"The world in which I exist is another world indeed but not to come." Coleridge

O what a wailing tragedy is this world considered in reference to money-matters. Read EBE's letter of 6 July, 1833 & the other to his mother.

Rather melancholy after asking the opinion of all living to

find no more receivers of your doctrine than your own three or four & sit down to wait until it shall please God to create some more men before your school can expect increase.

Show a head of Cuvier, Goethe, or Milton to vulgar people & they see nothing but resemblances to Deacon Gulliver or Mr Gibbons.

A year ago on 13 Nov. little Ezra Ripley started up in bed & told his father all the stars were falling down. His father bid him sharply go to sleep but the boy was the better philosopher.

What can be conceived so beautiful as actual Nature? I never see the dawn break or the sun set as last evening when from every grey or slate coloured cloud over the whole dome depended a wreath of roses or look down the river with its tree planted banks (from the bridge north of the house) absolutely *affecting* an elegancy, without a lively curiosity as to its reality & a self recollection that I am not in a dream. Well is this all superficial & is the earth itself unsightly? Look at a Narcissus or crocus or lily or petal or stamen or plumule, at any process of life and answer. What can be conceived so beautiful as an assemblage of bright & opake balls floating in space covered each with pretty races & each individual a counterpart & contemplator of the whole?

> How many events shall shake the earth
> Lie packed in silence waiting for their birth

Every thing to be appreciated must be seen from the point where its rays converge to a focus. This gorgeous landscape, these poetical clouds—what would they be if I should put my eye to the ground? a few pebbles: or into the cloud? a fog. So of human history, & of my own life. We cannot get far enough away from ourselves to integrate our scraps of thought & action & so judge of our tendency or ascend to our idea. We are in the battle, & cannot judge of its picturesque effect, nor how the day is going, nor at present of its consequences. The shepherd or the beggar in his red cloak little knows what a charm he gives to the wide landscape that charms you on the mountain top & whereof he makes the most agreeable feature, & I no more the part my individuality plays in the All.

"As he was inferior however in cavalry & the liver of the victim appeared without a head he retired to Ephesus &c, &c." Plutarch Life of Agesilaus p. 42

To an idle inquiry whether you are immortal, God maketh no answer. No argument of conviction can be found but do your duty, & you are already immortal: the taste, the fear of death has already vanished. We would study Greek & Astronomy if life were longer. Study them & life is already infinitely long.

1 December. Yesterday saw I at Waltham the eclipse of the Sun 10.45 digits. The fact that a prediction is fulfilled is the best part of it. Then the preternatural half night which falls upon the hills. & the violet shade which touches all the clouds. The fine fringes of the cloud made the best smoked glass thro' which to see the sun while the shadow encroached upon his face.

When the young philosopher forgets men's opinions nothing seems so worthy employment or rather life as religious teaching. If I could persuade men to listen to their interior convictions, if I could express, embody their interior convictions, that were indeed life. It were to cease being a figure & to act the action of a man. But for that work he must be free & true. He must not seek to weld what he believes, to what he does not wish publicly to deny. Nothing can compensate for want of belief—no accomplishments no talents. A believing man in a cause worthy of a Man gives the mind a sense of stability & repose more than mountains. I could not help calling the attention of my venerable neighbor to the different impression made by A Everett & J. Savage: one, very accomplished, but inspires no confidence; for he is not much of a man; the other, tolerably well equipped, but is himself an upright singlehearted man pursuing his path by his own lights & incapable of fear or favor. Columbus did not affect to believe in a new continent & make dinner speeches about it (other than his egg speech) and George Fox & Emanuel Swedenborg never advise people to go to church for the sake of example.

It would give scope for many truths in experimental religion to preach from the text of "There shall be new heavens & a new earth." Sometimes we perceive that God is wholly unknown in the world, that the church & the sermon & the priest & the alms are a profanation.

"We were early cast upon thy care," is a heathen expression.

—

December 2. Concord. The age of puberty is a crisis in the life of the man worth studying. It is the passage from the Unconscious to the Conscious; from the sleep of the Passions to their rage; from careless receiving to cunning providing; from beauty to use; from omnivorous curiosity to anxious stewardship; from faith to doubt; from maternal Reason to hard short-sighted Understanding; from Unity to disunion; the progressive influences of poetry, eloquence, love, regeneration, character, truth, sorrow, and of search for an Aim, & the contest for Property.

I look upon every sect as a Claude Lorraine glass through which I see the same sun & the same world & in the same relative places as through my own eyes but one makes them small, another large; one, green; another, blue; another, pink. I suppose that as an orthodox preacher's cry "the natural man is an enemy of God" only translates the philosopher's that "the instinct of the Understanding is to contradict the Reason"; so Luther's Law & Gospel (also St Paul's); Swedenborg's love of self & love of the Lord; William Penn's World & Spirit; the Court of Honor's Gentleman & Knave. The dualism is ever present through variously denominated.

The two conditions of Teaching are, 1. That none can teach more than he knows. 2. That none can teach faster than the scholar can learn. Two conditions more: 1. He must say that they can understand. 2. But he must say that which is given to *him*.

I have not so near access to Luther's mind through his works as through my own mind when I meditate upon his historical position.

It is true undoubtedly that every preacher should strive to pay his debt to his fellowmen by making his communication intelligible to the common capacity. It is no less true that unto every mind is given one word to say & he should sacredly strive to utter that word & not another man's word; his own, without addition or abatement.

'John Evang' says Luther, 'was simple & spake also simply but every word in John weigheth two Tons.' Table T.

When they jeered at the devil, Luther says, he went away. 'Quia est superbus spiritus & non potest ferre contemptum sui.'

My own picture was ugly enough to me. I read that when his own picture was shown to Erasmus he said "look I like this picture? so am I the greatest knave that liveth," which Luther relates with sharpness.

If we will lie, let us do it roundly. Captain   of Providence affirmed that he had pumped the Atlantic Ocean three times through his Ship on the passage, and that it was very common to strike porpoises in the Ship's hold.

Francis comes to Doctor Ripley at breakfast to know if he shall drive the cow into the battle-field?

A lockjaw which bended a man's head backward to his heels, and that beastly hydrophobia which makes him bark at his wife & children,—what explains these?

A real interest in your fellow creatures is of necessity reciprocal. For want of it how tragic is the solitude of the old man. No prayer, no good wish out of the whole world follows him into his sick chamber. It is as frightful a solitude as that which cold produces round the traveller who has lost his way. This comes of management, of cunning, & of vanity. Never held he intercourse with any human being with thorough frankness, man to man but always with that imp-like second thought. And so hath no friend. Yet I forget not his generosity, his tenderness to E. And his faults have not descended to his children. Blessed are the woods. In summer they shade the traveller from the sun, in Winter from the tooth of the wind. When there is snow it falls level: when it rains it does not blow in his face. There is no dust & a pleasing fear reigns in their shade. Blessed are the woods!

I think the most devout persons be the freest of their tongues in speaking of the Deity, as Luther, Fuller, Herbert, Milton whose words are an offence to the pursed mouths which make formal prayers; & beyond the word, they are free thinkers also. "Melancthon discoursed with Luther touching the prophets who continually do boast in this sort & with these words 'Thus saith the Lord' &c—whether God spake in person with them or no? Then Luther said, They were very holy spiritual people which seriously did contemplate on holy & divine causes: therefore God spake with them in their consciences which the prophets held for sure Revelations." Table talk p. 362 folio ed. So St. James he frankly called 'Epistola straminea.'

Bring men near one another & love will follow. Once the men of distant countries were painted as of monstrous *bodies* without necks, with tails, &c. But commerce contradicted the report. Then they were described as having monstrous *minds*: thieves, sottish, promiscuously mixed, destitute of moral sentiments. But commerce has exposed that slander too, & shown that as face answereth to face in water so the heart of man to man.

A man is a very vulnerable creature. His manners & dignity are conventional. Leave him alone & he is a sorry sight.

It seems as if a simple manly character should never make an apology but always regard his past action with the same marble calmness as Phocion when he admitted that the event was happy yet regretted not his dissuasion from the action. This supposes of course that the act *was* genuine.

How sad how disgusting to see this Neidrig air on the face, a man whose words take hold on the upper world whilst one eye is eternally down cellar so that the best conversation has ever a slight savor of sausages & soapbarrels. Basest when the snout of this influence touches the education of young women & withers the blessed affection & hope of human nature by teaching that marriage is nothing but housekeeping & that Woman's life has no other aim. Even G. was capable of saying 'the worst marriage is better than none'. & S. made a similar stab at the sanity of his daughter.

Concord 3 December. One morning Reason woke & exclaimed, "Demosthenes said well 'Whoso hath an evil cause

the same hath no good fortune.'" "Not so Gammer," replied
the Understanding, "The greater knave, the better luck."

The poor Irishman—a wheelbarrow is his country.

When I remember the twofold cord, then fourfold & go a
little back a thousand & a millionfold cord of which my being
& every man's being consists; that I am an aggregate of infini-
tesimal parts & that every minutest streamlet that has flowed
to me is represented in that man which I am, so that if every
one should claim his part in me I should be instantaneously
diffused through the creation & individually decease, then I
say if I am but an alms of All, & live but by the Charity of innumerable others, there is no peculiar propriety in wrapping
my cloak about me & hiding the ray that my taper may emit.
What is a man but a Congress of nations? Just suppose for one
moment to appear before him the whole host of his ancestors.
All have vanished; he—the insulated result of all that character,
activity, sympathy, antagonism working for ages in all corners
of the earth—alone remains. Such is his origin; well was his
nurture less compound. Who & what has not contributed
something to make him that he is? Art, science, institutions,
black men, white men, the vices & the virtues of all people, the
gallows, the church, the shop, poets, nature, joy, & fear, all
help all teach him. Every fairy brings a gift.

Deliver us from that intensity of character which makes all
its crows swans. So soon as I hear that my friend is engaged I
perceive at once that a very ordinary person is henceforward
adopted into that rose colored atmosphere which exhales from
his self love & every trait, every trifle, every nothing about the
new person is canonized by identifying the same with the positive Virtue to which it is related just as children refer the
moon to the same region of heaven with the stars. Talent
becomes genius; inoffensiveness, benevolence; wilfulness, character, & even stupidity simplicity. Poor dear human nature;
leave magnifying & caricaturing her. It frets & confuses us.
More winning, more sociable & society-making is she as she
stands, faults & virtues unpainted, confessed; then the fault
even becomes piquant & is seen to prop & underpin some ex-

cellent virtue. Let us deal so with ourselves & call a spade a spade.

6th Dec. Do you imagine that because I do not say Luther's creed all his works are an offence to me? Far otherwise. I can animate them all that they shall live to me. I can worship in that temple as well as in any other. I have only to translate a few of the leading phrases into their equivalent verities, to adjust his almanack to my meridian & all the conclusions, all the predictions shall be strictly true. Such is the everlasting advantage of truth. Let a man work after a pattern he really sees & every man shall be able to find a correspondence between these works & his own & to turn them to some account in Rome, London, or Japan, from the first to the hundredth century.

On reading yesterday P.M. to Aunt Mary Coleridge's defense of prayer against author of Nat. Hist Enthusiasm, she replied, "Yes, for our reason was so distinct from the Universal Reason that we could pray to it, & so united with it that we could have assurance we were heard."

8 December. The world looks poor & mean so long as I think only of its great men; most of them of spotted reputation. But when I remember how many obscure persons I myself have seen possessing gifts that excited wonder, speculation, & delight in me; when I remember that the very greatness of Homer, of Shakspeare, of Webster & Channing is the truth with which they reflect the mind of all mankind; when I consider that each fine genius that appears is already predicted in our constitution inasmuch as he only makes apparent shades of thought in us of which we hitherto knew not (or actualizes an idea,) and when I consider the absolute boundlessness of our capacity—no one of us but has the whole untried world of geometry, fluxions, natural philosophy, Ethics, wide open before him.

When I recollect the charms of certain women, what poems are many private lives, each of which can fill our eye if we so will, (as the swan, the eagle, the cedar bird, the canary each seems the type of bird-kind whilst we gaze at it alone,) and then remember how many millions I know not; then I feel the riches of my inheritance in being set down in this world gifted with organs of communication with this accomplished company.

Pray heaven that you may have a sympathy with all sorts of excellence even with those antipodal to your own. If any eye rest on this page let him know that he who blotted it, could not go into conversation with any person of good understanding without being presently gravelled. The slightest question of his most familiar proposition disconcerted him—eyes, face, & understanding, beyond recovery. Yet did he not the less respect & rejoice in this daily gift of vivacious common sense which was so formidable to him. May it last as long as the World.

The application of Goethe's definition of genius "That power which by working & doing gives laws & rules," to common life, to the art of living, is obvious. Deacon Warren, Mr Turner, Mr Crafts, and every new simple heart give us a new image of possible Virtues & Powers.

A fire is made to burn yet we do not like to have coals run behind the backlog.

If you ask me whether I will not be so good as to abstain from all use of ardent spirits for the sake of diminishing by my pint per annum the demand & so stopping the distiller's pernicious pump, I answer, Yes, with all my heart. But will I signify the same fact by putting my name to your paper? No. Be assured, I shall always be found on your side in discouraging this use & traffic. But I shall not deprive my example of all its value by abdicating my freedom on that point. It shall be always my example, the spectacle to all whom it may concern of my spontaneous action at the time.

Why, O diffuser of Useful K. do you not offer to deliver a course of lectures on Aristotle & Plato or on Plato alone or on him & Bacon & Coleridge? Why not strengthen the hearts of the waiting lovers of the primal philosophy by an account of that fragmentary highest teaching which comes from the half fabulous personages Heraclitus, Hermes Trismegistus, & Giordano Bruno, & Vyasa, & Plotinus, & Swedenborg? Curious now that first I collect their names they should look all so mythological.

I rejoice in Time. I do not cross the common without a wild poetic delight notwithstanding the prose of my demeanour. Thank God I live in the country. Well said Bell that no hour, no state of the atmosphere but corresponded to some state of the mind; brightest day, grimmest night.

9 December. The dear old Plutarch assures me that the lamp of Demosthenes never went out, that King Philip called his orations *soldiers*, & in a moment of enthusiasm on hearing the report of one of his speeches exclaimed "Had I been there I too should have declared war against myself." Flying before Antipater he wrote his own epitaph at Calabria. Ειχερ εισην ρωμην γνωμη Δημοσθενες εσχεσ Ουποτ αν Ελληνων ηρξεν Αρης Μακεδων. When Epicles twitted him upon his exact preparation he said "I should be ashamed to speak what comes uppermost to so great an assembly." One day his voice failing him, he was hissed, & he cried unto the people, "Ye are to judge of players indeed by the clearness & tuneableness of their voice, but of orators, by the gravity & excellency of their sentences." Despising other orators, when Phocion arose, Demosthenes was wont to say, "pruning knife of my orations, Arise!"

———

But it seemed to me that a fit question to handle in a public lecture is the one involved in the claims & apologies made by people & orators in this New England raft of ours every day.

It is said that the people can look after their own interests, that "Common sense, tho' no science, is fairly worth the seven," that a plain practical Man is better to the state than a scholar, &c.

He were a benefactor to his countrymen who would expose & pillory this stale sophism. We hold indeed that those reasons for a public action which are presented to us should be of that simple humane character as to be fully comprehensible by every citizen of good capacity as well the uneducated as the educated. That is a good test & condition of such reasons. They should not be addressed to the imagination or to our literary associations but to the ear of plain men. Therefore are they such as plain men—farmers, mechanics, teamsters, seamen, or soldiers—might offer, if they would gravely, patiently, humbly reflect upon the matter. There is nothing in their want of book-learning to hinder. This doctrine affirms that there is imparted to every man the Divine light of reason sufficient not only to plant corn & grind wheat by but also to illuminate all his life his social, political, religious actions. Sufficient according to its faithful use. Sufficient if faithfully used. The propositions are true to the end of the world with this inseparable condition. Every man's Reason is sufficient for his guidance, *if used*. But does it mean that because a farmer acting on deep conviction shall give a reason as good as Bacon could have given, that therefore the ordinary arguments of farmers are to be preferred to those of statesmen? that whatever crude remarks a circle of people talking in a bar room throw out, are entitled to equal weight with the sifted & chosen conclusions of experienced public men? And because God has made you capable of Reason therefore must I hear & accept all your selfish railing, your proven falsehoods, your unconsidered guesses as truth? No; I appeal from you to your Reason which with me condemns you from Philip drunk to Philip sober. It amounts to this; 'Every man's Reason can show him what is right. Therefore every man says what is right whether he use his Reason or no.' I hate this fallacy the more that it is, beside being dire nonsense, a profanation of the dearest of truths. Democracy has its root in the Sacred truth that every man hath in him the divine Reason or that though few men since the creation of the world live according to the dictates of Reason, yet all men are created capable of so doing. That is the equality & the only equality of all men. To this truth we look when we say, 'Reverence thyself. Be true to thyself.' Because every man has within him somewhat really divine therefore is slavery the unpardonable outrage it is.

—

I would add to what should have been inserted p. 371, that It is not for nothing that one word makes such impression & the other none; it is not without preestablished harmony this sculpture in the memory. The eye was placed where that ray should fall, to the end that it might testify of that particular ray.

There is great delight in learning a new language. When the day comes in the scholar's progress unawares when he reads pages without recurrence to his dictionary, he shuts up his book with that sort of fearful delight with which the bridegroom sits down in his own house with the bride, saying, 'I shall now live with you always.'

December 11. When the sick man came out of doors the stars seemed to shine through his eyes into his heart, & the blessed air that he inhaled seemed to lighten his frame from head to feet.

A little above I referred to one of my characters. It might be added that if he made his forms a strait jacket to others, he wore the same himself all his years & so reanimated for his beholders the order of La Trappe. Tread softly Stranger on the dust of one who showed ever in his fireside discourse traits of that pertinency & judgment softening ever & anon into elegancy, which make the distinction of the scholar, & which, under better discipline, might have ripened into a Salmasius or Hedericus. Sage & Savage strove harder in him than in any of my acquaintance, each getting the mastery by turns, & pretty sudden turns. "Save us" he said in his prayer, "from the extremity of cold, & violent sudden changes." "The society will meet after the Lyceum, as it is difficult to bring the people together in the evening, & no moon, &c." "Mr N.F. is dead, & I expect to hear the death of Mr B. It is cruel to separate old people from their wives in this cold weather." Thus is one reminded of the children's prayers who in confessing their sins, say, "Yes, I did take the jumprope from Mary." Pleasantly said he at supper, "that his last cup was not potent in any way, neither in sugar, nor cream, nor souchong; it was so equally & universally defective that he thought it easier to make another, than to mend that."

The Counsellor's fine simplicity & sweetness of character saved his speech the other evening from being distressful to the hearers. Charles is reminded by him of Edward. There are some points of resemblance. This for one, that neither was ever put out of countenance.

Concord. 14 December. Yesterday I sealed & despatched my letter to Carlyle. Today, riding to East Sudbury, I pleased myself with the beauties & terrors of the snow; the oak-leaf hurrying over the banks is fit ornament. Nature in the woods is very companionable. There, my Reason & my Understanding are sufficient company for each other. I have my glees as well as my glooms, alone. Confirm my faith (& when I write the word, Faith looks indignant.) pledge me the word of the Highest that I shall have my dead & my absent again, & I could be content & cheerful alone for a thousand years. I know no aisle so stately as the roads through the pine woods in Maine. Cold is the snowdrift topping itself with sand. How intense are our affinities: acids & alkalis. The moment we indulge our affections, the earth is metamorphosed; all its tragedies & ennuis vanish, all duties even, nothing remains to fill eternity with but two or three persons. But then a person is a *cause*. What is Luther but Protestantism? or Columbus but Columbia? And were I assured of meeting Ellen tomorrow would it be less than a world, a personal world? Death has no bitterness in the light of that thought.

In Boston C. was witty with his philosophy of caoutchouc & his inspired address to Mr. Gannett. Seize him Towzer! I cannot at all remember the instance I had alleged of false life where a man sees himself praised & exalted for that he is not; but C. said it was as if a man should see his shadow bowed to & honored & doing all for him.

And Hedge read me good things out of Schleiermacher concerning the twofold division of study, 1. Physics, or that which is; 2. Ethics, or that which should be. Also his definition of *Science* & *Art*—the one, *All things brought into the mind*; the other, *the mind* going *into things*. Then the Ascetic or the discipline of life produced by the opinions. Every man's system should appear in his ascetic. Scarce one man's does. I was reminded of Blanchard, that faithful man whose whole life & least part is conformed to his Reason, who upholds the Peace Society & works at the Bank Sundays & eschews the Communion & sweetens his tea with Canton sugar out of hatred to slavery & thinks Homer & Shakspeare to be the strongest War party.

1. The "savings bank": Emerson's journals and miscellaneous notebooks at Harvard University's Houghton Library.

'Mixing with the thousand pursuits & passions & objects of the world as personified by imagination' is profitable & entertaining These pages are intended at this their commencement to contain a record of new thoughts (when they occur) for a receptacle of all the old ideas that [...] partial but peculiar peepings at antiquity can furnish or furbish; for a tablet to save the wear & tear of weak Memory, & in short for all the various purposes & utility, real or imaginary, which are usually comprehended under that comprehensive title Common Place book Oye witches assist me! enliven or horrify some midnight lucubration or dream (whichever may be found most convenient) to supply this reservoir when other resources fail. Pardon me Fairy Land! rich region of fancy & gnomery elvery syllphery & Queen Mab! pardon me for presenting my first petition to your enemies but there is probably one in the chamber who maliciously influenced me to what is irrevocable; pardon & favour me! — & finally Spirits of Earth Air Fire Water wherever ye glow whatsoever you patronize whoever you inspire hallow hallow this devoted paper — Dedicated & — Jan 25. 1820. Junis. —

2. The opening page of the journal *Wide World 1* (January 1820).

3–4. Emerson's parents, Ruth Haskins Emerson and the Rev. William Emerson.

5. A sketch of 15 Hollis Hall at Harvard, where Emerson lived during his junior year, from his journal *Wide World I* (August 1820).

6. Alvan Fisher, *College Yard: A View from the President's House* (1821).

Books — Inquirenda

Subjects for themes

Destruction of a city. poetry

Mathers Magnalia.
Dunlop's history of Fiction.
Mattaire.
Swift.   Froissart.
Davy's Chemistry
Teignmouths life of Jones.
Simmons life of Milton — 3 Vol of
                        Brit. Plutarch
Chaucer
Montaigne's Essays
Germany (Stael)
Drummonds Academical Questions
Price on Morals
Humboldt's work on America
Smith's Virginia
Robertsons N. America
Hist of Philip 2
Life of Shakespeare

(Forensic) Whether Civil Government be
founded on a compact expressed
or implied. ——
The domestic relations as restraints on an adventurer
Influence of weather on intellec-
tual temperament.
Character of any fancy portrait as
/for instance

48
44
40
132

7. A reading list and fanciful sketch from *Wide World 2* (1820–21).

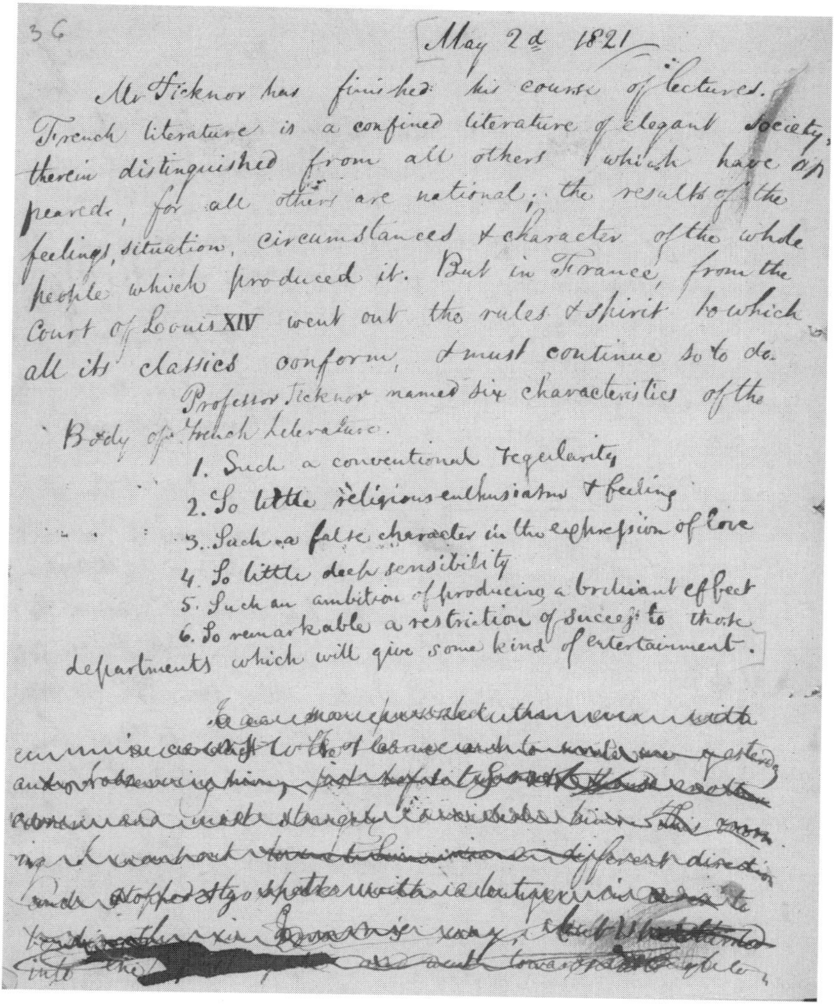
36

May 2d 1821

Mr Ticknor has finished his course of lectures. French literature is a confined literature of elegant society, therein distinguished from all others which have appeared, for all others are national; the results of the feelings, situation, circumstances & character of the whole people which produced it. But in France, from the Court of Louis XIV went out the rules & spirit to which all its classics conform, & must continue so to do.

Professor Ticknor named six characteristics of the Body of French literature.

1. Such a conventional regularity
2. So little religious enthusiasm & feeling
3. Such a false character in the expression of love
4. So little deep sensibility
5. Such an ambition of producing a brilliant effect
6. So remarkable a restriction of success to those departments which will give some kind of entertainment.

[illegible]

8. A heavily cancelled journal entry about Martin Gay (*Wide World 2*, 1821).

9–12. Family silhouettes (*clockwise from top left*): aunt Mary Moody Emerson as a young woman, Ralph Waldo Emerson in 1843, and brothers Edward and Charles.

13–14. Brothers Bulkeley (*top*) and William.

I feel the longevity of the mind; I admit the evidence of the immortality of the soul. Well as I said, I am afraid the season of this rare fruit is irrecoverably past; that the earth has made such a nutation of its nodes, that the heat has will never reach again that Hesperian garden in which alone these apricots & pomegranates grew.

Concord N. H. Dec. 21, 1828. I have now been four days engaged to Ellen Louisa Tucker. Will my Father in Heaven regard us with kindness, and as he hath, as we trust, made us for each other, will he be pleased to strengthen & purify & prosper & eternize our affection.

Sunday morning.

She has the purity & confiding religion of an angel. Are the words common? the words are true. Will God forgive me my sins & aid me to deserve this gift of his mercy. Jan. 17. 1829

15. Emerson records his engagement to Ellen in his journal (December 21, 1828).

16. A watercolor miniature of Emerson's first wife, Ellen Tucker (1830).

17. Charles Osgood, *Portrait of Nathaniel Hawthorne* (1840). In September 1842, Hawthorne and Emerson went on a 40-mile hike, visiting a local Shaker community.

18. Emerson met Charles King Newcomb (1820–1894) in 1840 and praised the "subtle genius" of his early manuscripts.

19. Emerson's son Waldo in October 1841.

28 January 1842

Yesterday night at 15 minutes after eight my little Waldo ended his life.

20. Emerson records the death of his son in his journal *J*: "Yesterday night at 15 minutes after eight my little Waldo ended his life." (January 28, 1842)

21. Emerson sat for this portrait in Edinburgh in 1848, during his second European tour. The clenched right hand was one of his characteristic gestures as a lecturer.

House of Seem & house of Be. Coleridge's four classes of Readers. 1. the Hour glass sort, all in & all out; 2 the Sponge sort, giving it all out a little dirtier than it took in; 3 of the Jelly bag, keeping nothing but the refuse; 4 of the Golconda, sieves picking up the diamonds only. Two sorts of diseases; those which kill & those that don't. Wordsworth, "whose thoughts acquaint us with our own." Francis Osborn 11th Edition Miscel. Works. "Wishers & woulders were never good householders."

Dec. 17. If it has so pleased God it is very easy for you to surpass your fellows in genius; but surpass them in generosity of sentiment; see not their meanness, whilst your eyes are fixed on everlasting virtues; being royal, being divine, in your sentiments: this shall be 'another morn risen on mid noon.' This shall be your own,—O no;—God forbid! not your own, but a vast accession of the Divinity into your trembling clay.

Michel Angelo sent to Florence for Granacci & others to come & help him in painting in fresco the Sistine Chapel as he knew not the art. But soon seeing that they wrought far enough from his desires, he shut himself up one morn in the chapel, & tore down all their work, & begun anew, nor would see them at his house. And they finding they could not get admission to him departed with mortification to Florence. This crisis is most unpleasing surely, but is in the nature of things; how could it be avoided? And such occur in the history of genius every day.

Every stroke of Michel Angelo's pencil moves the pencil in Raphael's hand.

How many states of mind have I & those which are intense even in their mournful or practick influence, which refuse to be recorded. I can not more easily recall & describe the feeling I had yesterday of limited power, & the small worth to me of a day, than I could recall a fled dream. Only the impression is left; the self-evidence is flown.

———

Loathsome lecture last eve. on precocity, & the dissection of the brain, & the distortion of the body, & genius, &c. A grim compost of blood & mud. Blessed, thought I, were those who, lost in their pursuits, never knew that they had a body or a mind.

19 Dec. He who makes a good sentence or a good verse exercises a power very strictly analogous to his who makes a fine statue, a beautiful cornice, a staircase like that in Oxford, or a noble head in painting.

One writes on air if he speaks, but no he writes on mind more durable than marble & is like him who begets a son, that is, originates a begetter of nations.

The maker of a sentence like the other artist launches out into the infinite & builds a road into Chaos & old Night & is followed by those who hear him with something of wild creative delight.

Dec. 20. I like well the doctrine 'that every great man, Napoleon himself, is an Idealist a poet with different degrees of Utterance'. As the love of flowers contains the Science of Botany, so the innate love of novelty, enterprize like that which delighted me when a boy in Atkinson st. with climbing by help of a small ladder & touching for the first time the shingles of the shed. Yes & makes every boy a poet when a fine morning in spring seducingly shows him the uplands in the neighboring towns on his way to school. This same desire of the untried, leads the young farmer in Maine to load his little wagon & rattle down the long hills on his way to Illinois.

A strictest correspondence ties all the arts. And it is as lawful and as becoming for the poet to seize upon felicitous expressions & lay them up for use as for Michel Angelo to store his sketchbook with hands, arms, triglyphs, & capitals to enrich his future Compositions. The wary artist in both kinds will tear down the scaffolding when the Work is finished & himself supply no clew to the curiosity that would know how he did the wonder.

Dec. 20. The chickadees are very busy & happy in Caesar's woods between the spots of snow. I met them yesterday. What is the green leaf under the snow resembling a potentilla?

Unitarianism & all the rest are judged by the standing or falling of their professors. I refuse that test to this. It is true. I see this to be true though I see it condemns my life & no man liveth by it. They are truth itself, they are the measure of truth & can no more be affected by my falling away or all men's denial than the law of gravity is changed by my acting as if it were not. Yet is it dangerous! It is very far from a system of negatives; it lowly earnestly sees & declares how its laws advance their reign forevermore into the Infinitude on all sides of us. Jesus was a setter up more than a puller down. Socrates was also. Both were spiritualists. George Fox, Wm Penn were urgent doers, hard livers. But they were of wrath. I see the World & its Maker from another side. It seems to me beauty. He seems to me Love.

Spiritual Religion has no other evidence than its own intrinsic probability. It is probable because the Mind is so constituted as that they appear likely so to be.

It never scolds. It simply describes the laws of moral nature as the naturalist does physical laws & shows the surprizing beauties & terrors of human life. It never scolds & never sneers.

It is opposed to Calvinism in this respect that all spiritual truths are self evident but the doctrines of C. are not, & are not pretended to be by their understanding defenders. Mystery.

This is the only live religion. All others are dead or formal. This cannot be but in the new conviction of the mind. Others may.

This produces instant & infinite abuses. It is a two-edged sword because it condemns forms but supplies a better law only to the living. It leaves the dead to bury their dead. The popular religion is an excellent constable, the true religion is God himself to the believer & maketh him a perfect lover of the whole world; but it is only a cloak of licentiousness to the rest. It would dismiss all bad preachers & do great harm to society by taking off restraints.

Spiritual religion is one that cannot be harmed by the vices of its defenders.

My Reason is well enough convinced of its immortality. It knows itself immortal. But it cannot persuade its downlooking brother the Understanding of the same. That fears for the cord

that ties them lest it break. Hence Miss Rotch affirms un-
doubtingly "I shall live forever," and on the other hand does
not much believe in her retaining her Personality.

21 Dec. Who says we are not chained? He lies. See how
greedily you accept the verse of Homer or Shakspear; the outline of M. Angelo; the strain of Handel; the word of Webster;
how thoroughly you understand and make them your own; &
are well assured, too, that they are only units from an infinite
store of the same kinds. Well, now put out your own hands &
take one more unit thence. I say you are chained.

M. Angelo was the Homer of Painting. Titian the Moore or
better the Spenser. The difference is the same betwixt this
stern Designer & the beautiful colorists that followed him, as
between the severe Aristotle & the ornate Cicero.

Go show me where to lay the first stone & I will build the
chapel.

Blessed is the day when the youth discovers that Within and
Above are synonyms.

That obscure experience which almost every person con-
fesses that particular passages of conversation & action have
occurred to him in the same order before, whether dreaming
or waking—What of that, Bishop Bruno!

Actio agentis nihil aliud est quam extrahere rem de potentia
ad actum. Aristotle

We can all put out our hands towards the desired truth but
few can bring their hands to meet around it.

He alone is an artist whose hands can perfectly execute what
his mind has perfectly conceived.

"Solo a quello arriva
La man che obbedisce all'intelletto"
Michel Angelo

The domestic man loves no music so well as his kitchen
clock and the airs which the logs sing to him as they burn in
the fire-place.

The best means of mending a bad voice is to utter judicious
remarks with it; the second best is to favor it by silence.

21 Dec. It is very easy in the world to live by the opinion of the world. It is very easy in solitude to be self-centered. But the finished man is he who in the midst of the crowd keeps with perfect sweetness the independence of solitude. I knew a man of simple habits & earnest character who never put out his hand nor opened his lips to court the public and having survived several rotten reputations of younger men, Honor came at last and sat down with him upon his private bench from which he had never stirred. I too can see the spark of Titan in that coarse clay.

—

The philosophy of *Waiting* needs sometimes to be unfolded. Thus he who is qualified to act upon the Public, if he does not act on many, may yet act intensely on a few; if he does not act much upon any but from insulated condition & unfit companions seems quite withdrawn into himself, still if he know & feel his obligations, he may be (unknown & unconsciously) hiving knowledge & concentrating powers to act well hereafter & a very remote hereafter. God is a rich proprietor who though he may find use for sprouts & saplings of a year's growth finds his account also in leaving untouched the timber of a hundred years which hardens & seasons in the cold & in the sun. But a more lowly use (& yet with right feelings all parts of duty are alike lowly) is pleasing, that of serving an indirect good to your friends by being much to them, a reserve by which their sallies of virtue are fortified & they cordially cheered by the thoroughness of a mutual understanding. How has Edward served us most in these last years? by his figures & invoices? or through the healthful influence of his perfect moral health? How serves the Aunt M.? How but by bearing most intelligible testimony which is felt where it is not comprehended.

—

If I were more in love with life & as afraid of dying as you seem to insinuate I would go to a Jackson Caucus or to the Julien Hall & I doubt not the unmixed malignity, the withering selfishness, the impudent vulgarity that mark those meetings would speedily cure me of my appetite for longevity. In the hush of these woods I find no Jackson placards affixed to the trees.

We republicans do libel the monarchist. The monarchist of
Europe for so many ages has really been pervaded by an Idea.
He intellectually & affectionately views the king as the State.
And the monarch is pervaded by a correspondent idea & the
worst of them has yet demeaned himself more or less faithfully
as a State. A crown then is by no means 'a strip of velvet with
jewels' nor is Louis XVI Mr Louis Capet, as we chuse to affirm. Certainly there is something that mightily tickles a
human ear in being named a nation as Elizabeth of England,
Mary of Scotland, Anne of Austria.

"His works do follow him," saith the blessed Revelation, &
the world echoes Amen. *What hath he done?* is the divine question which searches souls & transpierces the paper shield of
every false reputation. A fop may sit in any chair of the world
for his hour nor be distinguished from Homer or Washington,
but there never can be doubt concerning the respective ability
of human beings when we seek the truth. Pretension may sit
still, but cannot act. Pretension never feigned an act of real
greatness. Pretension never wrote an Iliad nor drove back
Xerxes nor Christianized the World nor discovered America
nor abolished Slavery. "The light of the public square will best
test its merit," said M. Angelo. Mr Coleridge has thrown many
new truths into circulation, Mr Southey never one.

—

Dec. 23. A good chapter might be writ of *Optical Deceptions.*
A sort of disappointment is felt by an ingenious man on hearing
opinions & truths congenial to his own announced with effect
in conversation. They are so near to his own thought or expression, that he thinks he ought to have spoken first. That is
an *optical deception* of the mind. If they had not been uttered
by this other, he would not have uttered them. It is merely
under the influence of this magnet that he becomes intensely
magnetic. Take it away & this effect will subside in him. Perhaps I shall never write of Shakspear's sonnets; yet let any critic
execute that work, & I should go to law with him for assault &
battery.

Bottom in Shakspear is a philosopher of this kidney. He
fathers each new part, the moment it is named. It fills his
whole horizon. He would be that alone. He mistakes his om-

nivolence for omnipotence. The only remedy is to present still a new thought to withdraw him from the last.

It results from the fact that every thought is one side of Nature, & really has the whole world under it.

This exclusive prominence of one thought is that which Bacon indicated by idols of the cave.

"Time & patience change a mulberry leaf into satin."

The disinterestedness of the truth-love is shown in this, that it only wants an intelligent ear. A good aunt is more to the young poet than a patron. Moliere had more happiness the year round from his old woman than from Louis.

———

Do, dear, when you come to write Lyceum lectures, remember that you are not to say, What must be said in a Lyceum? but what discoveries or stimulating thoughts have I to impart to a thousand persons? not what they will expect to hear but what is fit for me to say.

"No matter where you begin. Read anything five hours a day & you will soon be knowing." said Johnson.

Out of these fragmentary lobsided mortals shall the heaven unite Phidias, Demosthenes, Shakspear, Newton, Napoleon, Bacon, and St John in one person.

24 Dec. Him I call rich, that soul I call endowed whether in man or woman, who by poverty or affliction or love has been driven home so far as to make acquaintance with the spiritual dominion of every human mind. Hence forward he is introduced into sublime society; henceforward he can wave the hand of adieu to all the things he coveted most. Henceforward he is above compassion. He may it is true seldom look at his treasure; he may like one who has brought home his bride go apart & compose himself & only take furtive glances at his good with a fearful joy from the very assurance of confirmed bliss but him I leave within his heaven & all others I call miserably poor.

A singular equality may be observed between the great men of the first & the last ages. The Astronomy, the arts, & the history of sixty centuries give Lafayette, Canning, Webster no advantage over Saladin, Scipio, or Agesilaus. The reason is, the Arts, the Sciences are in man, & the Spartan possessed & used the very talent in his war that Watt used for economical ends & the pride & selfsufficiency of the Ancient was founded on this very consciousness of infinitely versatile resources. The beggars of Sparta & of Rome hurled defiance with as proud a tone as if Lysander's fleet of tubs had been an Armada or the rude walls of Sparta had been the bastions of Gibraltar. The resources of the mechanic arts are merely costume. If Fabricius had been shown instead of Pyrrhus's elephants Napoleon's park of artillery, he would have displayed no more emotion; he would have found a counterbalance in himself; all the finites cannot outweigh one infinite. All the erudition of an University of doctors is not a match for the mother wit of one Æsop. Hudson, Behring, Parry.

Raphael's three manners of painting may be matched in the biography of every genius.

Nature keeps much on her table but more in her closet.

A few words writ by a trembling hand of old Isaiah or Homer become an immoveable palisado to guard their sense against change or loss through all the storms & revolutions of time.

Dec. 25. Where there is D E F there must be A B C saith Sancho's aunt. For heaven's sake let me be alone to the end of the world unconsidered, unaided, rather than that my friend should affect an interest in me he does not feel or overstep by so much as one word or one expression of countenance his real sympathy. It turns my stomach, it cuts my throat where I looked for a manly furtherance or at least a manly resistance to find a mush of concession. Better be a nettle in the side of your companion than be his echo. I lament with a contrition too deep for groaning every sacrifice of truth to fat good nature & not less those where Custom has insensibly produced a great alteration in a wellfounded opinion. I am thankful that I was permitted to write G.B.E. in his bereavement that I lacked sympathy with the character of his wife. If I praise her virtues, he will now believe me. December 26. A good subject for book or lecture were it to read the riddle of the ancient Mythology; & show how far Minerva was only a fine word for wisdom. Bacon has done most & was fittest to do it. An obscure & slender thread of truth runs through all mythologies & this might lead often to highest regions of philosophy. Isis & Osiris. Eros & Anteros.

———

There is no object in nature which intense light will not make beautiful. & none which loses beauty by being nearer seen.

———

There are two kinds of blindness, one of incapacity to see; the other, of preoccupied attention. The prophet, the bard, the man of genius, absorbed with the Idea which haunts him ever, & which he is appointed to utter, as he can, to his age, may easily cast such careless glances at other men's works, as not to detect their superlative worth. A young man who falls in love with a maiden can easily set at nought all the advantageous or glorious offers that others may make him & perform prodigious acts of perseverance, courage, & self-denial in his quest. A nation of men unanimous & desperately bent on freedom or conquest can easily confound all calculation of statists & in defiance of superior potentates accomplish wild & extravagant actions out of all proportion to their numerical or fiscal strength, as the Greeks, the Saracens, the Swiss, the Americans, & the French did. Remember the 'Rostopchin' times & the 'last hoofs' of New England.

Their eyes were holden that they should not see.
Men of genius to be canonized after their death are disagreeable, sometimes hateful beggars in their lifetime. And when we see them there is no beauty that we should desire them.

Snow & moonlight make all landscapes alike.
Every thing may be painted, every thing sung, but to be poetized its feet must be just lifted from the ground.
The wind will go down with the sun.

I believe the Christian religion to be profoundly true; true to an extent that they who are styled its most orthodox defenders have never or but in rarest glimpses once or twice in a lifetime reached. I who seek to be a realist, to deny & put off every thing that I do not heartily accept, do yet catch myself continually in a practical unbelief of its deepest teachings. It taught, it teaches the eternal opposition of the world to the truth, & introduced the absolute authority of the spiritual law. Milton apprehended its nature when he said "For who is there almost that measures wisdom by simplicity, strength by suffering, dignity by lowliness?" That do I in my sane moments, & feel the ineffable peace, yea & the influx of God that attend humility & love, and before the cock crows, I deny him thrice.

"There's nothing good or bad but thinking makes it so."

A friend once told me that he never spent anything on himself without deserving the praise of disinterested benevolence.

Saturday night December 27. There is in every man a determination of character to a peculiar end, counteracted often by unfavorable fortune, but more apparent the more he is left at liberty. This is called his genius, or his nature, or his turn of mind. The object of Education should be to remove all obstructions & let this natural force have free play & exhibit its peculiar product. It seems to be true that no man in this is deluded. This determination of his character is to something in nature; something real. This object is called his Idea. It is that which rules his most advised actions, those especially that are most his, & is most distinctly discerned by him in those days or moments when he derives the sincerest satisfaction from his life. It can only be indicated by any action not defined by any thing less than the aggregate of all his genuine actions; perhaps then only approximated. Hence the slowness of the ancients to judge of the life before death. "Expect the end." It is most accurately denoted by the man's name, as when we say the Scipionism of Scipio; or "There spoke the soul of Caesar." The ancients seem to have expressed this spiritual superintendence by representing every human being as consigned to the charge of a Genius or Daemon by whose counsels he was guided in what he did best but whose counsels he might reject.

"Heathen philosophers taught that whosoever would but use his ear to listen might hear the voice of his guiding Genius ever before him, calling, &, as it were, pointing to that way which is his part to follow." *Milton* vol 1 p 251

December 28. Whenever I open my eyes I read that everything has expression, a mouth, a chin, a lock of hair, the lappel of a coat, the crimp or plait of a cap, a creampot, a tree, a stone. So much I concede to the physiognomist & craniologist. At the same time I see well enough how different is the expression of a pink ribbon upon one & upon another head.— But ah the pink ribbons of clouds that I saw last eve in the sunset modulated with tints of unspeakable softness and the air meantime had so much vivacity & sweetness that it was a pain to come in doors. C. saw the same flecks of cloud & likened them to gold fishes. Had they no expression? Is there no meaning in the live repose which that amphitheatre of a valley behind Ball's hill reflects to my eye & which Homer or Shakspeare could not re-form for me in Words? The leafless trees become spires of flame in the sunset with the blue East for their back ground & the stars of the dead calices of flowers & every withered stem & stubble rimed with frost with all their forms & hues contribute something to the mute music.

Rather let me be "a pagan suckled in a creed outworn" than cowardly deny or conceal one particle of my debt to Greek art or poetry or virtue. Certainly I would my debt were more, but it is my fault not theirs if 'tis little. But how pitiful if a mind enriched & infused with the spirit of their severe yet human Beauty modulating the words they spake, the acts they did, the forms they sculptured, every gesture, every fold of the robe; especially animating the biography of their men with a wild wisdom and an elegance as wild & handsome as sunshine; the brave anecdotes of Agesilaus, Phocion, & Epaminondas; the death of Socrates, that holy martyr, a death like that of Christ; the purple light of Plato which shines yet into all ages & is a test of the sublimest intellects—to receive the influences however partial of all this, & to speak of it as if it were nothing, or like a fool under praise it in a Sermon because the worshippers are ignorant, & incapable of understanding that there may be degrees & varieties of merit, & that the merit of Paul shall not be less because that of Aristotle is genuine & great,—I call that meanspirited, if it were Channing or Luther that did it. Be it remembered of Milton who drank deeply of these fountains that in an age & assembly of fierce fanatics he drew as freely from these resources & with just acknowledgment, as from those known & honored by his party. "His soul was like a Star & dwelt apart."

I honor him who made himself of no reputation. If I were called upon to charge a young minister, I would say Beware of Tradition: Tradition which embarrasses life & falsifies all teaching. The sermons that I hear are all dead of that ail. The preacher is betrayed by his ear. He begins to inveigh against some real evil & falls unconsciously into formulas of speech which have been said & sung in the church some ages & have lost all life. They never had any but when freshly & with special conviction applied. But *you* must never lose sight of the purpose of helping a particular person in every word you say. Thus my preacher summed the deaths of the past year & then reminded the bereaved that these were admonitions of God to them, &c. &c. Now all these words fell to the ground. They are Hamlet's "Many *As'es* of great charge"; mere wind. He ought to have considered whether it were true as his ear has always heard to be sure without contradiction, that deaths *were* admonitions. By enumerating in his mind the persons that would be included in this address, he would quickly perceive that there was great disparity in the cases, many had mourned but were not now mourners, that some of the deaths were to the survivors desireable, some quite indifferent, that some of these survivors were persons of that habitual elevation of religious view as to have just views of death & so were above this prose. Others were of such manifold business or preoccupation of mind as that any death must occupy but a subordinate place in their thoughts & if any where the words might be spoken with strict propriety, they were yet so general as not to be likely to strike that ear. I am prolix on this instance yet the fault is obvious to a discerning ear in almost every sentence of the prayers & the sermons that are ordinarily heard in the Church. Not so with Edward Taylor that living Methodist, the

Poet of the Church. Not so with the Swedenborgians if their pulpit resembles their book.

December 29. A critic pronounced that Wordsworth was a good man but no poet. "Ah!" said one present, "you know not how much poetry there is in goodness!"

C. says he has four stomachs like a camel & what law he reads in the morning he puts into the first stomach till evening; then it slides into the second.

Every truth is a full circle.

'He made himself of no reputation.' The words have a divine sound.

To the music of the surly storm that thickens the darkness of the night abroad & rocks the walls & fans my cheek through the chinks & cracks, I would sing my strain though hoarse & small. Yet please God it shall be lowly, affectionate, & true. It were worth trial whether the distinction between a spiritual & a traditional religion could not be made apparent to an ordinary congregation. There are parts of faith so great so self-evident that when the mind rests in them the pretensions of the most illuminated, most pretending sect pass for nothing. When I rest in perfect humility, when I burn with pure love what can Calvin or Swedenborg say to me?

But to show men the nullity of churchgoing compared with a real exaltation of their being I think might even promote parish objects & draw them to church. To show the reality & infinite depth of spiritual laws; that all the maxims of Christ are true to the core of the world; that there is not, can't be, any cheating of nature, might be apprehended.

Every spiritual law I suppose would be a contradiction to common sense. Thus I should begin with my old saws that nothing can be given; everything is sold; love compels love; hatred, hatred; action & reaction always are equal. No evil in society but has its check which coexists; the moral, the physical, the social world is a plenum & any strain in one place produces equal yielding in another. Nothing is free but the will of man & that only to procure his own virtue: on every side but that one, he beats the air with his pompous action; that punishment not follows but accompanies crime. They have said in churches in this age "Mere Morality". O God they know thee not who speak contemptuously of all that is grand. It is the distinction of Christianity, that it is moral. All that is personal in it is nought. When any one comes who speaks with better insight into moral nature he will be the new gospel; miracle or not, inspired or uninspired, he will be the Christ. Persons are nothing. If I could tell you what you know not, could by my knowledge of the divine being put that within your grasp which now you dimly apprehend, & make you feel the moral sublime, you would never think of denying my inspiration.

The whole power of Christianity resides in this fact, that it is more agreeable to the constitution of man than any other teaching. But from the constitution of man may be got better teaching still.

Morality requires purity, but purity is not it; requires justice, but justice is not that; requires beneficence, but is something better. Indeed there is a kind of descent & accommodation felt when we leave speaking of Moral Nature to urge a virtue it enjoins. For to the Soul in her pure action all the virtues are natural & not painfully acquired. Excite the soul & it becomes suddenly virtuous. Touch the deep heart and all these listless stingy beefeating bystanders will see the dignity of a sentiment, will say This is good & all I have I will give for that. Excite the soul, & the weather & the town & your condition in the world all disappear, the world itself loses its solidity, nothing remains but the soul & the Divine Presence in which it lives. Youth & age are indifferent in this presence.

Extremes meet. Misfortunes even may be so accumulated as to be ludicrous. To be shipwrecked is bad; to be shipwrecked on an iceberg is horrible; to be shipwrecked on an iceberg in a snowstorm, confounds us; to be shipwrecked on an iceberg in a storm and to find a bear on the snow bank to dispute the sailor's landing which is not driven away till he has bitten off a sailor's arm, is rueful to laughter.

Some people smile spite of themselves in communicating the worst news.

"Overturn, Overturn, and overturn," said our aged priest,

"until he whose right it is to reign, shall come into his kingdom."

The great willowtree over my roof is the trumpet & accompaniment of the storm & gives due importance to every caprice of the gale and the trees in the avenue announce the same facts with equal din to the front tenants. Hoarse concert: they roar like the rigging of a ship in a tempest.

The Unitarian preacher who sees that his orthodox hearer may with reason complain that the preaching is not serious, faithful, authoritative enough is by that admission judged. It is not an excuse that he can with clearness see the speculative error of his neighbor. But when a man speaks from deeper convictions than any party faith, when he declares the simple truth he finds his relation to the Calvinist or Methodist or Infidel at once changed in the most agreeable manner. He is of their faith, says each.

It is really a spiritual power which stopped the mouths of the regular priests in the presence of the fervent First Quaker & his friends. If the dead-alive never learned before that they do not speak with authority from the Highest, they learn it then when a commissioned man comes who speaks, because he cannot hold back, the message that is in his heart.

Certainly I read a similar story respecting Luther; that the preacher's heart, stout enough before, misgave him when he perceived Luther was in the audience.

The height of virtue is only to act in a firm belief that moral laws hold. Jesus & St Paul & Socrates & Phocion believed in spite of their senses that Moral law existed & reigned & so believing could not have acted otherwise. The sinner lets go his perception of these laws & then acts agreeably to the lower law of the senses. The logic of the sinner & of the saint is perfect. There is no flaw in either Epicureanism or Stoicism.

Does not Aristotle distinguish between Temperance for ends & Temperance for love of temperance? Each of these virtues becomes dowdy in a sermon. They must be practised for their elegance. The virtuous man must be a poet & not a drudge of his virtues, to have them perfect. If he *could by implication* perform all the virtues, that is not aim to be temperate nor aim to be honest nor aim to be liberal but in his lofty piety be all three without knowing it, then is he the good moralist. The Ecclesiastical dogma of 'Faith, not Works' is based on this truth.

Jesus believed in moral nature and he did not come in his own name. (When a preacher does not say he comes in his own name he generally looks it or speaks it plainer than by words.)

July 7. Rode up the river to the Mills. Noble sight is the saw mill of ten saws—the servitude of the river. It floats the timber down; then by the application of machinery the river hauls up the reluctant log into the mill as I have seen a halibut hauled into a ship; then the river saws the log into boards; then floats the raft into Bangor; then floats the brig or ship that receives the boards onward to the Ocean. The pride of the forest— White pines of four feet diameter which it cost a hundred years of sun & rain & cold to rear must end in a sawmill at last. Every body puts out a boom from his bank on the river, one man catches firewood. Another owns an eddy & catches logs & receives a fee for keeping them.

And all men are equally interested in the event of a full river. The lawyer, the physician, the bookseller all squint at the clouds & estimate the chance of a freshet.

As we sailed down the river in the steamboat the Indians who have a camp at High Head came to the shore & looked down upon the show as if their Genius looked its last.

Further down the river I saw a large white headed eagle sitting upon the bough of a pine.

———

Rode over to Exeter 23 miles to visit J.B. Hill, Esq. There sat my old classmate in his office with a client,—himself without coat or vest or neckcloth, unshaved, &, as he said, fat & rusty. He kept his countenance wondrously, & talked as of yore, & what a pile of forehead! A magnanimous man altogether incapable of pettifogging & stout hearted as of old; a whig in the midst of town where the tories are 300 to 30. Fine farming town, noble forest. You could drive a horse & chaise in the primitive forest of hard wood, so free of underwoods. No oak within 20 miles.

Death of Mr Loomis. "This year thou shalt die" was the text, & he presently fell down in the pulpit. He was carried home & put into a cold room, & proper means not used to restore him. On Tuesday noon a visiter found his stomach warm, & blood oozing from the arm and his head frozen.

5 Aug. This morn I went to Highgate & called at Dr Gillman's & sent up a note to Mr Coleridge requesting leave to see him. He sent me word that he was in bed but if I would call after 12 o'clock he would see me. I named one o'clock. At one I called & he appeared, a short thick old man with bright blue eyes, black suit & cane, & any thing but what I had imagined, a clear clean face with fine complexion—a great snuff taker which presently soiled his cravat & neat black suit. He asked me if I knew Allston & then launched into a discourse upon his merits & doings when he knew him in Rome, how Titianesque he was, &c. Then upon Dr Channing & what an unspeakable misfortune to him it was that he should have turned out an Unitarian after all. Thence he burst into a long & indignant declamation upon the folly & ignorance of Unitarianism, its high unreasonableness & took up Bp Waterland which lay (laid there I think for the occasion) upon the table & read me with great vehemence two or three pages of manuscript notes writ by him in the fly leaves, passages too which I believe are in the Aids to Reflexion.

As soon as he stopped a second to take breath, I remarked to him that it would be cowardly in me, after this, not to inform him that I was an Unitarian, though much interested in his explanations. Yes, he said, I supposed so, & continued as before. He spoke of the wonder that after so many ages of unquestioning acquiescence in the doctrine of St Paul, the doctrine of the Trinity, which was also according to Philo Judaeus the doctrine of the Jews before Christ—this handful of Priestleians should take upon themselves to deny it &c. Very sorry that Dr Channing a man to whom he looked up—no, to say he looked up to him, would be to speak falsely,—but a man whom he looked *at* with so much interest should embrace such views. But when he saw Dr C he hinted to him that he

was afraid he loved Christianity for what was lovely & excellent—he loved the good in it & not the true. And I tell you sir
that I have known many persons who loved the good, for one
person who loved the true. But it is a far greater virtue to love
the true for itself alone than to love the good for itself alone.
He knew all this about Unitarianism perfectly well because he
had once been an Unitarian & knew what quackery it was. He
had been called the rising Star of Unitarianism. Then he expa-
tiated upon the Trinitarian doctrine of the Deity as being Realism &c &c, upon the idea of God not being essential but
super essential &c, upon trinism & tetrakism, upon the *will*
being that by which a person is a person because if he should
push me in the street & so I should force the man next me into
the kennel I should at once exclaim to the sufferer 'I did not
do it sir,' meaning it was not done with my will. &c &c—I insisted that many Unitarians read Mr Coleridge's books with
pleasure & profit who did not subscribe to his theology.

He told me that if I should insist on my faith here in England & he should insist on his, his would be the hotter side of
the fagot.
I asked about the extract in the Friend; he said it was from a
pamphlet in his possession entitled the Protest of one of the
Independents or something to that effect. I said how good it
was. Yes, he said, the man was a chaos of truths, but lacked the
knowledge that God was a God of Order. But the passage no
doubt would strike me more in the quotation than in the original for he had filtered it. I rose to depart & he said, I do not
know whether you care about poetry but I will mention some
verses I lately made upon my baptismal anniversary & he recited with great emphasis, standing, ten or twelve lines that
were very interesting. Then he alluded to my visit to Malta &
to Sicily & compared one place with the other repeating what
he said to the Bp of London when he returned from that
country:
That Sicily was an excellent place to study political economy; for in any town there, it was only necessary to ask what
the government enacted & reverse that to know what ought to
be done. It was the most felicitously opposite course to every
thing good & wise. There were only three things which the
govt brought on that garden of delights, viz. Itch, Pox, &

Famine. Whereas in Malta the force of law & mind was seen in making that barren rock of Semi Saracen inhabitants, the seat of population & plenty. Going out, he showed me in the parlour Alston's picture, & told me that Montagu the famous picture dealer once came to see him & the moment he laid eyes upon this said "Well you have got a picture" thinking it a Titian or a Paul Veronese. Afterward as he talked with his back to the picture the said Montagu put up his hand & touched it & exclaimed "By —— this picture is not ten years old!" so intensely delicate & skilful was that man's touch.

I asked if he had had any correspondence with Marsh; he said No for he had received his book or letter at a time when he was incapable of any effort & soon should send him some new books & asked if I had seen his Church & State. He begged me to call upon Mr Alston from him & present him his regards. And so I left him wishing him renewed health.

But I have put down the least part of the conversation or rather discourse of Mr C. I was in the room an hour & much of the discourse was like so many printed paragraphs in his book, perhaps the same; not to be easily followed.

Almost nobody in Highgate knew his name. I asked several persons in vain; at last a porter wished to know if I meant an elderly gentleman with white hair? 'Yes, the same'—Why he lives with Mr Gillman. Ah yes that is he. So he showed me the way.

Dr Bowring says that Wilson & Hogg went to see Wordsworth & the morning was fine & then there was a rainbow & altogether it was genial. So Hogg said to Wordsworth this is a fit spot for poets to meet in. Wordsworth drew himself up with ineffable disdain saying "*Poets* indeed!"

"To think is to act."

Concord, 1 January, 1835.

January 6th. No doubt we owe most valuable knowledge to our conversation even with the frivolous, yet when I return as just now from more than usual opportunities of hearing & seeing, it seems to me that one good day here, is worth more than three gadding days in town. Sunday I went for the first time to the Swedenborg Chapel. The sermon was in its style severely simple & in method & manner had much the style of a problem in geometry wholly uncoloured & unimpassioned. Yet was it, as I told Sampson Reed, one that with the exception of a single passage might have been preached without exciting surprise in any church. At the opposite pole, say rather in another Zone from this hard truist was Taylor in the afternoon wishing his sons a happy new year praying God for his servants of the brine, to favor commerce, to bless the bleached sail, the white foam & through commerce to christianize the Universe. "May every deck," he said, "be stamped by the hallowed feet of godly captains, & the first watch, & the second watch be watchful for the Divine light." He thanked God he had not been in Heaven for the last twenty five years,—then indeed had he been a dwarf in grace, but now he had his redeemed souls around him.

And so he went on,—this Poet of the Sailor & of Ann street—fusing all the rude hearts of his auditory with the heat of his own love & making the abstractions of philosophers accessible & effectual to them also. He is a fine study to the metaphysician or the life philosopher. He is profuse of himself; he never remembers the lookingglass. They are foolish who fear that notice will spoil him. They never made him & such as they cannot unmake him; he is a real man of strong nature &

noblest richest lines on his countenance. He is a work of the same hand that made Demosthenes & Shakspear & Burns & is guided by instincts diviner than rules. His whole discourse is a string of audacious felicities harmonized by a spirit of joyful love. Every body is cheered & exalted by him. He is a living man & explains at once what Whitefield & Fox & Father Moody were to their audiences, by the total infusion of his own soul into his assembly, & consequent absolute dominion over them. How puny, how cowardly, other preachers look by the side of this preaching. He shows us what a man can do. As I sat last Sunday in my country pew, I thought this Sunday I would see two living chapels, the Swedenborg & the Seamen's, and I was not deceived.

7th January. Bitter cold days, yet I read of that inward fervor which ran as fire from heart to heart through England in George Fox's time. How precisely parallel are the biographies of religious enthusiasts. Swedenborg, Guyon, Fox, Luther & perhaps Bohmen. Each owes all to the discovery that God must be sought within, not without. That is the discovery of Jesus. Each perceives the worthlessness of all instruction, & the infinity of wisdom that issues from meditation. Each perceives the nullity of all conditions but one, innocence; & the absolute submission which attends it. All become simple, plain in word & act. Swedenborg & the Quakers have much to say of a new Name that shall be given in heaven.

———

January 8. There is an elevation of thought from which things venerable become less, because we are in the presence of their Source. When we catch one clear glimpse of the moral harmonies which accomplish themselves throughout the Everlasting Now & throughout the omnipresent Here how impertinent seem the controversies of theologians. God is before us & they are wrangling about dead gods. What matters it whether the inspiration was plenary or secondary; whether this or that was intended by the Prophet; whether Jesus worked a miracle or no; if we have access inwardly to the Almighty & all wise One, Inspirer of all Prophecy, Container of all Truth & Sole Cause of Causes? All the Godhead that was in either of those ages in either of those men was the perception of those resplendent laws which at this very moment draw me at the same time that they outrun & overwhelm my faculties. The Teacher that I look for & await shall enunciate with more precision & universality, with piercing poetic insight those beautiful yet severe compensations that give to moral nature an aspect of mathematical science. He will not occupy himself in laboriously reanimating a historical religion but in bringing men to God by showing them that he IS, not was, & speaks not spoke.

January 9. The only true economy of time is to rely without interval on your own judgment. Keep the eye & ear open to all impressions, but deepen no impression by effort, but take the opinion of the Genius within, what ought to be retained by you & what rejected by you. Keep, that is, the upright position. Resign yourself to your thoughts, & then every object will make that mark, that modification of your character which it ought. This were better advice to a traveller than Sir Henry Wotton's, 'il viso sciolto, i pensieri stretti.' All your time will be lived; the journey, the dinner, the waiting, will not need to be subtracted.

———

There are some occult facts in human nature that are natural magic. The chief of these is, the glance (oeillade). The mysterious communication that is established across a house between two entire strangers, by this means, moves all the springs of wonder. It happened once that a youth & a maid beheld each other in a public assembly for the first time. The youth gazed with great delight upon the beautiful face until he caught the maiden's eye. She presently became aware of his attention & something like correspondence immediately takes place. The maid depressed her eyes that the man might gaze upon her face. Then the man looked away, that the maiden might gratify her curiosity. Presently their eyes met in a full, front, searching, not to be mistaken glance. It is wonderful how much it made them acquainted. The man thought that they had come nearer together than they could by any other intercourse in months. But he felt that by that glance he had been strangely baulked. The beautiful face was strangely transformed. He felt the stirring of owls, & bats, & horned hoofs, within him. The face which was really beautiful seemed to him to have been usurped by a low devil, and an innocent maiden, for so she still seemed to him, to be possessed. And that glance was the confession of the devil to his inquiry. Very sorry for the poor maiden was the man, & when the assembly separated, & she passed him as a stranger in the crowd, her form & feet had the strangest resemblance to those of some brute animal.

It is remarkable too that the spirit that appears at the windows of the house does at once in a manner invest itself in a new form of its own to the mind of the beholder.

Jan. 12. Truth is beautiful. Without doubt; and so are lies. I have no fairer page in my life's album than the delicious memory of some passages at Concord on the Merrimack when affection contrived to give a witchcraft surpassing even the deep attraction of its own truth to a parcel of accidental & insignificant circumstances. Those coach wheels that rolled into the mist & darkness of the July Morning. The little piazza, a piece of silk, the almshouse, the Davison girl & such other things, which were not the charm, have more reality to this groping memory than the charm itself which illuminated them.

> — —"passing sweet
> Are the domains of tender memory."

Be assured. There is as deep a wisdom in embroidered coats & blue & pink ribbons, as is in truth & righteousness.

Is it not the stupendous riches of man's nature that gives an additional delight to every new truth? When I read a problem, I would be a geometer; poetry a poet; history, a historian; sermons, a preacher; when I see paintings I would paint; sculpture, carve; & so with all things, the manifold soul in me indicates its acquaintance with all these things. Similar delight we have in the admirable artist's, soldier's or sailor's life. We individuate ourselves with him & judge of his work. What is this but our first ride round our estate to take possession, promising ourselves withal after a few visits more, to have an insight & give a personal direction to all the affairs that go on within our domain, which is the All.

13 Jan. "Our very signboards show there has been a Titian in the world." Do you think that Aristotle benefits him only who reads the Ethics & the Rhetoric? Or Bacon or Shakspear or the Schools those only who converse in them? Far otherwise; these men acted directly upon the common speech of men & made distinctions which as they were seen to be just by all who understood them, were rigidly observed as rules in their conversation & writing; & so were diffused gradually as improvements in the vernacular language. Thus the language *thinks* for us as Coleridge said.

—

My friend Mr W. will be a good minister
   "When it shall please the Lord
   To make his people out of board."

—

The great value of Biography consists in the perfect sympathy that exists between like minds. Space & time are an absolute nullity to this principle. An action of Luther's that I heartily approve I do adopt also. We are imprisoned in life in the company of persons painfully unlike us or so little congenial to our highest tendencies & so congenial to our lowest that their influence is noxious & only now & then comes by us some commissioned spirit that speaks as with the word of a prophet to the languishing nigh dead faith in the bottom of the heart & passes by & we forget what manner of men we are. It may be that there are very few persons at any one time in the world who can address with any effect the higher wants of men. This defect is compensated by the recorded teaching & acting of this class of men. Socrates, St Paul, Antoninus, Luther, Milton have lived for us as much as for their contemporaries if by books or by tradition their life & words come to my ear. We recognize with delight a strict likeness between their noblest impulses & our own. We are tried in their trial. By our cordial approval we conquer in their victory. We participate in their act by our thorough understanding of it.

And thus we become acquainted with a fact which we could not have learned from our fellows, that the faintest sentiments which we have shunned to indulge from the fear of singularity are older than the oldest institutions,—are eternal in man; that we can find ourselves, our private thoughts, our preferences, & aversions, & our moral judgments perhaps more truly matched in an ancient Lombard, or Saxon, or Greek, than in our own family.

It is a beautiful fact in human nature that the roar of separating oceans no nor the roar of rising & falling empires cannot hinder the ear from hearing the music of the most distant voices; that the trumpet of Homer's poetry yet shrills in the closet of the retired scholar across three thousand years; that the reproof of Socrates stings us like the bite of a serpent, as it did Alcibiades.

These affinities atone to us for the narrowness of our society, & the prison of our single lot, by making the human race our society, & the vast variety of human fortune the arena of actions on which we, by passing judgment, take part.

History taken together is as severely moral in its teaching as the straitest religious sect.   And thus we are fortified in our moral sentiments by a most intimate presence of sages & heroes.

Pythagoras is said (falsely I suppose) to have declared that he remembered himself to have existed before under the name of Euphorbus at the Siege of Troy. Which of us who is much addicted to reading but recognizes his own saying or thinking in his favorite authors?

14 Jan. Apollo kept the flocks of Admetus, said the poets; another significant fable. Every man is an angel in disguise, a god playing the fool. It seems as if Heaven had sent its insane angels into our world as an asylum & here they will break out into rare music & utter at intervals the words they have heard in Heaven & then the mad fit returns & they mope & wallow like dogs. When the gods come among men they are not known. Jesus was not. Socrates & Shakspear were not.

My thoughts tame me. Proud may the bard be among his fellow men, but when he sits waiting his inspiration he is a child, humble, reverent, watching for the thoughts as they flow to him from their unknown source. The moment of inspiration I am its reverent slave. I watch & watch & hail its Aurora from afar.

—

My Grandfather William Emerson left his parish & joined the Northern Army in the strong hope of having great influence on the men. He was bitterly disappointed in finding that the best men at home became the worst in the camp, vied with each other in profanity, drunkenness & every vice, & degenerated as fast as the days succeeded each other & instead of much influence he found he had none. This so affected him that when he became sick with the prevalent distemper he insisted on taking a dismission not a furlough, & as he died on his return his family lost, it is said, a major's pension.

—

May I say without presumption that like Michel Angelo I only block my statues.

2 February. Let Christianity speak ever for the poor & the low. Though the voice of society should demand a defence of slavery from all its organs that service can never be expected from me. My opinion is of no worth, but I have not a syllable of all the language I have learned, to utter for the planter. If by opposing slavery I go to undermine institutions I confess I do not wish to live in a nation where slavery exists. The life of this world has but a limited worth in my eyes & really is not worth such a price as the toleration of slavery. Therefore though I may be so far restrained by unwillingness to cut the planter's throat as that I should refrain from denouncing him, yet I pray God that not even in my dream or in madness may I ever incur the disgrace of articulating one word of apology for the slave trader or slave-holder.

Yesterday had I been born & bred a Quaker, I should have risen & protested against the preacher's words. I would have said that in the light of Christianity is no such thing as slavery. The only bondage it recognizes is that of Sin.

—

February 11. It needs to say something, they tell me, of the French Revolution. Why, yes, I believe that it has been advantageous on the whole. I very readily seek & find reasons for any such proposition because whilst I believe that evil is to be hated & resisted & punished or at least forcibly hindered, yet offences must needs come & out of them comes good as naturally & inevitably as the beautiful flower & the nourishing fruit out of the dark ground. I believe that the tendency of all thought is to Optimism.

Now for the French Revolution. I believe in the first place that it would be an advantage though we were not able to point out a single benefit that had flowed thence & were able to show many calamities. I should still incline to think that we were too near to judge, like a soldier in the ranks who is quite unable amid the din & smoke to judge how goes the day or guess at the plan of the engagement.

If I could see no direct good which it had occasioned I should still say see what great lessons it has taught the governor & the subject. It has taught men how surely the relaxing of the moral bands of society is followed by cruelty. It taught men that there was a limit beyond which the terrors of a standing army & of loyal association could not avail; that there was a limit beyond which the patience, the fears of a down trodden people could not go.

—

17 March. I come back to my rare book scarce a journal. There is nothing so easy as to form friendships & connexions. Yet lies there unseen a gulf between every man & woman, & a Tragedy is the protection of what seemed so helpless. So thought I today, when I heard the details of M's danger.

Many days give me marine recollections as today. It is because when the wind is loud & the air clear, the great masses of cloud move so fast as to suggest immediately their vicinity to the sea. The wind blowing from the west they must reach the coast, & shade the sea in an hour. Instantly therefore comes up before the eye the cold blue sea gathered up into waves all rippled & scored over with wind lines & a few sail scudding on their several tracks though scarce seen to move over the broad black circle. But nature is a picture frame which fits equally well a comic or a mourning piece.

Taylor in the preface to this healthful poem, "Van Artevelde," says that Sense must be the basis of all consummate poetry. It is well & truly said. We have almost a theory of Shakspear,—the wonder of Shakspear is almost diminished when we say, Strong Sense is the staple of his verse. Because what is to be accounted for, is, the extent of the man, that he could create not one or two, but so manifold classes & individuals & each perfect. But we are quite familiar with the expertness & power of men of sense in every new condition, & this experience supplies us with a just analogy.

—

March 19. As I walked in the woods I felt what I often feel that nothing can befal me in life, no calamity, no disgrace, (leaving me my eyes) to which Nature will not offer a sweet consolation. Standing on the bare ground with my head bathed by the blithe air, & uplifted into the infinite space, I become happy in my universal relations. The name of the nearest friend sounds then foreign & accidental. I am the heir of uncontained beauty & power. And if then I walk with a companion, he should speak from his Reason to my Reason; that is, both from God. To be brothers, to be acquaintances, master or servant, is then a trifle too insignificant for remembrance. O keep this humor, (which in your lifetime may not come to you twice,) as the apple of your eye. Set a lamp before it in your memory which shall never be extinguished.

I think Taylor's poem is the best light we have ever had upon the genius of Shakspear. We have made a miracle of Shakspear, a haze of light instead of a guiding torch by accepting unquestioned all the tavern stories about his want of education, & total unconsciousness. The interval evidence all the time is irresistible that he was no such person. He was a man like this Taylor of strong sense & of great cultivation; an excellent Latin Scholar, & of extensive & select reading so as to have formed his theories of many historical characters with as much clearness as Gibbon or Niebuhr or Goethe. He wrote for intelligent persons, & wrote with intention. He had Taylor's strong good sense, & added to it his own wonderful facility of execution which aerates & sublimes all language the moment he uses it, or, more truly, animates every word.

I ought to have said in my wood-thoughts just now, that there the mind integrates itself again. The attention which had been distracted into parts, is reunited, reinsphered. The whole of Nature addresses itself to the whole man. We are reassured. It is more than a medicine. It is health.

In talking weeks ago with M. M. E. I was ready to say that a severest truth would forbid me to say that ever I had made a sacrifice. That which we are, in healthy times seems so great that nothing can be taken from us that seems much. I loved Ellen, & love her with an affection that would ask nothing but its indulgence to make me blessed. Yet when she was taken from me, the air was still sweet, the sun was not taken down from my firmament, & however sore was that particular loss, I still felt that it was particular, that the Universe remained to us both, that the Universe abode in its light & in its power to replenish the heart with hope. Distress never, trifles never abate my trust. Only this Lethean stream that washes through us, that gives sometimes a film or haze of unreality, a suggestion that, as C. said of Concord society, 'we are on the way back to Annihilation', only this threatens my Trust. But not that would certify me that I had ever suffered. Praise! Praise & Wonder! And oft we feel so wistful & babe-like that we cannot help thinking that a correspondent sentiment of paternal pleasantry must exist over us in the bosom of God.

———

This rebellious Understanding is the incorrigible liar. Convict him of perfidy, and he answers you with a new fib. No man speaks the truth or lives a true life two minutes together.

"Wrath is not worth carrying home, though a man should ride." Landor.

March 23d. There is no greater lie than a voluptuous book like Boccaccio. For it represents the pleasures of appetite which only at rare intervals a few times in a lifetime are intense, & to whose acme continence is essential, as frequent, habitual, & belonging to the incontinent. Let a young man imagine that women were made for pleasure & are quite defenceless, & act on that opinion, he will find the weakest of them garrisoned by troops of pains & sorrows which he who touches her, instantly participates. He who approaches a woman unlawfully thinks he has overcome her. It is a bitter jest of nature. He will shortly discover that he has put himself wholly in the power of that worthless slut. Montaigne, coarse as he is, is yet true.

Settle it in your mind that you must choose between your own suffrage & other people's. I used to think, all men used to think that you can have both, but you cannot. Secure your own, & you shall be assured of others, twenty years hence, but you must part with them so long. Before this Reason with bright eternal eyes, even merits that seem pure & saintlike compared with practices & reputations of the mob, are seen to be vulgar & vile. There are merits calculated on shorter & longer periods; better than those of the hour are the Benthamite & the Calvinist who keep the law all their life for pay; but these dwindle before the incalculable eternity which the lover of virtue embraces in the present moment.

The virtue of the intellect consists in preferring work to trade. Brougham, Canning, Everett, convert their genius into a shop, & turn every faculty upside down that they may sell well. Allston, Wordsworth, Carlyle, are smit with the divine desire of Creation, & scorn the auctioneers. Now what you do for the Shop is so much taken from science.

—

Cannot a man contemplate his true good so steadily as to be willing to renounce all thirst for display, & make all his doings tentative, imperfect, because aiming ever at truth & perfection lying out of himself; instead of tricking out what trifles he has picked up & disposing them to advantage in little popular poems or conversations or books? I think he had better live in the country, & see little society, & make himself of no reputation.

Sects fatten on each other's faults. How many people get a living in New England by calling the Unitarians prayerless, or by showing the Calvinists to be bigots. Hallet feeds on the Masons, & McGavin on the Catholics. The poor man that only sees faults in himself will die, in his sins.

Charles thinks the Unitarians pursue a low conservative policy.

The high, the generous, the selfdevoted sect will always instruct & command mankind.

Is it because I am such a bigot to my own whims, that I distrust the ability of a man who insists much on the advantage to be derived from literary *conversazioni*? Alone is wisdom. Alone is happiness. Society nowadays makes us lowspirited, hopeless. Alone is heaven.

In the Marquesas Islands on the way from Cape Horn to the Sandwich Islands 9° S. of the Equator they eat men in 1833.

March 26. The wild delight runs through the man in spite of real sorrows. Nature says he is my creature & spite of all his impertinent griefs he shall be glad with me. Almost I fear to think how glad I am.

I went by him in the night. Who can tell the moment when the pine outgrew the whortleberry that shaded its first sprout? It went by in the night.

March 27. He who writes should seek not to say what may be said but what has not been said that is yet true. I will read & write. Why not? All the snow is shovelled away, all the corn planted & the children & the creatures on the planet taken care of without my help. But if I do not read nobody will. Yet am I not without my own fears. Capt Franklin after 6 weeks travelling to the N. Pole on the ice found himself 200 miles south of the spot he set out from; the ice had floated. And I sometimes start to think I am looking out the same vocables in the Dictionary, spelling out the same sentences, solving the same problems.—My ice may float also.

———

March 28. If life were long enough among my thousand & one works should be a book of Nature whereof 'Howitt's Seasons' should be not so much the model as the parody. It should contain the Natural history of the woods around my shifting camp for every month in the year. It should tie their astronomy, botany, physiology, meteorology, picturesque, & poetry together. No bird, no bug, no bud should be forgotten on his day & hour. Today the chicadees, the robins, bluebirds, & songsparrows sang to me. I dissected the buds of the birch & the oak, in every one of the last is a star. The crows sat above as idle as I below. The river flowed brimful & I philosophised upon this composite collective beauty which refuses to be analysed. Nothing is beautiful alone. Nothing but is beautiful in the Whole. Learn the history of a craneberry. Mark the day when the pine cones & acorns fall.

A wonderful sight is the inverted landscape. Look at the prospect from a high hill through your legs & it gives the world a most pictorial appearance.

—

10 April. I fretted the other night at the Hotel at the stranger who broke into my chamber after midnight claiming to share it. But after his lamp had smoked the chamber full & I had turned round to the wall in despair the man blew out his lamp, knelt down at his bedside & made in low whisper a long earnest prayer. Then was the relation entirely changed between us. I fretted no more but respected & liked him.

Coleridge said it was no decisive mark of poetic genius that a man should write well concerning himself.

Is it not because the true genius the Shakspear & Goethe sees the tree & sky & man as they are, enters into them whilst the inferior writer dwells evermore with himself "twinkling restlessly"?

A man is seldom in the upright position two moments together, but when he is, let him record his observations & they shall be fit for "the Spiritual Inquirer."

—

I should be glad of a Catalogue of Ideas; objects of the Reason, as Conceptions are objects of the Understanding. Mr. Coleridge names a Point, a Line, a Circle, as Ideas in Mathematics. God, Free will, Justice, Holiness, as Ideas in Morals.

"Already my opinion has gained infinitely in force when another mind has adopted it." This is the reason why a writer appears ever to so much more advantage in the pages of another man's book than in his own. Coleridge, Wordsworth, Schelling are conclusive when Channing or Carlyle or Everett quote them, but if you take up their own books then instantly they become not lawgivers but modest peccable candidates for your approbation.

—

14 April. "Nec te, &c." Every Man is a wonder until you learn his studies, his associates, his early acts & the floating opinions of his times, & then he developes himself as naturally from a point as a river is made from rills. Burke's orations are but the combination of the Annual Register which he edited with the Inquiry on the Sublime & Beautiful which he wrote at the same time. Swedenborg is unriddled by learning the theology & philosophy of Continental Europe in his youth. Each great doctrine is then received by the mind as a tally of an Idea in its own reason & not as news.

Rev. Dr Freeman consoled my father on his deathbed by telling him he had not outlived his teeth, &c. & bid my mother expect now to be neglected by society.

You cannot show a head of Dante or Rousseau or Laplace to a company but one spectator shall see an exact resemblance to Deacon Bumstead, or Mr Kuhn, or Uncle Barrett; for common people will not make the effort to raise themselves to the great mind whose effigy is set before them, but must ever degrade that to the pinched circle of their habitual experience.

—

"That's indications of intemperance," said my fair stage companion to her friend.

Let the imaginative man deny himself & stick by facts. As a man must not bring his children into company naked, & must not bring more children into the world than he can clothe, so the idealist must retain his thoughts until they embody themselves in fit outward illustrations.

A courthouse is a good place to learn the limits of man. The best counsel are not orators, but very slovenly speakers: to use Mr Warren's fine apology for Baylies, "they spread their ability over the whole argument, & have not strong points." The interminable sentences of Mr H., clause growing out of clause "like the prickly pear," as Charles said, reminded me of nothing so much as certain vestry praelections. But in the courthouse the worth of a man is guaged.

An advantage shines on the abolition side that these philanthropists really feel no clog, no check from authority, no discord, no sore place in their own body which they must keep

out of sight or tenderly touch. People just out of the village or
the shop reason & plead like practised orators, such scope the
subject gives them, & such stimulus to their affections. The
Reason is glad to find a question which is not, like Religion or
Politics, bound around with so many traditions & usages that
every man is forced to argue unfairly, but one on which he may
exhaust his whole love of truth,—his heart & his mind. This is
one of those causes which will make a man.

Never is a good cause in facts long at loss for an ideal
equipment.

It was alarming to see the lines of sloth in so many faces in
the courthouse. The flame of life burns very dim. The most active lives have so much routine as to preclude progress almost
equally with the most inactive.

"Je défie un coeur comme le vôtre d'oser mal penser du
mien," writes Rousseau to Diderot.

———

22 April. I have made no record of Everett's fine Eulogy at
Lexington on the 20th. But he is all art & I find in him nowadays maugre all his gifts & great merits more to blame than
praise. He is not content to be Edward Everett, but would be
Daniel Webster. This is his mortal distemper. Why should such
a genius waste itself? Have we any to spare? Why should
Everett make grimaces? He will not deliver himself up to dear
Nature, but insists on making postures & sounds after his own
taste, & like those he has heard of, & now he does not know
there is any Nature *for him*. Neither has he any *faith*. Charles
proposed to read a sentence from the Phaedo, conceding that
the N. Testament was unfashionable. When he addressed the
Relics in the wooden box, he manifestly did not know what to
do with his eyes & looked out sideways at last to see how
people took it, so far has he got in his Lie, & so much of its
fruit may a man reap without yet suspecting it. Daniel Webster, Nature's own child sat there all day & drew all eyes. Poor
Everett! for this was it that you left your own work, your exceeding great & peculiar vocation, the desire of all eyes, the
gratitude of all ingenuous scholars—to stray away hither &
mimic this Man, that here & everywhere in your best & (for
work) unsurpassed exertions, you might still be mere secondary & satellite to him, & for him hold a candle?

Webster spoke at the Table few & simple words but from the old immoveable basis of simplicity & common natural emotion to which he instinctively & consciously adheres.

———

On the same auspicious morning I received a letter from Carlyle the wise, the brave, and his intimations of a visit to America, which purpose may God prosper & consummate. Better a great deal have friends full grown before they are made acquainted; like Moody & Webster they have the pleasant surprise of the bare result; a man meets a man. What fact is more valuable than the difference of our power alone & with others. The scholar sits down to write & all his years of Meditation do not furnish him with one good thought or happy expression but it is necessary to write a letter to his friend & forthwith troops of gentle thoughts embody themselves on every hand in chosen words. Blessed be the friend.

———

23 April. The order of things consents to virtue. Such scenes as luxurious poets & novelists often paint, where temptation has a quite overcoming force, never or very rarely occur in real life.

It is very hard to know what to do if you have great desires for benefitting mankind. But a very plain thing is your duty. It may be suspected then that the depth of wisdom & the height of glory is there. Self-Union,—never risk that. Neither lie nor steal nor betray, for you violate Consciousness. Nothing is self-evident but the commandments of Consciousness.

"The limbs of my buried ones," &c. I dislike the bad taste of almost every thing I have read of Jean Paul; this scrap for instance; Shakspear never said these hard artificial things.

We think we are approaching a star. I fear it is a nebula. At least individual aims are very nebulous.

———

Quite a piece of nature is my new acquaintance Mr Robbins of Lexington. A Man of genuine public spirit & profuse liberality yet out of his mouth runs ever this puddle of vitriol of spite "at the other village." The low slang which seasons all his conversation contrasts oddly enough with the nobleness of his sentiments. "They softsoaped me," &c. Whilst he plays the

Man of Ross, he says he does every thing "to please himself, that's all;" he doesn't care for liking or disliking, "he likes fair-weather," & "to see people work," & "to have all sort of 'amusements,'" by which he means churches, schools, lyceums, &c. It makes him sick to death to sit in the house, he goes every day to Boston, he pays $10,000. a year for labor in the town of Lexington.—And his fine grounds he has laid out for the public, & filled with pears & peaches & grapes for the boys, "enough for them & me too." & built the Hall, & put up clock & bell, & paid for singing & filled the punch pitcher, &c, &c, &c, but hates joint stock companies, & will do all himself, & 'to please himself.' He goes to Campmeeting "to see what the world is made on", & thinks a man may give away $100, & get no thanks or praise, but if he is guilty of a nine penny trick,—then is it proclaimed everywhere. Aunt M. asks if a star could be any thing to him & Herschel's mighty facts. I answer certainly if it were only possible to get his attention once to the facts, but the Pestalozzi is not born that could do this by art.

—

Anschauung   Truth first. Genius seems to consist merely in trueness of sight in using such words as show that the man was an eye-witness and not a repeater of what was told. Thus the girl who said "the earth was a-gee;" Lord Bacon when he speaks of exploding gunpowder as "a fiery wind blowing with that expansive force, &c"—these are poets. Aristotle

Hard Times. In this contradictory world of Truth the hard times come when the good times are in the world of commerce; namely, sleep, fulleating, plenty of money, care of it, & leisure; these are the hard times. Nothing is doing & we lose every day.

The young preacher is discouraged by learning the motives that brought his great congregation to church. Scarcely ten came to hear his sermon. But singing or a new pelisse or cousin William or the Sunday School or a proprietors' meeting after church or the merest anility in Hanover st were the beadles that brought and the bolts that hold his silent assembly in the Church. Never mind how they came my friend; never mind who or what brought them any more than you do who or what set you down in Boston in 1835. Here they are real men & women, fools I grant but potentially divine every one of them convertible. Every ear is yours to gain. Every heart will be glad & proud & thankful for a master. There where you are, serve them & they must serve you. They care nothing for you but be to them a Plato be to them a Christ & they shall all be Platos & all be Christs.

—

13 May. Do believe so far in your doctrine of Compensation as to trust that greatness cannot be cheaply procured. Selfdenial & persisting selfrespect can alone secure their proper fruits. Act naturally, act from within, not once or twice, but from month to month, without misgiving, without deviation, from year to year, & you shall reap the costly advantages of moral accomplishments. Make haste to reconcile you to yourself & the whole world shall leap & run to be of your opinion. Imprison that stammering tongue within its white fence until you have a necessary sentiment or a useful fact to utter, & that said, be dumb again. Then your words will weigh something,—two tons, like St John's.

What a benefit if a rule could be given whereby the mind could at any moment *east* itself, & find the sun. But long after we have thought we were recovered & sane, light breaks in upon us & we find we have yet had no sane moment. Another morn rises on mid noon.

Who is capable of a manly friendship? Very few. Charles thinks he can count five persons of *character*. & that Shakspear & the writers of the first class infused their character into their works & hence their rank. We feel an interest in a robust healthful mind, an Alfred, Chaucer, Dante, which Goethe never inspires.

The truest state of mind, rested in, becomes false. Thought is the manna which cannot be stored. It will be sour if kept, & tomorrow must be gathered anew. Perpetually must we East ourselves, or we get into irrecoverable error, starting from the plainest truth & keeping as we think the straightest road of logic. It is by magnifying God, that men become Pantheists; it is by piously personifying him, that they become idolaters.

(As the world signified with the Greek, Beauty, so Skepticism, alas! signifies Sight.) Not in his goals but in his transition man is great.

See the second Aphorism of the Novum Organon that neither the hand nor the mind of man can accomplish much without tools, &c. &c. "nec intellectus sibi permissus, multum valet." This is the defence of written or premeditated preaching, of the written book, of the composed poem. No human wit unaided is equal to the production at one time of such a result as the Hamlet or Lear, but by a multitude of trials & a thousand rejections & the using & perusing of what was already written, one of those tragedies is at last completed—a poem made that shall thrill the world by the mere juxtaposition & inter-action of lines & sentences that singly would have been of little worth & short date. Rightly is this art named composition & the composition has manifold the effect of the component parts. The orator is nowise equal to the evoking on a new subject of this brilliant chain of sentiments, facts, illustrations whereby he now fires himself & you. Every link in this living chain he found separate; one, ten years ago; one, last week; some of them he found in his father's house or at school when a boy; some of them by his losses; some of them by his sickness; some by his sins. The Webster with whom you talk admires the oration almost as much as you do, & knows himself to be nowise equal, unarmed, that is, without this tool of Synthesis to the splendid effect which he is yet well pleased you should impute to him.

No hands could make a watch. The hands brought dry sticks together & struck the flint with iron or rubbed sticks for fire & melted the ore & with stones made crow bar & hammer; these again helped to make chisel & file, rasp & saw, piston & boiler, & so the watch & the steam engine are made, which the hands could never have produced & these again are new tools to make still more recondite & prolific instruments. So do the collated thoughts beget more & the artificially combined individuals have in addition to their own a quite new collective power. The main is made up of many islands, the state of many men. The poem of many thoughts each of which, in its turn, filled the whole sky of the poet was day & Being to him.

May 14. There is hardly a surer way to incur the censure of infidelity & irreligion than sincere faith and an entire devotion.
For to the common eye, pews, vestries, family prayer, sancti-
monious looks & words constitute religion, which the devout
man would find hindrances. And so we go, trying always to
weld the finite & infinite, the absolute & the seeming, together.
On the contrary the manner in which religion is most posi-
tively affirmed by men of the world is barefaced skepticism.

When I write a book on spiritual things I think I will advertise the reader that I am a very wicked man, & that consistency
is nowise to be expected of me.

When will you mend Montaigne? When will you take the
hint of nature? Where are your Essays? Can you not express
your one conviction that moral laws hold? Have you not
thoughts & illustrations that are your own; the parable of
geometry & matter; the reason why the atmosphere is transparent; the power of Composition in nature & in man's
thoughts; the Uses & uselessness of travelling; the law of Compensation; the transcendant excellence of truth in character, in
rhetoric, in things; the sublimity of Self-reliance; and the rewards of perseverance in the best opinion? Have you not a testimony to give for Shakspear, for Milton? one sentence of real
praise of Jesus, is worth a century of legendary Christianity.
Can you not write as though you wrote to yourself & drop the
token assured that a wise hand will pick it up?

"My entrails I lay open to men's view." I recorded worse
things in my Italian Journal than one I omitted; that a lady in
Palermo invited me to come & ride out with her in her
barouche which I did, though the day was rainy & so the
coach was covered. She did not invite me to dine, so I made
my obeisance, when on our return I had waited upon her into
the house; then I *walked* home through a drenching rain in a
city where I was an entire stranger, but not until I had paid her
coachman my half dollar who waylaid me on the stairs. To as
fat an understanding as mine, I cannot but think it might have
occurred, that, to send the guest home or to pay one's servants, would really be a finer compliment. But it is a good
specimen of the misery of finery.

—

May 15. The thing set down in words is not therefore affirmed. It must affirm itself or no forms of grammar & no verisimilitude can give evidence; & no array of arguments. The sentence, the book must also contain its own apology for being writ.

—

The observation of a mere observer is more unsuspicious than that of a theorist. I ought to have no shame in publishing the records of one who aimed only at the upright position more anxious that the thing should be truly seen than careful what thing it was. As we exercise little election in our landscape but see for the most part what God sets before us, I cannot but think that mere enumeration of the objects would be found to be more than a catalogue;—would be a symmetrical picture not designed by us but by our Maker, as when we first perceive the meaning of a sentence which we have carried in the memory for years.

24 May. Coincidences, dreams, animal magnetism, omens, Sacred lots, have great interest for some minds. They run into this twilight & say "there's more than is dreamed of in your philosophy." Certainly these facts are interesting, and are not explained: they deserve to be considered. But they are entitled only to a share of our attention & not a large share. Nil magnificum nil generosum sapit. Read a page of Cudworth or Bacon, & we are exhilarated & armed to manly duties. Read Demonology or Colquhon's Report & you are only bewildered & perhaps a little besmirched. We grope. They who prefer these twilights to daylight say they are to reveal to us,—a world of unknown unsuspected truths. But suppose a diligent collection & study of these occult facts were made,—they could never do much for us. They are merely physiological, semi-medical; facts related to the machinery of man, opening to our curiosity how we live, but throwing no light & no aid on *what* we do. Whilst the dilettanti have been prying into the humors & muscles of the eye, simple active men will have helped themselves & the world by using their eyes.
In your Rhetoric notice that only once or twice in history can the words "dire" & "tremendous" fit.

We tell our charities because we see not how justice can be done us without. It is a capital blunder. For let another mention his, & you feel his mistake. Tell them not, & they will publish themselves by secret spiritual outlets. Fool, you have spoiled your good act by the boast. Hereby we discover that we always make a just impression.

29 May. He weakens who means to confirm his speech by vehemence, feminine vehemence.

"A tremendous faculty that of thinking on one's legs—" is a newspaper description of eloquence; & this is a tolerable use of the word noticed above.

—

> Happy the wit or dunce; but hard
> Is it to be half a bard.

May 30. There are two reasons why Wealth inspires respect in virtuous men; first, because wealth forms a strong will, which is always respectable. Second; because the rich man's state is a mockery of the true state of man. 'He speaks & it is done; he commands & it stands fast.' He has not fear. He has not shame. He has not meanness. He can be bountiful, & execute the conceptions of the Understanding, the fiat of the Reason. The aunt's amusing theory of the blood royal is the theory of the Angel.

The whole of Virtue consists in substituting *being* for *seeming*, & therefore God properly saith *I AM*.

The Ideal philosophy is much more akin to virtue than to vice. When the mountains begin to look unreal, the soul is in a high state, yet in an action of justice or charity things look solid again.

—

Mr Alston would build a very plain house & have plain furniture because he would hold out no bribe to any to visit him who had not similar tastes to his own. A good Ascetic.

—

The year is long enough for all that is to be done in it; it is long enough for Nature though not for Man.

If a conversation be prolonged which is not exactly on my key, I become nervous, & need to go out of the room, or to eat. And when my friend is gone, I am unfit for work. Society suffocates, as Lidian said, and irritates.

4 June. It seems as if every sentence should be prefixed with the word *True*, or, *Apparent*, to indicate the writer's intention of speaking after that which is, or that which seems. Thus, *truly*, our power increases exactly in the measure that we know how to use it, but *apparently*, Andrew Jackson is more powerful than John Marshall.

In Heaven, utterance is place enough. Heaven is the name we give to the True State, the World of Reason not of the Understanding, of the Real, not the Apparent. It exists always, whether it is ever to be separated from the Hell or not. It is, as Coleridge said, another world but not to come. The world I describe is that, where only the laws of mind are known, the only economy of time is saying & doing nothing untrue to self.

———

Away with this succumbing & servility forever. I will not be warned of the sacredness of traditions. I will live wholly from within. You say they may be impulses from below not from above. Maybe so. But if I am the Devil's child I will live from the Devil. I can have no law sacred but that of my nature.

Knowledge is hard to get & unsatisfying when gained. Knowledge is a pleasing provocation to the mind beforehand & not cumbersome afterwards.

Am I true to myself? Then Nations & ages do guide my pen. Then I perceive my commission to be coeval with the eldest causes.

Do Jim take your Mamma's porcelain waterpot, & go water the forests in Maine.

The clouds are our Water carriers,—and do you see that handbreadth of greener grass where the cattle have dropped dung? That was the first lecturer on Agriculture.

The sea is the ring by which the nations are married.

> "The privates of man's heart
>   They speaken & sound in his Ear
>   As tho they loud Winds were."   *Gower*

Do what we can, summer will have its flies. If we walk in the woods, we shall be annoyed by musquitoes. If we go a fishing we must expect a wet coat.

10 June

Aristotle Platonizes. Cudworth is like a cow in June which breathes of nothing but clover & scent grass. He has fed so entirely on ancient bards & sages that all his diction is redolent of their books. He is a stream of Corinthian brass in which gold & silver & iron are molten together out of anc. temples.

I endeavor to announce the laws of the First Philosophy. It is the mark of these that their enunciation awakens the feeling of the moral sublime, & great men are they who believe in them. Every one of these propositions resembles a great circle in astronomy. No matter in what direction it be drawn it contains the whole sphere. So each of these seems to imply all truth. Compare a page of Bacon with Swift, Chesterfield, Lacon, & see the difference of great & less circles. These are gleams of a world in which we do not live: they astonish the Understanding.

—

When we read a book in a foreign language we suppose that an English version of it would be a transfusion of it into our own consciousness. But take Coleridge or Bacon or many an English book besides & you immediately feel that the English is a language also & that a book writ in that tongue is yet very far from you being transfused into your own consciousness. There is every degree of remoteness from the line of things in the line of words. By & by comes a word true & closely embracing the thing. That is not Latin nor English nor any language, but *thought*. The aim of the author is not to tell truth—that he cannot do, but to suggest it. He has only approximated it himself, & hence his cumbrous embarrassed speech: he uses many words, hoping that one, if not another, will bring you as near to the fact as he is.

For language itself is young & unformed. In heaven it will be, as Sampson Reed said, "one with things." Now, there are many things that refuse to be recorded,—perhaps the larger half. The unsaid part is the best of every discourse.

The good of publishing one's thoughts is that of hooking to you likeminded men, and of giving to men whom you value, such as Wordsworth or Landor, one hour of stimulated thought. Yet, how few! Who in Concord cares for the first philosophy in a book? The woman whose child is to be suckled? the man at Nine-Acre-Corner who is to cart 60 loads of gravel on his meadow? the stageman? the gunsmith? O No! Who then?

21 June. Poetry preceded prose as the form of sustained thought, as Reason, whose vehicle poetry is, precedes the Understanding. When you assume the rhythm of verse & the analogy of nature it is making proclamation 'I am now freed from the trammels of the Apparent; I speak from the Mind.'
———

Persons
Some people in Rhode Island saying to G. Fox that if they had money enough they would hire him to be their Minister, he said, "Then it was time for him to be gone, for if their eye was to him, or to any of them, then would they never come to their own teacher."

June 24. "Three silent revolutions in England; first, when the professions fell from the Church. 2. When literature fell from the professions. 3. When the press fell from literature". *Coleridge*

I remembered to C. tonight the English gentleman whom I saw in the cold hostelrie at Simplon at the top of the mountain, & whose manners so satisfied my eye. He met there unexpectedly an acquaintance, & conversed with him with great ease & affectionateness, & as if totally unconscious of the presence of any other company, yet with highbred air.
The selfexistency of the gentleman is his best mark. He is to be a man first, with original perceptions of the true & the

beautiful, & thence should grow his grace & dignity. Then he is God's gentleman and a new argument to the Stoic.

"When I am purified by the light of heaven my soul will become the mirror of the world, in which I shall discern all abstruse secrets." Warton quotes this, he says, from an ancient Turkish poet. *Hist. Eng. Poetry*, vol. 2, p. 241

Books are not writ in the style of conversation. One might say they are not addressed to the same beings as gossip & cheat in the street. Neither are speeches, orations, sermons, academic discourses on the same key of thought or addressed to the same beings. The man that just now chatted at your side, of trifles, rises in the assembly to speak, & speaks to them collectively in a tone & with a series of thoughts he would never think of assuming to any one of them alone. Because man's Universal nature is his inmost nature.

I will no longer confer, differ, refer, defer, prefer, or suffer. I renounce the whole family of *Fero*. I embrace absolute life.

Idealism is not so much prejudiced by danger as by inconvenience. In our speculative habits we sometimes expect that the too solid earth will melt. Then we cross the ocean sweltering, seasick, reeling, week after week, with tar, harness-tub, & bilge, and, as an ingenious friend says, It is carrying the joke too far.

———

27 June, I wrote Hedge that good society seemed an optical illusion that ought to be classed with Bacon's Idols of the Cave. Carlyle affirms it has ceased to exist. C.C.E. affirms that it is just begun—Greek & Roman knew it not. To me it seems that it is so steadily & universally thwarted—by death, sickness, removals, unfitness, ceremony, or what not, that a design to hinder it, must be suspected. Every person is indulged with an opportunity or two of equal & hearty communication enough to show him his potential heaven. But between cultivated minds the first interview is the best, & it is surprizing in how few hours the results of years are exhausted. Besides though it seem ungrateful to friends whom the heart knoweth by name yet the value of the conversation is not measured according to the wisdom of the company but by quite other &

indefinable causes, the fortunate moods. I think we owe the most recreation & most memorable thoughts to very unpromising gossips. I copied the above from memory.

June 29. Geo. Fox's chosen expression for the God manifest in the mind is the Seed. He means that seed of which the Beauty of the world is the Flower & Goodness is the Fruit.

I replied this morn. to the Committee that I would do what I could to prepare a Historical Discourse for the Town Anniversary. Yet why notice it? Centuries pass unnoticed. The Saxon King was told that man's life was like the swallow that flew in at one window, fluttered around, & flew out at another. So is this population of the spot of God's earth called Concord. For a moment they fish in this river, plow furrows in the banks, build houses on the fields, mow the grass. But hold on to hill or tree never so fast they must disappear in a trice.

The contemplation of nature is all that is fine. Who can tell me how many thousand years, every day, the clouds have shaded these fields with their purple awning? The little river by whose banks most of us were born every winter for ages has spread its crust of ice over the great meadows which in ages it had formed. The countless families that follow or precede man keep no jubilee, mark no era, the fly & the moth in burnished armor. These little emigrants travel fast, they have no baggage wagon. All night they creep. The ant has no provision for sleep. The trees that surround us grew up in the days of Peter Bulkeley. This first celebration from the everlasting past. The oaks that were then acorns wave their branches in this morning's wind. The little flower that at this season stars the woods & roadsides with its profuse blooms won the eye of the stern pilgrim with its humble beauty. The Maple grew red in the early frost over those houseless men burrowing in the sand. The mighty Pine yet untouched towered into the frosty air. And yet another kind of permanence has also been permitted. Here are still the names of the first 50 years. Here is Blood, Willard, Flint, Wood, Barrett, Heywood Hunt, Wheeler, Jones, Buttrick.
And if the name of Bulkeley is wanting the honor you have done me this day shows your kindness for his blood.

—

Norris's first volume was an unexpected delight this P.M. He fights the battles & affirms the facts I had proposed to myself to do. But he falls, I so think, into the common error of the first philosophers, that of attempting to fight for Reason with the Weapons of the Understanding. All this polemics, syllogism, & definition is so much wastepaper & Montaigne is almost the only man who has never lost sight of this fact.

4 July. Talked last eve. with G.P.B. of Locke who, I maintained, had given me little. I am much more indebted to persons of far less name. I believe his service was to popularize metaphysics, allure men of the world to its study, if that indeed be a service. G. gave a good account of his friend Alcott who is a consistent spiritualist & so expects the influence of Christianity into trade, government, literature, & arts.

—

I study the art of solitude. I yield me as gracefully as I can to my destiny. Why cannot one get the good of his doom, & since it is from eternity a settled thing that he & society shall be nothing to each other, why need he blush so, & make wry faces & labor to keep up a poor beginner's place, a freshman's seat in the fine world?

Of Truth Norris said something like this that we could not disimagine its existence, but always the Mind recovers itself with a strong & invincible spring to its faith.

One of the good effects of hearing the man of genius is that he shows the world of thought to be infinite again which you had supposed exhausted.

"That inbred loyalty unto virtue which can serve her without a livery."

15 July. Why do I still go to pasture where I never find grass, to these actors without a purpose unless a poor mechanical one, these talkers without method, & reasoners without an idea? At the Divinity School this morning I heard what was called the best performance but it was founded on nothing & led to nothing & I wondered at the patience of the people. This P.M. the King of the House of Seem spoke & made as if he was in earnest with pathetic tones & gesture, & the most

approved expressions, and all about nothing; & he was answered by others with equal apparent earnestness & still it was all nothing. The building seemed to grudge its rent if the assembly did not their time. Stetson who jokes, seems the only wise man. It is pity 300 men should meet to make believe or play Debate.

They are all so solemn & vehement, that I listen with all my ears & for my life can't find any idea at the foundation of their zeal.

I forgive desultoriness, trifling, vice even in a young man so long as I believe that he has a closet of secret thoughts to which he retires as to his home & which have a sort of parents' interest in him wherever he is. At sight of them he bows. But if he is not in earnest about any thing, if all his interest is good breeding & imitation I had as lief not be as be him.

Great pudder make my philanthropic friends about the children. I should be glad to be convinced they have taught one child one thing. Gray & Barnard, no doubt, teach them just as much as the minister did before, not a jot more; for the children don't understand any thing they say.

Quotation.

Coleridge loses by Dequincey, but more by his own concealing uncandid acknowledgment of debt to Schelling. Why could not he have said generously like Goethe, I owe all? As soon as one gets so far above pride, as to say all truth that might come from him & that now does come from him as truth & not as *his* truth, as soon as he acknowledges that all is suggestion, then he may be indebted without shame to all.

—

Let not the voluptuary dare to judge of literary far less of philosophical questions. Let him wait until the blindness that belongs to pollution has passed from his eyes.

We all have an instinct that a good man good & wise shall be able to say intuitively i.e. from God what is true & great & beautiful. Never numbers but the simple & wise shall judge. Not the Wartons & Drakes but some divine savage like Webster, Wordsworth, & Reed whom neither the town or the college ever made shall say that we shall all believe. How we thirst for a natural thinker.

It is droll enough that when I had been groping for months after the natural process which I felt sure resembled in my experience the freedom with which at a certain height of excitement, thoughts pour into the mind, I should at last recognize it in so mean a fact as the passage of bile into the mouth in the retchings of seasickness. Better said Goethe when he spoke of filling the bottle under water than drop by drop. My illustration would be that the ornithologist from the city goes many miles to the woods & follows the bird all day long & cannot get a sight of him. But a farmer's boy passes thro' the wood & sees the whole manners of the bird in the next bush.

—

July 24. Hooker. "In the first age of the world—by reason of the number of their days, their memories served instead of books." There is no book like a Memory & none that hath such a perfect Index & that of every kind, alphabetical, systematic, & arranged by names of persons & all manner of associations.

"I say three persons, ingenuously confessed St Augustine (on the Trinity; v. 9) not that I may say something but that I may not say nothing." ap. Oegger

Most persons exist to us merely or chiefly in relations of time & space. Those whom we love, whom we venerate, or whom we serve, exist to us independently of these relations.

O Thou who drawest good out of the fury of devils save me.

Yesterday I visited Jonas Buttrick & Abel Davis the former aged 70 the latter 79 years. Both were present at Concord fight. Davis was one of the militia under command of   J.B. remembered Maj Hosmer & Capt Davis going back & forward often & said of Capt. Davis that "his face was red as a piece of broad cloth—red as a beet. He looked very much worried." I asked, 'Worried with fear?' No. Both agree that Capt. Davis had the right of the companies but know not why. J.B. thinks that he did not come up from Acton until after the consultation of the officers & the conclusion to fight & that he took the right because that was the side on which he most

conveniently joined the troops. A. Davis thinks that Maj.
having given up his company to   Capt. Davis had the
right in virtue of his rank.

The Indians said of the cannon they did not like those loud
speakers.

———

The Quarterly Review toils to prove that there is no selfish
aristocracy in America but that every man shakes hands
heartily with every other man & the chancellor says "My
brother, the grocer."
And to fix this fact will be to stamp us with desired infamy. I
earnestly wish it could be proved. I wish it could be shown
that no distinctions created by a contemptible pride existed
here & none but the natural ones of talent & virtue. But I fear
we do not deserve the praise of this Reviewer's ill opinion. The
only ambition which truth allows is to be the servant of all.
The last shall be first.

I read with great delight the "Record of A School." It aims
all the time to show the symbolical character of all things to
the children, & it is alleged, &, I doubt not, truly, that the
children take the thought with delight. It is remarkable that all
poets, orators, & philosophers, have been those who could
most sharply see & most happily present emblems, parables,
figures. Good writing & brilliant conversation are perpetual al-
legories. "My fortunes are in the moult" says Philip Van A.
Webster is such a poet in every speech. "You cannot keep out
of politics more than you can keep out of frost," he said to
Clifford. "No matter for the baggage so long as the troop is
safe" he said when he lost his trunk. "Waves lash the shore,"
&c Indian's whole speech. "Back of the hand" was Crockett's
expression. All the memorable words of the world are these
figurative expressions. Light & heat have passed into all speech
for knowledge & love. The river is nothing but as it typifies the
flux of time. Many of these signs seem very arbitrary & historical. I should gladly know what gave such universal acceptance
to Cupid's arrow for the passion of love; & more meanly the
horn for the shame of cuckoldom.

Ephraim Slow, says the newspaper, "was born on the last day of the year which gave occasion to a parish wit to remark that he came near not being born at all."

27 July. "One of those crystal days which are neither hot nor cold." Mrs R. cited a well known character to show that trick & pretension impose on nobody but that my friend is reverenced for his liberality.

Every body leads two or three lives, has two or three consciousnesses which he nimbly alternates. Here am I daily lending my voice & that with heat often to opinions & practices opposite to my own. Here is M.M.E. always fighting in conversation against the very principles which have governed & govern her.

Very good remark saw I in the very good Record of a School concerning Unity reproduced by the mind out of severed parts. Yes, all men have thoughts, images, facts, by thousands & thousands, but only one of many can crystallize these into a symmetrical one by means of the Nucleus of an Idea.

Humphrey Heywood showed me his fine toy cart which his father made for him. I see nothing of the farmer but his plain dealing & hard work; yet there are finer parts which but for this child would remain latent. His love & the taste which makes a fanciful child's wagon for its manifestation.

———

July 30th. It is affecting to see the old man's T. Blood's memory taxed for facts occurring 60 years ago at Concord fight. "It is hard to bring them up," he says "the truth never will be known." The Doctor like a keen hunter unrelenting follows him up & down barricading him with questions. Yet cares little for the facts the man can tell, but much for the confirmation of the printed History. "Leave me, leave me to repose."

Every principle is an eye to see with. Facts in thousands of the most interesting character are slipping by me every day unobserved, for I see not their bearing, I see not their connexion, I see not what they prove. By & by I shall mourn in ashes their irreparable loss.

No distinction in principle can be broader than that taken by the abolitionist against Everett. Everett said that in case of a servile war tho' a man of peace he would buckle on his

knapsack to defend the planter. The philanthropist who was
here this morning says that he is a man of peace but if forced
to fight on either side he should fight for the slave against his
tyrant.

I know nothing of the source of my being but I will not soil
my nest. I know much of it after a high negative way, but
nothing after the understanding. God himself contradicts
through me & all his creatures the miserable babble of Kneeland & his crew but if they set me to affirm in propositions his
character & providence as I would describe a mountain or an
Indian, I am dumb. Oft I have doubted of his person, never
that truth is divine.

You affirm that the moral development contains all the intellectual & that Jesus was the perfect man. I bow in reverence
unfeigned before that benign man. I know more, hope more,
am more because he has lived. But if you tell me that in your
opinion he has fulfilled all the conditions of man's existence,
carried out to the utmost at least by implication, all man's
powers, I suspend my assent. I do not see in him cheerfulness:
I do not see in him the love of Natural Science: I see in him no
kindness for Art; I see in him nothing of Socrates, of Laplace,
of Shakspeare. The perfect man should remind us of all great
men. Do you ask me if I would rather resemble Jesus than any
other man? If I should say Yes, I should suspect myself of
superstition.

Ages hence, books that cannot now be written may be possible. For instance a cumulative moral & intellectual science. If
I would know something of the elements & process of the
Moral sublime where shall I now seek the analysis? If I would
know the elementary distinction of spiritual & intellectual
where shall I inquire? A sentence showing a tendency is all that
a century contributes to psychology. Where shall I find the result of phrenology? of animal magnetism? of extacy?

By & by books of condensed wisdom may be writ by the
concentrated lights of thousands of centuries which shall cast
Bacon & Aristotle into gloom. As the Am. Encyc. said of Astron. "How many centuries of observation were necessary to
make the motion of the earth suspected!"

31 July. Every day's doubt is whether to seek for Ideas or to collect facts. For all successful study is the marriage of thoughts & things. A continual reaction of the thought classifying the facts & of facts suggesting the thought.

———

I wrote yesterday that these orators of a principle owed everything to it, & our good friend S.J. May may instruct us in many things. He goes everywhere & sees the leaders of society everywhere, his cause being his ticket of admission, and talks on his topic with no intelligent person who does not furnish some new light, some unturned side, some happy expression or strike off some false view or expression of the philanthropist. In this way his views are enlarged & cleared & he is always attaining to the best expressions. As when he said the Question between the Colonization & the Abolition men was "whether you should remove them (the negroes) from the prejudice or the prejudice from them."

It is, my God! an antidote to every fear, the conviction twice recently forced on me that men reverence virtue never by the appearance but accurately according to its weight. Nothing but an ounce will balance an ounce. Thus alone is the will strong: thus He whose right it is to reign shall reign. Spit at consequences; launch boldly forth into the pure element & that which you think will drown you, shall buoy you up.

If the stars should appear one night in a thousand years, men would believe & adore & for a few generations preserve the remembrance of the city of God which had been shown. But every night come out these preachers of beauty, & light the Universe with their admonishing smile.

Men believe that some of their fellows are more happily constituted than themselves after the pattern of themselves. They have in fortunate hours had the eye opened whereby the world was newly seen as if then first seen & which seemed to say that all prior life however loud & pretending was but death or sleep. They believe that some men add to this Eye a Tongue to tell their vision & a certain degree of control over these faculties, that the spirits of the prophets are subject to the prophets and they wish such men to take the chronicle of their parish or their age & in the auspicious hour let the facts pass thro' their mind & see if they will not take the form of a picture & song.

———

A systemgrinder hates the truth.
To make a step into the world of thought is given to but few men; to make a second step beyond his first, only one in a country can do; but to carry the thought out to three steps marks a great Teacher. Aladdin's Palace with its one unfinished window which all the gems in the royal treasury cannot finish in the style of the meanest of the profusion of jewelled windows that were built by the genie in a night, is but too true a picture of the efforts of Talent to add a scene to Shakspeare's Play or a verse to Shakspear's Songs.

August 1. A sparrow or a deer knows much more of nature's secrets than a man but is less able to utter them. And those men who know the most can say the least.

Jacob Behme is the best helper to a theory of Isaiah & Jeremiah. You were sure he was in earnest & could you get into his point of view the world would be what he describes. He is all imagination.

———

There sits the Sphinx from age to age, in the road Charles says, & every wise man that comes by has a crack with her. But this Oegger's plan & scope argue great boldness & manhood to depart thus widely from all routine & seek to put his hands like Atlas under Nature & heave her from her rest. Why the world exists & that it exists for a language or medium whereby God may speak to Man,—this is his query—this his answer.

Sat. Evg   August 1, 1835.   The distinction of fancy & imagination seems to me a distinction in kind. The fancy aggregates; the Imagination animates.

The Fancy takes the world as it stands & selects pleasing groups by apparent relations. The Imagination is Vision, regards the world as symbolical & pierces the emblem for the real sense, sees all external objects as types. A fine example is in the acct. of the execution of Lord Russell.

God hides the stars in a deluge of light. That is his chosen curtain. So he hides the great truths in the simplicity of the common consciousness. I am struck with the contrast which I have repeatedly noted before between the positiveness with which we can speak of certain laws, an evidence equal to that of consciousness, & the depth of obscurity in which the Person of God is hid. From month to month, from year to year I come never nearer to definite speaking of him. He hideth himself. I cannot speak of him without faltering. I unsay as fast as I say my words. He is, for I am. Say rather, He is. But in the depth inaccessible of his being he refuses to be defined or personified.

After thirty a man wakes up sad every morning excepting perhaps five or six until the day of his death.

It was strange after supposing for years that my respected friend was the heart of the county & blended thoroughly with the people to find him wholly isolated, more even than I, walking among them with these "monumental" manners unable to get within gunshot of any neighbor except professionally. Yet the fulness of his respect for every man & his self-respect at the same time have their reward & after sitting all these years on his plain wooden bench with eternal patience Honor comes & sits down by him.

2 Aug. Charles wonders that I don't become sick at the stomach over my poor journal yet is obdurate habit callous even to contempt. I must scribble on if it were only to say in confirmation of Oegger's doctrine that I believe I never take a step in thought when engaged in conversation without some material symbol of my proposition figuring itself incipiently at the same time. My sentence often ends in babble from a vain effort to represent that picture in words. How much has a figure, an illustration availed every sect. As when the reabsorption of the soul into God was figured by a phial of water broken in the sea. This morn. I would have said that a man sees in the gross of the acts of his life the domination of his instincts or

genius over all other causes. His Wilfulness may determine the character of moments but his Will determines that of years. While I thus talked I *saw* some crude *symbols* of the thought with the mind's eye, as it were, a mass of grass or weeds in a stream of which the spears or blades shot out from the mass in every direction but were immediately curved round to float all in one direction. When presently the conversation changed to the subject of Thomas a Kempis's popularity & how Aristotle & Plato come safely down as if God brought them in his hand (tho' at no time are there more than five or six men who read them) & of the Natural Academy by which the exact value of every book is determined maugre all hindrance or furtherance, then saw I as I spoke the old pail in the Summer street kitchen with potatoes swimming in it, some at the top, some in the midst, & some lying at the bottom; & I spoiled my fine thought by saying that books take their place according to their specific gravity "as surely as potatoes in a tub." And I suppose that any man who will watch his intellectual process will find a material image cotemporaneous with every thought & furnishing the garment of the thought.

It occurred with regard to A Kempis that it is pleasant to have a book come down to us of which the author has, like Homer, lost his individual distinctness, is almost a fabulous personage, so that the book seems to come rather out of the spirit of humanity & to have the sanction of human nature than to totter on the two legs of any poor Ego.

———

We have little control of our thoughts. We are pensioners upon Ideas. They catch us up for moments into their heavens & so fully possess us that we take no thought for the morrow, gaze like children without an effort to make them our own. By & by we fall out of that rapture & then bethink us where we have been & what we have seen & go painfully gleaning up the grains that have fallen from the sheaf.

When I see the doors by which God entereth into the mind, that there is no sot nor fop nor ruffian nor pedant into whom thoughts do not enter by passages which the individual never left open, I can expect any revolution.

Aug. 3. One of the poorest employments of the country gentleman is to sit sentinel at his window to watch every cow, baker, or boy that comes in at his gate. Better be asleep.

—

A thought comes single like a foreign traveller but if you can find out its name you shall find it related to a powerful & numerous family.

Uprose Shower-of-tears.

5 August. Our summer, Charles says, is a galloping consumption and the hectic rises as the year approaches its end.

—

Happy they & their counterparts in the intellectual kingdom, who sit down to write & lend themselves to the first thought & are carried whithersoever it takes them & solve the problem proposed in a way they could not have predicted & are not now conscious of their own action. Merely they held the pen. The problem whilst they pondered it confounded them.

The Battas in Sumatra are cannibals.

The birds fly from us & we do not understand their music. The squirrel, the musquash, the insect, have no significance to our blind eyes. Such is now the discord betwixt man & nature. Yet it is strange that all our life is accompanied by Dreams on one side & by the animals on the other as monuments of our ignorance or Hints to set us on the right road of inquiry.

The life of a contemplator is that of a reporter. He has three or four books before him & now writes in this now in that other what is incontinuously said by one or the other of his classes of thought.

It is a good trait of the manners of the times that Thaddeus Blood told me this morning that he (then 20 years old) & Mr Ball (50) were set to guard Lieut. Potter the Brit. Officer taken at Lexington 19 Apr '75 & whilst staying at Reuben Brown's Potter invited them both to dine with him. He, Lt. P. asked a blessing & after dinner asked Mr Ball to dismiss the table "which he did very well for an old farmer;" Lt. P. then poured out a glass of wine to each & they left the table. Presently came by a compy. from Groton, & Lt. P. was alarmed for his own safety. They bolted the doors &c &c. Bateman, he thinks, could not have made the deposition in Dr R.'s History. A ball passed thro' his cap & he cried A miss is as good as a mile. Immediately another ball struck his ear & passed out at the side of his mouth knocking out two teeth. He lived about 3 weeks & his wounds stunk intolerably. It was probably Carr or Starr's deposition.

———

The human mind seems a lens formed to concentrate the rays of the Divine laws to a focus which shall be the personality of God. But that focus falls so far into the infinite that the form or person of God is not within the ken of the mind. Yet must that ever be the effort of a good mind because the avowal of our sincere doubts leaves us in a less favorable mood for action & the statement of our best thoughts or those of our convictions that make most for theism induces new courage & force.

6 Aug. I think I may undertake one of these days to write a chapter on Literary Ethics or the Duty & Discipline of a Scholar. The camel & his four stomachs shall be one of his emblems.

———

8 August. Yesterday I delighted myself with Michel de Montaigne. With all my heart I embrace the grand old sloven. He pricks & stings the sense of Virtue in me, the wild gentile stock I mean, for he has no Grace. But his panegyric of Cato & of Socrates in his essay of Cruelty (Vol II) do wind up again for us the spent springs & make virtue possible without the discipline of Christianity or rather do shame her of her eyeservice & put her upon her honor. I read the Essays in Defence of Seneca & Plutarch; on Books; on Drunkenness; & on Cruelty. And at some fortunate line which I cannot now recal the Spirit of some Plutarch hero or sage touched mine with such thrill as the War-trump makes in Talbot's ear & blood.

15 August. 1835. I bought my house & two acres six rods of land of John T. Coolidge for 3500 dollars.

I know no truer poetry in modern verse than Scott's line "And sun himself in Ellen's eyes."

Every fact studied by the Understanding is not only solitary but desart. But if the iron lids of Reason's eye can be once raised, the fact is classified immediately & seen to be related to our nursery reading & our profoundest Science.

13 Augt. Add to what was said 6 Aug. concerning literary Ethics that no doubt another age will have such sermons duly preached and the immortality will be proved from the implication of the intellect. For who can read an analysis of the faculties by any acute psychologist like Coleridge without becoming aware that this is proper study for him & that he must live ages to learn anything of so secular Science?

August 14. We would call up him who

                         left half told
     The story of Cambuscan bold

but the great contemporary just now laid in the dust no man remembers; no man asks for him who broke off in the first sentences the Analysis of the Imagination on the warning of a friend that the public would not read the chapter. No man asks Where is the Chapter?

Joseph Lyman describes the iron bed at his residence at Farrandsville, Lycoming Co. Pa on the West Branch of the Susquehanna—a bed of iron ore a thousand acres in extent & four feet thick. The Compy bought it for 1500 dollars. "This whole region is filled with iron & coal. It is equal to the districts of Wales & Lancashire mile for mile but in extent it is larger than the British isles—extending from this place beyond Pittsburg & of the breadth of the Alleganny Mountains." Letter to CCE Apr. 1835.

25 Aug. Visited Miss Harriet Martineau at Cambridge today, a pleasant unpretending lady whom it would be agreeable to talk with when tired & at ease but she is too weary of society to shine if ever she does. She betrayed by her facile admiration

of books & friends her speedy limits. The ear trumpet acts as chain as well as medium, making Siameses of the two interlocutors. Henry Reeve, Henry Taylor, of Manchester, & John S. Mill, W.J. Fox, she regarded as the ablest young men in England. What pleased me most of her communications was that W.J. Fox though of no nerve, timid as a woman, yet had the greatest moral courage, as Charles said at my commentary, 'Go & be hanged but blush if spoken to on the tumbril.'

Aug. 31. Use of Harvard College to clear the head of much nonsense that gathers in the inferior colleges.

   Communicable attributes
It shall be a rule in my Rhetoric Before you urge a duty be sure it is one, Try Patriotism, for example.

   Edw. Taylor came to see us. Dr R. showed him the battle field. Why put it on this bank? he asked. "You must write on the monument, 'Here is the place where the Yankees made the British show the back seam of their stockings.'" He said he had been fishing at Groton & the fishes were as snappish as the people that he looked to see if the scales were not turned the wrong side &c.

   14 September 1835. I was married to Lydia Jackson.
                            —

   There is no gradation in feeble minds: they "laughed so that they thought they should have died," & five minutes after they have a regret or a vexation which they are sure "will kill them." The great mind finds ample spaces, vast plains, yea populous continents, & active worlds moving freely within these elastic limits & indeed never approaches the terminus on either side.

   Every man, if he lived long enough, would make all his books for himself. He would write his own Universal history, Natural History, Book of Religion, of Economy, of Taste. For in every man the facts under these topics are only so far efficient as they are arranged after the law of *his* being. But life forbids it & therefore he uses Bossuet, Buffon, Westminster Catechism as better than nothing, at least as memoranda &

badges to certify that he belongs to the Universe & not to his own house only and contents himself with arranging some one department of life after his own way. Our will never gave the images in our minds the rank they now take there. Anecdotes I read under the bench in the Latin School assume a grandeur in the natural perspective of memory which Roman history & Charles V &c have not.

The powers of poetry. It is said of the harper Glenkindie

> He'd harpit a fish out o' saut water
>   Or water out of a stane
> Or milk out o' a maiden's breast
>   That bairn had never nane.

10 Oct. This morning Mr May & Mr George Thompson breakfasted with me. I bade them defend their cause as a thing too sacred to be polluted with any personal feelings. They should adhere religiously to the fact & the principle, & exclude every adverb that went to colour their mathematical statement. As Josiah Quincy said in the eve of Revolution, 'the time for declamation is now over; here is something too serious for aught but simplest words & acts.' So should they say, I said also, what seems true, that if any man's opinion in the country was valuable to them that opinion would be distinctly known. If Daniel Webster's or Dr Channing's opinion is not frankly told, it is so much deduction from the moral value of that opinion & I should say moreover that their opinion *is* known by the very concealment. One opinion seeks darkness. We know what opinion that is.

—

Charles thinks there is no Christianity & has not been for some ages. And esteems Christianity the most wonderful thing in the history of the world. But for that, he can arrange his theory well enough of the history of man. It is, according to him, the first exalting of the bestial nature, the first allaying of clay with the Divine fire which succeeds in a few cases but in far the greater part the spirit is overlaid & expired. A few however under the benevolent aspect of heaven so cooperate with God as to work off the slough of the beast, & give evidence of arriving within the precincts of heaven. But the introduction of

Christianity seems to be departure from general laws & inter-position. Jesus seems not to be man.

Strange, thinks he, moreover, that so sensible a nation as the English should be content so long to maintain that old withered idolatry of their Church; with the history too of its whole manufacture, piece by piece, all written out.

Thompson the Abolitionist is inconvertible: what you say or what might be said would make no impression on him. He belongs I fear to that great class of the Vanity-stricken. An inordinate thirst for notice can not be gratified until it has found in its gropings what is called a Cause that men will bow to; tying him self fast to that, the small man is then at liberty to consider all objections made to him as proofs of folly & the devil in the objector, & under that screen, if he gets a rotten egg or two, yet his name sounds through the world & he is praised & praised.

The minister should be to us a simple absolute man; any trick of his face that reminds us of his family is so much deduction, unless it should chance that those related lineaments are associated in our mind with genius & virtue. But the minister in these days, how little he says! Who is the most decorous man? & no longer, who speaks the most truth? Look at the orations of Demosthenes & Burke, & how many irrelevant things—sentences, words, letters,—are there? Not one. Go into one of our cool churches, & begin to count the words that might be spared, & in most places, the entire sermon will go. One sentence kept another in countenance, but not one by its own weight could have justified the saying of it. 'Tis the age of Parenthesis. You might put all we say in brackets & it would not be missed.

Even Everett has come to speak in stereotyped phrase & scarcely originates one expression to a speech. I hope the time will come when phrases will be gazetted as no longer current and it will be unpardonable to say "the times that tried men's souls" or anything about "a Cause" & so forth. Now literature is nothing but a sum in the arithm. rule Permutation & Combination.

A man to thrive in literature must trust himself. The voice of society sometimes & the writings of great geniuses always, are so noble & prolific that it seems justifiable to follow & imitate. But it is better to be an independent shoemaker than to be an actor and play a king. In every work of genius you recognize your own rejected thoughts. It is here as in science, that the true chemist collects what every body else throws away. Our own thoughts come back to us in unexpected majesty. See the noble selfreliance of Ben Jonson. Shun manufacture or the introducing an artificial arrangement in your thoughts, it will surely crack & come to nothing, but let alone tinkering & wait for the natural arrangement of your treasures; that shall be chemical affinity, & is a new & permanent substance added to the world, to be recognized as genuine by every knowing person at sight. "A writer," says *Mme. de Stael*, "who searches only into the immutable nature of man, into those thoughts & sentiments which must enlighten the mind in every age, is independent of events; they can never change the order of those truths, which such a writer unfolds."

A meek self reliance I believe to be the law & constitution of good writing. A man is to treat the world like children who must hear & obey the spirit in which he speaks, but which is not his. If he thinks he is to sing to the tune of the times, is to be the decorous sayer of smooth things, to lull the ear of society, & to speak of religion as the great traditional things to be either mutely avoided or kept at a distance by civil bows he may make a very good workman for the booksellers but he must lay aside all hope to wield or so much as to touch the bright thunderbolts of truth which it is given to the true scholar to launch & whose light flashes through ages without diminution. He must believe that the world proceeds in order from principles. He must not guess but observe, without intermission, without end; and these puissant elements he shall not pry into who comes in fun, or in haste, or for show. The solemn powers of faith, of love, of fear, of custom, of conscience, are no toys to be shoved aside, but the forces which make & change society. They must be seen & known. You might as well trifle with time. They keep on their eternal way grinding all resistance to dust. If you will, you may read nothing but song books & fairy tales, all the year round, but if you would know the literature of any cultivated nation, you must meet the majestic ideas of God, of Justice, of Freedom, of Necessity, of War, & of Intellectual beauty, as the subject & spirit of volumes & eras.

What's a book? Everything or nothing. The eye that sees it is all. What is the heavens' majestical roof fretted with golden fire to one man, but a foul & pestilent congregation of vapors. Well a book is to a paddy a fair page smutted over with black marks; to a boy, a goodly collection of words he can read; to a halfwise man, it is a lesson which he wholly accepts or wholly rejects; but a sage shall see in it secrets yet unrevealed; shall weigh, as he reads, the author's mind; shall see the predominance of ideas which the writer could not extricate himself from, & oversee. The Belfast Town & County Almanack may be read by a sage; &, wasteful as it would be in me to read Antimasonic or Jackson papers, yet whoso pierces through them to the deep Idea they embody, may well read them.

———

My will never gave the images in my mind the rank they now take there. The four college years & the three years course of Divinity have not yielded me so many grand facts as some idle books under the bench at Latin School. We form no guess at the time of receiving a thought, of its comparative value.

———

Do not expect to find the books of a country written as an Encyclopedia by a society of savans on system to supply certain wants & fill up a circle of subjects. In French literature perhaps is something of this order of a garden where plat corresponds with plat & shrub with shrub. But in the world of living genius all at first seems disorder & incapable of methodical arrangement. Yet is there a higher harmony whereby 'tis set as in Nature the sea balances the land, the mountain, the valley & woods & meadows. And as the eye possesses the faculty of rounding & integrating the most disagreeable parts into a pleasing whole.

I listened yesterday as always to Dr Ripley's prayer in the mourning house with tenfold the hope, a tenfold chance of some touch of nature that should melt us, that I should have

felt in the rising of one of the Boston preachers of propriety—
the fair house of Seem. These old semi-savages do from the
solitude in which they live & their remoteness from artificial
society & their inevitable daily comparing man with beast, village with wilderness, their inevitable acquaintance with the
outward nature of man, & with his strict dependence on sun
& rain & wind & frost; wood, worm, cow, & bird, get an
education to the Homeric simplicity which all the libraries of
the Reviews & the Commentators in Boston do not countervail.

What a Tantalus cup this life is! The beauty that shimmers
on these yellow afternoons who ever could clutch it? Go forth
to find it, & it is gone; 'tis only a mirage as you look from the
windows of diligence.

Charles says that to read Carlyle in N A Review is like seeing
your brother in jail; & A Everett is the sheriff that put him in.

Far off no doubt is the perfectibility, so far off as to be ridiculous to all but a few. Yet wrote I once that God keeping a private door to each soul, nothing transcends the bounds of
reasonable expectation from a man. Now what imperfect tad-
poles we are! an arm or a leg, an eye or an antenna is unfolded;
all the rest is yet in the Chrysalis. Who does not feel in him
budding the powers of a Persuasion that by & by will be irresistible? Already how unequally unfolded in two men! Here is
a man who can only say yes & no in very slight variety of
forms. But to render a reason or to dissuade you by any thing
less coarse than interest he cannot & attempts not. But
Themistocles goes by & persuades you that he whom you saw
up was down, & he whom you saw down was up.

———

The objective religion of the Middle & after Age is well ex-
emplified in the spite which heightened Luther's piety. "We
cannot vex the devil more, said Luther, than when we teach,
preach, sing & speak of Jesus & his humanity. Therefore I like
it well, when with loud voices & fine, long & deliberately, we
sing in the church, 'Et homo factus est: et Verbum caro factum
est.' The devil cannot endure to hear these words; he flieth
away," &c. Table Talk

October 20. The hearing man is good. Unhappy is the speaking man. The alternations of speaking & hearing make our education.

October 21. Last Saturday night came hither Mr Alcott & spent the Sabbath with me. A wise man, simple, superior to display. & drops the best things as quietly as the least. Every man, he said, is a Revelation, & ought to write his Record. But few with the pen. His book is his school in which he writes all his thoughts. The spiritual world should meet men everywhere; & so the government should teach. Our life flows out into our amusements. Need of a drama here: how well to lash the American follies. Every man is a system, an institution. Autobiography the best book. He thinks Jesus a pure Deist. & says all children are Deists.

Charles remarks upon the nimbleness & buoyancy which the conversation of a spiritualist awakens; the world begins to dislimn.

It is the comfort I have in taking up those new poems of Wordsworth, that I am sure here to find thoughts in harmony with the great frame of Nature, the placid aspect of the Universe. I may find dulness & flatness, but I shall not find meanness & error.

Whence these oaths that make so many words in English books? The sun, the moon, St Paul, Jesus, & God, are called upon as witness that the speaker speaks truth. I suppose they refer to that conviction suggested by every object that something IS. And signify *If any thing is*, then I did so and so. Yet now they are all obsolete. Except for the court forms, I doubt if ever they would be used. They import something separate from the will of man. "By day & night" "by Jupiter" &c. By St Nicholas, &c i.e. my will which interferes to color & change all things interferes not here. This *is*.

—

What platitudes I find in Wordsworth. "I poet bestow my verse on this & this & this." Scarce has he dropped the smallest piece of an egg, when he fills the barnyard with his cackle.

In the hours of clear vision, how slight a thing it is to die. It is so slight that one ought not turn a corner or accept the least disgrace (so much as skulking) to avoid it. The mob may prove as kind & easy a deliverer as a pin or a worm. The mob seems a thing insignificant. It has no character. It is the emblem of unreason; mere muscular & nervous motion, no thought, no spark of spiritual life in it. It is a bad joke to call it a fruit of the love of liberty. It is permitted like earthquakes & freshets & locusts & is to be met like a blind mechanical force.

What of these atrocious ancestors of Englishmen—the Briton, Saxon, Northman, Berserkir? Is it not needful to make a strong nation that there should be strong wild will? If man degenerates in gardens he must be grafted again from the wild stock.

We all know how life is made up; that a door is to be painted; a lock to be repaired; a cord of wood is wanted; the house smokes; or I have a diarrhea; then the tax; & a hopeless visiter; & the stinging recollection of an injurious or a very awkward word. These eat up the hours. How then is any acquisition, how is any great deed or wise & beautiful work possible? Let it enhance the praise of Milton, Shakspear, & Laplace. These oppress & spitefully tyrannize over me because I am an Idealist.

The mob ought to be treated only with contempt. Phocion, even Jesus cannot otherwise regard it in so far as it is mob. It is mere beast; of them that compose it their soul is absent from it. It is to consider it too much to respect it, too much to speak of its terror in any other way than mere animal & mechanical agents. It has no will; oh no.

Sunday, 25 Oct. Every intellectual acquisition is mainly prospective. And hence the scholar's assurance of eternity quite aloof from his moral convictions.

Behind us, as we go, all things assume pleasing forms as clouds do far off. Even the corpse that has lain in our chambers has added a solemn ornament to the house. In this my new house no dead body was ever laid. It lacks so much sympathy with nature.

—

28 October. Plotinus says of the intuitive knowledge that "it is not lawful to inquire whence it sprang as if it were a thing subject to place & motion for it neither approached hither nor again departs from hence, to some other place, but it either appears to us, or it does not appear." Every man in his moment of reflection sees & records this vision & therefore feels the insufferable impertinence of contradiction from the unthinking as if had uttered a private opinion or caprice & not made himself a bare pipe for better wisdom to flow through.

—

'Tis a good thing for man that I am obliged to pick my words of low trades with so much care. In England you may say a sweep, a blacksmith, a scavenger, as synonym for a savage in civil life. But in this country I must look about me. I perhaps speak to persons who occasionally or regularly work at these works & yet do take as they ought their place as Men in places of manly culture & entertainment.

—

30 October. How hard it is to impute your own best sense to a dead author! The very highest praise we *think* of any writer, or painter, or sculptor, or builder, is, that he actually possessed the thought or feeling with which he has inspired us. We hesitate at doing Spenser so great an honor as to think that he meant by his allegory the sense which we affix to it.

We seem in this to believe that in a former age men could not attain that maturity of consciousness which we have,—& yet I do not know but we have the same infirmity respecting contemporary genius. We fear that Mr Alston did not foresee & design the effect he produces on us.

Familiar as it is to us, the highest merit we ascribe to Homer is that he forsook books & traditions & wrote not what men but what Homer thought.

Easy to enter into this region: every man has some moments of it in his years; but very very few men are able to speak & write those thoughts.

To the chaste man the white skin of the woman with whom he talks, appears to be distant by some miles.

—

When yesterday I read Antigone, at some words a very different image of female loveliness rose out of the clouds of the Past & the Actual. That poem is just what Winckelmann described the Greek beauty to be—"the tongue on the balance of expression." It is remarkable for nothing so much as the extreme temperance, the abstemiousness which never offends by the superfluous word or degree too much of emotion. How slender the materials! how few the incidents! how just the symmetry! C. thinks it as great a work of genius as any. Every word writ in steel. But that other image which it awakened for me brought with it the perception how entirely each rational creature is dowried with all the gifts of God. The Universe, nothing less, is totally given to each new being. It is his potentially. He may divest himself of it, he may creep into a corner as most men do, but he is entitled to deity by the Constitution: Only he must come & take it. "The winds & waves," says Gibbon, "are always on the side of the ablest navigators." What is not, I pray? When a noble act is done, perchance in a scene of great natural beauty, is not the hero entitled to the additional effect of the fine landscape? And when & where does not natural beauty—deep & high yea infinite beauty—steal in like air & envelope great actions? Nature alway stretcheth out her arms to embrace man; only let his thoughts be of equal grandeur & the *frame* will *suit the picture*. A virtuous man is in keeping with the works of nature & makes the central figure in the visible sphere. It is we who by error & crime thrust ourselves aside & make ourselves impertinent & inharmonious things.

But I thought thus yesterday in regard to the charming beauty which a few years ago shed on me its tender & immortal light. She needed not a historical name nor earthly rank or wealth. She was complete in her own perfections. She took up all things into her & in her single self sufficed the soul.

People think that husbands & wives have no *present time*, that they have long already established their mutual connexion, have nothing to learn of one another, & know beforehand each what the other will do. The wise man will discern the fact; viz, that they are chance-joined, little acquainted, & do observe each the other's carriage to the stranger as curiously as he doth.

———

Fine walk this P.M. in the woods with C.—beautiful Gothic arches yes & cathedral windows as of stained glass formed by the interlaced branches against the grey & gold of the western sky. We came to a little pond in the bosom of the hills, with echoing shores. C. thought much of the domesticity & comfort there is in living with one set of men; to wit, your cotemporaries: & thought it would be misery to shift them, & hence the sadness of growing old. Now, every newspaper has tidings of kenned folk. I projected the discomfort of our playing over again tonight the tragedy of Babes in the Wood. C. rejoiced in the serenity of Saturday Night. It was calm as the Universe. I told him what a fool he was not to write the record of his thoughts. He said it were an impiety. Yet he meant to, when he was old. I told him when Alcibiades turned author we worthies should be out of countenance. Yet I maintained that the Lycidas was a copy from the poet's mind printed out in the book, notwithstanding all the mechanical difficulties, as clear & wild as it had shone at first in the sky of his own thought. We came out again into the open world & saw the sunset as of a divine Artist & I asked if it were only brute light & aqueous vapor & there was no intent in that celestial smile? Another topic of the talk was that Lyceums,—so that people will let you say what *you* think—are as good a pulpit as any other. But C. thinks that it is only by an effort like a Berserkir a man can work himself up to any interest in any exertion. All active life seems an amabilis insania. And when he has done anything of importance he repents of it, repents of Virtue as soon as he is alone. Nor can he see any reason why the world should not burn up tonight. The play has been over, some time.

———

December 7. Last week Mr Alcott spent two days here. The wise man who talks with you seems of no particular size but like the sun & moon quite vague & indeterminate. His characterizing of people was very good. Hedge united strangely the old & the new; he had imagination but his intellect seemed ever to contend with an arid temperament.

G.P.B. was an impersonation of sincerity, simplicity, & humility without servility.

Dec. 7. Carlyle's talent I think lies more in his beautiful criticism in seizing the idea of the man or the time than in original speculation. He seems to me most limited in this chapter or speculation in which they regard him as most original & profound—I mean in his Religion & immortality from the removal of Time & Space. He seems merely to work with a foreign thought not to live in it himself.

In Shakspear I actually shade my eyes as I read for the splendor of the thoughts.

—

1836

16 January. Mr Meriam owns this field, Mr Bacon that, & Mr Butterfield the next, but the poet owns the whole. There is a property in the horizon which no man has but he whose eye can integrate all the parts. And the best part of all these men's farms, the face which they show to the poet's eye, they do not possess but he. The view of the field & wood at the distance of a quarter of a mile has no property in it.

There are parts of your nature deep & mysterious. I knew a man who stabbed the name & character of another; and at night he saw a murderer's face grinning & gibbering over him.

—

What can be more clownish than this foolish charging of Miss Martineau with ingratitude for differing in opinion from her southern friends. I take the law of hospitality to be this: I confer on the friend whom I visit the highest compliment, in giving him my time. He gives me shelter & bread. Does he therewith buy my suffrage to his opinions henceforward? No more than by giving him my time, I have bought his. We stand just where we did before. The fact is before we met he was bound to "speak the truth (of me) in love"; & he is bound to the same now.

———

The book is always dear which has made us for moments idealists. That which can dissipate this block of earth into shining ether is genius.

I have no hatred to the round earth & its gray mountains. I see well enough the sand hill opposite my window. I see with as much pleasure as another a field of corn or a rich pasture, whilst I dispute their absolute being. Their phenomenal being, I no more dispute than I do my own. I do not dispute but point out the just way of viewing them.

Religion makes us idealists. Any strong passion does. The best, the happiest moments of life are these delicious awakenings of the higher powers & the reverential withdrawing of nature before its god.

It is remarkable that the greater the material apparatus the more the material disappears, as in Alps & Niagara, in St Peter's & Naples.

———

Feb. 28. Cold bright Sunday morn white with deep snow.

C. thinks if a superior being should look into families, he would find natural relations existing, & man a worthy being, but if he followed them into shops, senates, churches, & societies, they would appear wholly artificial & worthless. Society seems noxious. I believe that against these baleful influences Nature is the antidote. The man comes out of the wrangling of the shop & office, & sees the sky & the woods, & is a man again. He not only quits the cabal but he finds himself. But how few men can see the sky & the woods!

———

13 Aug. Goethe the observer. What sagacity! What industry of observation! What impatience of words! To read Goethe is an economy of time; for you shall find no word that does not

stand for a thing, and he is of that comprehension as to see the value of truth. But I am provoked with his Olympian self complacency, "the damned patronizing air" with which he vouchsafes to tolerate the genius & performances of other mortals: the good Hiller, our costly Kant, &c &c. And excellent of this kind is his account of his philosophy in relation to the Kantian, 'that it was an Analogon of that by their confession.'

I read somewhere that "you might find in him sometimes a maxim, but never a sentiment."

I claim for him the praise of truth, of fidelity to his nature. We think when we contemplate the stupendous glory of the world, that it were life enough to one man merely to lift his hands & say Κοσμος! Beauty! Well, this he did. Here is a man who in the feeling that the thing itself was so admirable as to leave all comment behind, merely went up & down, from object to object, lifting the veil from every one & did no more. What he said of Lavater, I may better say of him, that "it was fearful to stand in the presence of one before whom all the boundaries within which Nature has circumscribed our being were laid flat ——" His are the "bright & terrible eyes" which meet you in every sacred as in every public enclosure.

This is his praise. There is in him nothing heroic. Epaminondas, Agis were greater men. Only he is the king of scholars.

———

Last week I went to Salem. At the Lafayette hotel where I lodged, every five or ten minutes the barkeepers came into the sitting room to arrange their hair & collars at the looking glass. So many joys has the kind God provided for us dear creatures.

———

March 11. All is in Each. Xenophanes complained in his old age that all things hastened back to Unity, Identity. He was weary of seeing the same thing in a tedious variety of forms. The Fable of Proteus has a cordial truth. Every natural form to the smallest, a leaf, a sunbeam, a moment of time, a drop, is related to the Whole, & partakes of the beauty of the Whole. This not only where the analogy is very strict, as when we detect the brother of the human Hand in the fin of the whale &

the flipper of the saurus, but between objects where the superficial dissimilarity is striking. Thus "Architecture is frozen
music" according to De Stael & Goethe. Haydn's Creation is
said to imitate not only movements as the stag's, the snake's,
& the elephant's but *colors* as the green grass. More sublimely
is this true in man & his action. "The wise man in doing one
thing, does all; or, in the one thing which he does rightly, he
sees the likeness of all which is done rightly." Hence I might
have said above the value of Proverbs or the significance of
every trivial speech as of a blacksmith or teamster concerning
his tools or his beasts, Namely, that the same thing is found to
hold true throughout Nature. Thus this morning I read in a
Treatise on Perspective that "the end of a Picture was to give
exclusive prominence to the object represented and to keep
out of sight the means whereby it was done." And change the
terms & of what art is not this true? It is an attribute of the
Supreme Being so to do & therefore will be met throughout
Creation. Every primal Truth is alone an expression of all
Nature. It is the absolute Ens seen from one side, and any
other truths shall only seem altered expression of this. A leaf is
a compend of Nature, and Nature a colossal leaf. An animal
is a compend of the World, and the World is an enlargement of
an animal. There is more family likeness than individuality.
Hence Goethe's striving to find the Arch-plant.

21 March. Only last evening I found the following sentence
in Goethe, a comment and consent to my speculations on the
All in Each in Nature this last week.

"Every existing thing is an analogon of all existing things.
Thence appears to us Being ever, at once sundered & connected. If we follow the analogy too far all things confound
themselves in identity. If we avoid it, then all things scatter
into infinity. In both cases, observation is at a stand, in the one
as too lively, in the other as dead." Vol. 22, p. 245

Man is an analogist. And therefore no man loses any time or
any means who studies that one thing that is before him,
though a log or a snail.

I *waste*, you say, an hour in watching one crab's motions, one
butterfly's intrigues; I learn therein the whole family of crab &
butterfly. I read Man in his remoter symbols.

Only trust yourself, and do the present duty, & God has provided for your access to infinite truths & richest opportunities.

I find an old letter to L. which may stand here—

Has not life woes enough to drug its children with without their brewing & seething such themselves? Shall they not forget all, renounce all, but the simple purpose to extort as much wit & worth from the departing hour as they jointly can?

It is strange—strangest—this omnipresent riddle of life. Nobody can state it. Speech pants after it in vain. All poetry, all philosophy, in their parts, or entire, never express it, tho' that is still their aim: they only approximate. Nobody can say what every body feels, & what all would jump to hear, if it should be said, and, moreover, which all have a confused belief *might be* said. Now this open secret, as he called it, is what our wise but sensual, loved & hated Goethe loved to contemplate, & to exercise his wits in trying to embody. I have been reading him these two or three days, & I think him far more lucky than most of his contemporaries at this game.

There sits he at the centre of all visibles & knowables, blowing bubble after bubble so transparent, so round, so coloured, that he thinks & you think, they are pretty good miniatures of the All. Such attempts are all his minor poems, proverbs, Xenien Parables. Have you read the Welt Seele?

The danger of such attempts as this striving to write Universal Poetry is,—that nothing is so shabby as to fail.

You may write an ill romance or play & 'tis no great matter. Better men have done so, but when what should be greatest truths flat out into shallow truisms, then are we all sick. But much I fear, that Time, the serene Judge, will not be able to make out so good a verdict for Goethe as did & doth Carlyle. I am afraid that under his faith is no-faith,—that under his love is love-of-ease. However his mind is catholic as ever any was. x x x x A human soul is an awsome thing, and when this point world, this something nothing of our life is re-absorbed into the

Infinite, let it be recorded of us that we have not defaced the page of Time with any voluntary blemish of folly or malignity.

Writ June, 1835. It is luxury to live in this beautiful month. One never dares expect a happy day, but the hardest ascetic may inhale delighted this breath of June. It is Devil's needle's Day;—I judge from the millions of sheeny fliers with green body & crape wing that overhang the grass and water. Then the inertia of my blue river down there in the grass, is even sublime. Does not this fine season help to edify your body & spirit?

———

"The light of the Public Square will best test its merit."*
I cultivate ever my humanity. This I would always propitiate. And judge of a book as a peasant does, not as a book by pedantic & individual measures, but by number & weight, counting the things that are in it. My debt to Plato is a certain number of sentences: the like to Aristotle. A large number, yet still a finite number, make the worth of Milton & Shakspeare, to me. I would therefore run over what I have written, save the good sentences, & destroy the rest. C. asks if I were condemned to solitude & one book,—which I would choose? We agreed that Milton would have no claims, & that the Bible must be preferred to Shakspear, because the last, one could better supply himself. The first has a higher strain.

A miracle is a patch. It is an after thought. The history of Man must be an Idea, a self-existent perfect circle, and admit of no miracle that does not cease to be such, & melt into Nature, when the wise eye is turned upon it.

All things are moral, & thereto is nature thus superfluously magnificent.

———

The Germans as a nation have no taste.———
The English are the tyrants of taste.

*M. Angelo Buonaroti.

Fine thought was this Chorus of the Greek Drama. It is like the invention of the cipher in Arithmetic; so perfect an aid and so little obvious. An elegant outer conscience to the interlocutors; Charles says it was the Not-Me.

—

How eagerly men seize on the classification of phrenology which gives them, as they think, an Idea, whereby the most familiar & important facts are arranged. Much more heartily do they open themselves to a true & divine Idea, as that of Freedom or Right. See the Orator, by a few sharp & skilful statements, unite his various audience, & whilst they stand mute & astonished, he touches their hearts as harp strings, until, in the presence of the aroused Reason, Good & Fair become practicable, and the gravest obstacles are swept away like the morning cloud. Under the stupendous dominion of Ideas, individual interests, even personal identity, melt into the swelling surges of the Universal Humanity. Eloquence is the voice of Virtue & Truth.

—

I thought yesterday morning of the sweetness of that fragrant piety which is almost departed out of the world, which makes the genius of A-Kempis, Scougal, Herbert, Jeremy Taylor. It is a beautiful mean, equidistant from the hard sour iron Puritan on one side, & the empty negation of the Unitarian on the other. It is the spirit of David & of Paul. Who shall restore to us the odoriferous Sabbaths which that Sweet Spirit bestowed on human life, and which made the earth and the humble roof a sanctity? This spirit of course involved that of Stoicism, as in its turn Stoicism did this. Yet how much more attractive & true that this Piety should be the Central trait and the stern virtues follow than that Stoicism should face the Gods & put Jove on his defence. That sentiment is a refutation of every skeptical doubt. David is a beauty, and read 3d chapter of Ephesians.

And yet I see not very well how the rose of Sharon could bloom so freshly in our affection but for these ancient men who like great gardens with banks of flowers do send out their perfumed breath across the great tracts of time. How needful is Paul & David, Leighton, A Kempis, & Fenelon to our Idea.

Of these writers, of this spirit that deified them, I will say with Confucius, "If in the morning, I hear about the right way, & in the evening die, I can be happy."

Idealism

Life, Action, is perfected Science. Under strong virtuous excitement, we contemn the body.

Without the ideas of God, Freedom, Virtue, Love, in his *head*, man would be vermin: but put them in his *heart* and he is one with God.

All is naught without the Idea which is its nucleus & soul: for this reason no natural fact interests until connected with man.

1836

22 March. It is now four months that we have had uninterrupted sleighing in Concord; and today it snows fast.

I admire specially three advantages of civilization: the post office, the newspaper, and the road. Hereby the human race run on my errands; the human race read & write of all that happens for me; the human race turn out, every morning, and shovel away the snow and cut a path for me.

It is a small & mean thing to attempt too hardly to disprove the being of Matter. I have no hostility to oxygen or hydrogen, to the sun or the hyacinth that opened this morning its little censer in his beam. This is not for one of my complexion who do expand like a plant in the sunshine, who do really love the warm day like an Indian or a bird. I only aim to speak for the Great Soul; to speak for the sovereignty of Ideas.

———

He only is a good writer who keeps but one eye on his page and with the other sweeps over things. So that every sentence brings us a new contribution of observation.

> This is spotless
> That is not less.

March 28. "All that frees Talent without increasing self command, is noxious." Thus the fabled ring of Gyges which is realized in a sort by the telescope as used by Schemel is only mischievous. A new language when it serves only low or political purposes; the balloon could it be guided; the steam battery so fatal as to end War by Universal Murder. Nature gives us no sudden advantages. By the time we have acquired great power, we have acquired therewith sufficient wisdom to use it well. Animal magnetism inspires us the prudent and moral with a certain terror. Men are not good enough to be trusted with such power.

—

1 April. Beautiful morn follower of a beautiful moon. Yet lies the snow on the ground. Birds sing, mosses creep, grass grows under the edge of the snow bank. Read yesterday Goethe's Iphigenia. A pleasing, moving, even heroic work yet with the great deduction of being an imitation of the antique. How can a great genius endure to make paste-jewels? It must always have the effect compared with the great originals of Franklin's or Taylor's apologue of Abraham or Everett's Burdens of the Nations compared with the comforting or alarming words of David & Isaiah. Yet when in the evening we read Sophocles, the shadow of a like criticism fell broad over almost all that is called modern literature. The words of Electra & Orestes are like actions. So live the thoughts of Shakspear. They have a necessary being. They live like men. To such productions it is obviously necessary that they should take that form which is then alive before the poet. The playhouse must have been the daily resort of Shakspear and that profession on which his circumstances had concentrated his attention. That is essential to the production of his plays. It is quite otherwise with Taylor & his Van Arteveldt. His playhouse & Muse is the reading of Shakspear. Sermons were thus a living form to Taylor, Barrow, South, & Donne. Novels & parliamentary speeches since Fielding & Burke. The Instauratio was a natural effect of the revival of ancient learning. But thus it always must happen that the true work of genius should proceed out of the wants & deeds of the age as well as the writer, & so be the first form with which his genius combines, as Sculpture was perfect in Phidias's age, because the marble was the first form with which the creative genius combined. Homer is the only true epic. Milton is to him what Michel Angelo is to Phidias. But Shakspear is like Homer or Phidias himself. Do that which lies next you, O Man!

Salem. 19 April. The philosopher should explain to us the laws of redeeming the time. The universal fact, says Goethe, is that which takes place once. Well, let us read in the same faith, that the sentence now under the eye is one of universal application, and the volume in our hand is for us the voice of God & Time. Many are the paths that lead to wisdom & honor: nay, every man hath a private lane thereto from his own door. Raphael paints wisdom, Handel sings it, Phidias carves it, Shakspear writes it, Washington enacts it, Columbus sails it, Wren builds it, Watt mechanizes it, Luther preaches it. Let us take Duty this serving angel for a God in disguise. Without telling us why, he bids us ever do this & that irksomeness. What if it should prove that these very injunctions so galling & unflattering are precisely the redemptions of time for us? These books thrust into our hands are books selected for us, & the persons who take up our time are picked out to accompany us. I at least fully believe that God is in every place, & that, if the mind is excited, it may see him, & in him an infinite wisdom in every object that passes before us.

22 April. I left Boston with Charles for New York where we arrived 26 April. I arrived in Salem again 2 May.

Salem, 4 May. The Marine Railway, the U.S. Bank, the Bunker Hill monument, are perfectly genuine works of the times. So is a speech in Congress, so is a historical discourse, a novel, Channing's Work on Slavery, & the Volume of Revised Statutes. But Taylor's Van Arteveldt, Byron's Sardanapalus, & Joanna Bailey's dramas are futile endeavors to revive a dead form & cannot succeed, nor I think can Greenough's sculpture. You must exercise your genius in some form that has essential life now; do something which is proper to the hour & cannot but be done. But what is once well done, lasts forever. As the gladiator, the Apollo, the Parthenon, the Iliad.

All the devils respect virtue.

Concord, 16 May, 1836. And here I am again at home but I have come alone. My brother, my friend, my ornament, my joy & pride has fallen by the wayside, or rather has risen out of this dust. Charles died at New York Monday afternoon, 9 May. His prayer that he might not be sick was granted him. He was never confined to a bed. He rode out on Monday afternoon with Mother, promised himself to begin his journey with me on my arrival, the next day; on reaching home, he stepped out of the carriage alone, walked up the steps & into the house without assistance, sat down on the stairs, fainted, & never recovered. Beautiful without any parallel, in my experience of young men, was his life, happiest his death. Miserable is my own prospect from whom my friend is taken. Clean & Sweet was his life, untempted almost, and his action on others all-healing, uplifting, & fragrant. I read now his pages, I remember all his words & motions without any pang, so healthy & humane a life it was, & not like Edward's, a tragedy of poverty & sickness tearing genius. His virtues were like the victories of Timoleon, & Homer's verses, they were so easy & natural. I cannot understand why his mss. journal should have so bitter a strain of penitence & deprecation. I mourn that in losing him I have lost his all, for he was born an orator, not a writer. His written pages do him no justice, and as he felt the immense disparity between his power of conversation & his blotted paper, it was easy for him to speak with scorn of written composition.

Now commences a new & gloomy epoch of my life. I have used his society so fondly & solidly. It was pleasant to unfold my thought to so wise a hearer. It opened itself genially to his warm & bright light, and borrowed color & sometimes form from him. Besides my direct debt to him of how many valued thoughts,—through what orbits of speculation have we not travelled together, so that it would not be possible for either of us to say, This is my thought, That is yours.

I have felt in him the inestimable advantage, when God allows it, of finding a brother and a friend in one. The mutual understanding is then perfect, because Nature has settled the constitution of the amity on solidest foundations; and so it admits of mercenary usefulness & of unsparing censure; there exists the greatest convenience inasmuch as the same persons & facts are known to each, and an occult hereditary sympathy underlies all our intercourse & extends farther than we know.

Who can ever supply his place to me? None. I may live long.

I may, (tho' 'tis improbable) see many cultivated persons, but his elegance, his wit, his sense, his worship of principles, I shall not find united—I shall not find them separate. The eye is closed that was to see Nature for me, & give me leave to see; the taste & soul which Shakspear satisfied; the soul that loved St John, & St Paul, Isaiah & David; the acute discernment that divided the good from the evil in all objects around him, in society, in politics, in church, in books, in persons; the hilarity of thought which awakened good humor wherever it came, and laughter without shame; and the endless endeavor after a life of ideal beauty;—these are all gone from my actual world & will here be no more seen.

I read with some surprise the pages of his journal. They show a nocturnal side which his diurnal aspects never suggested,— they are melancholy, penitential, self accusing; I read them with no pleasure: they are the creepings of an eclipsing temperament over his abiding light of character.

His senses were those of a Greek. I owe to them a thousand observations. To live with him was like living with a great painter. I used to say that I had no leave to see things till he pointed them out, & afterwards I never ceased to see them.

The fine humor of his conversation seemed to make the world he saw. His power of illustration & the facility of his association embroidered his sentences with all his reading & all his seeing. He could not speak but in cheerful figures. When something was said of maritime people, the pilots & fishermen, he said, "they were the fringes of the human race." When Miss Martineau was commended for the energy with which she had clung to society, despite her infirmity, he said "She *had* brushed pretty well thro' that drift of deafness." We complained much of the ugly mill they built over "Sleepy Hollow" in Concord. By & by they painted the vans red; Charles said, "This was adding insult to injury."

I conversed with him one day upon the agreement of so many thinkers in representing Nature as the symbol of the mind. He said "Yes there sits the Sphynx by the road-side, & every fine genius that goes by has a crack with her."

"The nap," he said "is worn off of the world."

He said of the unfortunate Mr. ———; 'As fast as Mrs ——— rows, Mr ——— backs water.'

"It is only by an effort like a Berserkir's," he said, "that a man can work himself up to an interest in any exertion. All active life seems an *amabilis insania*. And when I have done anything of importance I repent of it: I repent of virtue as soon as I am alone; nor can I see any reason why the world should not burn up tonight: the play has been over some time."

He said of our Concord Society, that "we seemed to be on the way back to annihilation."

He said he never spent anything on himself without thinking he deserved the praise of disinterested benevolence.

He said, The south wind made every body handsome.

Charles said, There were two ways of living in the world, viz. either to postpone your own ascetic entirely, & live among people as among aliens; or, to lead a life of endless warfare by forcing your Ideal into act. In either of these ways the wise man may be blameless.

Charles said, No speculation interested him that could not help him in action, & so become his daily bread.

Nothing disgusted him more than aimless activity.

Truth of character he worshipped; truth to one's self—& proportionally despised the excessive craving for sympathy & praise, the parasitic life.

He could not bear to think that he should degenerate into a householder & lead the base life.

He held at a very low rate the praise of fashionable people. He held at a very high rate the praise or gratitude of plain men whose habits of life, precluded compliment, & made their verdict unquestionable.

A man is sure of nothing, he said, but what he got himself. Let him count every thing else mere good fortune, & expect to lose it any moment.

He thought that Jeremy Taylor's sermons might be preached in an obscure country village with greatest advantage to the hearers; that they would be a sort of University; in themselves an education to those who had no other.

He thought that the religious sentiment was the right of the poor at Church; that any speculations merely ingenious, or literary merits of a discourse did not excuse the defect of this; but defrauded the poor of his Christianity.

He thought Christianity the philosophy of suffering; the religion of pain: that its motto was, "Thy Will be done"; and that the print of the bended head of Christ with hands folded on the breast should be the altar-piece & symbol in churches, & not the crucifixion.

He thought it a measure of any man's ability, the value he set upon his time.

———

He sympathized wonderfully with all objects & natures, & as by a spiritual ventriloquism threw his mind into them, which appeared in the warm & genial traits by which he again pictured them to the eye. I find him saying to E. H. 3 Apr. 1834 "I do not know but one of the ancient metamorphoses will some day happen to me, & I shall shoot into a tree, or flow in a stream. I do so lose my human nature & join myself to that which is without. Today even Goethe would have been satisfied with the temper in which I became identified with what I saw, a part of what was around me!"

———

Concord, 19 May, 1836. I find myself slowly, after this helpless mourning. I remember states of mind that perhaps I had long lost before this grief, the native mountains whose tops reappear after we have traversed many a mile of weary region from home. Them shall I ever revisit? I refer now to last evening's lively remembrance of the scattered company who have ministered to my highest wants. Edward Stabler, Peter Hunt, Sampson Reed, my peasant Tarbox, Mary Rotch, Jonathan Phillips, A.B. Alcott—even Murat has a claim—a strange class, plain & wise, whose charm to me is wonderful, how elevating! how far was their voice from the voice of vanity of display, of interest, of tradition! They are to me what the Wanderer in the Excursion is to the poet. And Wordsworth's total value is of this kind. They are described in the lines at the end of the Yarrow Revisited. Theirs is the true light of all our day. They are the argument for the spiritual world for their spirit is it. Nothing is impossible since such communion has already been. Whilst we hear them speak, how frivolous are the distinctions of fortune! and the voice of fame is as unaffecting as the tinkle of the passing sleigh bell.

—

The generic soul in each individual is a giant overcome with sleep which locks up almost all his senses, & only leaves him a little superficial animation. Once in an age at hearing some deeper voice, he lifts his iron lids, & his eyes straight pierce through all appearances, & his tongue tells what shall be in the latest times: then is he obeyed like a God, but quickly the lids fall, & sleep returns.

[Otherism]

Sunday, 22 May. We overestimate the conscience of our friend. His goodness seems better than our goodness. His nature finer, his temptation less. Every thing that was his, his name, his form, his dress, his books, fancy enhances. It is the action of the social principle "aiming above the mark that it may hit the mark." Our own expressed thought strikes us as new & of some more weight from the mouth of a friend.

Persons: the talk of the kitchen & the cottage is exclusively occupied with persons. It is the sickness, crimes, disasters, airs, fortunes of persons; never is the character of the action or the object abstracted. Go into the parlor & into fashionable society. The persons are more conspicuous but the fact is the same. The conversation still hovers over persons, over political connexions, over events as they related to individuals.—Go at last into the cultivated class who ask What is Beauty? How shall I be perfect? To what end exists the world? and you shall find in proportion to their cultivation a studious separation of personal history from their analysis of character & their study of things. Natural History is elegant, astronomy sublime for this reason, their impersonality. And yet when cultivated men speak of God they demand a biography of him as steadily as the kitchen & the bar room demand personalities of men. Absolute goodness, absolute truth must leave their infinity & take form for us. We want fingers & sides & hair. Yet certainly it is more grand & therefore more true to say 'Goodness is its own reward'; 'Be sure your sin will find you out,' than to say, God will give long life to the upright; God will punish the sinner in hell, in any popular sense of these words. But the angels will worship virtue & truth not gathered into a person but inly seen in the perspective of their own progressive being. They see the dream & the interpretation of the world in the faith that God is within them. As a spiritual truth needs no proof but is its own reason, so the Universe needs no outer cause but exists by its own perfection and the sum of it all is this, God is.

Theism must be & the name of God must be because it is a necessity of the human mind to apprehend the relative as flowing from the absolute & we shall always give the Absolute a name. But a storm of calumny will always pelt him whose view of God is highest & purest.

I heard today a preacher who made me think that the stern Compensations work themselves out in pulpits too, since if a preacher treats the people as children they too will treat him as a child.

It is strange how simple a thing it is to be a great man, so simple that almost all fail by over doing. There is nothing vulgar in Wordsworth's idea of Man. To believe your own thought, that is Genius. To believe that a man intended to produce the emotion we feel before his work is the highest praise, so high that we ever hesitate to give it.

———

Put in the Sermon to Scholars the brave maxim of the Code of Menu; "A teacher of the Veda should rather die with his learning than sow it in sterile soil, even though he be in grievous distress for subsistence."

*

Please God the curse of the carpenter shall never lie on my roof!

Fine thoughts flowing from an idea perceived by the mind, & fine thoughts wilfully recollected & exhibited, differ as leaves & flowers growing from a branch, & leaves & flowers tied together by a string.

31 May. All powerful action is by bringing the forces of nature to bear upon our objects. We do not grind corn or lift the loom by our own strength but we build a mill & set the North wind to play upon our instrument or the expansive force of steam or the ebb & flow of the ocean. So in our manipulations, we do few things by muscular force but we place ourselves in such attitudes as to bring the force of gravity, the weight of the planet, that is, to bear upon the spade or the axe we wield; in short in all our operations we seek not to use our own but to bring a quite infinite force to bear. In like manner are our intellectual works done. We are to hinder our individuality from acting; we are to bring the whole omniscience of Reason upon the subject before us. We are to aim at getting observations without aim, to subject to thought things seen without thought. What is it that gives force to the blow of ax or crowbar? Is it the muscles of the man's arm or is it the attraction of the whole globe below it on the ax or bar?

Yesterday in the wood it seemed to me that the three aspects of Natural Beauty might take this order. 1. The beauty of the world as a daily delight & luxury—rainbows, moonlight, & perspective; 2. The beauty of the world as it is—the drapery of Virtuous actions, Leonidas, Columbus, & Vane, & always the Unconscious Man; 3. The beauty of the World as it becomes an object of the intellect and so the foundation of Art or the voluntary creation of Beauty.

1 June.
Once there was an urn which received water out of a fountain. But sometimes the fountain spouted so far as to fall beyond the lips of the Urn, & sometimes not far enough to fill it; so that sometimes it was only sprinkled. But the Urn desired

to be always full and Nature saw the Urn, & made it alive, so
that it could move this way & that to meet the waterfall, and
even when the water did not rise out of the spring, it could
change its shape, & with a long neck suck up the water from
hollows with its lips. Then it began to go far from the fountain, looking in many places for wells, & sometimes when the
fountain was full, the Urn was gone, & did not come back until the fountain was a thread; and often, the walking Urn lost
its way & came into sands, & was long empty. Moreover
though Nature gave it life, she did not give it more body, so
that what was spent in making feet & legs was lost from the
belly of the Urn; and in the motion of going, much water was
spilled so that now it was never full as before. So the Urn came
to Nature, and besought her to take away its life, & replace it
at the old fountain.

2 June. It is another fact to be remembered in the scholar's
sermon that hard labor,—for example farm-work,—is not
favorable to thought. My friend Mr Wight tells me that it
blunts the sensibility of the upper system so that he sleeps &
not thinks in the study. And I have found the same thing true.
Therefore he thinks the farm schools will not succeed in
making scholars.

———

3 June. Shall I not treat all men as gods?

4 June. The painters have driven me from my apartment.
What a droll craft is theirs generically considered! There certainly is a ridiculous air over much of our life.

———

There is one mind. Inspiration is larger reception of it: fanaticism is predominance of the individual. The greater genius
the more like all other men, therefore. A man's call to do any
particular work as to go super cargo to Calcutta, or missionary
to Serampore, or pioneer to the Western country is his fitness
to do that thing he proposes. Any thought that he has a personal summons—

> signs that mark him extraordinary
> & not in the roll of common men

—is dreaming, is so much insanity. It denotes deficiency of perceiving that there is One Mind in all the individuals. In like manner guessing at the modes of divine action as Norton's about electricity, &c betrays ignorance of the truth that all men have access to the divine counsels, for God is the Universal mind.

5 June 1836. I have read with interest Mr Alcott's Journal in MS for 1835. He has attained at least to a perfectly simple & elegant utterance. There is no inflation & no cramp in his writing. I complained that there did not seem to be quite that facility of association which we expect in the man of genius & which is to interlace his work with all Nature by its radiating upon all. But the sincerity of his speculation is a better merit. This is no theory of a month's standing; no peg to hang fine things on; no sham enthusiasm; no cant; but his hearty faith & study by night & by day. He writes it in the book, he discourses it in the parlor, he instructs it in the school.
And whatever defects as fine writers such men may have it is because colossal foundation are not for summerhouses but for temples & cities. But come again a hundred years hence & compare Alcott & his little critics.

June 6. Last Saturday eve. I had a conversation with E. H. which I cannot recal but of which the theme was that when we deal truly & lay judgment to the line & rule we are no longer permitted to think that the presence or absence of friends is material to our highest states of mind. In those few moments which are the life of our life when we were in the state of clear vision, we were taught that God is here no respecter of persons, that into that communion with him which is absolute life, & where names & ceremonies & traditions are no longer known, but the virtues are loved for their loveliness alone, for their conformity to God;—in that communion our dearest friends are strangers. There is no personëity in it.

Yesterday I remembered the saying of Coleridge's friend Moxon that he would go to the Cabinet Ministers to read their faces, for Nature never lies. Also by writing is the character made known. And he who is dumb & motionless for fear of betraying his thought does by very silence & inaction tell it. Dum tacet clamat. So irresistibly does human nature ever publish itself.

June 7. Many letters from friends who loved or honored Charles. I know not why it is, but a letter is scarcely welcome to me. I expect to be lacerated by it & if I come safe to the end of it, I feel like one escaped.

The Use of Nature is to awaken the feeling of the Absolute. Nature is a perpetual effect. It is the great shadow pointing to an unseen Sun.

Why fret at particular events? For every thing you have missed, you have gained some thing else: And for every thing you gain, you lose something.

> "Wishing good & doing good
>   Is laboring Lord with thee
>   Charity is gratitude
>   And piety best understood
>   Is sweet humanity."

The value of so many persons is like that of an unit in decimal notation which is determined altogether by the *place* of the number.

"Why strew'st thou sugar on this bottled spider?"

Do not fear the multitude of books. They all have their place. Shakspear, Moses, Cicero, Bacon, A Kempis, Cervantes, Bunyan, dwell together without crowding in the Mind as in Nature there is room for all the succession of herbs & trees, of birds, & beasts. The world is large enough, the year is long enough for all that is to be done in it.

———

I become querulous, discontented, even garrulous. In that rare society of which I wrote above p. 457, I dilate and am wise, good, & hopeful by sympathy, but in ordinary company & what is not so, (non é nel mondo, se on volgo,) I shrink & patter & apologize. I know not why, but I hate to be asked to preach here in Concord. I never go to the Sunday School Teachers without fear & shame.

I take admonitions from every passenger with the attitude & feeling of a willow. I am like those opium eaters of Constantinople who skulked about all day the most pitifull drivellers, then at even when the bazars were open slunk to the opium shop & became glorious & great.

I am afraid that the brilliant writers very rarely feel the deepest interest in truth itself. Even my noble Scotchman, I fancy, feels so strongly his vocation to produce, that he would not listen with half the unfeigned joy to a simple oracle in the woods that Hosmer or Hunt would find. He is certainly dedicated to his book, to the communication & the form of that he knows. Yet he ought to feel more curious to know the truth than anxious to exhibit what he knows. Yet what is any man's book compared with the undiscoverable All?

14 June. What learned I this morning in the woods, the oracular woods? Wise are they the ancient nymphs. Pleasing sober melancholy truth say those untameable savages the pines. Under them bend & reign each in his tiny sphere surrounded by a company of his own race & family the violets, thesiums, cypripediums &c. The windflower (rue leaved) is the Bride. But thus they said.

Power is one great lesson which Nature teaches Man. The secret that he can not only reduce under his will, that is, conform to his character, particular events but classes of events & so harmonize all the outward occurrences with the states of mind, that must he learn.

Worship, must he learn.

Is the pretension of the Ideal Theory enormous? Every possible statement of the connexion between the world & you involves pretensions as enormous.

Have you been associated with any friend whose charm over you was coextensive with your idea that is, was infinite; who filled your thought on that side as most certainly befals us; &

so you was enamoured of the person. And from that person have you at last by incessant love & study acquired a new measure of excellence, also a confidence in the resources of God who thus sends you a real person to outgo your ideal, you will readily see when you are separated, as you shortly will be, the bud, flower, & fruit of the whole fact. As soon as your friend has become to you an object of thought, has revealed to you with great prominence a new nature, & has become a measure whereof you are fully possessed to guage & test more, as his character become solid & sweet wisdom it is already a sign to you that his office to you is closing; expect thenceforward the hour in which he shall be withdrawn from your sight.

To you he was manifest in flesh. He is not manifest in flesh. Has that portion of spiritual life which he represented to you any less reality? All which was, is now & ever shall be. See then whether you do not overesteem the greatness of your labors & instead of vaunting so loudly your mission to the world look perhaps if the world have not a mission to you.

It were a wise secret inquiry for the bosom to compare point by point especially at eras or remarkable events our own biography with the rise, progress, & practice of Ideas in us.

Truth & originality go abreast always.

June 16. Yesterday I went to Mr Alcott's school & heard a conversation upon the Gospel of John. I thought the experiment of engaging young children upon questions of taste & truth successful. A few striking things were said by them. I felt strongly as I watched the gradual dawn of a thought upon the minds of all, that to truth is no age or season. It appears or it does not appear, & when the child perceives it, he is no more a child; age, sex are nothing: we are all alike before the great Whole. Little Josiah Quincy now six years, six months old, is a child having something wonderful & divine in him. He is a youthful prophet.

The more abstract, the more practical.

Monsters & aberrations give us glimpses of the higher law;—let us into the secret of Nature, thought Goethe. Well. We fable to conform things better to our higher law, but when by & by we see the true cause, the fable fades & shrivels up. We see then the true higher law. To the wise therefore a fact is true poetry & the most beautiful of fables.

—

The εν και παν is the reason why our education can be carried on & perfected any where & with any bias whatsoever. If I study an ant hill & neglect all business, all history, all conversation yet shall that ant hill humbly & lovingly & unceasingly explored furnish me with a parallel experience & the same conclusions to which business, history, & conversation would have brought me. So the sculptor, the dragoon, the trader, the shepherd, come to the same conclusions. All is economized. When you are doing, you lose no time from your book, because you still study & still learn. Do what you will you learn, so that you have a right mind & a right heart. But if not, I think you still learn though all is mislearned. Pains & prayer will do any thing.

Debt makes a large part of our education.

—

A fact we said was the terminus of spirit. A man, I, am the remote circumference, the skirt, the thin suburb or frontier post of God but go inward & I find the ocean; I lose my individuality in its waves. God is Unity, but always works in variety. I go inward until I find Unity universal, that Is before the World was; I come outward to this body a point of variety.

Magnitude is nothing to science.

The drop is a small ocean, the ocean a large drop. A leaf is a simplified world, the world a compound leaf.

Matter is "the frail & weary weed in which God has drest the soul which he has called into time."

22 June. Mr Alcott has been here with his Olympian dreams. He is a world-builder. Ever more he toils to solve the problem,

Whence is the World? The point at which he prefers to begin is the Mystery of the Birth of a child. I tell him it is idle for him to affect to feel an interest in the compositions of any one else. Particulars,—particular thoughts, sentences, facts even, cannot interest him except as for a moment they take their place as a ray from his orb. The Whole,—Nature proceeding from himself, is what he studies. But he loses like other sovereigns great pleasures by reason of his grandeur. I go to Shakspear, Goethe, Swift, even to Tennyson, submit myself to them, become merely an organ of hearing, & yield to the law of their being. I am paid for thus being nothing by an entire new mind & thus a Proteus I enjoy the Universe through the powers & organs of a hundred different men. But Alcott cannot delight in Shakspear, cannot get near him. And so with all things. What is characteristic also, he cannot recal one word or part of his own conversation or of any one's let the expression be never so happy. He made here some majestic utterances but so inspired me that even I forgot the words often. The grass, the earth seemed to him "the refuse of spirit."

Jesus says, Leave father & mother, house & lands & follow me. And there is no man who hath left all but he receives more. This is as true intellectually as morally. Each new mind we approach seems to require an abdication of all our past & present empire. A new doctrine seems at first a subversion of all our opinions, tastes, & manner of living. So did Jesus, so did Kant, so did Swedenborg, so did Cousin, so did Alcott seem. Take thankfully & heartily all they can give, exhaust them, leave father & mother & goods, wrestle with them, let them not go until their blessing be won, & after a short season the dismay will be overpast, the excess of influence will be withdrawn, & they will be no longer an alarming meteor but one more bright star shining serenely in your heaven & blending its light with all your day.

I love the wood god. I love the mighty PAN.

Yesterday I walked in the storm. And truly in the fields I am not alone or unacknowledged. They nod to me & I to them. The waving of the boughs of trees in a storm is new to me &

old. It takes me by surprize & yet is not unknown. Its effect is like that of a higher thought or a better emotion coming over me when I deemed I was thinking justly or doing right. We distrust & deny inwardly our own sympathy with nature. We own & disown our relation to it. We are like Nebuchadnezzar cast down from our throne bereft of our reason & eating grass like an ox.

—

It is the property of the divine to be reproductive. The harvest is seed. The good sermon becomes a text in the hearer's mind. That is the good book which sets us at work. The highest science is prophecy. Jesus is but the harbinger & announcer of the Comforter to come, & his continual office is to make himself less to us by making us demand more.

The Understanding, the Usurping Understanding the lieutenant of Reason, his hired man, the moment the Master is gone steps into his place; this usher commands, sets himself to finish what He was doing, but instantly proceeds with his own dwarf Architecture & thoroughly cheats us until presently for a moment Reason returns & the slave obeys, & his work shrinks into tatters & cobwebs.

Not whilst the wise are one class & the good another, not whilst the physiologist & the psychologist are twain, can a Man exist, & Messiah come.

A man is a god in ruins. When men are childlike, life may be longer. Now the world would be more monstrous yet, if these disorganizations were more permanent. Infancy is the perpetual messiah which comes into the arms of these lost beings, & pleads with them to return to paradise.

How hard to write the truth. "Let a man rejoice in the truth and not that he has found it," said my early oracle. Well, so soon as I have seen the truth I clap my hands & rejoice & go back to see it & forward to tell men. I am so pleased therewith that presently it vanishes. Then am I submiss & it appears "without observation." I write it down, & it is gone. Yet is the benefit of others & their love of receiving truth from me the reason of my interest & effort to obtain it & thus do I double

& treble with God. The Reason refuses to play at couples with Understanding; to subserve the private ends of the Understanding.

June 24. I have read with great pleasure, sometimes with delight, No 5 of Mr Alcott's Record of Conversations in the Gospels. The internal evidence of the genuineness of the thinking on the part of the children is often very strong. Their wisdom is something the less surprizing because of the simplicity of the instrument on which they play these fine airs. It is a harp of two strings, Matter & Spirit, & in whatever combination or contrast or harmony you strike them, always the effect is sublime.

———

29 June. In this pleasing contrite wood life which God allows me, let me record day by day my honest thoughts, & the record ought to have the interest to a philosopher which the life of a gymnosophist or stylite had. The book should smell of pines & resound with hum of insects. I suppose no man can violate his nature. All the sallies of his will are rounded in by the law of his being as the inequalities of Andes & Himmaleh are insignificant in the curve of the sphere. Nor does it matter how you guage & try him. A character is like a quincunx or an Alexandrian stanza,—read it forward or backward or across, it still spells the same thing. So you may judge a man by his company or by his books, or by his expenditure, by his craniology, or his physiognomy—he will give the same result.

———

July 21. The worst guest is Asmodeus who comes into the quiet house sometimes in breeches sometimes in petticoats and demands of his entertainer not shelter & food, but to find him in work, and every body is on pins until some rope of sand is found for the monster to twist.

Respect yourself. You have first an instinct, then an opinion, then a knowledge, as the plant has root, bud, & fruit. Trust the instinct to the end, though you cannot tell why or see why. It is vain to hurry it. By trusting it, it shall ripen into thought & truth & you shall know why you believe.

Pleasant it is to see two persons acting habitually & harmoniously together of entirely different manner & voice; two strong natures neither of which impairs the other by any direct modification. The more perfect the Union, the concession at the same time of individual peculiarity being the least, makes the best society.

Make your own Bible. Select & Collect all those words & sentences that in all your reading have been to you like the blast of trumpet out of Shakspear, Seneca, Moses, John, & Paul.

30 July. Man is the point wherein matter & spirit meet & marry. The Idealist says, God paints the world around your soul. The spiritualist saith, Yea, but lo! God is within you. The self of self creates the world through you, & organizations like you. The Universal Central Soul comes to the surface in my body.

31 July. The wise man has no secrets. Secrets belong to the individual, local. He strives evermore to sink the individual in the universal. The friend who can bring him into a certain mood has a right to all the privacies that belong to that mood. Moreover, he believes that no secrets can be: that the nature of the man does forever publish itself and that all laborious concealments lose their labor.

6 August. The grey past, the white future.

A year ago I studied Ben Jonson a good deal. You may learn much from so complete records of one mind as his works are. There is something fearful in coming up against the walls of a mind on every side & learning to describe their invisible circumference.

"I know not what you think of me", said my friend. Are you sure? You know all I think of you by those things I say to you. You know all which can be of any use to you. If I, if all your friends should draw your portrait to you—faults & graces, it would mislead you, embarrass you; you must not ask how you please me for curiosity. You must not look in the glass to see how handsome you are but to see if your face is clean. Certainly I know what impression I made on any man, by remembering what communications he made to me.

———

I said once that if you go expressly to look at the moon, it becomes tinsel. A party of view hunters will see no divine landscape. There is however in moon gazing something analogous to Newton's fits of easy transmission & reflection. You catch the charm one moment, then it is gone, then it returns to go again. And spoken of it becomes flat enough. Perhaps the "fits" depend on the pulsations of the heart.

The best Service which history renders us is to lead us to prize the present.

I went to Walden Pond this evening a little before sunset, and in the tranquil landscape I behold somewhat as beautiful as my own nature.

———

How rarely can a female mind be impersonal. S.A.R. is wonderfully free from egotism of place & time & blood. M. F. by no means so free with all her superiority. What shall I say of MME!

17 August. "Our part in public occasions, says Goethe, is, for the most part, Philisterei". True of commencement & this Cambridge jubilee.
Criticism has this defence that, like poetry, it is an accomodation of the shows of things to the desires of the mind.

27 August. Today came to me the first proof-sheet of "Nature" to be corrected, like a new coat, full of vexations; with the first sentences of the chapters perched like mottoes aloft in small type! The peace of the author cannot be wounded by such trifles, if he sees that the sentences are still good. A good sentence can never be put out of countenance by any blunder of compositors. It is good in text or note, in poetry or prose, as title or corollary. But a bad sentence shows

all his flaws instantly by such dislocation. So that a certain sublime serenity is generated in the soul of the Poet by the annoyances of the press. He sees that the spirit may infuse a subtle
logic into the parts of the piece which shall defy all accidents to
break their connexion.

The man of talents who brings his poetry & eloquence to
market is like the hawk which I have seen wheeling up to
heaven in the face of noon—& all to have a better view of mice
& moles & chickens.

———

History. A great licentiousness seems to have followed directly
on the heels of the Reformation. Luther even had to lament
the decay of piety in his own household. "Doctor," said his
wife to him one day, "how is it that while subject to papacy, we
prayed so often & with such fervor, while now we pray with
the utmost coldness & very seldom?" Remember Luther's
wife!

———

Again I hear the melancholy sentence of Pestalozzi that he
had learned that no man in God's wide world is either able or
willing to help any other man.

How strongly it came to mind the other eve. at the Teachers'
Meeting (as oft before) that nothing needs so much to be
preached as the law of Compensation out of the nature of
things, that the good exalts & the evil degrades us not hereafter but in the moment of the deed.

G.P.B. says of Alcott that he destroys too many illusions.
At the age ludicrously called the age of discretion every
hopeful young man is shipwrecked. The burdensome possession of himself he cannot dispose of. Up to that hour, others
have directed him & he has gone triumphantly. Then he
begins to direct himself & all hope, wisdom, & power sink flat
down. Sleep creeps over him & he lies down in the snow.

One of us is received with favor & of another the world is
not worthy.

*

There is difference between the waiting of the prophet & the standing still of the fool.

2 September. We see much truth under the glitter & ribbons of a festival like Commencement. Each year the same faces come there, but each elongated or whitened or fallen a little. The courage too, that is felt at presenting your own face before the well known assembly, is not an extempore feeling, but is based on a long memory of studies & actions. An assembly is a sort of Judgment Day, before whose face every soul is tried. Fat & foolish faces, to be sure, there are in the forefront of the crowd, but they are only warnings & the imps & examples of doom. The scholar looks in at the door, but unwilling to face this ordeal to little purpose, he retreats & walks along solitary streets & lanes, far from the show.

Every principle is a war-note.

Sept. 13. I went to the College Jubilee on the 8th instant. A noble & well thought of anniversary. The pathos of the occasion was extreme & not much noted by the speakers. Cambridge at any time is full of ghosts; but on that day the anointed eye saw the crowd of spirits that mingled with the procession in the vacant spaces, year by year, as the classes proceeded; and then the far longer train of ghosts that followed the company, of the men that wore before us the college honors & the laurels of the state—the long winding train reaching back into eternity.—But among the living was more melancholy reflection, namely the identity of all the persons with that which they were in youth, in college halls. I found my old friends the same; the same jokes pleased, the same straws tickled; the manhood & offices they brought hither today seemed masks; underneath, we were still boys.

20 Sept. Yesterday despatched a letter to Thomas Carlyle—P.M. Attended a meeting of friends at Mr G Ripley's house—present, F. H. Hedge, C. Francis, A. B. Alcott, J. F. Clarke, O. A. Brownson, G. Ripley. The conversation was earnest & hopeful. It inspired hope. G. R. said that a man should strive to be an idea & merge all his personalities, in debate. We

agreed to bury fear even the fear of man & if Dr C. & Mr J. P. or Dr J. W. should join us, no man should look at the spout but only at the flowing water. Incidentally we had some character drawing. I said of Mr F. He has a French mind & should have been born at Paris in the era of brilliant conversation with the Diderots, Grimms, Rousseaus, DeStaels. Pit him against a brilliant mate & he will sparkle & star away by the hour together. But he is hopeless. He has no hope for society. The rule suggested for the club was this, that no man should be admitted whose presence excluded any one topic. I said in the beginning of the afternoon present only G R & J.F.C. that 'twas pity that in this Titanic Continent where Nature is so grand, Genius should be so tame. Not one unchallengeable reputation. I felt towards Allston as Landor said of his picture: "I would give 50 guineas to the artist would swear it was a Dominichino." So A. was a beautiful draughtsman but the soul of his picture is *imputed* by the spectator. His merit is like that of Kean's recitation merely outlinear, strictly emptied of all obtrusive individuality, but a vase to receive & not a fountain to impart *character*. So of Bryant's poems, chaste, faultless, beautiful, but uncharacterised. So of Greenough's Sculpture, picturesque but not creative & in the severe style of old art. So of Dr Channing's preaching. They are all *feminine* or receptive & not masculine or creative.

A rail road, State street, Bunker Hill monument are genuine productions of the age but no art.

The reason is manifest. They are not wanted. The statue of Jove was to be worshipped. The Virgin of Titian was to be worshipped. Jesus, Luther were reformers; Moses, David did something, the builders of cathedrals feared. Love & fear laid the stones in their own order.

What interest has Greenough to make a good statue? Who cares whether it is good? A few prosperous gentlemen & ladies, but the Universal Yankee nation roaring in the Capitol to approve or condemn would make his eye & hand & heart go to a new tune.

———

Sir Walter Raleigh's conclusion of his Hist. of the World is sublime only because it closes a history of the world. In a sermon it would not be of much mark; the topstone of the pyramid is sublime by position, so the sentence admired by Warburton in Milton's History.

I think two causes operate against our intellectual performances.
1. Our devotion to property. The love of Liberty in the Revolution made some great men. But now the sentiment of Patriotism can hardly exist in a country so vast. It can be fired in Carolina by contracting the country to Carolina. It might be here by separating Massachusetts from the Union.
However I confess I see nothing in the outward condition of a native of this country which any but a sickly effeminate person can arraign.
2. But the Influence of Europe certainly seems to me prejudicial. Genius is the enemy of genius.

Sunday Dec. 10.   Rhetoric
I cannot hear a sermon without being struck by the fact that amid drowsy series of sentences what a sensation a historical fact, a biographical name, a sharply objective illustration makes! Why will not the preacher heed the admonition of the silence momentary of his congregation & (often what is shown him) that this particular sentence is all they carry away? Is he not taught hereby that the synthesis is to all grateful & to most indispensable of abstract thought & concrete body? Principles should be verified by the adducing of facts & sentiments incorporated by their appropriate imagery. Only in a purely scientific composition which by its text & structure addresses itself to philosophers is a writer at liberty to use mere abstractions.
A preacher should be a live coal to kindle all the church.

Dec. 10. I wrote elsewhere of Composition. Yet today the old view came back again with new force on seeing & hearing about King's College, Cambridge—that it is what is already done that enables the artist to accomplish the wonderful. That hall is covered with a profusion of richest fan work in solid stone to which a charming tint is given by the stained glass windows. The artist who has this talent for delicate embellishment & splendid softening tints, has not usually the talent for massive masonry & Cyclopean architecture. One man built a church on solid blocks able to uphold a Mountain; another took advantage of this Alpine Mass to spring an airy arch thereon; a third adopted this foundation & superstructure, the fruit of talents not his own, & converted the rigid surface into garlands & lace; and thus is the Chapel a work of the human mind, & altogether transcending the abilities of any one man.

This is my belief of written Composition that it can surpass any unwritten effusions of however profound genius, for what is writ is a foundation of a new superstructure & a guide to the eye for new foundation, so that the work rises tower upon tower with ever new & total strength of the builder.

—

Mr Webster never loses sight of his relation to Nature. The Day is always part of him. "But, Mr President, the shades of evening which close around us, admonish me to conclude," he said at Cambridge.

I notice George Herbert's identification of himself with Jewish genius. "List, you may hear great Aaron's bell"— "Aaron's drest!" & the like. It reminds me of that criticism I heard in Italy of Michel Angelo, viz. that he painted prophets & patriarchs like a Hebrew; that they were not merely old men in robes & beards, but a sanctity & the character of the penta-teuch & the prophecy was conspicuous in them.

—

What is good that is said or written now lies nearer to men's business & bosoms than of old. What is good goes now to all. What was good a century ago is written under the manifest be-lief that it was as safe from the eye of the common people as from the Tartars. The Universal Man is now as real an existence as the Devil was then. Prester John no more shall be heard of. Tamerlane & the Buccaneers vanish before Texas, Oregon ter-ritory, the Reform Bill, the abolition of Slavery & of Capital Punishment, questions of Education & the Reading of Re-views; & in these all men take part. The human race have got possession, and it is all questions that pertain to their interest outward or inward, that are now discussed. And many words leap out alive from barrooms, Lyceums, Committee Rooms, that escape out of doors & fill the world with their thunder.

When I spoke or speak of the democratic element I do not mean that ill thing vain & loud which writes lying newspapers, spouts at caucuses, & sells its lies for gold, but that spirit of love for the General good whose name this assumes. There is nothing of the true democratic element in what is called Democracy; it must fall, being wholly commercial. I beg I may not be understood to praise anything which the soul in you does not honor, however grateful may be names to your ear & your pocket.

———

There is no concealment. There is no truth in the proverb that if you get up your name you may safely play the rogue. Thence the balancing proverb that in every wit is a grain of fool. You are known. The sly sin bedaubs you & weakens all your good impression. Men know not why they do not trust you but they do not trust you. The sin glasses your eye, furrows with vulgarity a celestial cheek, bestifies the back of the head, pinches the nose, & writes o fool! fool! fool! on the forehead of a king. On the other hand, can you not withhold the avowal of a just & brave act for fear it will go unwitnessed & unloved? One knows it. Who? Yourself & are pledged by it to sweetness of peace & to nobleness of aim & will not that be a better proclamation of it than the relating of the incident? Look into the stage coach & see the faces! stand in State street & see the heads & the gait & gesture of the men! They are doomed ghosts going under Judgment all day long. Brutus dying was the prince of fops.

This is the effervescence & result of all religions. This is what remains at the core of each when all forms are taken away. This is the Law of Laws, Vedas, Zoroaster, Koran, Golden Verses of Pythagoras, Bible, Confucius. This is that which is carved in mythology & the Undersong of Epics, & the genius of history & birth & marriage & war & trade do only typify this, and the world as it whirls round its solar centre sings this perpetual hymn & nature writes it in flaming characters of meteor & orb & system all throughout the Temple of Silent Space.

———

He who seeks self-union is accused of injustice & inhospitality. People stretch out to him their mendicant arms to whom he feels that he does not belong & who do not belong to him.

He freezes them with his face of apathy, & they very naturally tax him with selfishness. He knows it is unjust. Send me, he says cold, despised, & naked, the man who loves what I love, the man whose soul is regulated & great, & he shall share my loaf & my cloak. But people of this class do not approach him, but the most unfit associates hasten to him with joy & confidence that they are the very ones whom his faith & philosophy invites, they mar all his days with their follies & then with their tacit reproaches, so that his fair ideal of domestic life & serene household gods he cannot realize but is afflicted instead with censures from the inmate, censures from the observer, & necessarily if he be of a sympathetic character censures from himself also.

I suppose he must betimes take notice of this fact that the like-minded shall not be sent him; that Apollo sojourns always with the herd men of Admetus; that he must not be too much a utilitarian with too exact calculation of profit & loss but must cast his odors round broadcast to the Gods heedless if they fall upon the altar or upon the ground for all the world is God's altar. Let his music be heard, let his flowers open, let his light shine believing that invisible spectators & friends environ him & honorable afar is a kindness done to the obscure. Moreover when once he attains a spiritual elevation sufficient to understand his daily life & the ministry to him of this motley crew, this galling prose will be poetry.

For hospitality, however, the duties will clear themselves: give cake & lemons to those who come for such & give them nothing else, & account yourself cheaply let off. And if those seek you, whom you do not seek, hold them stiffly to their rightful claims. Give them your conversation; be to them a teacher, utter oracles, but admit them never into any infringement on your hours; keep state: be their priest not their companion, for you cannot further their plans, you cannot counsel them on their affairs, & you have never pledged yourself to do so by confounding your relation to them.

Every law will some time or other become a fact.

It is all idle talking to discourse of history unless I can persuade you to think reverently of the attributes of your own mind. If you persist in calling a quadrant a crooked stick, & will not sufficiently credit its relation to the sun & the celestial sphere to put it to your eye & to find the sun you can never learn your latitude. But true it is, that the intelligent mind is forever coming into relation with all the objects of nature & time until from a vital point it becomes a great heart from which the blood rolls to the distant channels of things & to which, from those distant channels, it returns.

The fine prints & pictures which the dentist hangs in his anteroom have a satirical air to the waiting patient.

—

Very strange & worthy of study is the pleasure we derive from a description of something we recognize in our past life as when I read Goethe's Account of the feelings of a bridegroom. The subjective is made objective. That which we had *only* lived & not thought & not valued, is now seen to have the greatest beauty as picture; and as we value a Dutch painting of a kitchen or a frolic of blackguards or a beggar catching a flea when the scene itself we should avoid, so we see worth in things we had slighted these many years. A making it a subject of *thought*, the glance of the Intellect raises it. We look at it now as a God upraised above care or fear. It admonishes us instantly of the worth of the present moment. It apprizes us of our wealth, for if that hour & object can be so valuable, why not every hour & event in our life if passed through the same process? I learn (such is the inherent dignity of all intellectual activity) that I am a being of more worth than I knew & all my acts are enhanced in value.

The deepest pleasure comes I think from the occult belief that an unknown meaning & consequence lurk in the common every day facts & as this panoramic or pictorial beauty can arise from it, so can a solid wisdom when the Idea shall be seen as such which binds these gay shadows together. It is the pleasure arising from Classification that makes Calvinism, Popery, Phrenology run & prosper. Calvinism organizes the best known facts of the world's history into a convenient mythus &, what is best, applied to the individual. We are always at the mercy of a better Classifier than ourselves.

—

How curious we are respecting the attainments of another mind in the knowledge of Deity is shown by our desire to know of Calvinism & Swedenborgianism. The man of another church is no nearer to God than you are, yet you feel so far from God as to be curious concerning what each bigot can say. In other words Sectarianism is the ignorance of God. When I am sane & devout, I see well what sort of revelation a good man hath. I see my curiosity concerning revivals & devotees to be vain. I oversee them.

Sept. 28. The world is full of Judgment Days. The event is always modified by the nature of the being on whom it falls. An assembly of men or a wise man do always try us. As a snowflake falling on the ground is white; falling on a man's hand becomes water; falling on the fire becomes steam.

Very disagreeable rencontres are there all the way. To meet those who expect light from you & to be provoked to thwart & discountenance & unsettle them by all you say is pathetical. Again to make an effort to raise the conversation of your company by communicating your recondite thought & to behold it received with patronizing interest by one of the company & with liberal & foolish illustration returned to you, may make you hang your head. My visit to Groton was variously instructive.

Nature occupies herself in beautiful contraventions of her own laws. Thus she takes pleasure in annihilating Space, for taking an animal she adds a few feathers to each side of his body & thereby makes all the fields of a thousand miles of the earth's surface equally present to him on the same day as the square feet of the barnyard are to the domestic fowl. See the passenger pigeon.

A vicious ornament is like those excrescences on plants which the ignorant may mistake for a flower, but which the botanist knows to be a diseased growth around the eggs of a worm.

The house praises the carpenter.

When we study Architecture every thing seems architectural
—the forms of animals, the building of the world, clouds, crystals, flowers, trees, skeletons. When we treat of poetry all these
things begin to sing. When of Music, Litchfield Cathedral is a
tune.
World is picturesque to Allston, dramatic to Garrick, symbolical to Swedenborg, Utilitarian to Franklin, a seat of war to
Napoleon &c, &c.

I observe that after looking at the print of a cathedral the
houseprints & trade illustrations are offensive, but a Greek
statue not; animals & plants not; & especially grateful & homogeneous was the print of organic remains of the Elder
world *restored*. Certainly in the forest, Architecture finds its
analogons in ferns, in spikes of flowers, in locust, in poplar, in
oak, in pine, in fir & spruce, and the Cathedral is a flowering of
Stone subdued by the insatiable demand of harmony in man.
The mountain of granite blooms into an eternal flower with
the lightness as well as aerial proportions & perspective of vegetable beauty.

The study of one man, of one object radically, is like the
study of one book in a foreign language: when he has
mastered that one book the learner finds with a joyful surprise
that he can read with equal facility in ten thousand books. A
half inch of vegetable tissue will tell all that can be known on
the subject from all the forests & one skeleton or a fragment of
animal fibre is an account of zoology.

If I read a poem or see a Temple I desire to make such; as
they say in Arabia 'a figtree looking on a figtree becometh
fruitful'.

———

Ellen

29 Sept.
                              Ellen

         Ellen

September 30. I dislike the gruff jacobin manners of our village politicians but I reconcile myself to them by the reflection

that Genius hurts us by its excessive influence, hurts the freedom & inborn faculty of the individual: &, if Webster, Everett, Channing, yea Plato & Shakspear, found such cordial adorers in the populace as in the scholars, no more Platos & Shakspears could arise. But by this screen of porcupine quills, of bad manners & hatred, is the sacred germ of individual genius concealed & guarded in Secular darkness. After centuries, will it be born a god. Out of Druids & Berserkirs were Alfred & Shakspear made.

Observe how strongly guarded is the Common Sense. If men were left to Contemplation, if the contemplative life were practicable, to what subtilties to what dreams & extravagancies would not all run! Laputa, a court of love, a college of Schoolmen, would be the result. How is this hindered? Poverty, Frost, Famine, Rain, Disease are the beadles & guardsmen that hold us to Common Sense.

———

Every thing is necessary in its foundation. The oath that is heard in the street & the jargon profanity of boys points not less distinctly than a church at the conviction in man of absolute nature as distinct from apparent & derivative nature.

October 6, 1836. I neglected on my return from Boston to record the pleasant impression made by the Monday afternoon Meeting at Mr Alcott's house. Present—Alcott, Bartoll, Brownson, Clarke, Francis, Hedge, Ripley, Emerson. Alcott maintained that every man is a genius, that he looks peculiar, individual, only from the point of view of others, that Genius has two faces, one towards the Infinite God, one towards men.—But I cannot report him. Bartoll too spake very well. And Clarke gave examples from the West of the Genesis of Art; as oratory & painting.

Transcendentalism means, says our accomplished Mrs B, with a wave of her hand, *A little beyond*.

Shall I call my subject The Philosophy of modern History, & consider the action of the same general causes upon Religion, Art, Science, Literature; consider the common principles

on which they are based; the present condition of these severally; and the intellectual duties of the present generation & the
tendencies of the times inferred from the popular science?

11 October. In the pulpit at Waltham, I felt that the composition of his audience was not of importance to him who possessed true eloquence. Smooth or rugged, good natured or ill
natured, religious or scoffers, he takes them all as they come,
he proceeds in the faith that all differences are superficial,
that they all have one fundamental nature which he knows
how to address. This is to be eloquent. And having this skill
to speak to their pervading soul he can make them smooth
or rugged, good-natured or ill natured, saints or scoffers at
his will. Eloquence always tyrannical never complaisant or
convertible.
In earlier days I wrote, "the high prize of eloquence may be
mine, the joy of uttering what no other can utter & what all
must receive."

———

October 18. When I see a man of genius he always inspires me
with a feeling of boundless confidence in my own powers.
   Yesternight I talked with Mr Alcott of education. He proposes still the old recipe the illustration of humanity in the life
of Jesus. I say, No, let us postpone everything historical to the
dignity & grandeur of the present hour. Take no thought for
"the great mass" and "the evil of being misunderstood" &c,
&c, & "what & how ye shall say", *In that hour it shall be given
you what ye shall say.*
   Say the thing that is fit for this new-born and infinite hour.
Come forsake, this once, this balmy time, the historical, & let
us go to the Most High & go forth with him now that he is to
say, Let there be Light. Propose no methods, prepare no
words, select no traditions, but fix your eye on the audience, &
the fit word will utter itself as when the eye seeks the person
in the remote corner of the house the voice accomodates itself
to the area to be filled.

   I rejoice in human riches when I see how manifold are the
gifts of men. He is the rich man who can see and avail himself
of all their faculties. What should I know of the world but that

one man is forever rubbing glass, grinding lenses, cutting with diamonds &c; another would always be mixing colors; another is a hunter, & puts his dog's nose into every thicket & knows what the partridge & the musquash are doing; another mines for coal; another makes almanacks; another traverses Iceland; another prints the book; & so I in my country farmhouse for 1500 dollars can have the good of all.

Oct. 19. As long as the soul seeks an external God, it never can have peace, it always must be uncertain what may be done & what may become of it. But when it sees the Great God far within its own nature, then it sees that always itself is a party to all that can be, that always it will be informed of that which will happen and therefore it is pervaded with a great Peace.

The individual is always dying. The Universal is life. As much truth & goodness as enters into me so much I live. As much error & sin so much death is in me.

Yet Reason never informs us how the world was made. I suppose my friends have some relation to my mind. Perhaps they are its thoughts, taking form & outness though in a region above my will & that in that fact, my plastic nature, I have a pledge of their restoration: that is again, hereafter, I shall be able to give my thoughts Outness & enjoy myself in persons again.

'Tis very strange how much we owe the perception of the absolute solitude of the Spirit to the affections. I sit alone & cannot arouse myself to thought, I go & sit with my friend & in the endeavor to explain my thought to him or her, I lay bare the awful mystery to myself as never before & start at the total loneliness & infinity of one man.

———

As History's best use is to enhance our estimate of the present hour, so the value of such an observer as Goethe who draws out of our consciousness some familiar fact & makes it glorious by showing it in the light of thought is this, that he makes us prize all our being by suggesting its inexhaustible wealth; for we feel that all our experience is thus convertible into jewels. He moves our wonder at the mystery of our life.

—

I have spoken of the power of nature as predominant over the human in all human works. It is remarkable that it also paints the best part of the picture, carves the best part of the statue, speaks the best part of the oration, &, in short, that the Universal lends to the individual ever his best ornament. The cheek of the maiden would be pale but for the sun & wind or for the glitter of the lighted & decorated hall filled with other beauty reflecting rays on her.

In like manner Madame de Stael said 'tis "tradition more than invention helps the poet to a good fable". How many things must combine to a good word or event! Webster is in a galvanized state.

The preponderance of Nature over Will in every life is great. There is less intention in history than we ascribe to it. We impute deeplaid farsighted plans to Napoleon & Caesar. The cement or the spine which gave unity to their manifold actions was not their logic but the concatenation of events. "My son cannot replace me. I could not replace myself. I am the child of circumstances," said Napoleon. My will never gave the images in my mind the rank they now take there. The four College years & the three years of Divinity have not yielded me so many grand facts as some idle books under the bench at Latin School. We form no guess at the time of receiving a thought of its comparative value.

It is remarkable also that we find it so hard to impute our own best sense to a dead author. The very highest praise we think of any writer, painter, sculptor, or builder is that he actually possessed the thought or feeling with which he has inspired us. We hesitate at doing Spenser so great an honor as to think that he intended by his allegory the sense which we affix to it. We have this infirmity of respect also to contemporary genius. We fear that Mr Allston did not foresee & design the effect he produces on us. Familiar as freedom of thought may be to us, the highest merit we ascribe to Homer, is, that he forsook books & traditions & wrote not what men but what Homer thought.

—

Solon said, "He that has better iron shall have all this gold." In modern times the nations that are the best manufacturers of iron are the most civilized & run away with all the gold. "And all that cowards have is mine." —

It seemed to me last night at the Teachers' Meeting, as so often before, that the mind is now mature enough to offer a consistent simple system of religious faith. What is true, is self-affirmed. There are two facts, the Individual and the Universal. To this belong the finite, the temporal, ignorance, sin, death; to that belong the infinite, the immutable, truth, goodness, life. In Man they both consist. The All is in Man. In Man the perpetual progress is from the Individual to the Universal, from that which is human, to that which is divine. "Self dies, & dies perpetually." The circumstances, the persons, the body, the world, the memory are forever perishing as the bark peels off the expanding tree. The facts so familiar to me in infancy, my cradle and porringer, my nurse and nursery, have died out of my world forever. The images of the following period are fading, & will presently be obliterated. Can I doubt that the facts & events & persons & personal relations that now apper-tain to me will perish as utterly when the soul shall have ex-hausted their meaning & use? The world is the gymnasium on which the youth of the Universe are trained to strength & skill. When they have become masters of strength & skill, who cares what becomes of the masts & bars & ropes on which they strained their muscle? —

29 October. This very plagiarism to which scholars incline, (& it is often hard to acknowledge a debt) arises out of the Community of Mind. There is one mind. The man of genius apprises us not so much of his wealth as of the commonwealth. Are his illustrations happy so feel we, do our race illustrate their thoughts. 'That's the way they show things in my coun-try.' Are his thoughts profound, so much the less are they his, so much more the property of all.

I have always distinguished Sampson Reed's Oration on Genius, and Collins' ode on the Passions, & all of Shakspear as being works of genius, inasmuch as I read them with extreme pleasure & see no clue to guide me to their origin, whilst Moore's poetry or Scott's was much more comprehensible & subject to me. But as I become acquainted with S. R.'s books

& teachers the miracle is somewhat lessened, in the same manner as I once found that Burke's was.

As we advance, shall every man of genius turn to us the axis of his mind; then shall he be transparent, retaining however always the prerogative of an original mind; that is, the love of truth in God & not the love of truth for the market. We shall exhaust Shakspear.

There is one advantage which every man finds in setting himself a literary task as these my lectures, that it gives him the high pleasure of reading which does not in other circumstances attain all its zest. When the mind is braced by the weighty expectations of a prepared work, the page of whatever book we read, becomes luminous with manifold allusion. Every sentence is doubly significant & the sense of our author is as broad as the world. There is creative reading as well as creative writing.

—

31 October, 1836, Concord.—

Last night at 11 o'clock, a son was born to me. Blessed child! a lovely wonder to me, and which makes the Universe look friendly to me. How remote from my knowledge, how alien, yet how kind does it make the Cause of Causes appear! The stimulated curiosity of the father sees the graces & instincts which exist, indeed, in every babe, but unnoticed in others; the right to see all, know all, to examine nearly, distinguishes this relation, & endears this sweet child. Otherwise I see nothing in it of mine; I am no conscious party to any feature, any function, any perfection I behold in it. I seem to be merely a brute occasion of its being & nowise attaining to the dignity even of a second cause no more than I taught it to suck the breast.

Please God, that "he, like a tree of generous kind,

By living waters set," may draw endless
nourishment from the fountains of Wisdom & Virtue!
Now am I Pygmalion.

Every day a child presents a new aspect, Lidian says, as the face of the sky is different every hour, so that we never get tired.

The truth seems to be that every child is infinitely beautiful, but the father alone by position & by duty is led to look near enough to see. He looks with microscope. But what is most beautiful is to see the babe & the mother together, the contrast of size makes the little nestler appear so *cunning*, & its tiny beseeching weakness is compensated so perfectly by the happy patronizing look of the mother, who is a sort of high reposing Providence toward it—that they make a perfect group.

—

It seemed yesterday morn as the snow fell, that the adult looks more sourly than the child at the phenomena of approaching Winter. The child delights in the first snow & sees with it the spruce & hemlock boughs they bring for Christmas with glee. The man sees it all sourly expecting the cold days & inconvenient roads & labors of Winter. But the experience of a thousand years has shown him that his faculties are quite equal to master these inconveniences & despite of them to get his bread & wisdom. Therefore the child is the wiser of the two.

> "Disasters do the best we can
> Will come to great & small,
> And he is oft the wisest man
> Who is not wise at all."

I remember with joy such aspects of nature as Bartram saw far from cabinets & cities, on the lonely canebrakes of Florida & the Mississippi; and such as we see in desert winter morns not on our pleasant walk peeping out of our warm houses half a mile or so, but in the deep echoing forest where the pines grow undisturbed from year to year & the eagle & the crow see no intruder; where the broad cold lowland forms its coat of vapor with the stillness of subterranean crystallization & the traveller amid the repulsive savages that are native in the swamp, thinks never of views but only of frozen fingers & distant towns. The moss hanging from cypresses so thick that a man would be concealed under the shade.

—

I ought not to forget in characterising Charles the things he remarked & loved in nature. G.B.E. truly said We shall think of him when the June birds return. The birds he loved & discriminated & showed them us. So the pleasing effect of the grey oakleaf on the snow pleased him well; next it was he said in liveliness to green & white of pine tree & snow. Like my brother Edward, Charles had a certain severity of Character which did not permit him to be silly—no not for moments, but always self possessed & elegant whether morose or playful; no funning for him or for Edward. It was also remarkable in C. that he contemplated with satisfaction the departure of a day. Another day is gone, I am thankful he said. And to E.H. "Put me by the world wheels, & if I wouldn't give them a twirl!"

—

5 Nov. I find my measures of the value of time differ strangely. At the close of the day, at the close of the week I am quite incompetent to say if it have been well or ill spent. When I have least to show for my time, no reading in English or German, no writing in Journal, & no work in the world, I have yet philosophised best, and arrived at some solid conclusions that become conspicuous thoughts in the following months & years.
This day I have been scrambling in the woods & with help of Peter Howe I have got six hemlock trees to plant in my yard which may grow whilst my boy is sleeping.

7 November. Sleep for five minutes seems an indispensable cordial to the human system. No rest is like the rest of sleep. All other balm differs from the balm of sleep as mechanical mixture differs from chemical. For this is the abdication of Will & the accepting a supernatural aid. It is the introduction of the supernatural into the familiar day.
If I have weak or sore eyes, no looking at green curtains, no shutting them, no cold water, no electuaries are of certain virtue; whatever My will doth, seems tentative, but when at last I wake up from a sound sleep then I know that he that made the eye has dealt with it for the time & the wisest physician is He.

8 November. I dislike to hear the patronizing tone in which the self sufficient young men of the day talk of ministers "adapting their preaching to the great mass." Was the sermon

good? "O yes, good for you & me, but not understood by the great mass." Don't you deceive yourself, say I, the great mass understand what's what, as well as the little mass. The selfconceit of this tone is not more provoking than the profound ignorance it argues is pitiable.

The fit attitude of a man is humble Wonder & gratitude, a meek watching of the marvels of the Creation to the end that he may know & do what is fit. But these pert gentlemen assume that the whole object is to manage "the great mass" & they forsooth are behind the curtain with the Deity and mean to help manage. They know all & will now smirk & manoeuvre & condescendingly yield the droppings of their wisdom to the poor people.

———

8 Nov. The man capable of bursts of prodigious eloquence gives no more intimation of his power talking with you in the street than the cannon on which you sit, or which you measure, does of the flash & report of its discharge. And very pleasant stimulus it is to the faculties to meet some great captain as Napoleon or Murat or Claverhouse in the lassitude & elegance of a parlor & from the sleeping lion judge of the aroused lion; as Caesar said that his soldiers were so well trained that though powdered & perfumed they ran like giants to battle.

The Antique.

A man is the prisoner of ideas & must be unconscious. Every man is unconscious, let him be as wise as he may, & must always be so until he can lift himself up by his own ears.
I have read in English (for want of thee, dear Charles!) this P.M. the Ajax & the Philoctetes of Sophocles, of which plays the costly charm is that the persons speak simply. A great boy, a great girl with good sense is a Greek.
Webster was a Greek when he looked so goodhumoredly at Major Ben Russell at a Caucus once. Beautiful is the love of nature in Philoctetes. But in reading those fine apostrophes to sleep, to the stars, rocks, mountains, & the sea, I feel Time passing away as an ebbing sea, I feel the eternity of man, the identity of the soul in every age. The Greek had, it seems, the same fellow beings as I; the sun & moon, water & fire met his

eye & heart as they do mine, precisely. Then the vaunted distinctions between Greek & English, between Classic & Romantic schools, seem superfluous & pedantic. When a thought of Plato becomes a thought to me, when a truth that fired the soul of Jesus Christ fires mine, Time is no more. When I feel that we two meet in a great truth, that our two souls are tinged with the same hue & do as it were run into one.

Under the great & permanent influences of nature all others seem insignificant. I think we make rather too much of the Greek genius. As in old botanical gardens they turn up in the soil every now & then seeds that have lain dormant for ages and as in families they say a feature will sometimes sleep for a hundred years & then reappear in a descendant of the line, so I believe that this Greek genius is ever reappearing in society, & that each of us knows one or more of the class. Aunt Mary is a Greek & I have more in memory. Every child is a Greek.

Yet as I looked at some wild tall trees this afternoon I felt that Nature was still inaccessible, that for all the fine poems that have been written the word is not yet spoken that can cover the charm of morning or evening or woods or lakes, & tomorrow something may be uttered better than any strain of Pindar or Shakspear.

A wife, a babe, a brother, poverty, & a country, which the Greek had, I have.

See the naiveté of Xenophon's account of horse troops.

Anabasis   vol p. 95

—

10 Nov. For form's sake or for wantonness I sometimes chaffer with the farmer on the price of a cord of wood but if he said twenty dollars instead of five I should think it cheap when I remember the beautiful botanical wonder—the bough of an oak—which he brings me so freely out of the enchanted forest where the sun & water, air & earth & God formed it. In like manner I go joyfully through the mire in a wet day and admire the inconvenience, delighted with the chemistry of a shower. Live in the fields & God will give you lectures on natural philosophy every day. You shall have the snow bunting, the chickadee, the jay, the partridge, the chrysalis & wasp for your neighbors.

Language clothes nature as the air clothes the earth, taking the exact form & pressure of every object. Only words that are new fit exactly the thing, those that are old like old scoriae that have been long exposed to the air & sunshine, have lost the sharpness of their mould & fit loosely. But in new objects & new names one is delighted with the plastic nature of man as much as in picture or sculpture. Thus Humboldt's "volcanic paps" & "magnetic storms" are the very mnemonics of Science & so in general in books of modern science the vocabulary yields this poetic pleasure.   "Veins inosculate."

[Compensation]

11 Nov. Every faculty which is a receiver of pleasure has an equal penalty put on its abuse. It is to answer for its moderation with its life.

The Idea is spiritual sight; the idealess research of facts is natural sight. Cannot the natural see better when assisted by the spiritual?

I read the Anabasis in English today with great pleasure. Xenophon draws characters like Clarendon. His speeches are excellent, none better than that upon *horses*, & that where having seen the Sea, he draws up his line against the opposing barbarians & tells them "that these being all the obstacle that is left, they ought to eat these few alive." He is an ancient hero;—he splits wood, he defends himself by his tongue against every man in his army as by his sword against the enemy.

I will tell you where there is music in those that cannot sing: in the mother's earnest talk to her baby, shouts of love.

———

Nov. 12. We scare ourselves by the names we give 'death watch' (ptinus); earwig; deathshead moth; St Anthony's fire; St Vitus's Dance.

How many attractions for us have our passing fellows in the streets both male & female, which our ethics forbid us to express which yet infuse so much pleasure into life. A lovely child, a handsome youth, a beautiful girl, a heroic man, a maternal woman, a venerable old man, charm us though strangers & we cannot say so, or look at them but for a moment.

15 November. On Sunday morn, 13th at 4 o'clock A.M. & again at 5 & at 6 o'clock I saw falling stars in unusual numbers & dropping all perpendicular to the horizon. It was a pleasing testimony to the theory of Arago.

Yesterday the election of state & town officers. One must be of a robust temper & much familiar with general views to avoid disgust from seeing the way in which a young fellow with talents for intrigue can come into a peaceful town like this, besot all the ignorant & simple farmers & laborers, & ride on their necks until as yesterday they reject their long honoured townsman who had become sort of second conscience to them, a Washington in his county & choose in his place an obscure stranger whom they know not & have no right to trust. Yet the philosopher ought to learn hence how greedy man is of fellowship & of guidance. The low can best win the low and all men like to be made much of.

When fear enters the heart of a man at hearing the names of candidates & the reading of laws that are proposed, then is the state safe, but when these things are heard without regard as above or below us, then is the commonwealth sick or dead.

———

There is room in the world for all men & all gifts.

Nov. 19. Went to see Alcott in town & heard him read his excellent Introduction to the new book he is printing of Recorded Conversations. An admirable piece full of profound anticipations. I listen with joy. I feel how much greater it is to hear & receive than to speak or do. Every description of Man seems at the moment to cover the whole ground & leave no room for future poets. But it is, as Goethe said, "Twenty great masters have painted the Madonna & Child, but not one can be spared," & no two interfere.

———

November 21. I read with pleasure this morning Everett's notice of Bentley in N. A. Review for Oct. 1836. The beautiful facts are that Bentley having published conjectural emendations of Homer, in opposition to all known manuscripts, his nephew finds at Rome, sixteen years afterwards, more correct MSS. in which his conjectural readings are exactly confirmed. And Wheeler & Spon two learned travellers having separately copied & published an inscription on an ancient temple of Jupiter at the entrance of the Euxine, Chishull corrected it & published it in his Antiquitates Asiaticae. Bentley undertook to restore the eight lines to their original form. Chishull received some & rejected some of his emendations. In 1731, the original marble was brought to England & found to coincide precisely with Bentley's conjectural emendations.

He had said he thought himself likely to live to fourscore which was long enough to read every thing that was worth reading,

> Et tunc magna mei sub terris ibit imago.

He died 1742 aet. 80.

He compared himself in old age to "an old trunk which, if you let it alone will last a long time, but if you jumble it by moving, will soon fall to pieces."

He had a club which consisted of Sir Christopher Wren, Sir Isaac Newton, Evelyn, John Locke, & himself. Here is his epitaph on Newton.

> Hic quiescunt ossa et pulvis
>   Isaaci Newtoni.
> Si quaeris, quis et qualis fuerit,
>   Abi:
> Sin ex ipso nomine reliqua novisti,
>   Siste paulisper
> Et mortale illud philosophiae numen
>   Gratâ mente venerare.

---

24 November. Talking tonight with E. H. I sought to illustrate the sunny side of every man as compared with his sour & pompous side by the two entrances of all our Concord houses. The front door is very fair to see, painted green, with a knocker, but it is always bolted, & you might as well beat on the wall as tap there; but the farmer slides round the house into a quiet back door that admits him at once to his warm fire & loaded table.

Nothing is useless

November 25. A superstition is a hamper or basket to carry useful lessons in.

I told Miss Peabody last night that Mr Coleridge's churchmanship is thought to affect the value of his criticism &c. I do not feel it. It is a harmless freak & sometimes occurs in a wrong place, as when he refuses to translate some alleged blasphemy in Wallenstein. Some men are affected with hemorrhage of the nose; it is of no danger but unlucky when it befals where it should not as at a wedding or in the rostrum. But Coleridge's is perfectly separable. I know no such critic. Every opinion he expresses is a canon of criticism that should be writ in steel, & his italics are italics of the mind.

25 Nov. Here are two or three facts plain & clear. That histories are not yet history; that the historian should be a philosopher, for surely he can describe the outward event better if assisted by the sight of the cause; historians are men of talents, & of the market, & not devout, benevolent, with eyes that make walls no walls; that history is written to enhance the present hour; that all history is to be written from man, is all to be explained from individual history or must remain words. We as we read must be Romans, Greeks, Barbarians, priest & king, martyr & executioner, or we shall see nothing, keep nothing, learn nothing. There is nothing but is related to us; nothing that does not interest the historian in its relation; tree, horse, iron, that the roots of all things are in man & therefore the philosophy of history is a consideration of science, art, literature, religion, as well as politics.

Sallust, I think, said that men would put down to the account of romance whatever exceeded their own power to perform. A very safe & salutary truth.

Otherism

I see plainly the charm which belongs to Alienation or Otherism. "What wine do you like best, O Diogenes?" "Another's," replied the sage. What fact, thought, word, like we best? Another's. The very sentiment I expressed yesterday without heed, shall sound memorable to me tomorrow if I hear it from another. My own book I read with new eyes when a stranger has praised it. It is, (is it not?) all one & the same radical fact which I noticed above, that the picture pleases when the original does not, that the subjective must be made objective for us & the soul, body.

Or is the charm wholly in the new method by which it was classified; for, a new mind is a new method. How often we repeat in vain the words or substance without conveying to others the genius of a friend's remark.

—

Edward Taylor is a noble work of the divine cunning who suggests the wealth of Nature. If he were not so strong, I should call him lovely. What cheerfulness in his genius & what consciousness of strength. "My voice is thunder," he said in telling me how well he was. And what teeth & eyes & brow & aspect—I study him as a jaguar or an Indian for his untamed physical perfections. He is a work, a man not to be predicted. His vision poetic & pathetic; sight of love, is unequalled. How can he transform all those whiskered shaggy untrim tarpaulins into sons of light & hope? By seeing the man within the sailor, seeing them to be sons, lovers, brothers, husbands.

But hopeless it is to make him that he is not; to try to bring him to account to you or to himself for aught of his inspiration. A creature of instinct, his colors are all opaline & doves'-neck-lustres & can only be seen at a distance. Examine them & they disappear. If you see the ignis fatuus in a swamp, & go to the place, the light vanishes; if you retire to the spot whereon you stood, it reappears. So with Taylor's muse. It is a panorama of images from all nature & art, whereon the sun & stars shine but go up to it & nothing is there. His instinct, unconscious instinct is the nucleus or point of view, & this defies science & eludes it. Do not forget Charles's love of him, who said if he were in town he would go & record all his fine sayings.

—

Come let us not be an appanage to Alexander, Charles V. or any of history's heroes. Dead men all! but for me the earth is new today, & the sun is raining light. The doctrine of the amiable Swedenborgian & of the subtle Goethe is, that "we murder to dissect," that nature has told everything once, if only we seek the fact where it is told in Colossal. Therefore are so manifold objects, to present each fact in capitals somewhere. What else is history? We see not the perspective of our own life. We see the ruts, pebbles, & straws of the road where we walk, but cannot see the chart of the land. "We are not sufficiently elevated with respect to ourselves to comprehend ourselves." Our own life we cannot subject to the eye of the intellect. What remedy? Why, history is the remedy. Its volumes vast have but one page; it writes in many forms but one record, this human nature of mine.

Like the signs of the Zodiac, the crab, the goat, the scorpion, the balance, the waterpot have lost all their meanness when hung in the blue spaces of the empyrean from an unrecorded age, so I can see the familiar & sordid attributes of human nature without emotion as objects of pure science when removed into this distant firmament of time. My appetite, my weaknesses, my vices I can see in Alexander, Alcibiades, & Catiline, without heat & study their laws, without anger or personal pique or contrition. Scythian, Hebrew, & Gaul serve as algebraic exponents in which I can read my own good & evil without pleasure & without pain.

—

29 November. There is no more chance goes to making towns than to making quadrants. Knowledge of business & the world tends to acquaint a man with values. Every minute of the day of a good workman is worth something in dollars & cents. The novice thinks this & that labor is of quite inappreciable value, it is so little like a bushel of corn or so short in time in the doing. So ought men to feel about character & history. The most fugitive deed or word, the mere air of doing a thing, the intimated purpose, expresses character & the remote results of character are civil history & events that shake or settle the world. If you act, you show character: if you sit still, you show it; if you sleep

But in analysing history do not be too profound, for often the causes are quite superficial. In the present state of Spain, in the old state of France, & in general in the reigns of Terror, every where, there is no Idea, no Principle. It is all scrambling for bread & Money. It is the absence of all profound views; of all principle. It is the triumph of the senses, a total skepticism. They are all down on the floor striving each to pick the pocket or cut the throat that he may pick the pocket of the other, & the farthest view the miscreants have is the next tavern or brothel where their plunder may glut them. If presently one among the mob possesses ulterior aims, & these inspire him with skill, he masters all these brutes as oxen & dogs are mastered by a man & turns them to work for him & his thought.

Nov. 30.

> Thus when the gods are pleased to plague mankind
> To our rash hands our ruin is assigned.

Moore's life of Sheridan is a flagrant example of a book, which damns itself. He writes with the manifest design of securing our sympathies for Sheridan, our tears for his misfortunes & poverty, our admiration for his genius, & our indignation against the king & grandees who befriended that butterfly in his prosperity & forsook him in his jail. He details the life of a mean fraudulent vain quarrelsome play-actor, whose wit lay in cheating tradesmen, whose genius was used in studying jokes & bonmots at home for a dinner or a club, who laid traps for the admiration of coxcombs, who never did anything good & never said anything wise. He came as he deserved to a bad end.

The contrast between him & Burke is very instructive & redounds to the praise of one & the infamy of the other.

Moore involves himself in the ruin & confusion of his culprit.

I heard of a dishclout gentleman yesterday of the Sheridan stamp who thus against his will unmasks himself & being a puppy cannot restrain his paw from doing the deeds of a puppy, & who affecting to keep the company of men & above all others wishing to be esteemed a man writes as on his own forehead every day, 'I am a whelp.'

2 December, 1836. The present state of the colony at Liberia is a memorable fact. It is found that the black merchants are so

fond of their lucrative occupations that it is with difficulty that any of them can be prevailed upon to take office in the colony. They dislike the trouble of it. Civilized arts are found to be as attractive to the wild negro, as they are disagreeable to the wild Indian.

December 3. I have been making war against the superlative degree in the rhetoric of my fair visiter. She has no positive degree in her description of characters & scenes. You would think she had dwelt in a museum where all things were extremes & extraordinary. Her good people are very good, her naughty so naughty that they cannot be eaten. But beside the superlative of her mind she has a superlative of grammar which is suicidal & defeats its end. Her minds are "most perfect" "most exquisite" & "most masculine." I tell her the positive degree is the sinew of speech, the superlative is the fat. "Surely all that is simple is sufficient for all that is good" said Mme. de Stael. And when at a trattoria at Florence I asked the waiter if the cream was good, the man replied 'yes, sir, stupendous': *Si, signore, stupendo.*

———

Dec. 10. Pleasant walk yesterday, the most pleasant of days. At Walden Pond, I found a new musical instrument which I call the ice-harp. A thin coat of ice covered a part of the pond but melted around the edge of the shore. I threw a stone upon the ice which rebounded with shrill sound, & falling again & again, repeated the note with pleasing modulation. I thought at first it was the 'peep' 'peep' of a bird I had scared. I was so taken with the music that I threw down my stick & spent twenty minutes in throwing stones single or in handfuls on this crystal drum.

At night, with other friends came Shackford with a good heart & inquisitive mind. He broached the question, out of Brownson's book, of the positiveness or entity of moral evil; which I gladly & strenuously denied,—as a corollary to my last night's discourse on the Unity of Mind. 'There is One mind in many individuals.' I maintained that evil is merely privative not absolute. It is like cold the privation of heat. All evil is death. Benevolence is absolute & real. So much benevolence & justice as a man hath, so much life hath he. For all things proceed out of this same spirit whose attributes are love, justice, & so on & all things conspire with them. Whilst a man seeks these ends he is strong by the whole strength of the Universe. In so far as he roves from these ends, he bereaves himself of power, of auxiliaries; his being shrinks out of all remote channels & he disuniversalises & he individualizes himself & becomes all the time less & less—a mote, a point. Until absolute badness is absolute privation. It is annihilation. Pure badness therefore could not exist. Do you not see that a man is a bundle of relations, that his entire strength consists not in his properties but in his innumerable relations? If you embrace the cause of right, of your country, of mankind, all things work with & for you, the sun & moon, stocks & stones. The virtuous man & the seeker of truth finds brotherhood & countenance in so far forth, in the stars, the trees, & the waters. All Nature cries to him All Hail! The bad man finds opposition, aversation, death in them all.

All mankind oppose him. No whisper from secret beauty or grandeur cheers him. The world is silent; the heaven frowns. What is that star to him which prompted a heroic sentiment of love in the hero? A white point. And being not in the current of things, an outlaw, a stoppage,—the wheels of God must grind him to powder in their very mission of charity.

We talked further of Christianity. I think that the whole modus loquendi about believing Xy is vicious. It has no pertinence to the state of the case. It grows out of the Calvinistic nonsense of a Gospel-Scheme, a dogmatic Architecture which one is to admit came from the God of Nature. Or it grows out of the figment that to believe a given miracle is a spiritual merit. Believe Xy. What else can you do? It is not matter of doubt. What is good about it is self affirming. When Jesus says Kingdom of God comes without observation; comes as a little child; is within you; &c these are not propositions upon which you can exercise any election but are philosophical verities quite independent of any asseveration or testimony or abnegation.

Never a magnanimity fell to the ground. Always the heart of man greets it & accepts it unexpectedly.

A thought in the woods was that I cannot marshal & insert in my compositions my genuine thoughts which are in themselves vital & life communicating. The reason is you do not yet take sufficiently noble & capacious views of man & nature whereinto your honest observation would certainly fall as physical phenomena under chemical or physiological laws.

One mind.

Once more. Add to what was said on last page. There is One Mind, & therefore the best minds who love truth for its own sake, think much less of property in truth. Thankfully they accept it everywhere & do not carefully label & ticket it with any man's name for it is theirs long beforehand. It is theirs from eternity.

Concord.

1 January, 1837. 3d Jan. It occurred last night in groping after the elements of that pleasure we derive from literary compositions, that it is like the pleasure which the prince Le Boo received from seeing himself for the first time in a mirror,—a mysterious & delightful surprise. A poem, a sentence causes us to see ourselves. I be & I see my being, at the same time.

It is not some wild ornithorhynchus nondescript that attracts the most attention but it was the *Man* of the New World that concentrated the curiosity of the contemporaries of Columbus. After I got into bed, somewhat else rolled through my head & returned betwixt dreams, which I fear I have lost. It seems as if it were to this purport; that every particular composition takes its fit place in the intellectual sphere, the light & gay a light & fugitive place; the wise a permanent place; but only those works are everlasting which have caught not the ephemeral & local but the universal symbols of thought & so written themselves in a language that needs no translation into the sympathies & intellectual habits of all men. Homer & Shakspear.

6 January. It occurred to me at midnight with more clearness than I can now see it, that not in nature but in man was all the beauty & worth he sees; that the world is very empty & is indebted to this gilding & exalting soul for all its pride so that Wordsworth might write Earth fills her lap with splendor not her own for his line, "Earth fills her lap with pleasures of her own." The vale of Tempe, Tivoli, & Rome are but earth & water, rocks & sky.

Jan. 7. Received day before yesterday a letter from Thomas Carlyle dated 5 November;—as ever,—a cordial influence.

Strong he is, upright, noble, & sweet, & makes good how much of our human nature. Quite in consonance with my delight in his eloquent letters I read in Bacon this afternoon this sentence, (of letters) "And such as are written from wise men are of all the words of man, in my judgment, the best; for they are more natural than Orations & public speeches, & more advised than conferences or present speeches." Works, Vol. 1. p. 89.

—

Jan. 8. Can you not show the man of Genius that always genius is situated in the world as it is with him?

   Lidian Emerson
   Waldo Emerson
   R. Waldo Emerson

I had come no farther in my query than this when mine Asia came in & wrote her name, her son's & her husband's, to warm my cold page.

—

Jan. 14. Lidian's grandmother had a slave Phillis whom she freed. Phillis went to the little colony on the outside of Plymouth which they called New Guinea. Soon after, she visited her old mistress. "Well, Phillis, what did you have for dinner on Thanksgiving Day?" "Fried 'taturs, Missy;" replied Phillis. "And what had you to fry the potatoes in?" said Mrs Cotton. "Fried in Water, Missy;" answered the girl. "Well Phillis," said Mrs Cotton, "how can you bear to live up there, so poor, when here you used to have every thing comfortable, & such good dinner at Thanksgiving?"—"Ah Missy, Freedom's sweet," returned Phillis.

A poor woman having covered her children in the winter nights with all the rags & bits of cloth and carpet she could find, was accustomed to lay down over all an old door which had come off its hinges. "Ah, dear mother," said her eldest daughter, "how I pity the poor children that haven't got any *door* to cover them."

—

21 January. Every change in the physical constitution has its external sign, although for the most part it is not heeded. Hemorrhage of the lungs or palsy does not suddenly overtake a

man, but after long warnings which he had disregarded. Look at the clock: you have only noticed the striking of the hours, but it struck the seconds, & showed the seconds & minutes on the dial, which were making up the hour; but you had no ears & no eyes.

I either read or inferred today in the Westminster Review that Shakspear was not a popular man in his day. How true & wise. He sat alone & walked alone a visionary poet & came with his piece, modest but discerning, to the players, & was too glad to get it received, whilst he was too superior not to see its transcendant claims.

January 22. Being a lover of solitude I went to live in the country seventeen miles from Boston, & there the northwest wind with all his snows took me in charge & defended me from all company in winter, & the hills & sand-banks that intervened between me & the city, kept guard in summer.

25 Jan. This evening the heavens afford us the most remarkable spectacle of Aurora Borealis. A deep red plume in the East & west streaming almost from the horizon to the zenith, forming at the zenith a sublime coronet; the stars peep delicately through the ruddy folds & the whole landscape below covered with snow is crimsoned. The light meantime equal nearly to that of full moon, although the moon was not risen.

27 Jan. "The best use of money is to pay debts with it."

The only aristocracy in this country is the editors of newspapers.

As Goethe says that any particular bone that is in one animal may be found in every other, however abridged or obscure, so I am never quite acquainted with my neighbor until I have found somewhat in his nature & life to tally with every thing I know of myself.

The true explanation of "Res nolunt diu male administrari" undoubtedly is that mischief is shortlived, & all things thwart

& end it. Napoleon's empire built up amid universal alarm—in how short space of time vanished out of history like breath into the air: but St Paul, the tent maker,—see what a tent he built.

January 29. One has patience with every kind of living thing but not with the dead alive. I, at least, hate to see persons of that lumpish class who are here they know not why, & ask not whereto, but live as the larva of the ant or the bee to be lugged into the sun & then lugged back into the cell & then fed. The end of nature for such, is that they should be fatted. If mankind should pass a vote on the subject, I think they would throw them in sacks into the sea.

—

Feb. 6. There is one memory of waking, & another of sleep. Certainly in my dreams the same scenes or fancies are associated & a whole crew of boarders at some dream house of which gentlemen & ladies I can trace no shadow of remembrance in any waking experience of mine. In sleep, I also travel certain roads in certain stage coaches, & walk alone in meadows whose archetype I wot not.

In these Lectures which from week to week I read, each on a topic which is a main interest of man, & may be made an object of exclusive interest I seem to vie with the brag of Puck "I can put a girdle round about the world in forty minutes." I take fifty.

—

Old & New put their stamp to every thing in Nature. The snowflake that is now falling is marked by both. The present moment gives the motion & the color of the flake: Antiquity, its form & properties. All things wear a lustre which is the gift of the present & a tarnish of time.

March 4. I have finished on Thursday evening last, my course of twelve Lectures on the Philosophy of History. I read the first on the 8 December, 1836—The audience attending them, might average 350 persons. I acknowledge the Divine Providence which has given me perfect health & smoothed the way unto the end.

*

March 14. Edward Taylor came last night & gave us in the old church a Lecture on Temperance. A wonderful man; I had almost said, a perfect orator. The utter want & loss of all method, the ridicule of all method, the bright chaos come again of his bewildering oratory, certainly bereaves it of power but what splendor! what sweetness! what richness what depth! what cheer! How he conciliates, how he humanizes! how he exhilarates & ennobles! Beautiful philanthropist! godly poet! the Shakspeare of the sailor & the poor. God has found one harp of divine melody to ring & sigh sweet music amidst caves & cellars.

He spent the night with me. He says "he lives a monarch's life, he has none to control him, or to divide the power with him." His word is law for all his people & his coadjutors. He is a very charming object to me. I delight in his great personality, the way & sweep of the man which like a frigate's way takes up for the time the centre of the ocean, paves it with a white street, & all the lesser craft "do curtsey to him, do him reverence." Every body plays a second part in his presence, & takes a deferential & apologetic tone. In the church, likewise, every body,—the rich, the poor, the scoffer, the drunkard, the exquisite, & the populace, acknowledge the Man, & feel that to be right & lordly which he doth,—so that his prayer is a winged ship in which all are floated forward. The wonderful & laughing life of his illustration keeps us broad awake. A string of rockets all night. He described his bar-room gentry as "hanging like a half dead bird over a counter." He describes Helen Loring as out on her errands of charity, & "running through the rain like a beech-bird." He speaks of poor ministers coming out of divinity schools, &c. as "poor fellows hobbling out of Jerusalem." "We'll give you hypocrites for honest men, two for one, & trade all night." "The world is just large enough for the people. There is no room for a partition wall."

March 18. A strong South wind today set all the hills & fields afloat under melting snow banks. Tempted out by the new brown of the hill-sides, I climbed for the first time since autumn the opposite hill to see if the snows were abated & my wood alleys open but there was too much winter left, & I retreated.

March 19. Today at Waltham I talked of the potential invention of all men. Caroline Sturgis can sketch with invention; others can draw as well, but cannot design. I call it self-distrust,—a fear to launch away into the deep which they might freely & safely do. It is as if the dolphins should float on rafts or creep & squirm along the shore in fear to trust themselves to the element which is really native to them.

—

March 19. Yesterday I read many of C.C.E.'s letters to E. H. I find them noble but sad. Their effect is painful. I withdrew myself from the influence. So much contrition, so much questioning, so little hope, so much sorrow, harrowed me. I could not stay to see my noble brother tortured even by himself. No good or useful air goes out of such scriptures, but cramp & incapacity only. I shall never believe that any book is so good to read as that which sets the reader into a working mood, makes him feel his strength, & inspires hilarity. Such are Plutarch, & Montaigne & Wordsworth.
But also Charles would say this, & his conversation was of this character; but when he shut his closet door, "a quality of darkness" haunted him.

—

March 29. Noble paper of Carlyle on Mirabeau. This piece will establish his kingdom, I forebode, in the mind of his countrymen. How he gropes with giant fingers into the dark of man! into the obscure recesses of power in human will, and we are encouraged by his word to feel the might that is in a man. "Come the ruggedest hour that time & fate dare bring to frown upon the enraged Northumberland." Indeed this piece is all thunder, gigantic portrait painting.
The "Diamond Necklace" too, I doubt not, is the sifted story, the veritable fact, as it fell out, yet so strangely told by a series of pictures, cloud upon cloud, that the eye of the exact men is speedily confused & annoyed. It seems to me, his genius is the redolence of London "the Great Metropolis." So vast, enormous, with endless details, & so related to all the world, is he. It would seem as if no baker's shop, no mutton stall, no Academy, no church, no placard, no coronation, but he saw & sympathized with all, & took all up into his omnivorous fancy, &

hence his panoramic style, & this encyclopediacal allusion to all knowables.

Then he is a worshipper of strength, heedless much whether its present phase be divine or diabolic. Burns, Geo. Fox, Luther, and those unclean beasts Diderot, Danton, Mirabeau, whose sinews are their own & who trample on the tutoring & conventions of society he loves. For he believes that every noble nature was made by God, & contains—if savage passions,—also fit checks & grand impulses within it, hath its own resources, &, however erring, will return from far. Then he writes English & crowds meaning into all the nooks & corners of his sentences. Once read he is but half read.

I rode well. My horse took hold of the road as if he loved it. I saw in Boston my fair young L. but so rashly grown that her sweet face was like a violet on the top of a pole.

A disaster at Lowell. The powder mill blew up & two men so shattered that their remains were gathered in a basket.

Carlyle again. I think he has seen as no other in our time how inexhaustible a mine is the language of Conversation. He does not use the *written* dialect of the time in which scholars, pamphleteers, & the clergy write, nor the parliamentary dialect, in which the lawyer, the statesman, & the better newspapers write, but draws strength & motherwit out of a poetic use of the *spoken* vocabulary, so that his paragraphs are all a sort of splendid conversation.

—

April 8. Ah! my darling boy, so lately received out of heaven leave me not now! Please God, this sweet symbol of love & wisdom may be spared to rejoice, teach, & accompany me.

People expect to read a lesson of the Divine Providence in a death or a lunacy as they would read a paragraph in a newspaper, & when they cannot, they say like my Irishman Roger Herring to the Probate Court, "Well, I am not satisfied." But one lesson we are to learn is the course or *genius* of the Divine Providence, which a malady or any fact cannot teach, but a sober view of the events of years, the action & reaction of character & events, may.

*

9 April. How many extraordinary young men we have seen or heard of who never ripened or whose performance in actual life was not extraordinary. When we see their air & expression, when we hear them speak of society, of books, of religion, we admire their superiority,—they seem to throw contempt on the whole state—of the world; it is the tone of a youthful giant who is sent to work revolutions. But the moment they enter an active profession, the forming colossus shrinks to the common size of man. The power & the charm they possessed was the ideal tendencies which always make the actual ridiculous; but the tough world had its revenge when once they put their horses of the sun to plough in its furrow. Then, if they die, we lose our admiration another way, for we say this superiority was not healthy, was not just, or it would have enabled the body to work.

April 10. Very just are the views of Goethe in Eckermann that the poet stands too high than that he should be a partisan. I thought as I rode through the sloughs yesterday that nothing is more untrue as well as unfavorable to power than that the thinker should open his mind to fear of the people among whom he works. Rather let him exult in his force. Whichever way he turns, he sees the pleasure & deference which these faculties of writing & speaking excite. The people call them out; the people delight in them; the better part of every man feels, 'This is my Music'; surely therefore the poet should respond & say, 'the people & not solitude is my home.' Never my lands, my stocks, my salary, but this power to help & to charm the disguised soul that sits veiled under this whiskered & that smooth visage, this is my rent & ration.

10 April.   Love an eye-water.

Love is fabled to be blind, but to me it seems that kindness is necessary to perception, that love is not an ophthalmia but an electuary. Let us never argue disputed points. The poet should never know an antagonist. Few men can be trusted, almost no man has temper enough to argue with an adversary. But meet joyfully on what common ground they can, & extend in love that area, and ere they know it the boundary mountains on which the eye had fastened have melted into air.

—

As smooth as a cat came W.

April 11. I wrote G. P. B. that Eckermann was full of fine things & helps one much in the study of Goethe. Always the man of genius dwells alone, & like the mountain pays the tax of snows & silence for elevation. It would seem as if he hunted out this poor Dutch Boswell for a thing to talk to, that his thoughts might not pass in smother. His thinking, as far as I read him, is of great altitude & *all level*. Dramatic power I think he has very little. The great felicities, the miracles of Poetry, he has never. It is all design with him, just thought, & instructed expression, analogies, allusion, illustration, which knowledge & correct thinking supply; but of Shakspeare & the transcendant muse no syllable. But he is a pledge that the antique force of nature is not spent & 'tis gay to think what men shall be.—

Is not life a puny unprofitable discipline whose direct advantage may be fairly represented by the direct education that is got at Harvard College? As is the real learning gained there, such is the proportion of the lesson in life.

April 12. I find it the worst thing in life that I can put it to no better use. One would say that he can have little to do with his time who sits down to so slow labor & of such doubtful return as studying Greek or German; as he must be an unskilful merchant who should invest his money at three per cent. Yet I know not how better to employ a good many hours in the year. If there were not a general as well as a direct advantage herein we might shoot ourselves.

Where I see anything done, I behold the presence of the Creator. Peter Howe knows what to do in the garden, & Sullivan at a ball, & Webster in the Senate, & I over my page. Exchange any of our works, & we should be to seek. And any work looks wonderful to me except that one which I can do.

How little of the man see we in his person. The man Minot who busies himself all the year round under my windows writes out his nature in a hundred works, in drawing water, hewing wood, building fence, feeding his cows, haymaking & a few times in the year he goes into the woods. Thus his human spirit unites itself with nature. Why need I ever hear him speak articulate words?

I listen by night I gaze by day at the endless procession of wagons loaded with the wealth of all regions of England, of China, of Turkey, of the Indies which from Boston creep by my gate to all the towns of New Hampshire & Vermont. With creaking wheels at midsummer & crunching the snows on huge sledges in January, the train goes forward at all hours, bearing this cargo of inexhaustible comfort & luxury to every cabin in the hills.

In life all finding is not that thing we sought, but something else. The lover on being accepted, misses the wildest charm of the maid he dared not hope to call his own. The husband loses the wife in the cares of the household. Later, he cannot rejoice with her in the babe for by becoming a mother she ceases yet more to be a wife. With the growth of children the relation of the pair becomes yet feebler from the demands children make, until at last nothing remains of the original passion out of which all these parricidal fruits proceeded; and they die because they are superfluous.

16 April. How little think the youth & maiden who are glancing at each other across a mixed company with eyes so full of mutual intelligence—how little think they of the precious fruit long hereafter to proceed from this now quite external stimulus. The work of vegetation begins first in the irritability of the bark & leaf buds. From exchanging glances they proceed to acts of courtesy & gallantry, then to fiery passion, then to plighting troth & to marriage. Immediately they begin to discover incongruities, defects. Thence comes surprise, regret, strife. But that which drew them at first was signs of loveliness, signs of virtue. These virtues appear & reappear & continue to draw, but the regard changes, quits the sign & attaches to the substance. This comes in to mitigate the disaffection. Meantime as life wears on it proves to be nothing but a game of permutation & combination of all possible positions

of the parties to extort all the resources of each & acquaint each with the whole strength & weakness of the other. All the angels that inhabit this temple of a human form show themselves at the doors & all the gnomes also. By all the virtues that appear, by so much kindness, justice, fortitude &c, by so much are they made one. But all the vices are negations on either part & they are by so much two. At last they discover that all that at first drew them together was wholly caducous, had merely a prospective end like the scaffolding by which a house is built, & the unsuspected & wholly unconscious growth of principles from year to year is the real marriage foreseen & prepared from the first but wholly above their consciousness. This is the boardingschool & God.

The Newspapers persecute Alcott. I have never more regretted my inefficiency to practical ends. I was born a seeing eye not a helping hand. I can only comfort my friends by thought, & not by love or aid. But they naturally look for this other also, & thereby vitiate our relation, throughout.

Sommering possessed in his cabinet the hand of a certain Paule de Viguier nearly 300 years old. This beautiful person was such an object of universal wonder to her contemporaries for her enchanting form, virtue, & accomplishments that according to the assurances of one of them the citizens of her native city Tholouse obtained the aid of the civil authorities to compel her to appear publicly on the balcony at least twice a week & as often as she showed herself the crowd was dangerous to life.

Good letter from Tischbein to Merck describing Michel Angelo's last Judgment which he had the opportunity of seeing very near, & was astonished at the minute finish of muscles & nerves. Finished like a miniature. "A group of the damned whom the devils drive into hell made me so much distress that I feared I should fall from the ladder. I was forced to hold on with both hands & to banish the shuddering thoughts."

Wieland says Goethe read to them his account of their (Granduke & G.) passage through Valois over the Furka & St Gothard & it was as good as Xenophon's Anabasis. "It was also a true fieldmarch against all the elements which opposed them. The piece is one of his most masterly productions & thought & written with the great mind peculiar to him. The fair hearers were enthusiastic at the Nature in this piece; I liked the sly Art in the composition whereof they saw nothing still better. It is a true poem so concealed is the art also. But what most remarkably in this, as in all his other Works distinguishes him from Homer & Shakspear, is, that to *ME* the *Ille ego* everywhere glimmers through, although without any boasting, & with an infinite fineness." *Merck* p. 236.

"I have sometimes (says the Grand duke) remarked before great works of art, & just now especially in Dresden, how much a certain property contributes to the lively effect which thrills our hearts, & makes us fall down upon our faces to worship, which gives life to the figures & to the life an irresistible truth. This property is the hitting in all the figures we draw the right centre of gravity. I mean the placing the people firm upon their feet, making the hands grasp, & fastening the eyes on the spot where they should look. Even lifeless figures as in geschlossenen pictures, vessels, stools, let them be drawn & painted ever so fine, lose all effect so soon as they lack the resting upon their centre of gravity, & have a certain swimming & oscillating appearance. The Raphael in the Dresden Gallery, the only greatly affecting picture which I have seen, is the quietest & most passionless picture you can imagine. A couple of saints who worship the Virgin & child. Nevertheless it makes a deeper impression than the contorsions of ten crucified martyrs. But it possesses besides all the resistless & instreaming beauty of form, in the highest degree the property of the perpendicularity of all the figures. The Virgin Mary walks the cloud so lightly & notwithstanding, you have no fear of a mis-step." Letter to Merck p. 362.

New England
21 April. It has been to me a sensible relief to learn that the destiny of New England is to be the manufacturing country of America. I no longer suffer in the cold out of morbid sympathy with the farmer. The love of the farmer shall spoil no more days for me. Climate touches not my own work. The foulest or

the coldest wind is as dear to the muses as the sweet southwest, & so to the manufacturer & the merchant. Where they
have the sun, let them plant; we who have it not, will drive our
pens & waterwheels. I am gay as a canary bird with this new
knowledge. In the Tyrolese mountains they do not plant corn,
but every man & woman carves wooden foxes, wolves, &
smoking Dutchmen or tends goats. I will write & so teach my
countrymen their office as Johan Mez did his by carving.

An opinion is seldom given; & every one we have heard of,
weighs with us. Let an opinion be given upon a book, the *vis
inertiae* of the general mind is proved by the circulation this
sentence has. It runs through a round of newspapers, & of social circles, & finds mere acquiescence in thousands. If the subject is one which has a political or commercial bearing, it
commonly happens that another individual protests against
the opinion, & affirms his own to be just the reverse. In that
case still I should think is there but one opinion affirmed &
denied: there is yet no new *quality* shown.

Wo unto you, critics! for an opinion is indeed not the safest
ware to deal in. It is a cotton-ball thrown at an object, but the
thread at the other end remains in the thrower's bag. Or rather
it is the harpoon thrown at the whale & if the harpoon is not
good, or not well thrown, it will go nigh to cut the steersman
in twain, or drown the boat.

In the Tyrol they carved & whittled until one morning they
went to the mountain & behold there was not one pine tree
left standing.

I learn evermore. In smooth water I discover the motion of
my boat by the motion of trees & houses on shore, so the
progress of my mind is proved by the perpetual change in the
persons & things I daily behold.

Beauty is ever that divine thing the ancients esteemed it. It
is, as they said "the flowering of Virtue." I see one & another,
& another fair girl, about whose form or face glances a nameless charm. I am immediately touched with an emotion of tenderness or complacency. They pass on, and I stop to consider

at what this dainty emotion, this wandering gleam points. It is no poor animal instinct, for this charm is destroyed for the imagination by any reference to animalism. It points neither to any relations of friendship or love that society knows & has, but as it seems to me to a quite other & now unattainable sphere, relations of transcendant delicacy & sweetness, a true faerieland to what roses & violets hint & foreshow. We cannot *get at* beauty. Its nature is evanescent.

———

Cold April; hard times; men breaking who ought not to break; banks bullied into the bolstering of desperate speculators; all the newspapers a chorus of owls. 'Tobacco, cotton, teas, indigo, & timber all at tremendous discount & the end not yet.' Eight firms in London gave the bank a round robin bond for £3 800 000 of discounts.—Such things I read in the papers specially "London Age" of March 12. Loud cracks in the social edifice.—Sixty thousand laborers, says rumor, to be presently thrown out of work, and these make a formidable mob to break open banks & rob the rich & brave the domestic government. May 5   In New York the president (Fleming) of the Mechanics Bank resigns, & the next morning is found dead in his bed "by mental excitement," according to the verdict of the Coroner. Added bitterness from the burning of the Exchange in New Orleans by an incendiary; the Park mobs, & the running on banks for specie in N.Y.

There is a crack in every thing God has made. Fine weather!—yes but cold. Warm day!—'yes but dry.'—'You look well'—'I am very well except a little cold.' The case of damaged hats—one a broken brim; the other perfect in the rim, but rubbed on the side; the third whole in the cylinder, but bruised on the crown.

I say to L. that in composition the *What* is of no importance compared with the *How*. The most tedious of all discourses are on the subject of the Supreme Being.

———

April 26. More conversation about the German Man. I perceived that he differed from all the great in a total want of frankness. Whoso saw Milton, whoso saw Shakspeare saw them do their best & utter their whole heart manlike among their brethren. No man was permitted to call Goethe brother. He hid himself & worked always to astonish, which is an egotism & therefore little.

Furthermore as he describes the Devil as the great Negation —or as Carlyle says the Lie is the Second Best, God & truth being the first—so it would appear as if he aimed himself to be the Third Term or the Universal Quiz, a sort of Bridge from the truth to the Lie. He thought it necessary therefore to dot round as it were the entire sphere of knowables & for many of his stories this seems the only reason: viz. Here is a piece of humanity I had hitherto omitted to sketch—take this. This, to be sure, he never expresses in words. Yet a sort of incumbency to be up to the Universe is the best account of many of them.

On the whole What have these German Weimarish Art friends done? They have rejected all the traditions & conventions, have sought to come thereby one step nearer to absolute truth. But still they are not nearer than others. I do not draw from them great influence. The heroic, the holy, I lack. They are contemptuous. They fail in sympathy with humanity. The voice of Nature they bring me to hear is not divine, but ghastly hard & ironical. They do not illuminate me: they do not edify me. Plutarch's heroes cheer, exalt. The old bloodwarm Miltons & Sidneys & Pauls help & aggrandize me. The roots of what is great & high must still be in the common life.

Christianity. To those fundamental natures that lie as the basis of the soul, truth, justice, love, &c, the idea of eternity is essentially associated. Jesus a pure intellect exclusively devoted to this class of abstractions (the ethical) did never yet utter one syllable about the naked immortality of the soul, never spoke of simple duration. His disciples felt as all must the coexisting perception of eternity & separated it & taught it as a doctrine & maintained it by evidences. It ought never to be. It is an impertinence to struggle up for the immortality. It is inevitable to believe it if you come down upon the conviction from the seeing these primary natures in the mind.

29 April. Warm & welcome blows the southwind at last, & the sun & moon shine again to raise the desponding hearts of

the people in these black times. Yet our idle dallying tentative conversation goes on, sunshine still lying kindly on my hearthstone. Therefor be lowly interceding praise from me & mine.

Mrs Lee gave me beautiful flowers. These gay natures contrast with the somewhat stern countenance of the world in these latitudes. They are like music heard out of a workhouse or jail. Nature does not cocker us. We are children, not pets. She is not fond. Everything is dealt to us without fear or favor after serene severe Universal laws. Yet these delicate flowers look like the frolic & interference of love & beauty. They use to tell us that we love flattery even which we see through because it shows that we are of importance enow to be courted. Something like that pleasure the star, the flower, & the tinted cloud give us. Well, what am I to whom these sweet & sublime hints are addressed!

How wild & mysterious our position as individuals to the Universe! Here is always a certain amount of truth lodged as intrinsic foundation in the depths of the soul, a certain perception of absolute being, as justice, love, & the like, natures which must be the God of God, and this is our capital stock. This is our centripetal force. We can never quite doubt, we can never be adrift; we can never be nothing, because of this Holy of Holies, out of sight of which we cannot go. Then on the other side all is to seek. We understand nothing; our ignorance is abysmal,—the overhanging immensity staggers us, whither we go, what we do, who we are, we cannot even so much as guess. We stagger & grope.

Fine manners present themselves first as formidable; they are primarily useful as the noble science of defence is, merely to parry & ward & intimidate, but once matched by our own skill they drop the point of the sword—points & shields all disappear & you find yourself in a perfectly transparent medium wherein life is a finer vehicle & not a cloud like that which Beckendorf's keen eye detected in his glass, is visible between man & man. They aim at good certainly. They aim to facilitate life; to get rid of chaff & husks & to bring the man pure to operate. They aid society as a railway aids travelling by getting rid

of all the details of the road & leaving nothing to be conquered but pure space.

Miss Fuller read Vivian Gray & made me very merry. Beckendorf is a fine teaching that he who can once conquer his
own face, can have no farther difficulty. Nothing in the world
is to him impossible. As Napoleon who discharged his face of
all expression whilst Mme de Stael gazed at him.

———

" 'The French,' said Goethe 'have understanding & talent
but no Foundation & no piety. What serves them for the
moment, what can benefit their party, is to them the Right.
They praise us, therefore, not out of recognition of our merit,
but only when they can strengthen their party through our
views.' "

Eckermann
Vol. 1 p. 168

"The French *esprit* said Goethe comes near that which we
Germans name *Witz*. Our *Geist* would the French perhaps express through *esprit* and *ame*. There lies in the word the import of productiveness which the French *esprit* has not."
Eckermann Vol. 2, p. 323.

———

A characteristic of Goethe is his choice of topics. What an
eye for the measure of things! Perhaps he is out in regard to
Byron, but not of Shakspear; & in Byron he has grasped all
the peculiarities. Paper-money; Periods of belief; Cheerfulness
of the poet; French Revolution; how just are his views of
these trite things! What a multitude of opinions & how few
blunders! The estimate of Sterne, I suppose to be one.

———

It is to me very plain that no recent genius can work with
equal effect upon mankind as Goethe, for no intelligent young
man can read him without finding that his own compositions
are immediately modified by his new knowledge.

I do not remember a joke or aught laughable in all Goethe
except Philina cracking nuts upon the trunk & perhaps
Friedrich's gibe at Natalia.

For the new Faust and the "classick Carnival," as Margaret
Fuller calls it, I seem to see some explanation in the man's

desire that every word should be a thing. These figures, he would say these Chirons, Sphinxes & Peneus, Helen & Leda, are somewhat & do exert a specific influence on the mind. So far they are eternal entities as real today as in the first Olympiad. Much revolving them he writes out freely his humor & having given them by successive efforts body to his own imagination he thinks they have humanity to other men to whom they are wholly fantastic.

———

"The faults" writes Goethe to Schiller (Briefe p. 66) "which you rightly indicate, come out of my inmost nature, out of a certain realistic whim, through which I find it pleasing to withdraw my existence, my actions, my writings out of the eyes of men. So I like ever to travel incognito, choose worse rather than better clothes & in intercourse with strangers or half strangers, prefer a trifling subject & common expressions, behave myself more capricious than I am, & place myself so to speak between me & my appearance."

Goethe prefers to drop a profound observation incidentally to stating it circumstantially: for example "Seneca sees nature as an uncultivated man; since not it, but its events interest him."

Nachg. W. vol. 13   p 68.

So, speaking of Bacon he says, "Revolutionary thoughts arise in individual men rather from single occasions than from the general state of affairs & so we meet in Bacon's writings some such axioms which he with special stress harps upon; e.g. the doctrine of final causes is particularly odious to him." Nachg. W. vol. 13. p. 157

———

May 1. I do not forgive in any man this forlorn pride as if he were an Ultimus Romanorum. I am more American in my feeling. This country is full of people whose fathers were judges, generals, & bank presidents & if all their boys should give themselves airs thereon & rest henceforth on the oars of their fathers' merit, we should be a sad, hungry generation. Moreover I esteem it my best birthright that our people are not crippled by family & official pride, that the best broadcloth coat in the country is put off to put on a blue frock, that the best man in town may steer his plough tail or may drive a milk cart. There is a great deal of work in our men & a false pride has not yet made them idle or ashamed. Moreover I am more philosophical than to love this retrospect. I believe in the being God not in the God that has been. I work; my fathers may have wrought or rested. What have I to do with them or with the Fellatahs or the great Khan! I know a worthy man who walks the streets with silent indignation as a last of his race quite contemptuously eyeing the passing multitude as if none of them were for him & he for none of them, as if he belonged to the club & age of Shakspear, Bacon, Milton, but by some untoward slip in old spiritual causes had been left behind by the etherial boat that ferried them into life & came now scornful an age too late. But what a foolish spirit to pout & sneer. That did not these able persons; & if some good natured angel should transport him into their serene company they would say unto him 'We know you not.' What if a man has great tastes & tendencies. Is not that the charm & wonder of time, the oil of life that in common men every where gleam out these majestical traits so wildly contrasting with their trivial employments, decking their narrow patch of black loam with sunshine & violets so that the lowest being, intimately seen, never suffers you to lose sight of his relations to the highest & to all?

Character is higher than intellect. And Character is what the German means when he speaks of the Daimonisches. A strong monad is strong to live as well as to think, & this is the last resource. Do I lack organ or medium to impart my truths? I can still retreat on this elemental force of living them. This is a total act; all thinking is a partial act. Webster in his speech does but half engage himself. I feel that there is a great deal of waste strength. Therefore I say let me not meet a great man in a drawing room or in an Academy or even in my own library but let him bound on his private errand meet me bound on mine in the stage coach our road being the same for two or three hundred miles, then will a right natural conversation grow out of our mutual want of relief & entertainment. Or better yet, put us into the cabin of a little coasting merchantman to roll & welter in the gulf Stream for a fortnight towards Savannah or St Croix. Then will two persons feel each the force of the other's constitution, the weight of each other's metal far better than it can be estimated from a speech or an Essay.

I went to see Mr Jonathan Phillips once & he said to me "when you come into the room, I endeavor to present humanity to you in a lovely & worthy form to put away every thing that can mar the beauty of the image." He also said that "life appeared to him very long; his existence had stretched over a vast experience."

May 4. I have copied into p. 33 of my Transcript, an account of the founding of an Alpine Hospital for travellers in 1386 by Heinrich the Foundling as a specimen of active beneficence. In this instance doing good is as clear & respectable as sunshine or self respect or aught else which the fastidious philosopher can still revere.

Margaret Fuller left us yesterday morning. Among many things that make her visit valuable & memorable, this is not the least that she gave me five or six lessons in German pronunciation never by my offer and rather against my will, each time, so that now spite of myself I shall always have to thank her for a great convenience—which she foresaw.

—

Be & Seem

Creation is genius, however, whenever. There are few actions. Almost all is appetite & custom. A new action commands us & is the Napoleon or Luther of the hour. So with manners. They are sometimes a perpetual creation & so do charm & govern us. So with opinions (as above, p. 513.). Miss Edgeworth has not *genius*, nor Miss Fuller; but the one has genius-in-narrative, & the other has genius-in-conversation. At Palermo I remember how shabby & pitiable seemed the poor opera company to me until the prima donna appeared & spoke. Presently she uttered cries of passion and the mimic scene becomes instantly real & vies at once with whatever is human & heroic. I have recorded an action p. 520.

The lady told me that she had never seen heroic manners. I think she has, in fragments, or the word would not be significant to her. I know them well yet am the least heroic of persons & I see well that my types of them are not one but many. Murat, Wordsworth. Sweet tempered ability & a scientific estimate of popular opinion, are essential.

The law of communication is this: Here am I a complex human being—Welcome to me all creatures; Welcome each of you to your part in me; St Paul to his; the eagle to his; the horse & the bat to theirs.

—

6 May. I see with joy the visits of heat & moisture to my trees & please myself with this new property. I strangely mix myself with Nature & the Universal God works, buds, & blooms in my grove & parterre. I seem to myself an enchanter who by some rune or dumb gesture compels the service of superior beings. But the instant I separate my *own* from the tree & the potato field, it loses this piquancy. I presently see that I also am but an instrument like the tree, a reagent. The tree was to grow; I was to transplant & water it, not for me, not for it, but for all.

A lesson learned late in life is that every line that one can draw on paper has expression. A boy making his first attempts at drawing thinks a neck is a neck, and that there is one right way for that part to be sketched. By & by he learns that every variation of the outline has meaning.

It occurred today how slowly we learn to trust ourselves as adepts of the common Nature. When a fashionable man, when a great judge or Engineer performs a charity, it gives us pause, it seems strange & admirable, we fear it will not last. Yet the same thing would appear not strange in me but quite natural. Slowly I learn with amazement that in my wildest dream, in my softest emotion, in my tear of contrition, I but repeat moment for moment the impulses & experience of the fashionist, the buccaneer, the slave, or whatever other Variety may be of the generic man.

The words "I am on the eve of a revelation," & such like, when applied to the influx of truth in ordinary life, sound sad & insane in my ear.

Sad is this continual postponement of life. I refuse sympathy
& intimacy with people as if in view of some better sympathy & intimacy to come. But whence & when? I am already
thirtyfour years old. Already my friends & fellow workers are
dying from me. Scarcely can I say that I see any new men or
women approaching me; I am too old to regard fashion; too
old to expect patronage of any greater or more powerful. Let
me suck the sweetness of those affections & consuetudes that
grow near me,—that the Divine Providence offers me. These
old shoes are easy to the feet. But no, not for mine, if they
have an ill savor. I was made a hermit & am content with my
lot. I pluck golden fruit from rare meetings with wise men. I
can well abide alone in the intervals, and the fruit of my own
tree shall have a better flavor.

7 May. The Sabbath reminds me of an advantage which education may give, namely a normal piety, a certain levitical education which only rarely devout genius could countervail. I
cannot hear the young men whose theological instruction is
exclusively owed to Cambridge & to public institution, without feeling how much happier was my star which rained on me
influences of ancestral religion. The depth of the religious sentiment which I knew in my Aunt Mary imbuing all her genius
& derived to her from such hoarded family traditions, from so
many godly lives & godly deaths of sainted kindred at Concord, Malden, York, was itself a culture, an education. I heard
with awe her tales of the pale stranger who at the time her
grandfather lay on his death bed tapped at the window &
asked to come in. The dying man said, 'Open the door;' but
the timid family did not; & immediately he breathed his last,
& they said one to another It was the angel of death. Another
of her ancestors when near his end had lost the power of
speech & his minister came to him & said, 'If the Lord Christ
is with you, hold up your hand'; and he stretched up both
hands & died. With these I heard the anecdotes of the charities
of Father Moody & his commanding administration of his holy
office. When the offended parishioners would rise to go out of
the church he cried "Come back, you graceless sinner, come
back!" And when his parishioners ventured into the ale house

on a Saturday night, the valiant pastor went in, collared them, & dragged them forth & sent them home. Charity then went hand in hand with zeal. They gave alms profusely & the barrel of meal wasted not. Who was it among this venerable line who whilst his house was burning, stood apart with some of his church & sang "There is a house not made with hands." Another was wont to go into the road whenever a traveller past on Sunday & entreat him to tarry with him during holy time, himself furnishing food for man & beast. In my childhood Aunt Mary herself wrote the prayers which first my brother William & when he went to college I read aloud morning & evening at the family devotions, & they still sound in my ear with their prophetic & apocalyptic ejaculations. Religion was her occupation, and when years after, I came to write sermons for my own church I could not find any examples or treasuries of piety so hightoned, so profound, or promising such rich influence as my remembrances of her conversation & letters.

This day my boy was baptized in the old church by Dr Ripley. They dressed him in the selfsame robe in which twenty-seven years ago my brother Charles was baptised. Lidian has a group of departed Spirits in her eye who hovered around the patriarch & the babe.

———

All this has my man done yet was there not a surmise, a hint in all the discourse that he had ever lived at all. Not one line did he draw out of real history.

8 May. It ought to have been more distinctly stated in "Nature" than it is that life is our inexhaustible treasure of language for thought. Years are well spent in the country in country labors, in towns, in the insight into trades & manufactures, in intimate intercourse with many men & women, in science, in art, to the one end of mastering in all their facts a language by which to illustrate & speak out our emotions & perceptions. I learn immediately from any speaker how much he has really learned, through the poverty or the splendor of his speech.

My garden is my dictionary.

*

There are three degrees of proficiency in this lesson of life. The one class live to the utility of the symbol as the majority of men do, regarding health & wealth as the chief good. Another class live above this mark, to the beauty of the symbol; as the poet & artist, and the Sensual school in philosophy. A third class live above the beauty of the symbol, to the beauty of the thing signified; and these are wise men. The first class have common sense; the second, taste; and the third spiritual perception.

I see in society the neophytes of all these classes, the class especially of young men who in their best knowledge of the sign have a misgiving that there is yet an unattained substance & they grope & sigh & aspire long in dissatisfaction, the sand-blind adorers of the symbol meantime chirping & scoffing & trampling them down. I see moreover that the perfect man— one to a millenium,—if so many, traverses the whole scale & sees & enjoys the symbol solidly; then also has a clear eye for its beauty; & lastly wears it lightly as a robe which he can easily throw off, for he sees the reality & divine splendor of the inmost nature bursting through each chink & cranny.

Dr R. has lived so long that he says things every now & then, with the most laudable impatience; but he idealizes nothing: out he comes with literal facts & does not dream among words. Homely & dry his things are because they are traditions accepted for nature & facts out of life crude & unassimilated, in short just as he found them. But you do not feel cheated & empty as when fed by the grammarians.

C.C.E. said when his friend was engaged, "At such times it is a comfort to feel that you are something to offer."

May 9. Two babies Willie & Wallie and excellent cousins they prove. Willie conscious of seniority in all the dignity of twentytwo months; Wallie six & a fortnight any thing but indifferent to his handsome cousin, whom he regards as a capital plaything, & his hair is divine to pull. So says Wallie's mamma, & moreover that he accounts her a porridgepot, & papa a prime horse.

Yesterday in the woods I followed the fine humble bee with rhymes & fancies fine.

May 14. Harder times. Two days since the suspension of specie payments by the New York & Boston Banks. William and his wife & child have spent a little time with us. F. H. Hedge was here day before yesterday. We walked in the wood & sat down there to discuss why I was I. Yesterday came Dr Channing & Mr Jonathan Phillips & honored our house with a call. But sages of the crowd are like kings so environed with deference & ceremony, that a call like this gives no true word for the mind & heart.

The true medicine for hard times seems to be sleep. Use so much bodily labor as shall ensure sleep, then you arise refreshed and in good spirits and in Hope. That have I this morn. Yesterday afternoon I stirred the earth about my shrubs & trees & quarreled with the piper-grass and now I have slept, & no longer am morose nor feel twitchings in the muscles of my face when a visiter is by. The humblebee & the pine warbler seem to me the proper objects of attention in these disastrous times*. I am less inclined to ethics, to history, to aught wise & grave & practick, & feel a new joy in nature. I am glad it is not my duty to preach these few sundays & I would invite the sufferers by this screwing panic to recover peace through these fantastic amusements during the tornado.

Our age is ocular.

May 19. Yesterday Alcott left me after three days spent here. I had "lain down a man & waked up a bruise" by reason of a bad cold, & was lumpish, tardy, & cold. Yet could I see plainly that I conversed with the most extraordinary man and the highest genius of the time. He is a Man. He is erect: he sees: let who ever be overthrown or parasitic or blind. Life he would have & enact, & not nestle into any cast off shell & form of the old time and now proposes to preach to the people or to take his staff & walk through the country conversing with the school teachers, & holding conversations in the villages. And so he ought to go publishing through the land his gospel like them of old time. Wonderful is his vision. The steadiness &

---

*The hollowness so sad we feel after too much talking is an expressive hint.

scope of his eye at once rebukes all before it, and we little men creep about ashamed. It is amusing even to see how this great visual orb rolls round upon object after object, & threatens them all with annihilation, seemeth to wither & scorch.

Coldly he asks 'whether Milton is to continue to meet the wants of the mind?' & so Bacon, & so of all.
He is, to be sure, monotonous: you may say, one gets tired of the uniformity,—he will not be amused, he never cares for the pleasant side of things, but always truth & their origin he seeketh after.

Is it not pathetic that the action of men on men is so partial? We never touch but at points. The most that I can have or be to my fellow man, is it the reading of his book, or the hearing of his project in conversation? I approach some Carlyle with desire & joy. I am led on from month to month with an expectation of some total embrace & oneness with a noble mind, & learn at last that it is only so feeble & remote & hiant action as reading a Mirabeau or a Diderot paper, & a few the like. This is all that can be looked for. More we shall not be to each other. Baulked soul! It is not that the sea & poverty & pursuit separate us. Here is Alcott by my door,—yet is the union more profound? No, the Sea, vocation, poverty, are seeming fences, but Man is insular, and cannot be touched. Every man is an infinitely repellent orb, & holds his individual being on that condition.

Conversation among the witty & well-informed hops about from spot to spot around the surface of life. Like the bird, we peck at this moss, & that bud, & that leaf upon the bark & the interior of the tree seems to us inedible, stringy, uniform, uninteresting. But the philosopher comes like the soul of vegetation itself & manifests great indifference at these excrescences, & the pretty colors & pretty organizations we magnify, & insists upon entering the sap that bubbles up from the root & accompanying it upward & outward, forms the bough, the bud, the leaf, the excrements & configures the rough rind as a mere superficial effect of its interior arrangements.

*

George Bradford compares the happiness of Gore R. riding the horse to plow, with boys in Boston of his age, who are too old to play on the common, and who can only dress & fix straps to their pantaloons.

Men are continually separating & not nearing by acquaintance. Once Dr Channing filled our sky. Now we become so conscious of his limits & of the difficulty attending any effort to show him our point of view, that we doubt if it be worth while. Best amputate. Then we come to speak with those who most fully accord in life & doctrine with ourselves, and lo! what mountains high & rivers wide. How still the word is to seek which can like a ferryman transport either into the point of view of the other. Invisible repulsions take effect also. The conversation is tentative, groping, only partially successful; and although real gratification arises out of it, both parties are relieved by solitude. I more. I hug the absolute being unbroken, undefined of my desart.

———

I see a good in such emphatic & universal calamity as the times bring, that they dissatisfy me with society. Under common burdens we say there is much virtue in the world & what evil coexists is inevitable. I am not aroused to say, 'I have sinned; I am in the gall of bitterness, & bond of iniquity'; but when these full measures come, it then stands confessed—Society has played out its last stake; it is checkmated. Young men have no hope. Adults stand like daylaborers idle in the streets. None calleth us to labor. The old wear no crown of warm light on their grey hairs. The present generation is bankrupt of principles & hope, as of property. I see man is not what man should be. He is the treadle of a wheel. He is a tassel at the apron string of Society. He is a money chest. He is the servant of his belly. This is the causal bankruptcy—this the cruel oppression that the ideal should serve the actual; that the head should serve the feet. Then first I am forced to inquire if the Ideal might not also be tried. Is it to be taken for granted that it is impracticable? Behold the boasted world has come to nothing. Prudence itself is at her wits' end. Pride, and Thrift, & Expediency, who jeered and chirped and were so well pleased with themselves and made merry with the dream as they termed it of philosophy & love: Behold they are all flat and here is the Soul erect and Unconquered still. What answer is it now to say—it has always been so.—I acknowledge that as far back as I can see the winding procession of humanity the marchers are lame & blind & deaf; but, to the soul, that whole past is but the finite series in its infinite scope. Deteriorating ever and now desperate. Let me begin anew. Let me teach the finite to know its Master. Let me ascend above my fate and work down upon my world.

May 22. Let us not sit like snarling dogs working not at all, but snapping at those who work ill.

I told the Sunday School yesterday that the misfortunes of the adult generation give a new interest to childhood as born to a new state of things, born to better fortunes. Let them learn that what we live to know is Ourselves. That out of every school-lesson, game, errand, friendship, quarrel, they come forth different persons from that they went in, with a new faculty unlocked. So let them behold themselves and their exercises with awe & hope.

The black times have a great scientific value. It is an epoch so critical a philosopher would not miss. As I would willingly carry myself to be played upon at Faneuil Hall by the stormy winds & strong fingers of the enraged Boston so is this era more rich in the central tones than many languid centuries. What was, ever since my memory, solid continent, now yawns apart and discloses its composition and genesis. I learn geology the morning after an earthquake. I learn fast on the ghastly diagrams of the cloven mountain & upheaved plain and the dry bottom of the Sea. The roots of orchards and the cellars of palaces and the cornerstones of cities are dragged into melancholy sunshine. I see the natural fracture of the stone. I see the tearing of the tree & learn its fibre & its rooting. The Artificial is rent from the eternal.

The world has failed. The pretended teachers who have scoffed at the Idealist, have failed utterly. The very adulation they offer to the name of Christ, the epithets with which they encumber his name, the ragged half screaming bass with which they deepen the sentences of sermons on purity, martyrdom, & spiritual life, do preach their hollowness & recoil upon them. They lash themselves with their satire.

The kingdom of the involuntary, of the not me. See they not how when the unfit guest comes in, the master of the house goes out? He is not at home, he cannot be at home whilst the guest stays. His body is there and a singular inconvenience to any family. Men & women should not contend with the laws of human nature. They sit at one board, but a cloud falleth upon their faces, that hinders them from seeing one another.

People are stung by a pregnant saying and will continue to repeat it without seeing its meaning. I said 'If you sleep, you show character'—and the young girls asked what it could mean. I will tell you. You think that because you have spoken nothing when others spoke and have given no opinion upon the times, upon Wilhelm Meister, upon Abolition, upon Harvard College, that your verdict is still expected with curiosity as a reserved wisdom. Far otherwise; it is known that you have no opinion: You are measured by your silence & found wanting. You have no oracle to utter, & your fellowmen have learned that you cannot help them; for oracles speak. Doth not wisdom cry & understanding put forth her voice?

Among provocatives, the next best thing to good preaching is bad preaching. I have even more thoughts during or enduring it than at other times.

I wrote above that life wants worthy objects: the game is not worth the candle: It is not that not I,—it is that *nobody* employs it well. The land stinks with suicide.

—

May 25. "My dear Sir, clear your mind of cant," said Dr Johnson. Wordsworth, whom I read last night, is garrulous & weak often, but quite free from cant. I think I could easily make a small selection from his volumes which should contain all their poetry. It would take Fidelity, Tintern Abbey, Cumberland

Beggar, Ode to Duty, September, The force of prayer, Lycoris, Lines on the death of Fox, Dion, Happy Warrior, Laodamia, the Ode.

Philosophical poetry. The extract at the close of the New volume.

There is still the Universal beyond and above. There is still room to say "What light shall be vouchsafed" as A. writes me today. I am never so much party as I am receiver.

Composition
Let not a man decline being an artist under any greenhorn notion of intermeddling with sacred thought. It is surely foolish to adhere rigidly to the order of time in putting down one's thoughts & to neglect the order of thought. I put like things together.

Let a man be a guest in his own house. Let him be a spectator of his own life. Let him heal himself not by drugs but by sleep. Let him not only do but be. Let him not vaticinate but hear. Let him bask in beauty & not always carry on a farm. I wrote at sea, Jan. 1833, "I am well pleased, yet I have nothing to record; I have read little; I have done nothing. What then? Need we be such barren dogs that the whole beauty of heaven, the main, & man, cannot entertain us unless we too must needs hold a candle & daub God's world with a smutch of our own insignificance? Not I, for one. I will be pleased though I do not deserve it. &c."

A young man told Edmund Hosmer that he had come for the honeysuckles because his father liked them but for his own part he would rather see a hill of potatoes. Hillman could not see in the yellow warbler on the fir tree, any more beauty than in a rat.

Still hard times. Yet how can I lament, when I see the resources of this continent in which three months will anywhere yield a crop of wheat or potatoes. On the bosom of this vast plenty, the blight of trade & manufactures seems to me a momentary mischance.

———

I behold; I bask in beauty; I await; I wonder; Where is my Godhead now? This is the Male & Female principle in Nature. One Man, male & female created he him. Hard as it is to describe God, it is harder to describe the Individual.

A certain wandering light comes to me which I instantly perceive to be the Cause of Causes. It transcends all proving. It is itself the ground of being; and I see that it is not one & I another, but this is the life of my life. That is one fact, then; that in certain moments I have known that I existed directly from God, and am, as it were, his organ. And in my ultimate consciousness Am He. Then, secondly, the contradictory fact is familiar, that I am a surprised spectator & learner of all my life. This is the habitual posture of the mind,—beholding. But whenever the day dawns, the great day of truth on the soul, it comes with awful invitation to me to accept it, to blend with its aurora.

Cannot I conceive the Universe without a contradiction?

Why rake up old MSS to find therein a man's soul? You do not look for conversation in a corpse.

To behold the great in the small, the law in one fact, the vegetation of all the forests on the globe in the sprouting of one acorn, this is the vision of genius.

I hail with glad augury from afar that kindred emotion which the grand work of genius awakens kindred with that awakened by works of Nature. The identity of their origin at the fountain head, I augur with a thrill of joy. Nature is too thin a screen; the glory of the One breaks through everywhere.

To run after one's hat is ludicrous.

———

July 17. Did I read somewhere lately that the sum of Virtue was to know & dare? The analogy is always perfect between Virtue & genius. One is ethical the other intellectual creation. To create, to create is the proof of a Divine presence. Whoever creates is God, and whatever talents are, if the man create not,

the pure efflux of Deity is not his. I read these Donnes &
Cowleys & Marvells with the most modern joy;—with a pleasure, I mean, which is in great part caused by the abstraction
of all *time* from their verses. What pleases most, is what is next
to my Soul; what I also had well nigh thought & said. But for
my faith in the oneness of Mind, I should find it necessary to
suppose some preestablished harmony, some foresight of souls
that were to be & some preparation of stores for their future
wants like the fact observed in insects who lay up food before
their death for the young grub they shall never see. Here are
things just hinted which not one reader in a hundred would
take, but which lie so near to the favorite walks of my imagination and to the facts of my experience that I read them with
a surprise & delight as if I were finding very good things in a
forgotten manuscript of my own.

Creation is always the style & act of these minds. You shall
not predict what the poet shall say and whilst ephemeral
poetry hath its form, its contents, & almost its phrase out of
the books & is only a skilful paraphrase or permutation of
good authors, in these the good human soul speaks because it
has something new to say. It is only another face of the same
fact to denominate them sincere. The way to avoid mannerism, the way to write what shall not go out of fashion is to
write sincerely, to transcribe your doubt or regret or whatever
state of mind, without the airs of a fine gentleman or great
philosopher, without timidity or display, just as they lie in your
consciousness, casting on God the responsibility of the facts.
This is to dare.

Cowley & Donne are philosophers. To their insight there is
no trifle. But philosophy or insight is so much the habit of
their minds that they can hardly see as a poet should the beautiful forms & colors of things, as a chemist may be less alive to
the picturesque. At the same time their poems like life afford the
chance of richest instruction amid frivolous & familiar objects;
the loose & the grand, religion & mirth stand in surprising
neighborhood and, like the words of great men, without cant.

Two proverbs I found lately; one; "He who would bring home
the wealth of the Indies, must carry out the wealth of the

Indies." The other may serve as foil to this magnificent sentence, "Small pot, soon hot." Then again I found in "the Phenix", the Persian sentence, "Remember always that the gods are good" which for genius equals any other golden saying.

At Plymouth which is one of the most picturesque of towns with its two hundred ponds, its hills and the great sea-line always visible from their tops I enjoyed the repose that seems native to the place. On the shore of Halfway Pond our party ate their gipsy dinner; the next day we rolled on the beach in the sun & dipped our spread fingers in the warm sand and peeped after bugs & botanized & rode & walked & so yielded ourselves to the Italian genius of the town, the dolce far niente. It is even so that the population of the historical town is on its back presently after dinner.

Lidian says that they who have only seen her baby well, do not know but half of his perfections; they do not how patient he is, & suffers just like a little angel: they must see him sick. If he should flap his little wings & fly straight up to heaven, he would not find there anything purer than himself. He coos like a pigeon house.

July 19. If you go into the garden & hoe corn or kill bugs on the vines or pick pease, when you come into the house you shall still for some time see simulacra of weeds, vines, or pea-pods as you see the image of the sun sometime after looking at the sun. Both are disagreeable phenomena, as bad as laughing.

The office of reading is wholly subordinate. I am certainly benefitted by each new mechanical or agricultural process. I see & do, chiefly as it affords me new language, & power of illustration. Precisely so am I gainer by reading history, by knowing the geography & civil annals of Arabia, of Germany; by knowing the systems of philosophy that have flourished under the names of Heraclitus, Zoroaster, Plato, Kant; by knowing the life & conversation of Jesus, of Napoleon, of Shakspear & Dante; by knowing chemistry & commerce; that I get thereby a vocabulary for my ideas. I get no ideas.

There is however one other service of good books. They provoke thoughts.

G.P.B. thought at Plymouth that the finest gifts for music yet always needed culture.

July 18, 1837. I wrote this P.M. to Miss Fuller, that Power & Aim seldom meet in one soul. The wit of our time is sick for an object. Genius is homesick. I cannot but think that our age is somewhat distinguished hereby, for you cannot talk with any intelligent company without finding expressions of regret & impatience that attack the whole structure of our Worship, Education, & Social Manners. We all undoubtedly expect that time will bring amelioration but whilst the grass grows, the noble steed starves—we die of the numb palsy.

But Ethics stand when wit fails. Fall back on the simplest sentiment, be heroic, deal justly, walk humbly, & you do something and do invest the capital of your being in a bank that cannot break & that will surely yield ample rents—

July 21. Abide by your spontaneous impression with good humoured inflexibility then most when the whole cry of voices is on the other side. Else, tomorrow a stranger will say with masterly good sense precisely what you have thought & felt all the time, & you will be forced to take with shame your own opinion from another.

Courage consists in the conviction that they with whom you contend, are no more than you. If we believed in the existence of strict *individuals*, natures, that is, not radically identical but unknown immeasureable, we should never dare to fight.

Crabbe knew men, but to read one of his poems seems to me all one with taking a dose of medicine.

Aristides was made "General Receiver of Greece" to collect the tribute which each state was to furnish Athens against the Barbarian. "Poor" says Plutarch, "when he set about it, but poorer when he had finished it."

Deb sent out little Faya into the garden to gather goose-berries & bade her pick the reddest & bring them in. Faya did as she was bid; but Deb knit her brows & drove her back to the bushes and told her to do as she had commanded her. Did I not tell you to pick the reddest? So now Faya gathered all the pink ones, and went in as before. But old Deb sent her again into the garden angrily with the like words. So now she picked those that were red on one side.

We are begirt with spiritual laws.

Epitaph
"Behold all you who now pass by!
As you are now, so once was I;
As I am now, so you shall be;
Prepare for death, and follow me."

July 26. Yesterday I went to the Atheneum, & looked thro' Journals & books—for wit, for excitement,—to awake in me the muse. In vain and in vain. And am I yet to learn that the God dwells within? that books are but crutches, the resorts of the feeble & lame, which if used by the strong, weaken the muscular power, & become necessary aids? I return home. Nature still solicits me. Overhead the sanctities of the stars shine forevermore & to me also, pouring satire on the pompous business of the day which they close & making the generations of men show slight & evanescent. A man is but a bug, the earth but a boat a cockle drifting under their old light.

27 July. A letter today from Carlyle rejoiced me. Pleasant would life be with such companions. But if you cannot have them on good mutual terms, you cannot have them. If not the Deity but our wilfulness hews & shapes the new relations their sweetness escapes as strawberries lose their flavor by cultivation.

The sublime envelopes us like air enters into every thing & recommends Peter Howe's employment as much to him as Webster's or Wordsworth's to them. Who can doubt that the clerk enjoys in the balance of his ledger the grandeur of the law of Compensation as really as the poet enjoys the same element in the ebb & flow of the sea, in the law of light & darkness, heat & cold? This is the tolerableness of servile or disagreeable vocations.

Every object in nature is a private door that lets in the wise to profound mystery, the music of numbers.

Richter said to Music, "Away! away! thou speakest of things which throughout my endless life I have found not & shall not find." The ancient British Bards had for the title of their order "Those who are free throughout the world," and their motto was "The truth against the world." "Poets are the natural guardians of admiration in the hearts of the people." "Es ist alles wahr wodurch du besser wirst." "An Epicure is a man that can eat anything."

"I turned from all she brought to all she could not bring."
Byron

I find these scraps in Chorley's Mrs Hemans.

Many trees bear only in alternate years. Why should you write a book every year?

29 July. If the Allwise would give me light, I should write for the Cambridge men a theory of the Scholar's office. It is not all books which it behooves him to know, least of all to be a bookworshipper, but he must be able to read in all books that which alone gives value to books—in all to read one, the one incorruptible text of truth. That alone of their style is intelligible, acceptable to him.

Books are for the scholar's idle times. When he can read God directly, the hour is too precious to be wasted on other men's transcripts of their readings. The poet, the prophet is caught up into the mount of vision, & thereafter is constrained to declare what he has seen. As the hour of vision is short & rare among heavy days & months so is its record perchance the least part of his volume. But the reverence which attaches to the record spreads itself soon over all his books especially for the bulk of mankind. Hence the book learned class who value books as such not as related to Nature & the human constitution but as making themselves a Third Estate. But the discerning man reads in his Shakspear or Plato only that least part, only the authentic utterances of the oracle, and all the rest he rejects were it never so many times Shakspear's & Plato's.

—

A beauty overpowering all analysis or comparison & putting us quite beside ourselves we can seldom see after thirty. Gertrude had a cheek like a sunset.

I find it to be a mischievous notion of our times that men think we are come late into nature, that the world is finished & sealed, that the world is of a constitution unalterable, and see not that in the hands of genius old things are passed a way & all things become new. Not he is great that can alter matter, but he that can alter my state of mind. But they are the kings of the world who give the color of their present thought to all nature & all art, & persuade men by the cheerful serenity of their carrying the matter that this is the apple which ages have aspired to pluck now at last ripe and inviting nations to the harvest. The great man makes the great thing. Linnaeus makes Botany the most attractive of studies & wins it from the farmer & the herbwoman. Genius makes the stony hours sing & shine for me. The day is always his who works in it with serenity. Wherever Macdonald sits, there is the head of the table. The pale young men diffident & complaisant who ride & walk into town in search of a place to fix themselves ought to feel that the differences between them & their proud patrons is slightest, that as infancy conforms to nobody, but all conform to it; so that one babe commonly makes four or five out of the adults who prattle & play to it; so God has armed youth & puberty and manhood with its own piquancy & charm & made it enviable & gracious and its claims not to be put by if it will stand by itself. The nonchalance of boys who are sure of a dinner & would disdain as much as a lord to do or say aught to conciliate one, is the healthy attitude of human nature, and the good youth & the good man though their pockets were empty would not bate one jot of assurance that bread was their due.

The two most noble things in the world are Learning & Virtue. The latter is health, the former is power; the latter is

Being, the former Action. But let them go erect evermore &
strike sail to none.

An enchanting night of southwind & clouds; mercury at
73°. All the trees are windharps. Blessed be light & darkness,
ebb & flow, cold & heat, these restless pulsations of Nature
which by & by will throb no more. Poetry I augur shall revive
and stamp a new age as the astronomers assure us that the star
in the constellation Harp shall be, in its turn, the Pole Star for
a thousand years.

I knew a man scared by the rustle of his own hatband.
    Scholars; who being poor made many rich. Eyes were they
to the blind, feet were they to the lame.

When the narrowminded & unworthy shall knock at my gate,
I will say 'Come now will I sacrifice to the gods below;' then
will I entertain my guests heartily & handsomely. Besides is it
for thee to choose what shadows shall pass over thy magical
mirror?

    Aug. 3. Hannah H. tells well the story of Aunt Mary's
watcher whilst she had a fellen on her thumb. She had never a
watcher in her life & was resolved to have one once. So seized
the chance. All day she was making preparations for her coming & requiring the family to have things in readiness. Twice
or thrice she sent messages over to the woman's house to tell
her to sleep & to fix the hour of her coming. When at last she
came she first put the watcher to bed that she might be ready
& watched her herself. But presently woke her because she
thought her head did not lie comfortably; then again because
she snored, to forbid her making such a shocking noise. At last
she became anxious lest her watcher should spend the night, &
day break before she had got any service from her, so she determined to get up & have her own bed made, for the sake of
giving her something to do. But at last growing very impatient
of her attendant, she dismissed her before light, declaring she
never would have a watcher again, she had passed the worst
night she remembered. On the other part Miss ——, the

Watcher declared that no consideration would tempt her to watch with Miss Emerson again.

—

The grass is mown; the corn is ripe; autumnal stars arise. After raffling all day in Plutarch's Morals, or shall I say angling there for such fish as I might find, I sallied out this fine afternoon through the woods to Walden Water. The Woods were too full of musquitoes to offer any hospitality to the muse & when I came to the blackberry vines the plucking the crude berries at the risk of splintering my hand and with a musquito mounting guard over every particular berry seemed a little too emblematical of general life whose shining & glossy fruits are very hard beset with thorns & very sour & good for nothing when gathered. But the pond was all blue & beautiful in the bosom of the woods and under the amber sky—like an sapphire lying in the moss. I sat down a long time on the shore to see the show. The variety & density of the foliage at the eastern end of the pond is worth seeing, then the extreme softness & holiday beauty of the summer clouds floating feathery overhead enjoying as I fancied their height & privilege of motion & yet & yet not seeming so much the drapery of this place & hour as forelooking to some pavilions & gardens of festivity beyond. I rejected this fancy with a becoming spirit & insisted that clouds, woods, & waters were all there for me. The waterflies were full of happiness. The frogs that shoot from the land as fast as you walk along, a yard ahead of you, are a meritorious beastie. For their cowardice is only greater than their curiosity & desire of acquaintance with you. Three strokes from the shore the little swimmer turns short round, spreads his webbed paddles, & hangs at the surface, looks you in the face & so continues as long as you do not assault him.

I sometimes fear that like those Savoyards who went out one day to find stock for their wooden images and discovered that they had whittled up the last of their pinetrees, so I careless of action, intent on composition, have exhausted already all my stock of experience, have fairly written it out.

—

8 August. I have read Miss Martineau's first volume with great pleasure. I growled at first at the difference betwixt it & the

Plutarch I had just left. The sailors refuse lemonade & cake & sugarplums and ask for pork & biscuit "something to line their ribs with"; and pleasant and exhilarating as the book is, I lacked the solids. It pleases like a novel, the brilliant pictures of scenery & of towns & things which she sketches, but I feel as I read I enrich myself not at all. Yet better pleased as I read on, I honored the courage & rectitude of the woman. How faithful is she found where to be faithful is praise enough. She gives that pleasure which I have felt before, when a good cause which has been trampled on is freshly & cheerily maintained by some undaunted man of good sense & good principle, and we are all contrite that we had not done it. As if we could have done it! This attribute of genius she has, that she talks so copiously & elegantly of subjects so familiar that they seemed desperate and writes evermore from one point of view. The *woman* is manifest, as she seems quite willing, in the superfluous tenderness for the fine boy & the snug farmhouse & other privacies. But the respect for principles is the genius of the book & teaches a noble lesson through every page. I will thank those who teach me not to be easily depressed.

———

I had a letter from Dr Frothingham today. The sight of that man's handwriting is parnassian. Nothing vulgar is connected with his name but on the contrary every remembrance of wit & learning & contempt of cant. In our Olympic Games we love his fame. But that fame was bought by many years' steady rejection of all that is popular with our saints & as persevering study of books which none else reads & which he can convert to no temporary purpose. There is a Scholar doing a Scholar's office.

Carlyle: how the sight of his handwriting warms my heart at the little post window. How noble it seems to me that his words should run out of Nithsdale or London over land & sea, to Weimar, to Rome, to America, to Watertown, to Concord, to Louisville, that they should cheer & delight & invigorate me: A man seeking no reward, warping his genius, filing his mind to no dull public but content with the splendors of Nature & Art as he beholds them & resolute to announce them if his voice is orotund & shrill, in his own proper accents—please or displease the World, how noble that he should trust his eye

& ear above all London & know that in all England is no man that can see so far behind or forward; how good & just that amid the hootings of malignant men he should hear this & that whispered qualification of praise of Schiller, Burns, Diderot, &c the commended papers being more every year & the commendation louder. How noble that alone & unpraised he should still write for he knew not who, & find at last his readers in the valley of the Mississippi, and they should brood on the pictures he had painted & untwist the many colored meanings which he had spun & woven into so rich a web of sentences and domesticate in so many & remote heads the humor, the learning, and the philosophy which year by year in summer & in frost this lonely man had lived in the moors of Scotland. This man upholds & propels civilization. For every wooden post he knocks away he replaces one of stone. He cleanses and exalts men & leaves the world better. He knows & loves the heavenly stars and sees fields below with trees & animals; he sees towered cities; royal houses; & poor men's chambers & reports the good he sees God thro' him telling this generation also that he has beholden his work & sees that it is good. He discharges his duty as one of the World's Scholars.

The farmer turns his capital once a year. The merchant many times oftener. The scholar cannot. The knowledge which he acquires will not become bread or reputation to him in a year or two years or ten. There is no doublespeeder, no railroad, no mechanical multiplication. He gives himself to the slow & un-honored task of observation. Flamsteed & Herschel in their glazed observatory may catalogue the stars with the good will of all men & the results being conspicuous, splendid, & useful honor is sure. But he in his private observatory cata-loguing obscure & nebulous stars of the human mind which as yet no man has thought of as such; & watching days & months sometimes for a few facts; correcting still his old records must sacrifice display & immediate fame; more than that, he must accept, often, a certain ignorance & shiftlessness in ordinary business incurring the disdain of the able who shoulder him aside. He must stammer in his speech, he must forego the living for the dead, he must accept poverty, obscurity, & solitude.

For robust health he becomes a valetudinarian; for the ease & pleasure of treading the beaten track accepting the fashions, the religion, the education of society he assumes the bold responsibility of making his own, & of course the self accusation, the faint heart, the frequent uncertainty & loss of time which are thorns & nettles in the way of the self relying & self-directed; and the state of virtual hostility in which he seems to stand to society & especially to educated society. For all this loss & scorn he is to find consolation in exercising the highest functions of human nature. He is to resist the prosperity that retrogrades ever to barbarism by preserving & communicating heroic sentiments, noble biographies, melodious verse, & the conclusions of history; whatsoever oracles the human heart in all emergences, in all solemn hours has uttered as its commentary on the storm of actions. The wisdom that he painfully gathers sweetens his own life. He is made gentle, noble, & self centred and who is so becomes in the heart of all clearseeing men venerable & salutary & oracular. He preserves for another generation the knowledge of what is noble & good.

———

If you gather apples in the sunshine or make hay or hoe corn and then retire within doors & strain your body or squeeze your eyes *six hours after* you shall still see apples hanging in the bright light with leaves & boughs thereto. There lie the impressions still on the retentive organ though I knew it not. So lies the whole series of natural images with which my life has made me acquainted in my memory, though I know it not and a thrill of passion, a sudden emotion flashes light upon their dark chamber & the Active power seizes instantly the fit image as the word of his momentary thought. So lies all the life I have lived as my dictionary from which to extract the word which I want to dress the new perception of this moment. This is the way to learn Grammar. God never meant that we should learn Language by Colleges or Books. That only can we say which we have lived.

Life lies behind us as the quarry from whence we get tiles & copestones for the masonry of today.

———

If Jesus came now into the world, he would say—You, YOU! He said to his age, I.

He that perceives that the Moral Sentiment is the highest in God's order, rights himself, he stands in the erect position, and therefore is strong, uses his hands, works miracles just as a man who stands on his feet is stronger than a man who stands on his head.

There never was a saint but was pleased to be accused of pride, and this because pride is a form of self-trust.

I like not to have the day hurry away under me whilst I sit at my desk; I wish not reveries; I like to taste my time & spread myself through all the hour.

Do they think the composition too highly wrought? A poem should be a blade of Damascus steel made up a mass of knife blades & nails & parts every one of which has had its whole surface hammered & wrought before it was welded into the Sword to be wrought over anew.

The least effect of the oration is on the orator. Yet it is something; a faint recoil; a kicking of the gun.

17 August. This morng. Mr Alcott & Mr Hedge left me. Four or five days full of discourse & much was seen. I incline to withdraw continually as from a surfeit, but the stomach of my wise guests being stronger, I strain my courtesy to sit by though drowsy. In able conversation we have glimpses of the Universe, perceptions of the soul's omnipotence but not much to record. I who enjoin on Alcott records, can attain to none myself,—to no register of these far darting lights & shadows or any sketch of the mountain landscape which has opened itself to the eye. It would be a valuable piece of literature, could a Report of these extended & desultory but occasionally profound, often ornamented, often sprightly & comic dialogues, be made, sinking some parts, fulfilling others, and chiefly, putting together things that belong together. I would rather have a perfect recollection of all this, of all that I have thought & felt in the last week, than any book that can now be published.

—

He who sees in the human mind the necessity of a French Revolution, the necessity of a generation of vain & selfish soldiers enamored of show & conquest, & of course that the most selfish, most showy, & most conquering man shall be the general & Napoleon of them, can outspeed in his intelligence newspapers & telegraphs.

I please myself with getting my nail box set in the snuggest corner of the barn chamber & well filled with nails & gimlet pincers, screw driver, & chisel. Herein I find an old joy of youth, of childhood which perhaps all domestic children share, —the cat-like love of garrets, barns, & corn chambers and of the conveniences of long housekeeping. It is quite genuine. When it occurs today, I ask—Have others the same? Once I should not have thought of such a question. What I loved, I supposed all children loved & knew, & therefore I did not name them. We were at accord. But much conversation, much comparison apprises us of difference. The first effect of this new learning is to incline us to hide our tastes. As they differ, we must be wrong. Afterwards some person comes & wins eclat by simply describing this old but concealed fancy of ours. Then we immediately learn to value all the parts of our nature, to rely on them as Self-authorised and that to publish them is to please others. So now the nailbox figures for its value.

We are indeed discriminated from each other by very slight inequalities which by their accumulation constitute at last broad contrasts. Genius surprises us with every word. It does not surprise itself. It is moving by the selfsame law as you obey in your daily cogitation & one day you will tread without wonder the same steps.

———

20 August. Many persons take pleasure in showing the differences that will never blend, the strong individualities of men. For these two years back, I incline more to show the insignificance of these differences as they melt into the Unity which is the base of them all. Aristotle & Plato are reckoned the respective heads of schools between which a yawning gulf lies. I like to see that Aristotle Platonizes.

Carlyle & Wordsworth now act out of England on us,—Coleridge also.

Lidian remembers the religious terrors of her childhood when *Young* tinged her day & night thoughts, and the doubts of *Cowper* were her own; when every lightning seemed the beginning of conflagration, & every noise in the street the crack of doom. I have some parallel recollections at the Latin School when I lived in Beacon street. Afterwards what remained for me to learn was cleansed by books & poetry & philosophy & came in purer forms of literature at College. These spiritual crises no doubt are periods of as certain occurrence in some form of agitation to every mind as dentition or puberty. Lidian was at that time alarmed by the lines on the gravestones quoted above p. 535.

The babe cheers me with his hearty & protracted laugh which sounds to me like thunder in the woods.

Aug. 21. A dream of a duel. Dreams may explain the magnetic *directed dream.* Dreams are the sequel of waking knowledge. Awake I know the character of Andrew, but do not think what he may do. In dream I turn that knowledge into a fact; and it proves a prophecy. In like manner the Soul contains in itself the event that shall presently befal it for the event is only the actualization of its thoughts. Why then should not symptoms, auguries, forebodings also be, and, as Hedge said, "the moanings of the spirit"?

What means all the monitory tone of the world of life, of literature, of tradition? Man is fallen Man is banished; an exile; he is in earth whilst there is a heaven. What do these apologues mean? These seem to him traditions of memory. But they are the whispers of hope and Hope is the voice of the Supreme Being to the Individual.

We say Paradise was; Adam fell; the Golden Age; & the like. We mean man is not as he ought to be; but our way of painting this is on Time, and we say *Was.*

I believe that I shall some time cease to be an Individual, that the eternal tendency of the soul is to become Universal to animate the last extremities of organization.

—

Yesterday as I watched the flight of some crows I suddenly discovered a hawk high over head & then directly four others at such a height they seemed smallest sparrows. There, on high, they swooped & circled in the pure heaven. After watching them for a time, I turned my eye to my path, & was struck with the dim & leaden color all unattractive & shorn of beams of this earth to him whose eye has conversed with heaven.

—

Sept. 18. In the woods today I heard a pattering like rain & looking up I beheld the air over & about the tops of the trees full of insects (the winged ant) in violent motion & gyrations and some of them continually dropping out of the flying or fighting swarm & causing the rain-like sound as they fell upon the oakleaves. The fallers consisted of little knots of two or three insects apparently biting each other & so twisted or holden together as to encumber the wings.

—

Sept. 19. There are few experiences in common life more mortifying & disagreeable than "the foolish face of praise"— the forced smile which we put on in company where we do not feel at ease in answer to conversation which does not interest us. The muscles not spontaneously moved but moved by a low usurping wilfulness, grow tight about the outline of the face & make the most disagreeable sensation—a sensation of rebuke & warning which no young man ought to suffer more than once.

—

We can hardly speak of our own experience & the names of our family sparingly enough. The rule seems to be that we should not use these dangerous personalities any more than we are sure the sympathies of the interlocutors will go along with us. In good company the individuals at once merge their egotism into a social soul exactly coextensive with the several consciousnesses there present. No partialities of friend to friend, no fondnesses of husband to wife are then pertinent, but quite otherwise. Only he may then speak who can sail as it were on the common thought of the party, & not poorly limited to his own.

—

On the 29 August, I received a letter from the Salem Lyceum signed I.F Worcester, requesting me to lecture before the institution next winter and adding "The subject is of course discretionary with yourself 'provided no allusions are made to religious controversy, or other exciting topics upon which the public mind is honestly divided.'" I replied on the same day to Mr W. by quoting these words & adding "I am really sorry that any person in Salem should think me capable of accepting an invitation so encumbered."

"The motto on all palace gates is *Hush*."
Lady Louisa Stuart Anecdotes of Lady
Mary Wortley Montagu.

Mr Lee said "Miss F. remembers; it is very ill bred to remember."

Nothing is more carefully secured in our constitution than that we shall not systematize or integrate too fast. Carry it how we will, always something refuses to be subordinated & to drill. It will not toe the line. The facts of Animal Magnetism are now extravagant. We can make nothing of them. What then? Why, own that you are a tyro. We make a dear little cosmogony of our own that makes the world & tucks in all nations like cherries into a tart, & 'tis all finished & rounded into compass & shape, but unluckily we find that it will not explain the existence of the African Race.

It was the happiest turn to my old thrum which Charles H Warren gave as a toast at the ΦBK Dinner. "Mr President," he said, "I suppose all know where the orator comes from; and I suppose all know what he has said. I give you *The Spirit of Concord. It makes us all of One Mind*."

That a man appears scornful & claims to belong to another age & race is only affirmation of weakness. A true man belongs to no other time or place but is the centre of things. He measures you & all men & all events. You are constrained to accept his standard.

Lidian's Aunt Sarah Cotton when washing clothes with her sisters was addressed by her father who passed thro' the kitchen "Girls, who that saw you now would think you the descendants of Robert Bruce?" "Father," said she, "if I knew in which of my veins his blood flowed, I would instantly let it out into the washtub."

20 Sept. I read this morning some lines written by Mr Allston to Mrs Jameson, on the Diary of the Ennuyée, very good & entirely self-taught, original—not conventional. And always we hear a sublime admonition in any such line. But the verses celebrate Italy not as it is, but as it is imagined. *That* Earth fills her lap with pleasures not her own, but supplied from self-deceived imaginations.

—

21 September. The autumnal equinox comes with sparkling stars and thoughtful days. I think the principles of the Peace party sublime and that the opposers of this philanthropy do not sufficiently consider the positive side of the spiritualist but only see his negative or abstaining side. But if a nation of men is exalted to that height of morals as to refuse to fight & choose rather to suffer loss of goods & loss of life than to use violence, they must be not helpless but most effective and great men; they would overawe their invader, & make him ridiculous; they would communicate the contagion of their virtue & inoculate all mankind.

—

September 23. I wrote long since thus.—When phrenology came, men listened with alarm to the adept who seemed to insinuate with knowing look that they had let out their Secret, that, maugre themselves, he was reading them to the bone & marrow. They were presently comforted by learning that their human incognito would be indulged to them a short time longer, until the artists had settled what allowance was to be made for temperament, & what for counteracting organs, which trifling circumstances hindered the most exact observation from being of any value.

*

28 Sept. I hope New England will come to boast itself in being a nation of servants, & leave to the planters the misery of being a nation of served.

30 September. The child delights in shadows on the wall. The child prattles in the house, but if you carry him out of doors, he is overpowered by the light & extent of natural objects & is silent. But there was never child so lovely but his mother was glad to get him asleep.

30 Sept. I get no further than my old doctrine that the Whole is in each man, & that a man may if he will as truly & fully illustrate the laws of Nature in his own experience as in the History of Rome or Palestine or England. A great deal of pregnant business is done daily before our eyes, of which we take very little note. Sift, for instance, what people say in reference to property, when the character of any man is considered. It will appear that it is an essential element to our knowledge of the man what was his opinion, practice, & success, in regard to the institution of property. It tells a great deal of his spiritual history, this part. He was no whole man until he knew how to earn a blameless livelihood. Society is barbarous until every industrious man can get his living without dishonest customs. When Eli Robbins insists that rules of trade apply to clergy as well as shopkeepers, he means no insult but a recognition only that there is a just law of humanity now hid under the canting of society.

—

The young man relying on his instincts who has only a good intention is apt to feel ashamed of his inaction & the slightness of his virtue when in the presence of the active & zealous leaders of the philanthropic enterprizes of Universal Temperance, Peace, & Abolition of Slavery. He only loves like Cordelia after his duty. Trust it nevertheless. A man's income is not sufficient for all things. If he spend here, he must save there. If he choose to build a solid hearth, he must postpone painting his house. Let each follow his taste, but let not him that loves fine porticoes & avenues, reprove him that chooses to have all weathertight & solid within. It is a grandeur of character

which must have unity, & reviews & pries ever into its domestic truth & justice, loving quiet honor better than a proclaiming zeal. I think the zealot goes abroad from ignorance of
the riches of his home.

But this good intention which seems so cheap beside this
brave zeal is the backbone of the world: When the trumpeters
& Heralds have been scattered, it is this which must bear the
brunt of the fight. This is the martyrable stuff. Let it, for
God's sake, grow free & wild, under wind under sun to be
solid heart of oak and last forever.

———

Lidian grieves aloud about the wretched negro in the horrors of the middle passage; and they are bad enough. But to
such as she, these crucifixions do not come. They come to the
obtuse & barbarous to whom they are not horrid but only a
little worse than the old sufferings. They exchange a cannibal
war for a stinking hold. They have gratifications which would
be none to Lidian. The grocer never damned L. because she
had not paid her bill; but the good Irish woman has that to
suffer once a month. She in return never feels weakness in her
back because of the slave-trade. The horrors of the middle passage are the wens & ulcers that admonish us that a violation of
nature has preceded. I should not—the nations would not
know of the extremity of the wrong but for the terrors of the
retribution.

———

Progress of the species. Every soul has to learn the whole lesson for itself. It must go over the whole ground. What it does
not see, what it does not live it will not know. What the former
age has epitomized into a formula or rule for manipular convenience, it will lose all the good of verifying for itself by
means of the wall of that Rule. Sometime or other, somewhere
or other, it will demand & find compensation for that loss by
doing the work itself. How then, since each must go over every
line of the ground can there be any progress of the Species?
Ferguson discovered many things which had long been very
well known. The better for him that he did not know.

———

The list of ships' names in the newspaper is worth considering. Like the moon, the sea seems the refuge of things

lost on earth. Fairy, Sylph, Neptune, Britomart, Ivanhoe, Rob
Roy.
                                    —

I wonder at the interest that Animal Magnetism inspires in
fine persons. Not at all that it startles the thoughtless. I feel no
strong interest in it. I do not doubt the wonder, but there is
wonder enough in my thumbnail already. Its phenomena belong to the copious chapter of Demonology under which category I suppose every body's experience might write a few
facts. These obscure facts are only to suggest that our being is
richer than we knew; & we are now only in the fore court or
portico. The hints we have, the dreams, the coincidences, do
make each man stare once or twice in a lifetime. But Animal
Magnetism seems the phenomena of Disease & too fuliginous
& typhoid in their character to attract any but the physician. I
suppose that as the marketplace & the alleys need to be stimulated by the raw head & bloody bones of a murder or piracy
with wood-cuts so our wise cotemporaries are glad to be made
to wonder by something that is wonderful to the *senses*. Animal magnetism is the shovel put under the feet to show how
poor our foundations are.

Laban Turner told me that the musicians of the Brigade
Band are paid six dollars a day, & their expenses, & that some
of them are employed almost every day of the year. Several of
them are men of good estate; & they are not dissipated.

8 October. Last evening, I had a good hour with Mrs Ripley.
The young Southerner comes here a spoiled child with
graceful manners, excellent self command, very good to be
spoiled more, but good for nothing else, a mere parader. He
has conversed so much with rifles, horses, & dogs that he is
become himself a rifle, a horse, & a dog and in civil educated
company where anything human is going forward he is dumb
& unhappy; like an Indian in a church. Treat them with great
deference as we often do, and they accept it all as their due
without misgiving. Give them an inch & they take a mile.
They are mere bladders of conceit. Each snippersnapper of
them all undertakes to speak for the entire Southern states.
"At the South, the reputation of Cambridge" &c. &c. which
being interpreted, is, In my negro village of Tuscaloosa or

Cheraw or St Marks I supposed so & so. "We, at the South,"
forsooth. They are more civilized than the Seminoles, however, in my opinion; a little more. Their question respecting
any man is like a Seminole's, How can he fight? In this country, we ask, What can he do? His pugnacity is all they prize, in
man, dog, or turkey. The proper way of treating them is not
deference but to say as Mr Ripley does "Fiddle faddle" in answer to each solemn remark about "The South." "It must be
confessed" said the young man, "that in Alabama, we are dead
to every thing, as respects politics." "Very true," replied Mr
Ripley, "leaving out the last clause."

I scarce ever see young women who are not remarkably
attractive without a wish an impulse to preach to them the
doctrine of character. I have sad foresight of the mortifications
that await them when I see what they look on. Could once
their eye be turned on the beauty of being as it outshines the
beauty of seeming, they would be saved.

When C.C E was newly engaged Aug 1833 he writes to E.H.
Do you know there seems to me a rose light shed on the very
pages of my law-books.

How is a man wise? by the perception of a principle.
The immortality is as legitimately preached from the intel-
lections as from the moral volitions. Every intellection is
prospective. Its present value is its least. It is a little seed. Each
principle that a man acquires is a lanthorn which he instantly
turns full on what facts & thoughts lay already in his mind and
instantly all the rubbish that had littered his garret becomes
precious. Every old & trivial fact in his private biography
becomes illustration of this new principle & is recalled into day
& delights all men by its piquancy & new charm. Men say
where did he get this? & think there was something divine in
his life. But no; they have myriads of facts just as good, would
they only get a lamp to ransack their attics withal.

Insist that the Schelling, Schleiermacher, Ackermann or
whoever propounds to you an Ontology, is only a more or less
awkward translator of entities in your consciousness which you

have also, your own way of seeing, perhaps of denominating. Say then, instead of too timidly pouring into his obscure sense that he has not succeeded in rendering back to you your consciousness: he has not succeeded, now let another try. If Spinosa cannot, perhaps Kant will: If Kant cannot, then perhaps Alcott. Any how, when at last it is done, you will find it no recondite but a simple common state which the writer restores to you.

—

October 12. I learn from the Westminster Review (July 1837) that the French make better gloves than the English because they have a better knowledge of the shape of the hand. That they also are never guilty of the inaccuracy of printing with a flower on silks or papers, leaves not belonging to that flower, as the English are. Also that the most beautiful scroll ornaments & indeed designs of every kind on a Cashmere shawl, on all upholstery, & furniture may be traced to the walls of Egyptian palaces & tombs whence first the Greeks borrowed them.

—

October 13. With much to say I put off writing until perhaps I shall have nothing in my memory. Now too soon then too late. I must try the pen & make a beginning.
At Boston Thursday I found myself nearly alone in the Athenaeum & so dropt my book to gaze at the Laocoon. The main figure is great: the two youths work harmoniously on the eye producing great admiration, so long as the eye is directed at the old man, but look at them & they are slight & unaffecting statues. No miniature copy and no single busts can do justice to this work. Its mass & its integrity are essential. At the Athenaeum, you cannot see it unless the room is nearly empty. For you must stand at the distance of nearly the whole hall to see it and interposing bystanders eclipse the statue. How is time abolished by the delight I have in this old work and without a name I receive it as a gift from the Universal Mind.

Then I read with great content the August number of the Asiatic Journal. Herein is always the piquancy of the meeting of civilization & barbarism. Calcutta or Canton are twilights where Night & Day contend. A very good paper is the Narrative of Lord Napier's mission to China (who arrived at Macao 15 July 1834 and died 11 October.) There stand in close contrast the brief wise English despatches with the mountainous nonsense of the Chinese diplomacy. The "red permit" writ by the vermilion pencil of the emperor, the superafrican ignorance with which England is disdained as out of the bounds of civilization, & her king called "reverently submissive" &c, &c. There is no farce in fiction better than this historical one of John Bull & the Yellow Man: albeit it ends tragically, as Lord Napier died of vexation apparently. I must get that book again.

Then I read an ascent of the Himmaleh mounts and the terror of the cold & the river seen bursting through caves of snow, and the traveller finding all over the desolate mountains bears' dung. Then, a duel: pistols for two and coffee for the survivor. Then an escape from a tiger in a cane-brake.

Then thinking of the trees which draw out of the air their food by their aerial roots the leaves, I mused on the strange versatility of the mind's appetite & food. Here were in the Reading Room some four or five men besides me, feeding on newspapers & Journals, unfolding our being thereby. Secluded from War, from trade, & from tillage, we were making amends to ourselves by devouring the descriptions of these things & atoning for the thinness by the quantity of our fare.

—

Oct. 16. The babe stands alone today for the first time.

—

Knowledge alters every thing & makes every thing fit for use. The vocabulary of two omniscient men would embrace words & images now excluded from all polite conversation. The wise will use the language which once he rejected. Wisdom is free.

Culture inspects our dreams also. The pictures of the night will always bear some proportion to the visions of the day.

I looked over the few books in the young clergyman's study yesterday till I shivered with cold. Priestley; Noyes; Rosenmuller; Joseph Allen, & other Sunday School books; Schleusner; Norton; & the Saturday Night of Taylor; the dirty comfort of the farmer could easily seem preferable to the elegant poverty of the young clergyman.

What a dream our Boston is, and New York will one day be an ancient illustration.

The great poets are content with truth. They use the positive degree. They seem frigid & phlegmatic to those who have been spiced with the frantic passion and violent coloring of the modern Byrons & Hemanses & Shelleys. But it is like taking a walk or drinking cold water, to the simple who read them. Such is Ben Jonson whose Epistles to Wroth & others; & Penshurst & a Masque in Vol 3 of Nature & Prometheus &c I read this morn. I call this their Humanity.

A lovely afternoon and I went to Walden Water & read Goethe on the bank.

In the present moment all the past is ever represented. The strong roots of ancient trees still bind the soil. The Provencal literature is not obsolete for me, for I have Spenser's Faerie Queen to read and all that faded splendor revives again in him for some centuries yet. Nor will Homer or Sophocles let me go though I read them not for they have formed those whom I read. Nor will the Egyptian designer die to me; my chair & tables forget him not.

Time is the principle of levity dissipating solidest things like exhalations. The monasteries of the Middle Ages were builded of timber, brick, & stone, so were the temples of Jove & those of Osiris, yet they dance now before me late come into their globe like words or less.

———

One of the last secrets we learn as scholars is to confide in our own impressions of a book. If Æschylus is that man he is taken for, he has not yet done his office when he has educated the learned of Europe for a thousand years; he is now to approve himself a master of delight to me also. If he cannot do that, all his fame shall avail him nothing. I were a fool not to sacrifice a thousand Aeschyluses to my intellectual integrity.

Skill in writing consists in making every word cover a thing. In the tragedies of Æschylus the thing is tragic and all the fine names of gods & goddesses stand for something in the reader's mind. The human mind is impatient of falsehood & drops all words that do not stand for verities: this by its instinct. Thus the Greeks called Jove, Supreme God, but having traditionally ascribed to him very bad & false actions, they involuntarily made amends to Reason by tying up the hands of so bad a god. He is like a king of England so helpless alone. Prometheus knows one secret which he is obliged to bargain for. He cannot get his own thunders. Minerva keeps the key of them,

> "Of all the Gods I only know the keys
>   That ope the solid doors within whose vaults
>   His thunders sleep."
>   *The Furies* of Aeschylus

A plain confession of the endless inworking of the All. & of its moral aim.

I went thro' the wood to Sleepy Hollow & sat down to hear the harmless roarings of the sunny Southwind. Into the narrow throat of the vale flew dust & leaves from the fields, & straggling leaves mounted & mounted to great heights. The shining boughs of the trees in the sun, the swift sailing clouds, & the warm air made me think a man is a fool to be mean & unhappy when every day is made illustrious by these splendid shows. If Nature relented at all from her transcending laws, if there were any traces in the daily Obituary that the yellow fever spared this doctor or that Sunday School teacher, if any sign were that a "good man" was governing, we should lose all our confidence, the world all its sublimity.

Oct. 19. We demand the sufficient reason for every fact. The Greek marbles amaze us until our knowledge or our reflection has supplied every step from the common human consciousness to such peculiar excellence, as, e.g. a religion asking Statues; Pentelican quarries; the Egyptian arts; the happy climate & presence of perfect naked forms in the games; the unchained imagination now experimenting in a new direction &

so unfettered by any conventions; the unreflecting genius of the people which permitted them to surrender themselves to the instincts of taste.

In skating over thin ice your safety is in your speed and a critical judgment would have checked & so broken the invention of Phidias, & his fellows.

A gothic cathedral affirms that it was done by us and not done by us. Surely it was by Man but we find it not in our man. Then we remember the forest dwellers, the first temples, the adherence to the first type, & the decoration of it as the wealth of the nation increased. The value which is given to wood by carving led to the carving over the whole mountain of stone of a cathedral. When we have gone through this process and added thereto the Catholic Church its Cross, its music, its processions, its Saints' days & image worship, we have, as it were, been the man that made the minster, we have seen how it could & must be, we have the sufficient reason.

So stand we before every public every private work; before an oration of Webster, before a victory of Napoleon; before a martyrdom of Sir Thomas More, of Sidney, of Marmaduke Robinson; before a French Reign of Terror and a Salem hanging of Witches; before a fanatic revival, and the Animal Magnetism in Paris or in Providence. We assume that we in like influence should be like affected & should achieve the like, & we aim to master intellectually the steps & reach the same height or the same degradation that our fellow our proxy has done.

—

A valuable fact is that mutual teaching which went on in Pestalozzi's School at Yverdon where the tutors quitted their chair at the end of an hour to go and become with their scholars a class to receive instruction of another teacher each being thus in turn teacher & pupil. This is natural & wise and every Man is for his hour, or for his minute, my tutor. Can I teach him something? as surely, can he me. The boy in the road of whom I ask my way is my tutor; knows that I do not, & cannot forego his tuition. But this relation is instantly vitiated the moment there is the least affectation. If an old man runs & sits down on the same bench with rosycheeked boys to hear some

formal not real teaching, for the sake of example, he is a fool
for his pains and they may well cry, Go up, thou baldhead go.
"Solus docet qui dat, et discit qui recipit."

I said when I awoke, After some more sleepings & wakings
I shall lie on this mattrass sick; then, dead; and through my
gay entry they will carry these bones. Where shall I be then?
I lifted my head and beheld the spotless orange light of the
morning beaming up from the dark hills into the wide
Universe.

It is well & truly said that proportion is beauty. That no ornament in the details can compensate for want of this, nay that
ornamented details only make disproportion more unsightly;
and that proportion charms us even more perhaps when the
materials are coarse & unadorned.

I see these truths chiefly in that species of architecture which
I study & practice, namely, Rhetoric or the Building of Discourse. Profoundest thoughts, sublime images, dazzling figures are squandered & lost in an immethodical harangue. We
are fatigued, & glad when it is done. We say of the writer, 'Nobody understood him: he does not understand himself.' But
let the same number of thoughts be dealt with by a natural
rhetoric, let the question be asked—What is said? How many
things? Which are they? Count & number them: put together
those that belong together. Now say *what your subject is*, for
now first you know: and now state your inference or perora-
tion in what calm or inflammatory temper you must, and behold! out of the quarry you have erected a temple, soaring in
due gradation, turret over tower to heaven, cheerful with thor-
ough-lights, majestic with strength, desired of all eyes. You
will find the matter less cumbersome, it even seems less when
put in order, and the discourse as fresh & agreeable at the conclusion as at the commencement. Moreover, if a natural order
is obediently followed, the composition will have an abiding
charm to your self as well as to others; you will see that you
were the scribe of a higher wisdom than your own, and it will
remain to you like one of nature's works pleasant & wholesome, & not as our books so often are, a disagreeable remembrance to the author.

A man may find his words mean more than he thought

when he uttered them & be glad to employ them again in a new sense.

October 23. It is very hard to be simple enough to be good.
An Individual is the All subordinated to a Peculium.

Montaigne, Alcott, M.M.E., and I, have written Journals; beside these, I did not last night think of another.

In conversing with a lady it sometimes seems a bitterness & unnecessary wound to insist as I incline to, on this self sufficiency of man. There is no society say I; there can be none. 'Very true but very mournful,' replies my friend; we talk of courses of action. But to women my paths are shut up and the fine women I think of who have had genius & cultivation who have not been wives but muses have something tragic in their lot & I shun to name them. Then I say Despondency bears no fruit. We do nothing whilst we distrust. It is ignoble also to owe our success to the coaxing & clapping of Society, to be told by the incapable, "That's capital. Do some more." That only is great that is thoroughly so and from the egg, a god.

Therefore I think a woman does herself injustice who likens herself to any historical woman, who thinks because Corinna or De Stael or M.M.E. do not satisfy the imagination and the serene Themis, none can, certainly not she. It needs that she feel that a new woman has a new as yet inviolate problem to solve: perchance the happiest nature that yet has bloomed is hers; let it not be ruined beforehand on despair grounded on their failure; but let the maiden with erect soul walk serenely on her way, accept the hint of each new pleasure she finds, try in turn all the known resources, experiments, pleasures that she may learn from what she cannot as well as what she can do, the power & the charm that—like a new dawn radiating out of the Deep of Space,—her new born being is.

Tears are never far from a woman's eye. The loveliest maiden on whom every grace sits, who is followed by all eyes, & never knew anything but admiration weeps much and if unexpected changes should blast her hopes then the tears fall so naturally as nothing but grief seems her native element.

—

October 24. I find in town the Φ.B.K. Oration, of which 500 copies were printed, all sold, in just one month.

The habitual attitude of the wise mind must be Adoration.

—

Iron if kept at the ironmonger's, will rust. Beer if not made in right state of the atmosphere will sour. Timber of ships will rot at sea, or if laid up high & dry, will strain, warp, & dry rot. Money if kept by us yields no rent & is liable to risk of loss; if invested, is liable to the depreciation of the particular kind of stock into which it is exchanged. Our New England trade is much of it on the extreme of this prudence. It saves itself by extreme activity. It takes banknotes good, bad, clean, ragged & saves itself by the speed with which it passes them off. Iron cannot rust nor beer sour nor timber rot nor calicoes go out of vogue nor money stocks depreciate in the few swift moments which the Yankee allows any one of them to remain in his possession. In skating over thin ice, our safety is in our speed.

Dr Bartlett has reclaimed a bog at the bottom of his garden ditching & earthing it for $27.08. A quarter of an acre.

When Monti's mother removed to Majano where the charitable habits of the family were unknown she complained in a sort of alarm that they were no longer visited by the poor.

How short is the distance from the two alarms. The ready hand is too frequently put under contribution until the man becomes prudent & refuses to give. Instantly pride, resentment, & inexpectancy hinder all petitioners from asking at his gate. Then the man selfreproached is alarmed on the other side, and saith, the curse of the poor is falling on my roof. This is progress. As it is progress from pride to humility.

—

Montaigne was an unbuttoned sloven.
A.H.E. & writers of his stamp, like Bolingbroke patronise Providence.

Let the air in. The Advertising is one of the signs of our times: the hanging out a showy sign with the hitherto unheard of name of the huckster flourished in letters more gorgeous than ever the name of Pericles or of Jove was writ in. They do wisely who do thus. It is a petty title of nobility. The man is made one of the public in a small way. What he doth is of some more importance; he is more responsible. His gay sign & far flying advertisement hold him at least to decency. So the publishing names of boys who have won school medals illustrates them, & bringing a petty Broad street scuffle into court lets the air in, & purges blind alleys.

October 28. The event of death is always astounding; our philosophy never reaches, never possesses it; we are always at the beginning of our catechism; always the definition is yet to be made, What is Death? I see nothing to help beyond observing what the mind's habit is in regard to that crisis. Simply, I have nothing to do with it. It is nothing to me. After I have made my will & set my house in order, I shall do in the immediate expectation of death the same things I should do without it. But more difficult is it to know the death of another. Mrs Ripley says that her little Sophia told the Mantuamaker this morning that "in heaven she was going to ask Dod to let her sit by Mother, all the time." And if this little darling should die, Mrs R thinks she could not live. So with the expectation of the death of persons who are conveniently situated, who have all they desire, & to whom death is fearful, she looks in vain for a consolation. In us there ought to be remedy. There ought to be, there can be nothing, to which the soul is called, to which the soul is not equal. And I suppose that the roots of my relation to every individual are in my own constitution & not less the causes of his disappearance from me.

Why should we lie so? A question is asked of the Understanding which lies in the province of the Reason and we foolishly try to make an answer. Our constructiveness overpowers our love of truth. How noble is it when the mourner looks for comfort in your face to give only sympathy & confession; confession that it is great grief & the greater because the apprehension of its nature still loiters.

Who set you up for Professor of omniscience? & cicerone to the Universe? Why teach? Learn rather.

When the conversation soars to principles, Unitarianism is boyish.

Nov. 2. I learn from my wise masters that Art does not love imitation, does not propose to make grapes that birds will peck, nor a cow that the gadfly will alight upon, but proposes to show the Mind of Nature in the work, and is therefore equally or better pleased with miniatures or colossal images, as with the size of life. Myron's Cow, according to Goethe, was so made as entirely to paint to the eye the beautiful instinct of the sucking calf & the sucked cow; and they mispraise it who say the herdman threw a stone at the cow to make her move.

———

Immense curiosity in Boston to see the delegation of the Sacs & Foxes, of the Sioux & the Ioways. I saw the Sacs & Foxes at the Statehouse on Monday,—about 30 in number. Edward Everett addressed them & they replied. One chief said "They had no land to put their words upon, but they were nevertheless true." One chief wore the skin of a buffaloe's head with the horns attached, on his head, others birds with outspread wings. Immense breadth of shoulder & very muscular persons. Our Picts were so savage in their headdress & nakedness that it seemed as if the bears & catamounts had sent a deputation. They danced a war-dance on the Common, in the centre of the greatest crowd ever seen on that area. The Governor cautioned us of the gravity of the tribe & that we should beware of any expression of the ridiculous; and the people all seemed to treat their guests gingerly as the keepers of lions & jaguars do those creatures whose taming is not quite yet trustworthy.

Certainly it is right & natural that the Indian should come & see the civil White man, but this was hardly genuine but a show so we were not parties but spectators.

———

November 6. M.M.E. says, "I hate to be expecting a cat."

So universal ought culture to be as to make no part of a man seem to be made in vain. Yet, I have seen men certainly who did not seem to use their legs, their hips, shoulders, & got the least service out of their eyes. So concentrated to some focal point was their vitality, that the limbs & constitution appeared supernumerary. Much oftener have I seen men whose emotive, whose intellectual, whose moral faculties lay dormant.

Fuller at Providence explained to me his plans, "that he was to keep the school 5 years—income so much; outlay so much; then he should be able to go to Europe; &c, &c." When I repeated all this to Alcott, he expressed chagrin & contempt. For Alcott holds the School in so high regard that he would scorn to exchange it for the Presidency of the United States. The School is his Europe. And this is a just example of the true rule of Choice of Pursuit. You may do nothing to get money which is not worth your doing on its own account. This is the sense of "he that serves at the altar shall live by it." Every vocation is an altar. There must be injury to the constitution from all false, from all half-action. Nor will the plainly expressed wishes of other people be a reason why you should do to oblige them what violates your sense, what breaks your integrity & shows you falsely not the man you are.

They do not know yet what their importunity hinders you from being. Resist their windy requests; give leave to Great Nature to unbind fold after fold, the tough integuments in which your secret character lies, & let it open its proud flower & fruitage to the day, and when they see what costly and hitherto unknown blessing they had well nigh defrauded the world, they will thank you for denying their prayer & will say, we would have used you as a handy tool, Now we worship you as a Redeemer. The difficulty in each particular case is the greater that the recusant himself seldom sees clearly enough what he wants, whither he tends, to be able to justify himself for shoving by gilded invitations & seems to his friends & sometimes to himself a tedious refiner & windy talker.

Here serves however the Spartan in us, the grit, the terror, the indomitable will. Let them denounce, let them laugh, let them scold, let them hint extreme measures & take extreme measures & if it come to that let the best friends you have shut the door in your face. And now under the cold heaven with literal grim poverty to meet as you can is something for a man to do; here is need for your pluck & kings for your competitors.

Poverty is commonly lamentable because there is no soul; the poor are chickenhearted people who desire to save appearances, to eat roast meat & dress in a gentlemanlike manner & be thought to have business in State Street and all the charity & all the sighing of his friends is directed to that end to new paint him. If poverty is merely culinary it is very sad, because it is very helpless. But if his poverty is want of bread to eat & clothes to wear simply because he will not sell his Will, his tastes, his honor for that pottage, & he keeps of course his will, his tastes, & his honor, it is very remediable & nowise lamentable poverty. It is a time, as Burke said, for a man to act in. He is now to convert the warlike part of his nature, always the attractive, always the salient; the almighty part, and which lies in the lukewarm milky dog days of common village life quite stupid, & so leaves common life so unattractive, he is to bring this artillery to bear, he is to "cry Havoc, & let slip the dogs of war." He has now field & hour & judges & is to fight out (with all gods to friend) his just cause with a resolution & address like Alexander's at Arbela. Caesar, Bonaparte, Alexander had not just cause; even Tell, Washington, & Miltiades in the judgment of William Penn & William Ladd had not just cause but he has.

In the common life a man feels hampered & bandaged: he cannot play the hero: there would be affectation in it: he must fight like poor   with his pump head. But if he is once rejected by all patrons & all relatives, is fairly set adrift, why then let him thank his gods that he has sea-room, & use his freedom so as never to lose it again. It is an immense gain if he reckon it well to have no longer false feelings & conventional appearances to consult. A few shillings a day will keep out cold & hunger & he will not need to study long how to get a few shillings a day honestly.

Why yes perhaps he said wisely who said that war is the natural state of man & the nurse of all virtues. I will not say man is to man a wolf, but man should be to man a hero.

———

It is a question of Culture which is best, a fair or a blotted page?

The ultra benevolence of mine Asia reminds me of the pretty fable of the seven cedar birds sitting on the bough who passed the morsel which one had taken from bird to bird with courtesy until it returned again to the first. None cared for the morsel: All are fed with love. Asia makes my gods hers.

Perhaps in the village we have manners to paint which the city life does not know. Here we have Mr S. who is man enough to turn away the butcher who cheats in weight & introduce another butcher into town. The other neighbors could not take such a step. Here is Mr. E. who when the Moderator of the Townmeeting is candidate for representative & so stands in the centre of the box inspecting each vote & each voter dares carry up a vote for the opposite candidate & put it in. There is the hero who will not subscribe to the flag staff or the engine though all say it is mean. There is the man who gives his dollar but refuses to give his name though all other contributors are set down. There is Mr H. who never loses his spirits though always in the minority & though the people behave as bad as if they were drunk, he is just as determined in opposition & just as cheerful as ever. Here is Mr C. who says "Honor bright" & keeps it so. Here is Mr S. who warmly assents to what ever proposition you please to make & Mr M. who roundly tells you he will have nothing to do with the thing. The high people in the village are timid, the low people are bold & nonchalant; negligent too of each other's opposition for they see the amount of it & know its uttermost limits which the more remote proprietor does not. Here too are not to be forgotten our two companies, the Light Infantry & the Artillery who brought up one the Brigade Band & one the Brass Band from Boston, set the musicians side by side under the great tree on the common, & let them play two tunes & jangle & drown each other & presently got the companies into actual hustling & kicking.

To show the force that is in you, (whether you are a philosopher & call it heroism, or are a farmer & call it pluck,) you need not go beyond the tinman's shop or the first corner; nay, the first man you meet who bows to you, may look you in the eye & call it out.

The stealthy Mr E. stealthiest of faces & forms. Here is J. M. not so much a citizen as a part of nature in perfect rapport with the trout in the stream, the bird in the wood or pond side, & the plant in the garden; whatsoever is early or rare or nocturnal; game or agriculture; he knows being awake when others sleep & asleep when others wake. Snipe, pelican, or breed of hogs; or grafting, or cutting; woodcraft; or bees.

"Miracles have ceased." Have they indeed? When? They had not ceased this afternoon when I walked into the wood & got into bright miraculous sunshine in shelter from the roaring wind. Who sees a pine cone or the turpentine exuding from the tree, or a leaf the unit of vegetation fall from its bough as if it said 'The Year is finished,' or hears in the quiet piny glen the Chickadee chirping his cheerful note, or walks along the lofty promontory-like ridges which like natural causeways traverse the morass, or gazes upward at the rushing clouds or downward at a moss or a stone & says to himself 'Miracles have ceased'?

Tell me good friend when this hillock on which your foot stands, swelled from the level of the sphere by volcanic force. Pick up that pebble at your feet, look at its gray sides, its sharp crystal, & tell me what fiery inundation of the world melted the minerals like wax & as if the globe were one glowing crucible gave this stone its shape. There is the truth-speaking pebble itself to affirm to endless ages the thing was so. Tell me where is the manufactory of this air so thin, so blue, so restless which eddies around you, in which your life floats, of which your lungs are but an organ, and which you coin into musical words. I am agitated with curiosity to know the secret of Nature. Why cannot Geology, why cannot Botany speak & tell me what has been, what is, as I run along the forest promontory & ask when it rose like a blister on heated steel? Then I looked up & saw the Sun shining in the vast Sky & heard the wind bellow above & the water glistened in the vale. These were the forces that wrought then & work now. Yes there they grandly speak to all plainly in proportion as we are quick to apprehend.

—

November 8. Yesterday William Channing & J.S. Dwight came here & found me just ready to go to Lowell to read the first Lecture of my Course. As they seemed to be bearers of the right Promethean fire I hated the contretemps. To Lowell also went wife & child. It seems to be worthy to be set down as a general rule of manners, In conversation never intimate that you ever was sick or ever shall be. So few people have dexterity enough to touch this dangerous topic without instantly becoming tedious, that I think the rule ought to stand without loopholes. If the unsavory corruption of lungs & stomach are alluded to, instantaneously change the conversation.

—

Lidian made a very just remark today that certainly she gave clothes, bedding, or money to her sick & poor neighbors lately with the greater confidence because of the written verse, "Give to him that asketh of thee & from him that would borrow of thee turn not thou away." It is true that the inclination to bestow gets edge from the time-honoured text in which it is embodied. As good a commentary as need be on the power of a sentence. As good a commentary on Christianity as is often to be found.

The eyes of men converse as much as their tongues, and the eyes often say one thing, & the tongues, another. A practised man relies always on the language of the first as it is very hard to counterfeit. And to what end all the forms of society, all these meetings & partings, these professions, invitations, courtesies if by them all a man cannot learn something vastly more weighty than the mere formal occasion & pretext of the hour. In every company into which a man goes there is he guaged, there he feels himself tried, assayed, & stamped with his right number. So long as there is about him any thing unreal anything factitious so long he feels unworthy & uneasy & afraid. However plausible & applauded his performance, he feels that he practises a degree of imposition upon men & stands on ticklish terms with them.

Milton's expression of "Music smoothing the raven down of darkness till it smiled" has great beauty. Nothing in nature has the softness of darkness. Ride in the night through a wood, and the overhanging boughs shall become to the eye lumps of darkness and of an unutterable gentleness to the sense.

To talk from the memory is the talk of display & you impress, you shine, & you lose all your time, for you have not had a thought, you have been playing a trick. A forfeit too which this sort of talk has often to pay is the agreeable fact of finding that you have repeated the same series of remarks to the same company before. But talk from the moment & do not shine but lie low in the Lord's power, wait & follow with endeavoring thoughts the incidents of the conversation, & you shall come away wiser than you went. You shall be uplifted into new perceptions.

Nov. 9. Differences. Take any collection of young men as West Point Academy or Harvard College: Do they all one thing? Or will you find one straggling off into remote pastures & to slaughterhouses for bones to make phosphorus with; & one scouring the woods with dog & rifle or down in the marsh for yellowlegs; and one tooting all day on a flute & one forever dressing & trimming himself for a party or a dance; & one with knife & gimlet making traps & boxes; & one with crayons & brushes sketching landscapes & caricatures; & one trading books, pictures, cloaks; & one always declaiming & acting plays where any can be found to listen?

How graceful & lively a spectacle is a squirrel on a bough cracking a nut! how sylvan beautiful a stag bounding through Plymouth Woods! how like a smile of the earth is the first violet we meet in spring! Well, it was meant that I should see these & partake this agreeable emotion. Was it not? And was it not further designed that I should thereby be prompted to ask the relation of these natures to my own, & so the great word Comparative Anatomy has now leaped out of the womb of the Unconscious. I feel a cabinet in my mind unlocked by each of these new interests. Wherever I go, the related objects crowd on my Sense & I explore backward & wonder how the same things looked to me before my attention had been aroused.

Goethe remarks that the face much magnified in a concave mirror, loses its expression.

Rightminded men have recently been called to decide for Abolition.

It is long ere we discover how rich we are. Our history we are sure is quite tame. We have nothing to write, nothing to infer. But our wiser years still run back to the before despised recollections of childhood & always we are fishing up some wonderful article out of that pond. Until by & by we begin to suspect that the foolish biography of the one foolish person we know is in reality nothing less than a miniature paraphrase of the Hundred Volumes of the Universal History.

11 November. In Boston yesterday heard Governor Everett read a Lecture to the Diffusion Society & thence went to Faneuil Hall where Webster presided at the caucus & heard Bell of Tenessee; Graves, & Underwood, of Kentucky; & Hoffmann, of New York. The speaking was slovenly, small, & tiresome, but the crowd exciting & the sound of the cheering extraordinarily fine. Webster said, when Bell ended, that "it was not a festive occasion, yet he would venture to propose a sentiment to the Meeting. The Health of Mr Bell & the Whigs of Tenessee and three times three." Then was heard the splendid voice of 4 or 5 000 men in full cry together. Such voice might well predominate over brute beasts. It was merely a spectacle to me. But the *Genius loci* is more commanding at Faneuil Hall than at any other spot in America. The air is electric. Every man thinks he can speak whilst he hears,—lifted off his feet oftentimes,—the multitude swaying alternately this side & that. In such crowds few old men, mostly young & middle aged, with shining heads & swoln veins. The mob is all the time interlocutor & the bucket goes up & down according to the success of the speaker. The pinched, wedged, elbowed, sweltering multitude as soon as the speaker loses their ear by tameness of his harangue feel all sorely how ill accommodated they are & begin to attend only to themselves & the coarse outcries made all around them. Then they push, resist, swear, & fill the hall with cries of tumult. The speaker stops; the moderator persuades, commands, entreats, "Order"; the speaker gets breath & a new hint & resumes, goes to the right place, his voice alters, vibrates, pierces the private ear of every one, the mob quiets itself somehow, every one being magnetized, & the hall hangs suspended on the lips of one man. A happy deliverance of common sentiments charms them. Never the fineness or depth of the thought but the good saying of the very few & very poor particulars which lie uppermost in every man's mind at the meeting. All appear struck with wonder &

delight at this cheap & mediocre faculty. So rarely is it found.
If the speaker become dull again, instantly our poor wedges
begin to feel their pains & strive & cry.

———

Music. Beethoven sat upon a stile near Vienna one hot summer's day & caught the tone of the choral flies whose hum
filled the air & introduced it with charming effect into his Pastoral Sinfony.

A page which is tedious to me today, tomorrow becomes
precious because I read in a book that it is precious to another
man. This vexes me, that I should be of that infirm temper as
to owe my ebbs & flows of estimation to any thing extrinsic.
Patience and the memory of these humiliations & the calm abstraction which detects at a distance the different depth of successive states of mind & of course the different authority of
these, will gradually invigorate the constitution of the mind to
a more prompt & genuine judgment, so that all men shall say,
There spoke the Truth.

———

The wise man always throws himself on the side of his assailants. It is more his interest than it is theirs to find out his
weak point; it falls from him like a dead skin & he passes on invulnerable.

He is not a skeptic who denies a miracle, who denies both
angel & resurrection, who does not believe in the existence of
such a city as ancient Rome or Thebes, but he is a skeptic & at-
tacks the constitution of human society who does not think it
always an absolute duty to speak the truth; who pretends not
to know how to discriminate between a duty & an inclination;
& who thinks the mind is not itself a perfect measure.

When a zealot comes to me & represents the importance of
this Temperance Reform my hands drop—I have no excuse—I
honor him with shame at my own inaction.
Then a friend of the slave shows me the horrors of Southern
slavery—I cry guilty guilty! Then a philanthropist tells me the
shameful neglect of the Schools by the Citizens. I feel guilty
again.

Then I hear of Byron or Milton who drank soda water & ate a crust whilst others fed fat & I take the confessional anew.

Then I hear that my friend has finished Aristophanes, Plato, Cicero, & Grotius, and I take shame to myself.

Then I hear of the generous Morton who offers a thousand dollars to the cause of Socialism, and I applaud & envy.

Then of a brave man who resists a wrong to the death and I sacrifice anew.

I cannot do all these things but these my shames are illustrious tokens that I have strict relations to them all. None of these causes are foreigners to me. My Universal Nature is thus marked. These accusations are parts of me too. They are not for nothing.

It seems to me that Circumstances of man are historically somewhat better here & now than ever. That more freedom exists for Culture. It will not now run against an axe at the first step. In other places it is not so: the brave Lovejoy has given his breast to the bullet for his part and has died when it was better not to live. He is absolved. There are always men enough ready to die for the silliest punctilio; to die like dogs who fall down under each other's teeth, but I sternly rejoice, that one was found to die for humanity & the rights of free speech & opinion.

———

I do not like to see a sword at man's side. If it threaten man, it threatens me. A company of soldiers is an offensive spectacle.

26 November. How can such a question as the Slave Trade be agitated for forty years by the most enlightened nations of the world without throwing great light on ethics into the general mind? The fury with which the slaveholder & the slavetrader defend every inch of their plunder, of their bloody deck, & howling Auction, only serves as a Trump of Doom to alarum the ear of Mankind, to wake the sleepers, & drag all neutrals to take sides & listen to the argument & to the Verdict which Justice shall finally pronounce. The loathsome details of the kidnapping; of the middle passage; six hundred living bodies sit for thirty days betwixt death & life in a posture of stone & when brought on deck for air cast themselves into the

sea—were these details merely produced to harrow the nerves of the susceptible & humane or for the purpose of engraving the question on the memory that it should not be dodged or obliterated & securing to it the concentration of the whole conscience of Christendom?

The Temperance question is that of no use, a question which rides the conversation of ten thousand circles, of every Lyceum, of every stage coach, of every church meeting, of every county caucus, which divides the whole community as accurately as if one party wore Blue coats & the other Red, which is tacitly present to every bystander in a bar room when liquor is drunk & is tacitly heeded by every visiter at a private table drawing with it all the curious ethics of the Pledge, of the Wine Question, of the equity of the Manufacture & of the Trade.

—

I magnify instincts. I believe that those facts & words & persons which dwell in a man's memory without his being able to say why, remain because they have a relation to him not less real for being as yet unapprehended. They are symbols of value to him as they can interpret parts of his consciousness which he would vainly seek words for in the conventional images of books & other minds. What therefore attracts my attention shall have it, as I will go to the man who knocks at my door, & a thousand persons as worthy go by it, to whom I give no heed.

Dec. 3. Lidian says, it is wicked to go to church Sundays.
Dec. 3. Waldo walks alone.

Whilst meditating on the Ideal, I hear today from the pulpit, "The friendship of the world is enmity with God," which thus translates itself into the language of philosophy; Harmony with the Actual is discord with the Ideal.

—

Dec. 8. The fair girl whom I saw in town expressing so decided & proud choice of influences, so careless of pleasing, so wilful & so lofty a will, inspires the wish to come nearer to & speak to this nobleness: So shall we be ennobled also. I wish to say to her, Never strike sail to any. Come into port greatly, or sail with God the seas. Not in vain you live, for the passing stranger is cheered, refined, & raised by the vision.

"Understanding"

The small man's part in the conversation seems to be to keep by him an ewer containing cold water, and as fast as in different parts of the room a little blaze is generated, he applies a little cold water with his hand to the place.

Sunday. I could not help remarking at church how much humanity was in the preaching of my good Uncle, Mr S. Ripley. The rough farmers had their hands at their eyes repeatedly. But the old hardened sinners, the arid educated men, ministers & others, were dry as stones.

Dec. 9. Truth is our element & life, yet if a man fasten his attention upon a single aspect of truth, & apply himself to that alone for a long time, the truth itself becomes distorted, &, as it were, false. Herein resembling the air which is our natural element & the breath of the nostrils, but if a stream of air be directed upon the body for a time it causes cold, fever, and even death. *The lie of One Idea.*

E. H. made a just remark the other evening about the fair girl I spake of, that among grown up or married women she knew no one who fulfilled the promise of that one. But there were idealizing girls when these women were young. She said she never knew a woman excepting M.M.E. who gave high counsels.

In the sunset against the sky, the stone wall looked like a locket of black beads.

—

Dec. 30. Remarkable weather for these many days past, mild, clear, & in the morning hoar frost. Mercury at noon today 44° in the shade. Jan 5; 9 P.M. mercury 42° 7th Mercury at 52 in shade. So on for seventeen days until 12 Jan.

Napoleon during his coronation, the whole time did nothing but gape.

1838

Jan. 26. All this mild winter, Hygeia & the Muse befriend with the elements the poor driven scribe. Eight lectures have been read on eight fine evenings; and today the mercury stands at 52° (3 o'clock P.M.) in the shade.

Today I send the Oration to press again.

Sleep & dreams. The landscape & scenery of dreams seem not to fit us but like a cloak or coat of some other person to overlap & encumber the wearer. So is the ground, the road, the house in dreams. Too long or too short. & if it served no other purpose would at least show us how accurately Nature fits man awake.

Jan. 27. How much superstition in the learned & the un-learned! All take for granted that a great deal,—nay, almost all—is known & forever settled. That which a man now says he merely throws in as confirmatory of this Corpse or Corpora-tion Universal of Science.

Whilst the fact is, that nothing is known: And every new mind ought to take the attitude of Columbus,—launch out from the ignorant gaping World, & sail west for a new world. Very, very few thoughts in an age. Now; Wordsworth has thought, & more truly Goethe has thought. Both have per-ceived the extreme poverty of literature. But all the rest of the learned were men of talents merely, who had some feat which each could do with words; Moore, Campbell, Scott, Mackin-tosh, Niebuhr; & the rest.

I think too that if there were philosophers, orators, men, to think boldly, there would be no difficulty in carrying with you the mind of any mixed audience. As soon as you become your-self dilated with a thought, you carry men with you as by miraculous uplifting; you lose them by your own want of thought, of which impotence they become instantly aware; simply as long as there is magnetism they are attracted—when there is no magnetism they are not.

Feb. 3. Five days ago came Carlyle's letter & has kept me warm ever since with its affection & praise. It seems his friend John Sterling loves Waldo Emerson also, by reason of reading

the book "Nature." I am quite bewitched maugre all my un-
amiableness with so dainty a relation as a friendship for a
scholar & poet I have never seen, and he Carlyle's friend. I
read his papers immediately in Blackwood & see a thinker if
not a poet. Thought he has & right in every line, but Music he
cares not for. I had certainly supposed that a lover of Carlyle &
of me must needs love rhythm & music of style.

So pleasant a piece of sentiment as this new relation, it does
not seem very probable that any harsh experience will be allowed to disturb. It is not very probable that we shall meet
bodily to put the ætherial web we weave to the test of any
rending or straining. And yet God knows I dare & I will boldly
impawn his temper that he dares meet & cooperate until we
are assayed & proven. I am not a sickly sentimentalist though
the name of a friend warms my heart & makes me feel as a girl,
but must & will have in my companion sense & virtue.

———

You must love me as I am. Do not tell me how much I
should love you. I am content. I find my satisfactions in a calm
considerate reverence measured by the virtues which provoke
it. So love me as I am. When I am virtuous, love me; when I
am vicious, hate me; when I am lukewarm, neither good nor
bad, care not for me.

But do not by your sorrow or your affection solicit me to be
somewhat else than I by nature am.

Love men, and do what you will with them.

Mrs W. lived with my wife as chambermaid & received nine
shillings a week for wages. She boarded her two children with
her sister in the neighborhood for eight shillings. She did not
go to church for six weeks because she said her sister would be
very much hurt if she should go to church without a black
ribbon on account of the death of the sister's little son, and
my wife could not for a week or two find a ribbon to lend her.
The best of it was, Mrs W. is a total stranger in the town of
Concord & not a soul would know whether she wore black
ribbons or spangles, and the sister poor woman is struggling
all the time with sickness & extreme poverty & a sot of a
husband.

11 February. At the "teachers' meeting" last night my good Edmund after disclaiming any wish to difference Jesus from a human mind suddenly seemed to alter his tone & said that Jesus made the world & was the Eternal God. Henry Thoreau merely remarked that "Mr Hosmer had kicked the pail over." I delight much in my young friend, who seems to have as free & erect a mind as any I have ever met. He told as we walked this afternoon a good story about a boy who went to school with him, Wentworth, who resisted the school mistress' command that the children should bow to Dr Heywood & other gentlemen as they went by, and when Dr Heywood stood waiting & cleared his throat with a Hem! Wentworth said, "You need not hem, Doctor; I shan't bow."

16 February. And what can you say for Milton, the king of song in the last ages, Milton the heroic, the continuator of the series of the Bards, the Representative of the Immortal Band with fillet & harp & soul all melody? To me he is associated with my family, with my two glorious dead—Edward & Charles,—whose ear tingled with his melodies—with Charles especially, who I think knew the delight of that man's genius as well or better than any one who ever loved it. It was worth Milton's labor on his poems to give so much clear joy & manly satisfaction to a noble soul in this distant time. Of this I am very sure, that Milton himself would more prize the admiration nay that is almost too strong a word, I may dare to say rather tho' even love of Charles than of any other person who has written about him. For Charles's severe delicate discriminating taste read in Milton what seemed I doubt not rather his own writing than another man's. Charles could not write as he could read and Milton wrote for Charles. My own ear still rings with the diamond sharpness of his poetic recitations of Samson Agonistes—

> "Is this he
> The renowned, the irresistible Samson
> Who tore the lion as the lion tears the kid"
> &c &c

and "the tame villatic fowl"
and "Held up their pearled wrists & took them in."

And so does Milton seem to me a poet who had a majestic ear & an ear for all the delicacies of rhythm   not at all squeamish.

17 February. My good Henry Thoreau made this else solitary afternoon sunny with his simplicity & clear perception. How comic is simplicity in this doubledealing quacking world. Every thing that boy says makes merry with society though nothing can be graver than his meaning. I told him he should write out the history of his College life as Carlyle has his tutoring. We agreed that the seeing the stars through a telescope would be worth all the Astronomical lectures. Then he described Mr Quimby's electrical lecture here & the experiment of the shock & added that "College Corporations are very blind to the fact that that twinge in the elbow is worth all the lecturing."

Tonight I walked under the stars through the snow & stopped & looked at my far sparklers & heard the voice of the wind so slight & pure & deep as if it were the sound of the stars themselves revolving.

How much self reliance it implies to write a true description of anything. For example Wordsworth's picture of skating; that leaning back on your heels & stopping in mid career. So simple a fact no common man would have trusted himself to detach as a thought.

19 February. Solitude is fearsome & heavy hearted. I have never known a man who had so much good accumulated upon him as I have. Reason, health, wife, child, friends, competence, reputation, the power to inspire, & the power to please. Yet leave me alone a few days, & I creep about as if in expectation of a calamity. My mother, my brother are at New York. A little farther,—across the sea,—is my friend Thomas Carlyle. In the islands I have another friend, it seems. I will love you all & be happy in your love. My gentle wife has an angel's heart; & for my boy, his grief is more beautiful than other people's joy. Carlyle too: Ah my friend! I thought as I looked at your book

today which all the brilliant so admire, that you have spoiled it for me. Why, I say, should I read this book? the man himself is mine: he can sit under trees of Paradise & tell me a hundred histories deeper, truer, dearer than this, all the eternal days of God. I shall not tire, I shall not shame him: We shall be children in heart, & men in counsel & in act. The pages which to others look so rich & alluring, to me have a frigid & marrowless air for the warm hand & heart I have an estate in & the living eye of which I can almost discern across the sea some sparkles. I think my affection to that man really incapacitates me from reading his book. In the windy night, in the sordid day, out of banks & bargains & disagreeable business, I espy you, & run to my pleasant thoughts.

23 February. Abel Adams told me that Boyden the late landlord of the Tremont House told him that he made forty five thousand dollars in one year in that establishment and was frightened at his success. Another year he made nearly so much. But it nearly killed him with care & confinement. He kept it eight years.

March 2. "Society," said M.M.E. in speaking of the malignity & meanness of conversation, "Society is like a corpse that purges at the mouth."

March 4. I told Alcott that in the city, Cousin & Jouffroy & the opinion of this & that Doctor showed very large; a fame of the bookstores seemed commanding; but as soon as we got ten miles out of town, in the bushes we whistled at such matters, cared little for Societies, systémes, or bookstores. God & the world return again to mind, sole problem, and we value an observation upon a brass knob, a genuine observation on a button, more than whole Encyclopaedias. It is even so; as I read this new book of Ripley's it looks to me, neat, elegant, accurate as it is, a mere superficiality: in my Jack Cade way of counting by number & weight, counting the things, I find nothing worth in the accomplished Cousin & the mild Jouffroy. The most unexceptionable cleanness, precision, & good sense,—never a slip, never an ignorance, but unluckily, never an inspiration. One page of Milton's poorest tract is worth the whole.

Last night a remembering & remembering talk with Lidian. I went back to the first smile of Ellen on the door stone at Concord. I went back to all that delicious relation to feel as ever how many shades, how much reproach. Strange is it that I can go back to no part of youth, no past relation without shrinking & shrinking. Not Ellen, not Edward, not Charles. Infinite compunctions embitter each of those dear names & all who surrounded them. Ah could I have felt in the presence of the first, as now I feel my own power & hope, & so have offered her in every word & look the heart of a man humble & wise, but resolved to be true & perfect with God, & not as I fear it seemed, the uneasy uncentred joy of one who received in her a good—a lovely good—out of all proportion to his deserts, I might haply have made her days longer & certainly sweeter & at least have recalled her seraph smile without a pang. I console myself with the thought that if Ellen, if Edward, if Charles could have read my entire heart they should have seen nothing but rectitude of purpose & generosity conquering the superficial coldness & prudence. But I ask now why was not I made like all these beatified mates of mine *superficially* generous & noble as well as *internally* so. They never needed to shrink at any remembrance; & I—at so many sad passages that look to me now as if I been blind & mad. Well O God I will try & learn, from this sad memory to be brave & circumspect & true henceforth & weave now a web that will not shrink. This is the thorn in the flesh.

At Church I saw that beautiful child A. P. & my fine natural manly neighbor who bore the bread & wine to the communicants with so clear an eye & excellent face & manners. That was all I saw that looked like God, at church: Let the clergy beware when the well disposed scholar begins to say, 'I cannot go to Church, time is too precious.'
That which was once a circumstance merely—that the best & the worst men in the parish met one day as fellows in one house, the eminent & the plain men,—has come to be a

paramount motive for going to Church,—that one should not shun the one opportunity of equal meeting with all citizens that is left!!! I go to be of one counsel, to own the sentiment of Holiness with Carr & Wright & Buttrick.

Bad to see a row of children looking old.

5 March. Yesterday (Sunday) was a beautiful day, mild, calm, & though the earth is covered with snow, somewheres two feet deep, yet the day & the night moonlit were as good for thought, if the man were rested & peaceful, as any in the year. The meteorology of thought I like to note.

They say of Alcott, & I have sometimes assented, that he is onetoned & hearkens with no interest to books or conversation out of the scope of his one commanding idea. May be so, but very different is his centralism from that of vulgar monomaniacs. For he looks with wise love at all real facts—at street faces, at the broad-shouldered long haired farmer, at the domestic woman, at the kitchen, at the furniture, at the season,—as related to Man, & so on. He can hear the voice which said to George Fox, "That which others trample on, must be thy food."

What shall I answer to these friendly Youths who ask of me an account of Theism & think the views I have expressed of the impersonality of God desolating & ghastly? I say that I cannot find when I explore my own consciousness any truth in saying that God is a Person, but the reverse. I feel that there is some profanation in saying He is personal. To represent him as an individual is to shut him out of my consciousness. He is then but a great man such as the crowd worships. Yet, yet, Cor purgat oratio.

Of the French Eclecticism & what Cousin thinks so conclusive (See G. Ripley's Specimens &c vol 1. p. 45) I would say there is an optical illusion in it. It looks as if they had got all truth in taking all the systems & had nothing to do but to sift & wash & strain, & the gold & diamonds would remain in the last cullinder. But in fact this is not so. For Truth is such a fly-away, such a slyboots, so untransportable & unbarrelable a commodity that it is as bad to catch as light. Shut the shutters never so quick to keep all the light in, 'tis all in vain, 'tis gone before you can say Jack. Well how is it with our philosophy? Translate, collate, distil all the systems, it steads you nothing, for truth will not be compelled in any mechanical manner. But the first observation you make in the sincere act of your nature, though on the veriest trifle may immediately open a new view of nature & of men that like a menstruum shall dissolve all systems in it; shall take up Greece, Rome, Stoicism, Eclecticism, & what not, as mere data & food for analysis and dispose of your world-containing system as a very little unit, (a kissed finger cannot write) Take Cousin's Philosophy. Well this book (if the pretension they make be good) ought to be wisdom's wisdom, & we can hug the volume to our heart & make a bonfire of all the libraries. But here are people who have read it & still survive, nor is it at once perceptible in their future reasonings that they have talked with God face to face. Indeed I have read it myself as I have read any other book. I found in it a few memorable thoughts, for philosophy does not absolutely hinder people from having thoughts, but by no means so many memorable thoughts as I have got out of many another book, say, for example, Montaigne's Essays. A profound thought anywhere classifies all things. A profound thought will lift Olympus. The book of philosophy is only a fact, & no more inspiring fact than another, & no less; but a wise man will never esteem it anything final or transcending. Go & talk with a man of genius & the first word he utters sets all your so called knowledge afloat & at large. Plato, Bacon, & Cousin condescend instantly to be men & mere facts.

I have read with astonishment & unabated curiosity & pleasure Carlyle's Revolution again half through the second volume. I cannot help feeling that he squanders his genius. Why should an imagination such as never rejoiced before the face of God since Shakspear be content to play? Why should he trifle & joke? I cannot see; I cannot praise. It seems to me, he should have writ in such deep earnest that he should have trembled to his fingers' ends with the terror & the beauty of his visions. Is it not true that with all his majestic toleration, his infinite superiority as a man to the flocks of clean & unclean creatures he describes, that yet he takes a point of view somewhat higher than his insight or any human insight can profitably use & maintain, that there is therefore some inequality between his power of painting which is matchless & his power of explaining which satisfies not. Somewhere you must let out all the length of all the reins. There is somewhat real; there is God.

We acquire courage by our success daily & have a daring from experience which we had not from genius. I regret one thing omitted in my late Course of Lectures; that I did not state with distinctness & conspicuously the great error of modern Society in respect to religion & say, You can never come to any peace or power until you put your whole reliance in the moral constitution of man & not at all in a historical Christianity. The Belief in Christianity that now prevails is the Unbelief of men. They will have Christ for a lord & not for a brother. Christ preaches the greatness of Man but we hear only the greatness of Christ.

6 March. Read in Montaigne's chapter on Seneca & Plutarch Vol II p. 624 a very good critique on the Systems & Methods on which I expended my petulance in these pages yesterday. Montaigne is spiced throughout with rebellion as much as Alcott or my young Henry T.

It is a mystery of numbers that in loss & gain, whether of finances or of political majorities, the transfer of one counts not one but two. Well in magnanimities it is not otherwise. I have generous purposes & go on benefitting somebody, wellpleased with myself. Presently I listen to the prudences, & say this person is heedless & ungrateful—I withhold my hand. Instantly the new coldness awakens resentment in the other party & all the feelings that naturally respond to selfishness. I who pleased myself with my generosity & am still the same person find no sort of complacency toward myself in the supposed beneficiary but only hard thoughts. And the difference of cost betwixt munificence & meanness may amount to one dollar fifty three cents.

I like, to be sure, Mrs Hoar's good saying that when that transcendant beggar Ma'am Bliss received the beefsteaks she had sent her, saying, "Yes, you can leave it; Mrs D. has sent me some turkey, but this will do for the cat;" Mrs H. told Elizabeth, that, "it would do her as much good as if she thanked us". Very true & noble, Mrs H! and yet I grudged the dollar & a half paid to my stupid beggar-mannered thankless, Mrs W. because all that I gave to this lump of tallow was so much taken from my friend & brother whom I ought to go labor on day-wages to help.

9 March. There was a simple man grew so suddenly rich that coming one day into his own stately door & hall in a reverie, he felt on his mind the accustomed burden of fear that now he should see a great person, & was making up his mouth to ask firmly if —— was at home, when he bethought himself, Who is ——? who is it I should ask for?, & on second thought, he saw it was his own house, & he was ——.

There was a lady who planted a parlor full of bulbs, & they all came up onions.

We take great pleasure in meeting a cultivated peasant, and think his independence of thought & his power of language surprising, but it is soon tedious to talk with him, for there is no progress in his conversation, no speed, no prompt intelligence, but a steady ox-team portage that you can see from where you stand where it will have got half an hour hence. The scholar is a comfort to your heart for he leaves all the details of the way & will jump with you over a few centuries when we have got into a bog.

———

14 March. Read a lecture on Peace at the Odeon on Monday evening, 12th. Yesterday saw Margaret Fuller and the Tremont Pictures & talked of Carlyle & Cousin & at the soiree saw Bancroft, & Ripley, & Loring, & so had a pleasant Boston visit. Bancroft talked of the foolish Globe Newspaper. It has a circulation of 30 000. & as he said each copy is read by ten persons so that an editorial article is read by 300 000 persons which he pronounced with all deepmouthed elocution. I only told him then I wished they would write better if they wrote

for so many. I ought to have said What utter nonsense to name in *my* ear this *number*, as if that were anything. 3,000 000 such people as can read the Globe with interest are as yet in too crude a state of nonage to deserve any regard. I ought to have expressed a sincere contempt for the Scramble newspaper.

18 March. I was so ungrateful in reading & finishing Carlyle's History yesterday as to say But Philosophes must not write history for me. They know too much. I read some Plutarch or even dull Belknap or Williamson & in their dry dead annals I get thought which they never put there. I hear a voice of great nature through these wooden pipes. But my wise poet sees himself all that I can see of the divine in events & however slightly says that he sees it. So is my subject exhausted & my end as an artist not furthered for do they not say that the highest joy is the creator's not the receiver's?

Yet wiser I have been & am whenever I sit & hear & wiser I am in this reading when my poet soars highest. It is strange how little moral sentence, how few moral sentences there are in literature. They affect us deeper, greatlier than all else. Yet how rare! The whole praise of Wordsworth is based on some ten pages or less of such matter. Herbert's is that; Shakspeare has spoken a little: & Carlyle has uttered both before & again in this book some immortal accents. Thus what is said of De Launay who could not fire the Bastille Magazine; what is said of Danton the realist & of the moral to go & do otherwise issuing from this era; abide in my memory with vital heat.
I have read the second volume of Poems by Tennyson with like delight to that I found in the first & with like criticism. Drenched he is in Shakspeare, born baptised & bred in Shakspear, yet has his own humor & original rhythm, music, & images. How ring his humorsome lines in the ear:

> "In the afternoon they came unto a land
> In which it seemed always afternoon."

The Old year's Death pleases me most. But why I speak of him now is because he had a line or two that looked like the moral strain amaranthine I spake of.

At Church all day but almost tempted to say I would go no more. Men go where they are wont to go else had no soul gone this afternoon. The snowstorm was real, the preacher merely spectral. Vast contrast to look at him & then out of the window. Yet no fault in the good man. Evidently he thought himself a faithful searching preacher, mentioned that he thought so several times; & seemed to be one of that large class, *sincere persons based on shams; sincere persons who are bred & do live in shams.* He had lived in vain. He had no one word intimating that ever he had laughed or wept, was married or enamoured, had been cheated, or voted for, or chagrined. If he had ever lived & acted we were none the wiser for it. It seemed strange they should come to church. It seemed as if their own houses were very unentertaining that they should prefer this thoughtless clamorous young person. I think it shows what I said on the last page to be true, that there is commanding attraction in the moral sentiment that can lend a faint tint of light to such dulness & ignorance as this coming in its place & name. What a cruel injustice it is to moral nature to be thus behooted & behowled, & not a law, not a word of it articulated.

But why do I blame the preachers? What is so rare among men may be rare among preachers: All men are bound to articulate speaking as well as they. I doubt I shall never hear the august laws of morals as I am capable of them. No pronouncer of them shall fill my ear.

Carlyle has too much reason for his insisting so oft on articulate speech as opposed to hysterics. There is but little. Even the few speeches he quotes from his great men in his History after the first or second sentence, do merely verb it. Verbs & not thoughts.

The Church is a good place to study Theism by comparing the things said with your Consciousness.

There is no better subject for effective writing than the Clergy. I ought to sit & think & then write a discourse to the American clergy showing them the ugliness & unprofitableness of theology & churches at this day & the glory & sweetness of the Moral Nature out of whose pale they are almost wholly shut.

Present Realism as the front face. & remind them of the fact that I shrink & wince as soon as the prayers begin & am very glad if my tailor has given me a large velvet collar to my wrapper or cloak, the prayers are so bad. A good subject, because we can see always the good ideal, the noble Ethics of Nature, as contrast to the poverty stricken pulpit. Tell them that a true preacher can always be known by this, that he deals them out his life, life metamorphosed; as Taylor, Webster, Scott, Carlyle do. But of the bad preacher, it could not be told from his sermon, what age of the world he fell in, whether he had a father or a child, whether he was a freeholder or a pauper, whether he was a citizen or a countryman, or any other fact of his biography. But a man's sermon should be rammed with life.

The men I have spoken of above—sincere persons who live in shams, are those who accept another man's consciousness for their own, & are in the state of a son who should always suck at his mother's teat. I think Swedenborg ought so to represent them or still more properly, as permanent embryos which received all their nourishment through the umbilical cord & never arrived at a conscious & independent existence.

Once leave your own knowledge of God, your own sentiment, & take a secondary knowledge as St Paul's, or George Fox's, or Swedenborg's, and you get wider from God with every year this secondary form lasts; & if, as now, eighteen centuries; why, the chasm yawns to that breadth that men can scarcely be convinced there is in them anything divine.

See how easily these old worships of Moses, of Socrates, of Zoroaster, of Jesus, domesticate themselves in my mind. It will be admitted I have great susceptibility to such. Will it not be as easy to say they are other Waldos?

A man comes now into the world a slave, he comes saddled with twenty or forty centuries. Asia has arrearages & Egypt arrearages; not to mention all the subsequent history of Europe & America. But he is not his own man but the hapless bondman of Time with these continents & aeons of prejudice to carry on his back. It is now grown so bad that he cannot carry the mountain any longer & be a man. There must be a Revolution. Let the revolution come & let One come breathing free into the earth to walk by hope alone. It were a new World & perhaps the Ideal would seem possible. But now it seems to me they are cheated out of themselves, & live on another's sleeve.

Astronomy is sedative to the human mind. In skeptical hours, when things go whirling, & we doubt if all is not an extemporary dream: the calm, remote, & secular character of astronomical facts composes us to a sublime peace.

19 March. Yesterday a snowstorm; lying today as in January banks; & the bluebirds have disappeared. If the best people I know, say, A. & B, & C, & L, & S, should meet with highest aims, should meet for worship I think they would say, Come, now let us join in Aspirations to the Soul—How little a portion is known of Him! What needs but lowly utter sincerity? And let us say together what we feel; then, let each if he be so happy as to have any moral sentiment, any moral law to announce, tell it, that we may animate each other's love & courage & hope.

To absolute mind, a person is but a fact, but consciousness is God.

Of the new testament the supreme value is the charm I wrote of yesterday which attaches to moral sentences, to the Veda, to Seneca, to all the Vaticinations, & highest to the Hebrew Muse: But it is true of the N. T. as of them all, that it has no epical integrity. I look for some moral Bard who shall see so far those shining laws that he shall see them come full circle & shall show them for their Beauty & not alone as Good. I call it fragmentary; & aver that the thought which can see their rounding complete grace & the identity of the law of gravitation with purity of heart has not yet come. God send me that Bard, Auspicious Babe be born!

21 March. Last night, George Minot says, he heard in his bed the screaming & squalling of the wild geese flying over between 9 & 10 o'clock. The newspaper notices the same thing. I riding from Framingham at the same hour heard nothing. The collar of my wrapper did shut out Nature.

24 March. The natural motions of the Soul are so much better than the voluntary ones that you will never do yourself justice in dispute. The thought is not then taken hold of by the "right handle", does not show itself proportioned & in its true bearings. It bears extorted, hoarse, & half witness.

I have been led yesterday in to a rambling exculpatory talk on Theism. I say that here we feel at once that we have no language; that words are only auxiliary & not adequate; are suggestions and not copies of our cogitation. I deny Personality to God because it is too little not too much. Life, personal life is faint & cold to the energy of God. For Reason & Love & Beauty, or, that which is all these, is the life of life, the reason of reason, the love of love.

———

March 27. This is one of the chilly white days that deform my spring.

It seems as if we owed to literature certain impressions concerning nature which nature did not justify.

By Latin & English poetry, I was born & bred in an oratorio of praises of nature, flowers, birds, mountains, sun & moon, and now I find I know nothing of any of these fine things, that I have conversed with the merest surface & show of them all; & of their essence or of their history know nothing. Now furthermore I melancholy discover that nobody,—that not these chanting poets themselves know anything sincere of these handsome natures they so commended; that they contented themselves with the passing chirp of a bird or saw his spread wing in the sun as he fluttered by, they saw one morning or two in their lives & listlessly looked at sunsets, & repeated idly these few glimpses in their song. But if I go into the forest, I find all new & undescribed. Nothing has been told me. The screaming of wild geese was never heard; the thin note of the titmouse & his bold ignoring of the bystander; the fall of the flies that patter on the leaves like rain; the angry hiss of

some bird that crepitated at me yesterday. The formation of
turpentine & indeed any vegetation, any animation, any & all,
are alike undescribed. Every man that goes into the wood
seems to be the first man that ever went into a wood. His sensations & his World are new. You really think that nothing new
can be said about morning & evening. And the fact is morning
& evening have not yet begun to be described. When I see
them I am not reminded of these Homeric or Miltonic or Shak-
spearian or Chaucerian pictures, but I feel a pain of an alien
world or I am cheered with the moist, warm, glittering, budding, & melodious hour that takes down the narrow walls of
my soul & extends its life & pulsation to the very horizon.
That is Morning. To cease for a bright hour to be a prisoner of
this sickly body & to become as large as the World.

Somewhere, as I have often said, not only every orator but
every man should let out all the length of all the reins, should
find or make a frank & hearty expression of himself. If G. P. B.
keeps school & in the details of his week loses himself or fails
to communicate himself to the minds of his scholars in his full
stature & proportion as a wise & good man, he does not yet
find his vocation: he must find in that an outlet for his character, so that he may justify himself to their minds for doing
what he does. He must take some trivial exercise or lesson, &
make it liberal. Whatever he knows & thinks, whatever in his
apprehension is worth his doing,—that let him communicate,
or they will never know him & honor him aright. G. B. E. is
more interested in his trees & cabinet of shells than in books;
he has not then given his lesson to his school until he has
shown them the shells & the shrubs.

I thought as I rode to Acton that we all betray God to the
devil, Being to Negation. I know well the value of a sentiment
& of sincerity yet how easily will any fop, any coat-&-boots
draw me to an appearance of sympathy with him & to an air of
patronising the sentiments; the commonest person of condition & fashion affects me more than is right, & I am mute,
passive, & let their world wag; let them make the world, I
being but a block of the same. I ought to go upright & vital &
say the truth in all ways. When the stiff, hard, proud, clenched

Calvinist takes up Abolition & comes to me with his last news from Montserrat; Why should I not say to him, Out upon this nonsense; hush. Go learn to love your infant, your wood-cutter; be good natured & modest; have that gleam of grace & not varnish over your hard uncharitable ambition with this incredible tenderness for black folks a thousand miles off. Why should all small, poor, disappointed bigots be so fierce in this philanthropy as languages, Frenchmen, & the cholera follow the watercourses? Rough & graceless would be such greeting nor indicate much love. Yet do not carry love to affectation & slaver.

Plain it is that our culture is not come, that none are culti-vated. That it could not be said by the traveller—I met in that country one highsouled & prevailing man. Foolish whenever you take the meanness & formality of what thing you do as a lecture, a preaching, a school, a teachers' meeting & do not rather magnify it to be the unwilling spiracle of all your char-acter & aims. Let their ears tingle, let them say, 'we never saw it in this manner.'

———

1 April. Cool or cold windy clear day. The Divinity School youths wished to talk with me concerning theism. I went rather heavyhearted for I always find that my views chill or shock people at the first opening. But the conversation went well & I came away cheered. I told them that the preacher should be a poet smit with love of the harmonies of moral na-ture: and yet look at the Unitarian Association & see if its as-pect is poetic. They all smiled No. A minister nowadays is plainest prose, the prose of prose. He is a Warming-pan, a Night-chair at sick beds & rheumatic souls; and the fire of the minstrel's eye & the vivacity of his word is exchanged for in-tense grumbling enunciation of the Cambridge sort, & for scripture phraseology.

Lidian said as I awoke this morning a lively verse enough of some hymn of Bunyan. There is no fanaticism as long as there is the creative muse. Genius is a character of illimitable free-dom. And as long as I hear one graceful modulation of wit I know the genial soul & do not smell fagots. The Bunyan, the

Boehmen is nearer far to Rabelais & Montaigne than to Bloody Mary & Becket & Inquisitions.

—

23 April. This tragic Cherokee business which we stirred at a meeting in the church yesterday will look to me degrading & injurious do what I can. It is like dead cats around one's neck. It is like School Committees & Sunday School classes & Teachers' meetings & the Warren street chapel & all the other holy hurrahs. I stir in it for the sad reason that no other mortal will move & if I do not, why it is left undone.

The amount of it, be sure, is merely a Scream but sometimes a scream is better than a thesis.

—

Young Eustis slightly said he had not read Bacon except the Apothegms, he had seen those, &c. So pass the Essays that were meat & drink to plodding me in early years over the gay brain of the juniors. Yet is this the right way for a Thinker to speak of them, slightingly—the apothegms,—Yes but after their value has been probed & settled by microscopic loving study then to be able to throw them into due perspective, & sternly refuse them for all our labor & old love any higher place than belongs to them in God & call them apothegms, & pass on—that were well. The glance of the ignorant gentleman has justice in it; and the sincere knowledge of the scholar has disproportion in it.

April 24. This cold, dreary, desponding weather seems to threaten the farmer who sourly follows his plough or drops pea seed in the garden. I like to think that instinct, impulse would carry on the world, that nature gives hints when to plant & when to stick poles & when to gather. But the turning out of the farmers in this November sky with coats & mittens to spring work, seems to show that calculation as well as instinct must be or that calculation must contravene instinct. Yesterday Peter Howe planted pease for me, & the garden was ploughed the 21st. Lidian says that when she gives any new direction in the kitchen she feels like a boy who throws a stone & runs.

26 April. The "Sirius" & the "Great Western," Steam packets, have arrived at New York from England, and so England is a thousand or 1500 miles nearer than it was to me, & to all.

Yesterday went the letter to V. B. a letter hated of me. A deliverance that does not deliver the soul. What I do, be sure, is all that concerns my majesty & not what men great or small think of it. Yet I accept the Dartmouth college invitation to speak to the boys with great delight. I write my journal, I read my lecture with joy—but this stirring in the philanthropic mud, gives me no peace. I will let the republic alone until the republic comes to me.

I fully sympathise, be sure, with the sentiment I write, but I accept it rather from my friends than dictate it. It is not my impulse to say it & therefore my genius deserts me, no muse befriends, no music of thought or of word accompanies. Bah!

As far as I notice what passes in philanthropic meetings & holy hurrahs, there is very little depth of interest. The speakers warm each other's skin & lubricate each other's tongue & the words flow, & the superlatives thicken, & the lips quiver, & the eyes moisten, & an observer new to such scenes would say, here was true fire; the assembly were all ready to be martyred, & the effect of such a spirit on the community would be irresistible. But they separate & go to the shop, to a dance, to bed, & an hour afterwards they care so little for the matter that on slightest temptation each one would disclaim the meeting. "Yes, he went, but they were for carrying it too far, &c. &c." The lesson is to know that men are superficially very inflammable but that these fervors do not strike down & reach the action & habit of the man.

Yesterday P.M. I went to the Cliff with Henry Thoreau. Warm, pleasant, misty weather which the great mountain amphitheatre seemed to drink in with gladness. A crow's voice filled all the miles of air with sound. A bird's voice, even a piping frog enlivens a solitude & makes world enough for us. At night I went out into the dark & saw a glimmering star & heard a frog & Nature seemed to say Well do not these suffice? Here is a new scene, a new experience. Ponder it, Emerson, &

not like the foolish world hanker after thunders & multitudes
& vast landscapes, the sea or Niagara.

Have I said it before in these pages, then I will say it again,
that it is a curious commentary on society that the expression
of a devout sentiment by any young man who lives in society
strikes me with surprise & has all the air & effect of genius; as
when J. Very spoke of "sin" & of "love" & so on.

In spite of all we can do, every moment is new.
Lidian came into the study this afternoon & found the tower-
let that Wallie had built half an hour before, of two spools, a
card, an awl-case, & a flourbox top—each perpendicularly balanced on the other, & could scarce believe that her boy had
built the pyramid, & then fell into such a fit of affection that
she lay down by the structure & kissed it down, & declared
she could possibly stay no longer with papa, but must go off to
the nursery to see with eyes the lovely creature; & so departed.

30 April. Saturday, Cyrus Warren set out 41 white pines, 2
hemlocks, 1 white maple & 2 apple trees, in my lot.
Yesterday at Waltham. The kindness & genius that blend their
light in the eyes of Mrs. Ripley inspire me with some feeling of
unworthiness at least with impatience of doing so little to deserve so much confidence.
Could not the natural history of the Reason or Universal Sentiment be written? One trait would be that all that is alive &
genial in thought must come out of that. Here is friend B. F.
grinds & grinds in the mill of a truism & nothing comes out
but what was put in. But the moment he or I desert the tradition & speak a spontaneous thought, instantly poetry, wit,
hope, virtue, learning, anecdote, all flock to our aid. This topic
were no bad one for the Dartmouth College boys whom I am
to address in July. Let them know how prompt the *limiting*
instinct is in our constitution so that the moment the mind by
one bold leap (an impulse from the Universal) has set itself free
of the old church and of a thousand years of dogma & seen the
light of moral nature, say *with Swedenborg*, on the instant the
defining lockjaw shuts down his fetters & cramps all round us,
& we must needs think in the genius & speak in the phrase-

ology of Swedenborg, & the last slavery is even worse than the first. Even the disciples of the new unnamed or misnamed Transcendentalism that now is, vain of the same, do already dogmatise & rail at such as hold it not, & can not see the worth of the antagonism also. The great common sense (using the word in its higher sense) is the umpire that holds the balance of these kingdoms. We come from the college or the coterie to the village & the farm & find the natural sentiment in the shrewd yet religious farmer, we see the manly beauty in his life, the tenderness (even) of his sense of right & wrong, of wise & silly, & we are ashamed of our pedantries & pitiful Chinese estimates. "Friends, sit low in the Lord's power". Precipitandus est liber spiritus.

It is perfectly legitimate to generalize in the common way & call Jesus a poet & his labor a poem. People very significantly distinguish betwixt Plato a thinker & Jesus a doer, & suppose that the former acts upon a few, the latter (through the difference of doing) upon millions & all history. The difference is in the thought still. The moral sentiment affects men omnipotently & instantly raises the receiving mind to the level of the supernatural & miraculous and it has upon all receivers abiding effect. Jesus taught that. But he was in love with his thought & quitted all for it. Any mind that *thought so* would have *acted so*. He must live somehow & his life can be discerned through the fragmentary & distorted story to have been just the life of a soul enamoured of moral truth. The difference betwixt the thinker & doer when it appears is that of the man of talents & of genius.

———

The advantage of the Napoleon temperament, impassive, unimpressible by others, is a signal convenience over this other tender one which every aunt & every gossipping girl can daunt & tether. This weakness be sure is merely cutaneous, & the sufferer gets his revenge by the sharpened observation that belongs to such sympathetic fibre. As even in college I was already content to be "*screwed*" in the recitation room, if, on my return, I could accurately paint the fact in my youthful Journal.

———

May 1. I sat in sunshine this P.M. beside my little pond in the woods & thought how wide are my works & my plays from those of the great men I read of or think of. And yet the solution of Napoleon whose life I have been reading, lies in my feelings & fancies as I loiter by this rippling water. I am curious concerning his day. What filled it? the crowded orders, the stern determinations, the manifold etiquette? The soul answers. Behold his day! In the sighing of these woods, in the quiet of these gray fields, in the cool breeze that sings out of those northwestern mountains, in the workmen, the boys, the girls you meet, in the hopes of the morning, the ennui of noon, & sauntering of the afternoon, in the disquieting comparisons, in the regrets at want of vigor, in the great idea & the puny execution, behold Napoleon's day; another yet the same; behold Byron's, Webster's, Canning's, Milton's, Scipio's, Pericles's day—Day of all that are born of woman. I am tasting the selfsame life, its sweetness, its greatness, its pain, which I so admire in other men. Do not foolishly ask of the inscrutable obliterated Past, what it cannot tell, the details of that nature, of that Day called Byron, or Burke, but ask it of the Enveloping Now; the more quaintly you inspect its evanescent beauties, its wonderful details, its astounding whole, its spiritual causes, so much the more you master the biography of this hero, & that, & every hero. Be lord of a day through wisdom & justice & you can put up your history books: they can teach you nothing.

———

Beautiful leaping of the squirrel up the long bough of a pine then instantly on to the stem of an oak & on again to another tree. This motion & the motion of a bird is the right perfection for foresters as these creatures are. They taste the forest joy. Man creeps along so slowly through the woods that he is annoyed by all the details & loses the floating exhaling evanescent beauty which these speedy movers find.

May 2. Homer's is the only Epic. How great a deduction do all the rest suffer from the fact of their imitated form. It is especially fatal to poetry, thought's chosen & beloved form,—the encroachment of these traditions.

May 4. Walter Scott says, that, "at night, the kind are savage." The French seem to have somewhat negrofine in their taste.

How much rhodomontade in Napoleon's & Las Cases's conversation. How much about glory & principles that is not glory & that are not principles. Sophomorical—repudiated by the stern English sense. Yet Napoleon now & then speaks with memorable vivacity. He was nicknamed *cent mille hommes.*

How painful to give a gift to any person of sensibility or of equality! It is next worse to receiving one. The new remembrance of either is a scorpion.

To keep a party conveniently small is the trick of our local politics.

May 5. Last night E.H described the apathy from which she suffers. I own I was at a loss to prescribe as I did not sufficiently understand the state of mind she paints. It seems to me as if what we mainly need, is the power of recurring to the sublime at pleasure. And this we possess. If the splendid function of seeing should lose its interest I can still flee to the sanctity of my moral nature & trust, renounce, suffer, bleed.

I complain in my own experience of the feeble influence of thought on life, a ray as pale & ineffectual as that of the sun in our cold & bleak spring. They seem to lie—the actual life, & the intellectual intervals, in parallel lines & never meet. Yet we doubt not they act & react ever, that one is even cause of the other; that one is causal, & one servile, a mere vesture. Yet it takes a great deal of elevation of thought to produce a very little elevation of life. How slowly the highest raptures of the intellect break through the trivial forms of habit. Yet imperceptibly they do. Gradually in long years we bend our living towards our idea. But we serve seven years & twice seven for Rachel. If Mr G that old gander (I owned) should now stop at my gate I should duck to him as to an angel & waste all my time for him &c. &c instead of telling him, as truth seems to require, that his visit & his babble was an impertinence, & bidding him Begone. Just so, when Miss W. & Mrs G. & Miss M. come, I straightway sit glued to my chair all thought, all action, all play departed & paralysed, & acquiesce & become less than they are, instead of nodding slightly to them & treating them like shadows & persisting in the whim of pathos or the whim of fun or the whim of poetry in which they found me & constraining them to accept the law of this higher thought (also theirs) instead of kneeling to their triviality.

I'll tell you what to do. Try to make Humanity lovely unto them.

—

Do not charge me with egotism & presumption. I see with awe the attributes of the farmers & villagers whom you despise. A man saluted me today in a manner which at once stamped him for a theist, a selfrespecting gentleman, a lover of truth & virtue. How venerable are the manners often of the poor.

—

Caricatures are often the truest history of the time for they only express in a pointed unequivocal action what really lies at the bottom of a great many plausible, public, hypocritical Manoeuvres.

The Bivouac or rest without lodging, is a trait of modern war. What are the bivouacs of literature? the Newspaper? & of the social economy?

11 May. Last night the moon rose behind four distinct pine tree tops in the distant woods & the night at ten was so bright that I walked abroad. But the sublime light of night is unsatisfying, provoking, it astonishes but explains not. Its charm floats, dances, disappears, comes & goes, but palls in five minutes after you have left the house. Come out of your warm angular house resounding with few voices into the chill grand instantaneous night, with such a Presence as a full moon in the clouds, & you are struck with poetic wonder. In the instant you leave far behind all human relations, wife, mother, & child, & live only with the savages—water, air, light, carbon, lime, & granite. I think of Kuhleborn. I become a moist cold element. "Nature grows over me." Frogs pipe; waters far off tinkle; dry leaves hiss; grass bends & rustles; & I have died out of the human world & come to feel a strange cold, aqueous, terraqueous, aerial, ethereal sympathy & existence. I sow the sun & moon for seeds.

*

May 12. Baby warbles quite irresistibly as if telling a secret too to all the house, "Mamma ky, Mamma ky!" thus blabbing Mamma's flebile tendencies.

—

A Bird-while.

In a natural chronometer, a Birdwhile may be admitted as one of the metres since the space most of the wild birds will allow you to make your observations on them when they alight near you in the woods, is a pretty equal & familiar measure.

Life & Death are apparitions.

Last night the Teachers' S. S. met here & the theme was Judgment. I affirmed that we were Spirits now incarnated & should always be Spirits incarnated. Our thought is the income of God. I taste therefore of eternity & pronounce of eternal law now & not hereafter. Space & time are but forms of thought. I proceed from God now & ever shall so proceed. Death is but an appearance. Yes & life's circumstances are but an appearance through which the firm virtue of this God-law penetrates & which it moulds. The inertia of matter & of fortune & of our employment is the feebleness of our spirit.

May 17. It is as easy to speak extempore as to be silent. A man sitting silent admires the miracle of free, impassioned, picturesque speech in the man addressing the assembly, a state of being & of power how unlike his own. Presently his own emotion rises to his lips & overflows in speech. He must also rise & say somewhat. Once embarked, once having overcome the novelty of the situation he finds it just as easy & natural to speak, to speak with thoughts, with pictures, with rhythmical balance of sentences—as it was to sit silent for it needs not to do but to suffer; he only adjusts himself to the free spirit which gladly utters itself through him. This is a practical lesson in the doctrine that there is but one Mind. Motion is as easy as rest.

We talked yesterday of Alcott's school. J. S. Dwight thought he should not feel the less certain of the good influence of his teaching on the boys though he never recognised it.—Yes, that is right. The unspoken influence of nature we know is greatest, yet we do not recognize & specify it in the man, & Alcott's aim is to make a spoken teaching that shall blend perfectly therewith.

—

26 May. Nettled again & nervous (as much as sometimes by flatulency or piddling things) by the wretched Sunday's preaching of Mr H. You Cambridge men affect to think it desireable that there should be light in the people. But the elevation of the people by one degree of thought would blow to shreds all this nightmare preaching. How miserable is that which stands only in the wooden ignorance of villages. As the dull man droned & droned & wound his stertorous horn upon the main doctrine of Xty the resurrection, namely, & how little it was remembered in modern preaching, & modern prayers, I could not help thinking that there are two emphases that distinguish the two sorts of teachers: 1. *Human life*. 2. *Thought*. Those who remain fast in the first, respect facts supremely; & thought is but a tool for them. Those who dwell in the second, respect principles;—& facts & persons & themselves they regard only as slovenly unperfect manifestations of these; they care not for Christ, nor for Death, nor for resurrection, except as illustrations.

I found Hedge the other day fully disposed to agree with me in regard to the social position of domestics.

22 May. Dr Jackson once said that the laws of disease were as beautiful as the laws of health. Our good Dr Hurd came to me yesterday before I had yet seen Dr Ripley (yesterday represented as in a dying condition)—with joy sparkling in his eyes. "And how is the Doctor, sir," I said. "I have not seen him today," he replied, "but it is the most correct apoplexy I have ever seen, face & hands livid, breathing sonorous, & all the symptoms perfect" & he rubbed his hands with delight.

The little village newspapers, I observe, stick in regularly every week paragraphs about the value of newspapers, which are true of the great newspapers as the National Gazette or Boston Advertiser but ludicrously untrue of these pert little country sheets. So Wordsworth, for a great man, has a great deal too much to say about what he the poet writes or does.

How noble a trait does Miss Sedgwick draw in her Mrs Hyde, when Lucy Lee says, "It makes people civil to speak to her."

How we glow over these novels! How we drivel & calculate & shuffle & lie & skulk, in life!

Democrat.

"My blood was not ditch water," said Napoleon in allusion to Duc d'Enghien.

In the wood, God was manifest as he was not in the sermon. In the cathedralled larches the ground pine crept him, the thrush sung him, the robin complained him, the catbird mewed him, the anemone vibrated him, the wild apple bloomed him; the ants built their little Timbuctoo wide abroad; the wild grape budded; the rye was in the blade; high overhead, high over cloud the faint sharphorned moon sailed steadily west through fleets of little clouds; the sheafs of the birch brightened into green below. The pines kneaded their aromatics in the sun. All prepared itself for the warm thunderdays of July. Riding with Dwight the other day I saw a broad cloud a quarter of a mile parallel to the horizon quite accurately in the form of the cherub as painted over churches, a round block in the centre which it was easy to animate with eyes & mouth supported on either side by widestretched symmetrical wings. I told D. who pointed it out that undoubtedly it was the archetype of that familiar ornament. In like manner I have myself seen in the sky a thunderbolt which satisfied me that the Greeks drew from nature when they painted that image in the hand of Jove. And I have seen a snowdrift along the wallsides that obviously gave the idea of a common architectural scroll to support a tower.

—

At dinner, today we wickedly roasted the martyrs. I say that nothing is so disgusting in our days as nothing is so dog-cheap as martyrdom. Dr A or Mr M the Messieurs Bookmakers should be requested to prepare a work immediately on the Duties of Martyrs of all sizes & sexes. Q., the Abolitionist, came here to Concord where every third man lectures on Slavery & being welcomed by some gentleman at the church to Concord replied "Yes we that turn the world upside down have come hither also." It reminds one of a sophomore's exclamation during a college rebellion, "Come, Bowers! let us go join these noble fellows." Next worst to the Martyrs are the officers of the philanthropic societies who have just got letters from Antigua & so on. These martyrs are such vermin that it needs to have a man of brawn & of virtue die, to put an end to them. These are dead already, & can as well be stoned or shot as not. But now let a man that is alive, laughing with life, all action, all power, who scorneth death, & who cannot die, let him meet the Axe's edge & thrill them with the conviction of immortality. Slay a gentleman, & put this gibbering rabble of ghosts out of countenance & out of misery forever—martyrs whose skin was never scratched, who have not a hang nail to show.

—

There is somewhat inconvenient & injurious in the position of the Scholar. They whom his thoughts have entertained or in-flamed seek him before yet they have learned the hard condi-tions of thought. They seek him that he may turn his lamp upon the dark riddles whose solution they think is scrawled on the Walls of their being. They find that he is a poor ignorant man in a seamed rusty coat like themselves nowise emitting a continuous stream of light but now & then a jet of luminous thought followed by total darkness, that he cannot make of his infrequent illumination a portable taper to carry whither he would, & explain now this dark riddle, then that Sorrow en-sues. The scholar regrets to damp the hope of ingenuous boys. The boy has lost a star out of his new flaming firmament. Hence the temptation to the scholar to mystify; to hear the question, to sit upon it, to give an answer of words in lieu of the lacking things.

June 6. Every body, I think, has sublime thoughts sometimes. At times they lie parallel with the world or the axes coincide so that you can see through them the great laws. *Then* be of their side. Let your influence be so true & simple as to bring them into these frames.

Another thing: We resent all criticism which denies us any thing that lies in our line of advance. Say that I cannot paint a Transfiguration or build a steamboat, or be a grand marshal, &

I shall not seem to me depreciated. But deny me any quality of metaphysical or literary power, & I am piqued. What does this mean? Why, simply that the soul has assurance by instincts & presentiments of *all* power in the direction of its ray, as well as the special skills it has already got.[*]

Another thing: A man that can speak well belongs to the new era as well as to the old. A revolution is welcome to him & oriental stability is friendly to him. I look with pity upon the young preachers who float into the profession thinking all is safe. But as soon as I hear one of them uttering out of the old velveted tub manly poetic words I see him to be Janus-faced & well to do in past or future.

7 June. I wish a church to worship in, where all the people are better than I am, & not spotted souls. Nothing shows more plainly the bad state of society than the difficulty or impossibility of representing to the mind any fit church or cultus.

Martyrs again

Take care oh ye martyrs! who like St Ursula & her choir, number Eleven Thousand, if of all one of you, one single soul is true take care not to snap in petulance instead of jetting out in spouts of true flame. Reserve your fire. Keep your temper. Render soft answers. Bear & forbear. Do not dream of suffering for ten years yet. Do not let the word *martyrdom* ever escape out of the white fence of your teeth. Be sweet & courtly & merry these many long summers & autumns yet, & husband your strength so that when an authentic inevitable crisis comes, & you are fairly driven to the wall, cornered up in your Utica, you may then at last turn fairly round on the baying dogs, all steel—with all Heaven in your eye & die for love, with all heroes & angels to friend.

———

[*]When I told Alcott, that, I would not criticise his compositions; that it would be as absurd to require them to conform to my way of writing & aiming, as it would be to reject Wordsworth because he was wholly unlike Campbell; that here was a new mind & it was welcome to a new style;—he replied, well pleased, "That is criticism."

It was observed that the Emperor was not fond of setting forward his own merits. "That is" said he, "because with me morality & generosity are not in my mouth but in my nerves. My hand of iron was not at the extremity of my arm, it was immediately connected with my head. I did not receive it from nature; calculation alone has enabled me to employ it."

"What," said he, "is the truth of history? A fable agreed upon."

Concord, June 7, 1838.

I told my friend last night I could think of nothing more deeply satisfactory than to be shut up in a little schooner bound on a voyage of three or four weeks with a man—an entire stranger—of a great & regular mind, of vast resources in his nature. I would not speak to him; I would not look at him; I would eat my supper; I would pack my trunk; I would read the newspaper; I would roll in my berth; so sure should I be of him, so luxuriously should I husband my joys that I should steadily hold back all the time, make no advances, leaving altogether to Fortune for hours, for days, for weeks even, the manner & degrees of intercourse. Yet what a proud peace would soothe the soul to know that heads & points as we lie & welter out at sea, all etiquette impossible, all routine far out of sight, here close by me, was grandeur of mind, grandeur of character; that here was element wherein all I am, & more than I am yet, could bathe & dilate, that here by me was my greater self; he is me, & I am him. Give me, not a thought but a magazine of a man.

8 June. A good deal of character in our abused age. The rights of woman, the antislavery,—temperance,—peace,—health,— and money movements; female speakers, mobs, & martyrs, the paradoxes, the antagonism of old & new, the anomalous church, the daring mysticism & the plain prose, the uneasy relation of domestics, the struggling toward better household arrangements—all indicate life at the heart not yet justly organized at the surface.

A man must have aunts & cousins, must buy carrots & turnips, must have barn & woodshed, must go to market & to the blacksmith's shop, must saunter & sleep & be inferior & silly.

I pleased myself in seeing the pictures brought in her port-folio S.M.F.; Guercino, Piranesi, Leyden, &c. It takes me long to know what to think of them, but I think I find out at last. I am quite confident in my criticism upon that infernal architecture of Piranesi & very delicious it is to me to judge them when at last I begin to see. The difficulty consists in righting one's self before them; in arriving at a quite simple conviction that the sketch appeals to me & coming at a state of perfect equilibrium leaving all allowance to spontaneous criticisms. Fear to judge or desire to judge, alike vitiate the insight. Many good pictures; as much knowledge of the artist & his times as can be; & perfect equilibrium of mind;—are the conditions of right judgment.

In this glorious summer day, I have taken a turn in my woods. How gaily the wind practises his graces there & every tree & all the woods bow with gentlest yet majestic elegance. & the pine shakes out its pollen for the benefit of the next century. There I feel the newness & prerogative of me & of today. I would say to the young scholar: Permit none to invade your mind. Live with God alone. See how the spirit does execute every presentiment in some gigantic fact. What else is Egypt, Greece, Rome, England, France, St Helena; what else are churches, & empires, & literatures? But I must & will have them subordinate & not masters, they shall accept & serve my point of view. If any person has less love of truth & less jealousy to guard his integrity than I have shall he dictate to me? Say to such, you are greatly obliged to them as you are to all the History, to the pyramids, & the Authors, but now are we here, now our day is come, we have been born out of the Eternal silence, & now will we live, live for ourselves & not as the pall-bearers of a funeral but as the upholders & creators of an age & neither Greece nor Rome nor the three kings of Cologne nor the three Unities of Aristotle nor the College of Sorbonne nor the Edinburgh Review is to command any longer. Now we are come & will put our own interpretation on things & more-over our own things for interpretation. Please himself with complaisance who will, for me things must take my scale, not I theirs. I will say with the warlike King, 'God gave me this crown & the whole world shall not take it away.'

June 9. We live in the sun & on the surface a thin, plausible, superficial existence & talk of prophet & priest, reform & revolution. But out of such shallow men as we, however solemn we look, how can greatness ever come? Come now let us go & be dumb. Let us sit with our hand on our mouths, & our mouths in the dust, a long, austere, Pythagorean lustrum. Let us live in corners & do chares & suffer & weep & drudge with eyes & hearts that love the Lord. Any thing that we may pierce deep into the grandeur & secret of our being & so diving bring up out of secular darkness the sublimities of the moral constitution. How contemptible & pernicious to go blazing in epaulettes & uniform of crimson & gold like a midshipman or a negro on a holiday & be a toy for babies & a mere piece of street furniture & foregoing the inestimable prerogative of the russet coat & the privacy of a citizen. Out of love & hatred, out of mortification & torment, out of earnings & borrowings & lending & loss of money, out of sickness & death, out of travelling & courting & worshipping & sinning, out of gardening & voting & watching & fearing, & out of disgrace & contempt—comes our tuition in the serene & beautiful laws. Not out of the empty city fashions of giving & receiving engraved cards of fashionable names, of dining & nocturnal visiting with well drest, mannerly, gentle folks. But Insight comes all ways. I refuse the insinuation that there is no perfect education of the genius but by violent passion.

—

Why do we seek this lurking beauty in skies, in poems, in drawings? Ah because there we are safe, there we neither sicken nor die. I think we fly to Beauty as an asylum from the terrors of finite nature. We are made immortal by this kiss, by the contemplation of beauty. Strange, strange that the door to it should thus perversely be through the prudent, the punctual, the frugal, the careful; & that the adorers of beauty, musicians, painters, Byrons, Shelleys, Keatses, & such like men, should turn themselves out of doors, & out of sympathies, out of themselves. Whilst I behold the holy lights of the June sunset last evening or tonight I am raised instantly & out of fear & out of time, & care not for the knell of this coughing body.— Strange the succession of humors that pass through this human spirit. Sometimes I am the organ of the Holy Ghost & some-times of a vixen petulance. I am a palace of sweet sounds & sights on Sunday morning, I dilate, I am twice a man. I walk with arms akimbo; I soliloquize; I accost the grass & the trees; I feel the blood of the violet, the clover, & the buttercup in my veins & in the afternoon I have not a thought.

I delight in our pretty country church music & to hear that poor slip of a girl without education, without thought, yet show this fine instinct in her singing, so that every note of her song sounds to me like an adventure & a victory in the *ton-welt*, & whilst all the choir beside stay fast by their leader & the bass viol, this angel voice goes choosing, choosing, choosing on & with the precision of genius keeps its faithful road & floods the house with melody.

—

10 June, Noon. Mercurcy 90° in the shade. Rivers of heat, yea, circumambient sea. Welcome as truly as finer & coarser in-fluences to this mystic solitary "purple island" that I am! I cel-ebrate the holy hour at church amid these fine creative deluges of light & heat which evoke so many gentle traits, gentle & bold, in man & woman. Man in summer is Man intensated. See how truly the human history is written out in the faces around you. The silent assembly thus talks very loud. The old farmer like Daniel Wood or David Buttrick carries as it were palpable in his face stone walls, rough woodlots, the meadows & the barnyard; the old Doctor is a gallipot; the bookbinder binds books in his face; & the good landlord mixes liquors yet in motionless pantomime. Beauty, softness, piety, & love come there also in female form & touch the heart. Vices even in slight degree improve the expression. Malice & scorn add to beauty. I see eyes set too near, & limited faces,—faces, I mean, of one marked but invariable expression. I wonder how such wear with the husband. They pique but must tire. I prefer uni-versal faces, countenances of a general humane type which pique less but to which I can always safely return home. I read plainly in these manifold persons the plain prose of life, timid-ity, caution, appetite, old houses, musty smells, stationary ret-rograde faculties *puttering round*, (to borrow Peter Howe's garden phrase,) in paltry routines from January to December.

And I see too, hope, & the far contributions of Europe, Palestine, & Egypt,—(so deep ingrained in American Education)—to the physiognomy of the house.

———

Every man sees his own past days marked with a slime which he does not see in another man's.

Everett has put more stories, sentences, verses, names, in amber for me than any other person.

"A wise Limitation."

Very refreshing it is to me to see Minot: he is a man of no extravagant expectations; of no hypocrisy; of no pretension. He would not have his corn eaten by worms,—he picks them out & kills them, he would have his corn grow, he weeds & hoes every hill; he would keep his cow well, & he feeds & waters her. Means to ends & Minot forever! They say he sleeps in his field. They say he hurts his corn by too much hoeing it.

———

Very pleasant to me were the glimpses I have got of the mind of C. S. who left us today, yet gave me only glimpses. Yet twice she engaged my cold pedantic self into a fine surprise of thought & hope. Today she would know who the geniuses were in history, & how many,—three, four, five, or six; & recognized the relation of Jesus to Shakspear, & lamented the impossibility of conversation in society; that in a dance they talked of miracles & at concerts of spiritualism. I replied that it was true that on certain topics it would not do to talk but for a very short time, then all thought deserted you, you fell into formalism, for it was necessary to think & live all the time & not to reproduce the same proposition. So I recommended crustiness & tartness, & lamented the lack of tart Luthers who know how to say No.

Michel Angelo was reduced to the dilemma of genius when he had procured fresco painters from Florence, to execute his designs in the Sistine Chapel (he not understanding the art) but after he had suffered much mortification from their imperfect & dwarf execution he got into the Chapel early & bolted them all out & scratched out all their picture. The painters came & knocked & complained, but Michel would not hear or relent, & they returned to Florence full of indignation. Thus he greatly *said No*; he could not help it. Then he went to work & *affirmed* all over the wall in grand strokes which are there still.

C.S. said that in society there was no variety of Character; the same person always said the same thing. & this P.M. she inquired whether conscious people were not they in whom the Understanding usurped the action of the Reason?

———

It is the distinction of genius that it is always inconceivable,—once & ever a surprise. Shakspeare we cannot account for, no history, no "life & times" solves the insoluble problem. I cannot slope things to him so as to make him less steep & precipitous; so as to make him one of many, so as to know how I should write the same things. Goethe, I can see, wrote things which I might & should also write, were I a little more favored, a little cleverer man. He does not astonish. But Shakspear, as Coleridge says, is as unlike his cotemporaries as he is unlike us. His style is his own. And so is Genius ever total & not mechanically composable. It stands there a beautiful unapproachable whole like a pinetree or a strawberry—alive, perfect yet inimitable; nor can we find where to lay the first stone, which given, we could build the arch. Phidias or the great Greeks who made the Elgin marble & the Apollo & Laocoon belong to the same exalted category with Shakspeare & Homer. And I imagine that we see somewhat of the same possibility boundless in countrymen & in plain motherwit & unconscious virtue as it flashes out here & there in the corners.

Time is optical. In the best thought, Time is no more & always it is full of illusion. To say that Life is long, is tedious; it is to say that it is in the Constitution that we should wear out every thought, should slowly roll it all round & see it to tediousness before we can be permitted to receive another. But the length of time or the prose of life accuses me. Once or twice I have been a poet, have been caught up on to a very high mountain. Why should I ever forego that privilege?

When I read the North American Review, or the London Quarterly, I seem to hear the snore of the muses, not their waking voice.

I was in a house where tea comes like a loaded wagon very late at night.

Read & think. Study now, & now garden. Go alone, then go abroad. Speculate awhile, then work in the world. Yours affectionately.

A sense of want & ignorance is a fine inuendo by which the great soul makes its enormous claim.

———

The far is holy, the near is economical. Go into the garden sunday morning & you may look across the fields to the distant woods. Monday morning you peep after weeds & bugs. Yet sunday morning you see the near flower with like emotion as the distant hill.

Health We must envy the great spirits their great physique. Goethe & Napoleon & Humboldt & Scott—what tough bodies answered to their unweariable souls! Now is there somewhat annoying & even comic in the fact that man may not sit down in the grass to inspect the wings, antennae, &c of his fellow creature nor yet on the stone wall in the June night to see the racing of the liquid lights in the nearing heavens, because he has consumption in his side, sciatica in his shoulder. Syria in a sensation. The iron hand must have an iron arm.

Alternation: the Bath & the Battle of Pisa as drawn by Michel Angelo, exhibited the extremes of relaxation & strength. We like the girding belt; we like to be dissolved in liberty. When we have seen friends & talked for days until we are turned inside out, then go lie down, then lock the study door; shut the shutters, then welcome falls the imprisoning rain, dear hermitage of nature. Recollect the spirits. Close up the too expanded leaves.

———

E.P.P. brought me yesterday Hawthorne's Footprints on the seashore to read. I complained that there was no inside to it. Alcott & he together would make a man.

The Unbelief of the age is attested by the loud condemnation of trifles. Look at our silly religious papers. Let a minister wear a cane, or a white hat, go to a theatre, or avoid a sunday school, let a school book with a Calvinistic sentence or a sunday schoolbook without one, be heard of, & instantly all the old grannies squeak & gibber & do what they call sounding an alarm, from Bangor to Mobile. Alike nice & squeamish is its ear; you must on no account say "stink" or "damn."

How rich the world is!
Yesterday E. H.'s letter from M.M.E. It was a sort of argument for the immortality of the soul to see such a scripture; for whilst the thing certainly interests, yet is not life long enough to study out the tendency & idea which subterraneously shines, sparkles, & glows in these sybilline leaves. It is a fragment of wisdom & poetry yet now gives me neither; only affirms that it came from these. Almost all souls intimate more of the Divine than they see. And Biography halts between that they were & that they suggested.

This afternoon, the foolishest preaching—which bayed at the moon. Go, hush, old man, whom years have taught no truth. The hardness & ignorance with which the threat that the son of man when he cometh in clouds will be ashamed of A. & B. because they are not members of Concord Church must have suggested to them 'Be it so: then I also will be ashamed of Him.' Such Moabitish darkness, well typified in the perplexity about his glasses, reminded one of the squash-bugs who stupid stare at you when you lift the rotten leaf of the vines.

What is so beautiful as the sobbing of a child, the face all liquid grief as he tries to swallow his vexation?

I feel also how rich the world is, when I read Ben Jonson's Masques or Beaumont & Fletcher; or when I go to the Athenaeum Gallery & see traits of grandeur & beauty which I am yet assured are not by the Masters & were done by I know not who. They were done by The Master.

17 June. A cool damp day, a cool evening, the first interruption we have had to the energy of the heat of the last 8 or 10 days

wherein the mercury has ranged from 70 to 90. When the cool wind blows, the serene muse parts her fragrant locks, & looks forth.

What canst thou say, high daughter of God! to the waiting son of man? What canst thou teach to elevate these low relations, or to interpret them; to fill the day; to dispel the languor & dulness; & bring heaven into the house-door? Ah! say it, & to me.

The pages of Swedenborg to one who does not yet penetrate to the man's thought, are as dull & stifling as a book describing the charlatanry of the freemasons.

18 June. C. S. protests. That is a good deal. In these times you shall find a small number of persons of whom only that can be affirmed that they protest. Yet is it as divine to say no, as to say yes. You say they go too much alone. Yea, but they shun society to the end of finding society. They repudiate the false out of love of the true. Extravagance is a good token. In an Extravagance, there is hope; in Routine, none.

And who would ask that on such a rare soul as is made to see beauty & announce it, the same culture should be applied & the same social demands made as on the crowd. One beholder of beauty is as much wanted as a scribe or a seamstress, o Jack Cade! I think the scholar, the artist must go alone & ask a somewhat dainty culture.

The art of writing consists in putting two things together that are unlike and that belong together like a horse & cart. Then have we somewhat far more goodly & efficient than either.

> "May makes the cheerful sure May breeds & brings
>   new blood
> May marcheth throughout every limb, May makes the
>   merry mood."
>   Richard Edwards
>   b. 1523 d. 1566

Ah my country! In thee is the reasonable hope of mankind not fulfilled. It should be that when all feudal straps & bandages were taken off an unfolding of the Titans had followed & they had laughed & leaped young giants along the continent & ran up the mountains of the West with the errand of Genius & of love. But the utmost thou hast yet produced, is a puny love of beauty in Allston, in Greenough; in Bryant; in Everett; in Channing; in Irving; an imitative love of grace. A vase of fair outline but empty, which whoso seeth may fill with what wit & character is in him but which does not like the charged cloud overflow with terrible beauty & emit lightnings on all beholders. Ah me! the cause is one; the diffidence of Ages in the Soul has crept over thee too, America. No man here believeth in the soul of man but only in some name or person old & departed. Ah me! No man goeth alone, all men go in flocks to this saint or that poet avoiding the God who seeth in secret. They cannot see in secret. They love to be blind in public. They think society wiser than their soul, & know not that one soul, & their soul is wiser than the whole world. See how nations & races flit by on the sea of time & leave no ripple to tell where they floated or sunk, & one good soul shall make the name of Moses or of Zeno or Zoroaster reverend forever. None assayeth the austere ambition to be the Man, the Self of the nation & of nature, but each would be an easy Secondary to some English Literature or Christian Scheme or American government.

—

19 June
Forget the past. Be not the slave of your own past. In your prayer, in your teaching cumber not yourself with solicitude lest you contradict somewhat you have stated in this or that public place. So you worship the dull God Terminus & not the Lord of Lords. But dare rather to quit the platform, plunge into the sublime seas, dive deep, & swim far, so shall you come back with self respect, with new power, with an advanced experience, that shall explain & overlook the old. Trust your emotion. If perchance you say in a metaphysical analysis I cannot concede personality to the Deity, yet when the devout motions of the soul come, yield to them heart & soul if they should clothe God with garments of shape & color.

—

A young lady came here whose face was a blur & gave the eye no repose.

21 June. Have you had doubts? Have you struggled with coldness; with apathy; with selfcontempt that made you pale & thin? George Fox perambulated England in his perplexity. In elegant Cambridge, have you walked a mile in perturbation of the spirit? Yet somehow you must come to the bottom of those doubts or the human soul in its great ebbs & flows asking you for its law will call you, Boy! Life, authentic life, you must have or you can teach nothing. There is more to be learned by the poor passions which have here exercised many a pale boy in the little strife for the college honors in the incommunicable irritations of hope & fear; of success, but still more of defeat; the remorse, the repentance, the resolution, that belong to conscientious youths in the false estimate they are apt to form here of duty & ambition, than there is in all the books of divinity.* I by no means believe in storms. Quite as much as Lord Byron I hate scenes. I think I have not the common degree of sympathy with dark, turbid, mournful, passionate natures, but in compunction, in a keen resentment of violation, in shame for idleness, in shame at standing still, in remorse for meanness, in remorse for wounded affection, in rolling in the dust & crying Unclean! Unclean! when we have debased ourselves to appetite, or undone ourselves with injustice;—I believe, I believe. I honor the retirements of men. I love the flush of hope. I love

Cyrus Warren says, that, "if you do not in hoeing corn, pull up every mite of the pipergrass, it will live till it rains, & then it will grow."

A church is a classification. Say rather a new mind is; Swedenborg is a new classification as Phrenology, as Benthamism,

---

*These trees, though not very old, if they could speak, could tell strange things. They could tell of tears; of the bright remembrance of domestic faces & virtues by young men who had just learned to wander; of homesickness; of piety that came after wine.

as Abolitionism, as Calvinism is; & the neophytes take the same delight in subordinating everything to their new terminology that a girl does who has just learned Botany, in seeing a new earth & new seasons thereby; which she does. But in all the unbalanced minds (& whose is not so?) the classification is idolized, passes for the end, not a speedily exhaustible means, so that the walls of the System blend to their eye in the remote horizon with the walls of the Universe & they cannot think how you aliens have any right to see,—how you can see. It must be that somehow you stole the light from us. They do not yet perceive that the Light, unsystematic, indomitable will break into any pen, even into theirs, & let them chirp awhile & call it their own. If they are honest & do well, presently their neat new pinfold will be wormeaten, will lean, will rot, & vanish, & the Immortal Light all young & joyful million-orbed, million-colored, will beam over the Universe as on the first morning.

They call it Christianity, I call it Consciousness.

Animal Magnetism peeps. If an adept should attempt to put me to sleep by the concentration of his will without my leave, I should feel unusual rights over that person's person & life. Keep away from keyholes. Do not write secrets on the walls of necessaries.

The ox lay down & died in the furrow.

G. Minot told me he gave 310 dollars for his field and Peter Howe gave 140 dollars for his triangle.

Day creeps after day each full of facts—dull, strange, despised things that we cannot enough despise,—call heavy, prosaic, & desart. And presently the aroused intellect finds gold & gems in one of these scorned facts, then finds that the day of facts is a rock of diamonds, that a fact is an Epiphany of God, that on every fact of his life he should rear a temple of wonder, joy, & praise, that in going to eat meat; to buy, or sell; to meet a friend; or thwart an adversary; to communicate a piece of news or buy a book; he celebrates the arrival of an inconceivably remote purpose & law at last on the shores of Being, & into the ripeness & term of Nature. And because nothing chances, but all is locked & wheeled & chained in Law, in these motes & dust he can read the writing of the True Life & of a startling sublimity.

22 June. Splendid summer, abounding in South Wind whose fine haze makes the distant woods look twice as distant; & man & beast & bird & insect see their corn & wine grow in beauty.

—

But you must treat the men & women of one idea, the Abolitionist, the Phrenologist, the Swedenborgian, as insane persons with a continual tenderness & special reference in every remark & action to their known state, which reference presently becomes embarrassing & tedious. "I am tired of fools," said once my sharpwitted Aunt to me with wondrous emphasis.

You admire your Etruscan vase, & with reason. But I have a cup & cover, also, that pleases me as well, to wit, the ocean & the sky.

Sampson Reed

I should like to get at S. R. very well, but entrenched as he is *in another man's mind*, it is not easy. You feel as if you conversed with a spy. He has you at advantages. He is not convertible. The frank & noble responses of a brother man I shall not hear from him. I cannot hope to shake, to convert him. A fine, powerful, imaginative soul that has thus bound itself hand & foot to serve another, is all the more intractable. And you have not the satisfaction of a good deliverance yourself because of the malign influences of this immense arrogancy & subtle bigotry of his church.

Saturday June 23. I hate goodies. I hate goodness that preaches. Goodness that preaches undoes itself. A little electricity of virtue lurks here & there in kitchens & among the obscure—chiefly women, that flashes out occasional light & makes the existence of the thing still credible. But one had as lief curse & swear as be guilty of this odious religion that watches the beef & watches the cider in the pitcher at table, that shuts the mouth hard at any remark it cannot twist nor wrench into a sermon, & preaches as long as itself & its hearer is awake. Goodies make us very bad. We should, if the race should increase, be scarce restrained from calling for bowl & dagger. We will almost sin to spite them. Better indulge yourself, feed fat, drink liquors, than go strait laced for such cattle as these.

24 June. Sunday. Forever the night addresses the imagination & the interrogating soul within or behind all its functions, and now in the summer night which makes the earth more habitable, the more. Strange that forever we do not exhaust the wonder & meaning of these stars, points of light merely, but still they speak & ask & warn, each moment with new mind.

In the garden, the eye watches the flying cloud & Walden woods, but turns from the village. Poor Society! what hast thou done to be the aversion of us all?

———

Alcott has the great merit of being a believer in the soul. I think he has more faith in the Ideal than any man I have known. Hence his welcome influence. A wise woman said to me that he has few thoughts, too few. She could count them all. Well. Books, conversation, discipline will give him more. But what were many thoughts if he had not this distinguishing Faith, which is a palpable proclamation out of the deeps of nature that God yet is? With many thoughts, & without this, he would be only one more of a countless throng of lettered men; but now you cannot spare the fortification that he is.

———

25 June. They said in the French Revolution there was a comte whose ruling passion was the fear of being guillotined. Civil life may show many men whose ruling passion is the fear of being robbed. I woke & watched one night a dull hour on hearing noises, steps below stairs or creaking of windows or doors. But the love of my spoons shall not again hinder me from sleep.

———

June 28. The moon & Jupiter side by side last night stemmed the sea of clouds & plied their voyage in Convoy through the sublime Deep as I walked the old & dusty road. The snow & the enchantment of the moonlight make all landscapes alike

& the road that is so tedious & homely that I never take it by day,—by night is Italy or Palmyra. In these divine pleasures permitted to me of walks in the June night under moon & stars I can put my life as a fact before me & stand aloof from its honor & shame.

Ideal Tendencies

A sentiment takes man by the hand & lifts him up out of the mire of circumstances. 'Make our life romantic', is the cry of boys & girls, or their wish if not their cry. This is the charm of tragedy, of novels, of Arcadia, & the forest of Ardennes. If I die in my bed amidst household friends & doctors & nurses, making my will, I see little joy, no perfume. 'Tis a dull Morgue. But if as in these dainty novellas I can fall struck by an eye-beam of some Cynthia or Pastorella, & this same fair cruel Diana shall come all life & witchcraft into my house of death, then is death dainty & will bear to be looked on, a curled minion, & we will not turn up the nose at him. Don't laugh. I am in earnest. I would verily be surrounded with forms of beauty & new & dainty life.

Sunday, 1 July. In Boston, Friday, 29 June, & rode to Charlestown & afterward to the Cambridge bushes with G.B.E. A beautiful thicket like a mat of South American vegetation; Arcadian ladders did the dead vines of the smilax make; a delicate fruit the pyrus villosus offered; the azalea was in profuse flower, the tupelo tree, & the ilex Canadensis I had never seen before. It seemed not June but August or September. The pines have a growth & twisted appearance that I do not remember elsewhere.

Hamamelis

Asper indentatus   Aralia nudicaulis

Most of the commonplaces spoken in churches every Sunday respecting the Bible & the life of Christ, are grossly superstitious. Would not, for example, would not any person unacquainted with the Bible, always draw from the pulpit the impression that the New Testament unfolded a system? and in the second place that the history of the life & teachings of Jesus were greatly more copious than they are? Do let the new generation speak the truth, & let our grandfathers die. Let go if you please the old notions about responsibility for the souls of your parishioners but do feel that Sunday is their only time for thought & do not defraud them of that, as miserably as two men have me today. Our time is worth too much than that we can go to church twice, until you have something to announce there.

If you rail at bodies of men, at institutions & use vulgar watchwords as Bank; aristocracy; agrarianism; &c, I do not believe you. I can expect no fruit. The true reformer sees that a soul is an infinite & addresses himself to one mind.

Look for a thing in its place and you will find it or tidings of it. The red leaf of the strawberry vines is mistaken for a berry; but go to it & you will find a real berry close by.

We want soul, soul, soul. A popedom of forms, one pulsation of virtue will uplift & vivify. Read Herbert. What Eggs & Ellipses, acrostics forward, backward, & across, could not his liquid genius run into, & be genius still & angelic love? And without soul, the freedom of our Unitarianism here becomes cold, barren, & odious. Nardini

Never compare. God is our name for the last generalization to which we can arrive & of course its sense differs today & tomorrow. But never compare your generalization with your neighbor's. Speak now, & let him hear you go his way. Tomorrow, or next year, let him speak, & answer thou not. So shall you both speak truth & be of one mind; but insist on comparing your two thoughts; or insist on hearing in order of battle, & instantly you are struck with blindness & will grope & stagger like a drunken man.

We think too lowly altogether of the scholar's vocation. To be a good scholar as Englishmen are, to have as much learning as our cotemporaries, to have written a successful book, satisfies us. And we say 'Now Lord we depart in peace!' A true man will think rather, All literature is yet to be written. Thucydides, Plutarch, have only provided materials of Greek history. There are few masters or none. Religion is to be settled on its everlasting foundations in the breast of man. And politics; & philosophy; & letters. As yet there is nothing but tendency & Indication.

I think Tennyson got his inspiration in Gardens & that in this country where there are no gardens his musky verses could not be written. The villa d'Esté is a memorable poem in my life.

—

16 July. The object catches your eye today, & begets in you lively thought & emotion which perchance arrives at expression. Tomorrow, you pass the same object,—it is quite indifferent: you do not see it, although once you have been religious upon it, & seen God through it, as we worship the moon with all the muses at midnight, &, when the day breaks, we do not even see that scanty patch of light that is fading in the west. They who have heard your poetry upon the thing are surprised at your negligence of a thing they have learned from you to respect. Tonight I saw fine trees. Trees look to me like imperfect men. It is the same soul that makes me, which, by a feebler effort arrives at these graceful portraits of life. I think we all feel so. I think we all feel a certain pity in beholding a tree: rooted there, the would-be-Man is beautiful, but patient & helpless. His boughs & long leaves droop & weep his strait imprisonment.

Little Waldo cheers the whole house by his moving calls to the cat, to the birds, to the flies,—"Pussy cat come see Waddow! Liddel Birdy come see Waddo! Pies! pies! come see Waddo!" His mother shows us the two apples that his Grandfather gave him, & which he brought home one in each hand & did not begin to eat till he got nearly home. "See where the dear little Angel has gnawed them. They are worth a barrel of apples that he has not touched."

July 17. In preparing to go to Cambridge with my speech to the young men, day before yesterday, it occurred with force that I had no right to go unless I were equally willing to be prevented from going.

August 6. At Dartmouth College Tuesday 24 July.

Lidian wonders what the phrenologists would pronounce on little Waldo's head. I reply, that, his head pronounces on phrenology. It is bad of poverty that it hangs on, after its lesson is taught. And it has a bad side; Poverty makes pirates. The senses would make things of all persons; of women, for example, or of the poor. The selfishness in the woman which hunts her betrayer, demands money of him, exposes him, swears a child on him, &c. is only the superficial appearance of Soul in her, resisting forevermore conversion into a thing.

As they said that men heard the music of the spheres always & never, so are we drunk with beauty of the whole, & notice no particular.

August 9. In hearing one of Wordsworth's poems read, I feel, as often before, that it has the merit of a just moral perception, but not that of deft poetic execution. How would Milton curl his lip at such slipshod newspaper style. The Rylston Doe might be all improvised. Nothing of Milton, nothing of Marvell, of Herbert, of Dryden, could be. These are such verses as in a just state of culture should be *vers de societé*, such as every gentleman could write, but none would then think of printing, or claiming a Poet's laurel for making. The Pindar, the Shakspear, the Milton, whilst they have the just & open soul, have also the eye to see the dimmest star that glimmers in the Milky Way, the notches of every leaf, the test objects of the microscope, and then the tongue to utter the same things in words that engrave them on all the ears of mankind. The poet demands all gifts & not one or two only. Yet see the frugality of nature. The men of strength & crowded sense run into affectation. The men of Simplicity have no density of meaning.

August 10. If that worthy ancient king in the school books who offered a reward to the inventor of a new pleasure could make his proclamation anew, I should put in for the first prize. I would tell him to write an oration & then *print* it & setting himself diligently to the correction let him strike out a blunder & insert the right word just ere the press falls, & he shall know a new pleasure.

Last Sunday a storm of heat.

Hateful is animal life resembling vegetable, as when a pear-worm is mistaken for a twig of the tree, or a snake for a stick.

Limitation

I told Mr Withington at the Medical Rooms in Hanover that this melancholy show of bones, of distortions & diseases, were one of the limitations which the man must recognize to draw his plan true.

14 August. Sanity is very rare: every man almost & every woman has a dash of madness, & the combinations of society continually detect it. See how many experiments at the perfect man. One thousand million, they say, is the population of the globe. So many experiments then. Well a few times in history a well mixed character transpires. Look in the hundreds of persons that each of us knows. Only a few whom we regard with great complacency, a few sanities.

———

Until History is interesting it is not yet written.

"Naturam expellas furca, tamen usque recurret."

Aug. 15. The sun & the moon are the great formalists.

I woke this morning with saying or thinking in my dream that every truth appealed to a heroic character. This does not seem to hold of mathematical as of ethical science.

The Understanding possesses the World. It fortifies itself in History, in Laws, in Institutions, in Property, in the prejudice of Birth, of Majorities, in Libraries, in Creeds, in Names; Reason, on the other hand, contents himself with animating a clod of clay somewhere for a moment & through a word withering all these to old dry cobwebs.

The little girl comes by with a brimming pail of whortleberries, but the wealth of her pail has passed out of her little body, & she is spent & languid. So is it with the toiling poet who publishes his splendid composition, but the poet is pale & thin.

*

"The columns of Persepolis shoot upwards with a slender yet firm elevation conveying a fit image of the stems of the lotus & palm from which they were probably copied." Heeren, (Persians) Vol. 1 p. 237

17 August. Saw beautiful pictures yesterday. Miss Fuller brought with her a portfolio of S. Ward, containing a chalk sketch of one of Raphael's Sibyls, of Cardinal Bembo, & the Angel in Heliodorus' profanation; and Thorwaldsen's Entry of Alexander, &c, &c. I have said sometimes that it depends little on the object, much on the mood, in art. I have enjoyed more from mediocre pictures casually seen when the mind was in equilibrium, & have reaped a true benefit of the art of painting,—the stimulus of color, the idealizing of common life into this gentle, elegant, unoffending fairy-land of a picture, than from many masterpieces seen with much expectation & tutoring, & so not with equipoise of mind. The mastery of a great picture comes slowly over the mind. If I see a fine picture with other people, I am driven almost into inevitable affectations. The scanty vocabulary of praise is quickly exhausted, & we lose our common sense, & much worse our reason, in our *superlative degrees.* But these pictures I looked at with leisure & with profit. In the antiques I love that grand style—the first noble remove from the Egyptian block-like images, & before yet freedom had become too free. The Phocion, the Aristides, & the like. The dying Gladiator, too, is of an architectural strength. What support of limbs in these works, & what rest therefore for the eye! A head of Julius Caesar suggested instantly "the terror of his beak, the lightning of his eye"—a face of command, & which presupposed legions & hostile nations.

Thorwaldsen is noble & inventive, & his figures are grand & his marchers march, but I see in him all the time the Greeks again & could wish him a modern subject & then an ignorance of Greek sculpture. Beside, it seemed to me that Alexander wanted a divine head.

Raphael's heads seem to show more excellent models in his time than any we have now. His Angel driving out Heliodorus is an ideal. The purity, the unity of the face is such that it is instantly suggested, *here is a vessel of God.* Here is one emptied of individuality. Nothing can be more impersonal. This is no

Gabriel nor Uriel, with passages of private experience, & a
long biography,—but is a dazzling creation of the moment, a
divine Wrath, as the resisted wave bursts into dazzling foam.
Again the expression of the face intimates authority impossible
to dispute. The crest of the angel's helmet is so remarkable,
that, but for the extraordinary energy of the face, it would
draw the eye too much; but the countenance of this god sub-
ordinates it, & we see it not.
The Sybil to whom the Messiah is announced is a noble daring
picture with a radiant eye, & a lovely youthful outline of head,
and admonishes us that there is a higher style of beauty than
we live in sight of. The Persian sybil of Guercino is an intellectual beauty. A. single expression lights the whole picture.
How much a fine picture seems to say. It knows the whole
world. How good an office it performs. What authentic mes-
sengers are these of a wise Soul, which thus stamped its
thought, & sends it out distinct, undecayed, unadulterated, to
me, at the end of centuries, & at the ends of the earth.

Life is a pretty tragedy especially for women. On comes a gay
dame of manners & tone so fine & haughty that all defer to
her as to a countess, & she seems the dictator of society. Sit
down by her, & talk of her own life in earnest, & she is some
stricken soul with care & sorrow at her vitals, & wisdom or
charity cannot see any way of escape for her from remediless
evils. She envies her companion in return, until she also dis-
burdens into her ear the story of *her* misery, as deep & hopeless as her own.

———

If the scholar would be true, instantly his natural & formidable position would appear, he would utter opinions upon all
passing affairs which being seen to be not private but eternal,
would sink like darts into the ear of men & put men in fear.
A Scholar is a selecting principle. He takes only his own out
of the multiplicity that sweeps & circles by him. He is like one
of these booms that are set out from the shore on rivers to
catch drift wood, &c. So in every community where aught
new or good is going on, God sets down one of these Per-
ceivers & Recorders. What he hears is homogeneous ever with
what he announces.

The length of the discourse indicates the distance of thought between the speaker & the hearer. If they were at a perfect understanding in any part, no words would be necessary thereon. If at one in all parts no words would be suffered.

I think myself more a man than some men I know, inasmuch as I see myself to be open to the enjoyment of talents & deeds of other men as they are not. When a talent comes by, which I cannot appreciate & other men can, I instantly am inferior. With all my ears I cannot detect unity or plan in a strain of Beethoven. Here is a man who draws from it a grand delight. So much is he more a man than I.

I noticed in fine pictures that the head subordinated the limbs & gave them all the expression of the face. In poor pictures the limbs & trunk degrade the face. So in women, you shall see one whose bonnet & dress are one thing & the lady herself quite another & wearing withal an expression of meek submission to her bonnet & dress; another whose dress obeys & heightens the expression of her form.

—

21 August. The Address to the Divinity School is published & they are printing the Dartmouth Oration. The correction of these two pieces for the press has cost me no small labor, now nearly ended. There goes a great deal of work into a correct literary paper, though of few pages. Of course, it cannot be overseen & exhausted except by analysis as faithful as this synthesis. But negligence in the author is inexcusable. I know & will know no such thing as haste in composition. All the foregoing hours of a man's life do stretch forth a finger & a pen & inscribe their several line or word into the page he writes today. I remember the impatience Charles expressed of the frolicking youth who had finished his College Oration a fortnight before the day & went about at his ease; remembering the pale boys who worked all the days & weeks of the interval between the appointment & the Exhibition & dreamed by night of the verses & images of the day.

—

25 August. What is more alive among works of art than our plain old wooden church built a century & a quarter ago with the ancient New England spire? I pass it at night & stand & listen to the beats of the clock like heartbeats; not sounding, as E. H. well observed, so much like tickings, as like a step. It is the step of Time. You catch the sound first by looking up at the clock face and then you see this wooden tower rising thus alone, but stable & aged, toward the midnight stars. It has affiance & privilege with them. Not less than the marble cathedral it had its origin in sublime aspirations, in the august religion of man. Not less than those stars to which it points, it begun to be *in the soul.*

———

The Whole History of the negro is tragedy. By what accursed violation did they first exist that they should suffer always? "They are particularly distinguished in the tombs of the kings, usually in such positions as to show that they have just been or are on the point of being executed; & the remembrance that it was customary to sacrifice black people immediately occurs." I think they are more pitiable when rich than when poor. Of what use are riches to them? They never go out without being insulted. Yesterday I saw a family of negroes riding in a coach. How pathetic!
The Negro has been from the earliest times an article of luxury.

One more black line of the negro's history is in Herodotus. Of the Garamantes he says "They are wont to hunt the Troglodyte Ethiopians in four horsed chariots."

———

There is history somewhere worth knowing; as, for example, Whence came the negro? Who were those primeval artists that in each nation converted mountains of earth or stone into forms of architecture or sculpture? What is the genealogy of languages? & When & What is the Genesis of Man?

"A man & his wife," says Menu "constitute but one person; a perfect man consists of himself, his wife, & his son."

28 August. It is very grateful to my feelings to go into a Roman Cathedral, yet I look as my countrymen do at the Roman

priesthood. It is very grateful to me to go into an English Church & hear the liturgy read. Yet nothing would induce me to be the English priest. I find an unpleasant dilemma in this, nearer home. I dislike to be a clergyman & refuse to be one. Yet how rich a music would be to me a holy clergyman in my town. It seems to me he cannot be a man, quite & whole. Yet how plain is the need of one, & how high, yes highest, is the function. Here is Division of labor that I like not. A man must sacrifice his manhood for the social good. Something is wrong, I see not what.

31 August. Yesterday at Φ.Β.Κ. anniversary. Steady, steady. I am convinced that if a man will be a true scholar, he shall have perfect freedom. The young people & the mature hint at odium, & aversion of faces to be presently encountered in society. I say no: I fear it not. No scholar need fear it. For if it be true that he is merely an observer, a dispassionate reporter, no partisan, a singer merely for the love of music, his is a position of perfect immunity: to him no disgusts can attach; he is invulnerable. The vulgar think he would found a sect & would be installed & made much of. He knows better & much prefers his melons & his woods. Society has no bribe for me, neither in politics, nor church, nor college, nor city. My resources are far from exhausted. If they will not hear me lecture, I shall have leisure for my book which wants me. Beside, it is an universal maxim worthy of all acceptation that a man may have that allowance which he takes. Take the place & attitude to which you see your unquestionable right, & all men acquiesce. Who are these murmurers, these haters, these revilers? Men of no knowledge, & therefore no stability. The scholar on the contrary is sure of his point, is fast-rooted, & can securely predict the hour when all this roaring multitude shall roar *for* him. Analyze the chiding opposition & it is made up of such timdities, uncertainties, & no opinions, that it is not worth dispersing.

We came home, E. H. & I, at night from Waltham. The moon & stars & night wind made coolness & tranquillity grateful after the crowd & the festival. E. H. in Lincoln woods said that the woods always looked as if they waited whilst you passed by—waited for you to be gone. But as you draw near

home you descend from the great self abandonment to Nature
& begin to ask What's o'clock? and will Abel be awake? & our
own doors unlocked?

———

I have usually read that a man suffered more from one hard
word than he enjoyed from ten good ones. My own experience does not confirm the saying. The censure (I either know
or fancy) does not hit me; and the praise is very good.

E. H.'s thought, as we rode, that the woods are suspending
their deeds until the wayfarer has passed by, is precisely that
thought which poetry has celebrated in the dance of fairies,
which breaks off on the approach of human feet.

Is it not better to live in Revolution than to live in dead
times? Are we not little & low out of goodnature now, when,
if our companions were noble, or the crisis fit for heroes, we
should be great also?

5 September. How rare is the skill of writing! I detected a certain unusual unity of purpose in the paragraph levelled at me
in the Daily Advertiser, & I now learn it is the old tyrant of the
Cambridge Parnassus himself, Mr Norton, who wrote it. One
cannot compliment the power & culture of his community so
much as to think it holds a hundred writers: but no, if there is
information & tenacity of purpose, what Bacon calls longanimity, it must be instantly traced home to some one known
hand.

———

George P. B. has been here to my great contentment & to
him I have owed the peace & pleasure of two strolls, one to
Walden Water, & one to the river & north meadows. I like the
"abandon" of a saunter with my friend. It is a balsam unparalleled. George says his intellect approves the doctrine of the
Cambridge Address, but his affections do not. I tell him I
would write for his epitaph "Pity 'tis, 'tis true."

I saw a maiden so pure that she exchanged glances only with
the stars.

*

Of proverbs, although the greater part have so the smell of current bank bills that one seems to get the savor of all the marketmen's pockets, & no lady's mouth may they soil, yet are some so beautiful that they may be spoken by fairest lips unblamed; and this is certain,—that they give comfort & encouragement, aid & abetting to daily action. For example. "There are as good fish in the sea as ever came out of it"—is a piece of trust in the riches of Nature & God, which helps all men always. Is it so? Is there another Shakspeare? Is there another Ellen?

Sept. 8. That which is individual & remains individual in my experience is of no value. What is fit to engage me & so engage others permanently, is what has put off its weeds of time & place & personal relation. Therefore all that befals me in the way of criticism & extreme blame & praise drawing me out of equilibrium,—putting me for a time in false position to people, & disallowing the spontaneous sentiments, wastes my time, bereaves me of thoughts, & shuts me up within poor personal considerations. Therefore I hate to be conspicuous for blame or praise. It spoils thought.

Henry Thoreau told a good story of Deacon Parkman, who lived in the house he now occupies, & kept a store close by. He hung out a salt fish for a sign, & it hung so long & grew so hard, black, & deformed, that the deacon forgot what thing it was, & nobody in town knew, but being examined chemically it proved to be salt fish. But duly every morning the deacon hung it on its peg.

—

How is a boy, a girl, the master, the mistress, of society independent, irresponsible,—Gore Ripley, for example, or A. P., or any other, looks out from his corner on such people & facts as pass by; tries, & sentences them on their merits, as good, bad, interesting, silly, eloquent, troublesome. He cumbers himself never about consequences, about interests; he gives an independent genuine verdict. You must court him, he courts not you. But the public man is as it were clapped into jail by his publicity. As soon as he has once spoken or acted with eclat, he is a committed man, watched by the sympathy or the hatred of hundreds, whose affections must now & will enter into his account. There is no Lethe for this. Ah that he could pass again into his neutral godlike independence. Who can lose all pledge thus & having observed, observe again from the same unaffected, unbiassed, unbribable, unterrified corner, must always be formidable, must always engage the poet's & the man's regards.

Teachers' meetings every where are disturbed by the question whether the man is not better who strives with temptation than the man whose virtue is constitutional: also whether any sin can be repented of so as to place the sinner where he had been if he had not sinned at all. In regard to the first, I think we love characters in proportion as they are impulsive & spontaneous. The less a man thinks or knows about his virtues the better I like them. Timoleon's victories are the best victories. When we see as we do see a soul whose acts are all regal, graceful, & pleasant as roses, we must thank God that such things can be & are, & not turn sourly on the angel & say—Peele Dabney is a better man with his grunting resistance to all his native devils. Greatness loves & accepts. The second question is answered by the consideration of the nature of Spirit. It is one & not manifold: when God returns & enters into a man, he does hallow him wholly, & in bringing him one good, brings him all good.

In all conversation between two persons tacit reference is made, as to a third party, to a common nature. That third party or common nature is not *social*; is impersonal; is God.

Sept. 12. Yesterday the Middlesex Association met here with two or three old friends beside. Yet talking this morning in detail with two friends of the proposition often made of a journal to meet the wants of the time, it seemed melancholy as soon as it came to the details. It is strange how painful is the actual world, the painful kingdom of time & place. There dwells care & canker & fear. With thought, with the ideal is immortal hilarity, the rose of joy. All the muses sing: but with names, & persons, & today's interests, is grief. Alcott wants a historical record of conversations holden by you & me & him. I say how joyful rather is some Montaigne's book which is full of fun, poetry, business, divinity, philosophy, anecdote, smut, which dealing of bone & marrow, of cornbarn & flour barrel, of wife, & friend, & valet, of things nearest & next, never names names, or gives you the glooms of a recent date or relation, but hangs there in the heaven of letters, unrelated, untimed, a joy & a sign, an autumnal star.

———

It is easy enough for a firm man who knows the world to brook the rage of the cultivated classes. Their rage is decorous & limitary for they are weak & their rage never very deep. They are timid as being very vulnerable themselves. But when to their feminine rage the indignation of the people is added, when the ignorant & the poor are aroused, when the unintelligent brute force that lies at the bottom of society is made to growl & mow, then it needs more than nerve, it needs the heights of magnanimity & religion to treat it godlike as a trifle of no concernment. Deep calls unto deep & Shallow to Shallow.

To raise yourself above the nonsense of our eleven hundred martyrs a man must know how to estimate a sour face. The by-standers look sourly on him in the public street or the friend's parlour. If this aversation had its origin in contempt & resistance like his own, he might well go home with a sad countenance. But the sour faces of the multitude like their sweet faces have no deep seat, disguise no god, but are put on & put off as the wind blows & a single newspaper directs. Yet it is difficult not to be affected by sour faces. Sympathy is a supporting atmosphere & in it we unfold easily & well. But climb into this thin iced difficult air of Andes of reform, & sympathy leaves you & hatred comes. The state is so new & strange & unpleasing that a man will, maugre all his resolutions, lose his sweetness & his flesh, he will pine & fret.

Animal Spirits

To pack a trunk for a journey is to me one of the most dispiriting employments. Another is to feel a necessity to laugh at fun & jokes which do not amuse you. I went to New Bedford & Mr D. was in a frolicsome mood, got up from supper in the evening, & said, "Come let us have some fun," & went about to tickle his wife & his sisters. I grew grave, & do what I could, I felt that I looked like one appointed to be hanged.

—

I please myself with the thought that my accidental freedom by means of a permanent income is nowise essential to my habits, that my tastes, my direction of thought is so strong that I should do the same things,—should contrive to spend the best of my time in the same way as now, rich or poor. If I did not think so, I should never dare to urge the doctrines of human Culture on young men. The farmer, the laborer, has the extreme satisfaction of seeing that the same livelihood he earns, is within the reach of every man. The lawyer, the author, the singer, has not.

Society seem to have lost all remembrance of the irresponsibility of a writer on human & divine nature. They forget that he is only a reporter, & not at all accountable for the fact he reports. If in the best use of my eyes, I see not something which people say is there, & see somewhat which they do not say is there, instantly they call me to account as if I had unmade or made the things spoken of. They seem to say, society is in conspiracy to maintain such & such propositions: & wo betide you, if you blab. This diffidence of society in authors seems to show that it has very little experience of any true observers,—of any who did not mix up their personality with their record. The Arabs of the desert would not forgive Belzoni with his spy glass for bringing their camp near to him.

Not the fact avails but the use you make of it. People would stare to know on what slight single observations those laws were inferred which wise men promulgate & which society receives later & writes down as canons. A single flute heard out of a village window, a single prevailing strain of a village maid, will teach a susceptible man as much as others learn from the orchestra of the Academy. One book as good as the Bodleian Library.

There must be somewhat unfair in entire literature. For every writer avoids of course to say what all think & say around him. This is his endeavor in every sentence,—to say that which is not thought & said. Because it is *not* said, therefore he says it. Of course that which he skipped, is precisely that which it now concerns us to know. He shunned the things of garish day & gave us the shades. He shunned the obvious & seized the rare & recondite.

I have learned in my own practice to take advantage of the aforesaid otherism that makes other people's bread & butter taste better than our own & books read better elsewhere than at home & now if I cannot read my German book I take it into the wood & there a few sentences have nothing lumpish but the sense is transparent & broad & when I come back I can proceed with better heart. So in travelling, how grateful at taverns is Goethe!

Sept. 16th. Dr R. prays "that the lightning may not lick up our spirits."

Mr Frost said very happily in today's sermon, "We see God in nature as we see the soul of our friend in his countenance."

You must read a great book to know how poor are all books. Shakspear suggests a wealth that beggars his own, & I feel that the splendid works which he has created & which in other hours we extol as a sort of self existent poetry take no stronger hold of real nature than the shadow of a passing traveller on the rock.

———

Sunday Eve. I went at sundown to the top of Dr Ripley's hill & renewed my vows to the Genius of that place. Somewhat of awe, somewhat grand & solemn mingles with the beauty that shines afar around. In the west, where the sun was sinking behind clouds, one pit of splendor lay as in a desert of space,— a deposite of *still light*, not radiant. Then I beheld the river like God's love journeying out of the grey past on into the green future. Yet sweet & native as all those fair impressions on that summit fall on the eye & ear, they are not yet mine. I cannot tell why I should feel myself such a stranger in nature. I am a tangent to their sphere, & do not lie level with this beauty.

And yet the dictate of the hour is to forget all I have mis-learned; to cease from man, & to cast myself again into the vast mould of nature.

It is singular how slight & indescribable are the tokens by which we anticipate the qualities of Sanity, of prudence, of probity, in the countenance of a stranger.

A stranger. We see with a certain degree of terror the new physique of a foreign man; as a Japanese, a New Zealander, a Calabrian. In a new country how should we look at a large Indian moving in the landscape on his own errand. He would be to us as a lion or a wild elephant.

———

Pericles was not yet ready. To keep order, & to give him time, a man of business was in the rostrum mumbling long initial statements of the facts before the people, & the state of Greek affairs. After what seemed a very long time the people grew nervous & noisy, &, at a movement behind him, he sat down. Pericles arose & occupied the rostrum. His voice was like the stroke of a silver shield. A cold mathematical statement warmed by imperceptible degrees into earnest announcements of a heroic soul. He conversed with the people, he told stories, he enumerated names & dates & particulars; he played; he joked, though coldly & reservedly, as it seemed to me; then having thus as it seemed drawn his breath, & made himself master of his place & work, he began to deal out his thoughts to the people: the conclusions of his periods were like far rattling storms. Every word was a ball of fire.

18 September. A stranger: What is the meaning of that? The fork falling sticks upright in the floor and the children say, a stranger is coming. A stranger is expected or announced & an uneasiness betwixt pleasure & pain invades all the hearts of a household. A commended stranger arrives and almost brings fear to the good hearts that would welcome him. The house is dusted; all things fly into their places; the old coat is exchanged for the new; & we must get up a dinner if we can. Of a commended stranger only the good report is told by others, only the good & new is heard by us. He stands to us then for

humanity. The stranger is *What we wish*:—the best possibilities of man. Having thus imagined & clothed him, we instantly enquire how we should stand related in conversation & action to such a man & are uneasy with fear. The same Idea exalts conversation with a stranger. We talk better than we are wont. We have no obstructions. For a long time we can continue a series of sincere, graceful, rich communications drawn from the oldest secretest experience, to a stranger, so that they who sit by of our own kinsfolk & acquaintance shall feel a lively surprise at our unusual powers. But as soon as the stranger begins to intrude his partialities, his definitions, his defects into the conversation, it is all over. He has heard the first, last, & best he will ever hear from us. He is no stranger now. Vulgarity, ignorance, misapprehension, are old acquaintances. Now when he comes he may get the order, the dress, & the dinner, but the throbbing of the heart & the communications of the soul, no more.

Housekeeping. If my garden had only made me acquainted with the muckworm, the bugs, the grasses, & the swamp of plenty in August, I should willingly pay a free tuition. But every process is lucrative to me far beyond its economy. For the like reason keep house. Whoso does, opens a shop in the heart of all trades, professions, & arts so that upon him these shall all play. By keeping house I go to a universal school where all knowledges are taught me & the price of tuition is *my annual expense*. Thus I want my stove set up. I only want a piece of sheet iron 31 inches by 33. But that want entitles me to call on the professors of tin & iron in the village Messrs Wilson & Dean & inquire of them the kinds of iron they have or can procure, the cost of production of a pound of cast or wrought metal, & any other related information they possess, & furthermore to lead the conversation to the practical experiment of the use of their apparatus for the benefit of my funnel & blower, all which they courteously do for a small fee. In like manner, I play the chemist with ashes, soap, beer, vinegar, manure, medicines; the naturalist with trees, shrubs, hens, pigs, cows, horses, fishes, bees, cankerworms, wood, & coal; the politician with the selectmen, the assessors, the Probate Court, the town-meeting.

Forget as fast as you can that you exist, if you would be beautiful & beloved. You do not tell me, young maiden, in words that you wish to be admired, that not to be lovely but to be courted, not to be mistress of yourself but to be mistress of me, is your desire. But I hear it, an ugly harlot sound in the recesses of your song, in the niceties of your speech, in the lusciousness (forgive the horrid word) of your manners. Can you not possibly think of any thing that you really & heartily want & can say so, & go the *straight* way in the face of God & men to effect, if it were only to raise a cucumber, or own a cat, or make a scratch cradle? Be it what it will, do that, chase your friend all over town; read, mark, *eat*, the book that interests you; any thing, no matter what, that interests you, that do, with a single aim, & forget yourself in it, & straightway you are a piece of nature & do share the loveliness & venerableness of nature. Therefore are tears *for another*, therefore is lively repartee, a good story, a fit action lovely & enlivening because in them the soul goes out of self & gives sign of relation to universal nature.

What is true of the stranger is true in its degree of the friends whom we occasionally see: they are new to us for the time: an oblivion has fallen upon their definitions, partialities, & defects, & we can talk with them better than we can with the housemates. But we could not live with them better.

Is not the beauty that piques us in every object, in a straw, an old nail, a cobble-stone in the road, the announcement that always our road lies *out* into nature, & not inward to the wearisome odious anatomy of ourselves & comparison of me with thee, & accusation of me, & ambition to take this from thee & add it to me?

Alcott is a ray of the oldest light. As they say the light of some stars that parted from the orb at the deluge of Noah has only now reached us.

—

It seems to be a rule of wisdom never to rely on your memory alone scarcely even in acts of pure memory. But bring the whole past into the full seen thousand-eyed Present, and live & live & live without interval.

—

19 September. I found in the wood this afternoon the drollest mushroom—tall, stately, pretending, uprearing its vast dome as if to say "Well I am something! Burst, ye beholders! thou lucky beholder! with wonder." Its dome was a deep yellow ground with fantastic starlike ornaments richly over wrought; so shabby genteel, so negro fine, the St Peter's of the beetles & pismires. Such ostentation *in petto* I never did see. I touched the white column with my stick,—it nodded like old Troy, & so eagerly recovered the perpendicular as seemed to plead piteously with me not to burst the fabric of its pride. Shall I confess it? I could almost hear my little Waldo at home begging me as when I have menaced his little block house, and the little puffball seemed to say "Don't, papa, pull it down!" So, after due admiration of this blister, this cupola of midges I left the little scaramouch alone in its glory. Goodbye Vanity, Goodbye Nothing! Certainly there is Comedy in the Divine Mind when these little Vegetable Selfconceits front the day as well as Newton or Goethe, with such impressive emptiness.

—

24 September. Nature is the beautiful asylum to which we look in all the years of striving & conflict as the assured resource when we shall be driven out of society by ennui or chagrin or persecution or defect of character. I say as I go up the hill & thro' the wood & see the soliciting plants I care not for you mosses & lichens, & for you, fugitive birds, or secular rocks! Grow, fly, or sleep there in your order, which I know is beautiful, though I perceive it not; I am content not to perceive it. Now have I entertainment enough with things nearer, homelier. Things wherein passion enters & hope & fear, have not yet become too dangerous, too insipid for me to handle. But by & by, if men shall drive me out, if books have become stale I see gladly that the door of your palace of Magic stands ajar, & my age

> Shall find the antique hermitage
> The hairy gown & mossy cell.

—

The Indians say, the negro is older than they, & they older than the white man. The negro is the preAdamite. But the great grandfather of all the races, the oldest inhabitant, seems to be the trilobite.

———

Sept. 25. The kiss of the Dryads is not soft. The kiss of the Oreads is harder still. A good woodland day or two with John Lewis Russell who came here, & showed me mushrooms, lichens, & mosses. A man in whose mind things stand in the order of cause & effect, & not in the order of a shop or even of a cabinet.

———

"Faction."
A foolish formula is "the Spirit of faction," as it is used in books old & new. Can you not get any nearer to the fact than that, you old granny? It is like the answer of children, who, when you ask them the subject of the sermon, say, it was about Religion.

———

To S.M.F.
There is no cheaper way of giving great pleasure than when we simply describe from our centre the disk, & direction of the ray of the surrounding orbs. How formidable it looks before-hand to estimate a fine genius & write down his value in words —Gibbon, Rousseau, or whosoever. Yet the whole charm of the historical part of Goethe's Farbenlehre, & charming it is, consists in the simplest statement of the relation betwixt the several grandees of European scientific history & John Wolfgang, the mere drawing of lines from John to Kepler, from John to Roger Bacon, from John to Newton. The drawing of the line is for the time & person a perfect solution of the for-midable problem & gives pleasure when Iphigenia & Faust do not, without any cost of labor comparable to that of Iphigenia & Faust.

I wrote Margaret Fuller today, that, "seeing how entirely the value of facts is in the classification of the eye that sees them I desire to study, I desire *longanimity*, to use Bacon's word. I verily believe that a philosophy of history is possible

out of the materials that litter & stuff the world that would
raise the meaning of Book, & literature. 'Cause & effect forever!' say I." Those old Egyptians built vast temples & halls in
some proportion to the globe on which they were erected &
to the numbers of the nation who were to hold their solemnities within the walls. They built them not in a day, nor in a single century. So let us with inveterate purpose write our history.
Let us not as now we do, write a history for display & make it
after our own image & likeness;—three or four crude notions of
our own & very many crude notions of old historians hunted
out & patched together without coherence or proportion &
no thought of the necessity of proportion & unity dreamed of
by the writer. A great conglomerate; or, at best, an Arabesque;
a Grotesque; containing no necessary reason for its being, nor
inscribing itself in our memory like the name & life of a friend.
But let us go to the facts of chronology as Newton went to
those of physics, knowing well that they are already bound together of old, & perfectly, & he surveys them that he may detect the bond. Let us learn with the patience & affection of a
naturalist all the facts & looking out all the time for the reason
that *was*, for the law that prevailed, & made the facts such, not
for one that we can supply & make the facts plausibly sustain.
We should then find abundant *aperçus* or lights self kindled
amid the antiquities we explored. Why should not history be
godly written, out of the highest Faith & with a study of what
really was? We should then have Ideas which would command
& marshal the facts, & show the history of a nation as accurately proportioned & necessary in every part as an animal.
The Connexion of Commerce & Religion explains the history
of Africa from the beginning until now. Nomadism is a law of
nature & Asia, Africa, Europe present different pictures of it.
The architecture of each nation had its root in nature. How
ample the materials show when once we have the true Idea
that explains all! Then the modern Man, the geography, the
ruins, the geology, the traditions as well as authentic history
recite & confirm the tale. I said above Cause & Effect forever!
in the thought that out of such incongruous patch work
thoughtlessly put together as our histories are, nothing can
come but incongruous impressions, obscure, unsatisfactory to

the mind; but that views obtained by patient wisdom drudging amidst facts, would give an analogous impression to the landscape.

They say the sublime silent desert now testifies through the mouths of Bruce, Lyon, Caillaud, Burkhardt to the truth of the calumniated Herodotus.

29 Sept. I have a full quiver of facts under that Sapphic & Adonian text of Every Dog, &c. We are ungrateful creatures. There is nothing we value & hunt & cultivate & strive to draw to us, but in some hour we turn & rend it. We sneer at ignorance & the life of the senses & the ridicule of never thinking & then goes by a fine girl like M. R., a piece of life gay because she is happy & making these very commonalties beautiful by the energy & heart with which she does them, & seeing this, straightway we admire & love her & them, & say, "lo! a genuine creature of the fair Earth, not *blasé*, not *fletri* by books, philosophy, religion, or care;" insinuating by these very words a treachery & contempt for all that we had so long loved & wrought in ourselves & others.

—

Censure & Praise

I hate to be defended in a newspaper. As long as all that is said is said *against* me, I feel a certain sublime assurance of success but as soon as honied words of praise are spoken for me, I feel as one that lies unprotected before his enemies.

29 September.

Blessed be the wife that in the talk tonight shared no vulgar sentiment, but said, In the gossip & excitement of the hour, be as one blind & deaf to it. Know it not. Do as if nothing had befallen.—And when it was said by the friend, The end is not yet: wait till it is done; she said, "It is done in Eternity." Blessed be the wife! I, as always, venerate the oracular nature of woman. The sentiment which the man thinks he came unto gradually through the events of years, to his surprise he finds woman dwelling there in the same, as in her native home.

30 September. P.M. 5 o'clock. The air delicious at 67° Fahr. & all day delicious.

*

Nearness & distinctness seem to be convertible. A noise, a jar, a rumble, is infinitely far off from my nature though it be within a few inches of the tympanum, but a voice speaking the most intelligible of propositions is so near as to be already a part of myself.

It seems as if a man should learn to fish, to plant, or to hunt, that he might secure his subsistence if he were cast out from society & not be painful to his friends & fellow men.

Royal Education

It would seem that in the Ancient Eastern kingdoms better views of an education at Court prevailed than in the kingdoms of modern Europe. "And the king spake unto Ashpenaz the master of his eunuchs that he should bring certain of the Children of Israel & of the king's seed & of the princes; children in whom was no blemish, but well favoured & skilful in all wisdom, & cunning in knowledge, & understanding science, & such as had ability in them to stand in the king's palace, & whom they might teach the learning & tongue of the Chaldeans." Daniel; I; 3, 4.

—

5 October. Once I thought it a defect peculiar to me, that I was confounded by interrogatories & when put on my wits for a definition was unable to reply without injuring my own truth: but now, I believe it proper to man to be unable to answer in terms the great problems put by his fellow: it is enough if he can live his own definitions. A problem appears to me. I cannot solve it with all my wits: but leave it there; let it lie awhile: I can by patient faithful truth live at last its uttermost darkness into light.

Books

It seems meritorious to read; but from every thing but history or the works of the old commanding writers I come back with a conviction that the slightest wood-thought, the least significant native emotion of my own, is more to me.

Compensation

I read today a horrid story of murder; it fills one with glooms, bludgeons & gibbets: then it turns out to be a systematic longsought accurately-measured revenge: instantly the gloom clears up; for in a degree the light of law & of cause & effect shines in.

How soon the sunk spirits rise again, how quick the little wounds of fortune skin over & are forgotten. I am sensitive as a leaf to impressions from abroad. And under this night's beautiful heaven I have forgotten that ever I was *reviewed*. It is strange how superficial are our views of these matters, seeing we are all writers & philosophers. A man thinks it of importance what the great sheet or pamphlet of today proclaims of him to all the reading town; and if he sees graceful compliments, he relishes his dinner; & if he sees threatening paragraphs & odious nicknames, it becomes a solemn depressing fact & sables his whole thoughts until bedtime. But in truth the effect of these paragraphs is mathematically measureable by their depth of thought. How much water do they draw? If they awaken you to think—if they lift you from your feet with the great voice of eloquence—then their effect is to be wide, slow, permanent over the minds of men: but if they instruct you not, they will die like flies in an hour.

October 9. They put their finger on their lip—the Powers above,—
I have intimations of my riches much more than possession, as is the lot of other heirs. Every object suggests to me in certain moods a dim anticipation of profound meaning, as if by & by it would appear to me why the apple tree, why the meadow, why the stump, stand there, & what they signify to me.

Vanburenism
I passed by the shop & saw my spruce neighbor the dictator of our rural jacobins teaching his little circle of villagers their political lessons. And here thought I is one who loves what I hate; here is one wholly reversing my code. I hate persons who are nothing but persons. I hate numbers. He cares for nothing but numbers & persons. All the qualities of man, all his accomplishments, affections, enterprises except solely the ticket he votes for, are nothing to this philosopher. Numbers of majorities are all he sees in the newspaper. All of North or South,

all in Georgia, Alabama, Pennsylvania, or New England that this man considers is what is the relation of Mr Clay or of Mr Van Buren to those mighty mountain chains, those vast fruitful champaigns, those expanding nations of men. What an existence is this to have no home, no heart, but to feed on the very refuse & old straw & chaff of man, the numbers & names of voters.

One thing deserves the thought of the modern jacobin. It seems the relations of society, the position of classes irk & sting him. He will one day know that this is not fluent or removeable but a distinction in the nature of things, that neither the caucus, nor the newspaper, nor the Congress, nor the tax, nor the mob, nor the guillotine, nor halter, nor fire, or all together can avail to outlaw, cut out, burn, or destroy the offence of superiority in persons. The manners, the pretension which annoy me so much, are not superficial but built on a real distinction in the nature of my companion. The superiority in him is an inferiority in me, & if he were wiped by a sponge out of nature, this my inferiority would still be made evident to me by other persons every where & every day.

[Self trust]
Persons

Every person is a new possibility unlimited. A man Caesar was born & for ages after we have a Roman Empire. Christ is born & millions of minds so cleave & grow to his genius, that he is confounded with Virtue & the possible of Man. We do not see what is equally true, that the persons around us are possibilities as vast, that we associate with many neuters out of any one of which, under right circumstances, a queen bee can be made. Scipio, Milton calls, "the height of Rome."

———

It seems not unfit that the Scholar should deal plainly with society & tell them that he saw well enough before he spoke the consequence of his speaking, that up there in his silent study by his dim lamp he fore-heard this Babel of outcries. The nature of man he knew, the insanity that comes of inaction & tradition, & knew well that when their dream & routine were disturbed, like bats & owls & nocturnal beasts they would howl & shriek & fly at the torch bearer. But he saw plainly that under this their distressing disguise of bird-form & beast-form, the divine features of man were hidden, & he felt that he would dare to be so much their friend as to do them this violence to drag them to the day & to the healthy air & water of God, that the unclean spirits that had possessed them might be exorcised & depart. The taunts & cries of hatred & anger, the very epithets you bestow on me are so familiar long ago in my reading that they sound to me ridiculously old & stale. The same thing has happened so many times over, (that is, with the appearance of every original observer) that if people were not very ignorant of literary history they would be struck with the exact coincidence. And whilst I see this that you must have been shocked & must cry out at what I have said I see too that we cannot easily be reconciled for I have a great deal more to say that will shock you out of all patience. Every day I am struck with new particulars of the antagonism between your habits of thought & action & the divine law of your being & as fast as these become clear to me you may depend on my proclaiming them.

Succession, division, parts, particles,—this is the condition, this the tragedy of man. All things cohere & unite. Man studies the parts, strives to tear the part from its connexion, to magnify it, & make it a whole. He sides with the part against other parts; & fights for parts, fights for lies. & his whole mind becomes an *inflamed part*, an amputated member, a wound, an offence. Meantime within him is the Soul of the Whole, the Wise Silence, the Universal Beauty to which every part & particle is equally related, the eternal One. Speech is the sign of partiality, difference, ignorance, and the more perfect the understanding between men, the less need of words. And when I know all, I shall cease to commend any part. An ignorant man thinks the divine wisdom is conspicuously shown in some fact or creature: a wise man sees that every fact contains the same. I should think Water the best invention, if I were not acquainted with Fire & Earth & Air. But as we advance, every proposition, every action, every feeling, runs out into the infinite. If we go to affirm anything we are checked in our speech by the need of recognizing all other things until speech presently becomes rambling, general, indefinite, & merely tautology. The only speech will at last be Action such as Confucius describes the Speech of God.

———

Here came on Sunday Morning (14th) Edward Palmer & departed today, a gentle, faithful, sensible, well-balanced man for an enthusiast. He has renounced since a year ago last April the use of money. When he travels he stops at night at a house & asks if it would give them any satisfaction to lodge a traveller without money or price? If they do not give him a hospitable answer he goes on but generally finds the country people free & willing. When he goes away he gives them his papers or tracts. He has sometimes found it necessary to go 24 hours without food & all night without lodging. Once he found a wagon with a good buffalo under a shed & had a very good nap. By the seashore he finds it difficult to travel as they are inhospitable. He presents his views with great gentleness; & is not troubled if he cannot show the way in which the destruction of money is to be brought about; he feels no responsibility to show or know the details. It is enough for him that he is sure it must fall & that he clears himself of the institution altogether.

Why should not I if a man comes & asks me for a book give it him? if he ask me to write a letter for him write it? if he ask me to write a poem or a discourse which I can fitly write, why should I not? And if my neighbor is as skilful in making cloth, why should not all of us who have wool, send it to him to make for the common benefit, & when we want ten yards or twenty yards go to him & ask for so much & he like a gentleman give us exactly what we ask without hesitation? And so let every house keep a store-room in which they place their superfluity of what they produce, & open it with ready confidence to the wants of the neighborhood, & without an account of debtor & credit. E. P. asks if it would be a good plan for a family of brothers & sisters to keep an account of Dr. & Cr. of their good turns, & expect an exact balance? And is not the human race a family? Does not kindness disarm? It is plain that if perfect confidence reigned, then it would be possible and he asks how is confidence to be promoted but by reposing confidence?

It seems to me that I have a perfect claim on the community

for the supply of all my wants if I have worked hard all day, or if I have spent my day well, have done what I could, though no meat, shoes, cloth, or utensils, have been made by me, yet if I have spent my time in the best manner I could, I must have benefitted the world in some manner that will appear & be felt somewhere. If we all do so, we shall all find ourselves able to ask & able to bestow with confidence. It seems too that we should be able to say to the lazy "You are lazy; you should work & cure this disease. I will not give you all you ask, but only a part. Pinch yourself today & ask me for more when you have labored more, as your brothers do, for them."

However I incline to think that among angels the money or certificate system might have some imporant convenience not for thy satisfaction of whom I borrow, but for my satisfaction that I have not exceeded carelessly my proper wants,—have not overdrawn.

———

October 19. Let me add of quoting Scripture, to what was said above, that I hate to meet this slavish custom in a solemn expression of sentiment like the late manifesto of the Peace Convention. It seems to deny with the multitude the Omnipresence, the Eternity of God. Once he spoke thro' good men these special words. Now if we have aught high & holy to do we must wrench somehow their words to speak it in. We have none of our own. Humbly rather let us go & ask God's leave to use the Hour & Language that now is. Cannot you ransack the graveyards & get your great-grandfather's clothes also? It is like the single coat in St. Lucie in which the islanders one by one paid their respects to the new Governor.

It is a poor-spirited age. The great army of cowards who bellow & bully from their bed chamber windows have no confidence in truth or God. Truth will not maintain itself, they fancy, unless they bolster it up & whip & stone the assailants; and the religion of God, the being of God, they seem to think dependent on what we say of it. The feminine vehemence with which the A. N. of the Daily Advertiser beseeches the dear people to whip that naughty heretic is the natural feeling in the mind whose religion is external. It cannot subsist, it suffers shipwreck if its faith is not confirmed by all surrounding persons. A believer, a mind whose faith is consciousness, is never disturbed because other persons do not yet see the fact which he sees. It is plain that there are two classes in our educated community; first; Those who confine themselves to the facts in their consciousness; & secondly; Those who superadd sundry propositions. The aim of a true teacher now would be to bring men back to a trust in God & destroy before their eyes these idolatrous propositions: to teach the doctrine of the perpetual revelation.

20 October. All inquiry into antiquity, all curiosity respecting the pyramids, the excavated cities, Stone-Henge, Rome, Babylon, is simply & at last the desire to do away this wild, savage, preposterous *Then*, & introduce in its place the *Now*: it is to banish the *Not Me* & supply the *Me*; it is to abolish *difference* & restore *Unity*. Belzoni digs & scratches & climbs & gropes, until he can see to the end of the difference between the monstrous work, & himself. When he has satisfied himself in general & in detail that it was made by such a person as himself, so armed & so motived, & to ends to which he himself in given circumstances should also have worked,—the problem is then solved; his *Me* lives along the whole line of temples, sphinxes, & catacombs; passes through them all like a creative soul with satisfaction, & they live again to the mind, or are *Now*. And this is also the aim in all science, in the unprofitable abysses of entomology, in the gigantic masses of geology, & spaces of astronomy,—simply to transport our consciousness of cause & effect into those remote & by us uninhabited members, & see that they all proceed from "causes now in operation" from one mind, & that Ours. I do not wish to know that my shell is a strombus, or my moth a Vanessa, but I wish to know what they are to me?

Signs. The long waves indicate to the mariner with certainty that there is no land in the neighborhood in the direction from which they come. Three marks Belzoni saw that led him to dig for a door to the Pyramid of Ghizeh. What thousands had beheld the same spot for so many ages, & seen no three marks.

Steady, steady! When this fog of good & evil Affections falls, it is hard to see & walk straight.

One Mind. The ancients exchanged their names with their friends, signifying that in their friend they loved their own soul.

What said my brave Asia concerning the paragraph writers, today? that "this whole practice of self justification & recrimination betwixt literary men seemed every whit as low as the quarrels of the Paddies." Then said I, But what will you say, excellent Asia, when my smart article comes out in the paper, in reply to Mr A & Dr B? "Why, then," answered she, "I shall feel the first emotion of fear & of sorrow on your account." But do you know, I asked, how many fine things I have thought of to say to these fighters? They are too good to be lost.—"Then" rejoined the queen, "there is some merit in being silent."

It is plain from all the noise that there is Atheism somewhere. The only question is now, Which is the Atheist?

It is observable, as I have written before, that even the science of the day is introversive. The Microscope is carried to perfection. And Geology looks no longer in written histories, but examines the earth that it may be its own Chronicle.

Live without interval: if you rest on your oars, if you stop, you fall. He only is wise who thinks now, who reproduces all his experience for the present exigency, as a man stands on his feet only by a perpetual play & adjustment of the muscles. A dead body or a statue cannot be set up in the upright posture without support. "To the persevering mortal, the blessed immortals are swift."

"Please, papa, tell me a story," says the child of two years; who will say then that the novel has not a foundation in nature?

Idols
    Men are not units but poor mixtures. They defend with heat doctrines wholly foreign from their nature & connexion of

opinions & which whilst for moments & externally they es-
pouse, —from year to year & in life & soul they reject &
abominate. They accept how weary a load of tradition from
their elders & more forcible neighbors. By & by, as the divine
effort of creation & growth begins in them, new loves, new
aversions, take effect,—the first radiation of their own soul
amidst things. Yet each of these outbursts of the central life is
partial, & leaves abundance of traditions still in force. Each
soul has its idols. The idol of Italy, of travelling, of England, &
Europe, remains for all educated Americans, & we worship it
in all unthinking weak hours. In the waking hour we see that
they who made England, Italy, or Greece venerable in the
imagination did so not by rambling round creation as a moth
round a candle, but by sticking fast where they were, like an
axis of the earth. But the new expansion & upthrusting from
the centre shall classify our facts by new radiation & will show
us idols in how many things which now we esteem part & parcel of our constitution & lot in nature. Property, Government,
Books, Systems of Education & of Religion will successively
detach themselves from the growing spirit. I call an Idol any
thing which a man honors, which the constitution of his mind
does not necessitate him to honor.

—

I think I learn as much from the sick as from the sound,—
from the insane as from the sane. Deal plainly, or as we say
roundly with every man, & you convert him instantly into an
invaluable teacher of *his Science*, and every man has one science. Every one then becomes a messenger of God to you. Insane men have a great deal to teach you.

Mine Asia says A human being should beware how he laughs,
for then he shows all his faults.

I have transcribed a grand sentence of Swedenborg. It indicates, had he left nothing else, his perception that the Soul is
capable of truth & it does utter a certain defiance to all such as
ask that foolish question, "But how do you know it is truth &
not an error of your own?" We know truth when we see it,
from opinion, as we know when we are awake that we are awake.
The sentence is this. "It is no proof of a man's understanding

to be able to *con*firm whatever he pleases, but to be able to discern that what is true is true, & that what is false is false, this is the mark & character of intelligence."

A great colossal soul, I fancy, was Swedenborg & lies vast abroad on his times, quite uncomprehended by them, or, I think, by us. He is one who like Plato requires a long focal distance to be seen. He suggests too as Shakspear, Aristotle, Bacon, & Linnaeus do, that a certain vastness of learning, an omnipresence of the human soul in nature is possible.

It was not possible to write the history of Shakspear until now. For it was on the translation of Shakspear into German by Lessing that "the succeeding rapid burst of German literature was most intimately connected." Here certainly is an important particular in the story of that great mind yet how recent! And is this the last fact?

I have no joy so deep as the stings of remorse.

E. P. asked me if I liked two services in a sabbath. I told him— Not very well. If the sermon was good, I wished to think of it; if it was bad, one was enough.

26 October. Jones Very came hither two days since & gave occasion to many thoughts on his peculiar state of mind & his relation to society. His position accuses society as much as society names it false & morbid. & much of his discourse concerning society, the church, & the college was perfectly just.

Entertain every thought, every character that goes by with the hospitality of your soul. Give him the freedom of your inner house. He shall make you wise to the extent of his own uttermost receivings. Especially if one of these monotones (whereof, as my friends think, I have a savage society, like a menagerie of monsters,) come to you, receive him. For the partial action of his mind in one direction is a telescope for the objects on which it is pointed. And as we know that every path we take is but a radius of our sphere, & we may dive as deep in every other direction as we have in that, a far insight of one evil suggests instantly the immense extent of that revolution that must be wrought before He whose right it is, shall reign, the All in All.

Vocabularies.

In going through Italy I speak Italian, thro' Arabia Arabic; I say the same *things*, but have altered my speech. But ignorant people think a foreigner speaking a foreign tongue a formidable odious nature, alien to the backbone. So is it with our brothers. Our journey, the journey of the Soul, is through different regions of thought, and to each its own vocabulary. As soon as we hear a new vocabulary from our own, at once we exaggerate the alarming differences,—account the man suspicious, a thief, a pagan, & set no bounds to our disgust or hatred, and, late in life, perhaps too late, we find he was loving & hating, doing & thinking the same *things* as we, under his own vocabulary.

Scholar

Every word, every striking word that occurs in the pages of an original genius will provoke attack & be the subject of twenty pamphlets & a hundred paragraphs. Should he be so duped as to stop & listen? Rather, let him know that the page he writes today will contain a new subject for the pamphleteers, & that which he writes tomorrow, more. Let him not be misled to give it any more than the notice due from him, viz. just that which it had in his first page, before the controversy. The exaggeration of the notice is right for them, false for him. Every word that he quite naturally writes is as prodigious & offensive. So write on, & by & by will come a reader and an age that will justify all your context. Do not even look behind. Leave that bone for them to pick & welcome.

Let me study & work contentedly & faithfully, I do not remember my critics. I forget them,—I depart from them by every step I take. If I think then of them, it is a bad sign.

In my weak hours I look fondly to Europe & think how gladly I would live in Florence & Rome. In my manly hours, I defy these leanings, these lingering looks *behind*, these fleshpots of Egypt, & feel that my duty is my place, & that the merrymen of circumstance should follow as they might. So is it with the world. In peace, in ease, in custom, in tradition, the soul sleeps, & lets itself be mastered & enslaved by the biggest tradition, the oldest city. In London, in Paris is the love of Egypt, of primeval India: in Boston & New York, new only in name, are minds & wills as old & dilapidated. They give the eye all the pain that we feel in seeing a row of children looking old & bad in stable yards & the precincts of theatres. Ruins to ruins. But if a crisis or a soul should call out the slumbering soul of this fat & prone people, instantly they would let dead history go,—would live with the living, &, as in camps & dangers, a hasty burial would be all that the crowded moment could afford to worthless ashes.

—

Converse with a soul which is grandly simple & literature looks like wordcatching. The simplest utterances are worthiest to be written yet are they so cheap & so things of course, that in the infinite riches of the soul, it is like gathering pebbles off the ground or bottling up a little air in a phial, when the whole earth & the whole atmosphere are yours. The mere author in such society is like a pickpocket amidst gentlemen, not their fellow, but came in to steal a gold button or a pin. Nothing can pass there or make you one of the circle but the casting off all your trappings & dealing man to man in naked truth— perfect confession & omnipotent affirmation. Therefore I feel that I ought to say amidst the clearest strain of my teaching— But be it known to you, there is higher teaching still:—Souls such as these, treat you as gods would, walk as gods amongst us; accepting without any admiration your wit, your bounty, your virtue even;—no, not your virtue; that they own as their proper blood, royal as themselves & over-royal and the father of the gods. But what rebuke their plain fraternal bearing casts upon the mutual flattery with which authors solace each other & wound themselves. These flatter not. I do not wonder that these men go to see Cromwell & Charles II & James I & the Grand Turk. They must always be a godsend to princes for they confront them—a king to a king,—without ducking or concession & give a high nature the refreshment & satisfaction of resistance; of plain humanity; of even companionship; & of new ideas. They leave them wiser & superior men.

*

O worthy Mr Graham! poet of branbread & pumpkins: There is limit to the revolutions of a pumpkin, project it along the ground with what force soever. It is not a winged orb like the Egyptian symbol of dominion, but an unfeathered, ridgy, yellow pumpkin, & will quickly come to a standstill.

Literature is a heap of verbs & nouns enclosing an intuition or two.

A few ideas & a few fables.

Literature is a subterfuge.

One man might have writ all the firstrate pieces we call English literature.

Literature is eavesdropping.

Literature is an amusement, virtue is the business of the universe.

—

Mrs Ripley is superior to all she knows. She reminds one of a steam mill of great activity & power which must be fed, & she grinds German, Italian, Greek, Chemistry, Metaphysics, Theology, with utter indifference which; something she must have to keep the machine from tearing itself.

The influence of an original genius is matter of literary history. It seems as if the Shakspear could not be admired, could not even be seen until his living, conversing, & writing had diffused his spirit into the young & acquiring class so that he had multiplied himself into a thousand sons, a thousand Shakspears & so *understands himself.*

Oct. 28. J. V. says it is with him a day of hate; that he discerns the bad element in every person whom he meets which repels him: he even shrinks a little to give the hand,—that sign of receiving. The institutions, the cities which men have built the world over, look to him like a huge blot of ink. His own only guard in going to see men is that he goes to do them good, else they would injure him. (Spiritually). He lives in the sight that he who made him, made the things he sees.

He would as soon embrace a black Egyptian mummy as Socrates. He would obey, obey. He is not disposed to attack

religions & charities though false. The bruised reed he would
not break; the smoking flax he would not quench. To L. he
says your thought speaks there, & not your life. And he is very
sensible of *interference* in thought & act. A very accurate discernment of spirits belongs to his state, & he detects at once
the presence of an alien element though he cannot tell
whence, how, or whereto it is. He thinks me covetous in my
hold of truth, of seeing truth separate, & of receiving or taking
it instead of merely obeying. The Will is to him all, as to me
(after my own showing,) Truth. He is sensible in me of a little
colder air than that he breathes. He says you do not disobey
because you do the wrong act, but you do the wrong act,
because you disobey. And you do not obey because you do the
good action, but you do the good action because you first
obey. He has nothing to do with time, because he obeys. A
man who is busy, says, he has no time,—he does not recognize
that element. A man who is idle, says, he does not know what
to do with his time. Obedience is in eternity. He says it is the
necessity of the Spirit to speak with Authority. What led him to
study Shakspeare was the fact that all young men say, Shakspeare was no saint,—yet see what genius. He wished to solve
that problem.

He had the manners of a man. One, that is, to whom life was
more than meat, the body than raiment. He felt it an honor,
he said, to wash his face, being as it was the temple of the
Spirit. And he is gone into the multitude as solitary as Jesus. In
dismissing him I seem to have discharged an arrow into the
heart of society. Wherever that young enthusiast goes he will
astonish & disconcert men by dividing for them the cloud
that covers the profound gulf that is in man.

———

The Correspondence of O'Connell & our American Stevenson indicates a new step taken in civilization. Our haughty feudal Virginian suddenly finds his rights to enter the society of
gentlemen questioned, & he obliged to mince & shuffle &
equivocate in his sentences, to deny that he is a slave breeder
without denying that he is a slaveowner. He finds that the eyes
of men have got so far opened that they must see well the dis-

tinction between a cavalier & the cavalier's negro-driver, a race abhorred.

The men you meet & seek to raise to higher thought, know as well as you know that you are of them & that you stand yet on the ground, whilst you say to them sincerely, let us arise, let us fly. But once fly yourself, & they will look up to you.

There is no terror like that of being known. The world lies in night of sin. It hears not the cock crowing: it sees not the gray streak in the East. At the first entering ray of light, society is shaken with fear & anger from side to side. Who opened that shutter? they cry, Wo to him! They belie it, they call it darkness that comes in, affirming that they were in light before. Before the man who has spoken to them the dread word, they tremble & flee. They flee to new topics, to their learning, to the solid institutions about them, to their great men, to their windows, & look out on the road & passengers, to their very furniture, & meats, & drinks, anywhere, anyhow to escape the apparition. The wild horse has heard the Whisper of the Tamer: the maniac has caught the glance of the Keeper. They try to forget the memory of the speaker, to put him down into the same obscure place he occupied in their minds before he spake to them. It is all in vain. They even flatter themselves that they have killed & buried the enemy when they have magisterially denied & denounced him. But vain, vain, all vain. It was but the first mutter of the distant storm they heard,—it was the first cry of the Revolution,—it was the touch, the palpitation that goes before the Earthquake. Even now Society is shaken because a thought or two have been thrown into the midst. The sects, the colleges, the church, the statesmen all have forebodings. It now works only in a handful. What does State street and Wall street and the Royal Exchange & the Bourse at Paris care for these few thoughts & these few men? Very little; truly; most truly. But the doom of State street, & Wall street, of London, & France, of the whole world, is advertised by those thoughts: is in the procession of the Soul which comes after those few thoughts.

—

I ought not to omit recording the astonishment which
seized all the company when our brave saint the other day
fronted the presiding preacher. The preacher began to tower
& dogmatize with many words. Instantly I foresaw that his
doom was fixed; and as quick as he ceased speaking, the Saint
set him right & blew away all his words in an instant—
unhorsed him I may say & tumbled him along the ground in
utter dismay like my Angel of Heliodorus. Never was discomfiture more complete. In tones of genuine pathos he "bid him
wonder at the Love which suffered him to speak there in his
chair, of things he knew nothing of; one might expect to see
the book taken from his hands & him thrust out of the room,
—& yet he was allowed to sit & talk whilst every word he
spoke was a step of departure from the truth, and of this he
commanded himself to bear witness!"

Soirée

October 31. Yesterday eve. Lidian's soirée. As soon as the
party is broken up, I shrink, & wince, & try to forget it. There
is no refuge but in oblivion of such misdemeanors.

God's dream

When I look at life, & see the snatches of thought, the
gleams of goodness here & there amid the wide & wild madness, I seem to be a god dreaming, & when shall I awake &
dissipate these fumes & phantoms?

Nov. 2. Heard I not that a fair girl said, She would not be
"charitable" as she wished to be, because it looked to her so
like *feeding*? "Rem acu tetigisti." To all let us be Men, & not
pastry cooks. In proportion to the nobleness of men nowadays
are they solitary, and in proportion to their virtue are they
negligent of the great charities of the day. Why should you descend to their measure, instead of raising them up to ours?

Our enjoyments are pagan. We separate ourselves from the
human family & from remembrance of debt above us, & say
"Shall I not take mine ease in mine inn?" Then are we pagans.
Only that good which we taste with all doors open, not separate, but *in the chain* of beings, so that the spark freely passes,
makes all happy as well as us,—only that is godly. Other enjoy-

ments,—enjoyments sought for enjoyment, are false, & degrade all the partakers & ministers. In the base hour, we become slaveholders. We use persons as things, & we think of persons as things.

—

I should not dare to tell all my story. A great deal of it I do not yet understand. How much of it is incomplete. In my strait & decorous way of living, native to my family & to my country, & more strictly proper to me, is nothing extravagant or flowing. I content myself with moderate languid actions, & never transgress the staidness of village manners. Herein I consult the poorness of my powers. More culture would come out of great virtues & vices perhaps, but I am not up to that. Should I obey an irregular impulse, & establish every new relation that my fancy prompted with the men & women I see, I should not be followed by my faculties; they would play me false in making good their very suggestions. They delight in inceptions, but they warrant nothing else. I see very well the beauty of sincerity, & tend that way, but if I should obey the impulse so far as to say to my fashionable aquaintance 'You are a coxcomb,—I dislike your manners,—I pray you avoid my sight,'—I should not serve him nor me, & still less the truth; I should act quite unworthy of the truth; for I could not carry out the declaration with a sustained, even-minded frankness & love, which alone could save such a speech from rant & absurdity.

We must tend ever to the good life.

I told J. V. that I had never suffered, & that I could scarce bring myself to feel a concern for the safety & life of my nearest friends that would satisfy them: that I saw clearly that if my wife, my child, my mother, should be taken from me, I should still remain whole with the same capacity of cheap enjoyment from all things. I should not grieve enough, although I love them. But could I make them feel what I feel—the boundless resources of the soul,—remaining entire when particular threads of relation are snapped,—I should then dismiss forever the little remains of uneasiness I have in regard to them.

*

Nov. 4.—I wish society to be a Congress of Sovereigns without the pride but with the power. Therefore I do not like to see a worthy woman resemble those flowers that cannot bear transportation, and when I behold her in a foreign house perceive instantly that she has lost an inch or two of height—her manners not so *tall* as they were at home. A woman should always challenge our respect & never move our compassion. If they be great only on their own ground, & demure & restless in a new house, they have all to learn. If people were all true, we should feel that all persons were infinitely deep natures. But now in an evening party you have no variety of persons, but only one person. For, say what you will, to whom you will,—they shall all render one & the same answer, without thought, without heart,—a conversation of the lips. So is a soirée a heap of lies; false itself it makes falsehoods. As when the sculptors carve a dragon they adorn his points & folds with little imps & toads & worms, so is this grand lie escorted in & out by scores of petty fibs of notes & compliments by way of garnish.

———

I am very sensible to beauty in the human form, in children, in boys, in girls, in old men, & old women. No trait of beauty, I think escapes me. So am I to beauty in Nature; a clump of flags in a stream, a hill, a wood, a path running into the woods, captivate me as I pass. If you please to tell me that I have no just relish for the beauty of man or of nature, it would not disturb me certainly. I do not know but it may be so, & that you have so much juster, deeper, richer knowledge, as that I, when I come to know it, shall say the same thing. But now your telling me that I do not love nature will not in the least annoy me. I should still have a perfect conviction that, love it, or love it not, every bough that waved, every cloud that floated, every water ripple is & must remain a minister to me of mysterious joy. But I hear occasionally young people dwelling with emphasis on beauties of nature which may be there or may not, but which I do not catch, & blind, at the same time, to the objects which give me most pleasure. I am quite unable to tell the difference, only I see that they are less easily satisfied than I; that they talk where I would be silent, & clamorously demand my delight where it is not spontaneous. I fancy the love of nature of such persons is rhetorical. If however, I tell them, as I am moved to do, that I think they are not susceptible of this pleasure, straightway they are offended, & set themselves at once to prove to me with many words that they always had a remarkable delight in solitude & in nature. They even affirm it with tears. Then can I not resist the belief that the sense of joy from every pebble, stake, & dry leaf is not yet opened in them.

"It is proverbial that the youngest son in a large family is commonly the man of the greatest talents in it."

Coleridge

Swedenborg thought that a man's character is usually fixed at the *age of discretion* forever.

After thirty a man wakes up sad every morning.

—

Freedom

Nov. 7. I will, I think, no longer do things unfit for me. Why should I act the part of the silly women who send out invitations to many persons, & receive each billet of acceptance as if it were a pistol shot? Why should I read lectures with care & pain & afflict myself with all the meanness of ticket mongering, when I might sit, as God in his goodness has enabled me, a free poor man with wholesome bread & warm clothes though without cakes or gewgaws, & write & speak the beautiful & formidable words of a free man? If you cannot be free, be as free as you can.

—

Let me never fall into the vulgar mistake of dreaming that I am persecuted whenever I am contradicted. No man, I think, had ever a greater well being with a less desert than I. I can very well afford to be accounted bad or foolish by a few dozen or a few hundred persons,—I who see myself greeted by the good expectation of so many friends far beyond any power of thought or communication of thought residing in me. Besides, I own, I am often inclined to take part with these who say I am bad or foolish, for I fear I am both. I believe & know there must be a perfect compensation. I know too well my own dark spots. Not having myself attained, not satisfied myself, far from a holy obedience,—how can I expect to satisfy others, to command their love? A few sour faces, a few biting paragraphs,—is but a cheap expiation for all these short-comings of mine.

9 November. With the vision of this world these fugitive measures of time & space shall vanish.

> "Spirits
> Can crowd eternity into an hour,
> Or stretch an hour to eternity."

This superstition about magnitude & duration is a classification for beginners introductory to the real classification of cause & effect, as the Linnean botany gives way to the natural classes of Jussieu. Why should that complex fact we call Assyria, with its hundreds of years, its thousands of miles, its millions of souls, be to me more than a violet which I pluck out of the grass? It stands for about so much; it awakens perchance not so much emotion & thought. I surely shall not cumber myself to make it more. Every thing passes for what it is worth.

SHAKSPEAR.

Read Lear yesterday & Hamlet today with new wonder & mused much on the great soul whose authentic signs flashed on my sight in the broad continuous *day light* of these poems. Especially I wonder at the perfect reception this wit & immense knowledge of life & intellectual superiority find in us all in connexion with our utter incapacity to produce anything like it. The superior tone of Hamlet in all the conversations how perfectly preserved without any mediocrity much less any dulness in the other speakers. How real the loftiness! an in-born gentlemen; & above that, an exalted intellect. What incessant growth & plenitude of thought,—pausing on itself never an instant,—and each sally of wit sufficient to save the play. How true then & unerring the *earnest* of the dialogue, as when Hamlet talks with the Queen! How terrible his discourse! What less can be said of the perfect mastery as by a superior being of the conduct of the drama as the free introduction of this capital advice to the players; the commanding good sense which never retreats except before the godhead which inspires certain passages—the more I think of it the more I wonder. I will think nothing impossible to man. No

Parthenon, no sculpture, no picture, no architecture can be named beside this. All this is perfectly visible to me & to many,—the wonderful truth & mastery of this work, of these works,—yet for our lives could not I, or any man, or all men, produce any thing comparable to one scene in Hamlet or Lear. With all my admiration of this life-like picture, set me to producing a match for it, & I should instantly depart into mouthing rhetoric. Now why is this that we know so much better than we do? that we do not yet possess ourselves, & know at the same time that we are much more? I feel the same truth how often in my merely trivial conversation or dealing with my neighbors, that somewhat higher in each of us over-looks this by-play, & Jove nods to Jove from behind each of us. Men descend to meet. They seem to me to resemble those Arabian sheikhs who dwell in mean houses & affect an external poverty to escape the rapacity of the pacha, & reserve all their display of wealth for their interior & guarded retirements. And what have I recorded respecting our a priori knowledge of drawing?

One other fact Shakspeare presents us; that not by books are great poets made. Somewhat—& much he unquestionably owes to his books; but you could not find in his circumstances the history of his poem. It was made without hands in his invisible world. A mightier magic than any learning, the deep logic of cause & effect he studied: its roots were cast so deep, therefore it flung out its branches so high.

I find no good lives. I would live well. I seem to be free to do so, yet I think with very little respect of my way of living; it is weak, partial, not full & not progressive. But I do not see any other that suits me better. The scholars are shiftless & the merchants are dull.

———

My brave Henry Thoreau walked with me to Walden this P.M. and complained of the proprietors who compelled him to whom as much as to any the whole world belonged, to walk in a strip of road & crowded him out of all the rest of God's earth. He must not get over the fence: but to the building of that fence he was no party. Suppose, he said, some great proprietor, before he was born, had bought up the whole globe.

So had he been hustled out of nature. Not having been privy to any of these arrangements he does not feel called on to consent to them & so cuts fishpoles in the woods without asking who has a better title to the wood than he. I defended of course the good Institution as a scheme not good but the best that could be hit on for making the woods & waters & fields available to Wit & Worth, & for restraining the bold bad man. At all events, I begged him, having this maggot of Freedom & Humanity in his brain, to write it out into good poetry & so clear himself of it. He replied, that he feared that that was not the best way; that in doing justice to the thought, the man did not always do justice to himself: the poem ought to sing itself: if the man took too much pains with the expression he was not any longer the Idea himself. I acceded & confessed that this was the tragedy of Art that the Artist was at the expense of the Man; & hence, in the first age, as they tell, the Sons of God printed no epics, carved no stone, painted no picture, built no railroad; for the sculpture, the poetry, the music, & architecture, were in the Man. And truly Bolts & Bars do not seem to me the most exalted or exalting of our institutions. And what other spirit reigns in our intellectual works? We have literary property. The very recording of a thought betrays a distrust that there is any more or much more as good for us. If we felt that the Universe was ours, that we dwelled in eternity & advance into all wisdom we should be less covetous of these sparks & cinders. Why should we covetously build a St Peter's, if we had the seeing Eye which beheld all the radiance of beauty & majesty in the matted grass & the overarching boughs? Why should a man spend years upon the carving an Apollo who looked Apollos into the landscape with every glance he threw?

Always pay, for first or last you must pay your entire expense. Uncles & Aunts, fathers & elder brothers, patrons & friends may stand for a time between you & justice; but it is only postponement—you must pay at last your own debt. If you are wise, you will dread a prosperity which only loads you with new debt. A whig victory, a rise of rents, the momentary triumph of a religious poet or some other quite outward event raises your spirits & you think easy days are preparing for you.

Do not believe it. It can never be so. Nothing can ever bring you peace but yourself. Nothing can bring you peace but the attainment of principles.

Should not the will be dramatised in a Man who, put him where you would, commanded, & who saw what he willed come to pass? Caesar said to Metellus, Young Man it is easier for me to put you to death than to say that I will, & the youth yielded. He was taken by Corsairs, but fell on his feet, told them stories, declaimed to them;—if they did not praise the speech, he threatened them with hanging, which he performed afterwards, & so, in a short time was master of things. A man this is who cannot be disconcerted & so can never play his last card but always has a reserve of power when he has shot his fatal bolt. With a serene face he rives a kingdom. What is told of him is miraculous. It affects men so. The confidence of men in him is lavish and he changes the face of the world & letters & science also & new philosophies must be to account for him. A supreme commander over all his passions & affections as much as Hampden yet the secret of his power is higher than that. It is God in the hands. Men & women are his game; where they are he cannot be without resource. Shall I introduce you to Mr A? to Madam B? 'No,' he replies, 'introduction is for dolls: I have business with A & with B'.

Will never consults the law or prudence or uses any paltry expedient like that falsely ascribed to St Paul about the 'Unknown God.' Tricks, saith Will, for little folks. I am dearer to you than your laws for which neither you nor I care a pin. He is a cool fellow. Every body in the street reminds us of somewhat else. Will or Reality reminds you of nothing else. It takes place of the whole creation.

> He'd harpit a fish out of saut water
>   Or water out of a stone
> Or milk out of a maiden's breast
>   That bairn had never none.

The counterpart to this master in my Drama should be a maiden, one of those natural magnets who make place & a court where they are. She should serve in menial office & they who saw her should not know it, for what she touched she decorated & what she did the stars & moon do stoop to see. But this magnetism should not be meant for him & he should only honor it as he went by. It is to work on others, on another as a balance to him or if I may refine so far another Richmond, a transmuted Will infused into *form* & now *unconscious* yet omnipotent as before & in a sweeter way.

—

Ah Memory! dear daughter of God! Thy blessing is million-fold. The poor short lone fact that dies at the birth, thou catchest up & bathest in immortal waters. Then a thousand times over it lives and & acts again, each time transfigured, ennobled. Then in solitude & darkness, I walk over again my sunny walks; in streets behold again the shadows of my grey birches, in the still river; hear the joyful voices of my brothers, a thousand times over; & vibrate anew to the tenderness & dainty music of the early poetry I fed upon in boyhood. As fair to me the clump of flags that bent over the water as if to see its own beauty below, one evening last summer, as any plants that are growing there today. At this hour, the stream is flowing, though I hear it not; the plants are drinking their accustomed life, & repaying it with their beautiful forms, but I need not wander thither. It flows for me, & they grow for me in the returning images of former summers.

'Fire', Aunt Mary said, 'was a great deal of company;' & so is there company, I find, in Water. It animates the solitude. Then somewhat nearer to human society is in the hermit birds that harbor in the wood. I can do well for weeks with no other society than the partridge & the jay, my daily company.

—

I remember that when I preached my first sermon in Concord, "on showing piety at home," Dr Ripley remarked on the frequent occurrence of the word *Virtue* in it, and said his people would not understand it, for the largest part of them when Virtue was spoken of understood *Chastity*. I do not imagine however that the people thought any such thing. It was an old-school preacher's contractedness.

—

Boys & girls.
The strong bent of nature is very prettily seen in the win-

ning half-artful half-artless ways of young girls in the middle
classes who go into the shops to buy a skein of silk or a sheet of
paper & talk half an hour about nothing with the broad-faced
good natured shop boy. Here in the country they are on a perfect equality & without any coquetry the happy affectionate
nature of woman flows out in this pretty gossip. The girls
whom I watched from behind my newspaper at the other end
of the shop were not pretty, yet plainly did they establish
between them & the good boy the most agreeable confiding
relations, what with their fun & their earnest about Henry &
Mary, & who was invited, & who danced at the dancing
school, & when the singing school should begin, & other
nothings, about which they cooed & wooed. By & by that boy
wants a wife & very truly & heartily will he know where to find
a sincere sweet mate, without any risque of mistake such as the
shy scholar or fashionable man may so easily make.

—

Ellen was never alone. I could not imagine her poor & solitary. She was like a tree in flower, so much soft budding informing beauty was society for itself and she taught the eye
that beheld her, why Beauty was ever painted with loves &
graces attending her steps.

—

The pathetic lies usually not in miseries but petty losses &
disappointments as when the poor family have spent their little
utmost upon a wedding or a christening festival, & their feast
is dishonored by some insult or petty disaster,—the falling of
the salver, or the spoiling of a carpet. When I was a boy, I was
sent by my mother with a dollar bill to buy me a pair of shoes
at Mr Baxter's shop, & I lost the bill; & remember being sent
out by my disappointed mother to look among the fallen
leaves under the poplar trees opposite the house for the lost
bank note.

My ambition.
When I was in College, Robert Barnwell, the first scholar in
my class put his hand on the back of my head to feel for the
bump of ambition, & pronounced that it was very very small.

Would you know if the man is just, ask of the tax gatherer.

Bambino

"Where's the cover that lives in this box?" asks little Waldo. When he saw the dead bird, he said "he was gone By-By"; then he said, "he was broke." When Dr J. smoked a cigar, Waldo said "See the cobwebs go up out of the gentleman's mouth."

25 February. Yesterday morning, 24 Feb. at 8 o'clock a daughter was born to me, a soft, quiet, swarthy little creature, apparently perfect & healthy. My second child. Blessings on thy head, little winter bud! & comest thou to try thy luck in this world & know if the things of God are things for thee? Well assured & very soft & still, the little maiden expresses great contentment with all she finds, & her delicate but fixed determination to stay where she is, & grow. So be it, my fair child! Lidian, who magnanimously makes my gods her gods, calls the babe Ellen. I can hardly ask more for thee, my babe, than that name implies. Be that vision & remain with us, & after us.

Memory.

3 March. The Memory plays a great part in settling the intellectual rank of men. A Seneschal of Parnassus is Mnemosyne. Thus am I a better scholar than one of my neighbors who visited me? I see how it is. We read the same books a year, two years, ten years ago; we read the same books this month. Well that fact which struck us both, then, with equal force, I still contemplate. He has lost it. He & the world have only *this* fact. I have that *and* this.

A fine voice in a choir seems to inundate the house with spouts & jets & streams of sound & to float the old hulk of the choir itself insinuating itself under all the droning groans & shrill screams & hurrying them all away the spoils of its own stream.

Byron says of Jack Bunting "He knew not what to say & so he swore." I may say it of our preposterous use of Books
He knew not what to do, & so he read.

I can think of nothing to fill my time with, & so without any constraint I find the Life of Brant. It is a very extravagant compliment to pay to Brant or to Gen Schuyler or to General Washington. My time should be good as their time. My world, my facts, all my net of relations, as good as theirs or either of theirs. Why should I forsake weaving of my web & run to stare & gossip on theirs? Rather let me do my work so well that other idlers, if they choose, may compare my texture with the texture of these, & find it identical with the best.

10 March. I charge the church with a want of respect to the soul of the worshipper. The question every worshipper should ask of the preacher is "What is that to me? what have I to do with thee? what with thy fact; what with thy history; thy person; thine alleged inclinations, & aversions? I am here. Behold thy tribunal. Come with thy persons & facts to judgment." And the church, the preacher should say, "Soul of my brother, methinks I have glad tidings for thee. Methinks I have found something of thine spoken by one Jesus, by one Zoroaster, by one Penn. Hear & judge."—But now we are a mob: man does not stand in awe of man; nor is the soul provoked & admonished to stay at home in God; to root itself; & accept the whole of nature, the whole of history, the whole of thought; but it shuts its organs of reception & goes gadding abroad, a valet & a loafer.

———

Isolation

Isolation must precede society. I like the silent church before the service begins better than any preaching. How far off, how cool & chaste the persons look, begirt each one with a precinct or sanctuary! So let us always sit. Why should we assume the faults of our friend or wife or mother or child because they sit around our hearth or are said to have the same blood? All men have my blood, & I have all men's. Not for that will adopt their petulance or fury or vulgarity even to the extent of being ashamed of it. If they will have it, let them; I will none of it.

At church P.M. I doubted whether that dislocation, disunion, reflex life, second thought, that mars all our simplicity, be not an universal disease, & whether all literary pictures of

Nathan the Wise, or whatever calm placid philosopher, be not false & overcharged. Howbeit, I thought it best to seek one peace by fidelity; & at least I would write my procrastinated letters. How dare you be reading Washington's Campaigns, when you have not even answered your own correspondents? Then again it seemed wise to sit at home contented with my work & word, & never rove into other men's acres more. Why this needless visiting? If you can really serve them, they will visit you.

> Their peace profound his features kept
> His purpose woke, his aspect slept;

One thing more. It is not by running after Napoleon that the corresponding element, the Napoleonism in you, is stimulated & matured; but by withdrawing from him, from all, back on the deeps of Home.

Conversation

13 March. The office of conversation is to give me self posses-sion. I lie torpid as a clod. Virtue, wisdom sound to me fabu-lous, all cant. I am an unbeliever. Then comes by a sage & gentle spirit who spreads out in order before me his own life & aims, not as experience but as Good & desireable. Straightway I feel the presence of a new & yet old, a genial, a native ele-ment. I am like a southerner who having spent the winter in a polar climate, feels at last the south wind blow, the rigid fibres relax, & his whole frame expands to the welcome heats. In this bland flowing atmosphere, I regain one by one, my facul-ties, my organs, life returns to a finger, a hand, a foot. A new nimbleness,—almost wings—unfold at my side, & I see my right to the heaven as well as the farthest fields of the earth. The effect of the conversation resembles the effect of a beauti-ful voice in a church choir as I have noted it above, which in-sinuates itself as water into all chinks & cracks & presently floats the whole discordant choir & holds it in solution in its melody. Well I too am a ship aground, & the bard directs a river to my shoals, relieves me of these perilous rubs & strains, & at last fairly uplifts me on the waters, & I put forth my sails, & turn my head to the sea. Alcott is the only majestic con-

verser I now meet. He gives me leave to be, more than all others. Alcott is so apprehensive that he does not need to be learned.

—

A man must consider what a rich realm he abdicates when he becomes a conformist. I hear my preacher announce his text & topic as for instance the expediency of the institution of Fast with a coldness that approaches contempt. For do I not know beforehand that not possibly can he say a new or spontaneous word? Do I not know that with all this affectation of *examining the grounds* of the institution he will do no such thing? Do I not know that he is pledged to himself beforehand not to look at but one side; the permitted side; not as a man, but as a parish minister in Concord? What folly then to say *let us examine*, & purse the mouth with the wrinkles of a judge. He is a retained attorney; and this air of *judgeship* is mere affectation. Even so is it with newspapers; & so with most politicians.

This conformity makes them not false in a few particulars, authors of a few lies, but false in all particulars. Their every truth is not quite true. Their two is not the real two; their four not the real four. So that every word they say chagrins me, and I protest against the entire speech.

March 26. A good man is contented. I love & honor Epaminondas, but I do not wish to be even Epaminondas. I hold it more just to love the world of this hour than the world of his hour. Nor can you, if I am true, excite me to the least uneasiness by saying, 'he acted & thou sittest still.' I see action to be good when the need is, & sitting still to be also good. Epaminondas, if he was the man I take him for, would have sat still with joy & peace, had his lot been mine. Heaven is large & affords space for all modes of love & fortitude. Why should we be busybodies & superserviceable? Action & inaction are alike to the true. One piece of the tree is cut for a weathercock & one for the sleeper of a bridge; the virtue of the wood is apparent in both.

I desire not to disgrace the soul. The fact that I am here, certainly shows me that the soul had need of an organ here. Shall I not assume the post? Shall I skulk & dodge, & imagine my being here, impertinent? less pertinent than Epaminondas

or Homer being there? & that the Soul did not know its own
needs? Besides, without any reasoning on the matter, I have
no discontent. The good soul nourishes me alway, unlocks
new magazines of power & enjoyment to me every day. I will
not meanly decline the immensity of good, because I have
heard it has come to others in another shape. But we are
always ducking with our unseasonable apologies. Shall the
priest or priestess on the tripod full of the God baulk the inquirer with nonsense of modesty?

To him who said it before. I see my thought standing, growing, walking, working, out there in nature. Look where I will,
I see it. Yet when I seek to say it, all men say "NO: It is not.
These are whimsies & dreams!" Then I think they look at one
thing, & I at others. My thoughts, though not false, are far, as
yet, from simple truth, & I am rebuked by their disapproba-
tion nor think of questioning it. Society is yet too great for me.
But I go back to my library & open my books & lo I read this
word spoken out of immemorial time, "God is the unity of
men." Behold, I say, my very thought! This is what I am rebuked for saying; & here it is & has been for centuries in this
book which circulates among men without reproof, nay, with
honor. But behold again here in another book "Man is good,
but men are bad." Why, I have said no more. And here again,
read these words, "Ne te quaesiveris extra." What, then! I have
not been talking nonsense. These lines of Greek & Latin
which pass now current in all literatures as proverbs of old wise
men are expressions of the very facts which the sky, the sea, the
plant, the ox, the man, the picture, said daily unto me, &
which I repeated to you. I see that I was right; that not only I
was right, which I could not doubt, but my language was
right; that the soul has always said these things; & that you
ought to hear it & say the same. And thou, good ancient
brother, who to ancient nations, to earlier modes of life & politics & religion, didst utter this my preception of today, I greet
thee with reverence, & give thee joy of that which thou so
long hast held, & which today a perfect blessing one & indi-
visible yields itself to me also, yields itself all to me, without
making thy possession less.

—

It is the best part of each writer which has nothing private in it. That is the best part of each which he does not know; that which flowed out of his constitution, & not from what he called his talents; that which in the study of a single artist, you might not so easily find, but in the study of many, would abstract as the spirit of them all. Phidias it is not but the work of Man in that early Hellenic World that I would know. The name & circumstance of Phidias, however convenient for history, embarrasses merely when we come to the highest criticism. We are to see that which Man was tending to do in a given period & was hindered or, if you will, modified in doing by the interfering volitions of Phidias, of Dante, of Shakspear, the Organ whereby Man at the moment wrought.

———

The philosopher has a good deal of knowledge which cannot be abstractly imparted, which needs the combinations & complexity of social action to paint it out, as many emotions in the soul of Handel and Mozart are thousand voiced & utterly incapable of being told in a simple air on a lute, but must ride on the mingling whirlwinds & rivers & storms of sound of the great orchestra of organ, pipe, sackbut, dulcimer, & all kinds of music. As the musician avails himself of the concert, so the philosopher avails himself of the drama, the epic, the novel, & becomes a poet; for these complex forms allow of the utterance of his knowledge of life by *indirections* as well in the didactic way, & can therefore express the fluxional quantities & values which the thesis or dissertation could never give. There is the courage of the cabinet as of the field. There is the courage of painting & of poetry as well as of siege & stake.

April 15. My books are my picture gallery. Every man has his fine recreations & elegancies allowed him by the liberal God as well as his chares. These noble English poems so rich, so sincere, so coloured in the grain, proceeding out of a depth of nature answering to the good Saxon heart in us, these are the Pitti palace & Vatican of me & my friends. Why should I grudge the Grandduke of Tuscany his gallery? The citizen of old Thebes needed not inquire after the young artists of Athens or Ionia as he stood in his gigantic palaces in the shadow of a sphinx. The Hindoo at Elephantina dwelt also with his own national ornaments. To each his own the liberal God supplies. Only accept your own. Drink deep of this enjoyment. Know your books & brilliant souls that soared & sang, yet kept their own law, & so tell of great Nature to you. Your native proper muses, your own cousins & college. They are the wild flowers that fringe your sod; but go sometimes, of a morning or evening, into this garden of delights.

Artificial Memory   Value of a Catalogue

The simple knot of Now & Then will give an immeasureable value to any sort of catalogue or journal kept with common sense for a year or two. See in the Merchant's compting room for his peddling of cotton & indigo, the value that comes to be attached to any Blotting book or Leger; and if your aims & deeds are superior, how can any record of yours (suppose, of the books you wish to read, of the pictures you would see, of the facts you would scrutinize)—any record that you are genuinely moved to begin & continue—not have a value proportionately superior? It converts the heights you have reached into table land. That book or literary fact which had the whole emphasis of attention a month ago stands here along with one which was as important in preceding months, and with that of yesterday; &, next month, there will be another. Here they all occupy but four lines & I cannot read these together without juster views of each than when I read them singly.

To know one you must know all

Nature hates finites & cripples. It is of no use to say because the world is represented in each particle as in a moss or an apple, Come I will dedicate myself to the study of botany in one thing, I will explore the dandelions. A dandelion shall be my meat & drink, house & home, & through that alone will I achieve nature.—It is all in vain, for the way Nature tells her secrets is by exposing one function in one flower, & another function in a different plant. If the spiral vessels are seen in bulbs, the vesicles are seen in others, stomata in another, pila in another, & chromule in a fifth, and to show all the parts of the one plant, she leads you all round the garden.

*

April 17. Am I a hypocrite who am disgusted by vanity everywhere, & preach self trust every day?

We give you leave to prefer your work to the whole world so long as you remain in it; but when uninvited you come to visit me, what was the praise of God, sounds in my ear like self praise.

I will assume that a stranger is judicious & benevolent. If he is, I will thereby keep him so. If he is not, it will tend to instruct him.

Self-reliance
Ask nothing of men & in the endless mutations, thou only firm column must presently appear on a throne the king of all men.

The author appeals to the judicious reader: but if he has prevailed so far with any reader that he is inflamed with a desire to behold & converse with this master, the author is shy, suspicious, & disdainful. Let him go into his closet & pray the Divinity to make him so great as to be good-natured.

———

May 10. The best conversation equally, I think, with the worst, makes me say, I will not seek society. At least I wish to hear the thoughts of men which differ widely in some important respect from my own. I would hear an artist or a wise mechanic, or agriculturist, or statesman, or historian, or wit, or poet, or scholar great in a peculiar department of learning, but not one who only gives me in a varied garb my own daily thoughts. I think it is better to sever & scatter men of kindred genius than to unite them.

I hate to quote my friend who, with all his superiority, still thinks like me. In quoting him, I am presently reduced to defend his opinion. Then I find it not only hard but impossible to seperate his view from mine, & am admonished to preach another time from God & not from a man. Hence came the Pereant qui ante nos nostra dixerunt.

*

May 12. Does it not seem imperative that the Soul should find
an articulate utterance in these days on man & religion? All or
almost all that I hear at Church is mythological; & of the few
books or preachers or talkers who pretend to have made some
progress, the most are in a transition state, Janus faced, &
speak alternately to the old & the new. It is manifest in every
word the man says whether he speaks truth or tradition. You
can tell by his pronunciation of God whether he is Theist or
Atheist.

Our aim in our writings ought to be to make daylight shine
through them.

Once I supposed that only my manner of living was superficial, that all other men's was solid. Now I find, we are all alike
shallow.

———

At Church today I felt how unequal is this match of words
against things. Cease, o thou unauthorized talker, to prate of
consolation, & resignation, and spiritual joys, in neat & balanced sentences. For I know these men who sit below, & on
the hearing of these words look up. Hush quickly; for care &
calamity are things to them. There is Mr Tolman the shoemaker, whose daughter is gone mad, and he is looking up
through his spectacles to hear what you can offer for his case.
Here is my friend, whose scholars are all leaving him, & he
knows not what to turn his hand to, next. Here is my wife who
has come to church in hope of being soothed & strengthened
after being wounded by the sharp tongue of a slut in her
house. Here is the stage driver who has the jaundice, & cannot
get well. Here is B. who failed last week, and he is looking up.
O speak things, then, or hold thy tongue.

There is no such thing as concealment: Every element hangs
out its flag. Health is a quality that cannot lie; so is disease.
The wild exotic which no man can tell of, at last puts out its
flower, its fruit, & the secret can be kept no longer. Ali may
keep the secret of his gold, but a bit will stick to the wax at
the bottom of the peck measure. You cannot wipe out the
foot track, you cannot draw up the ladder, so as to leave no

trace & no inlet. To those who have crimes to conceal, the simplest laws & elements of nature—fire, water, snow, wind, gravitation—become penalties & the sun & the moon are the frowns of God & lanthorns of his police.

In fable, again, there is the vindictive Circumstance in the old age of the Immortal Tithon.

In society, let this be thy aim, to put men in tune. Untune nobody. If, o Doctor Prose! the faces of thy friends do lengthen & quiver & gape, canst thou not retreat to thine own lexicons & grammars, to thy spade & poultry yard? The narrowest life is very wide, as wide as the largest.

May 23. The poor madman—whipped through the world by his thoughts.

Fear is an instructer who has a great talent. You may learn one thing of him passing well, this, namely, that there is certainly rottenness where he appears. He is a carrion crow; though you see not well what he hovers for, there is dead dog somewhere. Fear, for ages, has boded & mowed & gibbered over property & over social relations. I assure you that obscene bird is not there for nothing. These are great wrongs & need to be revised.

If you do not feel pleasantly toward your workman or workwoman, your kinsman or townsman, you have not dealt justly.

—

A College

My College should have Allston, Greenough, Bryant, Irving, Webster, Alcott, summoned for its domestic professors; & if I must send abroad, (& if we send for dancers & singers & actors, why not at the same prices for scholars) Carlyle, Hallam, Campbell should come & read lectures on History, Poetry, Letters. I would bid my men come for the love of God & man, promising them an open field & a boundless opportunity, & they should make their own terms. Then I would open my lecture rooms to the wide nation & they should pay, each man, a fee that should give my professors a remuneraton fit & noble. Then I should see the lecture room, the College filled with life & hope. Students would come from far; for who would not ride a hundred miles to hear some one of these men

giving his selectest thoughts to those who received them with
joy? I should see living learning; the muse once more in the
eye & cheek of the youth.

"If I love you, what is that to you?" We say so because what
we love is not in your will but above it. It is the lustre of you &
not you. It is that which you know not in yourself & can never
know.

May 26. At Waltham I repeated with somewhat more emphasis
perhaps than was needed the impression the Allston gallery
makes on me; that whilst Homer, Phidias, Dante, Shakspeare,
Michel Angelo, Milton, Raphael, make a positive impression,
Allston does not. It is an eyeless face. It is an altar without fire.
Beautiful drawing there is,—a rare merit;—taste there is; the
blandest, selectest forms & circumstance; a highly cultivated
mind; a beneficent genial atmosphere; but no man. And this it
does not seem unreasonable or ungrateful to demand, that the
artist should pierce the soul; should command; should not sit
aloof & circumambient merely, but should come & take me by
the hand & lead me somewhither. For it is the right & property of all natural objects, of all genuine talents, of all native
properties whatsoever, to be for their moment the top of the
world, to exclude all other objects, & themselves monopolize
the attention. A squirrel or a rabbit as I watch him bounding
in the wood, not less than a lion fills the eye, is beautiful, suf-
ficing, & stands then & there for nature; is the world. A ballad
if well done draws my ear & heart whilst I listen, as much as an
Epic has done before. A dog drawn by Landseer or a litter of
pigs satisfies & is a reality not less than the Transfiguration;
adds somewhat to my being.
Allston's pictures are Elysian; fair, serene, but unreal.

I extend the remark to all the American geniuses; Irving,
Bryant, Greenough, Everett, Channing, even Webster in his
recorded Eloquence, all lack nerve & dagger.

If as Hedge thinks I overlook great facts in stating the absolute laws of the soul; if as he seems to represent it the world

is not a dualism, is not a bipolar Unity, but is *two*, is Me and It, then is there the Alien, the Unknown, and all we have believed & chanted out of our deep instinctive hope is a pretty dream.

The poor mind does not seem to itself to be anything unless it have an outside oddity, some Graham diet, or Quaker coat, or Calvinistic Prayer-meeting, or Abolition Effort, or any how some wild contrasting action to testify that it is somewhat. The rich mind lies in the sun & sleeps & is Nature. Or Why need you rail, or need a biting criticism on the Church & the College to demonstrate your holiness & your intellectual aims? Let others draw that inference which damns the institutions if they will. Be thyself too great for enmity & fault-finding.

—

A great genius must come & preach self reliance. Our people are timid, desponding, recreant whimperers. If they fail in their first enterprises they lose all heart. If the young merchant fails, men say he is RUINED. If the finest genius studies at the Cambridge Divinity College, and is not ordained within a year afterwards in Boston, or New York, it seems to his friend & himself that he is justified in being disheartened & in complaining for the rest of his life.

A sturdy New Hampshire man or Vermonter who in turn tries *all* the professions, who *teams it, farms it, peddles*, keeps a school, preaches, edits a newspaper, goes to Congress, & so forth, in successive years, and always like a cat falls on his feet, is worth a hundred of these Boston dolls. My brave Henry here who is content to live now, & feels no shame in not studying any profession, for he does not postpone his life but lives already,—pours contempt on these crybabies of routine & Boston. He has not one chance but a hundred chances. Now let a stern preacher arise who shall reveal the resources of Man, & tell men they are not leaning willows, but can & must detach themselves, that a man, a woman, is a sovereign eternity, born to shed healing to the nations, that he should be ashamed of our compassion; & that the moment he acts from himself, tossing the laws, the books, the idolatries, the customs, out of the window, we pity him, we pity her no more, but thank & revere them; that with the exercise of self trust new powers shall appear.

A great fact of much import to the new philosophical opinions is the garden discovery, that, a potato put into a hole in six weeks becomes ten. This is the miracle of the multiplication of loaves.

May 28. There is no history: There is only Biography. The attempt to perpetuate, to fix a thought or principle, fails continually. You can only live for yourself: Your action is good only whilst it is alive,—whilst it is in you. The awkward imitation of it by your child or your disciple, is not a repetition of it, is not the same thing but another thing. The new individual must work out the whole problem of science, letters, & theology for himself, can owe his fathers nothing. There is no history; only biography.

———

The finite is the foam of the infinite. We stand on the shore & see the froth & shells which the sea has just thrown up, & we call the sea by the name of that boundary, as, the German Ocean,—the English channel,—the Mediterranean Sea. We do the like with the Soul. We see the world which it once has made, & we call that *God*, though it was only one moment's production, & there have been a thousand moments & a thousand productions since. But we are to learn to transfer our view to the Sea instead of the Shore, the living sea instead of the changing shore, to the energy instead of the limitation, to the Creator instead of the World. We must ever tend to a good life.

Nature will not have us fret or fume. When we come out of the Caucus or the Abolition Convention or the Temperance Meeting, she says to us, "So hot? my little Sir!" I fear the criticism of the Sun & moon.

I think we must hold a man amenable to reason for the choice of his profession. It is not an excuse any longer for his deeds that they are the custom of his trade. What business has he with an evil trade? Has he not a *Calling* in his character? Let him quit his foolish trade & embrace henceforward his Calling.

*

Travelling is a fool's paradise. We owe to our first travels the discovery that place is nothing. At home I dream that at Naples, at Rome, I can be intoxicated with beauty and lose my sadness. I pack my trunk, embrace my friends, embark on the sea, and at last wake up in Naples and there beside me is the Stern Fact, the Sad Self unrelenting, identical, that I fled from. I seek the Vatican & the palaces. I affect to be intoxicated but I am not intoxicated. Giant goes with me wherever I go.

How can I hope for a friend to me who have never been one?

29 May. The laws, literature, religion, at certain times appear but a sad travestie & caricature of nature, & so do our modes of living.

—

The lotus-eaters.

Reform always has this damper, that a new simplicity can be preached with equal emphasis (& who shall deny that it is preached with equal reason too) on the simplicity it preaches. Thus when we have come to live on the fruits of our own gardens, & begin to boast that we lead a man's life, then shall come some audacious upstart to upbraid us with our false & foreign taste which steadily plucks up every thing which nature puts in our soil & laboriously plants every thing not intended to grow there. Behold, shall that man of the Weeds say, the perpetual broad hint that nature gives you. Every day these plants you destroyed yesterday, appear again: and see a frost, a rain, a drought, has killed this exotic corn & wheat & beans & beets which luxurious man would substitute for his native & allowed table. Then too will arise the Society for preventing the murder of worms. And it will be asked with indignation what right have we to tear our small fellow citizens out of the sod and put them to death for eating a morsel of corn or a melon leaf or a bit of apple, whilst it can be proved to any jury by a surgical examination of their jaws & forceps & stomachs, that this is the natural food of this eater. In the same age a man will be reproached with simony & sacrilege because he took money of the bookseller for his poem or history.

We see all persons who are not natural with a certain Commiseration. We see that the avengers are on their track & that certain crises & purgatories they must pass through.

Compression.

There is a wide difference between compression and an elliptical style. The dense writer has yet ample room & choice of phrase & even a gamesome mood often between his noble words. There is no disagreeable contraction in his sentence any more than there is in a human face where in a square space of a few inches is found room for command & love & frolic & wisdom & for the expression even of great amplitude of surface.

Men do not converse; they chat.

Language is made up of the Spoils of all actions, trades, arts, games, of men. Every word is a metaphor borrowed from some natural or mechanical, agricultural or nautical process. The poorest speaker is like the Indian dressed in a robe furnished by a half a dozen animals. It is like our marble footslab made up of countless shells & exuviae of a foregone World.

June 3. Our young scholars read newspapers, smoke, & sleep in the afternoons. Goethe, Gibbon, Bentley, might provoke them to industry. Undoubtedly the reason why our men are not learned, why G.P.B., for instance, is not, is because the Genius of the age does not tend that way. This old learning of Bentley & Gibbon, was the natural fruit of the Traditional age in philosophy & religion. Ours is the Revolutionary Age, when man is coming back to Consciousness, & from afar this mind begets a disrelish for lexicons. Alcott therefore, and Very, who have this spirit in great exaltation, abhor books. But at least it behoves those who reject the new ideas, the sticklers of tradition to be learned. But they are not.

The Sabbath is painfully consecrated because the other days are not, and we make prayers in the morning because we sin all day. And if we pray not aloud & in form, we are constrained to excuse ourselves to others with words. O Son of man thou shouldst not excuse thyself with words. Thy doing or thy abstaining should preclude words, & make every contrary act from thine show false & ugly.

June 6. I suppose the number of reforms preached to this age exceeds the usual measure, and indicates the depth & universality of the movement which betrays itself by such variety of symptom: Anti-money, anti-war, anti-slavery, anti-government, anti-Christianity, anti-College; and, the rights of Woman.

Our conventional style of writing is now so trite & poor, so little idiomatic that we have several foreigners who write in our journals in a style not to be distinguished from their native colleagues, as Dr Follen, Maroncelli, Dr Lieber, Graeter. But whosoever draws on the language of conversation, will not be so easily imitated but will speak as the stream flows.

—

Two absolutions

June 11. You may fulfil acceptably your circle of duties by clearing yourself in the direct or in the reflex way. You may consider whether you have not satisfied all your relations to father, mother, cousin, neighbor, town, cat & dog; whether any of these can upbraid you. But I may also neglect this reflex standard & absolve me to myself. I have my own stern claims & perfect circle. It denies the name of duty to many offices that are called duties. But if I can discharge its debts, it enables me to dispense with the popular code.

Iteration

Walked to the two ponds yesterday with C. S. A beautiful afternoon in the woodlands & waters & aerial waters above; I thought how charming is always an analogy, as, for example, the iteration which delights us in so many parts of nature, in the reflection of the shore & the trees in water; in Architecture, in the repetition of posts in a fence, or windows or doors or rosettes in the wall, or still finer the pillars of a colonnade; in

poetry rhymes & still better the iteration of the sense as in
Milton's

> "though fallen on evil days
> On evil days though fallen & evil tongues"

and the sublime death of Sisera,—"At her feet he bowed, he
fell; where he bowed there he fell; where he bowed, there he
gave up the ghost;" where the fact is made conspicuous, nay
colossal, by this simple rhetoric. In society we have this figure
as soon as we put ten or twenty persons in one apartment; in a
regiment of soldiers in uniform; in a funeral procession, where
all wear black; in a bridal procession, where a choir of maidens
in white robes give the charm of living statues.

June 12. I know no means of calming the fret & perturbation
into which too much sitting, too much talking brings me so
perfect as labor. I have no animal spirits; therefore when surprised by company & kept in a chair for many hours, my heart
sinks, my brow is clouded, & I think I will run for Acton
Woods, & live with the squirrels henceforward.

But my garden is nearer, and my good hoe as it bites the
ground revenges my wrongs & I have less lust to bite my enemies. I confess I work at first with a little venom, lay to a little
unnecessary strength. But by smoothing the rough hillocks, I
smooth my temper; by extracting the long roots of the piper
grass, I draw out my own splinters; & in a short time I can
hear the Bobalink's song & see the blessed deluge of light &
colour that rolls around me.

In Allston's Lorenzo & Jessica, there is moonlight but no
moon; in the Jeremiah, the receiving Baruch is the successful
figure. His best figures read & hear: and always his genius
seems feminine & not masculine.

I said all History becomes subjective & repeats itself,
Parthia, Macedon, Rome, and Netherlands, in each man's life.
And now Alcott with his hatred of labor & commanding
contemplation, a haughty beneficiary, makes good to the 19th
Century Simeon the Stylite & the Thebaid, & the first
Capuchins.

The prayer of the farmer kneeling in his field to weed it, the prayer of the rower who kneels with the stroke of his oar, are true prayers & are answered. As Caratach in Fletcher's Bonduca says of the god Andate

> "His hidden meaning lies in our endeavors
>   Our valors are our best Gods."

14 June. Shall I not call God the Beautiful who daily showeth himself so to me in his gifts? I chide society, I embrace solitude, & yet I am not so ungrateful as not to see the wise, the lovely, & the noble minded as from time to time they pass my tent. Who hears me, who understands me becomes mine, a possession for all time. Nor is nature so poor but she gives me this joy several times. And thus we weave social threads of our own, a new web of relations, and, as many thoughts in succession substantiate themselves, we shall by & by stand in a new world of our own Creation, & no longer strangers & pilgrims in a traditionary globe. By oldest right, by the divine affinity of Virtue with itself, I find my friends, or rather not I but the deity in me & in them doth deride & cancel the thick walls of individual character, relation, age, sex, & circumstance, at which he usually conniveth, & now makes many one. High thanks I owe you, excellent lovers, who carry out the world for me to new & noble depths and enlarge the meaning of all my thoughts. These are not stark & stiffened persons, but the new born poetry of God, poetry without stop,—hymn, ode, and epic, poetry still flowing & not yet caked in dead books with annotation & grammar but Apollo & the Muses chaunting still.

16 June. Was not the motto of the Welch bards "Those whom truth had made free before the world"? Certainly the progress of character & of art teaches to treat all persons with an infinite freedom. What are persons but certain good or evil thoughts masquerading before me in curious frocks of flesh & blood. I were a fool to mind the color or figure of the frock & slight the deep aboriginal thought which so arrays itself. In this sense you cannot overestimate persons. And now in my house as I

see them pass or hear their step on the stair, it seems to me the step of Ages & Nations. And truly these walls do not lack variety in the few individuals they hold. Here is Simeon the Stylite, or John of Patmos in the shape of Jones Very, religion for religion's sake, religion divorced, detached from man, from the world, from science & art; grim, unmarried, insulated, accusing; yet true in itself, speaking *things* in every word. The lie is in the detachment; and when he is in the room with other persons, speech stops as if there were a corpse in the apartment. Then here is mine Asia not without a deep tinge herself of the same old land & exaggerated & detached pietism, and so she serves as bridge between Very & the Americans. Then comes the lofty maiden who represents the Hope of these modern days, whom the "limits of earthly existence", "the highest knowledge", "the fairest blessings cannot in the slightest degree satisfy", & whose beautiful impatience of these *dregs of Romulus* predicts to us a fairer future. And here are the two babes not yet descended into our sympathy or the world where we work, not yet therefore individualized & rigid, but a common property to all, which each can blend with his own ideas.

———

Be sacred. Do not let any man crowd upon you by peeping into him. No man can come near me unless I cumber myself about him. He comes too near by my act, not otherwise. Remember the great sentiment, "What we love that we have, but by Desire we bereave ourselves of the love," which Schiller said, or said the like.
I must be myself. I cannot disintegrate myself any longer for you or you. If you can love me for what I am, we shall be the happier. If you cannot, I will still seek to deserve that you should. I must be myself; I will not hide my tastes or my aversions. I will so trust that what is deep is holy, that I will do bravely before the sun & moon whatsoever inly rejoiceth me, & the heart appoints.

I do with my friends as I do with books. I would have them where I can get them, but I seldom use them. We must have society on our own terms and admit or exclude it on the slightest cause. I cannot afford to speak much with my friend.

If he is great he makes me so great that I cannot descend to converse. In the great days presentiments hover before me, far before me in the firmament. I ought then to dedicate myself to them. I go in that I may seize them; I go out that I may seize them. I fear only that I may lose them receding into the sky in which now they are only a patch of brighter light. Then though I prize my friends I cannot afford to talk with them and study their visions lest I lose my own. It would indeed give a certain household joy to quit this lofty seeking, this spiritual astronomy or search of stars, & come down into warm sympathies with you but then I know well I shall mourn always the vanishing of my Mighty Gods. 'Tis true, next week, I shall have languid times when I can well afford to occupy myself with foreign objects; then I shall regret the lost literature of your mind & wish you were here by my side again. But if you come, perhaps you will fill my mind only with new visions, not with yourself but with your lustres, & I shall not be able any more than now to converse with you. So I will owe to my friends this evanescent intercourse. I will receive from them not what they have, but what they are. They shall give me that which properly they cannot give, but which radiates from them. But they shall not hold me by any relations less subtle & pure. We will meet as though we met not, & part as though we parted not.

We should be all kings & all queens.

Idealism

There are degrees in idealism. We learn first to play with it academically, as the magnet was once a toy. Then we see in the heyday of youth & poetry that it may be true; that it is true in gleams & fragments. Then its countenance waxes stern & grand, & we see that it must be true. It now shows itself ethical & practical. We learn that God Is; that he is in me; & that all things are shadows of him.

There is no history, only biography. The private soul ascends to transcendental virtue. Like Very, he works hard without moving hand or foot; like Agathon, he loves the goddess & not the woman; like Alcott he refuses to pay a debt without injustice; but this liberty is not transferable to any disciple, no nor to the man himself when he falls out of his trance & comes down from the tripod.

I will surrender to the Divine—to nothing less, not to Jove, not to ephod or cross.

Beauty
I seek beauty in the arts & in song & in emotion for itself & suddenly I find it to be sword & shield. For dwelling there in its depths I find myself above the region of Fear, & unassailable like a god at the Olympian tables.

June 21. It may be said in defence of this practice of *Composition* which seems to young persons so mechanical & so *un*-inspired that to men working in Time all literary effort must be more or less of this kind, to Byron, to Goethe, to De Stael, not less than to Scott & Southey. Succession, moments, parts are their destiny & not wholes & worlds & eternity. But you say that so moving & moved on thoughts & verses gathered in different parts of a long life you sail no straight line but are perpetually distracted by new & counter currents, & go a little way north, then a little way north east, then a little north west, then a little north again; & so on. Be it so; Is any motion different? The curve line is not a curve but an infinite polygon. The voyage of the best ship is a zig zag line on a hundred tacks. This is only microscopic criticism. See the line from a sufficient distance & it straightens itself to the average tendency. All these verses & thoughts were as spontaneous at some time to that man as any one was. Being so, they were not his own but above him the voice of simple, necessary, aboriginal Nature & coming from so narrow an experience as one mortal, they must be strictly related, even the farthest ends of his life, and seen at the perspective of a few ages will appear harmonious & univocal.

—

Chance Pictures
An instructive picture gallery is the weather stains on a wall or the figures on a marbled paper for Chance is no mannerist & one instantly learns how free & bold the hand of a master might become. For here are outlines of knights & ladies &

beggar women & griffins & ghosts & trees that need but a stroke or two of an imaginative eye to fill up in to more commanding & graceful & various forms & attitudes beyond all the masters drew.

As I read Ben Jonson the other eve it seemed to me as before that there is a striking resemblance between the poetry of his age & the painting of the old masters in the depth of the style. With all the frolic & freedom the poetry is not superficial and with all the weight of thought it is not solemn. The beauty is necessary & the shadows are transparent.

As I looked into the river the other afternoon it struck me that the Rembrandts & Salvators who paint the dark pictures probably copied the *reflection* of the landscape in water. Certainly its charm is indescribable, and as I think, not to be painted.

Rhyme

27 June. Rhyme; not tinkling rhyme but grand Pindaric strokes as firm as the tread of a horse. Rhyme that vindicates itself as an art, the stroke of the bell of a cathedral. Rhyme which knocks at prose & dulness with the stroke of a cannon ball. Rhyme which builds out into Chaos & Old night a splendid architecture to bridge the impassable, & call aloud on all the children of morning that the Creation is recommencing. I wish to write such rhymes as shall not suggest a restraint but contrariwise the wildest freedom.

—

Belief. The man I saw believed that his suspenders would hold up his pantaloons & that his straps would hold them down. His creed went little farther.

Progress of the Species! Why the world is a treadmill.

A friend looks to the past & the future. He is the child of all my foregoing hours, the prophet of those to come. He is the harbinger of a greater friend. It is the property of the divine to be reproductive.

*

June 30. You dare not say 'I think', 'I am', but quote St Paul or Jesus or Bacon or Locke. Yonder roses make no reference to former roses or to better ones. They exist with God today.

It is proposed to form a very large Society to devise & execute means for propping in some secure & permanent manner this planet. It has long filled the minds of the benevolent & anxious part of the community with lively emotion, the consideration of the exposed state of the globe; the danger of its falling & being swamped in absolute space; the danger of its being drawn too near the sun & roasting the race of mankind & the daily danger of its being overturned & if a stage coach overset costs valuable lives what will not ensue on the upset of this Omnibus? It has been thought that by a strenuous & very extensive concert aided by a committee of master builders & blacksmiths, a system of booms & chains might be set round the exterior surface & that it might be underpinned in such a manner as to enable the aged & the women & children to sleep & eat with greater security henceforward. It is true that there is not a perfect unanimity on this subject at present & it is much to be regretted. A pert & flippant orator remarked to the meeting last Sunday, that the World could stand without linch pins & that even if you should cut all the ropes & knock away the whole underpinning, it would swing & poise perfectly for the poise was in the globe itself. But this is Transcendentalism.

3 July. In Boston yesterday & the day before, & saw the Allston Gallery, & the Atheneum, & met Margaret Fuller, Miss Clarke, Dwight, & young Ward, on that ground; & Alcott on the broader platform. In the Allston gallery the Polish Jews are an offence to me; they degrade & animalize. As soon as a beard becomes any thing but an accident, we have not a man but a Turk, a Jew, a satyr, a dandy, a goat. So we paint angels & Jesus & Apollo beardless, & the Greek & the Mohawk leave them to Muftis & Monks.

The landscapes pleased me well. I like them all: he is a fine pastoral poet & invites us to come again & again. The drawing also of the figures is always pleasing, but they lack fire & the impression of the gallery though bland is faint in the memory. Nothing haunts the memory, from it. It never quickens a

pulse of virtue. It never causes an emulous throb. Herein perhaps it resembles the genius of Spenser; & is, as I have said,
Elysian.

When I went to Europe, I fancied the great pictures were
great strangers; some new unexperienced pomp & show; a foreign wonder; 'barbaric pearl & gold'; like the spontoons &
standards of the militia which play such pranks in the eyes &
imaginations of schoolboys. I was to see & acquire I knew not
what. When I came at last to Rome & saw with eyes the pictures, I was suddenly taught better. I saw that the picture was
the reverse of all this; that it left for little people the gay & fantastic & ostentatious, & itself pierced directly to the simple &
true; that it was familiar & sincere; that it was the old eternal
fact I had met already in so many forms,—unto which I lived;
that it was the plain *You & Me* I knew so well,—had left at
home in so many conversations. That which had impressed me
in the pause before service in the English Ambassador's chapel
in Naples, on the first Sunday after my arrival in that City,
when I saw that nothing was changed with me but the place &
said to myself; 'Thou foolish Child, hast thou come out hither
over four thousand miles of salt water to find that which was
perfect to thee there at home?'—that fact I saw again in the
Academia of Naples where the sculptures were, & yet again
when I came to Rome & to the paintings of Raphael, Angelo,
Sacchi, Titian & Leonardo da Vinci. "What, old mole! workest
thou in the earth so fast?" It had travelled by my side;—that
which I fancied I had left in Boston was here in the Vatican
and again at Milan, & at Paris, & made all travelling ridiculous
as a treadmill.

I now require this of all pictures, that they domesticate me
not that they dazzle me. Allston's St Peter is not yet human
enough for me. It is too picturesque, & like a bronzed cast of
the Socrates or Venus.

Perception not whimsical but fatal. If I see a trait my children will see it after me & all men & all women for my perception is as much a fact as is the sun. Abolitionist. You have not
voted for Mr B because you have made so much of the slave

question. You have ceased to be a man that you may be an abolitionist.

Consistency! Nonsense with your wooden walls. Speak what you think today in words as strong as cannon balls & tomorrow speak what you think then in words as hard though it contradicts to the ear every thing you said today.

Beside a great man, by Napoleon or Scipio, all men look like shadows though they were solid enough a moment ago.

A cool fellow

How foolish this distrust of calling a meeting for lack of subject. That word or alphabetical letter that just skipped through your mind will be as large as Atlas if you let it grow.

How much we owe to poor pictures! that which nature paints. Hence we ask authentic proof that an artist has been there also.

Influence of Construction in Architecture

4 July. The doctrine of hatred must be preached as the counteraction of the doctrine of love when that pules & whines. I hate father & mother & wife & brother when my muse calls me & I say to these relatives that if they wish my love they must respect my hatred. I would write on the lintels of the doorpost, Whim. Expect me not to show cause why I seek or why I shun company. Then again do not tell me of the obligation on me to put all poor men in good situations. I tell thee, thou foolish philanthropist, that I grudge the dollar, the shilling, the cent I give to such men as do not belong to me & to whom I do not belong. There is a class of persons to whom by all spiritual affinity I am bought & sold; for them I will go to prison, if need be; but your nonsense of popular charity, the suckling of fools, the building of meetinghouses, the alms to sots,—though I confess with shame I sometimes succumb & give the dollar it is a wicked dollar which by & by I shall have the manhood to withhold. I have no duties so peremptory as my intellectual duties.

—

I like my boy with his endless sweet soliloquies & iterations and his utter inability to conceive why I should not leave all my nonsense, business, & writing & come to tie up his toy horse, as if there was or could be any end to nature beyond his horse.

And he is wiser than we when he threatens his whole threat 'I will not love you.'

Nature delights in punishing stupid people. The very strawberry vines are more than a match for them with all their appetites, & all their fumbling fingers. The little defenceless vine coolly hides the best berry now under this leaf, then under that, & keeps the treasure for yonder darling boy with the bright eyes when Booby is gone.

July 14. I desire that my housekeeping should be clean & sweet & that it should not shame or annoy me. I desire that it should appear in all its arrangements that human Culture is the end to which that house is built & garnished. I wish my house to be a college open as the air to all to whom I spiritually belong, & who belong to me. But it is not open to others or for other purposes. I do not wish that it should be a confectioner's shop wherein eaters & drinkers may get strawberries & champagne. I do not wish that it should be a playground or house of entertainment for boys. They do well to play; I like that they should, but not with me, or in these precincts. Nor do I wish that it should be a hospital for the sick excepting only *my* sick. Nor do I wish that it should be a tavern or house of convenience to harbour any one,—neither unwise, neither wise,—beyond the limit of their stay for the express end of conversation & study. All these other wants are, I know, natural & necessary, but they must be satisfied elsewhere: as potatoes, fuel, & broadcloth must be had, yet you would not go to a church to buy them. I do not wish to hear such words or sounds at my table as to overpersuade me that there is a pig sitting there in the disguise of a fine lady or a fine gentleman.

———

27 Aug. Yesterday ascended Red Hill & saw our Lake & Squam Lake, Ossipee, Conway, Gunstock, & one dim summit which stood to us for the White Hills. Mrs Cook lives in this Red mountain half a mile from the top & a mile from the bottom. We asked her what brought her here 51 years ago. She said "Poverty brought & poverty kept her here." For our parts, we thought that a poor man could not afford to live here, that it was to increase poverty tenfold to set one's cabin

at this helpless height. Her son makes 1000 lb. of maple sugar in a year. They use the coffee bean for coffee, and the Fever bush for tea.

The Hedysarum which they call wild-bean was the principal food of the cows when they first came here until grass grew.

There is no man in mountain or valley but only abortions of such, and a degree of absurdity seems to attach to nature.

On Sunday we heard sulphurous Calvinism. The preacher railed at Lord Byron. I thought Lord Byron's vice better than Rev. Mr M's Virtue. He told us of a man he had seen on Lake Michigan who saw his ship in danger & said, "If the Almighty would only stand neuter six months, it was all he asked." In his horror at this sentiment the preacher did not perceive that it was the legitimate inference from his own distorting creed; that it was the *reductio ad absurdum* of Calvinism.

—

1839

Concord 4 September. In the journey to the White Mountains from which I returned Monday evening 2d Sept. I found few striking experiences. Nature seems ashamed of man & stands away from him even while he lives from her bounty. The men & women whom we see, live in their sensations, & repeat in memory & talk their paltriest satisfactions. The Profile mountain was a pleasing wonder. I admire the great & grave expression of this Mountain Bust (where Nature herself has done what Lysippus (?) & Michel Angelo projected) which sternly gazes eastward to the sea. Black eagles were wheeling over the summit when I saw it. But I believe the most agreeable circumstance in the tour was the echo of the horn blown at the door of the White Mountain Hotel (Fabian's) which turned the Mountains into an Aeolian harp and instantly explained the whole Attic Mythology of Diana and all divine hunters & huntresses. How lofty, how haughtily beautiful is a musical note!

Burke is a rhetoric, a robe to be always admired for the beauty with which he drapes facts as we love light or rather colour with clothes all things. What rich temperance, what costly textures, what flowing variety.

*

Manners need somewhat negligent & even slow in the perceptions as Business requires quick perceptions. Manners must have an ignoring eye, a languid graceful hand, a sluggard knight who does not see the annoyances, inconveniences, shifts that cloud the brow & smother the voice of the sensitive. The popular men & women are oft externally sluggish lazy natures not using superlatives nor staking their all on every peppercorn.

5 Sept.
How tedious is the perpetual self preservation of the traveller. His whole road is a comparison of what he sees & does at home with what he sees & does now. Not a blessed moment does he forget himself & yielding to the new world of facts that environ him, utter without memory that which they say. Could he once abandon himself to the wonder of the landscape he would cease to find it strange: In New Hampshire the dignity of the landscape made more obvious the meanness of the tavern-haunting men.

I do not know that I can recall the thought of last Thursday which made the mountains greater.

—

12 September. How to spend a day nobly, is the problem to be solved, beside which all the great reforms which are preached seem to me trivial. If any day has not the privilege of a great action, then at least raise it by a wise passion. If thou canst not do, at least abstain. Now the memory of the few past idle days so works in me that I hardly dare front a new day when I leave my bed. When shall I come to the end of these shameful days, & *organize* honour in every day?

Sept. 14. Yesterday Mr Mann's Address on Education. It was full of the modern gloomy view of our democratical institutions, and hence the inference to the importance of Schools. But as far as it betrayed distrust, it seemed to pray, as do all our pulpits, for the consolation of Stoicism. A Life in Plutarch would be a perfect rebuke to such a sad discourse. If Christianity is effete let us try the doctrine of power to endure.

*

Education. Sad it was to see the death-cold convention yesterday morning as they sat shivering, a handful of pale men & women in a large church, for it seems the Law has touched the business of Education with the point of its pen & instantly it has frozen stiff in the universal congelation of society. An education in things is not: we all are involved in the condemnation of words, an Age of words. We are shut up in schools & college recitation rooms for ten or fifteen years & come out at last with a bellyfull of words & do not know a thing. We cannot use our hands or our legs or our eyes or our arms. We do not know an edible root in the woods. We cannot tell our course by the stars nor the hour of the day by the sun. It is well if we can swim & skate. We are afraid of a horse, of a cow, of a dog, of a cat, of a spider. Far better was the Roman rule to teach a boy nothing that he could not learn standing. Now here are my wise young neighbors who instead of getting like the wordmen into a railroad-car where they have not even the activity of holding the reins, have got into a boat which they have built with their own hands, with sails which they have contrived to serve as a tent by night, & gone up the river Merrimack to live by their wits on the fish of the stream & the berries of the wood. My worthy neighbor Dr. B. expressed a true parental instinct when he desired to send his boy with them to learn something. The farm, the farm is the right school. The reason of my deep respect for the farmer is that he is a realist & not a dictionary. The farm is a piece of the world, the School house is not. The farm by training the physical rectifies & invigorates the metaphysical & moral nature.

Now so bad we are that the world is stripped of love & of terror. Here came the other night an Aurora so wonderful a curtain of red & blue & silver glory that in any other age or nation it would have moved the awe & wonder of men & mingled with the profoundest sentiments of religion & love, & we all saw it with cold arithmetical eyes, we know how many colours shone, how many degrees it extended, how many hours it lasted, & of this heavenly flower we beheld nothing more: a primrose by the brim of the river of time. Shall we not wish back again the Seven Whistlers, the Flying Dutchman, the lucky & unlucky days, & the terrors of the Day of Doom?

I lament that I find in me no enthusiasm, no resources for the instruction & guidance of the people when they shall discover that their present guides are blind. This convention of Education is cold, but I should perhaps affect a hope I do not feel if I were bidden to counsel it. I hate preaching whether in pulpits or Teachers' meetings. Preaching is a pledge & I wish to say what I think & feel today with the proviso that tomorrow perhaps I shall contradict it all. Freedom boundless I wish. I will not pledge myself not to drink wine, not to drink ink, not to lie, & not to commit adultery lest I hanker tomorrow to do these very things by reason of my having tied my hands. Besides Man is so poor he cannot afford to part with any advantages or bereave himself of the functions even of one hair. I do not like to speak to the Peace Society if so I am to restrain me in so extreme a privilege as the use of the sword & bullet. For the peace of the man who has forsworn the use of the bullet seems to me not quite peace, but a canting impotence: but with knife & pistol in my hands, if I, from greater bravery & honor, cast them aside, then I know the glory of peace.

It was a fine corollary of Stoicism that Aristotle said that the honor of chastity consisted in selfsufficing.

It is among the shames of these days that we talk about them, about days & virtues & works & heroism, a thing as unfit as to talk about our food.

The mob are always interesting. We hate editors, preachers, & all manner of scholars, and fashionists. A blacksmith, a truckman, a farmer we follow into the barroom & watch with eagerness what they shall say, for such as they, do not speak because they are expected to, but because they have somewhat to say.

How sad a spectacle so frequent nowadays to see a young man after ten years' of college education come out ready for his voyage of life & to see that the entire ship is made of rotten timber, of rotten honey-combed traditional timber without so much as an inch of new plank in the hull.

It seems as if the present age of words should naturally be followed by an age of silence when men shall speak only through facts & so regain their health. We die of words. We are hanged, drawn, & quartered by dictionaries. We walk in the vale of shadows. It is an age of hobgoblins. Public Opinion is a hobgoblin, Christianity a hobgoblin, the God of popular worship a hobgoblin. When shall we attain to be real & be born into the new heaven & earth of nature & truth?

It is a disgrace to remember as we do. All our life is the pitifullest remembering. Memory is an indigestion, a flatulency of mind which eats over again its dinner all night with feverish disgust. Each man does but six or seven new things in all his lifetime; the smith, the joiner, the farmer repeat every day the same manipulations. The singer repeats his old song, the preacher his old sermon, the talker his old fact.

It is not good sense to repeat an old story to the same child. Yet the pulpit thinks there is some piquancy or rag of meat in his paragraph about the traitor Judas or the good Samaritan.

—

I heard with great pleasure lately the songs of Jane Tuckerman. The tone of her voice is not in the first hearing quite pure & agreeable. The tone of Abby Warren's voice is much more pure & noble; but the wonderful talent of Miss T.—her perfect taste, the sweetness of all her tones, & the rich variety & the extreme tenuity with which she spins the thread of sound to a point as fine as a ray of light—makes the ear listen to her with the most delicious confidence. Her songs were better with every repetition. I found my way about in the hollows & alleys of their music better each time. Yet still her music was a phenomenon to me. I admired it as a beautiful curiosity, as a piece of virtu. It does not marry itself to the mind & become a part of it. She composes me by the serenity of her manners.

All conversation among literary men is muddy. I derive from literary meetings no satisfaction. Yet it is pity that meetings for conversation should end as quickly as they ordinarily do. They end as soon as the blood is up, & we are about to say daring & extraordinary things. They adjourn for a fortnight & when we are reassembled we have forgot all we had to say.

—

"These men."

In Massachusetts a number of young & adult persons are at this moment the subjects of a revolution. They are not organized into any conspiracy: they do not vote, or print, or meet together, they do not know each others' faces or names. They are united only in a common love of truth & love of its work. They are of all conditions & natures. They are some of them mean in attire, & some mean in station, & some mean in body, having inherited from their parents faces & forms scrawled with the traits of every vice. Not in churches or in courts or in large assemblies, not in solemn holidays where men were met in festal dress have these pledged themselves to new life, but in lonely & obscure places, in solitude, in servitude, in solitary compunctions & fears & shames, in disappointments, in diseases, trudging beside the team in the dusty road or drudging a hireling in other men's cornfields, schoolmasters who teach a few children rudiments for a pittance, ministers of small parishes of the obscurer sects, lone women in dependant condition, matrons & young maidens rich & poor, beautiful & hard-favored, without concert or proclamation of any kind have silently given in their several adherence to a new hope.

Friendship

September 24. "If you do not like my friend at first sight you will never like him." Indeed! I had not thought so. I did not, I remember, like you at first sight, yet we manage to converse now without disgust. I do not wish to treat friendships daintily. They are not glass or cobwebs but the most robust things in nature when they are things. I have the most romantic relations precisely with my oldest friends. He who offers himself a candidate for that relation comes up like an Olympian to the great Games where the firstborn of the world are the competitors. He proposes himself for contests where Time, Want, Danger, are in the lists, and he alone is victor who has truth enough in his constitution to preserve the delicacy of his beauty from the wear & tear of all these. Who is rich, who is fashionable, who is high bred, has great hindrances to success. Very hardly will he attain to mastery with all these ribbons, laces, & plumes in a tug where all the hap depends on eternal facts, on intrinsic nobleness & the contempt of trifles. Genius & Virtue like diamonds are best plain set,—set in lead, set in poverty. And the highest Beauty should be plain set.

Those only can sleep who do not care to sleep & those only can act or write well who do not respect the writing or the act.

I have read Oliver Twist in obedience to the opinions of so many intelligent people as have praised it. The author has an acute eye for costume; he sees the expression of dress, of form, of gait, of personal deformities; of furniture, of the outside & inside of houses; but his eye rests always on surfaces; he has no insight into Character. For want of key to the moral powers the Author is fain to strain all his stage trick of grimace, of bodily terror, of murder, & the most approved performances of Remorse. It all avails nothing. There is nothing memorable in the book except the *flash*, which is got at a police office, & the dancing of the madman which strikes a momentary terror. Like Cooper & Hawthorne he has no dramatic talent. The moment he attempts dialogue the improbability of life hardens to wood & stone. And the book begins & ends without a poetic ray & so perishes in the reading.

——

Mr Dewey said to me that W. C. promised to be a great man twenty years hence. Mr Felt, then one of the parish Committee in the First Church in N.Y., observed "Yes but we want a minister ready grown. He must have his growing elsewhere." So it is with us all. Only fathers & mothers may contentedly be present at the growing. I hate to hear a singer who is learning, let her voice be never so sweet. I wish not to be asked in every note whether I will allow it; I wish every note to command me with sweet yet perfect empire.

Also I hate Early Poems.

——

When I was thirteen years old, my uncle S. R. one day asked me, "How is it, Ralph, that all the boys dislike you & quarrel with you, whilst the grown people are fond of you?"—Now am I thirty six and the fact is reversed,—the old people suspect & dislike me, & the young love me.

*

Never exhort, only confess. All exhortation, O thou hoarse preacher! respects others & not thyself, respects appearances & not facts & therefore is cant.

Shall I not once paint in these pages an experience so conspicous to me & so oft repeated in these late years as the Debating Club, now under the name of Teachers' Meeting, now a Conference, now an Aesthetic Club, & now a religious Association, but always bearing for me the same fruit; a place where my memory works more than my wit & so I come away with compunction?

In correcting old discourses to retain only what is alive I discover a good deal of matter which a strong common sense would exclude. I seem however to discover in the same passages which I condemn the commendation of the ideal & holy life & hence am annoyed by a discrepancy betwixt the two states. I love facts & so erase this preaching. But also I venerate the Good, the Better & did therefore give it place. Cannot Montaigne & Shakspeare consist with Plato & Jesus?

———

How we hate this solemn Ego that accompanies the learned like a double wherever he goes! Let us be ravished by the fact & the thought as these beautiful children are by the acorn, the hobby horse, & the doll, rush into the object, nor think of our existence, though by the laws of nature forever & ever only the *subject* is consulted let the *objects* be as many & as grand as they will.

I discern degrees in the proficiency of the malcontents of the day. I see some who though not arrived at the chamber called Peace, have yet such redundant health that no poverty or unfriendly circumstance could much affect them; and others who are still seeking in the saloons of the city what not even solitude can give them.

The Transcendant is Economy also.

*

The Woes of the time,—is not that topic enough? He that can enumerate their symptoms, expose their cause, & show how they contain their remedies comes to men from heaven with a palm branch in his hand.

7 October. Only this strip of paper remains to me to record my introduction to Anna Barker last Friday at Jamaica Plains. A new person is to me ever a great event and few days of my quiet life are so illustrated & cheered as were the two in which I enjoyed the frank & generous confidence of a being so lovely, so fortunate, & so remote from my own experiences.

Pick no locks. Check this low curiosity. An answer in words is really no answer to the questions you ask. Do not ask a description of the countries towards which you sail. The description does not describe them to you & tomorrow you arrive there & know them by having them. Men ask of the Immortality of the soul, & the Employments of heaven &c &c & dream that Jesus has answered their questions. His great soul never stooped a moment to their *patois*. Ask such questions a hundred years & accumulate all the ingenious answers & you know nothing about the matter. The soul answers never such meddlers. The only mode of obtaining an answer is to forego all such curiosity & accepting in a trance of praise the great tide of Being that floats us into the secret of nature, work & live, work & live, work & live, & all unawares we find we are heavenly & divine, the question & the answer are one.

She seemed to me a woman singularly healthful & entire. She had no detached parts or powers. She had not talents or affections or accomplishments or single features of conspicuous beauty, but was a unit & whole, so that whatsoever she did became her, whether she walked or sat or spoke. She had an instinctive elegance. She had too much warmth & sympathy & desire to please than that you could say her manners were marked with dignity, yet no princess could surpass her clear & erect demeanour on each occasion. She is not an intellectual beauty but is of that class who in society are designated as having a great deal of Soul, that is, the predominating character of her nature is not thought but emotion or sympathy, & of course she is not of my class, does not resemble the women whom I have most admired & loved, but she is so perfect in her own nature as to meet these by the fulness of her heart, and does not distance me as I believe all others of that cast of character do. She does not sit at home in her own mind as my angels are wont to do, but instantly goes abroad into the minds of others, takes possession of society & warms it with noble sentiments. Her simple faith seemed to be that by dealing nobly with all, all would show themselves noble, & so her conversation is the frankest I ever heard. She can afford to be sincere. The wind is not purer than she is.

Eloquence.   *Lyceum.*

Here is all the true orator will ask, for here is a convertible audience & here are no stiff conventions that prescribe a method, a style, a limited quotation of books, & an exact respect to certain books, persons, or opinions. No, here everything is admissible, philosophy, ethics, divinity, criticism, poetry, humor, fun, mimicry, anecdotes, jokes, ventriloquism. All the breadth & versatility of the most liberal conversation highest lowest personal local topics, all are permitted, and all may be combined in one speech; it is a panharmonicon,— every note on the longest gamut, from the explosion of cannon, to the tinkle of a guitar. Let us try if Folly, Custom, Convention & Phlegm cannot hear our sharp artillery. Here is a pulpit that makes other pulpits tame & ineffectual—with their cold mechanical preparation for a delivery the most decorous,—fine things, pretty things, wise things, but no arrows, no axes, no nectar, no growling, no transpiercing, no loving, no enchantment. Here he may lay himself out utterly, large, enormous, prodigal, on the subject of the hour. Here he may dare to hope for ecstasy & eloquence.

Concord, 11 October, 1839.

At Waltham, last Sunday, on the hill near the old meeting-house, I heard music so soft that I fancied it was a pianoforte in some neighboring Farmhouse, but on listening more attentively I found it was the church bells in Boston, nine miles distant, which were playing for me this soft tune.

Horace Walpole whose letters I read so attentively in the past summer is a type of the dominant Englishman at this day. He has taste, common sense, love of facts, impatience of humbug, love of history, love of splendor, love of justice, & the sentiment of honor among gentlemen, but no life whatever of the higher faculties, no faith, no hope, no aspiration, no question even touching the Secret of nature.

"Matter, which is itself privation, often scatters & dissolves what a more excellent Being than herself had wrought," says Plutarch (on Oracles Vol 4 p 12).

Those books which are for all time are written indifferently at any time. How can the Age be a bad one which conveys to me the joys of literature? I can read Plutarch & Augustine, & Beaumont & Fletcher, & Landor's Pericles, & with no very dissimilar feeling the verses of my young contemporaries, T. & C. Let those then make much of the different genius of different periods who suffer by them. I who seek enjoyments which proceed not out of time, but out of thought, will celebrate on this lofty Sabbath Morn the day without night, the beautiful Ocean which hath no tides. And yet literature too, this magical man-provoking talisman is in some sort a creature of time. It is begotten by Time on the Soul. And one day we shall forget this primer. But how obviously initial it is to the writer. It is only his priming. The books of the nations, the universal books, are long ago forgotten of him who spake them. We must learn to judge books by absolute standards. Criticism too must be transcendental. Society wishes to assign subjects & method to its writers. But neither it nor you may intermeddle. You cannot reason at will in this & that other vein, but only as you must. You cannot make quaint combinations, & bring to the crucible & alembic of truth things far fetched or fantastic or popular, but your method & your subject are foreordained in your nature, & in all nature, or ever the earth was—or it has no worth. All that gives currency still to any book published today by Little & Brown is the remains of faith in the breast of men that not adroit book-makers, but the inextinguishable soul of the Universe reports of itself in articulate discourse through this & that other man, today as of old. The ancients strongly expressed their sense of the unmanageableness of these words of the God, by saying that the God made his priest insane, took him hither & thither as leaves are whirled by the tempest. But we sing as we are bid. Our inspirations are very manageable & tame. Death & Sin have whispered in the ear of our wild horses & they are become drays & hacks.

It is very easy to hint keen replies to these statements of the independency of writers. It is easy to make persons ridiculous. Let us all or any who say so, be ridiculous. Grant that we have been vain, boastful, cunning, covering our wretched pride with this claim of inspiration. Still the fact holds forever & ever, that the soul doth so speak, & that the law of literature giving its exact worth to every ballad & spoken sentence is thus transcendant & only selfcontained. It certainly is never vitiated by any affectation, cant, dulness, or crime, of those who speak for it. Their lie or folly recoils on them. Point out what abuses you will that might flow from the reception of this doctrine in weak & wicked heads,—the wind will still blow where it listeth, & the Eternal Soul will overpower the men who are its organs, & enchant the ears of those who hear them by the same right & energy by which long ago & now it enchants the mountains, & the Sea, the air & the globes in their musical dance. "Thou shalt not plant a palm tree," said Pythagoras, intimating that, as that tree comes up best out of the ground self-sown, so Virtue & Wisdom are the direct proceeding of God, & are not to be overlaid & distorted by indiscreet meddling & art.

———

A question which well deserves examination now is the Dangers of Commerce. This invasion of Nature by Trade with its Money, its Credit, its Steam, its Railroad, threatens to upset the balance of man, & establish a new Universal Monarchy more tyrannical than Babylon or Rome. Very faint & few are the poets or men of God. Those who remain are so antagonistic to this tyranny that they appear mad or morbid & are treated as such. Sensible of this extreme unfitness they suspect themselves. And all of us apologize when we ought not & congratulate ourselves when we ought not.

———

Plutarch fits me better than Southey or Scott, therefore I say, there is no age to good writing. Could I write as I would, I suppose the piece would be no nearer to Boston in 1839 than to Athens in the fiftieth Olympiad. Good thought, however expressed, saith to us, "Come out of time, come to me in the Eternal."

We wish the man should show himself for what he is, though he be Iscariot. If the humor is in the blood bring it out to the skin by all means.

Friendship

Oct. 16. What needs greater magnanimity than the waiting for a friend; a lover, for years? We see the noble afar off & they repel us; they need not us; why should we intrude? Late, very late, we perceive that no arrangements, no introductions, no consuetudes, or habitudes of society would be of any avail to establish us in such relations with them as we desire, but solely the uprise of nature in us to the same degree it is in them, then shall we mix as water with water, & if we should not meet them then, we shall not want them, for we are already they. How sadly true all over human life is the saying,—"To him that hath shall be given; from him that hath not shall be taken." Attentions are showered on the powerful who needs them not. Friends abound for the self-trusting, & he retreats to his cliff.

—

Nature mixes facts & thought to evoke a poem from the poet, but our philosophy would be androgynous, & itself generate poems without aid of experience.

Lectures.

October 18. In these golden days it behoves me once more to make my annual inventory of the world. For the five last years I have read each winter a new course of lectures in Boston, and each was my creed & confession of faith. Each told all I thought of the past, the present, & the future. Once more I must renew my work and I think only once in the same form though I see that he who thinks he does something for the last time ought not to do it at all. Yet my objection is not to the thing but to the form; & the concatenation of errors called *society* to which I still consent, until my plumes be grown, makes even a duty of this concession also. So I submit to sell tickets again. But the form is neither here nor there. What shall be the substance of my shrift? Adam in the garden, I am

to new name all the beasts in the field & all the gods in the Sky.
I am to invite men drenched in time to recover themselves &
come out of time, & taste their native immortal air. I am to fire
with what skill I can the artillery of sympathy & emotion. I am
to indicate constantly, though all unworthy, the Ideal and
Holy Life, the life within life,—the Forgotten Good, the Unknown Cause in which we sprawl & sin. I am to try the magic
of sincerity, that luxury permitted only to kings & poets. I am
to celebrate the spiritual powers in their infinite contrast to the
mechanical powers & the mechanical philosophy of this time. I
am to console the brave sufferers under evils whose end they
cannot see by appeals to the great optimism self-affirmed in all
bosoms.

Jones Very only repeated in a form not agreeable the
thought which agitated me in earlier years when he said, "The
same spirit which brings me to your door prepares my welcome." Shall I not say this in its extent of sense to the men &
institutions of today? Think & you annihilate the times. Drink
of the cup which God proffers to your lips & these storming,
anxious, contradicting, threatening crowds which surround
you, mad with debt & credit, with banks & politics, with
books & churches & meats & drinks shall all flee away like
ghosts from the new born soul. They are much to you while
the same blood flows in your veins & theirs. But let the man
put off the merchant in you & all this shall be pictures merely.

—

Who can blame men for seeking excitement? They are polar &
would you have them sleep in a dull eternity of equilibrium?
Religion, love, ambition, money, war, brandy, some fierce antagonism must break the round of perfect circulation or no
spark, no joy, no event can be. As good not be. In the country
the lover of nature dreaming through the wood would never
awake to thought if the scream of an eagle, the cries of a crow,
or a curlew near his head did not break the continuity. Nay if
the truth must out the finest lyrics of the poet come of this
coarse parentage; the imps of matter beget such child on the
Soul, fair daughter of God.

And so I went to the Sham-Fight & saw the whole show
with pleasure. The officer instantly appears through all this

masquerade & buffoonery. I thought when I first went to the field that it was the high tide of nonsense and indeed the rag tag & bobtail of the County were there in all the wigs, old hats, & aged finery of the last generations. Then the faces were like the dresses—so exaggerated noses, chins, & mouths that one could not reconcile them with any other dress than that frippery they wore. Yet presently Nature broke out in her old beauty & strength through all this scurf. The man of skill makes his jacket invisible. Two or three natural soldiers among these merry captains played out their habitual energy so well that order & reason appeared as much at home in a farce as in a legislature. Meantime the buffoons of a sham fight are soon felt to be as impertinent there as elsewhere. This organization suffices to bring pioneers, soldiers, outlaws, & homicides distinct to view & I saw Washington, Napoleon, & Marat come strongly out of the mottled crew.

21 October. How can I not record though now with sleepy eye & flagging spirits so fair a fact as the visit of Alcott and Margaret Fuller who came hither yesterday & departed this morning. Very friendly influences these, each & both. Cold as I am, they are almost dear. I shall not however fill my page with the gifts or merits of either. They brought nothing but good spirits & good tidings with them of new literary plans here & good fellowship & recognition abroad. And then to my private ear a chronicle of sweet romance, of love & nobleness which have inspired the beautiful & brave. What is good to make me happy is not however good to make me write. Life too near paralyses Art. Long these things refuse to be recorded except in the invisible colors of Memory.

———

I heard with joy that which thou toldest me O eloquent lady, of thy friends & mine, yet with my joy mingled a shade of discontent. Things must not be too fine. Parian marble will not stand exposure to our New England weather, and though I cannot doubt the sterling sincerity of the mood & moment you describe, and though I am cheered to the bottom of my heart by these dear magnanimities which made their way to the light in the neighborhood of all that is common yet I dare not believe that a mood so delicate can be relied on like a

principle for the wear & tear of years. It will be succeeded by
another & another & the new will sport with the old. Yet as it
is genuine today, it will never be nothing.

A part of the protest we are called to make is to the popular
mode of virtuous endeavor. "Will you not come to this Convention & nominate a Temperance ticket? Let me show you
the immense importance of the step." Nay, my friend, I do not
work with those tools. The principles on which your church &
state are built are false & a portion of this virus vitiates the
smallest detail even of your charity & religion. Though I own
I sympathize with your desire & abhor your adversaries yet I
shall persist in wearing this robe, all loose & unbecoming as it
is, of inaction, this wise passiveness, until my hour comes when
I can see how to act with truth as well as to refuse.

———

In the statements we make so freely that books are for idle
hours, and when we flout all particular books as initial merely,
we truly express the privilege of spiritual nature, but alas not
the fact & fortune of this low Concord & Boston, of these
humble Octobers & Novembers of mortal life. Our souls are
not self fed, but do eat & drink of chemical water & wheat. We
go musing in to the vault of day & night, no star shines, no
muse descends, the stars are but white points, the roses but
brick colored leaves, & frogs pipe, mice cheep, & waggons
creak along the road. We return to the house & take up Plutarch
or Augustin & read a page or two, & lo! the air swarms with
life, the front of heaven is full of fiery shapes: secrets of magnanimity & grandeur invite us on every hand: Life is made up
of them. Such is our debt to Literature. Observe moreover
that we ought to credit literature with much more than the
just word it gives us. The poems I have just been reading of C.
are a certain steady autumnal light. That is not in them which
they give me. Over every true poem lingers a certain wild
beauty immeasureable; a happiness lightsome & delicious fills
my heart & brain; as they say every man is environed by his
proper atmosphere extending to some distance around him.
Well this beautiful result must be credited to literature too in
casting up the dread accounts.

The Christianity represents no absolute fact in history, but only the present & recent state of thought. The traditional or conventional language on the subject is very ignorant. We choose to speak as if only in one book or one life was the pure light but the wise know better, the experience of each intelligent reader belies the tale. Whenever we are wise, every book we read streams with an universal light. Whenever we are wise the whole world is wise & emblematic. The great books do in that hour give us in every page the most authentic tokens that they also recognize the holiest law, the Unutterable. They do not preach; they recognize it in strains of pure melody. The Greek Mythology—what a wonderful example is that of profound sense overmastering the finite speakers & writers of the fables. Always & never the World is wise.

23 October. Fact is better than fiction if only we could get pure fact. Do you think any rhetoric or any romance would get your ear from one who could tell straight on the real history of man, who could reconcile your moral character & your natural history, who could explain your misfortunes, your fevers, your debts, your temperament, your habits of thought, your tastes, & in every explanation not sever you from the Whole but unite you to it? Is it not plain that not in senates or courts or chambers of commerce but in the conversation of a true philosopher the eloquence must be found that can agitate, convict, inspire, & possess us & guide us to a true peace? I look upon the Lecture room as the true church of today & as the home of a richer eloquence than Faneuil Hall or the Capitol ever knew.

Michel Angelo is as well entitled to the surname Colossal as Charles to his *Magne* or Alfred to his *Great.* The genius of Michel aims at Strength in all figures, not in gods & prophets alone, but in women & in children. A divine Strength titanic aboriginal before the world was; a strength anterior to all disease. The Colossal in him is not in the outline or particular drawing but is intrinsic; & so appears in all. To this, Beauty is made incidental.

Michel esteemed the human form the best ornament & so uses no other in each cornice or compartment only a new & wondrous attitude of sleep or Energy.

See a knot of country people working out their road-tax or laying a new bridge. How close are they to their work. How they sympathize with every log & foreknow its every nod & stir with chain & crowbar & seem to see through the ground all the accidents of preservation & decay.

> "May I gaze upon thee when my latest hour is come!
> May I hold thy hand when mine faileth me!"

Truth of character.   *Temperance*

Truth will cure all our ails. I hate the giving of the hand unless the whole man accompanies it. I hate giving seven pounds of rice or sugar to a poor person whose whole character is disagreeable to me. I grudge ninepence to a child I do not like. My money, as every man's, represents to me the things I would willingliest do with it. I am not one thing & my expenditure another. My expenditure is me. That our expenditure & our character are twain is the vice of society.

But now men are multiplex. The good offices they do are not their genuine aim, the mere flower & perfume of their nature, but are a compliance & a compliment & contradicted by other actions on the same day. Their temperance is a plume, a feather in the cap; this ostentatious glass of cold water & dry raw vegetable diet that makes your blood run cold to see, is not the joyful sign that they have ceased to care for food in nobler cares, but no, they peak & pine & know all they renounce. Temperance when it is only the sign of intrinsic Virtue is graceful as the bloom on the cheek that betokens health, but temperance that is nothing else than temperance is phlegm or conceit. Is it not better they should do bad offices & be intemperate so long as that is their ruling love? So at least they should not be hypocrites. Also I lament that people without character seeing the homage that is paid to character demand the homage & feel seriously injured & bewail themselves if it is withholden; & then the silly friends affect to yield that homage

& so lie & steal & transform themselves into the similitude of apes & serpents.

—

Garrison

October 27. Don't seek to vamp & abut principles. They were before you were born & will be when you are rotten. You might as well paint the sky blue with a bluebag. The old thought which I loved in my youth when the roar of politics fell harshest on my ear—that presently Government would cease to be sought by gentlemen & would be despatched by a few clerks—is now embodied & as far as I heard last night very ably & truly preached by the Non Resistants with Garrison at their head, a man of great ability in conversation, of a certain longsightedness in debate which is a great excellence, a tenacity of his proposition which no accidents or ramblings in the conversation can divert, a calmness & method in unfolding the details of his argument, and an eloquence of illustration, which contents the ear & the mind—thus armed with all the weapons of a great Apostle—no not yet, until I have remembered his religion, which is manifest, his religious trust in his principle, & his clearness from any taint of private end. And yet the man teases me by his continual wearisome trick of quoting texts of scripture & his judaical Christianity & then by the continual eye to numbers, to societies. Himself is not enough for him.

But to the principle of non resistance again. Trust it. Give up the Government without too solicitously inquiring whether roads can be still built, letters carried, & title deeds secured when the government of force is at an end. There will always be a government of force whilst men are selfish, & when they are pure enough to abjure the code of force they will be wise enough to see how these public ends can be best answered of the Post Office, & the Road, of Commerce, & the division of Property.

Again it seems clear that we should never cumber ourselves with maintaining either popular religion or popular sabbaths or popular Laws if we do not want them ourselves. Are they now maintained by us because the world needs them? let the world maintain them. And you shall find if the deacons & priests all fail, the bank presidents & the chambers of commerce, yea the very inn holders & democrats of the county would muster with fury to their support.

—

Shall I not explore for the subject of my new lectures the character, resources, & tendencies of the Present Age? Such an argument will include what speculations I may have to offer on all my favorite topics. Nor will it cripple me by confining to any local or temporary limits discussions which I should rather extend to universal aims & bearings. For the Age—what is it? It is what the being is who uses it,—a dead routine to me, and the vista of Eternity to thee. One man's view of the Age is confined to his shop & the market, and another's sees the roots of Today in all the Past & beneath the Past in the Necessary & Eternal. Let us not dwell so fondly on the characteristics of a single Epoch as to bereave ourselves of the permanent privileges of Man.

We ought never to lose our youth. In all natural & necessary labors as in the work of a farm, in digging, splitting, rowing, drawing water, a man always appears young—is still a boy. So in doing anything which is still above him;—which asks all his strength & more;—somewhat commensurate with his ability, so that he works up to it, not down upon it,—he is still a youth. But if his work is unseasonable, as botany & shells or the Greek verbs at 80 years of age, or playing Blindman's Buff, we say, Go up thou baldhead!

The dreams of youth, the passion of love are the constant reproduction of the vision of the Ideal, which God will not suffer a moment to remit its presence or to relax its energy as a coagent in history.

Oct. 31. No article so rare in New England as Tom.

Nov. 3. In Boston, I visited the gallery of Sculpture & saw the Day & Night of Michel Angelo. I find in Michel more "abandon" than in Milton. Rather say, he lets out all the length of all the reins, & Milton does never. Wonderful figure & head of Day. The head suggests not only as when I first saw it in Florence the sun new risen resting over the brow of a hill, but when better seen a whole rough landscape of woods &

mountains. I see reason for this figure being called Day: and I called the Night Night. The Jove of Phidias pleases me well. In the afternoon I visited Alcott & in the evening Ward came to see me and the next morning again brought me Raphael's designs to show me that Raphael was greater than Angelo, great as Shakspeare. But in making this scale we must be very passive. The gods & demigods must seat themselves without seneschal in our Olympus, & as they can install themselves by seniority divine so will I worship them & not otherwise. I had told Alcott that my First Class stood for today perhaps thus; Phidias, Jesus, Angelo, Shakspeare: or, if I must sift more sternly still,—Jesus & Shakspeare were two men of genius.

The common reply to the physician is—'See how many healthy men use the foods & liquors & practices which you reprehend.' And men see in this fact a treachery in Nature herself instead of esteeming it the bending goodness of the God, the Resistance of the Soul, the moral purchase, the intercession of the spirit, the elasticity straining still against this noxious wrong & giving the poor victim still another & yet another chance of selfrecovery & escape.

Health.
Is it becoming or agreeable to your imagination that the bursts of divine poetry, that the new delineations of God & his world should be the inspirations of opium or tea?

The Physiognomy & Phrenology of today are rash & mechanical systems but they rest on everlasting foundations. The sacred form of man is not seen under all these whimsical, pitiful, & sinister masks, these carbuncles & bloated & shrivelled forms, these bald heads & bead eyes, these broken winds, puny & precarious healths, & early deaths. We live ruins among ruins. These are not the royal natures that take up the sweetness & the might of all the elements into themselves, whose eye is more sovereign than the sun, & whose cheek is tender as the sunset—no our dwindled natures report too truly of us to the incorrupt child. He respects us not. Our aspects warn & bode & gibber in his keen ear before we speak.

It is the condition of inspiration—Marry Nature & not use her for pleasure.

Friendship.

Be sure that greatness & goodness is economy forever. Why should you intermeddle with your fortunes? Why dare to intermeddle in so sacred a formation as Friendship? Leave to the diamond his ages nor expect to accelerate the births of the eternal. Who set you to cast about for what you should say to the select souls? or to say anything to such? No matter how ingenious,—no matter how graceful & bland. There are innumerable degrees of folly & wisdom, & for *you* to say aught, is to be frivolous. Wait until the necessary & everlasting overpowers you, until day & night avail themselves of your lips.

By persisting in your path, by holding your peace, though you forfeit the little you gain the great. You become pronounced. You demonstrate yourself so as to put yourself out of the reach of false relations & do draw to you the firstborn of the world, those rare pilgrims whereof only one or two wander in nature at once & before whom all the nations show as cowards & shadows.

A patience which is grand, a brave & cold neglect of the offices which prudence exacts and which the traditional conscience exacts so it be done in a deep upper piety, a consent to solitude & to inaction which proceeds out of an unwillingness to violate character is the century which makes the gem.

If a man undertake to instruct a superior mind Union cannot be between them.

He who has not yet departed from his innocence stands in the highway which all souls must travel, & solitary as he may at moments seem to himself, he is lovely, and that which we seek in society: so that he appears to all beholders to stand betwixt them & the sun a transparent object, and whoso journeys towards that person, journeys towards the Sun. But he who departs from his innocency, must be loved for himself & not for virtue: the time given to courting his affection, is lost to any other object, & the affection itself is a false & fugitive affection.

It is only known to Plato that we can do without Plato.

Being costs me nothing. I need not be rich nor pay taxes nor leave home nor buy books for that. It is the organizing that costs. And the moment I *am*, I despise the city & the seashore, yes earth & the galaxy also.

Older! Older! We wish sign in praising or describing aught that the eye has seen other things. Deep eyes that have drank more of this wine than others.

Nose & teeth

I saw at the Athenaeum with great pleasure that old head of Jove attributed to Phidias. It is sublime in general & in all the details except the nose, which did not beseem the Father of the Gods. Indeed it is not easy to imagine the shaping of that feature, (long ago excluded from Epic Poetry,) worthily for such a form. And this is strange. Yet the nose of Caesar & of Pitt suggest "the terrors of the beak." I have mentioned elsewhere that the teeth in the physiognomy express limitation. For that reason it is very plain that no painter could dare to show the teeth in a head of Jupiter.

There can be no greatness without abandonment.

The city delights the understanding. It is made up of finites; short, sharp, mathematical lines, all calculable. It is full of varieties, of successions, of contrivances. The country on the contrary offers an unbroken horizon, the monotony of an endless road, of vast uniform plains, of distant mountains, the melancholy of uniform & infinite vegetation; the objects on the road are few & worthless; the eye is invited ever to the horizon & the clouds. It is the School of the Reason.

———

Ward showed me a volume of Raphael's designs by way of evincing Raphael's title to stand in the first class of men of genius. The book did certainly surprise me with the opulence of his genius and if this were a question in which details of power had any place this would be unexceptionable evidence. But it is a question not of talents but of *tone*, and not particular merits but the mood of mind to which one & another can bring us is the only relevant testimony.

Prudence governs the world & not Religion or Science or Art. Mr Cunard sends the steampacket from Boston to England & not I. In order that principles should rig & man & sail the ship, it needs to begin far back, & bring about a new state of society. At present, a right minded individual can only live so as to point at these ends, to imply Love & Art & Knowledge in every moment of his life.

I have read somewhere that Raphael was accustomed to draw his figures nude before he draped them. And I have read in Vasari that Michel Angelo was accustomed when he would sketch a group to draw the skeleton first & afterward clothe it with flesh—which fact I suppose may express the difference in the drawing of the two.

———

Cavendish who was Wolsey's Gentleman Usher being sent before him when in France to secure lodgings at Champaigne relates that on his arriving at Champaigne being set at dinner in his inn over against the market place he "heard a great noise & clattering of bills and looking out I saw the officers of the town bringing a prisoner to execution and with a sword cut off his head. I demanded what was the offence, they answered me, for killing of red deer in the forest near adjoining. And incontinently they held the poor man's head upon a pole in the market place between the stag's horns, & his four quarters set up in four places of the forest." See Harl. Misc. Vol 4 p. 517.

Certainly this anecdote is not a specimen of Law as we know it in America. Government is here less ferocious but it has not yet become amiable. Does the Customhouse, does the Statute Book associate itself with any idea of gladness, genius, of Holiness, of the progress of Man? When we look at a plant, at a gem, at a landscape, we behold somewhat accordant with though inferior to our own nature. But I ask if a man should go to walk in the woods & should there find suspended on the oaks or bulrushes electioneering placards setting forth the pretensions of Mr Van Buren or Mr Harrison whether the new train of thoughts thus awakened would harmonize with the place or would exalt his meditation.

—

Our moods do not believe in each other. Today I am full of thoughts & can write what I please. I see no reason why I should not have the same thoughts & the same power of expression tomorrow. What I write whilst I write it seems the most natural thing in the world, but yesterday I saw only a dreary vacuity in this very direction in which I now see so much. And a month hence I doubt not I shall wonder who he was that wrote so many continuous pages.

I fancied that W's objection to the verses which pleased me so much was really levelled against ethical verses & not against these particular strains. "There was no progress." Very well. The moral poet is subjective, & every sentence of his a round poem.

—

It is only safe to do what you like. So are the natural motions of the soul invigorated, and so you demonstrate yourself. I suspect myself of being moulded by the times & by society, of acquiring popular virtues & popular vices. So run I into the danger of knowing never what the God would say. But when I see discrepancies in my pleasures, pains, works, words, hopes, & in those of my companions, & that I, in the formation of all mine, have consulted my native bias, then I attend with more faith to the spontaneous oracles of my thought.
Trust thyself. Every heart vibrates to that iron string.

Tantalus means the impossibility of drinking the waters of thought which are always gleaming & waving within sight of the soul.

13 November. Do something, it matters little or not at all whether it be in the way of what you call your profession or not, so it be in the plane or coincident with the axis of your character. The reaction is always proportioned to the action, and it is the reaction that we want. Strike the hardest blow you can, & you can always do this by work which is agreeable to your nature. This is economy.

Self-Culture

In hard times, cultivate yourself. And you cannot lose your labor. A just man, a wise man is always good property; the world cannot do without him be the fashions or the laws or the harvest what they may. But if he seek to suit the times he miserably fails.

Even Plato & Kant can hardly be trusted to write of God. As soon as one sets out to write in the course of his book of the Divine mind, the love of system vitiates his perception. He grows a little limitary. The truest account of that Idea would be got by an observation & record of the incidental expressions of the most intelligent men when they speak of God quite simply & without any second thought.

Hospitality

Who is timid & uneasy & fleeting but the master of the house when his house is full of company? He should be glad that such brave & wise men are happy around his hearth, and he is tormented instead with fantastic suppositions. He hates every civil thing that is said to him as if it implied that their freedom was less than he had wished it. He scorns to treat any one with particular kindness as if it were some encroachment on that rude freedom he desires should prevail. It would give him some contentment if they would put his real generosity to the proof by hard knocks & abusive personalities levelled at himself. What a fine sentiment lay under the bold usage of the Romans when they set buffoons & satirists about the triumphing consul to warn & insult him. So took they off this slight delirium & vacillation of success & gave to the day a solid content.

Temperance is an universal sign by which we communicate with the pure of every sect & tongue.

I dare not look for a friend to me who have never been one. Give me thy hand.—'O man hast thou not two of thine own?'

*

Alcott seems to need a pure success. If the men & women whose opinion is fame could see him as he is & could express heartily as these English correspondents their joy in his genius, I think his genius would be exalted & relieved of some spots, with which a sense of injustice & loneliness has shaded it.

But no great man will ever drill. None will ever solve the problem of his character according to our preconceived notions or wishes, but only in his own high unprecedented way.

A good sentence, a noble verse which I meet in my reading are an epoch in my life. From month to month, from year to year they remain fresh & memorable. Yet when we once in our writing come out into the free air of thought, we seem to be assured that nothing is easier than to continue this communication at pleasure indefinitely. Up, down, around, the kingdom of thought has no enclosures, but the Muse makes us free of her city. Well the world has a million writers. One would think then that thought would be as familiar as the air & water & the gifts of each new hour exclude the repetition of those of the last. Yet I remember a beautiful verse for twenty years.

Selfreliance   Mrs F.
      in the man of the world.
We are such entire lovers of selfreliance that every degree of it awakens our esteem even on the lowest scale. If I meet a man or woman of the world, well born & moving in good society, I will excuse in such person many sins if he will show me a compleat satisfaction in his position, the air of unquestionable well being which asks no leave to be of mine or any man's good opinion. But any deference to me or any deference to some eminent man or woman of the world forfeits instantly all privilege of nobility; the person is a secondary. I have nothing to do with him. I will speak with his master.

The source of information on which I most rely for unlocking for me the secret of the age is the acceptance of the nearest suggestion & the most faithful utterance of all that which is borne in upon my mind. I cast myself upon the Age & will not resist it. Passive I will think what it thinketh & say what it saith. All my hope of insight & of successful reporting lies in my consciousness of fidelity & the abdication of all will in the matter. Whilst those whom I see around me consulting the same auguries are first enamored of their own opinion, or of some past man's opinion, or of some institution, or of some favorite measure & are striving to do something with the Age, to make their mill go, to persuade the Vast Ocean of the Time to convert itself into a mill stream to turn their nice wheel, & to corrupt if it were possible the incorruptible Wind.

———

S.M.F. writes me that she waits for the Lectures seeing well after much intercourse that the best of me is there. She says very truly; & I thought it a good remark which somebody repeated here from S. S. that I "always seemed to be on stilts". It is even so. Most of the persons whom I see in my own house I see across a gulf. I cannot go to them nor they come to me. Nothing can exceed the frigidity & labor of my speech with such. You might turn a yoke of oxen between every pair of words; and the behavior is as awkward & proud. I see the ludicrousness of the plight as well as they. But having never found any remedy I am very patient with this folly or shame, patient of my churl's mask, in the belief that this privation has certain rich compensations inasmuch as it makes my solitude dearer & the impersonal God is shed abroad in my heart more richly & more lowly welcome for this porcupine impossibility of contact with men. And yet in one who sets his mark so high, who presumes so vast an elevation as the birthright of man, is it not a little sad to be a mere mill or pump yielding one wholesome product at the mouth in one particular mode but as impertinent & worthless in any other place or purpose as a pump or a coffee mill would be in a parlor or a chapel? I make rockets:— Must I therefore be a good senator?

mimicry.
We cannot hear any one mimic the notes & sounds of the lower animals as frogs, birds, insects without instantly conceiving a new & immense extension possible to the descriptiveness & energy of language.

*

One Mind.
All languages are inter-translateable.

Systems.

I need hardly say to any one acquainted with my thoughts that I have no System. When I was quite young I fancied that by keeping a Manuscript Journal by me, over whose pages I wrote a list of the great topics of human study, as, *Religion, Poetry, Politics, Love*, &c in the course of a few years I should be able to complete a sort of Encyclopaedia containing the net value of all the definitions at which the world had yet arrived. But at the end of a couple of years my Cabinet Cyclopaedia though much enlarged was no nearer to a completeness than on its first day. Nay somehow the whole plan of it needed alteration nor did the following months promise any speedier term to it than the foregoing. At last I discovered that my curve was a parabola whose arcs would never meet, and came to acquiesce in the perception that although no diligence can rebuild the Universe in a model by the best accumulation or disposition of details, yet does the World reproduce itself in miniature in every event that transpires, so that all the laws of nature may be read in the smallest fact. So that the truth speaker may dismiss all solicitude as to the proportion & congruency of the aggregate of his thoughts so long as he is a faithful reporter of particular impressions.

Plutarch is charming by the facility of his associations, so that it matters little where you open his book, you find yourself instantly at the Olympian tables. His memory is like the Olympic Games wherein all that was noble & excellent in all Greece was assembled, & you are stimulated & recruited by lyric verses, by philosophic sentiments, by the forms & behaviour of heroes, by the worship of the Gods, & by the passing of fillets, parsley, & laurel wreaths, chariots, & armour, sacred cups & the utensils of sacrifice.

Nature never rhymes her children, never makes two men precisely alike. Yet as soon as we see a great man we find or fancy in him a resemblance to some historical person &

hastily predict the sequel of his character & fortune, a result which he is sure to disappoint.

Literature is now critical. Well, analysis may be poetic. People find out they have faces & write Physiognomy; Sculls, & write Phrenology; mysteries of Volition & Supervolition, & explore Animal Magnetism. Chemistry is criticism on an apple & a drop of water & the glassy air which to our fathers were wholes but which we have resolved. Is not the sublime felt in an analysis as well as in a creation? It seems very impertinent in us to fear a hurt in this tendency as if the gastric juices were beginning to dissolve the stomach & so the belly eat up its master. Rather expect immense discoveries & a magazine of new elements to enrich the combinations of the philosopher & the man in the next centuries.

———

We are accustomed to speak of our National Union & our Constitution as of somewhat sacred. Individual character & Culture are sacred, but these bands are trivial in the comparison. The language of the newspapers will undergo a great change in fifty years. The precious metals are not quite so precious as they have been esteemed. The spirit of political Economy is low & degrading. Man exists for his own sake & not to add a laborer to the State. Therefore, I can never forgive a great man who succumbs so far to the mere forms of his day as to peril his integrity for the sake of adding to the weight of his personal character the authority of office, or making a real government titular. Adams, Clay, & Webster electioneer. And Nature does not forgive them, for thus they compromise their proper majesty, and are farther than ever from obtaining the adventitious.

———

Death
And where is he now?—O he is dead, poor fellow!—That is the sentiment of mankind upon death that the dead, be he never so wise, able, or contented, is a poor fellow.

Men kill themselves. And run the risk of great absurdity; for our faculties fail us here to say what is the amount of this freedom, this only door left open in all the padlocked secrets of nature, this single door ajar, this main entry & royal staircase admitting apparently to the Presence-Chamber, yet so designedly it seems left wide. It may be that he who sheathes his knife in his own heart does an act of grand issues, & it may be a preposterous one. I think I would not try it until I had first satisfied myself that I did not baulk & fool myself. The question is whether it is the way *out*, or the way *in*.

Board.

L.C.B. went to board in the country & complained that she got bad air, bad light, bad water, bad fire, bad sound, bad food & bad company. The house shook with rats & mice, smelt of onions, the oil in the lamp would not burn, the water was foul, the wood on the fire was soggy & made no flame, the children stunned her, the table was poverty itself & the people vulgar & knavish, & when she would walk abroad she could not draw the bolt. I advised her to publish her adventures under the name of Bad Board or the Baroness Trenck.

Homerides.

It is strange how hard we find it to conceive of the organization of any other Ideas than those under which we live. We do not see that what we call Church, State, School, are only ideas embodied which have succeeded to other ideas & must give place hereafter to new. A new thought will orb itself in a moment. Our savants cannot believe that the Greek bards should be able to carry in the memory several thousand lines as the Iliad & the Odyssey. For we have no need of such memories. As little could one of these minstrels conceive of the faculty of one of Whitwell & Bond's clerks who, I have heard, can add up five columns of figures by one numeration instead of five. Mr Chase, a clerk of Waterston Pray & Co, will with a ruler add up any number of columns 3, 4, or 5 figures at one ascent of the column.

Temperance.

Who argues so sourly for beef & mutton against the man of herbs & grains? The fat & ruddy eater who hath just wiped his lips from feeding on a sirloin whose blood is spouting in his veins & whose strength kindles that evil fire in his eye. It is not then the voice of man that I hear, but it is beef & brandy that roar & rail for beef & brandy. But shall these play the judge in their own cause?

The Bible

The transcendant, I have said, is economy also. Literary accomplishments, skill in grammar, logic, & rhetoric can never countervail the want of things that demand voice. Literature is but a poor trick when it busies itself to make words pass for things. The most original book in the world is the Bible. This old collection of the ejaculations of love & dread, of the supreme desires & contritions of men, proceeding out of the region of the grand & Eternal, by whatsoever different mouths spoken, & through a wide extent of times & countries, seems the alphabet of the nations & all posterior literature either the Chronicle of facts under very inferior Ideas, or when it rises to sentiment, the combinations, Analogies, or degradations of this. It is in the nature of things that the highest originality must be moral. The only person who can be entirely independent of this fountain of literature and equal to it, must be a prophet in his own proper person. Shakspeare, the first literary genius of the world, leans on the Bible: his poetry supposes it. If we examine this brilliant influence—Shakspeare—as it lies in our minds, we shall find it reverent, deeply indebted to the traditional morality, in short, compared with the tone of the prophets, *Secondary*. On the other hand, the prophets do not imply the existence of Shakspear or Homer,—advert to no books or arts,—only to dread Ideas & emotions. People imagine that the place which the Bible holds in the world, it owes to miracles. It owes it simply to the fact that it came out of a profounder depth of thought than any other book & the effect must be precisely proportionate. Gibbon fancied combinations of circumstances that gave Christianity its place in history. But in nature it takes an ounce to balance an ounce.

I have used in the above remarks the *Bible* for the Ethical Revelation considered generally, including, that is, the Vedas, the Sacred Writings of every nation & not of the Hebrews alone; although these last, for the very reason I have given, precede all similar writings so far as to be commonly called *The Book* or Bible alone.

Eyes.

Women see better than men. Men see lazily if they do not expect to act. Women see quite without any wish to act. Men of genius are said to partake of the masculine & feminine traits. They have this feminine eye, a function so rich that it contents itself without asking any aid of the hand. Trifles may well be studied by him for he sees nothing insulated, the plaid of a cloak, the plaits of a ruffle, the wrinkles of a face absorb his attention & lead it to the root of these matters in Universal Laws.

No property in Art.

It is a noble fact that Heeren infers in his 'Greece,' that in that country every statue & painting was public, it being considered as absurd & profane to pretend a property in a Work of Art,—which belonged to whosoever could see it.

———

The Circumcision is a good instance of the power of religion & poetry to raise the low & offensive.

20 November. Ah Nature the very look of the woods is heroical & stimulating. This afternoon in a very thick grove where H.D.T. showed me the bush of mountain laurel, the first I have seen in Concord, the stems of pine & hemlock & oak almost gleamed like steel upon the excited eye. How old, how aboriginal these trees appear, though not many years older than I. They seem parts of the eternal chain of destiny whereof this sundered Will of man is the victim. Is he proud, high thoughted & reserved sometimes? Let him match if he can the incommunicableness of these lofty natures beautiful in growth, in strength, in age, in decay. The invitation which these fine savages give as you stand in the hollows of the forest, works strangely on the imagination. Little say they in recommendation of towns or a civil Christian life. Live with us, they say, & forsake these wearinesses of yesterday. Here no history or church or state is interpolated on the divine sky & the immortal Year.

O Lord! Unhappy is the man whom man can make unhappy.

Burton's Anatomy of Melancholy is a wonderful work of a man. To read it however is much like reading in a dictionary. I think we read it as an inventory to be reminded how many classes & species of facts exist &, by observing in to what strange & multiplex byways learning hath strayed, agreeably infer our opulence. A dictionary however is not a bad book to read. There is no cant in it. No excess of explanation. And it is very suggestive, full of inferences undrawn. There is all poetry & all prose & needs nothing but a little combination. See what hosts of forgotten scholars he feeds us withal.

—

Unconsciousness
27 Nov. Happy is he who in looking at the compositions of an earlier date knows that the moment wrote them, & feels no more call or right to alter them than to alter his recollections of a day or a fact. We pretend sometimes to find somewhat of this sacredness in our Scrolls; but I speak of one who should know it.

When once & again the regard & friendship of the noble-minded is offered me, I am made sensible of my disunion with myself. The head is of gold, the feet are of clay. In my *worthiness* I have such confidence, that I can court solitude. I know that if my aspirations should demonstrate themselves, angels would not disdain me. Of my *unworthiness*, the first person I meet shall apprize me. I shall have so little presence, such pitiful gingerbread considerations, so many calculations, & such unconcealable weariness of my company—that in my heart I beseech them to begone & I flee to the secretest hemlock shade in Walden Woods to recover my selfrespect. Patimur quisque Suos Manes! But when I have shriven myself to the partridges, I am gay again & content to be alone. Then I am let into the secret daily history of others to whom that grace & conversation I covet is given, and find such savage melancholy, such passion, discontent, & despair that suddenly I count myself the happiest of men & will know the sweetness of bread & water & live with the jays & sparrows still.

28 Nov. It seems a matter of indifference what, & how, & how much, you write, if you write poetry. Poetry makes its own pertinence and a single stanza outweighs a book of prose. One stanza is complete. But one sentence of prose is not.

But it must be poetry.

I do not wish to read the verses of a poetic mind but only of a poet. I do not wish to be shown early poems, or any steps of progress. I wish my poet born adult. I do not find youth or age in Shakspeare, Milton, Herbert; & I dread minors.

Shelley is never a poet. His mind is uniformly imitative; all his poems composite. A fine English scholar he is, with taste, ear, & memory; but imagination, the original authentic fire of the bard, he has not. He is clearly modern & shares with Wordsworth, Coleridge, Byron, & Hemans, the feeling of the Infinite, which so labors for expression in their different genius. But all his lines are arbitary, not necessary, and therefore though evidently a devout & brave man, I can never read his verses.

The same secondariness pervades Wilson's poetry. Scott & Crabbe are objective & have not the feeling of the Infinite. But from Crabbe's poems may the Muses preserve me!

The question of genuineness is whether this verse I read was one of twenty which the author might have written as well, or whether this is what that man was created to say. But whilst every line of the poet will be genuine, he is in a boundless power & freedom to say a million things. And the reason why he can say one thing well is because his vision extends to the sight of all things; & so he describes one as one who knows many & all.

De Stael, Goethe, & all the Germans, Chateaubriand & Manzoni have the feeling of the Infinite.

No peace without self-possession

There is at least this satisfaction in crime, "Crimen quos inquinat aequat." You can speak to your accomplice on even terms. To those whom we admire & love we cannot. There can never be deep peace between two spirits, never mutual respect until in their dialogue each stands for the whole world. The least defect of self-possession vitiates the entire relation. "I will not dine in the house of a man who does not head his own table," said the Duke of Clarence to the hospitable mulatto; and I will not have that man my friend whom I or any man can daunt & silence by manners.

———

In taking this P.M. farewell looks at the sybils & prophets of Michel Angelo, I fancied that they all looked not free but necessitated; ridden by a superior Will, by an Idea which they could not shake off. It sits in their life. The heads of Raphael look freer certainly, but this Obedience of Michel's figures contrasts strangely with the living forms of this Age. These old giants are still under the grasp of that terrific Jewish Idea before which ages were driven like sifted snow, which all the literatures of the world,—Latin, Spanish, Italian, French, English, tingle with, but we sleek dapper men have quite got free of that old reverence, have heard new facts on metaphysics, & are not quite ready to join any new church. We are travellers, & not responsible.

Let the painter unroll his canvas; millions of eyes look through his.

We are not at home in Nature. We confess our unworthiness inadvertently in all we say of it. The unusual beauty of the sunset attracts us and the soul dares not say, 'Behold my peace passed into nature also!' but we mendicantly say, 'What a scene for a painter or for a poet'; or more superficially still, "What an Italian sky!"

My friends.
        Sunday, 8 Dec.
    I read with joy Sterling's noble critique on Carlyle in the Westminster Review. All intellectual ability seems to have somewhat impersonal & destructive of personality; & yet I read with warm pride because a man who has offered me friendship gives this unequivocal certificate of his equality to

that office. O friend! you have given me that sign which high friendship demands, namely, ability to do without it. Pass on, we shall meet again. I woke this morn with devout thanksgiving for my friends, the old & the new. I think no man in the planet has a circle more noble. They have come to me unsought: the great God gave them to me. Will they separate themselves from me again or some of them? I know not but I fear it not, for my relation to them is so pure that we hold by simple affinity; & the Genius of my life being thus social the same affinity will exert its energy on whosoever is as noble as these men & women, wherever I may be.

A man with his thoughts about him distinguishes at first sight those fancies which are momentary & the revelations of the soul, knows among his reveries which is a circumstance & which is a thought, a power, as well as a man walking knows which is the wall & which is the road. Well thus among my fancies it occurs that the Mind of this Age will endure no miracle & this not because of unbelief but because of belief. It begins to see that the sun & the moon & the man who walks under them are miracles that puzzle all analysis; & that to quit these & go gazing for I know not what parish circumstances or Jewish prodigies, is to quit the eternal signs scrawled by God along the dizzy spaces of the Zodiack, for a show of puppets & wax lights.

I say how the world looks to me without reference to Blair's Rhetoric or Johnson's Lives. And I call my thoughts The Present Age, because I use no will in the matter, but honestly record such impressions as things make. So transform I myself into a Dial, and my shadow will tell where the sun is.

It is dangerous to "crush the sweet poison of misused wine" of the affections. A new person is to me always a great event & hinders me from sleep; as I wrote to C. I have had such fine fancies about two or three persons lately, as have given me delicious hours, but the joy ends in the hour, it yields no fruit. Thought is not born of it, and with me action is very little modified.

—

It has seemed to me lately more possible than I knew to carry a friendship greatly *on one side*, without due correspondence on the other. Why should I cumber myself with the poor fact that the receiver is not capacious. It never troubles the sun that some of his rays fall wide & vain into ungrateful space and only a small part on the reflecting planet. Let your greatness educate the crude & cold companion. If he is unequal, he will presently pass away but thou art enlarged by thy own shining, and no longer a mate for worms & frogs, dost soar & burn with the gods of the empyrean. It is thought a disgrace to love unrequited. But the great will see that true love cannot be unrequited. True love transcends instantly the unworthy object & dwells & broods on the eternal, and when the poor interposed mask crumbles, it is not sad but feels rid of so much earth, and feels its independency the surer. Yet these things may hardly be said without a sort of treachery to the relation. The essence of friendship is entireness,—the most total & magnanimous trust. It must not surmise or provide for infirmity. Friendship treats its object as a god that it may deify both. And fine, subtle, dainty as is that web we call friendship it is the solidest thing we know. For now after so many ages of experience, not one step has man taken toward the actual solution of the overwhelming problem of his nature. In one condemnation of folly stand the whole universe of men. But the sweet sincerity of joy & peace which I draw from this alliance with my brother's soul, is the nut itself whereof all nature & all thought is but the husk & shell.

—

In my dream I saw a man reading in the library at Cambridge, and one who stood by said, "He readeth advertisements," meaning that he read for the market only & not for truth. Then I said,—Do I read advertisements?

Our friends are not their own highest form.

From the necessity of loving none are exempt, & he that loves must utter his desires. I must feel pride in my friend's accomplishments as if they were mine,—wild delicate throbbing property in his virtues. I feel as warmly when he is praised as the lover when he hears applause of his engaged maiden.

—

Treat your friend as a spectacle. Of course if he be a man he has merits that are not yours & that you cannot honour if you must needs hold him close to your person. Stand aside; give them room; let them mount & expand. Be not so much his friend that you can never know your man, like fond mammas who shut up their boy in the house until he is almost grown a girl. Reverence is a great part of friendship. There must be very two before there can be very one. Let it be an alliance of two large formidable natures, mutually beheld, mutually feared, before they yet recognize the deep identity which beneath these disparities blends in a sublime unity. Are you the friend of your friend's buttons, or of his thought? To a great heart he will still be a stranger in a thousand particulars, that he may come near in the holiest ground. Leave it to girls & boys to regard a friend as property, and suck a short & all-confounding pleasure instead of the pure nectar of God.

Whoso sees Law does not despond, but is inflamed with great desires & endeavors based on his perfect trust. Whoso desponds, therefore, instantly betrays his blindness.

Pleasant these jets of affection that relume a young world for me again. Delicious is a just & firm encounter of two in a thought, in a feeling. But we must be tormented presently by baffled blows, by sudden unseasonable apathies, by epilepsies of wit & of animal spirits in the heyday of friendship & thought. Our faculties do not play us true.

1840

Guy wished all his friends dead on very slight occasion. Whoever was privy to one of his gaucheries, had the honour of this Stygian optation. Had Jove heard all his prayers, the planet would soon have been unpeopled. At last it occurred to Guy, that instead of wringing this hecatomb of friends' necks every morning, he would dine better if he gave as much life as he now took. He found to his astonishment the embryos of a thousand friends lying hid under his own heart, and that for every offence he forgave, and for every great choice he made, suddenly from afar a noble stranger knocked at his street gate.

—

Feb. 19. I closed last Wednesday, 12th instant, my Course of Lectures in Boston, "On the Present Age;" which were read on ten consecutive Wednesday Evenings, (excepting Christmas Eve 25 Dec). 1839. 4 December;

I.	Introductory
II.	Literature
III.	Literature
IV.	Politics.
V.	Private Life
VI.	Reforms.
VII.	Religion.
VIII.	Ethics.
IX.	Education.
X.	Tendencies.

I judge from the account rendered me by the sellers of tickets, added to an account of my own distribution of tickets to my friends, that the average audience at a lecture consisted of about 400 persons. 256 course-tickets were sold and 305 evening tickets or passes. I distributed about 110 to 120 course-tickets.

These lectures give me little pleasure. I have not done what I hoped when I said, I will try it once more. I have not once transcended the coldest selfpossession. I said I will agitate others, being agitated myself. I dared to hope for extacy & eloquence. A new theatre, a new art, I said, is mine. Let us see if philosophy, if ethics, if chiromancy, if the discovery of the divine in the house & the barn, in all works & all plays, cannot make the cheek blush, the lip quiver, & the tear start. I will not waste myself. On the strength of Things I will be borne, and try if Folly, Custom, Convention, & Phlegm cannot be made to hear our sharp artillery. Alas! alas! I have not the recollection of one strong moment. A cold mechanical preparation for a delivery as decorous,—fine things, pretty things, wise things, —but no arrows, no axes, no nectar, no growling, no transpiercing, no loving, no enchantment.—

And why?

I seem to lack constitutional vigor to attempt each topic as I ought. I ought to seek to lay myself out utterly,—large, enormous, prodigal, upon the subject of the week. But a hateful experience has taught me that I can only expend, say, twenty one hours on each lecture, if I would also be ready & able for the next. Of course, I spend myself prudently; I economize; I cheapen: whereof nothing grand ever grew. Could I spend sixty hours on each, or what is better, had I such energy that I could rally the lights & mights of sixty hours into twenty, I should hate myself less, I should help my friend.

I ought to be equal to every relation. It makes no difference how many friends I have & what content I can find in conversing with each if there be one to whom I have not been equal. If I have shrunk unequal from one contest instantly the joy I find in all the rest becomes mean & cowardly. "All these things avail me nothing so long as I see Mordecai sitting in the King's gate."

> "The valiant warrior famoused for worth
> After a thousand victories once foiled
> Is from the book of honor razed quite.
> And all the rest forgot for which he toiled."

I saw a maiden the other day dressed so prettily & fancifully that she gave the eye the same sort of pleasure that a gem does, —a fine opal, or the coloured stones. When I remember what fairy pleasure I found in some cornelians or agates which I saw for an hour when a very little boy, I think none but children & savages enjoy gems.

I wrote S.G.W.

I see persons who I think the world would be richer for losing: and I see persons whose existence makes the world rich. But blessed be the Eternal Power for those whom my lawless fancy, even, cannot strip of beauty and who never for a moment seem to me profane.

1840, April. By confession we help each other; by clean shrift, and not by dictation.

I like manners and their aristocracy better than the morgue of wealth. It is a gay chivalry, a merit, & indicates certainly the presence of a sense of beauty. I am always a fool to these mannered men at the first encounter. The Southerner holds me at arm's length, he will not let me measure him, and after twenty four hours my opinion shall still not be worth the telling;— such a cloak is his politesse. And yet, O stately friend, do not presume on this gay privilege of thine. Yonder simple countryman, on whom you have yet bestowed no smile, strikes down all your glittering & serried points with a wave of his hand, and overawes you, as does some grey Friar a circle of armed Barons. He oversteps with a free stride all your spaces marked with ribbons & etiquette, for he does not respect them; he is dignified by a higher thought, viz. by a humanity which slights all this, & overstands it, as a sane man an insane.

At Providence Mr G. is quite too much an artist. If he tells the best story I see so much preparation that the fun always falls short. I grow grave in my efforts to meet so much display.

It was well said of Mr F. by one of his neighbors, "He strikes twelve the first time."

Death in a novel or a poem is but the mechanical sublime, manage it how you will. Lay any emphasis on it & it only betrays the poverty of the writer; the feeblest action, the faintest thought must always be superior to the most imposing death in fable.

Ah my poor countrymen! Yankees & Dollars have such inextricable association that the words ought to rhyme. In New York, in Boston, in Providence, you cannot pass two men in the street without the word escaping them in the very moment of encounter, "dollars," "two & a half per cent," "three percent."

April 7. What does that fact signify,—that no body in this country can draw a hand except Allston? asserted by Mr Cole I think.

At Providence I was made very sensible of the desire of all open minds for religious teaching. The young men & several good women freely expressed to me their wish for more light, their sympathy in whatever promised a better life They inquired about the new Journal of next July. I was compelled to tell them that the aims of that paper were rather literary than psychological or religious. But the inquiry & the tone of these inquirers showed plainly what one may easily see in Boston & Cambridge & the villages also—that what men want is a Religion.

The railroad makes a man a chattel, transports him by the box & the ton; he waits on it. He feels that he pays a high price for his speed in this compromise of all his will. I think the man who walks looks down on us who ride.

I see with great pleasure this growing inclination in all persons who aim to speak the truth, for manual labor & the farm. It is not that commerce, law, & state employments are unfit for a man, but that these are now all so perverted & corrupt that no man can right himself in them, he is lost in them, *he* cannot move hand or foot in them. Nothing is left him but to begin the world anew, as he does who puts the spade into the ground for food. When many shall have done so, when the majority shall admit the necessity of reform, of health, of sanity in all these institutions, then the way will be open again to the great advantages that arise from division of labor. & a man will be able to select employments fittest for him without losing his selfdirection & becoming a tool.

It is said—What! will you give up the immense advantage reaped from the division of labor & set every man to make his own shoes, bureau, wagon, knife, & needle? It puts men back into barbarism by their own act.—I answer, as above.

In all my lectures, I have taught one doctrine, namely, the infinitude of the private man. This, the people accept readily enough, & even with loud commendation, as long as I call the lecture, Art; or Politics; or Literature; or the Household; but the moment I call it Religion,—they are shocked, though it be only the application of the same truth which they receive everywhere else, to a new class of facts.

The case of the menaced & insulted monarch is not quite aloof from our own experience. We have tasted that cup too. For see this wide society in which we walk of laboring men. We allow ourselves to be served by them. We pay them money & then turn our backs on them. We live apart from them & meet them without a salute in the streets. We do not greet their talents, nor rejoice in their good fortune, nor foster their hopes, nor in the assembly of the people vote for what is dear to them. Thus we enact the part of the selfish noble & king from the foundation of the world. See this tree always bears one fruit. In every household the peace of a pair is poisoned by the malice, slyness, indolence, & alienation of domestics. In every knot of laborers or boys the rich man, the scholar, does not feel himself among his friends but his enemies & at the polls he finds them arrayed in a mass in distinct opposition to him. Yet all these are but signs of an opposition of interest more deep which give a certain insecurity & terror to all his enjoyments for he feels himself an insulted & hated noble.

April 27. My little boy says, 'I want something to play with which I never saw before'. And thus lives over already in his experience the proclamation of Xerxes advertising a reward for a new pleasure. I tell him that the sun & moon are good playthings still, though they are very old; they are as good as new. So are Eating & drinking, though rather dangerous toys, very good amusements though old ones; so is water which we wash & play with; but he is not persuaded by my eloquence.

There seems a strange propensity to egotism in the mind of several eminent spiritualists whom I have known, a disproportion, a sad exaggeration which disables them from putting their act & word aloof from them, detaching it, & seeing it as a pitiful shrivelled apple, at its best a disgrace to the tree & to nature, & this in souls of unquestionable power & greater nearness to the secret of God than others. It is sadly punished too, & that speedily, inasmuch as this habit always leads men to humour it, to treat the patient tenderly not roundly, & so shut him up gradually in a narrower selfism, & exclude him from the great world of God's cheerful though fallible men & women. I had rather be insulted whilst I am insultable.

James Naylor, George Fox, Luther, are eminent examples of it long ago; and now we have Poets, Critics, Abolitionists, Prophets, & Philosophers infected with the same elephantiasis.

There is an important *équivoque* in our use of the word Unconscious, a word which is much displayed upon in the psychology of the present day. We say that our virtue & genius are unconscious, that they are the influx of God, & the like. The objector replies that to represent the Divine Being as an unconscious somewhat, is abhorrent, &c. But the unconsciousness we spake of was merely relative to *us*; we speak, we act from we know not what higher principle, and we describe its circumambient quality by confessing the subjection of our perception to it, we cannot overtop, oversee it,—not see at all its channel into us. But in saying this, we predicate nothing of its consciousness or unconsciousness in relation to itself. We see at once that we have no language subtle enough for distinctions in that inaccessible region. That air is too rare for the wings of words. We cannot say God is self conscious, or not self-conscious; for the moment we cast our eye on that dread nature, we see that it is the wisdom of wisdom, the love of love, the power of power, & soars infinitely out of all definition & dazzles all inquest.

True Criticism is inexhaustible. Every new thought supersedes all foregone thought & makes a new light on the whole world.

All spontaneous thought is irrespective of all else. It is for those who come after to find its relation to other thoughts.

If there be need of a new Journal, that need is its Introduction: it wants no preface. It proceeds at once to its own ends which it well knows & answers now for the first time. That consummated fitness is a triumphant apology. It will ignore all the old long constituted public or publics which newspapers & magazines address. It ignores all newspapers & magazines. It is so real, so full of its own authentic aim which it exists to attain, that it knows them not; not seeing them to fill any place which this mind esteems real, it has no thought to waste on them. It speaks to a public of its own, a newborn class long already waiting. They least of all need from it any letters of recommendation.

It is of course too confident in its tone to comprehend an objection, & so builds no outworks for possible defence against contingent enemies. It has the step of Fate & goes on existing like an oak or a river because it must.

If the projected Journal be what we anticipate—& if not we should not care for it—it does not now know itself in the way of accustomed criticism; it cannot foretell in orderly propositions what it shall do; its criticism is to be poetic, not the peeping but the broad glance of the American man on the books & things of this hour. Its brow is not wrinkled with circumspection but serene, cheerful, adoring. It has all things to say, & no less than all the world for its final audience.

There are no doubt many dogs barking at the moon & many owls hooting in this Saturday night of the world, but the fair moon knows nothing of either.

Apr. 30. Waldo looks out today from my study window & says, "These are not the woods I like to look at."—And what woods do you like to look at?—"Those that I see from the window of the Nursery."

Literature

May 3. Our moods are never quite transferable by means of words. The best record I can make of a certain state of self-reliance, for example, being often read by me, does not make me less surprised when I observe in another man the beauty of that virtue, or when I experience in myself the same degree of trust I had known before. The *life* of it is untranslateable by words.

Consolation

Our friends die—husbands, wives, children,—and the finest things are said to console us. Presently the man is consoled, but not by the fine things; no, but perhaps by very foul things, namely, by the defects of the dead from which he shall no more suffer; or, what often happens, by being relieved from relations & a responsibility, to which he was unequal. The willingness to lose a man shows us what a sad dog he is.

May 4. "When pens are not cut to write with, then they are called quills," says Waldo this morning.

Waldo says, "God is very glorious, he always says his prayers, and never 'haves (behaves) naughty."

———

In conversation, Alcott will meet no man who will take a superior tone. Let the other party say what he will, Alcott unerringly takes the highest moral ground & commands the other's position, & cannot be outgeneralled. And this because whilst he lives in his moral perception; his sympathies with the present company are not troublesome to him, never embarrass for a moment his perception. He is cool, bland, urbane, yet with his eye on the highest fact. With me it is not so. In all companies I sympathize too much. If they are ordinary & mean, I am. If the company were great I should soar: in all mere mortal parties, I take the contagion of their views & lose my own. I cannot outsee them, or correct, or raise them. As soon as they are gone, the muse returns; I see the facts as all cultivated men always have seen them, and am a great man alone.

Every man supposes himself not to be fully understood or appreciated; and if there is any truth in him, if he rests at last on the divine soul, I see not how it can be otherwise: the last chamber, the last closet, he must feel, was never opened; there is always a residuum unknown, unanalysable.

Strange how hard it is for cultivated men to free themselves from the optical illusion by which a great man appears an institution. They know & have observed in particular instances that the demonstration of a strong will, of a vast thought, at once arrested the eyes & magnetized the wills of men, so that society & events became secondaries & satellites of a man; and the genesis of that man's thought is not now explored after the laws of thought, but externally in his parentage, in his country, climate, college, election by his fellow citizens, & the like,—as we know is the tenor of vulgar biography. And yet though familiar with this fact the moment Jesus is mentioned, they forget their knowledge, & accept the apparatus of prophecy, miracle, positive supernatural indication by name & place, & claim on his part to extraordinary outward relations;—all these, which are the prismatic hues & lights which play around any wonderful genius, they regard as of an adamantine reality, and in the selectest society where Beauty, Goodness, & the Soul are named, these men talk of 'preaching Christ,' & of 'Christ's being the ideal of Man', &c. &c. so that I told them it might become my duty to spit in the face of Christ as a sacred act of duty to the Soul, an act which that beautiful pilgrim in nature would well enough appreciate.

We are halves: we see the past in Memory, but do not see the future. They say, that, at times, this hemisphere completes itself, and Foresight becomes as perfect as Aftersight.

9 May. Is it not pedantry to insist that every man should be a farmer as much as that he should be a lexicographer? Suppose the doctrine of the right Estate of Man finds him at sea, shall he therefore scrape together what dust & refuse he can find on deck, & dibble in a flower pot, or shall he learn to use the ropes, to stand at the wheel, to reef a sail & draw a fish out of the sea & be a farmer of the sea? In like manner, if the doctrine of universal labor find him in the midst of books whose use he understands & whose use other men wish to learn of him, shall he cast away this his skill & usefulness to go bungle with hoe & harrow, with cows & swine which he understands not? should he not rather farm his books well & lose no hour of beneficent activity in that place where he now is? The Doctrine of the Farm is merely this, that every man ought to stand in primary relations with the work of the world, ought to do it himself & not to suffer the accident of his having a purse in his pocket or his having been bred to some dishonorable & injurious craft, to sever him from those duties; and for this reason, that labor is God's education, that he only is a sincere learner; he only can become a Master, who learns the secrets of labor

& who by his real cunning extorts from nature its sceptre. Where is the fertile earth? Where the farmer is. Where do books become great engines but where the scholar is?

—

18 May. The terror of reform, that is, of true obedience, lies in the discovery that we must cast our virtues also, or what we have always esteemed such, into the same flame that has consumed our grosser sins.

Criticism must be transcendental, that is, must consider literature ephemeral & easily entertain the supposition of its entire disappearance. In our ordinary states of mind, we deem not only letters in general but most famous books parts of a preëstablished harmony, fatal, unalterable, and do not go behind Dante & Shakspeare, much less behind Moses, Ezekiel, & St John. But Man is critic of all these also and should treat the entire extant product of the human intellect as only one age, revisable, corrigible, reversible by him.

It seems as if the Jewsharp had sounded long enough.

—

Hate this childish haste to print & publish; for the hours of light come like Days of Judgment at last & cast their glory backward, forward, above, below. Then, poor child, all the folly stands confessed in thy scrolls & detaches itself from the true words.

By help of tea, tea was renounced.

I went to the circus & saw a man ride standing on the back of two galloping horses, a third horse being interposed between the two. As he rode, the sinews of his limbs played like those of his beasts. One horse brought a basket in his teeth, picked up a cap, & selected a card out of four. All wonder comes of showing an effect at two or three removes from the cause. Show us the two or three steps by which the horse was brought to fetch the basket, and the wonder would cease. But I & Waldo were of one mind when he said, "It makes me want to go home."

A pleasant walk & sail this fine afternoon with George P. B. I threatened by way of Earnestpenny in this absorbing Reform to renounce beef & the Daily Advertiser. There is ever a slight suspicion of the burlesque about earnest good men. It is very strange, but we flee to the speculative reformer to escape that same slight ridicule. Therefore it is that we say the Beautiful is the Highest, because this appears the Golden Mean escaping the dowdiness of the good & the heartlessness of the true.

I think it ought to be remembered in every essay after the Absolute Criticism that one circumstance goes to modify every work of literature, this namely, that all books are written generally by the unmagnetic class of mankind, by those who have not the active faculties & who describe what they have never done. This circumstance must certainly color what they say of character & action.

I owe to these pleasant poems I was reading a solitary joy. This great fineness of perception, this entire trust of the poet's own feeling to that degree that there is an entire absence of all conventional imagery and a bold use of that which the moment's mood had made sacred to him quite careless that it could be sacred to no other & might even be slightly ludicrous to the first reader—this is a proud style of writing—it sounds to the intelligent. A stroke that pleases me much is—"I & my flowers receive the music well."

28 May. At Bartol's, our Club was enriched by Edward Taylor's presence. I felt in a higher degree the same happiness I have formerly owed to that man's public discourses, the exhilaration & cheer of so much love poured out through so much imagination. For the time his exceeding life throws all other gifts into deep shade, "philosophy speculating on its own breath," taste, learning & all, and yet how willingly every man is willing to be nothing in his presence, to share this surprising emanation & be steeped & ennobled by the new wine of this eloquence. He gives sign every moment of a certain prodigious nature. No man instructs like him in the power of man

over men. Instantly you behold that a man is a Mover,—to the extent of his being a Power, and in contrast with the efficiency thus suggested, our actual life & society appears a dormitory. We are taught that earnest impassioned action is most our own & invited to try the deeps of love & wisdom,—we who have been players & paraders so long. And yet I think I am most struck with the *beauty* of his nature. This hardfeatured, scarred, & wrinkled Methodist whose face is a system of cordage becomes whilst he talks a gentle, a lovely creature—the Amore Greco is not more beautiful.

—

Was it Aesop or Epictetus who being sold for a slave at the market, cried out to all comers, "Who'll buy a master?" I should like to buy or hire that article. My household suffers from too many servants. My cow milks me. A rope of sand for Asmodeus to spin I cannot find. Now if so many dollars as I could amass, would fetch the good husband or gardener who would tell me what I ought to do in garden & barnyard, would summon me out to do it, even with a little compulsion, when I resisted,—that would suit me well.

Wordsworth's Excursion awakened in every lover of nature the right feeling. We saw stars shine, we felt the awe of mountains, we heard the rustle of the wind in the grass, & knew again the sweet secret of solitude. It was a great joy. It was nearer to nature & verse that more commanded nature than aught we had before. But the promise was not fulfilled. The whole book was dull. These were gleams, the poetry ran in veins and did not pervade the man.

—

Our American letters are, we confess, in the optative mood; but whoso knows these seething brains, these admirable radical projects, these talkers who talk the sun & moon away will believe that this generation cannot pass away without leaving its mark.

The swallow over my window ought to weave that straw in his bill through all my web also of speculations.

—

June 4. But Goethe must be set down as the poet of the Actual not of the Ideal; the poet of limitation & not of possibility; of this world & not of religion & hope; in short, if I may say so, the poet of prose & not of poetry. He accepts the base doctrine of Fate & gleans what joys may yet remain accessible. He is like a banker or a weaver with a passion for the country, he steals out of Babylon before sunrise or after sunset or on a rare holiday to get a draught of sweet air and a gaze at the magnificence of summer, and does not dare to emancipate himself from his livelong slavery and lead a man's life in a man's relation to nature. In that which should be his own place he feels like a truant, and is whipped back presently to his task & his cell. Poetry is with Goethe thus external,—the gilding of the chain,—the recreation, the mitigation of his lot, but the Muse never assays those thunder-tones which cause to vibrate the sun & the moon, which dissipate by terrible melody all this iron network of circumstance, & abolish the old heavens & old earth before the freewill or Godhead of man. He was content to fall into the track of vulgar poets & spend on common aims his splendid endowments, and has declined the office proffered to now & then a man in many centuries,—in the power of his genius, of a Redeemer of the human mind. He has written better than other poets, but only that his talent was better but the ambition of creation he declined. Life for him is prettier, easier, wiser, decenter, has a gem or two more on its apparel, but its old eternal burden is not relieved, no drop of healthier blood flows yet in its veins. Let him pass. Humanity must wait for its physician still at the side of the road, & confess as this man passes, that they have served it better who assured it out of the innocent hope in their heart that a Physician will come, than this majestic Artist with all his wealth & all his eloquence.

—

Bat and Ball

Toys no doubt have their philosophy & who knows how deep is the origin of a boy's delight in a spinning top? In playing with bat-balls, perhaps he is charmed with some recognition of the movement of the heavenly bodies, and a game of base or cricket is a course of experimental astronomy, and my young master tingles with a faint sense of being a tyrannical Jupiter driving spheres madly from their orbit.

June 4. Selfreliance sanctifies the character, for whoso is of that habit does not gossip or gad, is not betrayed by excess of sympathy into trifles, but ignores what he should ignore.

—

In reading Meister, I am charmed with the insight; it is "rammed with life." I find there all my brothers & sisters, my uncles & aunts,—in short, all people. I am moreover instructed in the possibility of a highly accomplished society and taught to look for great talent & culture under a grey coat. But these are all. I am never lifted above myself. I am never transported above the dominion of the senses or cheered with an infinite tenderness or armed with a grand trust.

It is not merely then a detached fact that Goethe had not the usual sharpness of moral perception that belongs to genius as we might relate of a man that he had or had not the sense of tune or an eye for colours, but it is the cardinal fact of health or disease, since lacking this he failed in the high sense to be a creator and with divine endowments falls by irreversible decree into the common history of genius.

—

Waldo says, "the flowers talk when the wind blows over them." My little boy grows thin in the hot summer & runs all to eyes & eyelashes.

June 11. Who has more self repose than I masters me by eye & manner though he should not move a finger; who has less is mastered by me with the like facility.

—I finish this morning transcribing my old Essay on Love, but I see well its inadequateness. I am cold because I am hot, — cold at the surface only as a sort of guard & compensation for the fluid tenderness of the core,—have much more experience than I have written there, more than I will, more than I can write. In silence we must wrap much of our life, because it is too fine for speech, because also we cannot explain it to others, and because somewhat we cannot yet understand. We do not live as angels eager to introduce each other to new perfections in our brothers & sisters, & frankly avowing our delight in each new trait of character, in the magic of each new eyebeam, but that which passes for love in the world gets official, & instead of embracing, hates all the divine traits that dare to appear in other persons. A better & holier society will mend this selfish cowardice and we shall have brave ties of affection not petrified by law, not dated or ordained by law to last for one year, for five years, or for life; but drawing their date like all friendship from itself only; brave as I said because innocent & religiously abstinent from the connubial endearments, being a higher league on a purely spiritual basis. This nobody believes possible who is not good. The good know it is possible. Cows & bulls & peacocks think it nonsense.

——

21 June. Can we not be so great as to offer tenderness to our friend,—tenderness with self trust? Why should we desecrate noble & beautiful souls by intruding on them? Can we not guard them from ourselves? Why insist on these rash personal relations? Why go to the houses or know the mothers & brothers of our friend? Leave this touching & clawing. Let him be a soul to me. A message, a compliment, a sincerity, a glance from him,—*that* I want. I can get politics & news & convenience without these sunbright qualities. To my friend I write a letter, & from him I get a letter. That seems to you a little. Me it suffices. It is a spiritual gift worthy of him to give & of me to receive. It profanes nobody. In these warm lines the heart will trust itself as it will not to the tongue, and pour out the prophecy of a better & godlier existence than all the annals of heroism have yet made good. To us even the society of our friend is as yet far from poetic. We are not therein cold & great. We are not pure, impassive, universal as yonder bar of cloud that sleeps on the horizon or that clump of waving grass. Let us bring him & ourselves up to that standard of nature. Leave him alone. Defend him from yourself. That proud defying eye, that scornful beauty of his mien & action, do not pique yourself on reducing but rather fortify & enhance. Guard him as thy great counterpart: have a princedom a World to thy friend. Let him be to thee forever a sort of beautiful Enemy, untameable, infinitely revered, and not a trivial shift & convenience to be soon outgrown & cast aside. The hues of

the opal, the lights of the diamond are not to be seen if the eye is too near. And yet, as E. H. said, though I do not wish my friend to visit me, I wish to live with him.

Of a man we should ask, What has he invented? Has he invented a Day? an action? every act, every moment, every mode of being he showed us? Alas! often he invented nothing; he was a speaking ape; he did not rise to an original force,—not for an instant—and we are hardly able in thought to detach him from his body & we talk well pleased of having put him in the ground.

A lover does not willingly name his mistress; he speaks of all persons & things beside; for she is sacred. So will the friend respect the name of his friend. Name him for pride & he is already ceasing to be yours. The base lover is piqued by the natural dignity of the virgin which overawes & disconcerts him, do what he can. He desires to possess her that so at least he may recover his tongue & his behaviour in her presence. Thus he steals the victory which he ought greatly to earn by raising his own character to the royal level of hers. The same ethics hold of friendship. Worship the superiorities of thy friend. Wish them not less by thought but hoard & tell them all: they are the uplifting force by which you are to rise to new degrees of rank.

Selfreliance applied to another person is reverence, that is, only the selfrespecting will be reverent.

24 June. The least sense of power, as the newly attained skill to make corn grow, or to row a boat, raises the spirits & from it a new wisdom immediately flows.

We love to paint those qualities which we do not possess. The poet admires the man of energy & tactics; the merchant breeds his son for the church or the bar; and where a man is not vain & egotistic you shall find what he has not, by his praise. I who suffer from excess of sympathy, proclaim always the merits of selfreliance.

*

C's poetry & C. S.'s have a certain merit which unfits them for print. They are proper manuscript inspirations, honest, great, but crude. They have never been filed or defiled for the eye that studies surface: the writer was not afraid to write ill; had a great meaning too much at heart to stand for trifles, & wrote lordly for his peers alone. This is the right poetry of hope, no French correctness but Hans Sachs & Chaucer rather.

The soul puts forth friends as the tree puts forth leaves & presently by the germination of new buds it extrudes the old leaf. The law of nature is alternation forevermore. The soul environs itself with friends that it may enter into a grander self-acquaintance or solitude; & it goes alone for a season only that it may exalt its conversation or society. We are never so fit for friendship as when we cease to seek for it, & take ourselves to friend.

Once I was in love and whenever I thought of what should happen to me & the maiden, we were always travelling; I could not think of her otherwise. Again I was in love, and I always painted this maiden at home.

Why should I wish to do or write many things,—since any one well done contains my history? Why should I see with regret the felling of the woods, & fear lest my son should lack the lessons his father drew from nature, when I have known myself entertained by a single dewdrop or an icicle, by a liatris, or a fungus, and seen God revealed in the shadow of leaf? Nature is microscopically rich, as well as cumulatively. Why should I covet a knowledge of new facts & skills, when I know that they are only other illustration of laws daily playing before my eyes? Day & night, garden & house, art & books serve me as illustration just as well as would all trades, all skills. Indeed I am far from having exhausted the significance of the few symbols I use. I can come to use them yet with a terrible simplicity. Each new fact I look upon as this steaming of hot air from the wide fields upward, is a new word that I learn & hive, well assured the use for it will come presently, as the boy learns with good hope his Latin Vocabulary. What is it to be a poet? What are his garland & singing robes? What but a sensibility so keen that the scent of an elderblow or the timberyard & corporation works of a nest of pismires is event enough for him. The poet's wreath & robe is to do what he likes; is emancipation from other men's questions & glad study of his own: Emancipation from the gossip & forms of society & the allowed right & practice of making new. He is not affable with all.

Originality

Talent without character is friskiness. The charm of Montaigne's egotism, & of his anecdotes, is, that there is a stout cavalier, a seigneur of France, at home in his chateau, responsible for all this chatting. Now suppose it should be shown & proved, that the famous "Essays" were a jeu d'esprit of Scaliger, or other scribacious person, written for the booksellers, & not resting on a real status picturesque in the eyes of all men, would not the book instantly lose almost all its value?

Montaigne

The language of the street is always strong. What can describe the folly & emptiness of scolding like the word *jawing*? I feel too the force of the double negative, though clean contrary to our grammar rules. And I confess to some pleasure from the stinging rhetoric of a rattling oath in the mouth of truckmen & teamsters. How laconic & brisk it is by the side of a page of the North American Review. Cut these words & they would bleed; they are vascular & alive; they walk & run. Moreover they who speak them have this elegancy, that they do not trip in their speech. It is a shower of bullets, whilst Cambridge men & Yale men correct themselves & begin again at every half sentence. I know nobody among my contemporaries except Carlyle who writes with any sinew & vivacity comparable to Plutarch & Montaigne. Yet always this profane swearing & bar-room wit has salt & fire in it. I cannot now read Webster's speeches. Fuller & Brown & Milton are quick, but the list is soon ended. Goethe seems to be well alive, no pedant. Luther too. *Guts* is a stronger word than intestines.

—

Now for near five years I have been indulged by the gracious Heaven in my long holiday in this goodly house of mine entertaining & entertained by so many worthy & gifted friends and all this time poor Nancy Barron the madwoman has been screaming herself hoarse at the poorhouse across the brook & I still hear her whenever I open my window.

The Best are never demoniacal or magnetic but all brutes are. The Democratic party in this country is more magnetic than the Whig. Andrew Jackson is an eminent example of it. Van Buren is not,—but his masters are who placed him in his house. Amos Kendall & Woodbury. Mr Hoar is entirely destitute of this element. It is the prince of the power of the air. The lowest angel is better. It is the height of the animal; below the region of the divine.

Quotation
There is little good quotation. The speaker cannot think of the good texts he suggests to the hearer. The speaker does not quote well; the hearer quotes well.

What a joyful sense of freedom we have when a writer on architecture announces that old opinion of artists that no man can build any house well who does not know something of anatomy.

29 June. Today at the Cliff we held our villegiatura. I saw nothing better than the passage of the river by the dark clump of trees that line the bank in one spot for a short distance. There nature charmed the eye with her distinct & perfect painting. As the flowing silver reached that point, it darkened, & yet every wave celebrated its passage through the shade by one sparkle. But ever the direction of the sparkles was onward, onward. Not one receded. At one invariable pace like marchers in a procession to solemn music, in perfect time, in perfect order, they moved onward, onward, & I saw the Warning of their eternal flow. Then the rock seemed good to me. I think we can ever afford to part with Matter. How dear & beautiful it is to us! As water to our thirst, so is this rock to our eyes & hands & feet. It is firm water; it is cold flame. What refreshment, what health, what magic affinity! ever an old friend, ever

like a dear friend or brother when we chat affectedly with strangers comes in this honest face whilst we prattle with men & takes a grave liberty with us & shames us out of our nonsense. The flowers lately, especially when I see for the first time this season an old acquaintance, a gerardia, a lespedeza, have much to say on Life & Death. "You have much discussion," they seem to say, "on Immortality. Here it is: Here are we who have spoken nothing on the matter." And as I have looked from this lofty rock lately, our human life seemed very short beside this ever renewing race of trees. Your life, they say, is but a few spinnings of this top. Forever the forest germinates; forever our solemn strength renews its knots & nodes & leaf-buds & radicles. Grass & trees have no individuals as man counts individuality. The continuance of their race is immortality; the continuance of ours is not. So they triumph over us and when we seek to answer or to say something the good tree holds out a bunch of green leaves in your face, or the woodbine five graceful fingers, & looks so stupid beautiful, so innocent of all argument that our mouths are stopped & Nature has the last word.

—

Carlyle shall make a statement of a fact, shall draw a portrait, shall inlay nice shades of meaning, shall play, shall insinuate, shall banter, shall paralyze with sarcasm, shall translate, shall sing a Tyrtaean Song, & speak out like the Liturgy or the old English Pentateuch all the secrets of manhood. This he shall do & much more, being an upright, plain dealing, hearty, loving soul of the clearest eye & of infinite wit & using the language like a protean engine which can cut, thrust, saw, rasp, tickle, or pulverize as occasion may require. But he is not a philosopher: his strength does not lie in the statement of abstract truth. His contemplation has no wings.

He exhausts his topic; there is no more to be said when he has ended. He is not suggestive.

Every new history that shall be written will be indebted to him. It will not be stately but will go now into the street & sitting room & the alehouse & kitchen.

What he has said shall be proverb, no body shall be able to say it otherwise.

It does not need that a poem should be long. Life, I have written above, is unnecessarily long and poems are, as we learn when we meet with a line "In the large utterance of the early gods," or Milton's "beyond the manhood of a Roman recovery," moments of personal relation, smiles & glances how ample, borrowers of eternity, they are. Some mellow satisfying sessions we have in the woods in cool summer days.

We are all boarders at one table,—White man, black man, ox and eagle, bee, & worm.

Logic.
   We want in every man a long logic. We cannot pardon the absence of it; but it must not be spoken,—it must never come to speech, like the name of Jehovah among the Jews.

   Education aims to make the man prevail over the circumstance. The vulgar man is the victim of the circumstance. In the stagecoach he is no man but a tedious echo of each new accident of the journey, absorbed in the heat, in the cold, in the bad horses, in the fret of a crowded carriage. In the rain he can think of nothing but that he wishes it would stop; in the drought, he waits till the rain fall; in debt, he postpones his being until his note is paid; in dull company, until the company is gone; & never rallies himself to sink the circumstance these encroaching trifles into their proper nothingness before the energies, the sweetness, the riches, the aspirations of a human mind.
The common man has no time. One Circumstance delivers him over to another. Now he cannot be, for he is travelling. Then he cannot be for he has arrived in a new place; now, because he labors, then because he rests.

15 July. Behaviour seems to me to give a higher pleasure than statues, higher than pictures, it is the finest of the fine arts. I like to see a man or a woman who does not palter or dodge, whose eyes look straight forward, & who throws the wisdom he or she has attained into the address & demeanor. What blandishment in the pronouncing of your name. Your name is

commended to your ear ever after it has been spoken by a man like Otis or a woman like Anna Ward.

Higher natures overpower lower ones by affecting them with a sleep. The faculties are locked up & can offer no resistance. That is perhaps the universal law. When the high cannot bring up the low to itself, it benumbs it. We put the resistance of the horse & ox asleep.

Heroic

An able man is always an equilibrium to balance the extremes of the volatile around him.

> "Sunshine was he
> On the cold day
> And when the dogstar raged
> Shade was he & coolness" says the Arabic poet

translated by Goethe, vol 6 p. 13.

17 July. The hottest weather—so long continued—that I have noticed,—red hot noons—the mercury reaches 93° in the shade—the crops are drying up. Let me be coolness & shade. The gardener floods his vines with water out of the well sure that the good Rain will in the year fill his well, though it delays to feed his garden. So is he "coolness & shade." In the winter he covers his asparagus with straw & in the cold spring his young tomatos with glass, so is he to them "Sunshine." But I weep with the weepers & fear with the fearers & am not a tower of defence but a foolish sympathy.

—

Tantalus is but a name for you & me.

Transmigration of Souls: that too is no fable. I would it were; but look around you at the men & women, do you not see that they are already only half human; that every animal of the barnyard, the field, & the forest, of the earth, & of the waters that are under the earth, has contrived to get a footing & to leave the print of his features & form in some one or other of these upright heaven-facing walkers? Ah brother! wake the guardian gods who slumber in the bottom of thy heart to hold thee to the man, to awe the beast, to stop the ebb of thy soul —ebbing downward into the forms into whose habits thou hast now for many years slid.

Proteus; and what else am I, who wept yesterday, & laugh now; who slept last night like a corpse, and this morning stood & ran? And what see I on any side but the transmigrations of Proteus? I can symbolize my thought by using the name of any creature, of any fact, because every Creature is Man agent or patient. Do not kill any life, for thou strikest at thyself. The very musquito which sings & stings, bear with, for the little emissary is also a man, & comes to teach patience & benevolence.

——

31 July. Talked with E. H. last night on Landor whom I read for a few minutes yesterday. We agreed that here was a book of Sentiment; (in Pericles & Aspasia) sentiment in the high & strict sense that one could hardly read it without learning to write with more elegance. The inimitable neatness of the sentences and then the wonderful elegance of suppression & omission which runs through it might polish a dunce.

31 July. A newspaper in Providence contains some notice of Transcendentalism, & deplores Mr Emerson's doctrine that the argument for immortality betrays weakness. The piece seems to be written by a woman. It begins with round sentences but ends in Oh's & Ah's. Yet cannot society come to apprehend the doctrine of One Mind? Can we not satisfy ourselves with the fact of living for the Universe, of lodging our beatitude therein? Patriotism has been thought great in Sparta, in Rome, in New England even, only sixty years ago. How long before *Universalism* or Humanity shall be creditable & beautiful?

And now I think that our Dial ought not to be a mere literary journal but that the times demand of us all a more earnest aim. It ought to contain the best advice on the topics of Government, Temperance, Abolition, Trade, & Domestic Life. It might well add to such compositions such poetry & sentiment as now will constitute its best merit. Yet it ought to go straight into life with the devoted wisdom of the best men & women in the land. It should,—should it not?—be a degree nearer to the hodiurnal facts than my writings are? I wish to write pure mathematics, and not a culinary almanac or application of science to the arts.

Sometimes I wish to please: & sometimes I do not wish to please you, but I wish that you should wish to please me.

Every history in the world is my history. I can as readily find myself in the tragedy of the Atrides as in the Saxon Chronicle, in the Vedas as in the New Testament, in Aesop as in the Cambridge Platform or the Declaration of Independence. The good eye, the good ear can translate fast enough the slight varieties of dialect in these cognate tongues. The wildest fable, the bloodiest tragedy is all too true.

—

Waldo rolled over in the night on his trundle bed until he got quite under my bed & off his own. Then he broke out into loud cries, telling me, "I tried to get away from the bed, and the bed came."

The poet cannot spare any grief or pain or terror in his experience; he wants every rude stroke that has been dealt on his irritable texture. I need my fear & my superstition as much as my purity & courage, to construct the glossary which opens the Sanscrit of the world.

—

I went into the woods. I found myself not wholly present there. If I looked at a pine tree or an aster, *that* did not seem to be nature. Nature was still elsewhere: this or this was but outskirt & far off reflection & echo of the triumph that had passed by & was now at its glancing splendor & heyday,— perchance in the neighboring fields, or, if I stood in the field, then in the adjacent woods. Always the present object gave me this sense of the stillness that follows a pageant that has just gone by.

It was the same among men & women as among the silent trees. Always it was a referred existence; always an absence; never a presence & satisfaction. Thus I was looking *up to nature*.

Afterwards I was for a season active, devout, & happy, and

passing through the woods the trees & asters looked *up at me*. There was I & there were these placid creatures around, and the virtue that was in them seemed to pass from me into them.

Nature is thus a differential thermometer detecting the presence or absence of the divine spirit in man.

One leaves me my freedom but another gives me more freedom.

10 Sept.

What fact more conspicuous in modern history than the creation of the Gentleman? Chivalry is that, & loyalty is that; and how much of Shakspeare & all of Beaumont & Fletcher paints that. Sir Philip Sidney for a moment reflected these concentring rays. It was the oblique & covert way in which the good world was training to the discovery that a man must have the saintly, & the poetic character, that by taste he must worship beauty and by love of the invisible if it were only of Opinion, must carry his life in his hand to be risked at any instant.

Strange history this of *abolition*. The negro must be very old & belongs, one would say, to the fossil formations. What right has he to be intruding into the late & civil daylight of this dynasty of the Caucasians & Saxons? It is plain that so inferior a race must perish shortly like the poor Indians. S. C. said, "the Indians perish because there is no place for them". That is the very fact of their inferiority. There is always place for the superior. Yet pity for these was needed, it seems, for the education of this generation in ethics. Our good world cannot learn the beauty of love in narrow circles & at home in the immense Heart, but it must be stimulated by somewhat foreign & monstrous, by the simular man of Ethiopia.

—

11 September. See how fond of symbols the people are. See the Great Ball which they roll from Baltimore to Bunker Hill. See Lynn in a Shoe, & Salem in a ship. They say & think that they hate poetry and all sorts of moonshine; & they are all the while mystics & transcendentalists.

Retsch encumbers us with accessories. His men & animals all run to hair & nails.

11 September. Would it not be a good cipher for the seal of the Lonely Society which forms so fast in these days, Two Porcupines meeting with their spines erect, and the motto, "We converse at the *quill's* end."

I would labor cheerfully in my garden every day, if when I go there it did not seem trifling. It is so easy to waste hours & hours there in weeding & hoeing and as pleasant as any other play that I can impute to you no merit that you labor. Nothing is easier or more epicurean.

Character establishes itself & blows a grand music through whatever instrument, though it were an oatpipe or a cornstalk viol. If love be there I shall find it out though I only see you eat bread or make some trifling but necessary request. The reform that is ripening in your mind for the amelioration of the human race, I shall find already in miniature in every direction to the domestics, in every conversation with the assessor, with your creditor, & with your debtor.

The monastery, the convent did not quite fail. Many & many a stricken soul found peace & home & scope in those regimens, in those chapels & cells. The Society of Shakers did not quite fail but has proved an agreeable asylum to many a lonesome farmer & matron. The College has been dear to many an old bachelor of learning. What hinders them that this age better advised should endeavor to sift out of these experiments the false & adopt & embody in a new form the advantage?

12 Sept. S. C. who left us yesterday is a true & high minded person, but has her full proportion of our native frost.

She remarked of the Dial, that the spirit of many of the pieces was lonely.

14 September. You cannot surprise me with your love. Of that surely I was apprised in my own nature & yours.

17 September. I am only an experimenter. Do not, I pray you, set the least value on what I do, or the least discredit on what I do not as if I had settled anything as true or false. I

unsettle all things. No facts are to me sacred, none are profane;
I simply experiment, an endless seeker, with no past at my
back.

—

Sept. 20. Can we not trust ourselves? Must we be such coxcombs as to keep watch & ward over our noblest sentiments
even, lest they also betray us, & God prove a little too divine?
Dare we never say, this time of ours shall be the era of Discovery? These have been the ages of darkness. Wide Europe, wide
America lieth in night, turneth in sleep. The morning twilight
is grey in the East; the Columbuses, the Vespuccis, the Cabots
of moral adventure are loosening their sails & turning their
bowsprits to the main. Men have never loved each other. See
already they blush with a kindness which is pure, and Genius
the Inventor finds in Love the unknown & inexhaustible continent. Love which has been exclusive shall now be inclusive.
Love which once called Genius proud,—behold,—they have
exchanged names. Love which was a fat stupid Shaker or a
maudlin Methodist or Moravian, now is a brave & modest
man of light, sight, and conscience. God hateth the obscure.
On the last day as on the first day, he still says, Let there be
Light. Where there is progress in character, there is no confusion of sentiment, no diffidence of self, but the heart sails ever
forward in the direction of the open sea.

Perhaps after many sad doubting idle days, days of happy
honest labor will at last come when a man shall have filled up
all the hours from sun to sun with great and equal action, shall
lose sight of this sharp individuality which contrasts now so
oddly with nature, and ceasing to regard shall cease to feel his
boundaries, but shall be interfused by nature & shall interfuse
nature that the sun shall rise by his will as much as his own
hand or foot do now; and his eyes or ears or fingers shall not
seem to him the property of a more private will than the sea &
the stars, and he shall feel the meaning of the growing tree and
the evaporating waters with a more entire & satisfactory intelligence than now attends the activity of his organs of sense.
Every glance we give to the landscape predicts a better
understanding by assuring us we are not right now. When I am
quite alone in my morning walk if I lift up my eyes the goodly

green picture I see seems to call me hypocrite & false teacher —me who stood innocently there with quite other thoughts & had not spoken a word. For the landscape seems imperatively to expect a clear mirror, a willing reception in me, which, not finding, it lies obtrusive & discontented on the outward eye unable to pass into the inward eye & breeds a sense of jar & discord.

The most trivial & gaudy fable—Kehama, Jack Giantkiller, Red Ridinghood, every grandam's nursery rhyme—contains, as I have elsewhere noted, a moral that is true to the core of the world. It is because Nature is an instrument so omnipotently musical that the most careless or stupid hand cannot draw a discord from it. A devil struck the chords in defiance, & his malevolence was punished by a sweeter melody than the angels made.

"Love will creep where it cannot go," will accomplish that by imperceptible original incalculable methods, being his own lever, fulcrum, & moving power, which force could never achieve. Have you not seen in the woods in a late autumn morning a poor little fungus, an agaric, a plant without any solidity, nay, that seemed nothing but a soft mush or jelly, yet by its constant, total, & inconceivably gentle pushing had managed to break its way up through the frosty ground & actually to lift a pretty hard crust on its head?

I have no quarrel with the universe. My heart, when the noble love me, beats peacefully. If I am bashful I am serene.

Old R.—his eye always found in the landscape the graveyard like a jackal.

The first thing men think of, when they love, is, to exhibit their usefulness & advantages. Women refuse these, asking only love.

Is thine eye evil because I am good?

*

Between narrow walls we walk:—insanity on one side, & fat dulness on the other.

Nelly smells like a cakepan.

There is no leap—not a shock of violence throughout nature. Man therefore must be predicted in the first chemical relation exhibited by the first atom. If we had eyes to see it, this bit of quartz would certify us of the necessity that man must exist as inevitably as the cities he has actually built.

My good neighbor coarsely but truly complains that there are no men in the pulpit, that "the ministers are as fine as a fiddle."

Sept. 24. The victories of the Arabs after Mahomet interest me. They did they knew not what. The naked Derar horsed on an idea was an overmatch to a troop of cavalry. The women fought & conquered men. To read this, causes fear, or something like it. That is to say I am so effeminate at this moment that the staves of those women do reach unto & hit me too. This force is not in Arabs but in all women. Every noble maiden & dame will take up into herself the same might, although in proportioned & cultivated souls it will cease to be terrible and will become endurance & overcoming love.

Cities & coaches shall never impose on me again. I seem to see every solitary dream of mine rushing to fulfilment. That fancy I had and did not express because I supposed it would make thee laugh, thou O broker & thou O carpenter sayest now the same thing. Had I waited a day longer to speak I had been too late.

H. H. asks what facts confirm you, not what principles.

25 Sept. I make haste to speak lest I be found unworthy of my office. I am a fact which it cost all the foregoing ages to produce. I am strong not to do but to live, not in my arms but in my heart, not as an agent but as a fact: herein a difficult, inaccessible, unrivalled, unrivalable whole of fate & God. Away then with this pitiful ambition, this groping and shame, this calculation & frugality & service of the belly, this gazing into

the looking-glass of men's opinion, this asking leave to live. A man might as well be a post as an economist, a sluggard, or a lover of popularity. Leave thy reserves, thy peppercorn prudences, thy worldly management and let the almighty nature stream through every pore & channel of thy soul, body, & estate. Generously and as a child & heir of the Past Universe release the life on life, the wisdom on wisdom long hived & mellowed & mixed through ages & agents, and all the wild variety of event to arrive at last at their consummation & secular flower in your perfect nature. Hast thou friends? Do bright eyes & leading souls approach thee once & again, & now in companies? They so inform thee of the fact that you are not your own but a public & sacred property which it were profane in you to hinder in its effect or to degrade to base uses.

I read today in Ockley a noble sentence of Ali, son-in-law of Mahomet; "Thy lot or portion of life is seeking after thee; therefore be at rest from seeking after it."

Sept. 26. You would have me love you. What shall I love? Your body? The supposition disgusts you. What you have thought & said? Well, whilst you were thinking & saying them, but not now: I see no possibility of loving any thing but what now is, & is becoming; your courage, your enterprize, your budding affection, your opening thought, your prayer, I can love,—but what else?

"Paradise," said Mahomet, "is under the shadow of swords." "Omar's walking stick struck more terror into those that were present than another man's sword. His diet was barley bread; his sauce salt; & oftentimes by way of abstinence he eat his bread without salt. His drink was water. His palace was built of mud. And when he left Medina to go to the conquest of Jerusalem he rode on a red camel with a wooden platter hanging at his saddle with a bottle of water & two sacks one containing barley & the other dried fruits."

———

I spoke of myself to L. when first I awoke & I seemed to stain the grey cheek of the morning by any allusion to myself. These pitiful narrowing egotisms do insult the glory of nature.

*

I will not be chidden out of my most trivial native habit by your distaste, O philosopher, by your preference for somewhat else. If Rhetoric has no charm for you, it has for me; and my words are as costly & admirable to me as your deeds to you. It is all pedantry to prefer one thing that is alive to another thing which is also alive. The mystery of God inhabits a nursery tale as deeply as the laws of a state or the heart of a man.

—

The Whigs meet in numerous conventions & each palpitating heart swells with the cheap sublime of magnitude & number. The greater the concourse and with each new uproar of announcement, "The delegation from Essex!" "the delegation from Vermont!" "the Whigs of Maine!" the young patriot feels himself greater, stronger than before, by a new thousand of eyes & arms. In like manner the reformers summon Conventions and vote & resolve in multitude. But not so, O friends! will the God deign to enter & inhabit you, but by a method precisely the reverse. It is only as a man detaches himself from all support & stands alone, that I see him to be strong and to prevail. He is weaker by every recruit to his banner. Is not a man better than a town?

In the history of the world the doctrine of Reform had never such scope as at the present hour. Herrnhuters, Quakers, Monks, Swedenborgians,—all respected something: the church or the state, literature, history, the market town, the usages of living, the dinner table, coined money. But now all these & all else hear the trumpet & are rushing to judgment. Christianity must quickly take a niche that waits for it in the Pantheon of the Past, and figure as Mythology henceforward and not a kingdom, town, statute, rite, calling, man, woman, or child, but is threatened by the new spirit. Nations will not shield you, neither will books. How can nations, if there is not the most bronzed attorney or broker who does not, (to your consternation almost,) quail & shake the moment he hears a question prompted by the new Ideas? Vain is the cumulative fame of Tasso, of Dante,—vain the volumes of literature which entrench their sacred rhymes, if the passing mystic has no glance for them, not a motion of respect. Alas! too surely their doom is sealed.

Lidian gives the true doctrine of property when she says "No one should take any more than his own share, let him be ever so rich."

5 October, 1840. On Saturday evening I attended the wedding of Samuel Gray Ward and Anna Hazard Barker at the house of Mr Farrar in Cambridge. Peace go with you, beautiful, pure, & happy friends,—peace & beauty & power & the perpetuity and the sure unfolding of all the buds of joy that so thickly stud your branches.

Oct. 7. Circumstances are dreams which springing unawares from ourselves amuse us whilst we doze & sleep, but when we wake, nothing but causes can content us. The life of man is the true romance which when it is valiantly conducted, and all the stops of the instrument opened, will go nigh to craze the reader with anxiety, wonder, & love. I am losing all relish for books & for feats of skill in my delight in this Power. Do not accuse me of sloth. Do not ask me to your philanthropies, charities, & duties, as you term them;—Mere circumstances;— flakes of the snow cloud, leaves of the tree;—I sit at home with the cause grim or glad. I think I may never do anything that you shall call a deed again. I have been writing with some pains Essays on various matters as a sort of apology to my country for my apparent idleness. But the poor work has looked poorer daily as I strove to end it. My genius seemed to quit me in such a mechanical work, a seeming wise,—a cold exhibition of dead thoughts. When I write a letter to any one whom I love, I have no lack of words or thoughts: I am wiser than myself & read my paper with the pleasure of one who receives a letter, but what I write to fill up the gaps of a chapter is hard & cold, is grammar & logic; there is no magic in it; I do not wish to see it again. Settle with yourself your accusations of me. If I do not please you, ask me not to please you, but please yourself. What you call my indolence, nature does not accuse; the twinkling leaves, the sailing fleets of waterflies, the deep sky like me well enough and know me for their own. With them I have no em- barrassments, diffidences, or compunctions: with them I mean to stay. You think it is because I have an income which exempts me from your day-labor, that I waste, (as you call it,) my time in sungazing & stargazing. You do not know me. If my debts, as they threaten, should consume what money I have, I should live just as I do now: I should eat worse food & wear a coarser coat and should wonder in a potato patch instead of in the wood—but it is I & not my Twelve Hundred dollars a year, that love God.

We feel—do we not?—at every one of those remarkable effects in landscape which occasionally catch & delight the eye, as, for example, a long vista in woods, trees on the shore of a lake coming quite down to the water, a long reach in a river, a double or triple row of uplands or mountains seen one over the other,—and whatever of the like has much affected our fancy, must be the rhetoric of some thought not yet detached for the conscious intellect.

Virtues are among men rather the exception than the rule. They do what is called a good action as some deed of courage, or charity, much as they would pay a fine in expiation of daily non appearance on parade. I do not wish to do such penances. I wish my life to be sound & sweet & not to need diet & bleeding. My life should be unique; it should be an alms; a battle; a conquest; a medicine. I do not value their charities if I do not value the persons. Their works are done as an apology & extenuation of their living in the world, as invalids & insane people pay a high board. It makes no difference to me poor & feeble though I am whether I do or forbear these actions. I cannot consent to pay for a privilege where I have intrinsic right. I may be & am a person of few & feeble gifts but I actually *am*, & my fellows must know it.

—

17 Oct.
Yesterday George & Sophia Ripley, Margaret Fuller & Alcott discussed here the new social plans. I wished to be convinced, to be thawed, to be made nobly mad by the kindlings before my eye of a new dawn of human piety. But this scheme was arithmetic & comfort; this was a hint borrowed from the Tremont House & U.S. Hotel; a rage in our poverty & politics

to live rich & gentlemanlike, an anchor to leeward against a change of weather; a prudent forecast on the probable issue of the great questions of pauperisim & property. And not once could I be inflamed,—but sat aloof & thoughtless, my voice faltered & fell. It was not the cave of persecution which is the palace of spiritual power, but only a room in the Astor House hired for the Transcendentalists. I do not wish to remove from my present prison to a prison a little larger. I wish to break all prisons. I have not yet conquered my own house. It irks & repents me. Shall I raise the siege of this hencoop & march baffled away to a pretended siege of Babylon? It seems to me that so to do were to dodge the problem I am set to solve, & to hide my impotency in the thick of a crowd. I can see too afar that I should not find myself more than now,—no, not so much, in that select, but not by me selected, fraternity. Moreover to join this body would be to traverse all my long trumpeted theory, and the instinct which spoke from it, that one man is a counterpoise to a city,—that a man is stronger than a city, that his solitude is more prevalent & beneficent than the concert of crowds.

—

If you criticize a fine genius as Burns or Goethe, the odds are that you are quite out of your reckoning, and are only whipping your own false portrait of the man. For there is somewhat spheral & infinite in every man, especially in every genius, which if you can come very near him, sports with all your limitations. For rightly every man is but a channel through which the God floweth, & whilst I thought I was criticizing him, I was blaspheming my own soul. Thus when I have chided Goethe, & called him courtier, artificial, unbelieving, worldly, I take up this book of Helena and find him a Mohawk Indian, as much a piece of nature as an apple or an oak, large as the morning or the night, as beautiful & savage as a briar rose.

"Woe to the giver when the bribe's refused."
Middleton

1 Jan., 1841. I begin the year by sending my little book of Essays to the press. What remains to be done to its imperfect chapters

I will seek to do justly. I see no reason why we may not write with as much grandeur of spirit as we can serve or suffer. Let the page be filled with the character not with the skill of the writer.
                                               —

1841.
17 January. It appears sometimes what Prudence stands for. The true prudence is no derogation from the lofty character. The man who moved by interrupted impulses of virtue would lead a violent & unfortunate life. These continent, persisting, immoveable persons who are scattered up & down for the blessing of the world—howsoever named Osiris or Washington or Samuel Hoar, have in this phlegm or gravity of their nature a quality which answers to the flywheel in a mill which distributes the motion equably over all the wheels & hinders it from falling unequally & suddenly in destructive shocks. It is better that joy should be spread over all the day in the form of strength than that it should be concentrated into extacies, full of danger, & followed by reactions. A sublime Prudence can well be which postpones always the present hour to the whole life, always talent to genius, always special results to character, which always believes in a vast rich future & will sow the sun & moon for seeds.

He did not get it from books but where the bookmaker got it.

Books lead us from extasy.   —

20 January.
Of these unquiet daemons that fly or gleam across the brain what trait can I hope to draw in my sketch book? Wonderful seemed to me as I read in Plotinus the calm & grand air of these few cherubims—great spiritual lords who have walked in the world—they of the old religion—dwelling in a worship that makes the sanctities of Christianity parvenues & merely popular; for "necessity is in intellect, but persuasion in soul." This band of grandees, Hermes, Heraclitus, Empedocles, Plato, Plotinus, Olympiodorus, Proclus, Synesius, & the rest, have somewhat so vast in their logic, so primary in their thinking,

that it seems antecedent to all the ordinary distinctions of rhetoric & literature, & to be at once poetry & music & dancing
& astronomy & mathematics. I am present at the sowing of
the seed of the world. With a geometry of sunbeams the Soul
lays the foundations of nature. The truth & grandeur of their
thought is proved by its scope & applicability; for it commands
more even than our dear old bibles of Moses & Swedenborg
the entire Schedule & inventory of things for its illustration.
But what marks its elevation & has a comic look to us if we are
not very good when we read, is the innocent serenity with
which these babe-like Jupiters sit in their clouds & from age to
age prattle to each other and to no contemporary; perfectly assured that their speech is intelligible & the most natural thing
in the world, they emit volume after volume without one moment's heed of the universal astonishment of the poor human
race below, who do not comprehend a sentence, no not a
clause or a syllable; nor do they ever relent so much as to insert
a popular or explaining sentence; nor testify the least displea-
sure or petulance at the dulness of their amazed auditory. The
angels are so enamoured of the language that is spoken in
heaven that they will not distort their lips with the hissing &
unmusical dialects of men but speak their own whether there
be any near, who can understand it or not.

———

When I look at the sweeping sleet amid the pine woods, my
sentences look very contemptible, & I think I will never write
more: but the words prompted by an irresistible charity, the
words whose path from the heart to the lips I cannot follow,—
are fairer than the snow. It is pitiful to be an artist when by forbearing to be artists we might be vessels filled with the divine
overflowings, not at all Waldo or William but the Influenced,
enriched by the circulations of omniscience & omnipotence.
Are there not moments in the history of heaven when the
human race was not counted by individuals but was only God
in distribution, God rushing into multiform benefit? It is sublime to receive, sublime to love, but this lust of imparting, as
from *us*, the desire to be loved, the wish to be recognized as
individuals, is finite, comes of a lower strain. The increase of
faith disposes us ever to greater sacrifices, to count nothing
a sacrifice, to leave fame & the most wonderful powers of

production, to leave all in the insatiable thirst of the divine communication. A purer fame, a greater power rewards the sacrifice. It is but the conversion of our harvest into seed. Is there not somewhat sublime in the action of the husbandman who casts into the ground the finest ears of his grain? The time will come when we shall hold nothing back but eagerly convert more than we now possess to means & powers, and, as I have written before, shall sow the sun & moon for seeds.

—

31 January. Bancroft writes with research faithful no doubt the "Synopsis of the Indian Families"—but the ungrateful reader asks "Wherefore? Is it history, to give me facts which do not involve the reason of their being told?" Bancroft does not know any more than he tells. He sees no reason why these barren facts should be preserved in modern ink. There is a kind of mockery in printing out in Boston in 1841, these withered marrowless facts, like the dead body of an officer I saw at Naples dressed out in his regimentals, powdered & pomatumed, & sitting up in the bier, going to his own funeral. God gives us facts & does not tell us why; but the reason lives in the fact: we are sure their order is right: there is no interpolation: they only await our riper insight to become harmonious in their order & proportion. God knows all the while their divine reason. Swedenborg writes history after ideas. If he names Jew or Persian, Moravian or Lutheran, Papist or African he gives us the reason in their character for the fact he names. I hope that day will come when no man will pretend to write history but he who does so by divine right. A man being born to see the order of certain facts, is born to write that history. Every other person not so qualified who affects to do this work is a pretender & the work is not done. It is vain that you tell me the Algonquins multiply the consonants and the Iroquois have no labials, if you leave me with that frivolous fact, whereof the reason is all that concerns me.

All my thoughts are foresters. I have scarce a day-dream on which the breath of the pines has not blown, & their shadows waved. Shall I not then call my little book Forest Essays?

—

The Present.

Cannot all literature, and all our own remote experience avail to teach us that the Today which seems so trivial, the task which seems so un-heroic, the inexpressive blank look of the Present moment, which leads us ever to reply to the inquiry "What are you doing?" "O nothing: I have been doing thus, & I am going to do thus;" and furthermore that which Harriet Martineau well noted, that all martyrdoms at the moment when they were suffered, appeared mean;—cannot all avail to teach us that these are wholly deceptive appearances, & that as soon as the irrecoverable Years have placed their Blue between these & us, these things shall glitter & attract us, seeming to be the wildest romance; and, as far as we allowed them in passing to take their own way & natural shape,—the homes of beauty & poetry?

Novels. To find a story which I thought I remembered in Quentin Durward, I turned over the volume until I was fairly caught in the old foolish trap & read & read to the end of the novel. Then as often before I feel indignant to have been duped & dragged after a foolish boy & girl, to see them at last married & portioned & I instantly turned out of doors like a beggar that has followed a gay procession into the castle. Had one noble thought opening the abysses of the intellect, one sentiment from the heart of God been spoken by them, I had been made a participator of their triumph, I had been an invited and an eternal guest, but this reward granted them is property, all-excluding property, a little cake baked for them to eat & for none other, nay which is rude & insulting to all but the owner. In Wilhelm Meister, I am a partaker of the prosperity.

Yet a novel may teach one thing as well as my choosings at the corner of the street which way to go,—whether to my errand or whether to the woods,—this, namely, that action inspires respect, action makes character, power, man, God. These novels will give way by & by to diaries or autobiographies;—captivating books if only a man knew how to choose among what he calls his experiences that which is really his experience, and how to record truth truly!

Feb. 4. I am dispirited by the lameness of an organ: if I have a cold, and the thought I would utter to my friend comes forth in stony sepulchral tones, I am disgusted, & will not speak more. But, as the drunkard who cannot walk can run, so I can speak my oration to an assembly, when I cannot without pain answer a question in the parlor. But lately it is a sort of general winter with me. I am not sick that I know, yet the names & projects of my friends sound far off & faint & unaffecting to my ear, as do, when I am sick, the voices of persons & the sounds of labor which I overhear in my solitary bed. A puny limitary creature am I, with only a small annuity of vital force to expend, which if I squander in a few feast days, I must feed on water & moss the rest of the time.

Our virtues need perspective. All persons do. I chide & rate my wife or my brother on small provocation if they come too near me. If I see the same persons presently after in the road, in the meetinghouse, nay, about the house on their own affairs, heedless of me, I feel reverence & tenderness for them.

—

If I judge from my own experience I should unsay all my fine things, I fear, concerning the manual labor of literary men. They ought to be released from every species of public or private responsibility. To them the grasshopper is a burden. I guard my moods as anxiously as a miser his money. For, company, business, my own household-chores untune & disqualify me for writing. I think then the writer ought not to be married, ought not to have a family. I think the Roman Church with its celibate clergy & its monastic cells was right. If he must marry, perhaps he should be regarded happiest who has a shrew for a wife, a sharp-tongued notable dame who can & will assume the total economy of the house, and having some sense that her philosopher is best in his study suffers him not to intermeddle with her thrift. He shall be master but not mistress, as E. H. said.

6 Feb. *Art*

Our Arts, if we shall have any, will take us by surprise. The sophomores at college & the merchants in Beacon Street are looking for the American sculptor & painter who shall carve friezes of the Plymouth Pilgrims for the State House, & paint American subjects in the pannels of the Rotunda at Washington. But true art springs up between the feet. Somebody shall be born who shall turn to a divine use the railway or the Insurance Office or our caucus or our commerce, in which we seek now only the economical use.

Prudence

10 February. What right have I to write on Prudence whereof I have but little & that of the negative sort? My prudence consists in avoiding & going without, not in the inventing of means & methods, not in adroit steering, not in gentle repairing. I have no skill to make money spend well, no genius in my economy & whoever sees my garden discovers that I must have some other garden. Yet I love facts & hate lubricity & people without perception. Then I have the same title to write on prudence that I have to write on poetry or holiness. We write from aspiration & antagonism as well as experience. We paint those qualities which we do not possess. The poet admires the man of energy & tactics; the merchant breeds his son for the church or the bar; & where a man is not vain & egotistic, you shall find what he has not, by his praise.

There is no time.

12 February, 1841. If the world would only wait one moment, if a day could now & then be intercalated which should be no time but pause & landing place, a vacation during which sun & star, old age & decay, debts & interest of money, claims & duties should all intermit & be suspended for the halcyon trance, so that poor man & woman could throw off the harness & take a long breath & consider what was to be done without being fretted by the knowledge that new duties are gathering for them in the moment when they are considering the too much accumulated old duties. But this on, on, forever onward wears out adamant. All families live in a perpetual hurry. Every rational thing gets still postponed and is at last slurred & ill done or huddled out of sight & memory.

*

In the Feejee islands, it appears, cannibalism is now familiar. They eat their own wives and children. We only devour widows' houses, & great merchants outwit & absorb the substance of small ones and every man feeds on his neighbor's labor if he can. It is a milder form of cannibalism; a varioloid.

—

Apr. 10.

Do not judge the poet's life to be sad because of his plaintive verses & confessions of despair. Because he was able to cast off his sorrows into these writings, therefore went he onward free & serene to new experiences. You must be a poet also to draw any just inference as to what he was from all the records, be they never so rich, which he has left. Did you hear him speak? His speech did great injustice to his thought. It was either better or worse. He gave you the treasures of his memory, or he availed himself of a topic rich in allusions to express hopes gayer than his life entertains or sorrows poured out with an energy & religion which was an intellectual play & not the habit of his character. You shall not know his love or his hatred from his speech & behaviour. Cold & silent he shall be in the circle of those friends who when absent his heart walks with & talks with evermore. Face to face with that friend who for the time is unto him the essence of night & morning, of the sea & the land, the only equal & worthy incarnation of Thought & Faith, silence and gloom shall overtake him, his talk shall be arid & trivial. There is no deeper dissembler than the sincerest man. Do not trust his blushes for he blushes not at his affection but at your suspicion. Do not trust his actions for they are expiations & fines often with which he has amerced himself & not the indications of his desire. Do not conclude his ignorance or his indifference from his silence: Do not think you have his thought, when you have heard his speech to the end. Do not judge him worldly & vulgar, because he respects the rich & the well bred, for to him the glittering symbol has a surpassing beauty which it has not to other eyes, & fills his eye, & his heart dances with delight in which no envy & no meanness are mixed. Him the circumstance of life dazzles & overpowers whilst it passes because he is so delicate a meter of every influence. You shall find him noble at last, noble in his chamber.

—

I read with joy the life of Pythagoras by Iamblichus; and the use of certain melodies to awaken in the disciple now purity, now valor, now gentleness. That "*Life*" is itself such a melody, & proper to these holy offices. Especially I admire the patience & longanimity of the probation of the novice. His countenance, his gait, his manners, diet, conversation, associates, employments, were all explored & watched; then the long discipline, the long silence was imposed, the new & vast doctrines taught, & then his vivacity & capability of virtue explored again.—If all failed, then his property, (otherwise made common,) was restored to him, a tomb built to his memory, & he was thenceforward spoken of & regarded by the School as *dead*. The long patience in this fugitive world is itself an affecting argument of the eternity of soul and affirms the faith of those who thus greatly slight our swift almanacs. He who treats human beings as centennial millennial natures convinces me of his faith . . . Yet how much I admire their use of music as a medicine. But for me with deaf ears Order & selfcontrol are the "melodies" which I should use to mitigate & tranquillize the ferocity of my Animal and foreign elements.

—

I read alternately in Dr Nichol & in Saint Simon—that is, in the Heavens & in the Earth, and the effect is grotesque enough. When we have spent our wonder in computing this wasteful hospitality with which boon nature turns off new firmaments without end into her wide common as fast as the madrepores make coral—suns & planets hospitable to souls, & then shorten the sight to look into this court of Louis Quatorze & see the game that is played there, duke & marshal, abbé & madame, a gambling house where each is laying a trap for the other, where the end is ever by some lie or fetch to outwit your rival & ruin him with this solemn fop in a wig & stars, the king, one can hardly help asking if this planet is a fair specimen of the so generous astronomy, and, if so, whether the experiment have not failed, & whether it be quite worth while to make more, & glut the space with so poor an article.

But there are many answers at hand to the poor cavil. And all doubt is ribald. An answer,—certainly not the highest,—the astronomy itself may furnish,—namely, that all grows, all is nascent, infant. As soon as we have recovered ourselves from the dizziness which this immense parade of arithmetic gives us, (for astronomy gives us always the temptation of that dreadful GIRO at the top of the interior of the Cupola of St Peter's, where one shakes with the wish to throw himself over the balustrade onto the beautiful tesselations of the marble floor on which men are creeping below,) we are steadied by the perception that a great deal is doing, that indeed all seems just begun; remote aims are in active accomplishment. We can point nowhere to anything final, but distinct tendency appears on all hands; the planet, the system, the firmament, the nebula, the total appearance is growing like a field of maize, or a human embryo, or the grub of a moth; is becoming somewhat else; is in the most rapid & active state of metamorphosis.

Why then should not the little messieurs at Versailles strut & smile for smiles & ribbons, for a season, without prejudice to the faculty to run on better errands by & by?

Metamorphois is nature. The foetus does not more strive to be man than yonder bur of light we call a nebula tends to be a ring, a comet, a solid globe, a sun, & the parent of new stars.

Yet the whole code of nature's laws may be written on the thumb nail, or on the signet of a ring. The whirling bubble on the surface of a brook admits us to the secret of the mechanics of the sky. Every shell on the beach is a key to it. A little water made to rotate in a cup explains morphology. And so poor is nature with all her cunning, so irremediably poor is she that from the beginning to the end of all the universe she has but one stuff, but one stuff with its two ends, to serve up all her endless variety of dishes—toujours perdrix—vary it how she will, galaxy, star, moon, comet, rock, water, fire, tree, man—it is still one stuff & shows the same properties to the anointed eye; and every marshal that bristles, every valet that grimaces in the French Court is related bodily to that heaven which Lagrange has been searching & works every moment by the same laws we thought so grand up there.

—

Apr. 24. I beheld him and he turned his eyes on me, his great serious eyes. Then a current of spiritual power ran through me and I looked farther & wider than I was wont, & the visages of all men were altered & the semblances of things. The men seemed as mountains, & their faces seamed with thought, & great gulfs between them, & their tops reached high into the air. And when I came out of his sight, it seemed to me as if his eyes were a great river like the Ohio or the Danube which was always pouring a torrent of strong sad light on some men, wherever he went, & tinging them with the quality of his soul.

———

I frequently find the best part of my ride in the Concord coach from my house to Winthrop Place to be in Prince street, Charter street, Ann street, & the like places at the North End of Boston. The dishabille of both men & women, their unrestrained attitudes & manners make pictures greatly more interesting than the clean shaved & silk robed procession in Washington & Tremont streets. I often see that the attitudes of both men & women engaged in hard work are more picturesque than any which art & study could contrive, for the Heart is in these first. I say *picturesque*; because when I pass these groups, I instantly know whence all the fine pictures I have seen had their origin: I feel the painter in me: these are the traits which make us feel the force & eloquence of *form* & the sting of color. But the painter is only *in* me; it does not come to the fingers' ends. But whilst I see a true painting, I feel how it was made; I feel that genius organizes, or it is lost. It is as impossible for the aspirant to paint a right picture, as for grass to bear apples. But when the genius comes, it makes fingers, it is pliancy & the power of translating the circumstance in the street into oils & colors. Raphael must be born & Salvator must be born. It is the gift of God, as Fanny Elssler can dance & Braham can sing, when many a worthy citizen & his wife however disposed can by no culture either paint, dance, or sing. Do not let them be so ridiculous as to try, but know thou, know all, that no citizen, or citizen's wife, no soul, is without organ. Each soul is a soul or an individual in virtue of its having or I may say being a power to translate the universe into some particular language of its own; if not into a picture, a statue, or a dance, why then, into a trade, or an art, or a science, or a mode of living, or a conversation, or a character, or an influence—into something great, human, & adequate which, if it do not contain in itself all the dancing, painting, & poetry that ever was, it is because the man is faint hearted & untrue.

The difference between talent & genius is in the direction of the current: in genius, it is from within outward; in talent, from without inward. Talent finds its models & methods & ends in society, and goes to the soul only for power to work: genius is its own end & derives its means and the style of its architecture from within & only goes abroad for audience or spectator, as we adapt our voice & our phrase to the distance & to the character of the ear we speak to. Aunt Mary, whose letters I read all yesterday afternoon, is Genius always new, subtle, frolicsome, musical, unpredictable. All your learning of all literatures & states of society, Platonistic, Calvinistic, English, or Chinese, would never enable you to anticipate one thought or expression. She is embarrassed by no Moses or Paul, no Angelo or Shakspeare, after whose type she is to fashion her speech: her wit is the wild horse of the desert who snuffs the sirocco & scours the palm-grove without having learned his paces in the Stadium or at Tattersall's. What liberal, joyful architecture, liberal & manifold as the vegetation from the earth's bosom, or the creations of frost work on the window! Nothing can excel the freedom & felicity of her letters,—such nobility is in this self rule, this absence of all reference to style or standard: it is the march of the mountain winds, the waving of flowers, or the flight of birds. But a man can hardly be a reader of books without acquiring their average tone, as one who walks with a military procession involuntarily falls into step.

M.M.E.   C.C.E.

In every family is its own little body of literature, divinity, & personal biography,—a common stock which their education & circumstance have furnished, & from which they all draw allusion & illustration to their conversation whilst it would be unintelligible (at least in the emphasis given to it) to a stranger. Thus in my youth, after we had brought home "Don Juan" and learned to pester Aunt Mary with grave repetition of the lines from the Shipwreck

> "They grieved for those who perished in the cutter,
> And likewise for the biscuit casks & butter,"

these became the byword for the mean spirit of derision that characterised the present age in contrast with the alleged earnest & religious spirit of the puritans & especially the austere saints of Concord & Malden, she was so swift to remember. I find a letter of hers to C.C.E. dated Waterford, Oct., 1831. ("O could you be here this afternoon—not a creature but the dog & me—we don't go to four-days-meeting. There's been one at the methodists', closing today, & such a rush from the other society. But such a day! Here's one balm of gilead tree— but a few leaves left, as though on purpose to catch the eye to see them play in the wind day after day,—& the deserted nest. Ah where are its anxious parents & their loved brood? Dead? Where the mysterious principle of life? x x x x Past Nine o'clock. The vision of beauty has changed—a white mist has risen which hides the venerable mount, but shows the trees in fine picturesque, and the deserted nest is sheltered with a soft pall, like the oblivion which rests on the miseries of the wretched. Just after the house was left for the evening vigils at the chapel, a man came for me to write a note he was going to carry. The peculiarity of notes here, is, a friend asks for another's conversion—thus the best of human feelings are brought into action. But note the *Crackers*: I brought down by mistake the only pen which is good of the four (one which I don't use to you or Brother S.) and I persuaded him to shorten his petitions; and, as he was satisfied, surely there was no harm. And here comes a living voice—the charm too is gone from the moon—she rides full brightly—the tarn has gathered her misty wanderers in her bosom, & the trees stretch their naked arms to the skies like the scathed martyrs of Persecution.")

   M.M.E.   New England Theology
   The new relations we form we are apt to prefer as *our own* ties, to those natural ones which they have supplanted. Yet how strict these are, we must learn later, when we recall our childhood & youth with vivid affection, and feel a poignant solitude even in the multitude of modern friends. In reading these letters of M.M.E. I acknowledge (with surprise that I could ever forget it,) the debt of myself & my brothers to that

old religion which in those years still dwelt like a Sabbath peace in the country population of New England, which taught privation, self denial, & sorrow. A man was born not for prosperity, but to suffer for the benefit of others, like the noble rock-maple-tree which all around the villages bleeds for the service of man. Not praise, not men's acceptance of our doing, but the Spirit's holy errand through us, absorbed the thought. How dignified is this! how all that is called talents & worth in Paris & in Washington dwindles before it! How our friendships & the complaisances we use, shame us now—they withdraw, they disappear, the gay & accomplished associates, —and our elder company, the dear children & grave relatives with whom we played & studied & repented,—they return & join hands again. I feel suddenly that my life is frivolous & public; I am as one turned out of doors, I live in a balcony, or on the street; I would fain quit my present companions as if they were thieves or pot-companions & betake myself to some Thebais, some Mount Athos in the depths of New Hampshire or Maine, to bewail my innocency & to recover it, & with it the power to commune again with these sharers of a more sacred idea. I value Andover, Yale, & Princeton as altars of this same old fire, though I fear they have done burning cedar & sandal wood there also, & have learned to use chips & pine.— But I meant to say above, that we are surprised to find that we are solitary, that what is holiest in our character & faculty is unappreciated by those who stand around us & so lies uncalled for & dormant, and that it needs that our dear ghosts should return, or such as they, to challenge us to right combats.

C.C.E.   E.B.E.

I ought to record the pleasure I found amid all this letter reading, in some letters to C.C.E. from his college mates, in the uniform tone of affection & respect with which these boys—for such they still were—accost him. Edward also was respected, admired by his mates, but, I suspect, never loved—not comprehended, not felt,—he puzzled them. Yet I still remember with joy Charles's remark when he returned from visiting Edward at Porto Rico, that the tone of conversation there, was the most frivolous & low that could be, yet that Edward never suffered anything unworthy to be said in his presence, without speaking for the right, & so goodhumoredly & so well, as invariably to command respect, & be a check on the company. But Charles always from his school days had this *following*, & that of the best who were about him; it was true leal service, homage to something noble & superior which the giver felt it was a compliment to himself to pay. Thus he brought boarders to the houses where he went, to Danforth's in Cambridge, and Pelletier's in Boston.

C.C.E.   M.M.E.

May 6. These letters revive my faded purpose of writing the oft requested Memoir of Charles. That certainly would have been unfit: it was right for the young & the dear friend to ask: it had been wrong in me to undertake: the very nobleness of the promise should make us more reluctant to recite the disappointment of the promise. Let us not stoop to write the annals of sickness & disproportion. Charles delighted in strength, in grace, in poetry, in success:—shall we wrong him so far as to make him the unwilling object of pity, the centre of a group of pain, a caryatid statue in our temple of Destiny?—Yet now as I read these yellowing letters of M.M.E. I begin to entertain the project in a new form. I doubt if the interior & spiritual history of New England could be truelier told than through the exhibition of family history such as this, the picture of this group of M.M.E. & the boys, mainly Charles. The genius of that woman, the key to her life, is in the conflict of the new & the old ideas in New England. The heir of whatever was rich & profound & efficient in thought & emotion in the old religion which planted & peopled this land, she strangely united to this passionate piety the fatal gift of penetration, a love of philosophy, an impatience of words, and was thus a religious skeptic. She held on with both hands to the faith of the past generation as to the palladium of all that was good & hopeful in the physical & metaphysical worlds, and in all companies, & on all occasions, & especially with these darling nephews of her hope & pride, extolled & poetised this beloved Calvinism. Yet all the time she doubted & denied it, & could not tell whether to be more glad or sorry to find that these boys were irremediably born to the adoption & furtherance of the new ideas. She reminds me of Margaret Graeme, the enthusiast in Scott's

"Abbot," who lives to infuse into the young Roland her enthusiasm for the Roman Church, only that *our* Margaret
doubted whilst she loved. Milton & Young were the poets en-
deared to the generation she represented. Of Milton they were
proud, but I fancy their religion has never found so faithful a
picture as in the "Night Thoughts." These combined traits in
M.M.E.'s character gave the new direction to her hope; that
these boys should be richly & holily qualified & bred to purify
the old faith of what narrowness & error adhered to it & import all its fire into the new age,—such a gift should her
Prometheus bring to men. She hated the poor, low, thin, unprofitable, unpoetical Humanitarians as the devastators of the
Church & robbers of the soul & never wearies with piling on
them new terms of slight & weariness. "Ah!" she said, "what a
poet would Byron have been, if he had been born & bred a
Calvinist!"

———

6 June. The chief is the chief all the world over, & not his hat
or his shoes, his land, his title or his purse. He who knows the
most,—he who knows what sweets & virtues are in the ground
beneath him, the waters before him, the plants around him, the
heavens above him,—he is the enchanter, he is the rich & the
royal man.

I am sometimes discontented with my house because it lies
on a dusty road and with its sills & cellar almost in the water of
the meadow. But when I creep out of it into the Night or the
Morning and see what majestic & what tender beauties daily
wrap me in their bosom, how near to me is every transcendant
secret of Nature's love & religion, I see how indifferent it is
where I eat & sleep. This very street of hucksters & taverns the
moon will transform to a Palmyra, for she is the apologist of all
apologists & will kiss the elm-trees alone & hides every meanness in a silver edged darkness. Then the good river-god has
taken the form of my valiant Henry Thoreau here & introduced me to the riches of his shadowy starlit, moonlit stream,
a lovely new world lying as close & yet as unknown to this vulgar trite one of streets & shops as death to life or poetry to
prose. Through one field only we went to the boat & then left
all time, all science, all history behind us and entered into Nature with one stroke of a paddle. Take care, good friend! I said,

as I looked west into the sunset overhead & underneath, & he with his face toward me rowed towards it,—take care; you know not what you do, dipping your wooden oar into this enchanted liquid, painted with all reds & purples & yellows which glows under & behind you. Presently this glory faded & the stars came & said "Here we are," & began to cast such private & ineffable beams as to stop all conversation. A holiday, a villeggiatura, a royal revel, the proudest, most magnificent, most heart rejoicing festival that valor & beauty, power & poetry ever decked & enjoyed—it is here, it is this. These stars signify it & proffer it: they gave the idea & the invitation, not kings, not palaces, not men, not women, but these tender, poetic, clear, and auspicious stars, so eloquent of secret promises: we heard what the king or rich man said, we knew of his villa, his grove, his wine, & his company, but the provocation & point of the invitation came out of these beguiling stars soothsaying, flattering, persuading, who though their promise was never yet made good in human experience, are not to be contradicted, not to be insulted, nay not even to be disbelieved by us. All experience is against them, yet their word is Hope & shall still forever leave experience a liar. In the soft glances of these western stars I see well what men before me had also seen & then strove to realize in some Versailles or Paphos or Ctesiphon. Yes, bright Inviters! I accept your eternal courtesy and will not mistake it for a bidding to a foolish banquet with men & women called rich & beautiful.

But on us sitting darkling or sparkling there in the boat, presently rose the moon, she cleared the clouds & sat in her triumph so maidenly & yet so queenly, so modest yet so strong, that I wonder not that she ever represents the Feminine to men. There is no envy, no interference in nature. The beauty & sovereignty of the moon, the stars, or the trees do not envy: they know how to make it all their own. As we sail swiftly along, & so cause the moon to go now pure through her amber vault & now through masses of shade & now half hid through the plumes of an oak or a pine, each moment, each aspect is sufficient & perfect; there is no better or worse, no interference, no preference, but every virtuous act of man or woman accuses other men & women; shames me; and the person of every man or woman is in my varying love slighted or preferred. Blessed is Law. This moon, the hill, the plant, the air, obey a law; they are but animated geometry & numbers; to them is no intemperance; these are through law born & ripened & ended in beauty: but we through the transgression of Law sicken & inveterate.

—

We are too civil to books. For a few golden sentences we will turn over & actually read a volume of 4 or 500 pages. Even the great books. 'Come,' say they, 'we will give you the key to the world'—Each poet each philosopher says this, & we expect to go like a thunderbolt to the centre, but the thunder is a superficial phenomenon, makes a skin-deep cut, and so does the Sage—whether Confucius, Menu, Zoroaster, Socrates; striking at right angles to the globe his force is instantly diffused laterally & enters not. The wedge turns out to be a rocket. I have found this to be the case with every book I have read & yet I take up a new writer with a sort of pulse beat of expectation. Ever & forever Heraclitus is justified who called the world an eternal inchoation.

—

Critics.
The borer on our peachtrees bores that she may deposit an egg; but the borer into theories & institutions & books, bores that he may bore.

—

Our criticism on the times is that life is mean.
1842
14 April. If I should write an honest diary what should I say? Alas that Life has halfness, shallowness. I have almost completed thirty nine years and I have not yet adjusted my relation to my fellows on the planet, or to my own work. Always too young or too old, I do not satisfy myself; how can I satisfy others?

Christianity
I do not wonder that there was a Christ; I wonder that there were not a thousand.

*

Dull cheerless business this of playing lion & talking down to people. Rather let me be scourged & humiliated; then the exaltation is sure & speedy.

Gifts

Sept. The expectation of gratitude is mean & is continually punished by total insensibility. And truly considered it is a great happiness to get off without injury & heart burning from one who has had the ill luck to be served by you. For it is very onerous business—this of being served, & they naturally wish to give you a slap.

Aug., 1842.

The only poetic fact in the life of thousands & thousands is their death. No wonder they specify all the circumstances of the death of another person.

—

We stopped at a farmhouse at Lincoln, and asked for milk. When we came away, I offered money, but this was wrong. We injure everybody with this money, both ourselves & the receivers. We owe men a great behaviour & knowing that we have half a dollar in our pocket, we skulk & idle & misbehave, and do not put ourselves on our courtesy & sentiment.

The Understanding is the perennial skeptic. He sees this principle of population always reducing wages to the lowest pittance whereby life can be sustained; and thinks this selfishness which stores the corn, & holds it back for high prices the preventative of Famine, & that the law of self preservation is surer policy than any legislation can be. The Soul is unable to invalidate his reasoning and can only scorn it & search nature through with its own glance from its own centre, see all things in a new order from the spiritual side.

Never look at my book & perhaps it will be better worth looking at. My thought today was how rightly Swedenborg pictured each man with a sphere, for we use for moral qualities the word *great*, & really conceive of Socrates, Milton, or Goethe, as a *large* personality. But this also occurred as the security of the institution of Marriage against the Shelleys of the time, that we need in these twilights of the gods all the

conventions of the most regulated life to crutch our lame &
indigent loves. The least departure from the usage of Marriage
would bring too strong a tide against us for so weak a reed as
modern love to withstand. Its frigidities, its ebbs already need
all the protection & humoring they can get from the forms &
manners.

1 September. A walk in the most wonderful sunset this P.M.
with W.E.C. The sunset is very unlike anything that is underneath it. But it must always seem unreal, until it has figures
that are equal to it. The sunset wanted men. But unutterable is
all we know of nature. How well we know certain winds, certain lights, certain aspects of the soil & the grove. Yet no words
can begin to convey that which they express to us monthly &
daily.

—

Nature & Literature prove subjective phenomena. It depends on the mood of the man whether he shall see the sunset
or the fine play. There are always sunsets and there is always
genius. But only a few hours so serene in our lives, that we are
lovers of nature or criticism.

There is an optical illusion about every new person we see.
In reality they are all creatures of given temperament which
will appear in a given character whose boundaries they will
never pass. But we look at them; they seem alive, and we presume Impulse in them. In the moment, it seems impulse; that
is the optical illusion; in the mass of moments, that is, in the
years, in the lifetime, it stands revealed to be a certain exact
tune which the revolving barrel of the music box must play.

I remember that Mr R. said to the young coxcomb from the
South, 'Fiddle faddle', in reply to all his brag. Pity that we do
not know how to say *Fiddle Faddle* to people who take our
time & do not exercise our wit. Most men are dupes of the
hour, dupes of the nearest object; they cannot put things in
perspective; but the nearest is still the largest. They talk with
inferiors & do not know it, do not know that they are talking
down. As on a mountain you must level your gun at another
mountain & see if the shot run out of the barrel, to know that
the summit is lower than yours. The eye cannot measure it.

The poor Irish Mary Corbet whose five weeks' infant died here 3 months ago, sends word to Lidian that "she cannot send back her bandbox (in which the child's body was carried to Boston): she must plase give it to her; & she cannot send back the little handkerchief (with which its head was bound up): she must plase give it to her."

N. Hawthorn's reputation as a writer is a very pleasing fact, because his writing is not good for anything, and this is a tribute to the man.

S. W. says, "I like women, they are so finished."

E. H.'s suffrage on Sunday eve. to A.B.A. was good, so qualified & so strong. I said to him what is really A's distinction, that, rejoicing or desponding, this man always trusts his principle, never deserts it, never mistakes the convenient customary way of doing the thing for the right & might, whilst all vulgar reformers, like these Community people, after sounding their sentimental trumpet, rely on the arm of money & the law. It is the effect of his nature, of his natural clearness of spiritual sight which makes this confusion of thought impossible to him. I have a company who travel with me in the world & one or other of whom I must still meet, whose office none can supply to me: Edward Stabler; my Methodist Tarbox; Wordsworth's Pedlar; Mary Rotch; Alcott; Manzoni's Fra Cristoforo; Swedenborg; Mrs Black; and now Greaves, & his disciple Lane. Supreme people who represent with whatever personal defects, the Ethical Idea. El. H, the true E. H., that is, felt the element of self in her intellectual & in her devout friends: the former loved truth but loved self in the truth; the latter would make sacrifices but never forgot their claims. Strange, all is strange, O Edith small, thyself strange, life is strange, & God the greatest strange & stranger in his Universe.

The lady said that S. never forgot himself; he was affected, but his affectation was natural to him; and that the only thing she was afraid of was of being frightened.

Mr. C. sold his Boston house, & went to live in the country, because he found he could not make a bow. It was a very sensible reason, & yet C.C.E's criticism on it was, that he should have raised his ceiling & made his rooms larger; because an aukward man in the area of the State House, or on the Common, is no longer aukward. Large space, high rooms, have the same exhilarating & liberating quality as great light. A dance in a half lighted ballroom would be a sad affair, but make the light intense, & the spirits of the party all rise instantly. There are two choices for one who is unhappy in an evening party; one to go no more into such companies, which is flight; the other to frequent them until their law is wholly learned & they become indifferent, which is conquest! O fine victim, martyr-child! clowns & scullions are content with themselves and thou are not.

Intellect always puts an interval between the subject & the object. Affection would blend the two. For weal or for woe I clear myself from the thing I contemplate: I grieve, but am not a grief: I love, but am not a love.

Marriage in what is called the spiritual world is impossible, because of the inequality between every subject & every object. The subject is the receiver of Godhead, & at every moment of his existence must feel his being infinitely enhanced by that cryptic energy: though not in energy yet by presence: it cannot be otherwise than felt; the immense magazine of Substance. But the object is only a reflection of the same energy for one moment of its action; nor can any power of intellect attribute to the object the proper immensity, the proper Deity which sleeps or wakes forever in every subject. Never can love make consciousness and ascription equal in force. There will always be the same gulf between every me & thee as between the original and the picture.

Moreover, sympathy is always partial. Two human beings are like globes which can touch only in one point, and whilst they remain in contact, all the other points of each of the spheres are inert, their turn must also come & the longer a particular union lasts, the more energy of appetency the parts not in union acquire.

It is the nature of love meantime to unite and not to disunite: therefore it believes in the permanency of the present relation, & does not conceive of its fracture. Whilst I love, whilst I apply my vision to a particular beloved object, I find in it a capacity of immortality. But when apart from names & persons, I yield to the nature of the Soul, I see why Nature hurries us out of these connubial unions which, short as they are, are long enough to fix what should be flowing, to petrify what should be flesh.

Young Simmons went out tutor in the family travelling through Italy. It would have been so easy to have made his life joyful;—one human creature made happy; yet they contrived to make him feel that he was a servant, & poisoned every day and he has come back with a fixed disgust at aristocracy. Too happy if he has. Too cheap the price he paid, if he has really attained to despise or to pity their joyless joys. But I doubt, I doubt.

I hate this sudden crystallization in my poets. A pleasing poem, but here is a rude expression, a feeble line, a wrong word. I am sorry, returns the poet, but it stands so written. 'But you can alter it,' I say. Not one letter, replies the hardened bard. I question when I read Tennyson's Ulysses, whether there is taste in England to do justice to the poet, whether the riches of Dante's greatness would find an equal apprehension. Yet it seems feeble to deny it. The poet, & the lover of poetry are born at one instant, twins; and when Wordsworth wrote Laodamia, Landor found it out & celebrated it, & so did an Edinbro' critic.

———

1841, September.   W. Ellery Channing, jun.
A poet is very rare. I spoke the other day to E's ambition & said, Think that in so many millions, perhaps there is not another one whose thought can flow into music. Will you not do what you are created to do? The poet seems the true & only doctor. He knows & tells. The great opaque opens for him in veins & vistas, & in the common & the highway he shows recesses of wisdom & love. But E. though he has fine glances and a poetry that is like an exquisite nerve communicating by thrills, yet is a very imperfect artist, and, as it now seems, will never finish anything. He does not even like to distinguish between what is good, & what is not, in his verses, would fain have it all pass for good,—for the best,—& claim inspiration for the worst lines. But he is very good company, with his taste, & his cool hard sensible behaviour, yet with the capacity

of melting to emotion, or of wakening to the most genial mirth. It is no affectation in him to talk of politics, of knives & forks, or of sanded floors, if you will; indeed the conversation always begins low down, &, at the least faltering or excess on the high keys, instantly returns to the weather, the Concord Reading Room, & Mr Rice's shop. Now & then something appears that gives you to pause & think. First I ask myself if it is real, or only a flitting shade of thought, spoken before it was half realized; then, if it sometimes appear, as it does, that there is in him a wonderful respect for mere humours of the mind, for very gentle & delicate courses of behaviour, then I am tempted to ask if the poet will not be too expensive to the man; whether the man can afford such costly selfdenials & finenesses to the poet. But his feeling, as his poetry, only runs in veins, & he is much of the time a very common & unedifying sort of person.

(Dr Channing died Oct 2: 1842)   Reverend Dr Channing Oct. 19, 1842. To M.M.E. Nothing has occurred to interest us so much as Dr Channing's departure, & perhaps it is saddest that this should interest us no more. Our broad country has few men; none that one would die for; worse, none that one could live for. If the great God shined so near in the breast that we could not look aside to other manifestations, such defamation of our Channings & Websters, would be joy & praise; but if we are neither pious, nor admirers of men,——. I wish you would write me what you think after so long a perspective as his good days have afforded, of your old preacher. For a sick man, he has managed to shame many sound ones, and seems to have made the most of his time, & was bright to the last month & week. A most respectable life; and deserves the more praise that there is so much merely external, and a sort of creature of society, in it;—that sort of merit of which praise is the legitimate fee. He seems sometimes as the sublime of calculation, as the nearest that mechanism could get to the flowing of genius. His later years,—perhaps his earlier,—have been adorned by a series of sacrifices which unhappily he rated high, & knew every pennyworth of their cost. His intellect dispensed its stores with the same economy; & he did not omit to intimate to the humble hearer that this truth was only seen by himself. Yet although thus stopping short in both respects of the generosity of genius, he has been, whilst he lived, the Star of the American Church, & has left no successor in the pulpit. He can never be reported, for his eye & his voice cannot be printed, & his discourses lose what was best in wanting them. He was made for the Public; he was the most unprofitable private companion, but all America would have been impoverished had it wanted him. I think we cannot spare a single word he uttered in public,—not so much as the reading a lesson in scripture, or a hymn. The sternest Judges of the Dead, who shall consider our wants & his austere self application to them, & his fidelity to his lights, will absolve this Soul as it passes, and say, This man has done well. Perhaps I think much better things of him too. His Milton & Napoleon were excellent for the time (the want of drill & thorough breeding as a writer, from which he suffered, being considered) & will be great ornaments of his biography.

We are very ungrateful but we do not willingly give the name of poet to any but the rarest talents or industry & skill in metre. Here is Tennyson a man of subtle & progressive mind, a perfect music-box for all manner of delicate tones & rhythms, to whom the language seems plastic, so superior & forceful is his thought.—But is he a poet? We read Burns & said, he is a poet. We read Tennyson & do him the indignity of asking the question, Is he poet? I feel in him the misfortune of the time. He is a strict contemporary, not Eternal Man. He does not stand out of our low limitations like a Chimborazo under the line,—running up from the torrid base through all the climates of the globe with rings of the herbage of every latitude on its high & mottled sides; but in him as in the authors of Paracelsus, & Festus, I hear through all the varied music the native tones of an ordinary, to make my meaning plainer, say, of a vulgar man. They are men of talents who sing, but they are not the children of Music. The particular which under this generality deserves most notice is this (and it is a black ingratitude to receive it so,) that the purpose of the poem is secondary, the finish of the verses primary. It is the splendor of the versification that draws me to the sense, and not the reverse. Who that has read the "Ode to Memory," the "Poet," the

"Confessions of a Sensitive Mind," the "Two Voices,"—remembers the scope of the poem when it is named, and does not rather call to mind some beautiful lines; or, when reading it, does not need some effort of attention to find the thought of the writer, which is also rather poor & mean. Even in "Locksley Hall," which is in a prouder tone, I have to keep a sharp lookout for the thought, or it will desert me. It is the merit of a Poet to be unanalysable. We cannot sever his word & thought. We listen because we must, & become aware of a crowd of particular merits, after we have been thoroughly commanded & elevated. I should not go to these books for a total diversion, & the stimulus of thought, as I should go to the Catskills, Nantasket or the Sea, or to Homer, Chaucer, or Shakspeare.

To the makers of artificial flowers, we say "the better the worse." The best verse-maker not inspired is accountable for the sentiment and spirit of his piece; it never exceeds his own dimensions. But the inspired writer, let his verse be never so frivolous in its subject or treatment,—a mere catch or street verse,—is yet not accountable for the piece, but it came as if out of a spiracle of the great Animal World. Therefore these little pieces about owls & autumn gardens, & the sea, are not tinged with London philosophy, which makes all the best pieces "disconsolate preachers," but are quite independent of Mr Alfred Tennyson, & are natural.

A poor man had an insufficient stove which it took him a great part of the winter to tend: he was up early to make the fire and very careful to keep it from going out. He interrupted his work at all hours of the day to feed it: he kept it late into the night that the chamber walls need not get hopelessly cold, but it never warmed the room; he shivered over it hoping it would be better, but he lost a great deal of time & comfort.

—

Our young Abolitionists vapor at the North, and in the streets of Boston with Massachusetts at their back, they are hot for an encounter with Mr Gray of Virginia. Him they will shove, him they will hustle, him they will utterly vanquish & drive out of the city. But if they go into the southern country, these young men are at once hushed by the "chivalry" which they sneer at, at home. For these southerners are haughty, self-ish, wilful, & unscrupulous men, who will have their way, & have it. The people of New England with a thousand times more talent, more worth, more ability of every kind, are timid, prudent, calculating men who cannot fight until their blood is up, who have consciences & many other obstacles betwixt them & their wishes. The Virginian has none, & so always beats them today, & is steadily beaten by them year by year.

Life is so much greater than thought, that when we talk on an affair of grave personal interest with one with whom hith-erto we have had only intellectual discourse, we use lower tones, much less oratory, but we come much nearer, and are quickly acquainted.

December, 1842.   Buddhism.

The trick of every man's conversation we soon learn. In one this remorseless Buddhism lies all around, threatening with death & night. We make a little fire in our cabin, but we dare not go abroad one furlong into the murderous cold. Every thought, every enterprise, every sentiment, has its ruin in this horrid Infinite which circles us and awaits our dropping into it. If killing all Buddhists would do the least good, we would have a slaughter of the Innocents directly.

—

There was a conversation last eve. at our good Mrs B.'s on "the Family" which was quite too narrowing & exclusive. There was a very unnecessary hostility in a great deal of the talk. A hostility in the hearers was presumed, & we were valiant men full of fight ready & able to break a lance for our faith. L. is so skilful, instant, & witty—there is no loitering or repetition in his speech—that I delight to hear him & forgive every thing to so much ability: yet he is very provoking & war-like in his manner. He rails at trade & cities & yet it is obvious in every word he says how much he is the debtor to both. There is a wisdom of life about them, a toughness & solidity of experience that makes them always entertaining & makes A.'s words look pale & lifeless. I came away from the company in better spirits than from any party this long time, for I did not speak one word. Perhaps the proper reply to the tone of dogmatism should have been, Shall there be no more cakes & ale? Why so much stress?

I hear the whistle of the locomotive in the woods. Wherever that music comes it has a sequel. It is the voice of the civility of the Nineteenth Century saying "Here I am." It is interrogative: it is prophetic: and this Cassandra is believed: "Whew! Whew! Whew! How is real estate here in the swamp & wilderness? Swamp & Wilderness, ho for Boston! Whew! Whew! Down with that forest on the side of the hill. I want ten thousand chestnut sleepers. I want cedar posts and hundreds of thousands of feet of boards. Up my masters, of oak & pine! You have waited long enough—a good part of a century in the wind & stupid sky. Ho for axes & saws and away with me to Boston! Whew! Whew! I will plant a dozen houses on this pasture next moon and a village anon; and I will sprinkle yonder square mile with white houses like the broken snow-banks that strow it in March."

January 11, 1841. Does Nature, my friend, never show you the wrong side of the tapestry? never come to look dingy & shabby? Do you never say "Old Stones! Old rain! old landscape! you have done your best; there is no more to be said. Praise wearies: you have pushed your joke a little too far."—Or, on the other hand, do you find nature always transcending and as good as new every day? I know, I know, how nimble it is,— the good monster; You have quite exhausted its power to please & today you come into a new thought & lo! in an instant there stands the entire world converted suddenly into the cipher or exponent of that very thought & chanting it in full chorus from every leaf & drop of water. It has been singing that song ever since the creation in your deaf ears.

How much we augur in seeing an usual natural phenomenon as for instance an electric spark. Already we are groping for its ethics.

What absence of all sadness in the drops of the snow bank!

—

Some men can write better than they speak. Of such I had rather see the manuscript than see the man. For what he speaks he says to me but what he writes he says to God.

I said to C. S.

The difference between persons is not in wisdom but in knack. I know twenty persons who defer to me, who think my experiences have somewhat superior, whilst I see that their experiences are quite as rich as mine. Give them to me I would make as effective a use of them. I have the talent of tacking together the old & the new, which they do not seem to exercise. I think if we should meet Shakspeare, we should not be conscious of any steep inferiority. No; but a great equality: only he possessed a strange, skill of using, of classifying his facts which we lacked.

9 April. We walked this P.M. to Edmund Hosmer's & Walden Pond—The south wind blew & filled with bland & warm light the dry sunny woods. The last year's leaves flew like birds through the air. As I sat on the bank of the Drop or God's Pond & saw the amplitude of the little water, what space what verge the little scudding fleets of ripples found to scatter & spread from side to side & take so much time to cross the pond, & saw how the water seemed made for the wind, & the wind for the water, dear playfellows for each other,—I said to my companion, I declare this world is so beautiful that I can hardly believe it exists. At Walden Pond, the waves were larger and the whole lake in pretty uproar. Jones Very said, "See how each wave rises from the midst with an original force, at the same time that it partakes the general movement!"

He said that he went to Cambridge, found his brother reading Livy—"I asked him, if the Romans were masters of the world? My brother said they had been: I told him, they were still. Then I went into the room of a senior who lived opposite, & found him writing a theme. I asked him, what was his subject? and he said, *Cicero's Vanity*. I asked him if the Romans were masters of the world? he replied, they had been: I told him, they were still. This was in the garret of Mr Ware's house. Then I went down into Mr Ware's study, & found him reading Bishop Butler. And I asked him if the Romans were masters of the world? he said, they had been; I told him, they were still."

Very obvious is the one advantage which this singular man has attained unto, that of bringing every man to true relations with him. No man would think of speaking falsely to him. But every man will face him & what love of nature or what symbol of truth he has, he will certainly show him. But to most of us society shows not its face & eye but its side & its back. To stand in true relations with men in a false age, is worth a fit of insanity, is it not?

May 10. I begin to dislike animal food. I had whimsies yesterday after dinner which disgusted me somewhat. The man will not be much better than the beast he eats.

—

It is the highest power of divine moments that they abolish even our contritions. I accuse myself of sloth & unprofit-ableness day by day but when these waves of God flow into me, I no longer reckon lost time. I no longer poorly compute my possible achievement by what remains to me of the month or the year, for these moments confer a sort of Omnipresence & omnipotence on me which asks nothing of duration but sees that the energy of the mind is commensurate to the work to be done without time.

Can we never extract this maggot of Europe out of the brains of our countrymen? Plato & Pythagoras may travel, for they carry the world with them and are always at home but our travellers are moths & danglers.

We are sure that we have all in us. We go to Europe or we pursue persons or we read books in the instinctive faith that these will call it out & reveal us to ourselves. Beggars all. The persons are such as we; poor as we; the Europe an old faded garment of dead persons; the books their ghosts. Let us drop this idolatry. Let us bid our dearest friends farewell, & say to them, Who are you? Unhand me; I will be dependent no more. Ah! seest thou not, brother, that thus we part only to meet again on a higher platform & only be more each others' because we are more our own.

In common hours nature accuses us. When shall we shame nature? We see the running brook with a compunction. But if our own life flowed with the right energy we should shame the brook. The brook of energy sparkles with real fire, & not with poor reflex rays of sun or moon.

Wordsworth has done as much as any living man to restore sanity to cultivated society.

Beware when the great God lets loose a new thinker on this planet. Then all things are at risk. It is as when a conflagration has broken out in a great city, & no man knows what is safe, or where it will end. There is not a piece of science but its flank may be turned tomorrow; there is not any literary reputation, not the so called eternal names of fame that may not be revised & condemned. The very hopes of man, the thoughts of his heart, the religion of nations, the manners & morals of mankind are all at the mercy of a new generalization.

But ah we impute the virtues to our friends and afterwards worship the face & feature to which we ascribe these divine tenants.

Labor with the hands that you may have animal spirits. Be not an opium eater. Cold water has no repentance. But do not let debt & the bondage of housekeeping fret you out of the knowledge of the value of house, husbandry, property. Suppose you have reformed & live on grains & black birch bark & muddy water that you may have leisure; well, what then? What will you do with the long day? think?—what! all day? Do you not see that instantly taste & arithmetic & power will plan plantations & build summer-houses & carve gods? We must have a basis for our delicate entertainments of poetry & philosophy, in our handicraft. We must have an antagonism in the tough world for all the variety of our spiritual faculties or they will not be born.

In regard to this Goethe I have to add that a man as gifted as he should not leave the world as he found it. There is something sad in this that every fine genius teaches us how to blame him. Being so much we cannot forgive him for not being more. When one of these grand monads is incarnated whom nature seems to design as eternal men & draw to her bosom we think that the old wearinesses of Europe & Asia, the trivial forms of life will now end, and a new morning break on us all. What is Austria? What is England? Shall not a poet redeem us from these idolatries & pale their legendary lustre before the kindling fires of the Divine Wisdom which burn in his heart for the light of the world? All that in our sovereign moments each of us has divined of the powers of thought, all the hints of omnipresence & energy which we have caught, this man should unfold & constitute facts. Yet how is the world better for Goethe? What load has he lifted from men or from women?

There is Austria; & England—the old & the new—full of old effete institutions & usages, full of men born old and the question still incessantly asked by the young "What shall I do?" with forlorn aspect. But let some strong Zeno, some nervous Epaminondas come into our society & see how he defies it & enables us to brave it, to come out of it & remake it from the cornerstone. There is hardly a life in Plutarch that does not infuse a new courage & prowess into the youth & make him gladder & bolder for his own work.

—

Whenever I read Plutarch or look at a Greek vase, I am inclined to accept the common opinion of the learned that the Greeks had cleaner wits than any other people in the universe. But there is anything but time in my idea of the Antique. A clear & natural expression by word or deed is that which we mean when we love & praise the Antique. In Society I do not find it; in modern books seldom; but the moment I get into the pastures I find Antiquity again. Once in the fields with the lowing cattle, the birds, the trees, the waters & satisfying outlines of the landscape, and I cannot tell whether this is Tempe and Enna, or Concord & Acton.

What is so bewitching as the experiments of young children on grammar & language? The purity of their grammar corrects all the anomalies of our irregular verbs & anomalous nouns. They carry the analogy thorough. *Bite* makes *bited*, and *eat eated* in their preterite. Waldo says there is no "telling" on my microscope meaning no name of the maker as he has seen on knifeblades, &c. "Where is the wafer that *lives* in this box?" &c. They use the strong double negative which we English have lost from our books, though we keep it in the street. "I wish you would not dig your leg," said Waldo to me. Ellen calls the grapes "green berries" & when I asked Does it rain this morning? she said "There's tears on the window."

But what is so weak & thin as our written style today in what is called literature? We use ten words for one of the child's. His strong speech is made up of nouns & verbs & names the facts. Our writers attempt by many words to suggest, since they cannot describe.

There is a difference between one & another moment of life in their authority & subsequent effect. Our faith comes in moments, our vice is habitual. Yet is there a depth in those brief moments which constrains us to ascribe more reality to them than to all other experiences. For this reason the argument which is always forthcoming to silence those who conceive extraordinary hopes of man, viz., the appeal to Experience, is forever invalid & vain. A mightier hope abolishes despair. We give up the Past and yet we hope. You must explain this Hope. We grant that human life is mean but how did we find out it was mean?

Waldo asks if the strings of the harp open when he touches them!

As for walking with Heraclitus, said Theanor, I know nothing less interesting: I had as lief talk with my own Conscience.

You fancy the stout woodchopper is thinking always of his poverty compared with the power & money of the capitalist who makes the laws. I will not deny that such things have passed thro' his mind for he has been at a Caucus with open mouth & ears. But now he is thinking of a very different matter, for his horse has started in the team & pulled with such a spring that he has cleared himself of the harness—hames & all—and he, as he mends the broken tackle is meditating revenge on the horse—"Well you may draw as fast as you like up the mile hill: you shall have enough of it if you like to draw, Damn you"—the horse, that is, and not the capitalist.

Let every man shovel out his own snow and the whole city will be passable.

Read a translation of the Prometheus Chained. It is a part of the history of Europe. The Mythology thinly veils authentic history & there is the story of the invention of the mechanic Arts. It seems to be the first chapter of Hist. of the Caucasian Race.

It is, beside, a grand effort of Imagination. Imagination is not good for anything unless there be enough. That a man can make a verse or have a poetic thought avails not, unless he has such a flow of these that he can construct a poem, a play, a discourse. Symmetry, proportion, we demand, and what are these but the faculty in such intensity or amount as to avail to create some whole. Man asks of man to be somewhat; to take a place; to prevail. The prudent father is willing that his son should be a poet, if he will be that, & by the evolution of his poetic force make good a place, satisfy all men that here is poetry. But he does not wish him to have a dash of poetry in his constitution just sufficient to spoil him for every thing else & not sufficient for its own end.

—

Prometheus is noble. He is the Jesus of the old mythology & plays with much exactness the part assigned to the Nazarene in the Genevan theology. He is the friend of man, stands between the *unjust justice* of the Eternal Father & the frail race of man, then readily suffers all things on their account. It is a pity he should be so angry: Anger continued & indulged becomes spleen. A single burst of indignation is heroic enough, but a persisting expression of it degenerates fast into scolding. Prometheus scolds; & Eteocles in "the Seven"; & Electra in Sophocles.

> Let the dreams of night recall
> Shadows of the thoughts of day
> And see thy fortunes as they fall
> Each secret of thy will betray

Sleep lurks all day about the corners of my eyes as night lurks all day about the stem of a pinetree.

I believe it will be found that poets have betrayed their genius first by their delight in mere music & rhythm, & later in thought.

—

16 Aug. After seeing A. B. I rode with M Fuller to the plains. She taxed me, as often before, so now more explicitly with inhospitality of soul. She & C. would gladly be my

friends, yet our intercourse is not friendship, but literary gossip. I count & weigh but do not love. They make no progress with me, but however often we have met, we still meet as strangers. They feel wronged in such relation, & do not wish to be catechised & criticised. I thought of my experience with several persons which resembled this: and confessed that I would not converse with the divinest person more than one week. M. insisted that it was no friendship which was so soon thus exhausted, & that I ought to know how to be silent & companionable at the same moment. She would surprise me, —she would have me say & do what surprised myself. I confess to all this charge with humility unfeigned. I can better converse with G. B. than with any other. E. H. & I have a beautiful relation not however quite free from the same hardness & fences. Yet would nothing be so grateful to me as to melt once for all these icy barriers, & unite with these lovers. But great is the law. I must do nothing to court their love which would lose my own. Unless that which I do to build up myself, endears me to them, our covenant would be injurious. Yet how joyfully would I form permanent relations with the three or four wise & beautiful whom I hold so dear, and dwell under the same roof or in a strict neigborhood. That would at once ennoble life. And it is practicable. It is easier than things which others do. It is easier than to go to Europe, or to subdue a forest farm in Illinois. But this survey of my experience taught me anew that no friend I have surprises, none exalts me. This then is to be set down, is it not? to the requirements we make of the friend, that he shall constrain us to sincerity, & put under contribution all our faculties.

—

1 September. One fact the fine conversations of the last week, —now already fast fading into oblivion,—revealed to me not without a certain shudder of joy—that I must thank what I am & not what I do for the love my friends bear me. I, conscious all the time of the short coming of my hands, haunted ever with a sense of beauty which makes all I do & say pitiful to me, & the occasion of perpetual apologies, assure myself to disgust those whom I admire, and now suddenly it comes out that they have been loving me all this time, not at all thinking of my hands or my words, but only of that love of something

more beautiful than the world, which, it seems, being in my heart, overflowed through my eyes or the tones of my speech.

Gladly I learn that we have these subterranean,—say rather, these supersensuous channels of communication, and that spirits can meet in their pure upper sky without the help of organs.

—

16 September. The questions which have slept uneasily a long time are coming up to decision at last. Men will not be long occupied with the Christian question, for all the babes are born infidels; they will not care for your abstinences of diet, or your objections to domestic hired service; they will find something convenient & amiable in these. But the question of Property will divide us into odious parties. And all of us must face it & take our part. A good man now finds himself excluded from all lucrative works. He has no farm & he cannot get one, for to earn money enough to buy one requires a sort of concentration toward money which is the selling himself for a number of years, and to him the present hour is as sacred & inviolable as any future hour.

Of course, whilst another man has no land, my title to mine is at once vitiated. The state then must come to some new division of lands and all voices must speak for it. Every child that is born must have a chance for his bread. Inextricable seem to be the twinings & tendrils of this evil and we have all involved ourselves the more in it by wives & children & debts. There is so much to be done that we ought to begin quickly to bestir ourselves. Lidian says well that it is better to work on institutions by the sun than by the Wind:—As Palmer remarked, that he was satisfied what should be done must proceed from the concession of the rich, not from the grasping of the poor. Well then, let us begin by habitual imparting. Let us make this day labor of mine which I confess has hitherto a certain emblematic air like the annual ploughing of the Emperor of China, an honest sweat. Let us diminish our debt to our corrupt Commerce, knowing how much perjury & fraud I buy in my sugar & tea. Let my ornamental austerities become natural & dear. The state will frown; the state must learn to humble itself, repent & reform.

A sleeping child gives me the impression of a traveller in a very far country.

"He can toil terribly," said Cecil of Sir Walter Raleigh. Is there any sermon on Industry that will exhort me like these few words? These sting & bite & kick me. I will get out of the way of their blows by making them true of myself.

The conversion of a woman will be the solidest pledge of truth & power.

30 September. Yes, I resent this intrusion of a few persons on my airy fields of existence. Shall our conversation when we meet O wife, or sister E., still return like a chime of seven bells to six or seven names, nor we freemen of nature be able long to travel out of this narrow orbit? Rather I would never name these names again. They are beautiful & therefore we have given them place; but they affront the sun & moon & the seven stars when they are remembered once too often. Beware of walls; let me keep the open field. Douglas-like I had rather hear the lark sing than the mouse cheep. Yet though I start like a wild Arab at the first suspicion of confinement, I have drank with great joy the contents of this golden cup hitherto. With great pleasure, I heard G.P.B. say that this romance took from the lustre of the Reformers who alone had interested him before. I felt that what was private & genuine in these rare relations was more real, and so more public & universal than conventions for debate, and these weary speculations on reform. The call of a heart to a heart, the glad beholding of a new trait of character,—freedom (derived from the friendly presence of a fellow being) to do somewhat we have never done,—freedom to speak what I could never say,—these are discoveries in the Ocean of Life, these are Perus, Brazils, & Plymouth Rocks, which to me were the more inestimable that I had been such a homekeeper, & knew nothing beyond the limits of my own forest & village fair.

———

Life only avails, not the having lived. Happiness is only in the moment of transition from a past to a new state, the shooting of the gulf, the darting onward. There is nothing so precious that it can be stored. Neither thought nor virtue will keep, but must be refreshed by new today. But we get forward by hops & skips. Shall we not learn one day to walk a firm continuous step?

If we could see we should know that we had nothing to do with our sins. The possibilities of man are so vast that he can ill afford to waste a moment in compunction over his past evils. Forward, forward!

As nothing will keep, but the soul demands that all shall be new today, therefore we reject a past man, or a past man's teaching. Who is Swedenborg? A man who saw God & nature for a fluid moment. His disciples vainly try to make a fixture of him, his seeing, & his teaching, & coax me to accept it for God & Nature.

Dependence is the only poverty.

—

Osman

24 October. Fine people do not prosper with me: they are so curious & busy with their Claude Lorraine glasses, and their exploration of doves' necks & peacocks' tails, that they do not see the road, & the poor men who go up & down on it. I must go back to my cabin, & be as before the trusty associate of those whom a household & highway experience has chastened, & be the poor man's poet. I should break with *one* fine person if I did not see or think I see my own rude self hid under the present mask.

—

Jan. 13.

The fate of the poor shepherd who blinded & lost in the snowstorm perishes in a drift within a few feet of his own cottage door, is a faithful emblem of the state of man. Here are we all on the brink of the waters of life & truth miserably dying. The inaccessibleness of every thought but that we are in is wonderful & it matters not how near you come to it, you are just as remote when you are nearest as when you are farthest, because you are riding on another track. Every thought is a prison; Every heaven is a prison also. Therefore we love the poet, the inventor, who in any form whether in an ode or a benefit or a grace has yielded us a new thought: he unlocks our chains & admits us to a new apartment.

Out of doors, in the snow, in the fields, death looks not funereal, but natural, elemental, even fair. In doors it looks disagreeable; I think who will have my coats. I do not wish to know that my body will be the subject of a funeral.

—

What a pity that we cannot curse & swear in good society. Cannot the stinging dialect of the sailors be domesticated? It is the best rhetoric and for a hundred occasions those forbidden words are the only good ones. My page about "Consistency" would be better written thus; Damn Consistency. And to how many foolish canting remarks would a sophomore's ejaculation be the only suitable reply, "The devil you do;" or, "You be damned."

The method of advance in nature is perpetual transformation. Be ready to emerge from the chrysalis of today, its thoughts & institutions, as thou hast come out of the chrysalis of yesterday.

And fear not the new generalizations. Does the fact look crass & material? Resist it not; it will refine & raise matter as much as it seems to degrade spirit.

Every new thought which makes day in our souls has its long morning twilight to announce its coming.

I dreamed that I floated at will in the great Ether, and I saw this world floating also not far off, but diminished to the size of an apple. Then an angel took it in his hand & brought it to me and said "This must thou eat." And I ate the world.

I see, I see.

Oct. 26. Theanor said that he saw too much; that he could no longer live at peace with other men for what he saw & they saw not. He said he went to the house of a man who in a dark & stormy night killed his enemy with a sword, and I, said Theanor, through the darkness & the storm sitting myself by the murderer's hearth saw him go along the road to his victim's house. I saw the sword & the thrust that reached his heart;

then new vision came to my eyes & I saw that the sword had a new length which he saw not beyond its visible point and bent about like a cow's horn and when the short point struck the sleeping enemy, I saw the elongated invisible point reach far back to his own house in which I sat & to the body of his own child. The child started in the adjoining room with a loud wailing & when the haggard man came back, his child was dying with black fever. And another man I knew who solaced himself with voluptuous imaginations and I saw that every pleasure he seemed to himself to steal from his paramours he was tearing away from the scanty stock of his own life.

When I go into my garden with the spade & dig a bed, I feel such an exhilaration & health from the work that I discover that I have been defrauding myself all this time in letting others do for me what I should have done with my own hands. But not only the health but the education is in the work. Is it possible that I who get indefinite quantities of sugar, hominy, cotton, buckets, crockery ware, & letter paper by simply signing my name once in three months to a cheque in favor of R. N. Rice & Co., get the fair share of exercise to my faculties by that act which the good Soul prepares for me in making all these far fetched matters important to my comfort? It is Rice himself & his carriers & dealers & manufacturers,—it is the sailor & the hide drogher, the butcher, the negro, the hunter & the planter that have intercepted the sugar of the sugar & the cotton of the cotton. They have got the education, I nothing but the commodity. This were all very well if I were necessarily absent, being detained by work of my own, work like theirs, work of the same faculties: then should I be sure of hands & feet; but now I have a pen & learned eyes & acute ears, yet am ashamed before my wood chopper, my ploughman, & my cook, for they have some sort of self sufficiency. They can contrive without my aid to make a whole day & whole year; but I depend on them, & have not earned by use a right to my fingers or toes. If a palsy should mortify them it were just.

—

Art is cant & pedantry if it is not practical & moral, that is, if it do not make the poor & uncultivated feel that it addresses them also, & brings with it the oracle of Conscience. And I find this power of art in the fact that human power grows with virtue; that virtue transfigures the face into its own glorious likeness, & of course redeems & purifies & beautifies posterity. A grand soul flings your gallery into cold nonsense, & no limits can be assigned to its prevalency, & to its power to adorn.

There is an appearance of paltriness as of toys & the trumpery of a theatre about Sculpture when compared with a rosebud or the egg of a sparrow.

—

Nov 21.

Swedenborg exaggerates the Circumstance of marriage. All loves, all friendships are momentary. *Do you love me?* means at last *Do you see the same truth I see?* If you do, we are happy together: but when presently one of us passes into the perception of new truth, we are divorced and the force of all nature cannot hold us to each other. I well know how delicious is this cup we call Love,—I existing for you, you existing for me,—but it is a child's apotheosis of his toy; it is an attempt to fix & eternize the fireside & nuptial chamber, to fasten & enlarge these fugitive clouds of circumstance, these initial pictures through which our first lessons are prettily conveyed. In vain & in vain. The Eden of God is naked & grand: Cold & desolate it seems to you whilst you cower over this nursery fire. But one to one, married & chained through the eternity of Ages, is frightful beyond the binding of dead & living together, & is no more conceivable to the soul than the permanence of our little platoon of gossips, Uncles, Aunts, & cousins. No, Heaven is the marriage of all souls. We meet & worship an instant under the temple of one thought & part as though we parted not, to join another thought with other fellowships of joy.

So far from there being any divine meaning in the low & proprietary sense of *Do you love me?* it is only when you leave & lose me by casting yourself on a noble sentiment which is higher than both of us that I draw near to you & find myself at your side. And I leave you & am repelled the moment you fix your eye on me & demand my love. In fact in the spiritual world we seem to change sexes every moment. You love the worth that is in me, therefore am I your husband; but it is not me but the worth that really fixes your love: well, that which is in me is but a drop of the Ocean of Worth that is behind me. Meantime I adore the greater worth that is in another; so I become his wife & he again aspires to a higher worth which dwells in another spirit & so is wife or receiver of that spirit's influence. Every soul is a Venus to every other soul.

—

Present a poetic design to people & they will tear it to mammocks. Yet how subtle an auxiliary is Nature! I knew a man who learned that his modes of living were false & mean by looking at the hill covered with wood which formed the shore of a small but beautiful lake which he visited in his almost daily walk. He returned to his gossips & told them his schemes of reform and they contradicted & chided & laughed & cried with vexation & contempt and shook his confidence in his plans. But when he went to the woods & saw the mist floating over the trees on the headland which rose out of the water, instantly his faith revived. But when he came to his house he could not find any words to show his friends in what manner the beautiful shores of the lake proved the wisdom of his economy. He could not show them the least connexion between the two things. When he once tried to speak of the bold shore, they stared as if he were insane. Yet whenever he went to the place & beheld the landscape his faith was confirmed.

Beauty can never be clutched; in persons & in nature is equally inaccessible. The accepted & betrothed lover has lost the wildest charm of his maiden in her acceptance of him. She was Heaven whilst he pursued her as a star: She cannot be Heaven if she stoops to such an one as he. So is it with these wondrous skies & hills & forests. What splendid distance, what recesses of ineffable pomp & loveliness in that sunset! But who can go where it is, or lay his hand or plant his foot thereon? Off they fall from the round world forever & ever. Glory is not for hands to handle.

The past is squalid. There is a poet in every broker. I shed all influences. A. is a tedious archangel. How few have faith enough to treat a man of genius as an exiled prince of the blood who must presently come to his own & it will then

appear that it had been best to have been of the same household all the time. *Yet if you have not faith in you, how can I have
faith in you?* But they are indefensible & unpresentable.

———

Waldo declines going to church with Mrs Mumford "because
Mrs M. is not beautiful. She has red hands & red face." The
next week when reminded that he does not like Mrs M. he tells
Louisa "I have made a little prayer that Mrs Mumford might
be beautiful, & now I think her beautiful."

Louisa proposed to carry W. to church with her & he
replies, 'I do not wish to go to church with you because you
live in the kitchen.'

———

People are uneasy because the philosopher seems to compromise their personal immortality. Mr Quin thinks that to affirm
the eternity of God & not to affirm the reappearance of Mr
Quin bodily & mentally with all the appearances & recollections of Mr Q. excepting of course his green surtout & his
bankstock scrip, is to give up the whole ship. But Mr Quin is a
sick God. All that sin & nonsense of his which he parades these
many summers & winters so complacently which seem to him
his life, his stake of being, in losing which he would lose all, are
the scurf & leprosy which do not perish & smell in the nostril
only because the divine Life has not yet ebbed quite away from
them. But it is the Life, it is the incoming of God by which
that Individual exists. It is the god only which he values &
pleads for, though to his diseased eye that poor skin & raiment
seem to have an intrinsic price. When that Divine Life shall
have more richly entered & shed itself abroad in him he will
no longer plead for life, he will live. Do not imagine that the
Universe is somewhat so vague & aloof that a man cannot be
willing to die for it. If that lives, I live. I am the Universe. The
Universe is the externisation of God. Wherever he is, that
bursts into appearance around him. The sun, the stars, physics
& chemistry we sensually treat as if they were selfexistences
and do not yet see that these are the retinue of that Being we
are, the signs of that Substance, translation into picture language of our sacred sense.

But there is no interval between this perception of Identity
of the growing God & littleness. If you do not see your right

to all, & your being reflected to you from all things, then the world may easily seem to you a hoax, & man the dupe. Yet the little fellow takes it so innocently, works in it so earnest & believing, blushes & turns pale, talks & sweats, is born red & dies gray, thinking himself an adjunct to the world which exists from him, that until he is explained to himself he may well look on himself as the most wronged of victims.

—

A droll dream last night, whereat I ghastly laughed. A congregation assembled, like some of our late Conventions, to debate the Institution of Marriage; & grave & alarming objections stated on all hands to the usage; when one speaker at last rose & began to reply to the arguments, but suddenly extended his hand & turned on the audience the spout of an engine which was copiously supplied from within the wall with water & whisking it vigorously about, up, down, right, & left, he drove all the company in crowds hither & thither & out of the house. Whilst I stood watching astonished & amused at the malice & vigor of the orator, I saw the spout lengthened by a supply of hose behind, & the man suddenly brought it round a corner & drenched me as I gazed. I woke up relieved to find myself quite dry, and well convinced that the Institution of Marriage was safe for tonight.

And why as I have written elsewhere not be Universalists or lovers of the Whole World? Why limit our zeal & charity to such narrow parochial bounds? Are there black, bilious, sad temperaments? They accuse me & thee. Let us arise & redeem them & purge this choler & sediment out of nature by our calmness & immoveable love.

Is there somewhat overweening in this claim? It is the fault of our rhetoric which cannot strongly state one fact without seeming to belie some other. I set the limits of our actual attainment very speedily. See the lizard on the fence, hear the rats in the wall, the fungus under foot, the lichen on the stone. What do I know of either of these worlds of life? As long as the Caucasian Man, perhaps longer, these creatures have kept their counsel beside his, yet not within recorded time has any word or sign passed from one to the other.

I am ashamed to see what a shallow local village tale our so called History is. How many times we must say Rome & Paris, yet what is Rome to the rat & lizard, what are Olympiads & Consulates to these neighboring regions of nature, nay what are they to the Esquimaux sealhunter, the Canàka in his canoe? Broader & deeper we must write our annals, from an ethical reformation, a new & vast sanative principle instead of this old chronology of selfishness & pride to which we have too long lent our homage & injured ourselves by our admiration. In that day the reader will stand for man & not as now for a shivering, imbecile, supplicating fraction of a man. Already that day exists for us, shines in on us at unawares but the path of science is not the way to these natures but from it rather; the idiot, the Indian, the child & rude boy all hand come much nearer to these, understand them better than the dissector or the lexicographer.

EDITOR'S AFTERWORD

CHRONOLOGY

NOTE ON THE TEXTS

NOTE ON THE ILLUSTRATIONS

NOTES

BIOGRAPHICAL NOTES

INDEX

Editor's Afterword

Ralph Waldo Emerson began keeping a journal when he was 18. By the time he was 30, in 1833, he had turned it into his most successful experiment in creating a literary form. He continued writing in that form for most of the rest of his life, with the last datable entry in 1877: "all writing should be affirmative." He left 182 individual volumes, some regular journals and some miscellaneous notebooks, some bought ready-made and some hand-sewn; these together fill 16 volumes in the great Harvard edition of the work, the *Journals and Miscellaneous Notebooks of Ralph Waldo Emerson* (*JMN*), begun in 1960 and completed in 1982. This Library of America edition contains approximately one third of what Emerson wrote in his regular journals, and is the most comprehensive selection ever made from that work.

The editor's goals in making the selection were two-fold: to present Emerson's best and most vital writing, and to retain what was most significant biographically and historically in the journals. Proportionality of representation was not a goal; by and large the selection draws more heavily on the mature journals, those in which Emerson was writing in a form he had mastered, than on the early journals or the very late ones, before Emerson had found his form or after he had lost some of his power.

The fact that Emerson often used passages from the journals in his lectures and in essays has led some to view them as primarily a literary quarry, a mine of rough material to be refined into finished products. But the journals should rather be approached as a great literary work in themselves, a different kind of literary work perhaps: more intimate, conversational, spontaneous, aleatoric, and indecorous than the lectures and essays.

The text of the present edition is based on, and deeply indebted to, the Harvard edition mentioned above, one of the great triumphs of modern scholarship. Our principles of adaptation have been simple. The *JMN* editors devised typographical conventions for showing the reader not only what Emerson wrote but also what he crossed out and what he added later, thus revealing much about the sentence-by-sentence process of Emerson's writing. We have not retained this editorial apparatus. From *JMN*'s densely marked-up process text we have produced clear text, omitting what Emerson crossed out and adding what he added.

This edition's order of presentation reflects *JMN*'s practice. The earlier large-scale edition of Emerson's journals, the 1909–14 *Journals* in ten volumes edited by his son Edward Waldo Emerson and grandson Waldo Emerson Forbes, rearranged the entries in the separate and often overlapping journal volumes into a single chronological sequence, and some previously published selections from the journals have followed the same principle. *JMN* offers, instead, each of Emerson's individual volumes in its original order of pagination, and presents the individual volumes themselves in rough chronological order. The present edition does the same.

A major advantage of keeping the individual journals separate is the opportunity it affords to reveal Emerson's art as a diarist, which was preeminently an art of transition and juxtaposition. The reader's illumination and pleasure in reading the journals lie in watching the movement of Emerson's thought from subject to subject and mood to mood. That such an approach is consistent with Emerson's thinking can be gauged from the compelling claims that he himself made for the aesthetic value of transition: "The experience of poetic creativeness . . . is not found in staying at home, nor yet in travelling, but in transitions from one to the other, which must therefore be adroitly managed to present as much transitional surface as possible" (*Selected Journals 1841–1877*, p. 289), he wrote in 1845. The present edition seeks precisely to "present as much transitional surface as possible," to show what Emerson in 1857 called one of his "few laws" in inexhaustibly vivid action: "Flowing, or transition, or shooting the gulf, the perpetual striving to ascend to a higher platform, the same thing to new and higher forms" (*Selected Journals 1841–1877*, p. 695).

The present edition is a selection from the journals, not the whole of them. Some of the transitions from one paragraph to the next, therefore, are not Emerson's but ours, produced by the elimination of the material originally separating them. Wherever we have omitted material, the omission is indicated with a centered em-dash, so that the reader can easily see which transitions are Emerson's and which are ours.

Because Emerson was a master of two related forms within the journal—the entry and the paragraph—we have seldom made cuts within entries (although it is, to be sure, not always clear when one entry ends and the next begins) and still more seldom within paragraphs.

A further principle has been to accept the distinction made by the *JMN* editors between regular journal and miscellaneous notebook, and to include only material from the former category. The distinction is fluid, and some individual volumes are hard to classify; but the distinction is broadly applicable and worth applying. It is, moreover, a distinction that Emerson himself seems to have been aware of and to have used; his titles differentiate the one category from the other, as do the epigraphs and concluding passages of most regular journal volumes.

The distinction matters because the miscellaneous notebooks are for the most part *topical* notebooks. In setting them up, Emerson determined in advance his principles of inclusion and exclusion, and limited in advance his freedom of intellectual movement. Often such notebooks are entirely what the regular journals are only secondarily, namely, collections of raw material of which finished essays or speeches are to be made. Often they bring together material written at multiple periods and in multiple volumes; sometimes it is precisely their purpose to accumulate previously written material on a defined subject. There is distinguished new writing in some of these, but in them Emerson is doing something different from what he is doing in the regular journals, and the movement of his mind is less exhilaratingly free and surprising. (Occasionally within a regular journal volume Emerson gets obsessed with a topic, and for a while writes about that topic. These sequences are some of his best writing, and we have sought to retain them; if in the topical notebooks one is reading Emerson the collector, in these intense sequences of reflection, about Thoreau or slavery or friendship, one is reading Emerson possessed.)

In 1841, Emerson offered a prophecy: "novels will give way by and by to diaries or autobiographies; captivating books if only a man knew how to choose among what he calls his experiences that which is really his experience, and how to record truly!" (in this volume, p. 769) If Emerson was wrong about novels "giving way," he was right about diaries, or at least about his own. Emerson was as good at the tasks he defined—to choose "that which is really his experience, and how to record truly!"—as any diarist before him or since. The present edition of his journals offers a capacious opportunity to watch him explore the full implications of those tasks in the extraordinary form he created.

Chronology

1803   Born May 25, Election Day, in Boston, Massachusetts, the fourth child of William (pastor of Boston's First Church) and Ruth Haskins Emerson, both of English descent. Described by father at age two as "rather a dull scholar." From age three attends nursery and then grammar school.

1811   Father dies May 12 of stomach tumor at age 42, leaving children to be raised by his widow with help from his sister, Mary Moody Emerson, whose idiosyncratic religious orthodoxy and acute critical intelligence were a lifelong influence. Of eight children, only Ralph Waldo and four brothers survive childhood: William (b. 1801), Edward Bliss (b. 1805), Charles Chauncy (b. 1808), and the mentally retarded Robert Bulkeley (b. 1807), named for illustrious ancestor Peter Bulkeley, first-generation Puritan minister and a founder of Concord, Massachusetts.

1812   Enters Boston Public Latin School; begins writing poetry.

1817–21   Attends Harvard College and lives in President Kirkland's lodgings as his "freshman" or orderly; waits on table and teaches during vacations to pay costs. Begins keeping a journal to record his "luckless ragamuffin ideas." By junior year prefers the name Waldo. Wins prizes for oratory and for essays on Socrates and ethical philosophy; graduates 30th in a class of 59 and delivers class poem at graduation after six others decline the honor. Following graduation teaches in brother William's school for young ladies in Boston.

1822   Continues to teach. Dedicates his seventh "Wideworld" journal to "the Spirit of America." Publishes essay on "The Religion of the Middle Ages" in *The Christian Disciple*, a leading Unitarian religious review.

1823   Takes walking trip to the Connecticut Valley. Runs school alone when William departs to study theology in Germany. Childhood dreams, he complains, "are all fading away & giving place to some very sober & very disgusting views of a quiet mediocrity of talents and condition."

1824   Dedicates himself to the study of divinity; complains in journal of his lack of warmth and self-confidence, but hopes "to put on eloquence as a robe."

1825   Closes school. Notes in journal that his "unpleasing boyhood is past" and enters middle class at Harvard Divinity School. When studies are interrupted by eye trouble, resumes teaching, this time in Chelmsford, Massachusetts. Edward sails for Europe for his health; William, back from Germany, decides against ministerial career because of religious doubts.

1826   Begins year with "mended eyes," but afflicted by rheumatism of the hip. Teaches in Roxbury, then opens school in Cambridge (a student later describes him as "not inclined to win boys by a surface amiability, but kindly in explanation or advice"). William and Edward study law, the former on Wall Street and the latter in Daniel Webster's office. Impressed by Sampson Reed's *Observations on the Growth of the Mind*, a treatise that discusses "correspondences" between nature and spirit. Approbated to preach in October, but with onset of lung trouble, voyages to Charleston, South Carolina, financed by uncle Samuel Ripley.

1827   "I am not sick; I am not well; but luke-sick," he writes William in January, complaining of "a certain stricture" in his lungs. Sails for St. Augustine, Florida; establishes friendship with Napoleon's nephew Achille Murat, and is intrigued by this "consistent Atheist." Returns to Boston in spring and continues to preach. In December, while preaching in Concord, New Hampshire, meets Ellen Louisa Tucker.

1828   Edward becomes deranged; Waldo links this collapse to his brother's "preternatural energy" and assures himself that he is protected from a similar fate by the "mixture of *silliness*" in his character. Made honorary member of Phi Beta Kappa. Engaged to Ellen Tucker in December.

1829–30   Invited in January to become junior pastor of Boston's Second Church—the church of the Mathers. Becomes chaplain of state senate, as his late father had been. Although Ellen is ill with tuberculosis, they marry in September. Elected to Boston School Committee in December. In November 1830, Edward, his health failing, sails for Puerto Rico.

1831   Ellen dies on February 8 at age 19. Waldo notes the reli-
          gious resignation of her last hours and writes, "My angel
          is gone to heaven this morning & I am alone in the world
          & strangely happy"; five days later he prays, "God be
          merciful to me a sinner & repair this miserable debility in
          which her death has left my soul." Begins walking to her
          tomb every morning. Charles' health begins to fail, and
          he sails for Puerto Rico where Edward is employed at the
          American consulate.

1832   Uneasy with role as minister; feels "the profession is anti-
          quated" and "in an altered age we worship in the dead
          forms of our forefathers." Writes Second Church govern-
          ing board requesting changes in communion service and,
          when denied, decides to resign. Suffers from persistent
          diarrhea. In September delivers sermon "The Lord's
          Supper" explaining his objections to the rite and con-
          cludes he is "not interested in it." In poor health, sails for
          Europe on December 25.

1833   Lands in Malta in February much improved in health.
          Enthusiastically travels north through Italy, spending
          Easter week in Rome and meeting Walter Savage Landor
          in Florence; describes religious pomp at Sistine Chapel as
          "millinery & imbecility," but finds Pope's Easter benedic-
          tion at St. Peter's "a sublime spectacle." Arrives in Paris
          in June. Complains it is "a loud modern New York of a
          place" but enjoys cafés and liveliness; visits Jardin des
          Plantes and decides to become "a naturalist." In London
          in July; meets John Stuart Mill, Coleridge, and Words-
          worth, and begins lifelong friendship with Carlyle, whom
          he visits in Craigenputtock, Scotland. Sails for home in
          September and notes, "I like my book about nature &
          wish I knew where & how I ought to live." Preaches at
          Boston Second Church in October and in November lec-
          tures on "The Uses of Natural History."

1834   Lectures in Boston on natural history and continues to
          preach nearly every Sunday; begins to correspond with
          Carlyle. In spring receives first half of Ellen's estate
          (about $11,600). In October moves with mother to
          Emerson family home in Concord (later named by
          Hawthorne the Old Manse). Decides "not to utter any
          speech, poem, or book that is not entirely & peculiarly
          my work." Edward dies in Puerto Rico on October 1.

1835   Lectures in Boston on lives of great men. In January feels
          "very sober joy" on being engaged to Lydia Jackson of

Plymouth; buys house in Concord for $3,500 and then marries Lydia (whom he calls "Lidian") in September. Declines pastorate in East Lexington, Massachusetts, but agrees to preach there every Sunday or procure a substitute. Delivers address on Concord history for the town's second centennial; begins winter lecture series on "English Literature" in Boston.

1836 Pronounces it a "gloomy epoch" when Charles dies of tuberculosis on May 9. Margaret Fuller visits the Emerson home for three weeks in July. Informal group (later dubbed Transcendental Club)—including Fuller, Orestes Brownson, Theodore Parker, Bronson Alcott, James Freeman Clarke, among others—organized for discussions and continues to meet until 1843. His "little azure-coloured *Nature*" published anonymously, a common practice, in September. Sees American edition of Carlyle's *Sartor Resartus* through press at own expense. (Although advances for this and future American editions of Carlyle's works are a financial hardship, Emerson will eventually recover his investment and send Carlyle nearly $3,000 in profits.) Son Waldo born October 30. Gives lecture series on "Philosophy of History" in winter.

1837 Notes in journal that "the land stinks with suicide" as American economy slides into severe depression. Receives final portion of Ellen's estate, bringing total to about $23,000, yielding an annual income of some $1,200. "Concord Hymn" sung July 4 at unveiling of monument to Revolutionary soldiers. Delivers "The American Scholar" as Harvard's Phi Beta Kappa oration in August and is toasted as "the Spirit of Concord" who "makes us all of One Mind." Lectures in winter on "Human Culture," defined as "educating the eye to the true harmony of the unshorn landscape."

1838 Finding the pulpit a constraint, asks East Lexington church committee to relieve him of responsibilities in February. In April writes open letter to President Van Buren protesting displacement of Cherokee Indians from their ancestral lands. Delivers address at Harvard Divinity School (July 15), subsequently attacked as "the latest form of infidelity." Though defended by George Ripley, Orestes Brownson, J. F. Clarke, and Theodore Parker, he is not invited back to Harvard for nearly 30 years. Dartmouth Oration ("Literary Ethics") delivered July 24. Meets Jones Very and develops close friendship with

Thoreau, with whom he takes walks in the woods. Winter lecture series on "Human Life" includes such topics as "Head," "Home," "Love," "Duty," "Genius," "Demonology," and "Animal Magnetism."

1839   Preaches his last sermon in January. Daughter Ellen born February 24, with Thoreau's mother serving as midwife. Visits from Very, Fuller, Alcott, and Carolyn Sturgis lead Emerson to note his "porcupine impossibility of contact with men," although of Alcott and Fuller he writes, "Cold as I am, they are almost dear." Edits and finds publisher for Very's poems and essays. Lectures on "The Present Age" in winter on a widening circuit.

1840   With Margaret Fuller, brings out first issue of *The Dial* in July, hoping it will be "one cheerful rational voice amidst the din of mourners and polemics." Strives to write "with some pains Essays on various matters as a sort of apology to my country for my apparent idleness." Attends reformers' Chardon Street Convention, but when invited to join Brook Farm community declines "to remove from my present prison to a prison a little larger."

1841   First series of *Essays* published in March, and aunt, Mary Moody Emerson, pronounces it a "strange medly of atheism and false independence"; favorable reviews in London and Paris lay basis for international reputation. Invites Thoreau to join household in spring, offering room and board in exchange for gardening and household chores. In summer delivers "The Method of Nature" at Waterville College in Maine. Daughter Edith born November 22. Lectures on "The Times" in winter.

1842   Devastated by death of five-year-old Waldo from scarlet fever on January 27, avers that he comprehends "nothing of this fact but its bitterness." Succeeds Margaret Fuller as editor of *The Dial* when she resigns. Raises money to send Bronson Alcott to England. Takes walking trip in September with Hawthorne, now living at the Old Manse, to visit Shaker community in village of Harvard, Massachusetts. On lecture tour in New York City—the lecture "Poetry of the Times" is reviewed by young editor Walter Whitman—dines with Horace Greeley and Albert Brisbane and visits between lectures at home of Henry James, Sr.

1843   In spring, finds Thoreau employment in Staten Island as tutor to children of his brother William, now a New York

State district judge. Completes a translation of Dante's *Vita Nuova*. Summer, entertains Daniel Webster at his home and pronounces him "no saint . . . but according to his lights a very true & admirable man."

1844   Last issue of *The Dial* appears in April. Son Edward Waldo born July 10. Purchases land on shore of Walden Pond. Contributes $500 toward land for the Alcott family when they purchase a house in Concord (later Hawthorne's Wayside). Opposes annexation of Texas and war with Mexico: "Mexico will poison us." Delivers address attacking slavery in the West Indies. *Essays: Second Series* published in October.

1845   Gives Thoreau permission to build hut on Walden property. His discourse at Middlebury College provokes a local minister to ask God "to deliver us from ever hearing any more such transcendental nonsense." Refuses to lecture at the New Bedford Lyceum when informed that Negroes are excluded from membership. In winter delivers "Representative Men" lecture series.

1846   April, hears Edward Everett's inaugural discourse as president of Harvard and decries "the corpse-cold Unitarianism & Immortality of Brattle street & Boston." In July feels limited sympathy for Thoreau's night in jail ("this prison is one step to suicide"). *Poems* published in December, including "Threnody," an elegy for his son Waldo.

1847–48 Sails for Liverpool in October, having been invited to lecture in various British industrial cities; Thoreau leaves Walden Pond to take charge of the Emerson household. November to February, lectures extensively on various topics, including "Natural Aristocracy," in an England and Scotland disturbed by political unrest. Sees Carlyle, Wordsworth, Harriet Martineau, Dickens, and Tennyson. May, visits Paris during attempted revolution, where he meets Alexis de Tocqueville. Returns to England in June, dines with Chopin, and visits Stonehenge with Carlyle. Disembarks in Boston in late July.

1849   Offers winter lecture series on "Mind and Manners in the Nineteenth Century," drawing on English experiences, and a spring series on "Laws of the Intellect." Begins smoking cigars. *Nature; Addresses, and Lectures* published in September.

1850   January, *Representative Men* published. Winter–spring, extensive lecturing in New England, New York, Phila-

delphia, Cleveland, and Cincinnati. July, mourns death of
Margaret Fuller Ossoli in shipwreck ("I have lost in her
my audience") and sends Thoreau to Fire Island beach to
search for her effects. Winter, lectures on "The Conduct
of Life."

1851   Outraged by Webster's March 7 speech defending Fugitive Slave Law, fills journal with passionate condemnation
of this former hero ("all the drops of his blood have eyes
that look downward") and speaks against the law.

1852   Contributes to *Memoirs of Margaret Fuller Ossoli*. Praises
Uncle Tom's Cabin. During winter, 1852–53, lectures to enthusiastic crowds from Boston to St. Louis, Philadelphia
to Maine and Montreal.

1853   Mother dies on November 16 at age 84; she had lived
with Waldo and Lidian since their marriage in 1835.

1854   Demanding lecture schedule throughout country includes attack on Fugitive Slave Law in New York City.

1855   Anti-slavery lectures in Boston, New York, and Philadelphia. Writes Whitman praising *Leaves of Grass* ("I give
you joy of your free & brave thought. . . . I greet you at
the beginning of a great career"). Helps F. B. Sanborn establish the Concord Academy, whose pupils will include
the children of Emerson, Hawthorne, and Henry James,
Sr. Saturday Club founded, with Emerson as a charter
member, for informal literary discussions. Addresses
Woman's Rights Convention in Boston.

1856   Lecture schedule ranges from New England to the Middle West. *English Traits* published in August. Speaks in
favor of Kansas Relief, a fund raised to help Kansans impoverished by marauding pro-slavery advocates.

1857   Listens approvingly to Captain John Brown's speech in
Concord. Moves remains of mother and Waldo ("I ven-
tured to look into the coffin") to Sleepy Hollow
Cemetery.

1858   Declares himself an abolitionist "of the most absolute
abolition." Spends two weeks in August camping in the
Adirondacks with Louis Agassiz, Oliver Wendell Holmes,
and others. Calculates his income for the year at $4,162.11.

1859   Brother Bulkeley dies at age 52. Records in journal his fear
that he has "no new thoughts, and that [his] life is quite
at an end." Much agitated by capture and execution of

John Brown, and predicts that his hanging will make the gallows "sacred as the cross."

1860 Lectures throughout New York, New England, the Middle West, and at Toronto. Walks on Boston Common with Whitman for two hours on a March day trying to persuade him to tone down the "sex element" in *Leaves of Grass*. William Dean Howells visits in August as part of the itinerary of his literary pilgrimage. Declares in November that news of Lincoln's election is "sublime." *Conduct of Life* published in December.

1861 Told to "dry up" by unruly pro-Union crowd while attempting to speak at Massachusetts Anti-Slavery Society ("the mob roared . . . and after several beginnings, I withdrew"). Roused by unity and patriotism of New England following attack on Fort Sumter, visits Charlestown Navy Yard and declares "sometimes gunpowder smells good." Says of war that "amputation is better than cancer."

1862 Lectures on "American Civilization" in Washington and meets Lincoln. Reads address at Thoreau's funeral averring that "the country knows not yet, or in the least part, how great a son it has lost." Celebrates Emancipation Proclamation in an address printed in the *Atlantic Monthly*.

1863 Aunt Mary dies at age 89 on October 3. Appointed to committee to review standards of U.S. Military Academy at West Point. Lectures throughout Midwest.

1864 Attends Hawthorne's funeral and laments "the painful solitude of the man—which, I suppose, could not longer be endured, & he died of it." Lectures on "American Life" and the "Fortune of the Republic," exhorting Americans to "wake" and correct the injustices of the political system "with energy"; declares "this country, the last found, is the great charity of God to the human race." Elected to newly formed American Academy of Arts and Sciences.

1865 Eulogizes martyred Lincoln as "the true representative of this continent." Thinks Grant's terms for Lee's surrender too lenient. Daughter Edith engaged to Col. William Forbes, later president of Bell Telephone Co., son of railroad magnate John Murray Forbes. Lectures 77 times.

1866 Receives honorary Doctor of Laws degree from Harvard. Reads to son Edward Waldo his poem "Terminus" ("It is time to be old, / To take in sail.").

1867   *May-Day and Other Pieces* published in April. Delivers Phi
        Beta Kappa oration at Harvard, ending 29-year exile.
        Named an overseer of Harvard College. Lectures 80
        times, the peak of his platform career, traveling west twice
        as far as Minnesota and Iowa.

1868   William dies in New York on September 13.

1870   *Society and Solitude* published in March; writes preface for
        edition of *Plutarch's Morals*. Lectures at Harvard on
        "Natural History of Intellect" and is much occupied with
        university affairs.

1871   Repetition of Harvard course cut short due to fatigue;
        April–May, travels to West Coast, in a private Pullman car
        leased by John Forbes, for relaxation and relief with fam-
        ily and friends. Meets naturalist John Muir and notes that
        California "has better days, & more of them" than any
        other place. Back in Concord, visited by Bret Harte.

1872   Health declines; suffers lapses of memory while lecturing.
        House in Concord badly damaged by fire on July 24; James
        Russell Lowell and other friends raise $17,000 to repair
        house and send Emerson abroad for a vacation. Travels to
        Egypt and Europe with daughter Ellen in October. In
        Paris, Henry James, Jr., guides them through the Louvre;
        sees Carlyle for last time. Meets Hermann Grimm, Hip-
        polyte Taine, Ivan Turgenev, Robert Browning, Friedrich
        Max Müller, Benjamin Jowett, and John Ruskin.

1873   Returns in May to cheering crowd in Concord and dis-
        covers house has been restored by friends.

1874   Publishes *Parnassus*, an anthology of his favorite poetry
        (Whitman and Poe are not included).

1875   Ceases writing new entries in his private journals, but
        rereads and comments on old ones; *Letters and Social
        Aims* published in December with editorial assistance of
        Ellen and James Elliot Cabot.

1876   Emma Lazarus visits, and this "real unconverted Jew" cre-
        ates much interest in household. *Selected Poems* published.

1877–82 Lives last years serenely in mental twilight (at Long-
        fellow's funeral in his own last year, Emerson is reported
        to have said, "That gentleman was a sweet, beautiful soul,
        but I have entirely forgotten his name"). Dies of pneu-
        monia on April 27, 1882, in Concord.

Note on the Texts

Emerson's career as a journal writer extended, with few significant periods of inactivity, for almost 60 years. He began his first journal, *Wide World 1*, in January 1820; his last, *ST*, includes an entry dated January 1877. Not counting a few journals known to have been lost, or items such as account books and engagement diaries, he completed 182 journals and miscellaneous notebooks during his lifetime, all but one of these now in the collections of the Houghton Library at Harvard University. Emerson used some of these manuscript volumes exclusively as commonplace books, poetry notebooks, composition books (in which he drafted works for publication), or record books of various kinds; others were journals in the more ordinary sense of the term, to which he added thoughts and observations over time; and in others, he mixed these modes to varying degrees.

The present volume contains selections from 35 manuscript journals, with entries written between 1820 and 1842. A companion volume, *Ralph Waldo Emerson: Selected Journals, 1841–1877*, contains selections from 46 journals. All told, the selections in these two volumes represent approximately a third of the contents of Emerson's regular journals, excluding his miscellaneous notebooks and mixed journals, in which regular journal writing is not the predominant mode. Both volumes present Emerson's manuscript journals as distinct works, in order of the date on which each is known or can be inferred to have been begun; entries within each journal are printed in the order in which they appear in Emerson's manuscripts (except in a few cases, where Emerson left some clear indication that he was writing in continuation of a remotely preceding entry). The resulting order of entries is not strictly chronological, though it is loosely so. Emerson sometimes began a new journal before he had finished a current one and would keep two or more journals at the same time; he also sometimes revisited earlier journals, revising or adding to them. Some entries bear a date, others do not.

Emerson did not attempt to publish his journals, but he drew on them extensively in his other writings, borrowing and adapting phrases, sentences, or longer passages from his journals. For a detailed account of his subsequent use of those parts of the journals included in the present volume, see www.loa.org/emerson-notes.

After Emerson's death, his son Edward Waldo Emerson and nephew Waldo Emerson Forbes collaborated in editing the journals for publication. Their 10-volume *Journals of Ralph Waldo Emerson*

(Boston: Houghton Mifflin, 1909–14) contains much of the text of Emerson's regular manuscript journals but omits passages printed elsewhere, rearranges entries from many separate journals into new chronological and thematic sequences, and also occasionally bowdlerizes.

The text of the journals presented here is a newly prepared clear text, based on the genetic text of Emerson's manuscript journals published in the 16-volume *Journals and Miscellaneous Notebooks of Ralph Waldo Emerson* (Cambridge: Harvard University Press, 1960–82), hereafter *JMN*. Where the editor of the present volume has omitted an entry or entries within the text of a journal, this fact is indicated with a centered em dash. (A centered asterisk at the bottom of a page indicates a line space in Emerson's manuscript journal.) *JMN* represents Emerson's cancellations and revisions and other features of the manuscript journals using a system of editorial marks to indicate rewriting, interlinear and marginal interpolation, original pagination, erasure, and manuscript mutilation. The present volume silently accepts a number of textual emendations included in *JMN* within these editorial marks and prints them plainly, such as restored or corrected punctuation; letters or words omitted or repeated by a likely slip of the pen; interlinear insertions; dates supplied for particular entries; matter interpolated from the margins or conjecturally recovered from illegible or damaged sections of the manuscripts. Canceled matter is silently omitted in all but a few cases; whatever text has been restored in these cases is described in the Notes. Also silently omitted in the present volume are *JMN*'s expansions of abbreviated names and other annotative additions, such as the identification of quotations; Emerson's brief cross-references to other journal passages; and uncanceled variant words or phrases. For the identification of abbreviated names or of quotations, see the Notes to the present volume; for further information about Emerson's cross-references and uncanceled textual variants, see www.loa.org/emerson-notes.

The list below offers further detail about the individual volumes of *JMN* from which the texts of the journals in the present volume have been taken. All volumes are reprinted by arrangement with Harvard University Press:

Wide World 1 to *Wide World 6*: *JMN* I (1819–1822), William H. Gilman, Alfred R. Ferguson, George P. Clark, Merrell R. Davis, eds. (1960).
Wide World 7 to *No. XV*: *JMN* II (1822–1826), William H. Gilman, Alfred R. Ferguson, Merrell R. Davis, eds. (1961).

Journal 1826 to *Blotting Book III*: *JMN* III (1826–1832), William H. Gilman, Alfred R. Ferguson, eds. (1963).

Q to *France and England*: *JMN* IV (1832–1834), Alfred R. Ferguson, ed. (1964).

B to *C*: *JMN* V (1835–1838), Merton M. Sealts, Jr., ed. (1965).

D to *F2*: *JMN* VII (1838–1842), A.W. Plumstead, Harrison Hayford, eds. (1969).

This volume presents the texts of *JMN* in clear form, but does not attempt to reproduce every feature of its typographic design, such as its display capitalization, or all representations of holographic features, such as variation in the length of dashes. A small number of emendations have been necessary in the preparation of a clear text from the genetic text of *JMN*, due to the unfinished nature of Emerson's manuscript. In some cases, for instance, Emerson added or canceled a word or phrase but did not subsequently correct a corresponding part of a sentence. Such emendations are listed below. The texts are otherwise presented without change, except for correction of typographical errors. Spelling, punctuation, and capitalization are often expressive features, and they are not altered, even when inconsistent or irregular. The following is a list of emendations and of typographical errors corrected, cited by page and line number: 24.18, child I; 45.29, an friendship; 68.5, ground the; 76.2, intentions though; 77.22, time,; 99.3, of homes.; 106.31, strange ↑gratifying↓; 122.13, course forgets; 127.16, every; 129.37, contrivances has; 129.38, chambers stocked; 142.11, minds the; 154.9, ↑litany↓ epitome; 181.33, cheerless the; 182.38, suceed; 201.7, it"; 233.16, shafts the; 237.13, scare; 241.6, Hussey fond; 252.28, Deus, &c. The; 269.3, those; 282.10, impracticable &; 306.12, flower so; 308.9, lay who; 319.26, we much; 349.4, itself.; 365.32, him [no period]; 418.3, memory [no period]; 484.20, said.; 530.3, Ode [no period]; 540.27, & and; 552.27, become; 717.23, discrepances; 734.36, think [no period]; 745.30, am cold; 749.6, all [no period]; 779.33, metephysical; 789.18, any the.

Note on the Illustrations

1. Emerson's journals and miscellaneous notebooks at Harvard's Houghton Library.
    Frontispiece photograph, *The Journals and Miscellaneous Notebooks of Ralph Waldo Emerson* (Cambridge: Harvard University Press, 1960), vol. 1: William H. Gilman, George P. Clark, Alfred R. Ferguson, Merrell R. Davis, eds.

2. The opening page of Emerson's journal *Wide World 1* (January 1820).
    MS Am 1280H (2). Houghton Library, Harvard University.
    Reprinted by permission of the Houghton Library, Harvard University.

3. Ruth Haskins Emerson, c. 1848.
    MS Am 1280.235 (706.16). Ralph Waldo Emerson Memorial Association deposit, Houghton Library, Harvard University. Not to be reproduced in whole or in part without permission.
    Reprinted by permission of the Houghton Library, Harvard University.

4. The Rev. William Emerson, c. 1812.
    Engraved portrait originally published in *The Polyanthos*, May 1812; from a copy trimmed and bound into William Taylor Newton's extra-illustrated copy of *A Memoir of Ralph Waldo Emerson* (1887), by James Elliot Cabot.
    Courtesy Concord Free Public Library.

5. A sketch of 15 Hollis Hall at Harvard, from Emerson's journal *Wide World 1* (August 1820).
    MS Am. 1280H (2). Houghton Library, Harvard University.
    Reprinted by permission of the Houghton Library, Harvard University.

6. Alvan Fisher, *College Yard: A View from the President's House* (1821).
    Oil on canvas; photo: David Mathews.
    Harvard University Art Museums, Fogg Art Museum, Harvard University Portrait Collection. Presented for the use of Harvard College by Henry Pickering, Harvard University Portrait Collection, 1823, L3.
    Copyright © President and Fellows of Harvard College.

7. A reading list and sketch from Emerson's journal *Wide World 2* (1820–21).
   MS Am 1280H (5). Houghton Library, Harvard University.
   Reprinted by permission of the Houghton Library, Harvard University.

8. A heavily canceled journal entry about Martin Gay (*Wide World* 2, 1821) MS Am 1280H (12a). Houghton Library, Harvard University.
   Reprinted by permission of the Houghton Library, Harvard University.

9. Mary Moody Emerson as a young woman (silhouette portrait).
   Courtesy Concord Free Public Library.

10–12. Ralph Waldo Emerson in 1843; Edward Emerson; Charles Emerson (silhouette portraits).
   David G. Haskins, *Ralph Waldo Emerson: His Maternal Ancestors, with Some Reminiscences of Him* (Boston: Cupples, Upham, 1886).

13. Robert Bulkeley Emerson, c. 1853?
   Addison A. Fish, photographer.
   MS Am 1280.235 (706.14). Ralph Waldo Emerson Memorial Association deposit, Houghton Library, Harvard University. Not to be reproduced in whole or in part without permission.
   Reprinted by permission of the Houghton Library, Harvard University.

14. William Emerson, c. 1833.
   Miniature portrait, watercolor on ivory, attributed to Thomas Seir Cummings.
   Courtesy of the Massachusetts Historical Society.

15. Emerson records his engagement to Ellen (December 21, 1828).
   MS Am 1280H (21). Houghton Library, Harvard University.
   Reprinted by permission of the Houghton Library, Harvard University.

16. Sarah Goodridge, *Ellen Louisa Tucker Emerson* (c. 1830).
   Watercolor on ivory, 3″ x 2.5″; photograph by David Bohl.
   Pi806. Concord Museum Collections, Gift of Dr. Augusta G. Williams. Label: "This miniature is that of Ralph Waldo Emerson's first wife. She gave it to her great friend Lucy

Ann Withington of Park St, Boston, Mass. Lucy Ann
Withington married Theodore Gardner of Bolton, Mass.
These were my grandparents. (Signed) Augusta G.
Williams."

Courtesy of the Concord Museum, Concord, Massachusetts;
www.concordmuseum.org.

Reproduced by permission of Concord Museum.

17.   Charles Osgood, *Portrait of Nathaniel Hawthorne* (1840).
Oil on canvas; photograph by Sexton/Dykes.
Peabody Essex Museum.

Copyright © 2009 Peabody Essex Museum. All rights reserved. Courtesy of the Peabody Essex Museum, Salem,
MA.

18.   Charles King Newcomb.
Edward Waldo Emerson and Waldo Emerson Forbes, eds.,
Journals of Ralph Waldo Emerson (Boston: Houghton
Mifflin, 1912), vol. 8 (frontispiece).

19.   Emerson's son Waldo in October 1841.
MS Am 1280.235 (706.17). Ralph Waldo Memorial Association
deposit. Houghton Library, Harvard University. Not to
be reproduced in whole or in part without permission.

Reprinted by permission of the Houghton Library, Harvard
University.

20.   Emerson records the death of his son Waldo in his journal *J*
(January 28, 1842).
MS Am 1280H (41). Houghton Library, Harvard University.
Reprinted by permission of the Houghton Library, Harvard
University.

21.   David Scott, *Ralph Waldo Emerson* (1848).
Oil on canvas.
Courtesy Concord Free Public Library.

Notes

In the notes below, the reference numbers refer to page and line of this volume; the line count includes titles, headings, and thin rules dividing entries, but not blank lines. No note is made for material found in standard desk-reference works. Biblical quotations are keyed to the King James Version. Quotations from Shakespeare are keyed to *The Riverside Shakespeare*, ed. G. Blakemore Evans (Boston: Houghton Mifflin, 1974).

For further information about Emerson's use of his journals in his other literary works, the journals' internal cross-references, and un-canceled variant words and phrases, see www.loa.org/emerson-notes, which presents a detailed account of such uses, references, and vari-ants, keyed to the present volume.

For biographical details about individuals in Emerson's family and his immediate circle, see the Biographical Notes. For more detailed notes, references to other studies, and further biographical informa-tion than is presented in the Biographical Notes or Chronology, see the 16-volume *Journals and Miscellaneous Notebooks of Ralph Waldo Emerson* (Cambridge: Harvard University Press, 1960–1982), and also: Gay Wilson Allen, *Waldo Emerson: A Biography* (New York: Viking Press, 1981); Maurice Gonnaud, *An Uneasy Solitude: Individ-ual and Society in the Work of Ralph Waldo Emerson*, tr. Lawrence Rosenwald (Princeton: Princeton University Press, 1978); Walter Harding, *Emerson's Library* (Charlottesville: University Press of Vir-ginia, 1967); Joel Myerson, *Ralph Waldo Emerson: A Descriptive Bib-liography* (Pittsburgh: University of Pittsburgh Press, 1982); Ralph H. Orb et al., eds., *The Topical Notebooks of Ralph Waldo Emerson*, 3 vols. (Columbia: University of Missouri Press, 1990–94); Barbara L. Packer, *Emerson's Fall* (New York: Continuum, 1982) and *The Tran-scendentalists* (Athens: University of Georgia Press, 2007); Joel Porte, ed., *Emerson in His Journals* (Cambridge: Harvard University Press, 1982); Joel Porte and Saundra Morris, eds., *The Cambridge Companion to Ralph Waldo Emerson* (New York: Cambridge Univer-sity Press, 1999); Robert D. Richardson Jr., *Emerson: The Mind on Fire* (Berkeley: University of California Press, 1995); Lawrence Rosenwald, *Emerson and the Art of the Diary* (New York: Oxford University Press, 1988); Ralph L. Rusk, *The Life of Ralph Waldo Emerson* (New York: Charles Scribner's Sons, 1949); Stephen E. Whicher, *Freedom and Fate: An Inner Life of Ralph Waldo Emerson* (Philadelphia: University of Pennsylvania Press, 1953).

from WIDE WORLD 1

1.23   Junio]   A pen name Emerson used in his journals through the end of his junior year at Harvard.

1.25   Edward Search]   A pen name of English philosopher Abraham Tucker (1705–1774).

3.6–11   Everett's . . . calling it fame"]   Edward Everett (1794–1865) was a Harvard professor of Greek and a Unitarian minister; Emerson quotes from a sermon he had recently preached in Boston's Brattle Street Church.

3.32–33   "Mount on thy . . . Samor)]   See *Samor, Lord of the Bright City* (1818), an epic poem by Henry Hart Milman (1791–1868).

5.20–21   Burke's regicide Peace]   Edmund Burke's *Thoughts on the Prospect of a Regicide Peace: In a Series of Letters* (1796).

5.22–23   The Pythologian Poem]   Emerson served as secretary for the Pythologian, a short-lived undergraduate literary society, while at Harvard.

6.36–37   "mewing his mighty . . . beam"]   See *Areopagitica* (1644), a pamphlet petitioning for freedom of publication, by John Milton (1608–1674).

7.9   Dr. Warren's]   John C. Warren (1778–1856), professor of anatomy.

8.10–12   Fontenelle . . . against him."]   French writer Bernard le Bovier de Fontenelle (1657–1757) was among those writers supporting the merits of the modern in a paper war against Boileau and others in the Académie française, who insisted on the superiority of classical models. He was eventually elected to the Academy in 1691.

8.15–16   Sir William Temple . . . Wattle]   See Temple's *Essay upon the Ancient and Modern Learning* (1690), and *Reflections upon Ancient and Modern Learning* (1694), by William Wotton (1666–1727).

9.1–2   page 47 . . . page 44]   The page numbers refer to pages of Emerson's manuscript journal not included in the present volume.

9.23   accursed Enfield lesson]   William Enfield (1741–1797), whose *Institutes of Natural Philosophy* (1785) was a required text in the Harvard curriculum.

10.29–33   the two questions . . . claim thy care.]   Emerson's search for answers in randomly chosen lines from Virgil follows the ancient divinatory practice of the *Sortes Virgilianae*. The lines he happens upon are from the *Eclogues* (II.6: "O cruel Alexis, care you naught for my songs?") and the *Aeneid*, VII.443.

12.5–6   "Mentem . . . arce,"]   See Juvenal, *Satires*, XV.146: "We have drawn from on high that gift of feeling."

13.18   "to swerve . . . forthright"] Shakespeare, *Troilus and Cressida*, III.iii.158.

14.4–5   Sterne . . . provoking."] See Laurence Sterne's novel *Tristram Shandy* (1759–69).

14.9   is Gay] Martin Gay (1803–1850), a classmate of Emerson's; the name is canceled in his manuscript journal.

14.29   life of Marlborough] William Coxe's *Memoirs of John Duke of Marlborough* (1817–19) was reviewed in the *Quarterly* in May 1820.

15.3   "Sed fugit . . . tempus."] See Virgil, *Georgics* (III.284): "But time meanwhile is flying, beyond recall."

from WIDE WORLD 2

17.7–8   "And forever . . . this spell."] See *Manfred*, I.i.210–11, an 1817 closet drama by George Gordon, Lord Byron (1788–1824), which features a Faust-like anti-hero.

17.23   Dr. Blair's] Hugh Blair (1718–1800), whose *Lectures in Rhetoric and Belles Lettres* (1783) was among Emerson's college textbooks.

17.30–31   the elegant Professor . . . Literature.] George Ticknor (1791–1871), professor of French and Spanish at Harvard.

19.13–18   Barnwell's . . . Barnwell & Upham] "Barnwell's," "Barnwell," and "Upham" are canceled in Emerson's manuscript journal; they attended Harvard with him.

20.12   "Delivery . . . Moonblasting."] See Milton's *An Apology against a Pamphlet Called a Modest Confutation* (1642).

22.3–4   Dominie Sampson] A schoolteacher in *Guy Mannering* (1815), an 1815 novel by Sir Walter Scott.

22.24   Sybilline Collections] The Sybilline Oracles, a 12-book anthology of utterances ascribed to the Greek sybils but actually drawn from a variety of classical and Christian sources.

22.32   Cowper's Task] 1785 epic-length poem by William Cowper (1731–1800).

23.36   Adelaide de Guesclin] Voltaire's play was first performed in 1734.

24.26–27   Let those now cough . . . the more.] With "cough" substituted for "love," the refrain from the 4th-century Latin poem *Pervigilium Veneris* ("The Vigil of Venus").

25.6   Martial . . . Epigrams] See *Epigrams*, book XIV.cxc.

25.9–10   Mr Channing] Edward Tyrrell Channing (1790–1856), a professor of rhetoric and oratory at Harvard.

26.8–15   When I saw . . . dozen words.] These two sentences are partially canceled in Emerson's manuscript journal, as follows: "When I saw—'s
~~pale but expressive face & large eye, I instantly invested him with the
complete character which fancy had formed and though entirely unacquainted with him was pleased to observe the notice which he appeared to
take of me. For a year I have entertained towards him the same feelings &
should be~~ sorry to lose him altogether before we have ever exchanged above
a dozen words."

26.21–29   I am more puzzled . . . tremendous affair.] These four sentences are heavily canceled in Emerson's manuscript journals.

from WIDE WORLD 3

28.23   "Men said . . . were asleep."] See Henry Hallam's *View of the
State of Europe during the Middle Ages* (1818), Vol. II, Ch. VIII, Pt. II, which
quotes the Saxon Chronicle on the condition of England during the reign of
Stephen.

30.30   Η γαρ . . . χρηματα] 'Tis character abideth, not possessions.

from WIDE WORLD 4

33.19–26   Etsi mearum . . . uti solet.] Although the praise and honor
of my thoughts has not been as great as before, yet it acquires a greater joy
and pleasure, since I believed I felt the beginnings of love. I saw a friend
(male), though an old one, unknown; I saw another (female) known and to
be known; both, perhaps, if it pleases God, will make a part of life, a part of
me. I regret telling important matters with the words that a beginner is accustomed to use.

34.14   scripsi nomen, supra] I have written the name above.

34.27–29   Animi ardor . . . ut viveret.] The ardor of spirit of which I
spoke above is not extinguished, but seems to me not to be as powerful, as
brilliant, as great, as before. I am afraid it may fade. I hope it will live.

35.32–36.3   one of Ben Jonson's . . . betide you."] See Jonson's
masque *The Gypsies Metamorphosed* (1621).

37.11–12   "Time . . . rollest now."] See Byron's quasi-autobiographical
long poem *Childe Harold's Pilgrimage* (1812–18), IV.clxxxii.

from WIDE WORLD 6

38.4   "Maximus partus temporis,"] "The greatest production of your
time."

38.6–9   "There the Northern . . . Night"] The quatrain is Emerson's.

40.5–6   "Jesuits . . . Abbé Boileau] See Charles Boileau (1648–1704), author of *Pensées choisies sur différents sujets de morale* (1707), *Homélies et sermons prononcés devant le Roi et leurs Majestés brittaniques* (1712), and other works, quoted in Jean le Rond d'Alembert's *Account of the Destruction of the Jesuits in France* (1766) and elsewhere.

41.20–22   Seneca . . . semel jussit."] See Seneca's *Dialogues*, I.5, 8: "Although the great creator and ruler of the universe himself wrote the decrees of Fate, yet he follows them. He obeys forever, he decreed but once."

42.2   with Gay;] "Gay" is canceled in Emerson's manuscript.

42.24–25   "And there is a great difference . . . unhurt."] See Francis Bacon's letter to the Earl of Essex, his patron, after the latter was appointed Lord Lieutenant of Ireland in March 1599.

42.29–32   Marchand . . . of the sea.] Étienne Marchand (1775–1793); his sighting was noted in *The Edinburgh Review* in June 1815, in a review of Alexander von Humboldt's *Personal Narrative of Travels to the Equinoctial Regions of the New Continent* (1814–19).

43.25–30   John of Cappadocia . . . Byron's kind] Emerson's list of villains includes John of Cappadocia, who became praetorian prefect in 531 CE during the reign of Justinian I and was noted for his cruelty (his career is described in Edward Gibbon's 1776–89 *History of the Decline and Fall of the Roman Empire*); Gilbert Glossin, a scheming lawyer in Scott's *Guy Mannering* (1815); Publius Clodius Pulcher (92–52 BCE), Roman politician notorious for his use of violence against his opponents; Robert Lovelace, in Samuel Richardson's novel *Clarissa* (1748); and Captain Clement Cleveland, in Scott's novel *The Pirate* (1821).

44.21   I have a nasty . . . gratify.] This sentence is heavily canceled in Emerson's manuscript journal.

46.2–3   Mr Otis] Harrison Gray Otis (1765–1848), U.S. senator from Massachusetts from 1817 to 1822.

48.27–30   "Let us plait . . . ruined land."] From "The Banquet Song of the Tonga Islanders," an anonymous 1818 versification of a song first published in prose in *An Account of the Natives of the Tonga Islands* (1818) by William Mariner (1791–1853). Emerson later included the poem in his anthology *Parnassus* (1874) as "Song of the Tonga Islanders."

49.7   "Let me not . . . Chaucer] See *The Clerk's Tale*, line 880.

from WIDE WORLD 7

50.4–5   Ζητῶ . . . ANTONINUS] From the *Meditations* (c. 170–180) of Marcus Aurelius (121–180): "For I seek the truth, whereby no one was ever harmed."

51.16–20   "Judgement . . . Fontenelle.] From Fontenelle's *Entretiens sur la pluralité des mondes* (1686).

from WIDE WORLD 8

63.5–6   Whilst the fat . . . back.] The couplet is Emerson's.

from WIDE WORLD 9

64.10–11   Cyropaedia] Semi-fictional biography of Cyrus the Great (c. 576–530 BCE) by Greek historian Xenophon (c. 430–354 BCE).

64.11–13   Sharon Turner . . . *facts*.] See Turner's *History of the Anglo-Saxons* (1802–5).

65.16   a book . . . translates] Alfred's account of Wulfstan's voyage appears in his translation of *Historiarum Adversum Paganos Libri VII*, by Paulus Orosius (c. 375–418).

67.1–5   "If 20,000 . . . Essays p. 104] See "The Dangers of an Honest Man in Much Company," by Abraham Cowley (1618–1667); Emerson cites an 1819 edition of Cowley's *Essays*.

67.16–17   Professor Playfair] John Playfair (1748–1819), professor of natural philosophy at the University of Edinburgh.

67.27–28   Falstaff . . . another."] See Shakespeare, *2 Henry IV*, V.i.75–77.

from WIDE WORLD 10

71.21–22   at ille . . . aevum.] See Horace, *Epistles*, I.ii.42–43: "yet on it glides, and on it will glide, rolling its flood forever."

71.33–34   Modern Mr Lancaster . . . schools] Joseph Lancaster (1778–1838), author of *Improvements in Education, As It Respects the Industrious Classes of the Community* (1803), founded schools in Britain, Canada, and the United States.

73.11   "Faber quisque fortunae suae."] "Every man is the maker of his own fortune," a proverb quoted at the beginning of Francis Bacon's essay "Of Fortune."

74.1–2   door be shut.—] In his manuscript journal, Emerson adds a flourish to his concluding dash so that it resembles the open mouth of a snake.

from WIDE WORLD 11

76.33   Dr Channing] William Ellery Channing (1780–1842), Unitarian theologian and preacher.

82.3   Dr Black] See Joseph Black, *Lectures on the Elements of Chemistry* (1803).

82.4   Mrs. Grant on Highlanders] See Anne Grant, *Essays on the Superstitions of the Highlanders of Scotland* (1811).

82.7–8   Alison . . . his theory.] See Archibald Alison, *Essays on the Nature and Principles of Taste* (1811).

from WALK TO THE CONNECTICUT

84.14   the Mogul] Emerson's brother William, also a teacher.

87.22   'vestigia ruris.'] Traces of the rustic. (See Horace, *Epistles*, II.i.160.)

90.2   'fit for the mast . . . Admiral.'] See Milton, *Paradise Lost*, I.293–94.

from WIDE WORLD 12

91.9–10   Alas our young . . . desert] See *Childe Harold's Pilgrimage*, IV.cxx.

92.3–4   'Animasque . . . Virgil] *Georgics*, IV.238: "lay down their lives in the wound."

93.29–30   The theory . . . beholder] See note 82.7–8.

93.36–37   "There lives . . . mate."] See "The Wife of Bath her Prologue, from Chaucer" (1713) by Alexander Pope (1688–1744).

94.4   "A friend . . . infirmities."] Shakespeare, *Julius Caesar*, IV.iii.86.

98.8–9   "born . . . mankind."] See "Retaliation: A Poem" (1774), by Oliver Goldsmith (c. 1730–1774).

98.19–20   "the pilot . . . storm."] See "The Pilot that Weathered the Storm," an 1802 song in praise of William Pitt, by George Canning (1770–1827).

99.7   "Humanity . . . Fox.] From a speech given by Charles James Fox (1749–1806) during British parliamentary debate in 1806 over the abolition of the slave trade.

99.11–12   "A Great empire . . . Franklin.] From the opening of Franklin's satirical article "Rules by Which a Great Empire May Be Reduced to a Small One" (1773).

from WIDE WORLD XIII

100.4–6   "La nature . . . composition.] See Pascal's *Pensées* (1670): "Nature confounds the Pyrrhonists, and reason the dogmatists." Mackintosh cites the sentence in the *Edinburgh Review* in October 1813.

100.18–19   Nihil est . . . Juv.] Juvenal, *Satires*, IV.70–71: "There is nothing which a man won't believe about himself."

101.10–11   "Praise . . . Young] See *Night Thoughts* (1742–45), by Edward Young (1683–1765).

101.17–18   Dat veniam . . . columbas] Juvenal, *Satires*, II.63: "Our censor absolves the crow and passes judgment on the pigeon."

101.19–20   'Somebody . . . Wollaston] See *The Religion of Nature Delineated* (1722), by William Wollaston (1659–1724).

101.21–22   uxorem . . . colubris?] Juvenal, *Satires*, IV.28–29: "Postumus, are you . . . taking to yourself a wife? Tell me what Tisiphone, what snakes are driving you mad?"

101.29   Perkin's] Jacob Perkins (1766–1849) invented a machine for making nails.

104.35–36   'sleep that knits . . . care,'] Shakespeare, *Macbeth*, II.ii.34.

105.2–3   'how beautiful . . . feet'] Isaiah 52:7.

105.3–4   'The world . . . Saurin.] See *Eleven Select Sermons* (1806) and *Sermon on the Repentance of the Unchaste Woman* (1823), by French Protestant preacher Jacques Saurin (1677–1730).

106.7–8   Such a change . . . James I] See *The History of Great Britain* (1754–62), by David Hume (1711–1776).

108.34   "Nil fuit . . . Hor.] Horace, *Satires*, I.iii.18: "Never was a creature so inconsistent."

110.7   Rienzi] Cola di Rienzi (c. 1313–1354), Roman politician.

110.17–18   Bell . . . Celsus] Brothers Charles Bell (1774–1842) and John Bell (1763–1820), Scottish anatomists; John Hunter (1728–1793), Scottish physician; Aulus Cornelius Celsus (c. 25 BCE–c. 50 CE), Roman author on medicine.

110.22–23   'aliquid . . . infinitumque'] "Something great and immeasureable."

111.7   "Spare Fast . . . diet,"] From Milton's "Il Penseroso," line 56.

111.34–35   Mokannah's . . . veil] Hakim ibn-Otta, al Mokanna (d. 780), "The Veiled Prophet of Khorassan" in *Lalla-Rookh* (1817), by Thomas Moore (1779–1852).

114.6–7   'the glow . . . low'] See *Childe Harold's Pilgrimage*, IV.clxxxv.

114.11   'She is not dead, but sleepeth.'] See Matthew 9:24 and Luke 8:52.

114.33   worse than vain.] In the margin of his manuscript, Emerson wrote, "'Twas a custom of philos. to describe a perfect man in his age; now we'll try."

115.36   Philip]   Philip II (382–336 BCE), king of Macedon.

115.38–116.2   Misery . . . aged cramps]   See Shakespeare, *The Tempest*, II.ii.39–40; III.i.3–4; IV.i.258–60.

116.10   Obsta principiis]   "Resist at the start."

from NO. XV

119.4–6   "To be no more . . . eternity?"]   Milton, *Paradise Lost*, II.146–48.

120.19   Dies delet . . . opiniorum]   See Cicero, *De Natura Deorum*, II.2, 5: "The years obliterate the inventions of the imagination, but confirm the judgments of nature."

120.38   No thought . . . cheek]   Milton, *Paradise Lost*, V.384–85.

121.1   the Simple Cobler of Agawam]   See *The Simple Cobler of Aggawam in America* (1646–47), by Nathaniel Ward (1578–1652).

121.3   Sophroniscus]   Father of Socrates.

121.6   Porphyrogenet]   One born into royalty.

122.25   Jack Cade]   Leader of Kentish peasants in a 1450 rebellion against Henry VI.

124.2–4   The Mind . . . the same?]   See Milton, *Paradise Lost*, I.254–56.

124.8–9   "so forcible . . . our own."]   Milton, *Paradise Lost*, IX.955–56.

124.13   Men may be read . . . too much]   See Alexander Pope, *Moral Essays*, Epistle I, "Of the Knowledge and Characters of Men" (1734), line 10.

127.17   the new novels . . . Saratoga]   James Fenimore Cooper had recently published *The Spy* (1821), *The Pioneers* (1823), and *The Pilot: A Tale of the Sea* (1824). *A Peep at the Pilgrims in Sixteen Hundred Thirty-Six*, by Harriet Vaughan Cheney, and *Saratoga: A Tale of the Revolution*, by Eliza Lanesford Foster Cushing, were both published in 1824.

from JOURNAL 1826

131.11   "aliquid immensum &c"]   See note 110.22–23.

131.20   "Est deus . . . illo."]   Ovid, *Ars Amatoria*, III.549, and *Fasti*, VI.5: "There is a god within us. It is when he stirs that our bosom warms."

132.20–21   Pulchrum est . . . known something.]   The Latin sentence, by poet and dramatist Gnaeus Naevius (c. 264–201 BCE), may be translated: "It is glorious to be praised by one who has himself been praised." Newton's appears in *Memoirs of the Life, Writings, and Discoveries of Sir Isaac Newton* (1855), by David Brewster (1781–1868).

133.34   Erostratus the Ephesian incendiary]   Also known as Herostratus, a fame-seeking young man who set fire to the Temple of Artemis in Ephesus in 356 BCE.

134.36–37   "the unreached . . . despair."]   *Childe Harold's Pilgrimage*, IV.cxxii.

135.32–33   "A straw . . . stone."]   Jurist and scholar John Selden (1584–1654) is quoted in these words in an April 1825 *Edinburgh Review* review-essay on Thomas Roscoe's *The Italian Novelists*.

136.7–10   as Milton . . . uproar."]   See *Paradise Lost*, VI.667–68.

136.11–15   "The Translator . . . brought over."]   From "A Translater," by Samuel Butler (1612–1680), collected posthumously in *Characters* (1759).

137.5–6   The world's . . . scorned."]   From Edward Young's *Night Thoughts*.

137.26   Seth Robinson]   The name is canceled in Emerson's manuscript journal.

137.28–30   Dr Priestly . . . Life p. 49).]   See Joseph Priestly, *Memoirs of Dr. Joseph Priestly to the Year 1795* (1806–7).

137.32–34   Miranda . . . you."]   Shakespeare, *The Tempest*, III.i.18–19.

137.35   "Pelican island."]   James M. Montgomery, *The Pelican Island* (1827).

from JOURNAL 1826–1828

140.9–10   'Poison expels . . . pride.']   See Francis Bacon, *De Augmentis Scientiarum* ("On the Improvement of Science," 1623).

140.11–13   "The aenigma . . . De Stael]   See *Germany* (*De l'Allemagne*, 1813), by Germaine de Staël (1766–1817).

146.22–23   "They also . . . wait."]   The final line of Milton's Sonnet XIX, "When I Consider How My Light Is Spent" (1655).

148.1–2   the amazing Conference . . . Lebanon.]   The New Lebanon Conference of July 1827 was organized in an attempt to resolve differences among Presbyterian churches, but instead helped to confirm them.

148.3–4   the convicted ignorance . . . Symmes]   John Cleves Symmes Jr. (1779–1829) proposed in 1818 that the earth was hollow, and went on to lecture widely about his theory.

148.5–6   Lord Bacon . . . the wise]   See Bacon's essay "Of Boldness" (1625).

from MEMO ST. AUGUSTINE

153.16   "Quousque Catilina."]   See Cicero's *Oratio in Catalinam Prima,* which in translation begins "In heaven's name, Catiline, how long will you abuse our patience?"

from SERMONS AND JOURNAL

154.5–6   Inter se . . . Juvenal]   *Satires,* XV.164.

154.7   The world . . . Locke]   From *Some Thoughts Concerning Education* (1693) by John Locke.

154.10–11   A single house . . . Juv.]   *Satires,* XIII.159–60.

154.17–20   In few words . . . Bacon]   See Bacon's "Of Simulation and Dissimulation" (1625).

156.34   melancholy Jaques]   See Shakespeare's *As You Like It* (1599).

157.11–15   "I will be flesh . . . sufferance."]   Shakespeare, *Much Ado About Nothing,* V.i.34–38.

157.22   Est deus in nobis, &c.]   See note 131.20.

157.27–29   Locke . . . skill in a duel."]   See *Some Thoughts Concerning Education* (1693).

158.10–11   J'attends toujours . . . pour Jackson]   I still await the time when my friend shall raise the battle standard for Jackson.

158.12   "The face . . . Plut.]   See "Of Herodotus's Malice" in Plutarch's *Morals.*

158.13   The echo . . . Essays.]   See Cotton Mather's *Bonifacius: An Essay upon the Good* (1710): "For, as of old the poet observed, on mentioning the name of Plutarch, that the *Echo* answered *Philosophy.*"

158.14–15   I read things . . . said himself.]   See Montaigne's "Of the Education of Children" (1580).

158.15   Scougal]   Henry P. Scougal, author of *The Life of God in the Soul of Man* (1823).

160.28–29   Vivian Gray . . . Pelham]   Apart from the historical Beau Brummel (1778–1840), the "fashionists" Emerson lists are characters in novels: Grey in Benjamin Disraeli's *Vivian Grey* (1824), Etherington in Scott's *St. Ronan's Well* (1824), Dalgarno in Scott's *The Fortunes of Nigel* (1822), and Pelham in Edward Bulwer-Lytton's *Pelham* (1828).

from BLOTTING BOOK Y

163.4   Quantum sumus scimus.]   We are what we know; see Samuel Taylor Coleridge's *Aids to Reflection* (1825).

163.15   που στω   Place to stand on.

163.24   Omnia . . . mysterium]   A scholastic adage: everything ends up in a mystery.

163.33–34   the saying of Wotton . . . clothes."]   Sir Henry Wotton (1568–1639) in the *Apophthegms* ("Aphorisms," 1625) of Bacon.

163.35   "The Eternal . . . slaughter"]   See *Hamlet*, I.ii.131–32.

164.13–14   Mr Webster's . . . Hayne]   See the "Second Speech on Foot's Resolution," delivered in the Senate on January 26, 1830, by Daniel Webster (1782–1851), in response to a speech by Robert Young Hayne (1791–1839) on the same subject.

164.29–31   Johnson says . . . in vain."]   See Samuel Johnson's "Life of Pope" in *Lives of the Most Eminent English Poets* (1779–81).

164.34   to write a Life . . . as T.]   George Ticknor published his *Outlines of the Principal Events in the Life of General Lafayette* in 1825.

165.4–5   "he taught . . . authority"]   See Matthew 7:29.

165.27   Buckminster . . . F.m]   Joseph S. Buckminster (1784–1812), a Unitarian minister, and Francis W. P. Greenwood (1797–1843), pastor at King's Chapel in Boston. Emerson's manuscript journal may read "F.m", "F.ln", or "F.tn"; his handwriting is ambiguous.

166.12–13   this in Stewart]   See *The Philosophy of the Active and Moral Powers of Man* (1828), by Dugald Stewart (1753–1828).

167.3–6   Dr Clarke's . . . shops.]   See Edward D. Clarke, *Travels in Various Countries of Europe, Asia, and Africa* (1816–24).

from BLOTTING BOOK PSI

172.21   The Bride of Lammermoor]   1819 novel by Sir Walter Scott.

173.17   "High over the full toned Sea."]   From the poem "Song" (later retitled "The Sea-Fairies"), by Alfred, Lord Tennyson (1809–1892).

from BLOTTING BOOK III

175.6–7   "All Error . . . mean."]   See Samuel Johnson's contribution to *The Rambler*, no. 31, for July 3, 1750.

175.23–25   Guesses at Truth . . . Plato."]   See *Guesses at Truth* (1827) by Augustus William Hare and Julius Charles Hare.

177.5–7   Sampson . . . S.A.R.]   According to Edward Emerson, George Sampson, Barnes, and Mrs. Lee were among Emerson's Boston parishoners; Mellish Irving Motte was a Harvard classmate. Sarah Alden Ripley (1793–1867), a protégé of Emerson's aunt Mary Moody Emerson, was a longtime family friend.

177.21–23   Young's line . . . the right"] See Edward Young's *Night Thoughts*.

177.24–27   Shakespeare's "*The More* . . . αριστος &c] Coleridge quotes *Othello*, V.ii.130, in *The Friend* (1809–10, 1812; 1818). Bacon's Latin, from *De Augmentis Scientiarum*, may be translated: "The mind that chooses generous ends to aim at shall have not only the virtues but the deities to help." The Greek phrase, from the *Iliad*, XII.243, means "one omen is best" in fighting for country.

177.29–30   "non verba . . . audio"] "It is not words but thunder that I hear." Coleridge praises Wordsworth's poetry in similar terms in *The Friend*.

177.30–31   C.G.L.'s . . . J. A.'s] Charles Greely Loring's or John Quincy Adams's. Loring (1794–1867) was a prominent Boston lawyer.

179.21–28   my old gossip Montaigne . . . 261 Vol. I.] Emerson's page reference is to Charles Cotton's 1693 translation of Montaigne's *Essays*, which quotes all three Latin authors and translates them as follows: "When once a thing conceived is in the wit, / Words soon present themselves to utter it" (Horace, *De Arte Poetica*, V.311); "When things are once in mind, the words offer themselves readily" (Seneca, *Controversiae*, III, proem); "The things themselves force words to express them" (Cicero, *De Finibus*, III.5).

180.31   "The more falls . . . on."] From an untitled puzzle poem in "On Riddles" (1825), by Anna Laetitia Barbauld (1743–1825).

182.31–33   Coleridge's compliment . . . tonitrua."] See note 177.29–30.

183.3–4   the two lines . . . Vol. 3. p. 27] Citing Wordsworth's *Poetical Works* (1824), Emerson refers to two lines in "To the Reverend Dr. Wordsworth": "Than fabled Cytherea's zone / Glittering before the Thunderer's sight."

183.5   He calls . . . poet."] See "Poems on the Naming of Places," VI.80.

183.21   "& live . . . thing?"] From "The Violet," a poem by Ellen Tucker Emerson.

185.7–8   "Always be sticking . . . advice.] See Scott, *The Heart of Midlothian* (1818).

185.18–19   horresco referens] Virgil, *Aeneid*, II.204: "I shudder as I tell the tale."

187.14–15   "Regard not . . . Proverbs.] See Thomas Fielding's *Select Proverbs of All Nations* (1824).

188.16–17   "Say not then . . . Herbert] From "The Church-Porch" (1633), by George Herbert (1593–1633).

188.18–22   Hotspur's avowal? . . . a hair.] Shakespeare, *1 Henry IV*, III.i.135–38.

188.31   Cousin]   Victor Cousin, *Introduction à l'histoire de la Philosophie* (1828).

189.7–8   Due to J. P. . . . 25.09]   A record of a debt to Joseph Putnam, who cared for Emerson's brother Bulkeley.

from Q

191.4   my food . . . 14 ¼ oz]   In his entry for March 28, 1832, in another journal, *Scotland and England*, Emerson similarly notes the weight of his food, and mentions Luigi Cornaro (c. 1463–1566?), who "satisfied himself with 12 oz. solid food & 14 oz. wine per day. He passed his 100th year." See *An Abridgment of the Writings of Lewis Cornaro, a Nobleman of Venice, on Health and Long Life*, ed. Herman Daggett (1824), which Emerson cites.

191.13–14   Sir J. Mackintosh . . . mind.]   See *A General View of the Progress of Ethical Philosophy, Chiefly during the Seventeenth and Eighteenth Centuries* (1832).

191.16–17   Fontenelle . . . see it."]   See de Staël's *Germany*.

191.26   *Mutato . . . narratur.*]   Horace, *Satires*, I.i.69-70: "Change but the name and the tale is told of you."

192.2   "Truth never . . . a-being."]   A translation by Thomas Carlyle (1795–1881), in his essay "Characteristics" (1831), of a sentence attributed to Friedrich von Schiller.

196.26–27   "Eyes that the beam . . . new."]   From "Morning," the first poem in *The Christian Year* (1827), by English clergyman John Keble (1792–1866).

196.36   Montaigne Vol 3. p. 548]   Emerson cites Charles Cotton's 1693 translation of the *Essays*.

197.12–13   George Fox . . . Swedenborg]   See William Sewel, *The History of the Rise, Increase, and Progress of the Christian People Called Quakers* (1722), and Nathaniel Hobart's "Life of Swedenborg" in *New Jerusalem Magazine* (1828–29).

197.19–21   this paper on Corn . . . whoever he be.]   Carlyle's "Corn Law Rhymes" appeared in the *Edinburgh Review* in July 1832.

198.7–8   what is said . . . Restraint]   See "External Restraint," *New Jerusalem Magazine*, September 1832.

199.1–2   "The mighty tread . . . liberty."]   John Wilson (1785–1854, writing under his pseudonym "Christopher North"), "On Reading Mr. Clarkson's History of the Abolition of the Slave Trade" (1812).

199.3–4   "Wisdom & goodness . . . themselves"]   Shakespeare, *King Lear*, IV.ii.38–39.

199.5   "The true Philosophy . . . prophet"] From "Barrow and Newton," one of the *Imaginary Conversations* (1824–29; 1853) by Walter Savage
Landor (1775–1864).

199.14–200.6   I will not live . . . the Deity.] The poem is Emerson's; it
was later published in *Poems* (1847) as "Self-Reliance."

203.14–16   that fine promising passage . . . *benedictions.*"] See "Lines
composed a few miles above Tintern Abbey" (1800).

203.31–32   'Tout commence' . . . says.] See *Discours sur l'histoire uni-
verselle* (1679) by Jacques Bénigne Bossuet (1627–1704).

204.6–7   'Time' said friend . . . Roses.'] Carlyle's phrase, from a German proverb, appears in "German Literature in the Fourteenth and Fifteenth
Century" (1831).

206.28–29   "un tale le cui . . . p. 121] See Alessandro Manzoni, *I
Promessi Sposi* (1827): "one whose hands could often reach beyond the views
of others."

206.31–32   On bravely . . . ours.] The lines are Emerson's.

207.1–4   Il tempo . . . obbedire.] From *I Promessi Sposi*: "let the
weather do its own business, and I mine"; "we ought to aim rather at doing
well, than being well"; "a studious man, he loved neither to command nor
obey."

208.28–29   Architecture . . . frozen music] See de Staël's *Germany*.

210.18–19   Peter Hunt] Benjamin Peter Hunt (1808–1877), a notable
student in Emerson's school at Chelmsford, in 1825, and a subsequent
correspondent.

215.17–18   Tis the most difficult . . . gain.] See Wordsworth's *The Excursion* (1814), IV.138–39.

from SICILY

218.20–21   'The clouds . . . love.']   *The Excursion*, I. 225–27.

219.6–7   Dr Johnson . . . weather] See *The Idler* (1758–60), No. 11.

220.1   Scelta di Goldoni] See *Scelta di alcune commedie per uno di dilettanti della lingua Italiana* (1813), a student's edition of Carlo Goldoni (1707–
1793).

220.5   Perrin] See John Perrin, *The Elements of French and English Conversation* (1807).

220.9–10   "A prison . . . drowned."] See Boswell's *The Life of Samuel
Johnson* (1791).

220.23   Bigelow] Andrew Bigelow (1795–1877), author of *Travels in Malta and Sicily with Sketches of Gibraltar in 1827* (1831).

228.5   Mr H.] Silas P. Holbrook (c. 1796–1835?), a Boston merchant and travel writer.

228.23–24   "Indulgentia . . . defunctis."] "Indulgence, full, daily, perpetually, for the living and the dead."

230.34–35   "Urbem Syracusas elegerat."] "He selected the city of Syracuse."

231.31–33   "Opus est ingens . . . *Cicero.*] See Cicero, *Against Verres*, II.v.27: "An immense and splendid piece of work, carried out by kings and tyrants. The whole thing is a profound excavation in the rock. . . ."

from ITALY

239.4   the Viceroy's Palace] In Palermo, Sicily.

239.25   their sad malady] Tuberculosis.

240.27   Ποιημα] Poem.

242.17   mariolo.] Swindler, rascal.

242.26   "ladre"] Pickpocket, thief.

243.30–31   Mac Guffog . . . Alsatia] McGuffog, a jailor in Scott's *Guy Mannering* (1815) and Duke Jacob Hildebrod, Lord of Whitefriars (Alsatia), a thieves' refuge in Scott's *The Fortunes of Nigel* (1822).

244.29–30   Goethe says . . . Naples.'] See *Aus meinem Leben: Dichtung und Wahrheit* (1811–33).

251.15   'the wealthiest Roman's wife'] *Childe Harold's Pilgrimage*, IV.ciii.

252.22–23   "Traditor autem . . . tenete eum,"] See Matthew 26:48: "Now he that betrayed him gave them a sign, saying, Whomsoever I shall kiss, the same is he: hold him fast."

254.31–34   Alas the young men . . . *nice* place.] These two paragraphs have been canceled in Emerson's manuscript journal.

255.8   ποιημα πραξεως] "A poem of action."

from ITALY AND FRANCE

259.31–32   "dazzled & drunk with beauty."] *Childe Harold's Pilgrimage*, IV.l.

264.1   "Ne sutor"] "Ne sutor ultra crepidam": the cobbler should stick to his last.

264.1–2   the story . . . Congreve.] In his *Letters Concerning the English Nation* (1733) and elsewhere, Voltaire recounts Congreve's "one defect," after a visit to the dramatist: his deprecation of the literary profession. Congreve asked to be treated as a simple gentleman; Voltaire, in disgust, answered "had he been so unfortunate as to be a mere gentleman, I should never have come here to see him."

264.22–24   As Don Ferrante says . . . piu."] See *I Promessi Sposi*: "He is neither ancient nor modern; he is the philosopher, nothing more."

266.8   "Birbo . . . Machiavelli.] "A rascal, but profound."

266.28   G.A.S.] George A. Sampson; see note 177.5–7.

279.23   Pere Enfant & Le Templier] Barthélemy Prosper Enfantin (1796–1864), "Le Père Enfantin," a leader of the utopian socialist Saint-Simonian sect, and Bernard-Raymond Fabré-Palaprat (1773–1838), a former associate of the Abbe Chatel who revived the medieval "culte Templier" or Knights Templar.

from SCOTLAND AND ENGLAND

284.10   Nero's death . . . perio'.] See Suetonius, *De Vita Caesarum*: "What an artist the world is losing!"

284.30–31   Stuart's book . . . his labor.] See James Stuart, *Three Years in North America* (1833).

286.27   prophesied by De Lolme] Jean Louis De Lolme (c. 1740–1807), author of *The Constitution of England & an Account of the English Government* (1775).

from SEA 1833

290.25–26   Milton says . . . the man."] See Milton's Letter VII (September 23, 1637) to Charles Diodati.

291.24   B. J.] Ben Jonson.

from A

293.4   Ch' apporta . . . sera.] See Dante, *Paradiso*, canto 27, line 138: "Who brings morning and leaves evening."

293.5   Not of men . . . man.] Galatians 1:1.

293.6–8   May I "consult . . . listen"] See Wordsworth's sonnet "Not 'mid the World's vain objects that enslave" (1808).

293.18–19   Richard Reynolds] A Quaker ironmaster and philanthropist (1735–1816), born in Bristol.

293.20–23   The elder Scipio . . . ridicule."] For Scipio's phrase, see Montaigne's "Of Vanity" (1580); for Fontenelle, see de Staël's *Germany* (1813).

294.9–18   Reaumur's angles . . . Bell on the Hand.]   Emerson refers in this paragraph to René de Réaumur (1683–1757), a French entomologist and physicist; John Smeaton (1724–1792), an English civil engineer; John Dollond (1706–1761), a pioneering optical instrument maker; Jean-Pierre-François Guillot-Duhamel (1730–1816), French engineer; and Sir Charles Bell (1774–1842), author of *The Hand: Its Mechanism and Vital Endowments, As Evincing Design* (1833).

295.10–11   "Newton . . . really great."]   See "Éloge historique de M. le Marquis de la Place," in *Mémoires de l'institut* (1831), by Jean Baptiste Joseph Fourier (1768–1830).

295.12–15   Herbert . . . thee not."]   See Herbert's "Affliction" (1633).

296.4   Jeffery's . . . Playfair]   See "Notice and Character of Professor Playfair," by Francis Jeffrey, included in *The Works of John Playfair* (1822).

296.27–28   treatises . . . Edwards's]   See *An Inquiry into the Modern Prevailing Notions of the Freedom of the Will* (1754), by Jonathan Edwards (1703–1758).

296.31–32   "Men have . . . mind."]   See "The Life of Michael Angelo Buonaroti," in *Lives of Eminent Persons* (1833).

298.4–5   my admirable Persian . . . command]   Otanes, a Persian nobleman who in 522 BCE aided in the ascension of Darius the Great, is described in William Beloe's 1830 translation of Herodotus' *History* as "equally averse to govern or obey."

298.5–6   Don Ferrante . . . ubbedire.']   See note 207.1–4.

298.8–9   "Bel fin . . . Petrarch]   See Petrarch's Rima 140: "For he makes a fine end who dies loving well."

298.27   "l'amor che move . . . stelle."]   See the last line of Dante's *Paradiso* (XXXIII.145): "the love that moves the sun and the other stars."

299.1   Anakim]   A pre-Canaanite tribe of reputed giants.

299.15   Corinne]   *Corinne, ou l'Italie* (1807), a novel by de Staël.

300.2–3   Webster's speech . . . Wright]   Webster defended the United States Bank against a resolution by New York senator Silas Wright Jr. on January 31, 1834, in "On the Removal of the Deposits."

300.15   G.A.S]   George A. Sampson; see note 177.5–7.

301.7   B. R.]   Benjamin Rodman, a prominent New Bedford, Massachusetts, merchant and banker.

303.16–17   "The day . . . said Goethe.]   See Friedrich von Müller and Johann Daniel Falk, *Characteristics of Goethe*, tr. Sarah Austin (1833).

303.35–36   Goethe . . . every thing once;"]   See note 303.16–17.

305.11–17   the old verse . . . be."] From *The Brus*, a long narrative poem by John Barbour (c. 1320–1395).

307.10–11   "My Heritage . . . Time."] Lines originally from Goethe's *West-Östlicher Divan* (1819), translated variously in several publications by Carlyle.

308.30–31   " 'Tis the most . . . gain."] See Wordsworth's *The Excursion*, IV.139–40.

309.24–26   Goethe . . . not speak."] See *Tag und Jahres Hefte* (1803).

309.29   'Husks, Husks . . . words!] See William Sewel, *The History of the Rise, Increase and Progress of the Christian People Called Quakers* (1722).

313.20   Kneelands] Albert Kneeland (1774–1844), an atheist, led the First Society of Free Enquirers in Boston; he was charged with blasphemy in 1833 and was ultimately imprisoned.

314.21–24   Milton . . . distresses."] See "The Doctrine and Discipline of Divorce" (1643).

315.34   Mirabeau . . . Dumont] Swiss writer Pierre Étienne Louis Dumont (1759–1829) wrote and aided in the writing of many of the speeches of Honoré-Gabriel Riqueti, Comte de Mirabeau (1749–1791).

318.18   Swammerdam] Jan Swammerdam (1637–1680), Dutch natural historian and author of *Historia Insectorum Generalis* (1669).

319.5   truths, these] Emerson left a considerable blank space between "truths," and "these" in his manuscript journal.

319.16–18   A German . . . Nature."] See de Staël's *Germany*.

321.10–11   "Our first . . . coincide."] See Dugald Stewart, *Elements of the Philosophy of the Human Mind* (1792–1827).

321.15–16   Dr Darwin's work . . . Brown] Erasmus Darwin (1731–1802) was author of *Zoönomia* (1794–96) and other works (including book-length poems) which foreshadowed his grandson Charles Darwin's theories of evolution. Dr. James Currie (1756–1805) was an enthusiastic advocate of and contributor to the elder Darwin's work; Thomas Brown (1778–1820), author of *Observations on the Zoönomia of Erasmus Darwin* (1798), a critic.

322.6–7   et ce que . . . l'autre] "And what women say about one another."

322.13–14   Iarno] See *Wilhelm Meisters Lehrjahre* (*Wilhelm Meister's Apprenticeship*, 1795–96).

324.19–20   'visiting the spirits . . . *preach*.'] See I Peter 3:19.

326.20–22   "Lingered among . . . beautiful."] See *The Excursion*, VII.1014–16.

327.22–25   'When a daughter . . . good.'] See *Shi Jing* (c. 1000 BCE), a collection of Chinese poems predating any other known to be extant.

327.28–31   "Happy, happier . . . earth"] From "To Corinna at the Capitol" (1827), by Felicia Hemans (1793–1835).

327.34   smilax peduncularis] *Smilax herbacea* (smooth carrionflower), a malodorous perennial.

328.34   *Entsagen*] Renunciation.

329.19–20   'He knows you . . . sorrow.'] See note 322.13–14.

330.6–7   "Lincoln bell . . . alarum."] From Wordsworth's "Peter Bell: A Tale" (written 1798; published 1819).

331.19–20   Come dal fuoco . . . *M. Angelo B*] See Michaelangelo's sonnet "La vita del mie amor": "As from fire the heat cannot be separated, neither can beauty from the eternal."

331.21–35   The great Spirit . . . given us rum.] See William D. Williamson, *The History of the State of Maine* (1832).

332.9–17   "We look upon . . . can render."] See note 331.21–35.

332.21–22   "Indeed all . . . humanity."] From Edmund Burke's speech before the House of Commons on February 11, 1780, recommending "A Plan, for the Better Security of the Independence of Parliament, and the Economical Reformation of the Civil and Other Establishments."

333.9–10   "Hold thy tongue . . . clearer."] See Carlyle, *Sartor Resartus* (1833–34).

334.7–8   'It is no more . . . to me.] See Montaigne's "On the Education of Children" (1580).

334.34   Quam parva sapientia.] How little wisdom.

335.19–20   "Honorable age . . . Solomon] Wisdom of Solomon (Apocrypha) 4:8.

335.37–38   Prince Hal's . . . doublet] See *II Henry IV*, II.ii.15–20.

336.6–8   "I tax you . . . subscription &c."] See *King Lear*, III.ii.16–18.

336.11–12   "so difficult . . . mistakes."] See Carlyle's review of J. G. Lockhart's *The Life of Robert Burns*, in the *Edinburgh Review* (1828).

336.14   Maelzel machine] Johann Neopmuk Mälzel (1772–1838), who visited Boston in 1826 while on an American tour, invented a mechanical musical instrument able to imitate a military band and the Panharmonicon, which mimicked a chamber orchestra; he also exhibited a fraudulent chess-playing automaton.

336.36–38   Edward Emerson . . . Oration'?] Edward Bliss Emerson gave his masters' oration on "The Importance of Efforts and Institutions for the Diffusion of Knowledge" in August 1827.

337.26–27   a Connecticutt Sunday]   Connecticut's "blue laws" regulating Sunday business had been notably restrictive since the colonial era.

339.23–24   Miss Barbauld's line . . . faster on."]   See note 180.31.

340.29–30   Iarnos & Abbés]   See note 322.13–14.

341.15   Nec te . . . extra]   See Persius, *Satires*, I.7: "Look to no one outside yourself."

342.3–5   Carlyle's justification . . . clothes.]   See *Sartor Resartus*.

344.28   He knew . . . man.]   John 2:25.

344.32   Abernethy . . . Hunter book]   See John Abernethy, *An Enquiry into the Probability and Rationality of Mr. Hunter's Theory of Life* (1814).

346.20–23   "One first question . . . question."]   See Carlyle's "Count Cagliostro, in Two Flights" (1833).

346.32–33   "Whatever fortunes . . . not."]   See Friedrich von Schiller's *The Death of Wallenstein*, in Coleridge's translation (both 1800).

347.4   "Let them . . . Dirge.]   From Tennyson's "The Dirge" (1830).

347.17–18   "Hope the paramount . . . heart."]   See Wordsworth's "Poems dedicated to National Independence and Liberty," II. 33.

347.20   Julien Hall]   A Boston hall which hosted meetings of the Society of the Free Enquirers.

347.29–30   "Where every man . . . any man."]   See Coleridge's *On the Constitution of Church and State* (1829).

349.11–12   "—plainest taught . . . so."]   Milton, *Paradise Regained*, IV.361–62.

350.20   "Who injures . . . all."]   See Publilius Syrus, *Sententiae*, 164.

350.32–33   Sublimely . . . combatants."]   See Isaac Taylor, *Fanaticism* (1833).

351.22–25   Humboldt's . . . paps."]   See von Humboldt's *Personal Narrative of Travels to the Equinoctial Regions of the New Continent*.

355.26–28   Bacon's Primae . . . habent]   See "For Youth," in *De Augmentis Scientiarum*: "First thoughts and the contemplations of youth are from God."

355.29   aged grandsire]   Ezra Ripley, D.D. (1751–1841), pastor of the First Church of Boston and Emerson's step-grandfather.

355.35–36   "—if those great Doctors . . . *Donne*."] See "An Anatomy of the World: The First Anniversary" (1621).

356.27   stirps generosa seu historica] "A race noble or historical."

357.5   (V. Seckendorf p. 204)] See Veit Ludwig von Seckendorf, *Commentarius Historicus et Apologeticus de Lutheranismo* (1692).

357.18–21   "If the heavens . . . in the way" &c] See John Scott, *Luther and the Lutheran Reformation* (1832).

357.24–25   Landor says . . . sublime."] See "Duke de Richelieu, Sir Fire Coats, and Lady Glengrin," in *Imaginary Conversations*.

358.6–7   "How is the king . . . more just?"] See Plutarch's *Morals*.

358.29–31   Goethe says . . . clear."] See "Goethe's Posthumous Works" as reviewed in the 1834 *Foreign Quarterly Review*.

358.32–33   "The world . . . Coleridge] From *On the Constitution of Church and State*.

360.29   A Everett & J. Savage] Alexander Everett (1790–1847), a diplomat, and James Savage (1784–1873), a bank president and co-founder of the Boston Athenaeum.

361.2–3   "There shall be . . . earth."] See II Peter 3:13.

362.6–7   'Quia est superbus . . . contemptum sui.'] "Because he is an arrogant spirit and cannot endure being scorned."

362.9–11   "look I like . . . sharpness.] See *Colloquia Mensalia; or Dr. Martin Luther's Divine Discourses at His Table*, tr. H. Bell (1652).

362.22   the old man] See note 355.29.

363.9–10   "Epistola straminea.'] "Epistle of straw."

363.26   Neidrig] *Niedrig*, low.

364.1   "Not so Gammer,"] See the anonymous medieval comedy *Gammer Gurton's Needle* (1533).

365.14–15   Coleridge's defense . . . Enthusiasm] "Notes on Isaac Taylor's History of Enthusiasm," in *On the Constitution of Church and State* (1826).

366.15–16   Goethe's definition . . . laws & rules,"] See note 244.29–30.

367.13–15   his own epitaph . . . Μακεδων] "Hadst thou, Demosthenes, an outward force great as thy inward magnanimity, Greece should not wear the Macedonian yoke."

369.11   A little above . . . characters] See note 355.29.

369.18–19   Salmasius or Hedericus]   Scholars Claudius Salmasius (Claude de Saumaise, 1588–1653) or Benjamin Hedericus (1675–1748).

371.6–7   Wordsworth . . . our own."]   See "The Village Patriarch" (1829), by Ebenezer Elliott (1781–1849).

371.14   'another morn . . . noon.']   Milton, *Paradise Lost*, V.310–11.

372.15–17   'that every great . . . Utterance']   See Carlyle's "Luther's Psalm" (1831).

374.22   Bishop Bruno]   See "Bishop Bruno" (1798) by Robert Southey (1774–1843).

374.23–24   Actio agentis . . . Aristotle]   See Aristotle's *Physics*: "The action of the mover is nothing other than the releasing of a thing from potentiality to motion."

374.29–31   "Solo a quello . . . Michel Angelo]   See Michaelangelo's Sonnet VII. In Emerson's own translation of the sonnet, these lines are rendered: "only the hand secure and bold / which still obeys the mind."

376.6–7   'a strip of velvet . . . jewels']   See Edward Everett, *An Oration Pronounced at Cambridge* (1824).

376.21–22   "The light . . . M. Angelo]   See note 296.31–32.

377.18–19   "No matter . . . Johnson.]   See Boswell's *Life of Johnson*.

378.23–24   Where there is D E F . . . aunt.]   See J. W. Cunningham, *Sancho, or the Proverbialist* (1819).

379.27   'Rostopchin' times]   Fyodor Vasilievich Rostopchin (1763–1828), military governor of Moscow during the French invasion of 1812, is noted for the drastic measures he ordered in defense of the city.

380.9–11   Milton apprehended . . . lowliness?"]   See Milton's *Reason of Church Government Urged Against Prelaty* (1642).

380.14   "There's nothing . . . makes it so."]   Shakespeare, *Hamlet*, II.ii.249–50.

381.1–5   "Heathen . . . *Milton* vol 1 p 251]   See "An Apology for Smectymnuus" (1642).

381.24   "a pagan . . . outworn"]   From Wordsworth's sonnet "The world is too much with us" (1802–4; published 1807).

382.22   "Many *As'es* . . . charge"]   Shakespeare, *Hamlet*, V.ii.43.

384.37   our aged priest,]   See note 355.29.

from MAINE

388.1   Mr Loomis . . . die"]   The Rev. Harvey Loomis, of the First Congregational Society of Bangor; see Jeremiah 28:19.

from FRANCE AND ENGLAND

389.18   Bp Waterland]   Bishop Daniel Waterland (1683–1740) was author of *A Vindication of Christ's Divinity* (1719) and other works.

391.26   Wilson & Hogg]   John Wilson (1785–1854) author of *The Isle of Palms* (1812) and other works under the pseudonym "Christopher North," and James Hogg (1772–1835), Scottish poet and novelist.

from B

392.17   Taylor]   Edward Thompson Taylor (1793–1871), pastor of Seamen's Bethel on Ann Street in Boston.

394.17–18   Sir Henry . . . stretti.']   "An open countenance, closed thoughts": advice from Sir Henry Wotton (1568–1639) to John Milton, prior to a journey to Italy.

395.21–22   "passing sweet . . . memory"]   From Wordsworth's "Ode to Lycoris" (1817).

396.1–2   "Our very signboards . . . world."]   See Coleridge's *Biographia Literaria* (1817).

396.12–13   "When it shall . . . board."]   See *Lyric Odes to the Royal Academicians* (1782–83) by Peter Pindar, a pseudonym of satirist John Wolcot (1738–1819).

399.35–36   Taylor in the preface . . . Artevelde,"]   See Henry Taylor, *Philip van Artevelde; a Dramatic Romance* (1835).

401.14   C.]   Charles Emerson.

401.24–25   "Wrath . . . Landor.]   See Landor's *Imaginary Conversations.*

403.26–27   'Howitt's Seasons']   William Howitt, *The Book of the Seasons, or The Calendar of Nature* (1831).

404.29–30   "Already my opinion . . . adopted it."]   See Carlyle's "Characteristics" (1831).

405.1   "Nec te, &c."]   See note 341.15.

406.15–16   "Je défie un coeur . . . du mien,"]   "I defy a heart like yours to dare to think ill of mine."

407.28–29   "The limbs . . . Jean Paul]   See Jean Paul Friedrich Richter, *The Life of Quintus Fixlein* (*Leben des Quintus Fixlein*, 1796), as translated in Carlyle's *German Romance* (1827).

408.1   Man of Ross]   See Pope's *Moral Essays*, Epistle III, "Of the Use of Riches" (1733), which includes a tribute to the philanthropic John Kyrle (1637–1724) as "the Man of Ross."

408.21   Anschauung]   Perspective; intuition; sense-perception.

409.20–21   two tons, like St John's.]   As Martin Luther is reported to have said of the words in the fourth gospel; see note 362.9–11.

411.26   "My entrails . . . view."]   See Cotton's 1738 translation of *Montaigne's Essays*, and ultimately Persius, *Satires*, V.22.

412.20–21   "there's more . . . your philosophy."]   Shakespeare, *Hamlet*, I.v.166–67.

412.23–24   Nil magnificum . . . sapit.]   "He knows nothing rich, nothing noble."

412.26   Demonology . . . Report]   Scott, *Letters on Demonology and Witchcraft* (1830); John C. Colquhoun, tr., *Report of the Experiments on Animal Magnetism* (1833).

413.18–19   'He speaks . . . fast.']   See Psalm 33:9.

414.14–15   as Coleridge said . . . come.]   See *On the Constitution of Church and State*.

415.2–4   "The privates . . . *Gower*]   See *Confessio Amantis*, by John Gower (c. 1330–1408).

415.21   Lacon]   See Charles Caleb Colton, *Lacon; or, Many Things in Few Words* (1820–22).

416.2   Sampson Reed . . . things."]   See Reed's "Oration on Genius" (1821).

416.20–24   G. Fox . . . teacher."]   See *A Journal or Historical Account of the Life, Travels, Sufferings, Christian Experiences, and Labour of Love in the Work of the Ministry, of . . . George Fox* (1694).

416.25–28   "Three silent . . . *Coleridge*]   See *Specimens of the Table Talk of the Late Samuel Taylor Coleridge* (1835).

416.29   C.]   Charles Emerson.

417.3–6   "When I am . . . vol. 2, p. 241]   See Thomas Wharton, *The History of English Poetry, from the Close of the Eleventh to the Commencement of the Eighteenth Century* (1824).

417.25   Hedge]   Frederic Henry Hedge (1805–1890), a Unitarian minister and founding member of Hedge's Club, also known as the Transcendental Club.

418.9–11   The Saxon King . . . at another.]   See Sharon Turner, *The History of the Anglo-Saxons* (1807).

418.25–26   Peter Bulkeley]   Bulkeley (1583–1659), a founder of Concord, was an ancestor of Emerson's.

419.2   Norris first volume]   See John Norris, *An Essay Towards the Theory of the Ideal or Intelligible World* (1701–4).

419.29–30   "That inbred loyalty . . . livery."]   See *Religio Medici* (1643), by Sir Thomas Browne (1605–1682).

420.18   Gray & Barnard]   Frederick T. Gray and Charles F. Barnard, ordained as "ministers at large" in Boston in 1834.

420.22–23   Coleridge loses . . . Schelling]   In "Samuel Taylor Coleridge," published in 1834 in *Tait's Edinburgh Review*, Thomas De Quincey accuses Coleridge of "barefaced plagiarism" of the works of Friedrich von Schelling in *Biographia Literaria*.

421.13–15   Hooker . . . books."]   See "Of the Lawes of Ecclesiastical Politie" (1593), by Richard Hooker (1554–1600).

421.19–21   "I say three . . . Oegger]   See *Le Vraie Messie* (1829), by Guillaume Oegger (c. 1790–c. 1853), which Emerson was reading in a manuscript translation by Elizabeth Palmer Peabody, later published in part as *The True Messiah; or, The Old and New Testaments, Examined According to the Principles of the Language of Nature* (1842).

422.7–10   The Quarterly Review . . . grocer."]   See *The Quarterly Review* (April 1835) quoting *Marie, or l'Esclave aux États-Unis* (1835), by Gustave de Beaumont.

422.18   "Record of A School."]   *Record of a School; Exemplifying the General Principles of Spiritual Culture* (1835), by Elizabeth Palmer Peabody.

422.25   "My fortunes . . . Philip Van A.]   See note 399.35–36.

423.5   Mrs R.]   Sarah Alden Ripley; see note 177.5–7.

423.31   "Leave me . . . repose."]   From "The Descent of Odin. An Ode" (1768), by Thomas Gray (1716–1771).

424.8–9   the miserable babble . . . his crew]   See note 313.20.

425.7   S. J. May]   Samuel Joseph May (1797–1871), a Unitarian minister active in the abolitionist and women's rights movements.

426.20   Jacob Behme]   Jacob Boehme (c. 1575–1624), German Lutheran mystic and author of *Aurora: Die Morgenröte im Aufgang* (*Aurora: The Rising Dawn*, 1612).

427.2   the acct. . . . Russell.]   In *Nature* (1836), Emerson explains that on the way to his execution in 1683, William Russell, riding in an open coach, was observed by "the multitude" to have "liberty and virtue sitting by his side."

427.17–18   my respected friend] According to Edward Emerson, the friend was Samuel Hoar (1778–1856), a prominent lawyer and politician and co-founder of the Concord Academy.

430.4   Dr R.'s History.] Ezra Ripley, *A History of the Fight at Concord* (1832).

430.36   Talbot's] See Shakespeare's *1 Henry VI* (c. 1588–90).

431.1–2   Scott's line . . . eyes."] See *The Lady of the Lake*, VI.xxiv.18.

431.15–16   left half . . . bold] From Milton's "Il Penseroso," lines 109–10.

433.8–12   It is said . . . never nane.] From a collection of traditional Scottish ballads and songs published in 1806 as *Popular Ballads and Songs from Tradition, Manuscripts, and Scarce Editions*, by Robert Jamieson (c. 1780–1844).

434.34–35   "the times . . . men's souls"] See Thomas Paine's *The American Crisis*, No. 1 (1776).

435.14–18   "A writer . . . unfolds."] See de Staël's *The Influence of Literature upon Society* (1800).

437.32–38   "We cannot vex . . . Table Talk] See note 362.9–11; the Latin quotation combines phrases about the incarnation from the Nicene Creed and the last gospel, "And He was made man; and the Word was made flesh."

438.18–19   those new poems of Wordsworth] *Yarrow Revisited, and Other Poems* (1835).

440.7–11   Plotinus . . . appear."] See *Enneads*, V.v, as quoted in Coleridge's *Biographia Literaria*.

441.9–11   what Winckelmann . . . expression."] See Augustus William Schlegel, *A Course of Lectures on Dramatic Art and Literature*, tr. John Black (1833).

441.22–23   "The winds . . . navigators."] See Chapter 68 of *The History of the Decline and Fall of the Roman Empire* (1776–88), by Edward Gibbon (1737–1794).

442.34   amabilis insania] "Fond illusion."

444.3   "speak the truth . . . love"] See Ephesians 4:15.

445.17–20   What he said . . . laid flat—] See note 358.29–30.

445.28–29   So many joys . . . creatures.] A canceled sentence concludes this entry in Emerson's manuscript journal: "Other men wait upon their bowels most of the day."

446.24   Goethe's striving . . . Arch-plant.] See note 303.16–17.

446.25–33   the following sentence . . . Vol. 22, p. 245] Emerson cites
Goethe's 40-volume *Werke* (1828–1833); the sentence also appears in Goethe's
posthumously published *Maximen und Reflexionen* (*Maxims and Reflections*).

447.3   L.] Lidian.

450.36   Schemel] See "Peter Schlemihls Wundersame Geschichte"
("Peter Schlemihl's Amazing History") an 1814 tale by Adelbert von
Chamisso (1781–1838).

451.31   Instauratio] The *Instauratio Magna*, a systematic work projected
by Francis Bacon and completed in part by the publication of his *Novum Organum* ("A New Instrument," 1620) and *De Augmentis Scientiarum* (1623).

456.13   "Thy Will be done"] See Matthew 6:10.

456.23   E. H.] Elizabeth Hoar (1814–1878), daughter of Samuel Hoar
(see note 427.17–18). She was engaged to Emerson's brother Charles
Chauncy before his death, and later worked with Emerson on *The Dial*.

457.1–3   Edward Stabler . . . even Murat] The company Emerson lists
includes Edward Stabler (1769–1831), a Quaker preacher from Alexandria, Virginia, whose counsel impressed Emerson when they met in 1827; Peter Hunt,
a former student of Emerson's (see note 210.18–19); Sampson Reed (1800–
1880), whose 1821 Harvard master's oration ("Oration on Genius") Emerson
claimed as a lasting influence; "Tarbox," a Methodist laborer Emerson met
while working on an uncle's farm in 1825, from whom he reported he learned
that "men were always praying" and that "their prayers were answered";
Mary Rotch (1777–1848) a New Light Quaker and religious schismatic Emerson met in 1833; Jonathan M. Phillips (1778–1861), a family friend, philanthropist, and member of the Transcendental Club; A. Bronson Alcott (1799–
1888), a longtime friend whom Emerson once credited with "natural clearness
of spiritual sight"; and Achille Murat (1801–1847), a nephew of Napoleon
whose skepticism in matters of religion was revelatory to Emerson when the
two met in 1827.

458.11   'Be sure . . . you out,'] See Numbers 32:23.

458.36–39   the brave maxim . . . subsistence."] See *Institutes of Hindu
Law; or, The Ordinances of Menu*, tr. Sir William Jones (1825).

460.36–37   signs that mark . . . common men] See Shakespeare, *1
Henry IV*, III.i.40–42.

461.34–36   the saying . . . never lies] See Edward Moxon (1801–1858),
in *Letters, Conversations, and Recollections of S. T. Coleridge* (1836).

462.2   Dum tacet clamat.] "While he is silent he cries out."

462.14–18   "Wishing good . . . humanity."] See "Winter Evening's
Song" by Dutch poet Hendrik Tollens (1780–1856), as translated in John
Bowring, *Sketch of the Language and Literature of Holland* (1829).

462.22 "Why strew'st . . . spider?"] See Shakespeare, *Richard III*, I.iii.241.

462.33 non é nel . . . volgo,] See *The Prince* (1513) by Niccolò Machiavelli (1469–1527): "and in the world there are only the vulgar."

465.32–33 "the frail & weary . . . time."] See Michaelangelo's Sonnet LI.

466.20–21 Jesus says . . . follow me.] See Matthew 19:28–29; Mark 10:29–30; Luke 18:29–30.

467.30–31 "Let a man . . . oracle.] See note 416.2.

470.24–25 "Our part . . . Philisterei".] See Goethe's posthumously published *Maximen und Reflexionen* (*Maxims and Reflections*), no. 788.

471.19–21 the melancholy sentence . . . other man.] See Edward Biber, *Henry Pestalozzi and His Plan of Education* (1831).

472.32 a meeting . . . Ripley's house] The first meeting of Hedge's Club—referred to by others as the Transcendental Club—a changing and occasional group subsequently responsible for the founding of *The Dial* (1840–44). The friends Emerson lists—apart from A. Bronson Alcott, all Unitarian ministers—include Frederic Henry Hedge (1805–1890), Convers Francis (1795–1863), James Freeman Clarke (1810–1888), Orestes Brownson (1803–1876), and George Ripley (1802–1880).

473.1–2 Dr C. . . . Dr J. W.] William Ellery Channing (1780–1842), Jonathan M. Phillips (1778–1861), and James Walker (1794–1874); Phillips was a family friend (see note 457.1–3), Channing and Walker were Unitarian ministers.

475.17–18 "List, you may . . . drest!"] From Herbert's 1633 poems "Decay" and "Aaron."

475.29 Prester John] Ruler of a Christian kingdom imagined in medieval and subsequent legend to have existed in the Orient.

484.10–11 Madame de Stael . . . fable."] See *The Influence of Literature upon Society*.

486.31–32 "he, like a tree . . . set,"] See Psalm 1:3.

487.20–23 "Disasters do . . . at all."] See Wordsworth, "The Oak and the Broom. A Pastoral" (1800).

487.24–26 as Bartram saw . . . Mississippi] See *Travels Through North and South Carolina, Georgia, East and West Florida* (1792).

487.38 G.B.E.] George Barrell Emerson, Emerson's geometry tutor at Harvard, and a second cousin.

491.6–7 Humboldt's "volcanic . . . storms"] See note 351.22–25.

492.6   Arago] François Arago (1786–1853), French astronomer and mathematician.

493.14   Et tunc . . . imago.] Virgil, *Aeneid*, IV.654: "And now in majesty my shade shall pass beneath the earth."

493.22–29   Hic quiescunt . . . venerare.] "Here repose the bones and dust of Isaac Newton. If you wish to know who and of what sort he was, go away: but if from the name itself you know the rest, linger a little while and worship with thankful mind that famous moral authority of philosophy."

495.13   Edward Taylor] See note 392.17.

496.36   if you sleep] Left unfinished in Emerson's manuscript journal, this sentence is completed in the essay "Spiritual Laws" (1841): "you show it."

497.12–13   Thus when the gods . . . assigned] From Lucan's *Pharsalia* (61–65 CE), as translated by Nicholas Rowe (1674–1718).

498.31   Shackford] Charles Chauncy Shackford, a teacher at the Concord Academy.

498.33   Brownson's book] Orestes A. Brownson, *New Views of Christianity, Society, and the Church* (1836).

from C

501.7–8   prince Le Boo . . . mirror] See George Keate, *The History of Prince Lee Boo, Son of Abba Thulle, King of the Pelew Islands* (1823).

501.28–30   Wordsworth might write . . . of her own."] See "Ode: Intimations of Immortality" (1807).

502.3–8   in Bacon . . . Vol. 1. p. 89.] See *The Proficience and Advancement of Learning*, book II (1605).

503.32   "Res nolunt . . . administrari"] See Jonathan Swift, Letter XXXVII (To Lord Bolingbroke, April 5, 1729): "Things refuse to be ill administered."

504.23–24   the brag of Puck . . . minutes."] See Shakespeare, *A Midsummer Night's Dream*, II.i.175–76.

505.18–19   "do curtsey . . . reverence."] See Shakespeare, *The Merchant of Venice*, I.i.13–14.

506.20–21   "a quality of darkness"] See note 458.36–39.

506.28–29   "Come the ruggedest . . . Northumberland."] See Shakespeare, *2 Henry IV*, I.i.150–52.

508.16   Goethe in Eckermann] See Johann Peter Eckermann's *Conversations with Goethe* (1836–48).

511.31–37   letter from Tischbein . . . shuddering thoughts."] See *Briefe an Johann Heinrich Merck von Goethe, Herder, Wieland und andern bedeutenden Zeitgenossen* (1835).

512.20   geschlossenen pictures] Cabinet pictures. Emerson added the word "geschlossenen," literally meaning "closed," in pencil.

516.34   Beckendorf's keen eye] See Disraeli's *Vivian Grey* (1826–27).

517.35–36   Philina cracking nuts . . . Natalia.] See *Wilhelm Meisters Lehrjahre* (1795–96).

518.31   Ultimus Romanorum] Last of the Romans.

520.7   my Transcript] A notebook in which Emerson copied passages from his reading.

523.24–26   All this has my man done . . . the discourse] In a passage earlier in Journal *C* not included in the present volume, Emerson noted the shortcomings of a young preacher: "He has read books, & eaten & drunk; his cow calves; his bull genders; he smiles & suffers & loves. *Yet*, all this experience is still aloof from his intellect; he has not converted one jot of it all into wisdom."

527.22–23   'I have sinned . . . iniquity'] See Acts 8:23.

530.4–5   the New volume.] *Yarrow Revisited* (1835).

533.2–4   "the Phenix . . . good"] See *The Phenix; A Collection of Old and Rare Fragments* (1835).

534.30–33   Aristides . . . finished it."] See "The Life of Aristides" in Plutarch's *Lives*.

535.1   Deb] Probably Deborah Colesworthy, the Emersons' maid.

535.32   Peter Howe's employment] Peter Howe, a Concord neighbor, worked occasionally as the Emersons' gardener.

536.11–12   "Es ist alles . . . wirst."] A German proverb: "Everything is true, by which thou art made better."

536.14–15   I turned . . . *Byron*] See *Childe Harold's Pilgrimage*, III.xxx.270.

536.16   Chorley's Mrs Hemans] Henry F. Chorley, *Memorials of Mrs. Hemans* (1836).

538.18   Hannah H.] Hannah V. Haskins (Mrs. Augustus Parsons), who cared for Emerson's aunt Mary Moody Emerson.

538.19   fellen] Felon; small abcess or boil.

539.38   Miss Martineau's first volume] *Society in America* (1837), by Harriet Martineau (1802–1876).

546.19   "the foolish face of praise"]   See Pope's "Epistle to Dr. Arbuthnot" (written 1731–34; published 1735).

548.7–8   line written . . . Ennuyée]   See "To the Author of 'The Diary
of an Ennuyée,'" by Washington Allston (1799–1843), published posthumously in *Lectures on Art, and Poems* (1850).

549.31   like Cordelia]   See Shakespeare, *King Lear*, I.i.95–98.

550.36   Ferguson]   James Ferguson (1710–1776), Scottish astronomer.

558.3   "Solus docet . . . recipit."]   From Sermon XX of Scottish scholar
and prelate Robert Leighton (1611–1684): "He alone teaches who gives, and
he who receives, learns."

560.30   A.H.E.]   Alexander Hill Everett (1792–1847), author of *Europe;
or, a General Survey of the Present Situation of the Principal Powers* (1822) and
other works.

562.6   Myron's Cow . . . Goethe]   In his 1816 essay on "Myron's Cow,"
a sculpture by Myron of Eleutherae (fl. c. 480–440 BCE) now lost, Goethe
argues against a tradition in antiquity which praised the work for its realism.

563.1   Fuller]   Hiram Fuller (1815–1880) ran the Green Street School in
Providence following Alcott's methods.

564.11–12 "cry Havoc . . . war."]   Shakespeare, *Julius Caesar*, III.i.273.

567.7–9   the written verse . . . away."]   See Matthew 5:42.

567.28–29 Milton's expression . . . it smiled"]   From Milton's masque
Comus (1834).

571.17   the brave Lovejoy]   The Rev. Elijah P. Lovejoy (1802–1837), a Presbyterian minister and editor of an abolitionist newspaper in Alton, Illinois,
was attacked by an anti-abolitionist mob and shot on November 7, 1837.

578.31   this new book of Ripley's]   George Ripley, tr., *Philosophical Miscellanies. Translated from the French of Cousin, Jouffroy, and B. Constant*
(1838).

578.32   Jack Cade way]   See note 122.25.

580.19–20 the voice which said . . . food."]   See William Sewel, *The
History of the Rise, Increase, and Progress of the Christian People Called
Quakers* (1823).

580.28–29 Cor purgat oratio.]   Prayer purifies the heart.

584.9–10   Belknap or Williamson . . . dead annals]   See Jeremy Belknap, *History of New Hampshire* (1784–92) and William Durkee Williamson,
History of the State of Maine (1832).

584.32–33 "In the afternoon . . . afternoon."]   From Tennyson's "The
Lotos-Eaters" (1832).

592.4   the letter to V. B.]   Emerson agreed to write a letter to President Van Buren after the Concord town meeting of April 23; it was published in the *Daily National Intelligencer* on May 14.

593.7   J. Very]   Jones Very (1813–1880), a clergyman and poet; Emerson aided in the publication of his *Essays and Poems* in 1839.

593.25   B. F.]   Barzillai Frost (1804–1858), a minister at the First Church in Concord.

594.12–13   Precipitandus . . . spiritus.]   From the *Satyricon* of Petronius Arbiter (c. 27–66): "The free spirit of genius must plunge headlong."

595.37   Walter Scott . . . savage."]   In a letter of January 25, 1820, to Willie Scott, published in John Gibson Lockhart, *Memoirs of the Life of Sir Walter Scott* (1837): "all the kind are savage at night."

597.31   Kuhleborn]   A water-spirit in the novella *Undine* (1811) by Friedrich de la Motte Fouqué (1777–1843).

598.3   flebile]   Of style: plaintive, doleful.

600.1   Miss Sedgwick . . . Hyde]   See *Live and Let Live; or, Domestic Service Illustrated* (1837), by Catherine Maria Sedgwick (1789–1867).

603.1–7   It was observed . . . agreed upon."]   See *Mémorial de Sainte Hélène: Journal of the Private Life and Conversations of the Emperor Napoleon at Saint Helena* (1823), by Emanuel, comte de Las Cases (1766–1842).

from D

605.2   S.M.F.]   Sarah Margaret Fuller.

608.19   C. S.]   Caroline Sturgis.

610.32–33   Hawthorne's . . . seashore]   A short story first published in January 1838.

612.29–33   "May makes . . . Edwards]   From "M Edwardes May," in *The Paradise of Dainty Devises* (1576), compiled by Richard Edwards.

618.21   G.B.E.]   George Barrell Emerson; see note 487.38.

621.16   Rylston Doe]   See Wordsworth's *The White Doe of Rylstone; or, The Fate of the Nortons* (1807–8).

621.30–31   that worthy ancient king . . . pleasure]   Xerxes.

622.19   "Naturam expellas . . . recurret."]   Horace, *Epistles*, I.x.24: "You may drive out Nature with a pitchfork, yet she will ever hurry back."

623.6   S. Ward]   Samuel Gray Ward (1817–1907), a financier and art patron.

623.28   "the terror . . . eye"]   See "The Progress of Poesy" (1757), by Thomas Gray.

626.35–36   "A man & his wife . . . son."]   See note 458.36–39.

628.25   Norton]   Andrews Norton (1786–1853), a professor at the Harvard Divinity School who had called Emerson's 1838 "Divinity School Address" a "great offence" and an "incoherent rhapsody."

630.18   Peele Dabney]   Jonathan Peele Dabney (1793–1868), an 1811 Harvard graduate and editor of *A Selection of Hymns and Psalms for Social and Private Worship* (1824) and *Annotations on the New Testament* (1829).

637.38–39   Shall find . . . mossy cell.]   See Milton's "Il Penseroso," line 169.

638.7–8   John Lewis Russell]   Russell (1808–1873) was a Unitarian minister who in 1833 became Professor of Botany and Horticultural Physiology at the Massachusetts Horticultural Society.

638.20   S.M.F.]   Sarah Margaret Fuller.

640.7–8   that Sapphic . . . Every Dog &c.]   See Thomas Fielding, *Select Proverbs of All Nations* (1824): "Every dog has his day, and every man his hour."

640.12   M. R.]   Mary Ripley, daughter of Sarah & Samuel Ripley.

643.30   Milton calls . . . Rome."]   See *Paradise Lost*, IX.510.

646.36   A. N.]   Andrews Norton; see note 628.20.

648.26–27   "To the persevering . . . swift."]   See "The Oracles of Zoroaster," in *The Phenix; a Collection of Old and Rare Fragments* (1835).

649.30   Asia]   Lidian Emerson.

650.17   E. P.]   Edward Palmer (1802–1886), an itinerant idealist preacher whose *Letter to Those Who Think* (1840) was reviewed in *The Dial*.

653.1   Mr Graham! . . . pumpkins]   Sylvester Graham (1794–1851), dietary reformer.

653.16   Mrs Ripley]   Sarah Alden Ripley; see note 177.5–7.

653.31   J. V.]   Jones Very; see note 593.5.

654.32–33   The Correspondence . . . Stevenson]   An exchange of letters between Andrew Stevenson (1784–1857), a Virginian and U.S. Minister to Great Britain, and Daniel O'Connell (1775–1847), an Irish political leader in the House of Commons, appeared in British and American newspapers after the latter called the former a "slave-breeder" in a speech on August 1, 1838.

656.2   our brave saint]   Jones Very; see note 593.7.

656.28   "Rem acu tetigisti."]   Literally, "you have touched the thing with a needle" (i.e. "you've hit the nail on the head").

659.7–9   "It is proverbial . . . Coleridge]   See "Lear," in *The Literary Remains of Samuel Taylor Coleridge* (1836–39).

660.6–8   "Spirits . . . to eternity."]   See Byron's 1822 closet drama *Cain*, I.i.533–34.

663.25–26   'Unknown God.']   See Acts 17:23.

663.31–34   He'd harpit . . . never none]   See note 433.8–12.

664.4   another Richmond]   See Shakespeare, *Richard III*, V.iv.10: "I think there be six Richmonds in the field."

666.33–34   Byron says . . . swore."]   See *The Island* (1823), III.v.

667.2   Life of Brant]   William L. Stone, *Life of Joseph Brant, Thayendanega: Including the Indian Wars of the American Revolution* (1838).

668.1   Nathan the Wise]   See *Nathan the Wise* (1779), a play by Gotthold Ephraim Lessing (1729–1781).

668.10–11   Their peace . . . aspect slept;]   Emerson adapted these lines for his poem "In Memoriam," for his brother Edward Bliss Emerson, who died in 1834.

670.24   "Ne te . . . extra."]   See note 341.15.

673.34   Pereant qui . . . dixerunt.]   See Aelius Donatus in St. Jerome's "Commentary on Ecclesiastes": "May they perish who said our good things before us."

676.34   Hedge]   See note 417.25.

680.23   G.P.B.]   George Partridge Bradford (1807–1890), a former Divinity School classmate of Emerson's, and a Concord schoolteacher.

681.15   Dr Follen . . . Graeter]   The foreigners Emerson refers to include Charles T. C. Follen, author of *A Practical Grammar of the German Language* (1828); Piero Maroncelli, of *Additions to "My Prisons, Memoirs of Silvio Pellico"* (1836); Frances Lieber, editor of the *Encyclopaedia Americana*; and Francis Graeter, author of the novel *Mary's Journey* (1829).

682.2–4   Milton's . . . evil tongues"]   See *Paradise Lost*, VII.25–26.

682.5–7   death of Sisera . . . ghost;"]   See Judges 5:27.

683.3–6   As Caratach . . . best Gods."]   See *Bonduca* (c. 1613), a tragedy by John Fletcher (1579–1625).

683.29–30   the motto . . . world"?]   See note 536.16.

684.26–28   "What we love . . . Schiller said]   See the poem "Love and Desire" by Friedrich von Schiller.

688.29   the Polish Jews]   Allston's exhibition included three works entitled "A Sketch of a Polish Jew."

689.6   'barbaric pearl & gold']   See *Paradise Lost*, II.4.

689.25–26   "What, old mole! . . . fast?"] See *Hamlet*, I.v.162.

698.22   W. C.] Probably William Henry Channing (1810–1884), philosopher and Unitarian clergyman, nephew of William Ellery Channing ("Dr. Channing"; see note 76.32).

698.33   S. R.] Samuel Ripley.

700.6   Anna Barker] A New Orleans socialite (1813–1900) and friend of Margaret Fuller.

from E

703.12   T. & C.] Thoreau and William Ellery Channing (1818–1901), the poet, nephew of theologian William Ellery Channing (see note 76.33).

705.16–17   "To him that hath . . . taken."] See Matthew 25:29, Mark 4:25, Luke 8:18 and 19:26.

710.9–10   "May I gaze . . . faileth me!"] See Landor's *Citation and Examination of William Shakespeare Touching Deer-Stealing* (1834).

715.16   "the terrors of the beak"] See note 623.28.

717.12   W's] Samuel Gray Ward's. See note 623.6.

723.9   L.C.B.] Lucy C. Brown, one of Lidian's sisters.

725.14   Heeren . . . 'Greece,'] Arnold H.L. Heeren, *Reflections on the Politics of Ancient Greece* (1824).

726.31–32   Patimur . . . Manes!] See Virgil, *Aeneid*, VI.743: "We bear each one our own destiny."

727.35–36   "Crimen quos . . . aequat."] Lucan, *Pharsalia*, V.290: "Crime makes equal those whom it taints."

729.30   crush . . . wine] See Milton's *Comus*, line 47.

731.30   Guy] See Emerson's poem "Guy" (1847).

733.16–18   "All those things . . . gate."] See Esther 5:13.

733.19–22   "The valiant warrior . . . toiled."] See Shakespeare, Sonnet XXV, lines 9–12.

742.23–24   "I & my flowers . . . well."] See William Ellery Channing's "Sonnet V," later published in *Poems* (1843).

742.25   At Bartol's, our Club] The Transcendental Club met occasionally at the home of Cyrus Augustus Bartol (1813–1900), a Unitarian clergyman.

743.10   the Amore Greco] One of two "Loves"—the other by Raphael—included in Samuel Gray Ward's portfolio of engravings; Emerson was introduced to Ward's collection in August 1838 by Margaret Fuller.

745.8 "rammed with life."] See Ben Jonson's play *The Poetaster* (1602).

748.7 Hans Sachs] German meistersinger and dramatist (1494–1576).

749.12 Scaliger] Joseph Justus Scaliger (1540–1609), French Protestant scholar and religious leader.

752.1–2 I have written above] Emerson refers to a paragraph in Journal *E* not included in the present volume. It reads: "I owe to Landor's Pericles & Aspasia the feeling that life is needlesly long; for every moment of a hero so raises & cheers us that a twelvemonth were an age. 'In the heat of the battle Pericles smiled on me & passed on to another detachment.'"

752.3–5 "In the large . . . recovery,"] See John Keats's abandoned long poem *Hyperion* (1819), I.51, and Milton's *Areopagitica*.

753.2 Otis . . . Anna Ward] Harrison Gray Otis and Anna Barker Ward.

753.11–15 "Sunshine was . . . p. 13.] Emerson cites Goethe's *Werke* (1828–1833); see also *Noten und Abhandlungen zu besserem Verständnis des West-östlichen Divans* (1828).

756.22 S. C.] Sarah Freeman Clarke (1808–1896), a former pupil of Emerson's and a friend of Margaret Fuller.

756.36 Retsch] Friedrich August Moritz Retzsch (1779–1857), painter and engraver of book illustrations.

760.12 naked Derar] See Simon Ockley, *The History of the Saracens* (1718).

765.35–36 "Woe to . . . *Middleton*] See *The Phoenix* (1603–4), I.iv.218, by Thomas Middleton (1580–1627).

766.35 "necessity is in . . . soul."] From Plotinus' *Enneads*, as translated by Thomas Taylor in *Select Works of Plotinus* (1817).

768.10–11 Bancroft . . . Indian Families"] See "Synopsis of the Tribes East of the Mississippi," in George Bancroft's *History of the United States*, vol. 3 (1840).

773.22 Dr Nichol & in Saint Simon] See *Views of the Architecture of Heaven* (1840), by John Pringle Nichol (1804–1859), and the posthumously published *Mémoires* of Louis de Rouvroi, Duc de Saint-Simon (1675–1755).

783.36 Shelleys] The poet Percy Bysshe Shelley (1792–1822) was noted for his opposition to the institution of marriage.

785.26 El. H.] Elizabeth Hoar; see note 456.23.

785.35 C.] John Perkins Cushing (1787–1862), a Boston philanthropist.

791.29 L.] Charles Lane (1800?–1870), an English reformer who established a utopian community, Fruitlands, with Bronson Alcott in the summer of 1843.

from F2

793.4   January 11, 1841] Subsequent entries in Journal F2 are dated
between February 1840 and March 1841; Emerson may have added this initial
entry at a later date, or "1841" may have been a slip of the pen for 1840.

798.14   Theanor] A Pythagorean philosopher; see Plutarch's *Morals.*

798.29   the Prometheus Chained] A Greek tragedy attributed in antiquity to Aeschylus but now often considered the work of a writer active as late
as 415 BCE.

799.34   A. B.] Anna Barker.

799.36   C.] Caroline Sturgis.

800.8   M.] Margaret Fuller.

801.29–31   As Palmer remarked . . . the poor!] See note 650.17.

802.3   "He can toil . . . Raleigh.] See Thomas Peregrine Courtenay,
"Robert Cecil, Earl of Salisbury," in *Cabinet Cyclopaedia: Lives of Eminent
British Statesmen*, vol. V (1836).

803.17   Osman] A name Emerson uses variously to refer to himself, to an
ideal man or poet, or sometimes to Jones Very.

Biographical Notes

AMOS BRONSON ALCOTT (1799–1888), the son of poor Connecticut farmers, was largely self-educated. He began working in a local clock factory at age 14, and left home at 17, earning a living as an itinerant peddler in the Carolinas and Virginia. He returned to Connecticut in 1823, and accepted several teaching positions. Soon after his marriage to Abigail May in 1830, he began to set up experimental schools, doing away with rote learning and corporal punishment. The most successful of these, his Temple School (where he was assisted by Elizabeth Peabody and Margaret Fuller), operated from 1835 to 1839; it closed amid controversies over his heretical methods and his admission of an African-American girl. Emerson met Alcott in 1835 and soon after called him "the most extraordinary man, and the highest genius of the time." After the failure of his experiment in communal living, Fruitlands, in 1844, Alcott and his family barely managed to make ends meet (in the mid-1850s, Emerson helped to raise money from local citizens to help support them). These circumstances were relieved in 1859, with his appointment as Concord's superintendent of schools. Though Emerson was sometimes irritated by Alcott's egotism (he "never loses sight of his own personality," he noted), they remained close friends throughout their lives; the day Emerson died, Bronson's daughter Louisa May Alcott wrote in her journal that Emerson had been "the nearest and dearest Friend father has ever had."

GEORGE PARTRIDGE BRADFORD (1807–1890), the youngest of several children of Captain Gamaliel Bradford and Elizabeth Hickling, was raised largely by his older sister, Sarah. In 1818, she married Emerson's uncle, the Rev. Samuel Ripley, of Waltham, Massachusetts, and he moved with her to Waltham. Bradford graduated from Harvard in 1825 and the Divinity School three years later. Forgoing the pulpit (Andrews Norton, a Divinity School professor, told him that one of his sermons was "marked by the absence of every qualification a good sermon ought to have"), he earned a living as a teacher in Plymouth. He was one of the original residents of Brook Farm, where he was assigned the task, with Nathaniel Hawthorne, of milking the cows. When the farm was converted into a Fourierist phalanx, Bradford confessed he was too much a "genuine descendant of the old Puritans" to participate fully in the Brook Farm experiment; he returned to Plymouth, where he worked briefly as a market gardener before returning to teaching. Emerson praised Bradford's "beautiful conscience," and wrote in 1840: "I can better converse with G. B. than with any other."

THOMAS CARLYLE (1795–1881) first attracted Emerson's attention as the anonymous writer of "Germanick new-light" essays in English periodicals; "The State of German Literature" (1827), "Signs of the Times" (1829), and "Characteristics" (1831) so struck him that, after he discovered the author's identity just prior to his 1833 European tour, he went out of his way to visit him at his farm, Craigenputtock, in Scotland. The two men favorably impressed each other. Carlyle, writing to John Stuart Mill, praised Emerson as "a most gentle, recommendable, amiable, wholehearted man." Emerson wrote of Carlyle: "He talks finely, seems to love the broad Scotch, & I loved him very much, at once." Thereafter, the pair began what would become a 38-year correspondence. Beginning in 1835, Emerson helped gather subscriptions for an American edition of *Sartor Resartus*, and wrote a preface. Carlyle had been unable to find an English publisher for his unconventional book; in 1836, Emerson proudly sent him the first edition, printed in Boston. He later served as Carlyle's American literary agent, reading proofs and sending royalty payments. The friendship grew strained after Emerson visited Carlyle during his 1848 lecture tour of England. In his journal, he wrote: "Carlyle is no idealist in opinions, but a protectionist in political economy, aristocrat in politics, epicure in diet, goes for murder, money, punishment by death, slavery, & all the pretty abominations, tempering them with epigrams. His seal holds a griffin with the word, *Humiliate*." In spite of increasing philosophical and political differences, the two continued to correspond and to follow each other's careers. In 1859, the year after its publication, Emerson described Carlyle's *History of Frederick the Great* in his journal as "infinitely the wittiest book that was ever written." A few days before his death, having lost much of his memory, he is reported to have noticed a photograph of Carlyle in his study and to have remarked: "That is my man, my good man!"

WILLIAM ELLERY CHANNING (1780–1842)—sometimes referred to as "Dr. Channing," to distinguish him from his nephew and namesake, poet William Ellery Channing (1817–1901)—was born into a prominent Rhode Island Federalist family and raised by his maternal grandfather, William Ellery, a signer of the Declaration of Independence, after the premature death of his father. He graduated from Harvard in 1798. After spending a miserable year as a tutor in Richmond, Virginia, Channing—now a determined opponent of slavery —returned North, and accepted the ministry of the Federal Street

Church in Boston. Over the coming years, in his essays and sermons, he would outline the central tenets of American Unitarianism. In 1816, he helped found Harvard's Divinity School; in 1820, he organized the Berry Street Conference, a forerunner of the American Unitarian Association. Though reclusive and reserved, Channing exercised a profound influence on the younger generation of Unitarians. Emerson called him "our Bishop" and claimed him, along with his aunt Mary Moody Emerson, as one of his principal early influences.

WILLIAM ELLERY CHANNING (1817–1901)—often known as "Ellery Channing" to distinguish him from his more famous uncle, the prominent Unitarian—was sent to live with relatives after his mother died when he was five. He entered Harvard in the fall of 1834, but dropped out three months later, feeling its attendance regulations constrained his freedom. He tried homesteading in Illinois for a few months, but soon moved to Cincinnati, where he met and married Ellen Fuller, Margaret's sister. In the summer of 1842, Channing came to Concord and met Emerson for the first time; the following spring, his wife joined him and they moved into Red Lodge, the cottage next to Emerson's garden. A frequent contributor of verse to *The Dial*, he published his *Poems* in 1843. (Edgar Allan Poe wrote a lacerating review: Channing's poems were "full of all kinds of mistakes, of which the most important is that of their having been written at all.") Never a consistent breadwinner, Channing often left his family—ultimately including five children—to wander ("whim, thy name is Channing," his friend Bronson Alcott would write in his journal). He worked at the *Tribune* in New York from November 1844 to March 1845, and in 1846 traveled in Europe. Returning to Concord, he spent much of his time rambling through the woods with Alcott, Emerson, and (most frequently) Thoreau. In 1855, he attempted to make amends with his family (his wife had gone to live with her sister-in-law Mary and her husband, Thomas W. Higginson, two years earlier) but Ellen Fuller died that same year; relatives agreed to take care of his children. After the death of Thoreau, his closest friend, he helped, along with Thoreau's sister, Sophie, to prepare Thoreau's *The Maine Woods* (1864) and *Cape Cod* (1865) for publication; in 1873, Channing's biography, *Thoreau, the Poet-Naturalist*, was published. Channing spent his last years living off the income from a trust fund, reading and writing, and dining with the Emersons on Sundays.

WILLIAM HENRY CHANNING (1810–1884), was, like Ellery Channing, a nephew of the theologian William Ellery Channing, who oversaw his education. He graduated from Harvard in 1829 and the Harvard Divinity School in 1833. After serving as the Unitarian minister of the First Congregational Church of Cincinnati, from 1838 to 1841, he moved to New York and became involved in a variety of social reform projects, serving as the head of congregations informed by Christian and Fourierist ideas. He edited two periodicals, *The Present* (1840) and *The Spirit of the Age* (1849–50), while contributing to the Fourierist journals *The Phalanx* and *The Harbinger*. He also lived briefly at Brook Farm in 1846 and in 1850 at the North American Phalanx, a Fourierist community in New Jersey. In 1851 he co-edited, along with Emerson and James Freeman Clarke, the *Memoirs of Margaret Fuller Ossoli*. After ministering to a Unitarian congregation in Rochester, New York, he accepted an appointment to a church in England. Channing returned to America on the outbreak of the Civil War, eventually becoming chaplain to the House of Representatives. Unable to find work after the war, he returned to England where he would live for the rest of his life, coming back to America occasionally for lecture tours.

CHARLES CHAUNCY EMERSON (1808–1836), the youngest of the Emerson brothers, was thought by many during his lifetime—including his aunt Mary Moody—to be the most promising. After graduating from Harvard, where he won the Bowdoin Prize his sophomore year, he studied law and in 1832 took a Harvard law degree. Daniel Webster was impressed enough by his performance to exclaim, when Charles was debating where he should practice, "Let him settle anywhere! . . . the clients will throng after him." Around this time he fell in love with Elizabeth Hoar, the daughter of Samuel Hoar, in whose Concord office he beginning his legal career; a wedding date was set for September 1836. Five months before the scheduled date, Charles died of tuberculosis at his brother William's house in Staten Island. Emerson wrote to his wife, Lidian, soon after: "I can never bring you back my noble friend who was my ornament my wisdom & my pride . . . You must be content henceforth with only a piece of your husband."

EDITH EMERSON (1841–1929), the third child of Emerson and Lidian, married William Hathaway Forbes, a Civil War veteran, in 1865. Forbes eventually became president of Bell Telephone; they raised seven children. She assisted her father in editing his 1874 poetry anthology *Parnassus*, and in 1916 herself edited *Favorites of a Nursery School Seventy Years Ago*.

EDWARD BLISS EMERSON (1805–1834), born two years after his brother Ralph Waldo, excelled at Harvard, where he delivered a commencement oration attended by the Marquis de Lafayette. After his graduation, he entered the law office of Daniel Webster, supplementing his income by teaching. All the while, his health was gradually deteriorating, a year abroad failed to improve his condition. "Edward hardly seems to have the strength necessary for the race he ought to run," wrote brother William. In the spring of 1828, he had a complete mental breakdown and was committed to the McLean Asylum—a "constitutional calamity," Emerson wrote, that "has buried at once so many towering hopes." He eventually recovered his sanity, sailed for Puerto Rico, and got a job as a clerk at the American consulate. He never fully recovered his health, however, and soon died of tuberculosis.

EDWARD WALDO EMERSON (1844–1930), the fourth and last child of Emerson and Lidian, graduated from Harvard in 1866 and Harvard Medical School in 1874. He practiced medicine in Concord from 1874 to 1882. After his father's death, he spent the rest of his life painting, writing, and editing his father's works. His 10-volume *Journals of Ralph Waldo Emerson* was published between 1909 and 1914.

ELLEN TUCKER EMERSON (1811–1831) was raised by her mother and stepfather in Concord, New Hampshire; her father, who owned a rope factory, died prematurely. She met Emerson on the day after Christmas, 1827, through his Harvard classmate Edward Kent, her stepbrother. By the end of the next year they were engaged and were married in September 1829, six months after Emerson was ordained as minister at the Second Church in Boston. They moved into a house in Chardon Street in Boston, and though she was consumptive, lived very happily together. She died of tuberculosis in February 1831. The income from her estate allowed Emerson a measure of financial independence in the years following her death.

ELLEN TUCKER EMERSON (1839–1909) was Emerson and Lidian's second child. She lived a quiet and religious life, assisting her father. Her *Life of Lidian Jackson Emerson* was published posthumously in 1980, followed by *The Letters of Ellen Tucker Emerson*, in two volumes, in 1982.

LIDIAN JACKSON EMERSON (1802–1892), a native of Plymouth, Massachusetts, saw Emerson for the first time in Boston in 1834, during a visit to her sister; after hearing him preach, she told a friend: "that man is certainly my predestined husband." She met him later the same year and they married the next, soon moving into their new Concord home, Bush, where they would spend the rest of their lives. Although an active and sympathetic participant in Emerson's social life (she regularly attended Margaret Fuller's "Conversations," and Emerson's friend Sarah Freeman Clarke called her a "searing transcendentalist"), Lidian was never fully content in Concord. Ellen Emerson, in her biography of her mother, wrote: "In her fifty-seven years of life in Concord she had never taken root there, she was always a sojourner," and that from 40 to 70 "sadness was the ground color of her life."

MARY MOODY EMERSON (1774–1863), Emerson's deeply pious, sharply satirical, and always unconventional paternal aunt, was one of his most formative influences. She was born in Concord to the Rev. William Emerson and Phebe (Bliss) Emerson, but lived after her father's death in 1776 and her mother's remarriage in 1780 with poor relatives in Maine. Though she spent much of her life in Maine— residing sometimes with her sister's family at Elm Vale in Waterford, a property she eventually owned—she also moved frequently, boarding with relatives and acquaintances. At 17, she returned to Concord to help raise her half-siblings. At 37, after the death of Emerson's father, she came to educate her nephews, with whom she also corresponded extensively in her absence. She lived again in the Emerson household for about a year in her early 60s, leaving in 1836. After staying with her in Maine some ten years later, Elizabeth Palmer Peabody called her "an extraordinary creature," but noted "she does stick hard things in all tender places." She quarreled with Emerson as his religious beliefs grew increasingly unorthodox (for his part, he felt that she was "not a Calvinist," only that she "wished everyone else to be one"). But they made amends, and Emerson eventually received from her some of her extensive manuscript writings, which he copied—along with recollections of her conversation—into four notebooks, totaling almost 900 manuscript pages.

ROBERT BULKELEY EMERSON (1807–1859), the second youngest of Emerson's siblings, was mentally retarded; he required constant care and supervision all his life, sometimes by the family, sometimes by hired helpers, and finally at the McLean Asylum. He is seldom mentioned in the journals. In a letter to his brother William describing Bulkeley's funeral, Emerson wrote: "His face was not much changed by death, but sadly changed by life from the comely boy I can well remember . . . it did not seem so odious to be laid down there under the oak trees in as perfect an innocency as was Bulkeleys, as to live corrupt & corrupting with thousands. What a happiness, that, with his infirmities, he was clean of all vices!"

RUTH HASKINS EMERSON (1768–1853), Emerson's mother, was born into a prosperous Boston Episcopalian family. She married William Emerson in 1796, and in 1799 they moved from Harvard, Massachusetts, to Boston. After the death of her husband in 1812, she earned enough money by taking in boarders to send four of her sons (including Ralph Waldo) to Harvard. She moved in with Emerson permanently after his second marriage in 1835. Emerson wrote of her soon after her death that her manners and character were "the fruit of a past age," and praised "her punctilious courtesy extended to every person." In June 1851 she demonstrated this in an extreme way: after falling out of bed in the middle of the night and breaking her hip, she refused to call for help so as not to wake anyone. Emerson wrote to Carlyle following her death: "in my journeyings lately, when I think of home, the heart is taken out."

WALDO EMERSON (1836–1842), Emerson's youngest child, died of scarlet fever soon after his fifth birthday. "His image, so gentle, so rich in hopes," Emerson wrote to Caroline Sturgis a few days later, "blends easily with every happy moment, every fair remembrance, every cherished friendship, of my life." Waldo's death was the occasion of one of Emerson's most famous poems, "Threnody."

WILLIAM EMERSON (1769–1811) died before his son, Ralph Waldo, had reached the age of eight. He was born in Concord, his father a minister; he graduated from Harvard in 1789, taught school for two years, studied divinity, and himself became a minister at the Unitarian church of Harvard, Massachusetts. He married Ruth Haskins in 1796, and besides Ralph Waldo they had seven other children, so he taught school in addition to preaching, and the family took in boarders. In 1799, he accepted the pulpit of Boston's First Church, and began an active literary and civic life in Boston, joining the Massachusetts Historical Society and becoming an overseer of Harvard College, founding the Anthology Club, and editing the *Monthly Anthology*. He published orations and sermons, and was the author of *An Historical Sketch of the First Church in Boston* (1812).

WILLIAM EMERSON (1801–1868), the oldest of Emerson's brothers, graduated from Harvard in 1818, just as Emerson was finishing his freshman year. For five years afterward he taught high school in Kennebunk, Maine, to help support the educations of his younger brothers, who called him "his Deaconship" and "our Sultan." In 1823, William left for Göttingen, Germany, to study theology, but his studies weakened his resolve to be a minister, and he soon returned to America with the intention of pursuing law. He moved to Staten Island, married, and raised a family; Thoreau was briefly a tutor to his children. Eventually he became a judge. He remained close to Emerson to the end of his life.

MARGARET FULLER (1810–1850) was born in Cambridgeport, Massachusetts, the daughter of Margaret Crane Fuller, a teacher, and congressman Timothy Fuller; she studied at Dr. Park's Boston Lyceum for Young Ladies. After her father's death in 1835, she began writing articles and teaching, to help support the family. She succeeded Elizabeth Palmer Peabody as an assistant at Bronson Alcott's controversial Temple School, and then taught in Providence, Rhode Island. Her writings brought her to Emerson's attention, and he invited her to his house for three weeks in the summer of 1836 as he was finishing *Nature*. In the coming years, she introduced Emerson to many of her friends, including Charles King Newcomb and Samuel Gray Ward. In 1839, she published a translation of Johann Eckermann's *Conversations with Goethe*, and in 1840 she became editor of *The Dial*, to which she made extensive contributions. She also began the first of her series of "Conversations for Women" (1839–44), gatherings that addressed the "great questions." Emerson described Fuller at one of these events: "She rose before me at times into heroical and godlike regions, and I could remember no superior woman, but thought of Ceres, Minerva, Proserpine." In 1844, her book *A Summer on the Lakes* prompted Horace Greeley to invite her to serve as literary critic for the *New-York Tribune*. After 18 months there reviewing books and reporting on slum conditions, lunatic asylums, and prisons—and having published her groundbreaking *Woman in the Nineteenth Century* (1845)—she traveled through England and France as a foreign correspondent. In 1847, she arrived in Italy, where she met and fell in love with Giovanni Angelo, Marchese d'Ossoli. In 1848 she had a son and became involved with the Italian revolution of 1848–49, which she described with enthusiasm in articles for the *Tribune*. After the fall of the Roman republic in 1849, she relocated with her family to Florence, and in 1850 they sailed for the United States. Within sight of Fire Island, their ship sank and all three drowned. Emerson, Henry Channing, and James Freeman Clarke immediately set about collaborating on a biography of her, published in 1852 as *Memoirs of Margaret Fuller Ossoli*.

MARTIN GAY (1803–1850) entered Harvard in 1819, when Emerson was a sophomore. Emerson was instantly drawn to this "strange face in the Freshman class" and would chronicle the development of his fascination with Gay over the next two years. After receiving his M.D. degree from Harvard in 1826, Gay became a prominent Boston physician, mineralogist, and chemist, occasionally lecturing on these subjects. He was one of the original members of the Boston Society of Natural History and a fellow of the American Academy of Arts & Sciences.

NATHANIEL HAWTHORNE (1804–1864) was a graduate, along with his friends Henry Wadsworth Longfellow and Franklin Pierce, of

Bowdoin College. His book of stories, *Twice-told Tales* (1837), brought him to the attention of Elizabeth Palmer Peabody, through whom he met his future wife, Sophia, her sister. In 1841, he became a resident at Brook Farm, mainly to save money while writing, but he found that farm work exhausted him and he left later that year. After his marriage to Sophia in 1842, he moved with her to the Old Manse in Concord (built by Emerson's grandfather William). He spent the next several years taking walks with Emerson, Channing, and Thoreau, and writing most of the stories that would be published in *Mosses from an Old Manse* (1846). Of Emerson at this time, he wrote: "It was impossible to dwell in his vicinity without inhaling the mountain-atmosphere of his lofty thought." Emerson was incompletely convinced of Hawthorne's abilities as a writer, but admired him personally: soon after Hawthorne's death, he wrote "I found in him a greater man than any of his works betray."

FREDERIC HENRY HEDGE (1805–1890), one of the leading New England disseminators of German thought, was the son of Levi Hedge, a Harvard professor of Natural Religion and Moral Philosophy. In his early teens, he accompanied historian George Bancroft to Germany, and studied for four years at schools in Hanover and Saxony. He took his bachelor's degree from Harvard in 1825, and graduated from the Divinity School in 1829; in the same year he married Lucy Pierce and was ordained a Congregational minister in West Cambridge. In 1833, he published "Coleridge's Literary Character," an essay sometimes cited as the first recognition of German transcendentalism in the United States; Emerson read it avidly, calling it "a living, leaping logos." In 1836, a year after becoming minister of the Independent Congregational Church in Bangor, Maine, Hedge's return visits to Massachusetts served as occasions for the meetings of Hedge's Club—later known as the Transcendental Club—which met regularly over the next four years at George Ripley's house in Boston. The meetings ended in 1840, Hedge feeling that the younger generation of Unitarians had "slipped their moorings" in abandoning the call for Unitarian church reform. In an 1840 letter to Margaret Fuller, Emerson wrote that though he and Hedge "never quite meet . . . he has such a fine free wit, such accomplishments & talents & then such an affectionate selfhealing nature that I always revere him." Hedge eventually settled in Brookline, Massachusetts, and in 1872 became professor of German at Harvard.

ELIZABETH SHERMAN HOAR (1814–1878) was the oldest child of Samuel Hoar, a wealthy Concord lawyer and politician. After graduating from Concord Academy, she was engaged to Emerson's brother Charles Chauncy, who was then working in her father's firm.

Five months before their wedding, her fiancé died of tuberculosis, but she remained closely connected with the Emersons. When Lidian was sick or indisposed, Hoar would manage the household; Emerson's mother, Ruth, died in her arms, and his children would call her "Aunt Lizzie." In 1841, Emerson wrote of her: "I have no friend whom I more wish to be immortal than she." A love of learning, cultivated at a young age, drew her into the circles of both Margaret Fuller, whose "Conversations" she regularly attended, and Sarah Alden Ripley, with whom she visited frequently after the Ripleys moved to Concord in 1846.

EDMUND HOSMER (1798–1881), a farmer, lived about half a mile east of the Emerson household. According to Edward Emerson, he was "the oracle constantly consulted" by his father and "the ally called in, dealing with the interesting but to him puzzling management of his increasing acres." Emerson was drawn instantly to Hosmer, whom he praised as "a man of strongly intellectual taste . . . of much reading, and of an erect good sense and independent spirit." Hosmer was not only a frequent guest at Emerson's house, but also a welcome visitor to Thoreau's Walden cabin, which he and his sons helped to build.

CHARLES THOMAS JACKSON (1805–1880), Lidian Emerson's brother, expressed an interest in mineralogy from an early age and published his first study (on the minerals of Nova Scotia) in the *American Journal of Science* in 1829, a year after graduating from Harvard Medical School. He studied medicine and mineralogy in Paris, and in 1836, four years after his return and two years after his marriage, he retired from medicine to set up a commercial chemical laboratory in Boston. Jackson later served as state geologist of Maine, New Hampshire, and Rhode Island, and as U.S. geologist for the Lake Superior region. His career was overshadowed, however, by his habit of claiming credit and priority for scientific advances not his own: at various points, he claimed to have discovered the telegraph, guncotton, the digestive action of the stomach, and the medical applications of ether. These and other controversies contributed to a mental breakdown in 1873, after which he was committed to the McLean Asylum, where he lived until his death.

HENRY JAMES SR. (1811–1882)—a recently married writer, lecturer, and Calvinist theologian—attended a lecture of Emerson's in New York in 1842 and sought him out. After they met, Emerson wrote Lidian that James seemed "a very manlike thorough seeing person," and they became lifelong friends, despite James's frustration at Emerson's unwillingness to defend or explain his religious views

("Oh you man without a handle!" he at one point exclaimed in their conversations). In 1844, during an extended trip to England, James experienced a "vastation" and spiritual crisis and turned increasingly to the works of Emanuel Swedenborg for his religious self-understanding. On his return to New York in 1845, he threw himself into social reform, associating with Albert Brisbane and the Fourierist movement and contributing reviews to the Fourierist organ *The Harbinger*. His *Moralism and Christianity* (1850) and other works that questioned conventional ideas of marriage and morality earned him considerable notoriety. James spent the rest of his life expounding Swedenborgian theology in books and articles. Though he continued to correspond with Emerson, their friendship became more distant after the Civil War; in 1868, James wrote his son William that Emerson's writings were "wholly destitute of spiritual flavor, being at most carbonic acid gas and *water*." In spite of philosophical differences, he always praised Emerson the man, writing in 1872: "Mr. Emerson's authority consists, not in his ideas, not in his intellect, not in his culture, not in his science, but simply in himself, in the form of his natural personality."

CHARLES LANE (1800–1870) was a member of the circle centered around James Pierrepont Greaves, an English mystic and former merchant who founded a small community and school in Ham, Surrey, known as "Alcott House" in honor of Bronson Alcott and informed by his progressive writings on education. Lane served as editor of a number of reformist magazines including *The Healthian*, which promoted spiritual enrichment through a wholesome diet, and contributed ten articles to *The Dial*. When Alcott returned from his trip to England in 1842, he brought Lane with him, along with Lane's son and Henry G. Wright, founder of *The Healthian*. In May of 1842, Lane purchased a 90-acre farm near Harvard, Massachusetts, where they founded Fruitlands, an experiment in communal living that forbade all ownership of property, the consumption of animals, animal products, and any liquid but water. It also enforced a rigorous celibacy. After seven months, the farm failed, having attracted no more than a dozen occasional members. After this, Lane lived briefly in the Harvard Shaker community; he eventually returned to England, resuming his job as manager of the *London Mercantile Price Current*.

CHARLES KING NEWCOMB (1820–1894) and his mother moved to Providence, Rhode Island, soon after his father died in 1825. After graduating from Brown in 1837, he abandoned plans to join the navy, then the Episcopal ministry. He met Emerson in 1840 through Margaret Fuller, a friend of his mother who had become a close correspondent. Newcomb's moral and intellectual leanings made him the ideal boarder at Brook Farm, where he lived more or less continuously from May 1841 to December 1845. During his residence there he wrote the only work published during his lifetime, "The Two Dolons," which appeared in the July 1842 issue of *The Dial*. Emerson drew comfort from it in the wake of his son's death, saying it had "more native gold than anything . . . since Sampson Reed's Oration on Genius." Soon after moving back to Providence with his mother, Newcomb began keeping a journal, eventually filling 27 manuscript volumes. This journal, excepting a three-month stint with Tenth Rhode Island Volunteer Infantry in 1862, would become the main focus of his life until he departed for Europe in 1871. Emerson's feelings toward him fluctuated from adoration (in the beginning, he called Newcomb his "key to Shakespeare" and the "brightest star" of the younger generation of Transcendentalists) to extreme impatience (after a visit in 1850, Emerson wrote in his journal, "He wastes my time . . . Destroyed three good days for me!"). In spite of what he felt was wasted potential in Newcomb, Emerson still thought highly enough of him in 1858 to agree with Caroline Sturgis when she said "no one could compare with him in original genius."

THEODORE PARKER (1810–1860), a native of Lexington, Massachusetts, was ordained as a Congregational minister in 1837, a year after graduating from Harvard Divinity School. In the same year he married Lydia Dodge Cabot and associated himself with the Transcendental Club, meeting Emerson and his circle; in 1838, he praised Emerson's controversial "Divinity School Address." His own preaching, influenced by the German higher criticism of the Bible, increasingly offended mainstream Unitarians, and in the wake of his 1841 sermon *The Transient and Permanent in Christianity* and 1842 lecture *A Discourse of Matters Pertaining to Religion*, he was publicly criticized and excluded from church functions. His parishoners opted to secede and in 1845 offered him the pulpit of the newly formed Twenty-Eighth Congregational Society of Boston. His following grew in size and enthusiasm. Parker railed against the political corruption and moral abuses of his day (Emerson called him "our Savonarola"), including slavery and the Mexican War. From 1850 onward, slavery became his central issue: he assisted many fugitive slaves, and was one of the "Secret Six," helping to fund John Brown's raid on Harpers Ferry. In 1857, after years of frenetic activity as a lecturer and writer, he fell ill and gradually withdrew from public life; he died of tuberculosis in Florence.

ELIZABETH PALMER PEABODY (1804–1894), born in Billerica, Massachusetts, moved with her family to Lancaster after her father's dental practice collapsed. Her mother soon set up a school, which Elizabeth at 15 was obliged to help run. Emerson, around this time, tutored her in Greek. From 1834 to 1836, along with Margaret Fuller, she taught at Bronson Alcott's controversial Temple School, where he attempted to arouse children's interest in religion by engaging them in conversation. When she transcribed and published these conversations in 1837 as *Conversations with Children on the Gospels*, some outraged parents pulled their children out of the school. Three years later Peabody opened a bookstore and lending library in the parlor of the family home in Boston; one of the few bookstores in the city that carried a substantial stock of foreign literature, it became, in the words of George Bradford, a "Transcendentalist exchange." She hosted Margaret Fuller's "Conversations," beginning in 1839, and helped plan the publication of *The Dial*, of which she served as business manager; she also published books by her brother-in-law Nathaniel Hawthorne and by the elder William Ellery Channing, under her imprint. Inspired by her reading of Friedrich Froebel, the creator of the Kindergarten, she opened the first English-language kindergarten on Pinckney Street in Boston in 1861. The rest of her life was spent promoting the kindergarten and training young women to teach in it, through books like *Moral Culture of Infancy and Kindergarten Guide* (1866) and *Lectures in Training Schools for Kindergartners* (1888) and her magazine the *Kindergarten Messenger* (1873–77). Miss Birdseye, in the younger Henry James's novel *The Bostonians* (1885–86), was taken by contemporaries as a caricature of Peabody, though James himself disclaimed this intention.

SAMPSON REED (1800–1880), the son of a Unitarian minister, gave up his own plans to join the ministry soon after his graduation from Harvard in 1818, in the wake of his encounter with the writings of Emanuel Swedenborg. Reed's "Oration on Genius," delivered three years later when he received his M.A., was admired by an 18-year-old Emerson, who was in the audience. His *Observations on the Growth of the Mind* (1826), a distillation of Swedenborg's thoughts, affected Emerson even more profoundly; it came to him with "the aspect of a revelation, such is the wealth & such is the novelty of the truth unfolded in it." (Bronson Alcott would later note that *Nature* "reminds me more of Sampson Reed's *Growth of the Mind* than any other work.") Reed apprenticed himself to an apothecary and later opened an apothecary shop in Boston, working in this profession until 1860. Although he would spend his life advancing the cause of the Swedenborgian church, he distanced himself from the Transcendentalists, explicitly denying any connection with them in his preface to the 1838 edition of his *Growth of the Mind*. Reed would prove to be a huge disappointment to Emerson when he came out in support of Daniel Webster and the Fugitive Slave Law of 1850. "There were my two greatest men," Emerson reflected in 1870, "both down in the pit together."

EZRA RIPLEY (1751–1841) was born in Woodstock, Connecticut, the fifth of 19 children. He graduated from Harvard in 1776. Two years later, he was ordained minister of the First Church of Concord, taking over from Emerson's recently deceased grandfather, William, whose widow, Phebe Bliss, he soon married, and whose son—Emerson's father—he would go on to raise. He would serve as pastor of the First Church for almost 63 years. In 1834, he invited Emerson and his mother, Ruth, to live with him in Concord's Old Manse, where Emerson remained until his marriage the next year, working on the essay *Nature* (1836). "He ever reminds one," Emerson noted during his stay there, "both in his wisdom & in the faults of his intellect, of an Indian Sagamore, a sage within the limits of his own observation, a child beyond." After his death, Emerson wrote, "I am sure all who remember . . . will associate his form with whatever was grave and droll in the old, cold, unpainted, uncarpeted, square-pewed meetinghouse."

GEORGE RIPLEY (1802–1880), son of Jerome Ripley, a businessman, and Sarah Franklin, was born in Greenfield, Massachusetts. He entered Harvard in 1819, graduated first in his class, and went on to Divinity School. In 1826, he became a minister at the Purchase Street Church in Boston and married Sophia Willard Dana. In 1836, along with his cousin Emerson, Frederick Henry Hedge, and George Putnam, he met to form an occasional discussion group. Nicknamed Hedge's Club, and later referred to as the Transcendental Club, the group gradually expanded to include Orestes Brownson, William Henry Channing, Margaret Fuller (with whom he worked on *The Dial*, as managing editor), Elizabeth Palmer Peabody, Sophia Ripley, Henry David Thoreau, Jones Very, and others. Also in 1836, after publishing articles that questioned the tenets of Unitarianism, he was attacked in print by theologian Andrews Norton (for whom the Transcendentalist movement was "the latest form of infidelity"), sparking a four-year paper war. He defended Emerson in 1838 after Norton criticized Emerson's "Divinity School Address" as heretical. Looking for a means of support after quitting the ministry in 1840 and wanting to put the Transcendentalists' ideas into practice, he came up with the idea of a community that would "combine the thinker and the worker as far as possible." The result was Brook Farm in West Roxbury, a six-year experiment in communal living that attracted hundreds of boarders, including George Bradford, Nathaniel Hawthorne, Charles King Newcomb, and Caroline Sturgis. In 1844, the Brook Farmers began building a "Phalanstery or Unitary dwelling," inspired by the writings of Charles Fourier; the nearly completed structure burned down in 1846, and the community was finally dissolved in 1847. Afterward, Ripley and his wife moved to New York City, where he found work as a critic for Horace Greeley's *Tribune*, filling a position Margaret Fuller had recently left. He soon established himself as one of New York's leading editors and critics, helping to found *Harper's Magazine* in 1850, and publishing the lucrative *New American Cyclopedia* (1858–63). After his wife, Sophia, died in 1861, he married Louisa Schlossberger; for the remainder of his life he was a convivial fixture of New York's literary scene.

SAMUEL RIPLEY (1783–1847) was born at Concord's "Old Manse," the son of the Rev. Ezra Ripley and Phebe Emerson, and a half-brother of Emerson's father, the Rev. William Emerson, and Emerson's aunt Mary Moody Emerson. He graduated from Harvard in 1804, and in 1809 became minister of the First Congregational Society in Waltham, Massachusetts. He continued to serve his parish there for over three decades. He married Sarah Alden Bradford in 1818, and they had nine children; they also, together, helped local students prepare for college. After his death, Emerson wrote: "I know not where we shall find in a man of his station & experience a heart so large, or a spirit so blameless & of a childlike innocence."

SARAH ALDEN BRADFORD RIPLEY (1793–1867) was the oldest daughter of Gamaliel Bradford, a prison warden and former sea-captain, and Elizabeth Hickling. With her mother incapacitated by tuberculosis, the responsibility for managing the household and six younger siblings often fell to her. Despite this, she learned Latin and Greek and studied physics, chemistry, and botany. When her brothers went to college, she read all of their books and, with the guidance of Mary Moody Emerson (who would later accuse her of leading Emerson into heterodoxy), gave herself a college education. In 1818, she married Emerson's uncle Samuel Ripley, the Unitarian minister at Waltham, Massachusetts, and moved into his parsonage along with four of her brothers and sisters, including George P. Bradford; she tutored in Latin and Greek. In 1846 the family moved to the Old Manse in Concord, recently vacated by the Hawthornes, her husband accepting a post in nearby Lincoln. The younger members of Emerson's circle, including Fuller, Hedge, Parker, Peabody, and Thoreau, were all frequent visitors. Emerson, who had known her since he was 11, wrote that despite her vast learning, she was "absolutely without pedantry." At her burial service, Frederic Henry Hedge said although she'd never written a book, "in the hearts of those who knew her, she wrote a book whose substance they will remember as long as they remember anything, & whose contents are a commentary on the text: 'A perfect woman nobly planned.'"

SOPHIA WILLARD DANA RIPLEY (1803–1861) was born in Cambridge, Massachusetts, to Francis Dana Jr. and Sophia Willard Dana. After graduating from Dr. Park's Lyceum in Boston, she and her sister began teaching in Fay House, a school near Harvard that her mother had opened some years earlier. In 1825, through her extensive network of Unitarian friends, she met George Ripley, whom she married two years later. She became friends with Margaret Fuller in the 1830s, and participated in Fuller's series of "Conversations" (1839–44); she also attended meetings of the Transcendental Club. In 1841, she contributed a letter to *The Dial* on the communistic "Separatists" of Zoar, Ohio, and a feminist essay entitled "Woman"; along with her husband, she formed a joint stock company to procure the funds to purchase Brook Farm. She envisioned the Brook Farm community as a place where she could realize her ideals of womanhood, but the experiment proved a disappointment as the scheme limited her to taking care of sick children and boarders, teaching elementary school, and working at menial chores in the kitchen and around the house. After Brook Farm collapsed she suffered an emotional breakdown, realizing "that I do not love anyone and never did, with the heart, & of course could never have been worthy in any relation." She converted to Catholicism in 1847, partly due to the influence of Orestes Brownson who had himself converted three years earlier. She spent the last decade of her life in New York with her husband, translating devotional tracts, praying, and visiting hospitals, prisons, and lunatic asylums.

GEORGE A. SAMPSON (d. 1834), a Boston merchant, was a parishioner of the Second Church and the closest of Emerson's friends during his pastorate there. Emerson lived briefly in the Sampson household in 1829, and later relied on his advice in business and financial matters. Eulogizing his friend in 1834—in his final sermon at the Second Church—Emerson described Sampson as "a man without a fault—I might almost say—so utterly unable am I, after five years intercourse with him, to remember in him anything to censure."

CAROLINE STURGIS TAPPAN (1819–1888) was the fourth of six children of William Sturgis, a Boston merchant who had built a large trading empire in the Far East, and Elizabeth Marston Davis. She and her sisters were encouraged to think for themselves and read widely in various disciplines. At 13, she met Margaret Fuller, who was deeply impressed by her; Caroline and her sister Ellen would be the first friends Fuller invited to her series of "Conversations," begun in 1839. When *The Dial* began publication, the Sturgis sisters would be among its most frequent contributors. Around this time, Fuller introduced her to Emerson, inaugurating a lifelong friendship. In 1847, Sturgis married William Aspinwall Tappan, the son of New York merchant and abolitionist Lewis Tappan. In 1850, when Sophia and Nathaniel Hawthorne were looking for a house to rent for the summer, the Tappans, now with two children, offered them their home in Lenox, Massachusetts, where Hawthorne would write *The House of the Seven Gables* (1851), *The Blithedale Romance* (1852), and *Tanglewood Tales* (1853). From 1855 to 1861 the Tappans lived in Europe, where they met the young William and Henry James; the latter later described Caroline as being of the "incurable ironic or mocking order." They returned to the United States to support the Union cause during the Civil War, and after ten more years in Europe, moved home permanently in 1880.

EDWARD THOMPSON TAYLOR (1793–1871)—the "Father Taylor" of Emerson's journals—was born in Richmond, Virginia. Orphaned and homeless by age seven, he went to sea as a cabin boy. At 17, he had a religious awakening after hearing a Methodist preacher and developed his own preaching skills as a British prisoner during the War of 1812. He eventually made his way to Boston, where he began preaching to sailors. In 1833, he was installed as pastor of Seaman's Bethel and would hold his pulpit there for almost 40 years. Emerson had sometimes preached at Bethel during his own ministry nearby in Boston's North End and was a great admirer, calling Taylor the "Shakspeare of the sailor & the poor." In a letter to Margaret Fuller, Emerson wrote, "There is beauty in that man & when he is well alive with his own exhortations it flows out from all the corners of his great heart & steeps the whole rough man in its gracious element." Dickens wrote about Taylor in his *American Notes for General Circulation* (1842), and he inspired the character of Father Mapple in Melville's *Moby-Dick* (1851). Taylor, though not impressed with Emerson's particular theological views or Transcendentalism more generally, is reported to have said that Emerson was "more like Jesus Christ than anyone he had ever known"; he had "seen him where his religion was tested, and it bore the test."

HENRY DAVID THOREAU (1817–1862), the son of a pencil manufacturer, was born in Concord. He graduated from Harvard in 1837 and taught briefly at a local school, resigning after he was ordered to flog students against his wishes; he later taught with his brother John at Concord Academy until John fell ill with tetanus in 1841. Emerson, greatly impressed by the young Thoreau, introduced him to his Concord circle and encouraged his writing: Thoreau began his ultimately voluminous journals in 1837 at Emerson's suggestion, and published his first essay, on the dramatist Aulus Persius Flaccus, in *The Dial* in 1840. For most of 1841–44, and occasionally thereafter, Thoreau lived in the Emerson household, acting as a tutor to Emerson's children and as a handyman and assistant. (He subsequently worked as a surveyor, and, for much of his life, in his father's pencil factory, suggesting innovations that made Thoreau pencils the best in the country.) In July 1845, Thoreau built his famous cabin on Emerson's land beside Walden Pond and lived there until September 1847, drafting *A Week on the Concord and Merrimack Rivers* (1849) and beginning *Walden, or Life in the Woods* (1854). The friendship between the two men cooled somewhat in 1849, Emerson critical of Thoreau's lack of ambition ("instead of engineering for all America," he later wrote, "he was the captain of a huckleberry party"), and Thoreau unhappy at being considered a mere follower of Emerson. But they continued to meet often for walks and conversation, read each other's works as they appeared, and had many friends in common, including Bronson Alcott and Ellery Channing. Thoreau traveled widely, writing accounts that would be published posthumously in his *Excursions* (1863), *The Maine Woods* (1864), *Cape Cod* (1865), and *A Yankee in Canada* (1866). During the 1850s his involvement in the abolitionist cause intensified; he aided fugitive slaves, spoke publicly, and wrote "Slavery in Massachusetts" (1854) and "A Plea for John Brown" (1859). He died of tuberculosis in 1862.

JONES VERY (1813–1880) was the oldest of six children of Jones Very, a ship's captain, and Lydia Very. He entered Harvard his sophomore year and finished second in his class in 1836, then served as a tutor in Greek while he studied at Harvard Divinity School. In April 1838, he met Emerson through Elizabeth Palmer Peabody. Emerson took an instant liking to him, and wrote to Peabody that he felt "anew" in his company. In the fall of 1838, college authorities decided that Very—overcome with religious enthusiasm—had gone insane, relieved him of his duties, and committed him to the McLean Asylum for a month. Over the next year and a half Very would produce a unique body of religious poetry—all a product, he would claim, of the "holy spirit." In 1839, Emerson selected and edited these poems and saw them through the press; Very's *Essays and Poems* received almost no critical attention at the time but was highly regarded by Emerson and his circle. By the mid-1840s, Very's religious enthusiasm had waned; he moved back in with his family in Salem, filling temporarily vacant pulpits in the neighboring towns when need arose, and continuing to write poetry.

ANNA HAZARD BARKER WARD (1813–1900), the sixth of 12 children, was born into a prosperous Quaker family. Her father moved the family to New Orleans while she was an infant, his insurance company having failed, and he built another fortune there. Barker met Emerson through Margaret Fuller, with whom she had been friendly for several years, in the fall of 1839. "So lovely, so fortunate," he wrote after their first meeting, "and so remote from my own experiences." After her marriage to Samuel Ward the next year, she and her husband moved to a farm in the Berkshires, but they moved back to Boston in the early 1850s so he could run his father's banking firm. Several years later, she suffered an attack of neuralgia following the death of her daughter and traveled to Europe alone to recover. In March 1858, while in Rome, she converted to Catholicism. On receiving this news, Emerson drafted a letter—never sent—lamenting "the chance-wind that has made a foreigner of you—whirled you from the forehead of the morning into the medievals." Samuel Ward accepted his wife's decision, and had a chapel built for her near their country house in Lenox, Massachusetts. After the war, the Wards moved to New York City, where they became prominent patrons of the arts.

SAMUEL GRAY WARD (1817–1907) was the son of banker Thomas Wren Ward and Lydia Gray Ward. After graduating from Harvard in 1836, he traveled in Europe for two years, studying art and architecture; while abroad, he met Anna Hazard Barker, whom he married in 1840. He met Emerson soon after he returned, and the two became fast friends, Emerson eager to draw on the knowledge and judgment of art his friend had acquired in Europe. Ward loaned him sketches and books, and Emerson spent time with Margaret Fuller looking through Ward's portfolios of prints. At Emerson's suggestion, Ward wrote poems and essays for *The Dial*. After his father's retirement in the early 1850s, he took over as the American agent for the London banking house of Baring Brothers, which was to be his main occupation, first in Boston, then in New York City. In 1869, he became one of the founders of the Metropolitan Museum of Art, later serving on its Board of Trustees and eventually becoming its treasurer. Emerson's correspondence with Ward was collected in 1899 as *Letters to a Friend*.

Index

Abernethy, John, 344
Abolitionism, 423–25, 434, 475, 529, 549, 568, 571, 589, 600, 615–16, 677–78, 681, 689–90, 711, 737, 754, 756, 790
Abraham, 451
Ackermann, Herr, 552
Acton, Mass., 421, 589, 797
Adam, 129, 222, 241, 276, 290, 545, 705
Adams, Abel, 578
Adams, John, 98, 106–7, 126–27, 135, 196, 296, 349
Adams, John Quincy, 126–27, 146–47, 177–79, 722
Addison, Joseph, 8, 164, 291
Admetus, 397, 477
Adorno, Anselmo, 235–36
Aeolus, 220
Aeschylus, 555–56; *The Furies*, 556; *Prometheus Unchained*, 798; *Seven against Thebes*, 799
Aesop, 203, 378, 743, 755
Africa, 40, 54–55, 122, 152, 225, 497–98, 639, 768
African-Americans, 57–59, 142, 310, 324, 364, 425, 502, 547, 550–52, 626, 638, 752, 756
Agathon, 685
Agesilaus, 183, 360, 378, 381
Agis, 445
Ahriman, 129
Alabama, 17, 552, 643
Alaric, 332
Albigenses, 133
Alcibiades, 397, 442, 496
Alcott, Bronson, 419, 438, 443, 457, 461, 464–66, 471–72, 481–82, 492, 511, 525–26, 530, 543, 553, 559, 563, 578, 580, 582, 598–99, 602, 610, 617, 630, 668–69, 675, 680, 682, 685, 713, 739, 785, 791, 799
Alexander, Francis, 253
Alexander the Great, 10, 62, 165, 246, 262–63, 293, 326, 355, 495–96, 564, 623
Alexandria, Va., 146–47

Alfieri, Vittorio, 260
Alfred the Great, 64–65, 196, 298, 339, 409, 481, 709
Algonquin tribes, 768
Ali, 761
Alison, Archibald, 82, 93
Allen, Joseph, 554
Allston, Washington, 389, 391, 402, 413, 440, 473, 480, 484, 613, 675–76, 682, 688–89, 734; "To the Author of 'The Diary of an Ennuyée,' " 548
Alps, 270–72, 315, 416, 444, 511, 513, 520
Ambleside, England, 284
America, 50–51, 53, 62–63, 67, 106–7, 133, 142, 144, 162, 166, 204, 209, 211, 217–18, 222, 225–26, 236, 254, 265, 270–71, 284–86, 324, 340, 348, 353, 379, 422, 474, 512, 518, 586, 613, 649, 716, 743, 758
American Quarterly Review, 307
Amherst, Mass., 85–87, 89
Amherst, N.H., 90
Amherst College, 85–87
Amici, Giovanni Battista, 260–61
Anapus River, 232–33
Anasagunticook tribe, 329
Anaxagoras, 169
Andover Theological Seminary, 778
Anglo-Saxon Chronicle, 755
Anne of Austria, 376
Anteros, 379
Antigua, 601
Antinous (statue), 248
Apennines, 255, 265
Apollo, 321, 397, 477, 683, 688
Apollo (statue), 207, 248, 259, 452, 609, 662
Apollodorus the Ephesian, 48
Appleton, Mr., 315
Aquila, Signor, 247
Arabia, 30, 40, 480, 533, 651
Arabs, 27, 69, 632, 661, 753, 760, 802
Arago, Dominique-François, 492
Arbela, Persia, 564
Arcadia, 618
Archimedes, 229–30
Arethusa fountain, 228, 231

Aristides, 107, 241, 324, 534, 623
Aristophanes, 9, 571
Aristotle, 102, 137, 164, 189, 264, 349, 355, 366, 374, 382, 385, 396, 408, 415, 424, 428, 448, 544, 605, 650, 695
Arno River, 260
Arrian, 114
Arthur, King, 5, 9
Asia, 108, 122, 165, 586, 639, 641, 796
Asiatic Journal, 553
Askew, Mr., 261
Asmodeus, 468, 743
Assacombuit, 329
Asser, 65
Assyria, 37, 67, 660
Atheism, 77, 145, 193, 648
Athens, Greece, 133, 149, 162, 231, 233, 314, 452, 534, 671, 704
Athos, Mount, 778
Atlantic Ocean, 214, 218–16, 290–92
Atlantis, 314
Atlas, 426
Atreus, house of, 755
Attila the Hun, 332
Augustine (saint), 421, 703, 708
Augustus Caesar, 64, 114
Australia, 144, 352
Austria, 117, 252, 269, 376, 796–97
Avernus, Lake, 245
Azores, 221

Babylon, 647, 704, 744, 765
Bacon, Francis, 8, 14, 71, 84–85, 95, 102, 120, 123, 148, 154, 168, 196–97, 346, 350, 355, 366, 368, 377, 379, 396, 408, 412, 415, 417, 424, 462, 518–19, 526, 581, 628, 638, 650, 688; *Advancement of Learning*, 502; *De Augmentis Scientiarum*, 177; *Essays*, 115, 591; *Novum Organum*, 13, 410
Bacon, Roger, 72, 315, 638
Baiae, 241, 245
Baillie, Joanna, 452
Baker, Mr., 232
Balloch, Scotland, 282
Baltimore, Md., 756
Bancroft, George, 583; *History of the United States*, 768
Bangor, Me., 333, 387, 611
"Banquet Song of the Tonga Islanders," 48

Barbauld, Anna Letitia, 137, 339; "On Riddles," 180
Barbour, John: *The Brus*, 305
Barclay, Mr., 241
Barnard, Charles F., 420
Barnes, Mr., 177
Barnwell, Robert Woodward, 19, 665
Barron, Nancy, 750
Barrow, Henry, 451
Barrow, Isaac, 10
Bartlett, Josiah, 560, 694
Bartlett, Mr., 86
Bartol, Cyrus, 481, 742
Bartram, William, 487
Batavia, 150
Bateman, John, 430
Bates, James, 216
Battas, 429
Baylies, Mr., 405
Beaumont, Francis, 206, 263, 610, 703
Becket, Thomas à, 590
Beecher, Edward, 342
Beecher, Lyman, 342
Beethoven, Ludwig van, 272, 570, 625
Belchertown, Mass., 85
Beleo, Michele, 240
Belisarius, 107
Belknap, Jeremy, 584
Bell, Charles, 110, 294, 367
Bell, John, 110, 569
Bellini, Vicenzo: *La Straniera*, 206, 261
Belzoni, Giovanni, 632, 647
Benedictines, 235–36, 240
Bennett's Memorial, 46
Bentham, Jeremy, 196, 284, 347, 402, 614
Bentley, Richard, 8, 492–93, 680
Béranger, Pierre-Jean de, 328
Bering, Vitus, 378
Bernard of Clairvaux, 214
Berni, Francesco, 298
Bethune, J.E.D.: "Life of Galileo," 189
Bible, 132, 154–55, 167, 180, 189, 224, 311, 357, 376, 406, 413, 426, 448–49, 451, 466, 469, 476, 486, 587, 618, 646, 705, 724–25, 755
Bible Society, 152–53
Bigelow, Andrew: *Travels in Malta and Sicily*, 220
Bisbie, Rev., 84
Biscari, Prince of, 236

Bisset, Robert: *Life of Edmund Burke*, 5
Black, Joseph, 82
Black, Rebecca, 785
Blackwood's Edinburgh Magazine, 575
Blagden, George Washington, 342
Blair, Hugh, 17; *Lectures on Rhetoric and Belles Lettres*, 729
Blanc, Mont, 272
Blanchard, Joshua P., 370
Blood, Oliver, 90
Blood, Thaddeus, 423, 429
Boccaccio, Giovanni, 215; *Decameron*, 401
Bodenstein, Andreas (Bodenstein von Karlstadt), 356
Bodleian Library, 632
Boethius, 101
Böhme, Jakob, 393, 426
Boileau, Charles, 40
Boileau, Nicolas, 8
Bolingbroke, Henry St. John, 560
Bolton, Mass., 90
Bombay, India, 315
Bond, George, 299
Bonifacio, 268
Bora, Katherina von, 355
Borgia, Cesare, 249
Bossuet, Jacques-Bénigne, 203, 432
Boston, Mass., 27, 38, 48, 50, 53-54, 70, 88, 142, 148, 150, 172, 174, 184-85, 217, 226, 230, 265, 293, 302, 307, 311, 332-33, 339, 343, 346, 409, 437, 452, 481, 503, 507, 510, 525, 527-28, 553, 555, 562, 565, 569, 578, 583, 618, 652, 655, 677, 688-89, 702, 704-5, 708, 712, 716, 732, 734-35, 756, 768, 770-71, 775, 779, 785, 792
Boston Athenaeum, 611, 688, 712, 715, 728
Boston Globe, 583-84
Boswell, James, 342
Botany Bay, Australia, 352
Boulogne, France, 209, 280
Bowring, John, 391
Boyden, Dwight, 578
Boyle, Charles, 8
Bradford, Gamaliel, 295
Bradford, George P., 302-3, 316, 419, 443, 471, 509, 527, 534, 589, 628, 680, 742, 800, 802
Bradford, William, 106

Braham, John, 775
Brant, Joseph, 667
Brazil, 802
Brescia, Italy, 269
Bridgen, Anna, 262, 265, 270, 272
Bridgewater, Mass., 342
Britain. *See* England; Scotland; Wales
Brookfield, Mass., 84
Brookline, Mass., 167
Brougham, Henry Peter, 340, 348, 402
Brown, John, 321
Brown, Lucy C., 723
Brown, Mr., 749
Browne, Thomas: *Religio Medici*, 419
Brownson, Orestes, 472, 481; *New Views of Christianity, Society, and the Church*, 498
Brozas y Garay, Pedro de, 150
Bruce, James, 640
Bruce, Robert, 305, 548
Brummel, George Bryan (Beau), 160
Bruno, Giordano, 366
Brutus, Marcus Junius, 149, 310, 476
Bryant, William Cullen, 473, 613, 675-76
Buchanan, Claudius, 43-44
Buckminster, Joseph S., 165
Buddhism, 791
Buffon, comte (Georges-Louis Leclerc), 335, 432
Bulkeley, Peter, 418
Bulwer-Lytton, Edward: *Pelham*, 160
Bunyan, John, 172, 462, 590
Burckhardt, John Lewis, 640
Burke, Edmund, 97-98, 107, 117, 141, 197, 263, 332, 351, 434, 451, 486, 497, 564, 595, 692; *Inquiry on the Sublime and Beautiful*, 405; *Letters on a Persian Peace*, 5
Burns, Robert, 284, 287, 393, 507, 541, 765, 789
Burton, Robert, 344; *Anatomy of Melancholy*, 726
Butler, Bishop, 794
Butler, Joseph, 53, 109, 168, 213, 215
Butler, Samuel, 136
Buttera, Prince of, 239
Buttrick, David, 607
Buttrick, Jonas, 421
Byron, Lord (George Gordon), 43, 124-25, 158, 249, 255, 258-59, 263,

269, 272, 312, 338, 517, 555, 571, 595, 606, 614, 686, 692, 727, 780; *Cain*, 660; *Childe Harold's Pilgrimage*, 37, 91, 259, 536; *Don Juan*, 776; *The Island*, 666; *Manfred*, 17; *Sardanapalus*, 452
Byzantium, 162

Cabot, John, 758
Cade, Jack, 95, 122, 316, 578, 612
Cadmus, 42
Caillaud, Frédéric, 640
Cairo, Egypt, 330
Calabria, 634
Calcutta, India, 553
Calhoun, John C., 296
Californ (giant), 38, 48
Callender, Scotland, 281
Calvin, John, 164, 249, 272, 383
Calvinism, 84, 181, 193, 212–13, 216, 272–73, 333, 342, 358, 373, 385, 402, 478–79, 499, 589, 611, 615, 676, 692, 776, 779–80, 799
Cambridge, Mass., 5, 87, 89, 105, 126–27, 134–35, 140, 159, 307, 310, 431, 470, 472, 475, 522, 536, 551, 590, 599, 614, 618, 620, 628, 677, 730, 735, 749, 755, 763, 779, 794
Cambridge University, 474–75
Campbell, Thomas, 574, 602, 675
Canning, George, 162, 340, 377, 402, 595
Canossa, Italy, 13
Canova, Antonio, 248, 268
Canterbury, Mass., 75, 90, 125, 291
Canton, China, 553
Cape Cod, 343
Capri, 245
Capuchins, 231–33, 239, 682
Carbery, Countess of (Alice Egerton), 215
Carbery, Countess of (Frances Vaughan), 215
Caribs, 294
Carlisle, England, 283
Carlyle, Jane Welsh, 283–84
Carlyle, Thomas, 192, 209–12, 262, 283–85, 308–9, 327–28, 332, 342, 347, 370, 402, 407, 417, 437, 443, 447, 463, 472, 501–2, 506, 515, 526, 535, 540–41, 545, 574–75, 577, 583–86, 675, 728–29,

749, 751; "Characteristics," 319, 404; "Corn Law Rhymes," 197; "Count Cagliostro, in Two Flights," 346; *The French Revolution*, 581, 584–85; "German Literature in the 14th and 15th Century," 204; *Sartor Resartus*, 328, 333
Carmelites, 256
Carnot, Lazare-Nicolas, 99
Carr, Robert (Viscount Rochester), 107
Carthage, 231, 233
Casal, marchese di, 232
Cassandra, 792
Castalia, 6
Castelli, Benedetto, 189
Castillo San Marcos, 152–53
Catania, Italy, 234–38
Catholicism, 66, 151–53, 204–5, 228, 237, 239, 244, 250, 356, 402, 557, 626–27, 762, 768, 770, 780
Catiline, 496
Cato, 114, 140, 187–88, 430
Catskill Mountains, 790
Catullus, 258
Cavendish, George, 716
Céard, Nicholas, 271
Cecil, Robert (Earl of Salisbury), 802
Celsus, Aulus Cornelius, 110
Cenci, Beatrice, 249
Cervantes, Miguel de, 215, 462
Cethegus, 249
Chaldeans, 317, 641
Champlain, Lake, 173
Channing, Edward Tyrrell, 26
Channing, William Ellery ("Dr. Channing," 1780–1842), 25, 76–77, 93, 109, 164, 174, 213, 287, 313, 338, 347, 365, 382, 389–90, 404, 433, 473, 481, 525, 527, 566, 613, 676, 788–89; *Negro Slavery*, 452
Channing, William Ellery ("Ellery," 1818–1901), 703, 708, 748, 784, 787–88
Channing, William Henry, 698
Charlemagne, 709
Charles II (of England), 652
Charles V (Holy Roman emperor), 227, 330, 433, 495
Charleston, S.C., 142–43, 145–46, 291
Charron, Pierre, 262
Chase, Mr., 723

Chateaubriand, François-René de, 3, 23, 727

Chatel, Ferdinand-Toussaint-François, 279

Chaucer, Geoffrey, 409, 589, 748, 790; *Canterbury Tales*, 49, 93

Cheney, Harriet Vaughan: *A Peep at the Pilgrims*, 127

Cheraw, Miss., 552

Cherokee tribe, 591

Chesterfield, Earl of (Philip Dormer Stanhope), 206, 263, 415

Chimborazo, 38, 789

China, 68, 104, 108, 114, 224, 510, 553–54, 594, 776, 801

Chishull, Edmund, 493

Chod, 42

Chorley, Henry F., 536

Christian III (of Denmark), 357

Christianity, 53, 66, 92, 110, 137, 180, 185, 193, 197, 209, 213, 231, 234, 314, 322, 334, 376, 380, 384, 390, 398, 411, 419, 430, 433–34, 456, 499, 515, 567, 582, 599, 613, 615, 681, 693, 696, 709, 711, 724–25, 762, 766, 782, 801

Cicero, 8, 62, 66, 110, 117, 197, 229–30, 234, 241, 243, 291, 296, 374, 462, 571, 794; *Contra Verres*, 231; *De Finibus*, 179; *De Natura Deorum*, 120; *Oratio in Catalinam Prima*, 153

"Cinderella," 160

Clarence, Duke of, 728

Clarendon, Earl of (Edward Hyde), 491

Clarke, Edward D.: *Travels in Various Countries*, 167

Clarke, James Freeman, 472–73, 481

Clarke, Samuel, 53, 109, 215

Clarke, Sarah Freeman, 688, 756–57

Clay, Henry, 124–25, 296, 643, 722

Cleopatra, 62

Clifford, Nathan, 422

Clodius, Publius, 43

Cobbett, William, 95

Cobham, Baron (John Oldcastle), 196

Colburn and Bentley, 283

Coleridge, Samuel Taylor, 177, 181–82, 210, 285, 336, 346–47, 353, 357, 366, 371, 376, 389–91, 404, 414–15, 420, 431, 461, 494, 545, 609, 727; *Biographia Literaria*, 396, 404; *The Friend*, 169, 319, 390; "Lear," 659; *On the Constitution of Church and State*, 347, 358, 365; *Table Talk*, 416

Cole, Thomas, 734

Colesworthy, Deborah, 535

Collignon, Auguste-Charles, 277

Collins, William: "The Passions," 485

Cologne, Germany, 605

Colonization movement, 425, 497–98

Colquhoun, John C.: *Report on the Experiments on Animal Magnetism*, 412

Colton, Charles Caleb: *Lacon*, 415

Columbus, Christopher, 103, 133, 221, 360, 370, 452, 459, 501, 574, 758

Concord, Mass., 353, 357, 361, 363, 370, 392, 395, 401, 416, 418, 421–23, 429–30, 432, 450, 452, 454–56, 463, 486, 492–93, 501, 522, 540, 547, 565, 575, 579, 600, 604, 611, 664, 669, 692, 702, 708, 725, 775, 777, 788, 797

Concord, N.H., 148, 159

Confucius, 450, 476, 645, 782

Congress, U.S., 53, 98, 343, 452, 509, 643, 677

Congreve, William, 22, 264

Connecticut, 273, 337, 643

Connecticut River, 87–89

Constantinople, 463

Constitution, U.S., 51, 132, 352–53, 358, 722

Contino, Antino, 236

Conway, N.H., 193, 691

Cook, Mrs., 691–92

Coolidge, John T., 430

Cooper, James Fenimore, 127, 698

Copenhagen, Denmark, 315

Copernicus, Nicolaus, 189

Corbet, Mary, 785

Cordis, Mr., 273

Corinth, Greece, 37

Correggio (Antonio Allegri), 241

Cortona, Italy, 271

Cotes, Roger, 132

Cotton, John, 106

Cotton, Sarah, 502, 548

Cousin, Victor, 188, 286, 466, 578, 580–81, 583

Cowley, Abraham, 532; "The Dangers of an Honest Man in Much Company," 67

Cowper, William, 545; *The Task*, 22
Coxe, William: *Memoirs of John Duke of Marlborough*, 15
Crabbe, George, 534, 727
Crafts, Mr., 366
Cranch, John, 209, 253, 258
Crawford, Ethan Allen, 194
Cremona, Italy, 46
Crockett, Davy, 422
Cromwell, Oliver, 652
Crosby, Mr., 152
Crusades, 71, 332
Ctesiphon, 781
Cudworth, Ralph, 113, 412, 415
Cunard, Samuel, 716
Cunningham, J. W.: *Sancho, or the Proverbialist*, 378
Currie, James, 321
Cushing, Caleb, 322
Cushing, Eliza Lanesford: *Saratoga*, 127
Cushing, John P., 785
Cuvier, Georges, 196, 215, 295, 312, 359
Cyrus the Great, 64

Dabney, Jonathan Peele, 630
Dalton, John, 286
Daniel, 641
Dante Alighieri, 158, 260, 262, 405, 409, 533, 671, 676, 741, 762, 787; *Divine Comedy*, 215; *Paradiso*, 293, 297
Danton, Georges-Jacques, 507, 584
Danube River, 775
Darius the Great, 246
Dartmouth College, 592–93, 620, 622, 625
Darwin, Erasmus, 321
David, 449, 451, 454
Davis, Abel, 421–22
Davison, Miss, 395
Davy, Humphrey, 263
De Lolme, John Louis, 286
De Quincey, Thomas, 420
Dean, G. E., 635
Declaration of Independence, 56, 176, 755
Deerfield, Mass., 89
Defoe, Daniel: *Robinson Crusoe*, 95, 147
Deism, 438, 580, 585, 590

Delavigne, Casimir: *Les Enfants d'Édouard*, 278
Delphi, Greece, 37
Delsere, Signora, 261, 265
Demades, 149
Demerara, 144
Democratic Party, 352–53, 750
Demosthenes, 8, 133–34, 363–64, 367, 377, 393, 434
Denmark, 315, 357
Derry Academy, 182
Dewey, Orville, 631, 698
Dial, The, 735, 737–38, 754, 757
Dickens, Charles: *Oliver Twist*, 698
Diderot, Denis, 406, 473, 507, 526, 541
Diodati, Charles, 214
Diogenes Laertius (Bias), 223, 293, 330, 494
Dion, 230
Disraeli, Benjamin: *Vivian Grey*, 160, 516–17
Dollond, John, 294
Domenichino (Domenico Zampiere), 473
Domodossola, Italy, 270
Donatus, Aelius, 236, 263, 673
Donne, John, 451, 532; "An Anatomy of the World," 355
Drake, Joseph Rodman, 420
Dresden, Germany, 512
Dryden, John, 10, 117, 137, 621; "Ode on St. Cecilia's Day," 123
Druids, 481
Dumbarton, Scotland, 282
Dumfries, Scotland, 283
Dumont, Jacques-Edme, 315
Durante, Mr., 243
Dwight, John Sullivan, 566, 598, 600, 688
"Dying Gladiator," 248, 258, 452, 623

East Indies, 105, 150, 429, 510, 532–33
East Sudbury, Mass., 370
Ecbatana, Persia, 330
Eckermann, Johann Peter, 508–9, 517
Eden, 40, 545, 806
Edgeworth, Maria, 520
Edinburgh, Scotland, 209, 281
Edinburgh Review, 82, 93, 98, 165, 197, 605

Edwards, Jonathan, 106; *Freedom of the Will*, 296
Edwards, Richard, 612
Egypt, 9, 37, 67, 314, 553, 555–56, 586, 605, 608, 623, 639, 647, 651–53
Elephanta, India, 671
Eleusinian mysteries, 66
Elijah, 311
Eliot, John, 106
Elisha, 311
Elizabeth I (of England), 93, 106, 376
Elliott, Stephen, 84
Ellis, Cornelius, 217, 223–26
Elssler, Fanny, 775
Emerson, Charles Chauncy (brother), 176, 178, 181, 184, 191, 205, 294, 300, 317, 322, 339, 342, 358, 369–70, 380–81, 383, 401–2, 405–6, 409, 416–17, 426–27, 429, 431–34, 437–38, 441–42, 444, 448–49, 452–55, 462, 487–89, 495, 506, 523–24, 552, 576, 579, 583, 625, 776–79, 785, fig. 12
Emerson, Edith (daughter), 785
Emerson, Edward Bliss (brother), 69, 121, 126, 156–57, 336, 346–47, 350, 358, 369, 375, 453, 488, 576, 579, 778–79, fig. 11
Emerson, Ellen (daughter), 797
Emerson, Ellen Tucker (first wife), 159–61, 164, 169–73, 177–80, 191, 202, 205, 301, 327, 362, 370, 401, 480, 579, 629, 665–66, fig. 15, fig. 16; "The Violet," 183
Emerson, George Barrell (cousin), 378–79, 487–88, 589, 618
Emerson, Lydia (Lidian) Jackson (second wife), 414, 432, 447, 486, 502, 507, 523–24, 533, 545, 548, 550, 564, 566–67, 572, 575, 577, 579, 591, 593, 598, 620–21, 648–49, 654, 656, 666, 761, 763, 785, 801
Emerson, Mary Moody (aunt), 24, 121, 147, 201, 309, 311, 327, 365, 375, 401, 408, 413, 423, 470, 490, 522–23, 538–39, 559, 562, 573, 578, 611, 616, 664, 776–80, 788, fig. 9
Emerson, Ralph (cousin), 274, 331
Emerson, Ralph Waldo
    ADDRESSES: "The American Scholar," 536, 559, 574; "Divinity School Address," 620, 625; "Literary Ethics," 620, 625
    BOOKS: *Essays* (First Series), 763, 765–66, 768; *Nature*, 470, 523, 575
    JOURNALS/NOTEBOOKS: fig. 1, fig. 2, fig. 7, fig. 8, fig. 15, fig. 20
    LECTURES: "On the Present Age," 732; "Philosophy of History," 504, 566
    POEMS: "Always day & night," 288; "The days pass over me," 173; "Dost thou not hear me Ellen," 171; "Hark rascal!" 33–34; "How many events shall shake the earth," 359; "I will not live out of me," 199–200; "Let the dreams of night recall," 799; "O keep the current of thy spirits even," 77; "On bravely thro' the sunshine or the showers," 206; "Pride carves rich emblems on its seals," 77; "Pythologian Poem," 5, 15; "She never comes to me," 179–80; "There died an old man at St. Mary's the Pier," 40–41; "There the Northern light reposes," 38; "When bounding Fancy leaves the clods of earth," 18; "Whilst the fat fool prates nonsense to the pack," 63; "Wishing good & doing good," 462
    PORTRAITS: fig. 10, fig. 21
Emerson, Robert Bulkeley (brother), 189, fig. 13
Emerson, Ruth Haskins (mother), 95, 147, 170, 183, 350, 358, 405, 453, 577, fig. 3
Emerson, Susan Haven (sister-in-law), 525
Emerson, Waldo (son), 502, 523–24, 533, 566, 572, 577, 593, 598, 620–21, 637, 666, 690–91, 736, 738–39, 741, 745, 755, 797–98, 808, fig. 19, fig. 20
Emerson, William (brother), 84, 121, 523, 525, 577, fig. 14
Emerson, William (father), 110, 405, fig. 4
Emerson, William (grandfather), 110, 398
Emerson, William (nephew), 524–25

Empedocles, 766
Encyclopaedia Americana, 424
Enfantin, Barthélemy-Prosper, 279
Enfield, William, 9
Enghien, duc d' (Louis de Bourbon-Condé), 600
England, 8, 13, 37, 47, 62, 64–65, 68, 92–93, 95, 97–98, 106, 131, 133, 137, 142, 144, 158, 176, 196, 203, 209–12, 223, 226, 232, 239–40, 254, 259, 265, 280, 283–89, 301, 315, 325, 330–31, 340, 353, 376, 389–91, 393, 415–16, 432, 434, 439–40, 448, 493, 510, 536, 540–41, 545, 549, 553–54, 556, 588, 591, 596, 605, 613–14, 619, 627, 649, 653, 655, 671, 702, 716, 719, 776, 787, 796–97
England, John, 250
English Channel, 678
English language, 144, 153, 728
Enna, 797
Epaminondas, 381, 445, 669, 797
Epicles, 367
Epictetus, 344, 743
Epicureanism, 157, 224, 329, 385
Epicurus, 198
Erasmus, Desiderius, 362
Erminia, 264
Eros, 379
Eskimos, 810
Ethiopia, 756
Etna, Mount, 231, 234–35, 237, 241
Euclid, 349
Euler, Leonhard, 348, 351
Eumenides, 147
Euripides, 232
Europe, 62, 106–8, 164–65, 207, 212–13, 217–18, 222, 225–26, 236, 270, 376, 474, 555, 563, 586, 608, 639, 641, 649, 651, 758, 795–96, 798, 800
Eustis, Frederic A., 591
Eustis, William, 87
Evelyn, John, 215, 493
Everett, Alexander, 360, 437, 560
Everett, Edward, 3, 7–9, 17–18, 22, 24, 66, 117, 122, 127, 178, 180, 296, 341, 402, 404, 406, 423–24, 434, 451, 481, 562, 569, 613, 676
Exeter, Me., 387
Eynard, Paul, 227
Ezekiel, 741

Fabricius, Gaius, 378
Faliero, Marino, 268
Falkland, Viscount (Lucius Cary), 188, 196, 349
Falmouth, Mass., 332
Farley, Frederick A., 734
Farrar, Eliza Rotch, 301
Farrar, John, 301, 322, 763
Faya, 535
Felt, Mr., 698
Fénelon, François de, 213, 328, 339, 449
Ferdinand VI (of Spain), 150
Ferguson, James, 550
Ferney, Switzerland, 272
Ferrara, Abate, 240
Fichte, Johann Gottlieb, 302
Fielding, Henry, 451
Fielding, Thomas: *Select Proverbs of All Nations*, 187
Fiesole, Italy, 262
Fiji, 772
Fisher, Alvan, fig. 6
Flamsteed, John, 541
Flaxman, John, 186
Fleming, Mr., 514
Fletcher, John, 206, 263, 610, 703; *Bonduca*, 683
Florence, Italy, 205–8, 215, 259–68, 371, 498, 608, 651, 712
Florida, 144–45, 150–53, 487
Follen, Charles, 681
Fondulo, Cabrino, 46
Fontenelle, Bernard de, 8, 51, 140, 191, 293, 315
Fourier, Jean-Baptiste, 295
Fox, Charles James, 97–99, 107
Fox, George, 196–97, 339, 342, 349, 355, 360, 373, 393, 416, 418, 507, 580, 586, 614, 737
Fox, William J., 432
Fox tribe, 562
Framingham, Mass., 21, 83, 588
France, 8, 64, 92, 131, 133, 136, 142, 144, 174, 209–10, 254, 260, 269, 271–80, 307, 318, 326, 329, 343, 379, 436, 473, 496, 517, 553, 580, 590, 595, 605, 655, 716, 748–49, 773–74
Francis, Convers, 472, 481
Franklin, Benjamin, 98–99, 103–4, 106, 168, 197, 272, 339, 356, 451, 480
Franklin, John, 403

Frascati, M., 279
Fraser's Magazine, 201
Freeman, Reverend, 405
Freemasonry, 402
French Academy, 122
French language, 17–18, 331, 728
French Revolution, 94–95, 98, 318, 398–99, 496, 517, 544, 557, 617
Frisbie, Levi, 51
Frost, Barzillai, 633
Frothingham, Nathaniel L., 311, 473, 540
Fuller, Hiram, 563
Fuller, Margaret, 470, 517, 520, 534, 583, 605, 623, 638, 688, 720, 764, 799–800
Fuller, Mr., 749
Fuller, Thomas, 362

Gadsden, James, 151
Gaetano, Lorenzo, 237
Galen, 349
Galignani, John and William, 278
Galileo Galilei, 72, 103, 189, 215, 259–60, 264
Gannett, Ezra Stiles, 370
Garamantes, 626
Gardner, Mr., 239
Garofalo, Italy, 343
Garrick, David, 480
Garrison, William Lloyd, 711
Gaul, 496
Gay, Martin, 14, 19–20, 26, 41–42, 61, fig. 8
Gay, Mr., 150
Gay-Lussac, Joseph-Louis, 274, 349
Gelo, 233
Geneva, Switzerland, 271–73, 799
Geneva (Leman), Lake, 271–72
George, Duke of Saxony, 356–57
George, Lake, 231
George IV (of England), 206
Georgia, 643
Gérando, Marie-Joseph de, 262, 347
Gerard, Alexander, 349
German language, 509, 520, 633, 650
Germanic tribes, 68
Germany, 18, 144, 151, 189, 254, 316, 350, 356–57, 448, 514–15, 517, 519, 533, 650, 727
Giardini, Italy, 237–38
Giarre, Italy, 237

Gibbon, Edward, 66, 68, 92, 99, 107, 137, 271–72, 284, 288, 400, 638, 680, 724; *History of the Decline and Fall of the Roman Empire*, 43, 271, 441
Gibbons, Mr., 359
Gibraltar, 214, 222, 225, 378
Gillman, James, 389, 391
Giotto di Bondone, 262–63
Giovanni da Bologna, 263
Giovanni da San Giovanni, 265
Giramo, Squarcia, 46
Gissot, M., 272
Giza, pyramid at, 647
Glasgow, Scotland, 281–83
Glauber, Johann Rudolf, 295
Gloriana, 5
God, 4, 23, 28–29, 45, 59–61, 66, 76–77, 125, 129, 135, 142, 146, 149, 155, 159, 177, 191, 213, 218, 333–34, 337, 354, 357, 390, 393, 427, 430, 458, 586–88, 600, 613, 718, 737, 795, 808
Godwin, William, 165
Goethe, Johann Wolfgang von, 196–97, 242, 244, 261, 267, 284, 288, 295, 297–98, 303, 309, 314, 318–19, 325–29, 355, 358–59, 366, 400, 404, 409, 420–21, 444–47, 452, 456, 465–66, 470, 483, 492, 496, 503, 508–9, 511–12, 515, 517–18, 555, 562, 568, 609–10, 633, 637, 680, 686, 727, 744–45, 749, 753, 765, 783, 796; *Dichtung und Wahrheit*, 478; *Farbenlehre*, 638; *Faust*, 517, 638, 765; *Iphigenia auf Tauris*, 451, 638; *Tag und Jahres Hefte*, 312, 325, 328; *West-Östlicher Divan*, 307; *Wilhelm Meister*, 208, 285, 325–26, 517, 529, 745, 769
Golden Age, 545
Goldoni, Carlo, 220
Goldsmith, Oliver: "Retaliation," 98
Gordon, George, 95
Gorham, John: *Elements of Chemical Science*, 21
Gower, John: *Confessio Amantis*, 415
Graeter, Francis, 681
Grafton, Joseph, 333
Graham, Sylvester, 653, 677
Graham of Claverhouse, John, 489
Granacci, Francesco, 371
Grant, Anne, 82
Grant, Patrick, 249

Graves, William J., 569
Gray, Frederick T., 420
Gray, Mr., 790
Gray, Thomas: "The Descent of
    Odin," 423; "The Progress of
    Poesy," 623, 715
Greaves, James Pierrepont, 785
Greece, 103, 122, 649; ancient, 6–9, 30,
    37, 47–48, 51, 62, 66–68, 70, 92–93,
    102, 114, 117, 133, 189, 231–34, 236,
    240, 248, 263, 314, 335–36, 344, 378–
    79, 381, 397, 417, 441, 449, 451, 454,
    480, 489–90, 494, 534, 553, 555–56,
    581, 600, 605, 609, 619, 623, 634, 671,
    688, 709, 721, 723, 797
Greek language, 117, 360, 410, 509,
    670, 712
Green Mountains, 173
Green River, 89
Greene, Albert Groton, 734
Greenfield, Mass., 89
Greenough, Horatio, 452, 473, 613,
    675–76
Greenough, Thomas, 87, 90, 263
Greenwood, Francis W. P., 165
Gregory VII (pope), 12, 14
Gregory XVI (pope), 250, 252–54
Grimm, Jacob and Wilhelm, 473
Grotius, Hugo, 189, 571
Groton, Mass., 430, 432, 479
Guelph, William and Adelaide, 284
Guercino, Giovanni, 605, 624
Guicciardini, Francesco: History of
    Italy, 265
Gulliver, Deacon, 359
Gunstock, N.H., 691
Guy, 731–32
Guyana, 144, 294

Hadley, Mass., 88
Hallam, Arthur Henry, 675
Hallett, Benjamin Franklin, 402
Hamel, Jean-Pierre du, 294
Hampden, John, 196, 324, 349, 663
Hancock, John, 98
Handel, George Frederick, 374, 452,
    671
Hanover, N.H., 622
Happoldt, Mr., 151
Hare, Augustus W.: Guesses at Truth,
    175–76

Hare, Julius C., 264; Guesses at Truth,
    175–76, 263
Harlein Miscellany, 716
Harrison, William Henry, 716
Harvard College, 5, 14–15, 18–20, 33,
    41–42, 61, 87, 89, 105, 126, 310, 321,
    432, 470, 472, 475, 484, 509, 529, 536,
    545, 551, 568, 577, 594, 665, 749, fig. 5,
    fig. 6
Harvard Divinity School, 125, 156–57,
    159, 419–20, 484, 522, 590, 620, 625,
    677
Haskins, Hannah, 538–39
Haskins, Robert, 185
Hastings, 64–65
Hatsfield, Mass., 89
Haven, Mr., 90
Hawthorne, Nathaniel, 698, 785, fig.
    17; "Foot-prints on the Sea-shore,"
    610
Haydn, Joseph: The Creation, 123, 446
Hayne, Robert Y., 164
Heari, Professor, 277
Heber, Reginald, 315
Hebrew language, 117
Hebrews, ancient, 37, 189, 335–36, 475,
    496, 587, 641, 724
Hederich, Benjamin, 369
Hedge, Barnabas, 299
Hedge, Frederic H., 370, 417, 443,
    472–73, 481, 525, 543, 545, 676
Hedge, Levi, 321
Heeren, Arnold: Historical Researches,
    623; Reflections on the Politics of
    Ancient Greece, 725
Hegel, Georg Wilhelm Friedrich, 196
Heinrich the Foundling, 520
Hemans, Felicia, 536, 555, 727; "To
    Corinna at the Capitol," 327
Henry IV (of France), 97, 273
Henry IV (Holy Roman emperor), 12
Heraclitus, 366, 533, 766, 798
Herbert, George, 158, 179, 362, 449,
    584, 619, 621, 727; "Aaron," 475;
    "Affliction," 295, 297; "The Church-
    Porch," 188; "Decay," 475
Herculaneum, 241, 246
Hercules (statue), 248
Herder, Johann Gottfried von, 137, 328
Heredia, Alonzo Fernández de, 150
Hermes, 42

Hernhutters, 762
Herodotus, 9, 349, 626, 640
Herostratus, 133
Herrick, Robert, 158, 352
Herring, Roger, 507
Herschel, William, 193, 260, 263, 289, 408, 541
Heywood, Abiel, 576
Heywood, Humphrey, 423
Hiero, 229
Hill, John Boynton, 387
Hiller, Johann Adam, 445
Hillman, Mr., 301, 530
Himalayas, 554
Hinduism, 93, 310
Hoar, Elizabeth, 456, 461, 488, 493, 506, 522, 573, 583, 596, 611, 626–28, 747, 754, 770, 785, 800
Hoar, Mrs. Samuel, 583
Hoar, Samuel, 405, 427, 750, 766
Hobbes, Thomas, 134
Hoffmann, Josiah O., 569
Hogg, James, 391
Holbrook, Silas P., 228
Holyoke, Mount, 87
Homer, 137, 158, 298, 316, 336, 365, 370, 374, 378, 381, 397, 428, 437, 440, 451, 453, 484, 492, 501, 555, 589, 595, 609, 670, 676, 724, 790; *Iliad*, 376, 452, 723; *Odyssey*, 723
Hone, Philip, 348
Hooker, Richard: *Of the Lawes of Ecclesiastical Politie*, 421
Horace, 8, 258; *Art of Poetry*, 179; *Epistles*, 71, 622; *Satires*, 108, 191
Hosmer, Edmund, 463, 530, 576, 794
Howard, John, 339
Howard Benevolent Society, 24
Howe, Peter, 488, 509, 535, 591, 607, 615
Howe, Samuel, 167
Howitt, William: *Book of the Seasons*, 403
Hoxie, Captain, 289, 291–92
Hubbardstown, Mass., 90
Hudson, Henry, 378
Humboldt, Alexander von, 312, 349, 351, 491, 610
Hume, David, 66, 92, 106, 109, 185, 215; *Of the Idea of Necessary Connexion*, 77

Humphreys, Colonel, 152
Hungary, 166
Hunt, Benjamin Peter, 210, 457, 463
Hunter, John, 110
Hus, Jan, 46
Hussey, Mr., 241

Iamblichus: *Life of Pythagoras*, 773
Illinois, 372, 800
India, 6, 9, 19, 25, 43–44, 57, 93, 144, 162, 315, 460, 652, 671
Indians. *See* Native Americans
Inquisition, 590
Inversnaid, Scotland, 282
Ionia, 671
Iowa tribe, 562
Ipswich, Mass., 343
Ireland, 283–84, 289–90
Irish immigrants, 352, 364, 550, 785
Iroquois tribes, 768
Irving, Washington, 613, 675–76
Isabella (of Spain), 109
Isaiah, 378, 426, 451, 454
Isis, 217, 379
Islam, 760–61
Italian language, 728
Italy, 46, 204–10, 215, 220, 228–71, 273, 280, 315, 342–43, 390–91, 411, 475, 533, 618, 649, 651, 728, 787
Itellario, Signor, 237

"Jack the Giant-Killer," 759
Jackson, Andrew, 148, 151, 313, 317, 325, 352, 358, 375, 414, 436, 750
Jackson, Charles Thomas, 599, 606
Jackson, Lydia. *See* Emerson, Lydia Jackson
Jamaica, 144
James (saint), 363
James I (of England), 106–7, 111, 192, 652
Jameson, Anna Brownell Murphy: *The Diary of an Ennuyée*, 548
Jamieson, Robert, 433, 663
Japan, 365, 634
Jarvis, Edward, 261
Jefferson, Thomas, 107, 126, 135, 174, 356
Jeffrey, Francis, 131, 296
Jeremiah, 426
Jerry, Mr., 153

Jerusalem, 505, 761
Jesuits, 40
Jesus, 28, 77, 140–42, 149, 151, 165, 191, 195–98, 249–50, 252, 283, 304, 314, 317, 323, 334, 339, 350, 373, 381, 383–86, 393, 397, 409, 411, 424, 434, 437–39, 466–67, 473, 482, 490, 499, 515, 533, 542, 576, 582, 586, 594, 599, 608, 618, 643, 654, 667, 688, 699–700, 713, 740, 782, 799
Jews, 37, 155, 180, 189, 191, 253, 314, 333, 335, 389, 688, 728–29, 752, 768
John (saint), 314, 362, 377, 409, 454, 464, 469, 684, 741
John of Cappadocia, 43
John XXIII (anti-pope), 46
Johnson, Adams, 87
Johnson, Samuel, 99, 164–65, 175, 219, 355, 377, 529; Lives of the Poets, 117, 729
Jonson, Ben, 10, 22, 158, 291, 435, 469, 555, 611, 687; The Alchemist, 137; The Gypsies Metamorphosed, 35–36
Joseph II (Holy Roman Emperor), 252
Jouffroy, Théodore, 274, 578
Judas Iscariot, 696, 705
Juggernaut temple, 43–44
Julius Caesar, 12, 36, 62, 197, 251, 263, 300, 380, 484, 489, 564, 623, 643, 663, 715
Julius II (pope), 298
Jupiter (Jove), 117, 119, 233, 321, 449, 473, 555–56, 560, 600, 661, 715, 767
Jussieu, Antoine-Laurent de, 276, 660
Justinian, 111
Juvenal: Satires, 12, 100–1, 154

Kant, Immanuel, 202, 445, 466, 533, 553, 718
Kean, Edmund, 473
Keats, John, 606
Keble, John: "Morning," 196
Kendall, Amos, 750
Kent, Margaret Tucker, 202, 205
Kentucky, 253
Kepler, Johannes, 638
Kingston, Mr., 247
Kneeland, Abner, 313, 424
Knights Hospitalers, 203, 227
Knox, John, 283

Koran, 180, 476
Kyrle, John, 408

La Fontaine, Jean de, 22; Fables, 277
La Rochefoucauld, François de, 149
La Valette, Jean Parisot de, 227
Ladd, William, 564
Lafayette, Marie-Joseph-Paul de, 164, 275, 326, 349, 377
Lancaster, Joseph, 71
Landor, Walter Savage, 206, 209–10, 262–65, 284, 357, 416, 473, 787; "Barrow and Newton," 199–200; "Citation and Examination of William Shakespeare Touching Deer-Stealing," 710; "Epicurus, Leontion, and Ternissa," 198, 200–1; Imaginary Conversations, 401; Pericles and Aspasia, 703, 754; "William Penn and Lord Peterborough," 200
Landseer, Thomas, 676
Lane, Charles, 785, 791
"Laocoön," 248, 259, 553, 609
Laplace, Pierre-Simon de, 77, 131, 295, 405, 424, 439
Lapland, 14, 69, 142
Las Cases, comte de (Emmanuel-Augustin Dieudonné), 595, 603
Latin language, 17, 153, 237, 286, 588, 670, 728, 748
Launay, Bernard-René de, 584
Lausanne, Switzerland, 271–72
Lavater, Johann Kaspar, 358, 445
Le Boo, Prince, 501
Lechmere, Mr., 126
Leclerc, Jean, 117
Lee, Mrs., 177, 516
Leibniz, Gottfried Wilhelm, 68, 348
Leicester, Mass., 84
Leighton, Robert, 449, 558
Leipzig, Germany, 356
Lentulus, 249
Leo Bizantinus, 162
Leonardo da Vinci, 274, 689; "Last Supper," 270
Leonidas, 219, 459
Lessing, Gotthold Ephraim, 650; Nathan the Wise, 668
Levi, Lieutenant, 275
Lexington, Mass., 406–8, 429

Liberia, 497–98
Lieber, Francis, 681
Linberg, Henning Gotfried, 341
Lincoln, England, 330, 343
Lincoln, Mass., 627, 783
Linnaeus, Carolus (Carl von Linné), 314–16, 335, 537, 650, 660
Litchfield, England, 480
Little, Brown (publisher), 703
"Little Red Riding Hood," 160, 759
Liverpool, England, 209–11, 283–84, 287, 289, 353
Livy, 25, 794
Locke, John, 8, 109, 113, 154, 166–67, 419, 493, 688; *Essay Concerning Human Understanding*, 36; *Thoughts Concerning Education*, 157
Lombards, 397
Lombardy, 270–71
Lomond, Loch, 282
London, England, 95, 209, 260, 280, 283–84, 365, 389–91, 506, 514, 540–41, 652, 655, 790
London Age, 514
London Literary Gazette, 353
London Quarterly, 609
London and Westminster Review, 503, 553, 728
Longinus, 357
Lonsdale, Earl of, 283
Loomis, Harvey, 388
Lord's Prayer, 189
Loring, Charles G., 177
Loring, Ellis Gray, 583
Loring, Helen, 505
Lorrain, Claude (Claude Gellée), 252, 361, 803
Louis XIV (of France), 329, 773
Louis XVI (of France), 376
Louis-Philippe, 273
Louisiana, 47
Louisville, Ky., 540
Lovejoy, Elijah P., 571
Lowell, Mass., 507, 566
Lucan: *Pharsalia*, 497, 727
Lucas, Richard, 262
Lucas van Leyden, 605
Lucretius, 286
Luther, Martin, 71, 164, 196, 201, 207, 249, 295–96, 349–50, 353, 355–57, 361–

63, 365, 370, 382, 385, 393, 396, 437, 452, 471, 507, 520, 608, 737, 749
Lutherans, 768
Lyman, Joseph, 431
Lynn, Mass., 235, 756
Lyon, George Francis, 640
Lysippus, 692

Macao, 554
Macedon, 682
Machiavelli, Niccolò, 252, 259, 266, 462
Mackintosh, James, 100, 117, 131, 196, 215, 262, 574; *General View of the Progress of Ethical Philosophy*, 191
Madison, James, 126
Madrid, Spain, 150
Maecenas, 188, 258
Maezel, Johann Nepomuk, 336
Maggiore, Lake, 270
Maine, 105, 329–32, 370, 372, 387–88, 414, 643, 778
Malden, Mass., 522, 777
Malta, 203–5, 209, 217, 226–28, 260, 282, 390–91
Manchester, England, 432
Mann, Horace, 693
Manzoni, Alessandro, 727; *I Promessi Sposi*, 206–7, 264, 266, 298, 785
Marat, Jean-Paul, 707
Marathon, battle of, 133
Marcellus, 234
Marchand, Étienne, 42
Marcus Aurelius, 50, 114, 396
Marlborough, Duke of (John Churchill), 14
Maroncelli, Piero, 681
Marquesa Islands, 403
Mars, Madame, 278
Marsh, James, 391
Marshall, John, 414
Martial: *Epigrams*, 25, 117
Martineau, Harriet, 431–32, 443, 454, 769; *Society in America*, 539–40
Marvell, Andrew, 158, 196, 532, 621
Mary, Queen of Scots, 376
Mary I (of England), 590
Massachusetts, 84–90, 106, 307, 351, 474, 643, 697, 790
Massinger, Philip, 206, 263
Mather, Cotton, 106; *Essays To Do Good*, 158

Mather, Increase, 106
Mauna Loa, 42
May, Edwardes, 612
May, Samuel J., 425, 433
McGavin, William, 402
Medina, Arabia, 761
Mediterranean Sea, 225–26, 230, 678
Melanchthon, Philipp, 363
Mellili, Italy, 234
Mendelssohn, Moses: *Phédon*, 186
Menu, 626, 782
Merck, Johann Heinrich, 511–12
Merrimack River, 395
Messina, Italy, 236–38, 270
Mestre, Italy, 267
Metella, Cecilia, 251
Metellus, 663
Methodists, 151, 153, 181, 314, 382, 385, 743, 758, 777, 785
Methuselah, 102
Mexico, 144
Mez, Johan, 513
Michael II (of Greece), 103
Michelangelo Buonarroti, 251–52, 256, 259–60, 263–64, 267, 297–99, 315, 331, 349, 371–72, 374, 376, 398, 448, 451, 465, 475, 511, 608–10, 676, 689, 692, 709–10, 712–13, 716, 728, 776
Michigan, Lake, 692
Middle Ages, 114, 122–23, 136, 174, 437, 555
Middlesex Association, 630
Middleton, Thomas: *The Phoenix*, 765
Milan, Italy, 46, 208, 270, 689
Mill, John Stuart, 284, 432
Milman, Henry Hart: *Samor*, 3
Milo, 12
Miltiades, 564
Milton, John, 3, 8, 71, 75, 101, 117, 136–38, 158, 189, 196, 214–15, 290, 309, 314, 336–37, 349, 355, 359, 362, 382, 396, 411, 439, 448, 451, 514–15, 519, 526, 571, 576–77, 579, 589, 595, 621, 676, 712, 727, 749, 752, 780, 783, 789; *Apology against a Pamphlet Called a Modest Confutation*, 20; *Apology for Smectymnus*, 381; *Areopagitica*, 6; *Comus*, 111, 215, 567, 576; *History of Britain*, 474; *Lycidas*, 217, 224, 442; *Paradise Lost*, 119, 122, 124, 136, 138, 160, 193, 643, 682, 689; *Paradise

Regained*, 349; "Il Penseroso," 111, 431, 637; *Reason of Church Government Urged against Prelaty*, 82, 240; *Samson Agonistes*, 576; sonnets, 146
Mind, 20, 59–60, 68, 73, 81, 97, 104, 124–25, 139–40, 173–74
Minerva, 54, 229–30, 326, 379, 556
Minorcans, 151
Minott, George, 509–10, 588, 608, 615
Mirabeau, marquis de (Victor Riqueti), 315, 506–7, 526
Mississippi River, 487, 541
Mitford, William, 117
Mobile, Ala., 611
Modena, Duke of, 258
Mohammed, 27, 164, 357, 760–61
Mohawk tribe, 113, 688, 765
Molière (Jean-Baptiste Poquelin), 377
Monk, James Henry (Bishop of Gloucester), 209
Monroe, James, 126, 175, 179
Montagu, Mary Wortley, 547
Montagu, Mass., 89
Montague, Basil, 391
Montaigne, Michel de, 134, 196, 262, 339, 401, 419, 506, 559–60, 590, 630, 699; *Essays*, 115, 117, 149, 158, 179, 196, 204, 277, 306, 308, 411, 430, 581–82, 749
Montesquieu, baron de (Charles-Louis de Secondat): *Lettres Persanes*, 100
Montfort, Simon de, 133
Montgomery, James M.: *The Pelican Island*, 137–38
Monti, Vicenzo, 560
Montserrat, 590
Moody, Paul, 407
Moody, Samuel, 393, 522
Moore, Dr., 87
Moore, Thomas, 374, 485, 497, 574
Moravians, 758, 768
Mordecai, 733
More, Thomas, 196, 557
Moreau, Jean-Victor, 99
Morocco, 225
Morton, Ichabod, 571
Moscow, Russia, 167
Moses, 259, 304, 462, 469, 586, 613, 741, 767, 776
Motte, Mellish Irving, 14, 177

Motte-Guyon, Jeanne-Marie de la, 393
Moxon, Edward, 461
Mozart, Wolfgang Amadeus, 252, 671
Mumford, Luise, 808
Muqanna, al- (Hashim ibn Hakim), 111
Murat, Achille, 145–46, 291, 457, 489, 521
Murillo, Bartolomé Esteban, 274
Muslims, 180, 338, 760–61
Mycale, battle of, 133

Nahant, Mass., 245
Nantasket, Mass., 790
Napier, William John, 554
Naples, Bay of, 235, 241, 245
Naples, Italy, 205, 226, 240–47, 249, 259–60, 343, 444, 679, 689, 768
Napoléon Bonaparte, 64, 67, 99, 165–66, 270–71, 295–96, 330, 372, 377–78, 480, 484, 489, 504, 517, 520, 533, 544, 557, 564, 573, 594–96, 600, 603, 610, 668, 690, 707, 789
Nardini, 619
Narses, 107
Natick, Mass., 83
Native Americans, 17, 105–6, 113, 133, 151–52, 329, 331–32, 356, 387, 422, 498, 551–52, 562, 591, 634, 638, 688, 756, 765, 768, 810
Nayler, James, 737
Nebuchadnezzar, 467
Needham, Mass., 83
Negroes. See African-Americans
Nelson, Horatio, 67
Nero, 233, 284
Netherlands, 17, 150, 478, 682
New Bedford, Mass., 297, 299, 301–5, 343, 631
New Hampshire, 193–95, 510, 643, 677, 691–93, 778
New Holland, 144
New Jersey, 315
New Jerusalem Magazine, 186, 198
New Lebanon Conference, 148
New Orleans, La., 514
New Salem, Mass., 90
New Testament. See Bible
New York City, 267, 274, 289, 346, 348, 351, 452–53, 514, 525, 555, 591, 652, 655, 677, 734
New Zealand, 634

Newcomb, Charles King, fig. 18
Newhall, Mary, 304–5
Newton, Isaac, 45, 53, 71, 77, 82, 123, 132, 166, 168, 196, 215, 286, 288, 295, 317, 377, 470, 493, 637–39
Newton, Mass., 83, 216, 313, 317, 332, 339
Niagara Falls, 330, 444, 592
Nicholas I (of Russia), 297
Nichol, John Pringle, 773
Nichols, Ichabod, 84
Nicolini, Signor, 232, 234
Nicolosi, Francesco, 237
Niebuhr, Barthold Georg, 400, 574
Nineveh, 102
Nithsdale, Scotland, 540
Noah, 102, 276, 636
Norris, John: Essay Towards the Theory of the Ideal or Intelligible World, 419
North America, 144
North American Review, 437, 492, 609, 749
North Brookfield, Mass., 84
North Carolina, 151, 351, 474
North Pole, 403
North Sea, 678
Northampton, Mass., 88
Norton, Andrews, 554, 628, 646: Statement of Reasons, 212
Norway, 47, 142
Novalis (Friedrich von Hardenberg), 327–28
Noyes, George Rapall, 554

Oberlin, Jérémie-Jacques, 315
Ockley, Simon: History of the Saracens, 760–61
O'Connell, Daniel, 654
Odin, 345
Oegger, Guillaume: The True Messiah, 421, 426
Ohio, 351
Ohio River, 775
Old Testament. See Bible
Olympiodorus, 766
Oregon, 475
Oromasdes, 129
Orosius, Paulus: Historiarum Adversum Paganos, 65
Osborn, Francis, 371
Osgood, Charles, fig. 17

Osiris, 217, 379, 555, 766
Ossipee, Lake, 691
Otanes, 298
Otis, Harrison Gray, 46, 753
Otis, James, 106
Otway, Thomas, 22
Ovid: *Art of Love*, 157; *Fasti*, 131
Owen, Robert, 347
Oxford University, 64, 315, 372, 632

Pacific islanders, 810
Pacini, Giovanni: *Ivanhoe*, 265
Padua, Italy, 215, 268
Painting, 29, 36, 123
Palermo, Italy, 239–40, 411, 520
Palestine, 549, 608
Paley, William, 53
Palma Giovane (Jacopo Palma), 268
Palma Vecchio (Jacopo Palma), 268
Palmer, Edward, 645, 650, 801
Palmer, Mass., 85
Palmyra, 30, 618, 780
Pantheism, 145
Papacy, 12, 71, 250, 252–54
Paphos, 781
Paris, France, 23, 209, 272–80, 307, 331,
    473, 557, 605, 652, 655, 689, 778, 810
Parkman, Francis, 178
Parkman, William, 629
Parliament, 97–98
Parnassus, 6, 29, 123
Parry, William E., 378
Parthia, 682
Pascal, Blaise, 100
Passions, 42–43, 79–80
Paul (saint), 224, 249, 334, 339, 349,
    361, 382, 385, 389, 396, 438, 449,
    454, 469, 504, 515, 521, 586, 663, 688,
    776
Paul III (pope), 256
Peabody, Elizabeth Palmer, 494, 610;
    Record of a School, 422–23
Peace Society, 174, 370, 646, 695
Pelham, Mass., 87
Pelletier, James, 293
Pendragon, 5, 9
Penn, William, 180, 191, 213, 361, 373,
    564, 667
Pennsylvania, 431, 643
Penobscot tribe, 105–6, 387
Pepperell, William, 332

Pericles, 560, 595, 634
Perkins, Jacob, 101, 211
Perkins, Reverend, 89
Perrin, John: *Elements of French and
    English Conversation*, 220
Persepolis, 30, 623
Persia, 51, 298, 330, 533, 768
Peru, 802
Perugino (Pietro Vannucci), 263
Pestalozzi, Johann Heinrich, 347–48,
    408, 471, 557
Peter (saint), 249
Peter the Hermit, 71–72
Petrarch, Francesco, 215, 236, 298
Petronius Arbiter: *Satyricon*, 594
Phenix, The, 533, 648
Phidias, 377, 451–52, 557, 609, 671, 676,
    713, 715
Philip II (of Macedon), 115, 262, 367
Philippe Marie, 46
Phillips, Jonathan, 457, 473, 520, 525
Phillips, William, 87
Phillis, 502
Philo Judaeus, 389
Phipps, William, 106
Phocion, 134, 263, 324, 344, 363, 367,
    381, 385, 439, 623
Phoenicians, 7
Picts, 562
Pilgrims, 771
Pindar, 490, 621, 687
Piranesi, Giambattista, 605
Pitt, William (the Elder) (Earl of
    Chatham), 97–98, 197, 296, 715
Pitt, William (the Younger), 97–98
Plataea, battle of, 133
Plato, 8, 45, 58, 62, 133, 175, 299, 314,
    319, 334, 366, 381, 409, 415, 428, 448,
    481, 490, 533, 537, 544, 571, 581, 594,
    650, 699, 715, 718, 766, 776, 795;
    Phaedo, 406
Platonism, 104, 173, 297–99
Platt, Mr., 180
Playfair, John, 67, 117, 296, 304
Pliny (the Elder), 101–2
Plotinus, 366; *Enneads*, 440, 766
Plutarch, 51, 149, 158, 162, 196, 315, 339,
    346, 358, 360, 367, 430, 506, 515, 534,
    582, 584, 619, 693, 703–4, 708, 721,
    749, 797; *Morals*, 539–40
Pluto, 233

Plymouth, Mass., 299, 302–4, 502, 533–34, 568, 802
Poland, 166–67, 297
Pompeii, 241, 246–47
Pompey, 12, 251
Pope, Alexander, 117, 137, 164; "Epistle to Dr. Arbuthnot," 546; "Essay on Man," 115; *Moral Essays*, 115, 117, 124
Porta, Giacomo della, 256
Portici, Italy, 246
Portland, Me., 84
Posilippo, 241–42
Posterla, Giovanni di, 46
Potomac River, 146–47
Potter, Lieutenant, 429–30
Pozzuoli, 242–43, 245
Pratt, William, 249
Presbyterians, 283, 290
Prester John, 475
Priestley, Joseph, 137, 554
Princeton, Mass., 90
Princeton College, 778
Proclus, 766
Prometheus, 134, 555–56, 566, 780, 798–99
Proserpine, 233
Protestantism, 66, 151, 228, 244, 370
Proteus, 345, 445, 466, 754
Providence, R.I., 557, 563, 734–35, 754
Publius Syrus, 350
Puerto Rico, 184, 191, 346, 778
Puritans, 106, 332, 449
Putnam, Joseph, 189
Pygmalion, 486
Pyrrhus, 378
Pythagoras, 318, 397, 476, 606, 704, 773, 795
Pythologian Club, 5, 15

Quakers, 106, 165, 191, 215, 301, 304–5, 312, 385, 393, 398, 557, 677, 762
Quarterly Review, 7, 9, 14, 349, 422
Quebog River, 84
Queen Mab, 1, 9
Quimby, Mr., 577
Quin, Mr., 808
Quincy, Josiah, 433
Quincy, Josiah Phillips, 464
Quincy, Mass., 126
Quintilian, 8

Rabelais, François, 19, 590
Racine, Jean, 8
Radici, Signor, 297
Raimondo, 240
Raleigh, Walter, 802; *History of the World*, 473
Rambler, 101, 117
Rammohun Roy, 315
Raphael (Raffaello Sanzio), 241, 247–49, 251, 263, 267, 275, 371, 452, 512, 623–24, 676, 689, 713, 715–16, 728, 775
Ravenna, Italy, 215, 260
Réamur, René-Antoine de, 294
Reason, 42, 57–58, 103, 109, 326, 368, 373
Reed, Sampson, 144, 165, 354, 392, 420, 457, 616; *Observations on the Growth of the Mind*, 139–40; "Oration on Genius," 416, 467, 485
Reeve, Henry, 432
Reformation, 67, 106, 133, 144, 471
Regulus, 324
Rembrandt van Rijn, 687
Reni, Guido, 241, 249
Resina, Italy, 246–47
Retzsch, Friedrich August, 756
Revolutionary War, 51, 67, 95, 98, 106, 332, 421–23, 429–30, 432–33, 474
Reynolds, Richard, 293
Rhode Island, 416, 643
Rhodes, 227
Ricciardi, Giuseppe, 232, 234–35
Rice, M., 85
Rice, Reuben Nathaniel, 788, 805
Richardson, Samuel: *Clarissa*, 43; *Sir Charles Grandison*, 157
Richter, Jean Paul, 34
Rienzi, Cola di, 110, 248
Rinaldi, 256
Ripley, Christopher Gore, 527, 629
Ripley, Ezra (Dr.), 355–56, 362, 384–85, 432, 436, 523–24, 599, 633, 664; *History of the Fight at Concord*, 430
Ripley, Ezra (grandson), 359
Ripley, George, 89, 472–73, 481, 462, 764, 784; *Philosophical Miscellanies*, 578, 580
Ripley, Lincoln, 89
Ripley, Mary, 640
Ripley, Noah, 164
Ripley, Phebe Bliss Emerson, 356

Ripley, Samuel, 90, 359, 552, 573, 698
Ripley, Sarah Alden, 177, 327, 423, 470, 551, 561, 593, 653
Ripley, Sophia, 561, 764
Robbins, Eli, 549
Robbins, Mr., 407–8
Robertson, William, 92
Robinson, Seth, 137
Robinson, William, 557
Rochester, Earl of (Henry Wilmot), 328
Rodman, Benjamin, 301
Rodman, Elizabeth, 304
Rogers, Mr., 243
Rome, ancient, 3, 6, 8, 12–13, 36–37, 43, 47, 62, 66–68, 93, 102, 114, 117, 140, 189, 231, 233, 235–38, 240, 242–48, 315–16, 378, 417, 433, 494, 549, 570, 581, 588, 605, 643, 647, 682, 694, 704, 718, 752, 754, 794
Rome, Italy, 205, 208–9, 220, 247–60, 262, 266, 268, 298, 328, 365, 389, 444, 493, 501, 540, 608, 626, 651, 679, 689, 774, 810
Romulus, 684
Rosa, Salvator, 687
Roscoe, William, 236
Rosenmüller, Johann Georg, 554
Rostopchin, Fyodor Vasilyevich, 379
Rotch, Mary, 301–2, 304, 374, 457, 785
Rousseau, Jean-Jacques, 272, 405–6, 473, 638
Roxbury, Mass., 83, 119, 125, 308
Russell, Ben, 489
Russell, John Lewis, 638
Russell, William, 427
Russia, 10, 47

Sac tribe, 562
Sacchi, Andrea, 256, 689
Sachs, Hans, 748
Sadducees, 145
Said Ibn Haer, 154
St. Augustine, Fla., 144–45, 150–53, 291
St. Croix, 519
St. Helena, 605
St. Lucia, 646
St. Marks, Fla., 552
Saint-Simon, duc de (Louis de Rouvroy), 773
Sais, 323

Saladin, 378
Salamis, battle of, 133
Salem, Mass., 445, 452, 547, 557, 756
Sallust, 494
Samaritans, 155, 696
Sampson, George A., 177, 266, 300, 303, 332, 334, 346–47
San Juan, Puerto Rico, 346
Sandwich Islands, 42, 193, 318, 403
Saracens, 379, 391
Sarto, Andrea del (Andrea d'Agnolo), 249
Satan, 350, 362
Saul, 347
Saumaise, Claude de, 369
Saurin, Jacques, 105
Savage, James, 360
Savannah, Ga., 519
Savoy, 539
Saxons, 188, 397, 418, 439, 671, 755–56
Saxony, 357–58
Scaliger, Julius Caesar, 749
Schelling, Friedrich Wilhelm von, 404, 420, 552
Schiller, Friedrich von, 192, 202, 355, 518, 541, 684; Death of Wallenstein, 346, 494
Schlegel, August Wilhelm von or Friedrich von, 175, 308
Schleiermacher, Friedrich, 370, 552
Schleusner, Johann Friedrich, 554
School for Young Ladies, 119
Schubert, Daniel, 319, 324
Schuyler, Philip, 667
Scipio Africanus, 197, 236, 251, 293, 378, 380, 595, 643, 690
Scotland, 210, 281–83, 376, 540–41
Scott, Walter, 116–17, 131, 160, 196, 215, 312, 335–36, 340, 485, 574, 586, 595, 610, 686, 704, 727; The Abbot, 779–80; The Bride of Lammermoor, 22, 172–73; The Fortunes of Nigel, 160; Guy Mannering, 22, 43; The Heart of Midlothian, 185; "The Lady of the Lake," 431; Letters on Demonology and Witchcraft, 412; The Pirate, 43; Quentin Durward, 769; Rob Roy, 283; St. Ronan's Well, 160
Scougal, Henry P., 449; The Life of God in the Soul of Man, 158
Scythians, 113, 496

Search, Edward (Abraham Tucker), 1
Sebastian (saint), 249
Seckendorf, Veit Ludwig von, 357
Sedgwick, Catherine Maria: *Live and Let Live*, 600
Selbourne, England, 315
Selden, John, 135
Seminole tribe, 552
Seneca, 242, 430, 469, 518, 582, 587; *Controversiae*, 179; *Dialogues*, 41
Severini family, 244
Sewall, Jonathan, 127
Shackford, Charles Chauncy, 498
Shakers, 757–58
Shakespeare, William, 8, 62, 71, 116–17, 123, 136–37, 158, 176, 181, 196–97, 206, 215, 291, 309, 312, 315, 336, 338, 365, 370, 374, 376–77, 381, 393, 396–97, 399–400, 404, 407, 409, 411, 424, 426, 439, 443, 448, 451–52, 454, 462, 466, 469, 481, 485–86, 490, 501, 503, 505, 509, 514, 517, 519, 533, 537, 581, 584, 589, 608–9, 621, 629, 633, 650, 653–54, 660–61, 671, 676, 699, 713, 724, 727, 741, 776, 790, 793; *Antony and Cleopatra*, 192, 335, 339; *As You Like It*, 156; *Hamlet*, 163, 192, 336, 380, 382, 410, 412, 660–61, 689; *1 Henry IV*, 188, 201; *2 Henry IV*, 67, 335, 506; *1 Henry IV*, 430; *Julius Caesar*, 94, 564; *King Lear*, 140, 199, 335–36, 410, 549, 660–61; *Macbeth*, 104, 336; *A Midsummer Night's Dream*, 324, 504; *Much Ado about Nothing*, 157; *Othello*, 177, 336, 505; *Richard III*, 462; sonnets, 181, 316–17, 733; *The Tempest*, 115–16, 137, 192; *Troilus and Cressida*, 13; *Two Gentlemen of Verona*, 759
Shelley, Percy Bysshe, 555, 606, 727, 783
Shenstone, William, 171
Sheridan, Richard Brinsley, 497
Sherlock, William, 53
Shi Jing, 327
Sicily, 210, 217, 228–40, 246, 390–91, 411
Siculi, 236
Sidney, Philip, 515, 557
Sigismund (Holy Roman emperor), 46
Silenus, 345
Simeon the Stylite, 682, 684

Simmons, George Frederick, 787
Simonides, 130
Simplon Pass, 270–71, 416
Sioux tribe, 562
Sisera, 682
Sismondi, Jean-Charles de, 46, 220, 267
Skepticism, 186, 410–11
Slave trade, 67, 131, 550, 571–72
Slavery, 40, 55–61, 152, 169, 176, 191, 300, 310, 368, 376, 398, 423–25, 452, 475, 502, 549, 568, 570, 600, 654–55, 681, 689–90, 756, 790–91
Slow, Ephraim, 423
Smeaton, John, 294
Smith, John, 106
Smith, Mr., 258
Snow, Louisa, 808
Socialism, 571
Socrates, 15, 72, 103, 149, 168, 179, 186, 193, 196, 206, 213, 263, 288, 302, 326, 328, 334, 339, 342–43, 350, 355, 373, 381, 385, 396–97, 424, 430, 586, 653, 689, 782–83
Solomon, 38, 115, 335, 337
Solon, 484–85
Somerville, Mary, 193
Sophocles, 555; *Ajax*, 489; *Antigone*, 441; *Electra*, 30–31, 451, 799; *Philoctetes*, 489
Sorbonne, 605
South America, 62, 122
South Brookfield, Mass., 85
South Carolina, 142–43, 145–46, 351, 474
Southey, Robert, 262, 376, 686, 704; "Bishop Bruno," 374
Spain, 62, 67, 133, 142, 150–53, 225, 496
Spanish language, 728
Spalatin, Georg, 357
Sparta, Greece, 68, 128, 378, 563, 754
Spencer, Mass., 84
Spenser, Edmund, 317, 374, 440, 689; *The Faerie Queene*, 555
Sphinx, 426, 454, 671
Spinoza, Baruch, 553
Spurzheim, Johann Kaspar, 347
Stabler, Edward, 165, 457, 785
Stackpole, Joseph Lewis, 249
Staël, Anne-Louise-Germaine de, 140, 144, 173, 272, 319, 324, 346–47, 355,

435, 446, 473, 484, 498, 517, 686, 727; *Corinne*, 208, 299, 559

Standish, Miles, 106

Stanley, Edward George, 296

Staples, Samuel, 720

Stearns, Samuel H., 311

Stebbins, Artemas, 305

Sterling, John, 574–75, 728

Sterling, Mass., 90

Sterne, Laurence, 517; *Tristram Shandy*, 14

Stetson, Caleb, 420

Stevens, Mr., 84

Stevenson, Andrew, 654

Stevenson, Marmaduke, 557

Stewardson, Thomas, 270, 272

Stewart, Dugald, 117, 166–67

Stirling, Scotland, 281

Stoicism, 114, 139, 157, 385, 417, 449, 581, 693, 695

Stone, Reverend, 84

Stonehenge, 647

Strong, Allen, 88

Strong, Theodore, 88–89

Stuart, Louisa, 547

Sturgis, Caroline, 506, 608–9, 612, 681, 748, 793, 799–800

Sturgis, William, 193

Sullivan, Mr., 296

Sumatra, 429

Susa, Persia, 330

Swain, William W., 315

Swammerdam, Jan, 318

Swedenborg, Emanuel, 144, 197, 213, 341, 360–61, 366–67, 383, 393, 405, 466, 480, 586, 593, 612, 649–50, 659, 767–68, 783, 785, 803, 806

Swedenborgians, 189, 305, 318, 358, 383, 392–93, 479, 496, 614, 616, 762

Swift, Jonathan, 415, 466, 503; "The Battle of the Books," 8

Switzerland, 77, 105, 132, 210, 240, 270–73, 379, 511

Sybilline Oracles, 22

Symmes, John Cleves, 148

Synesius, 766

Syracuse, Italy, 228–35

Talma, François-Joseph, 278

Tamerlane, 475

Tantalus, 753

Taormina, Italy, 238

Tarbox, Mr., 457, 785

Tartars, 68, 300, 475

Tasso, Torquato, 158, 256, 762

Taunton, Mass., 342

Taylor, Edward, 382, 392–93, 432, 495, 505, 586, 742

Taylor, Henry, 432; "Philip van Artevelde," 399–400, 422, 451–52

Taylor, Isaac: *Fanaticism*, 352; *Saturday Evening*, 554

Taylor, Jeremy, 215, 449, 451, 456

Tell, William, 564

Tempe, vale of, 501, 797

Temperance movement, 549, 572, 678, 754

Temple, William, 8

Tennyson, Alfred, 466, 620, 789–90; "Confessions of a Sensitive Mind," 789; "The Dirge," 347; "Locksley Hall," 789; "The Lotos-Eaters," 584; "Ode to Memory," 789; "The Poet," 789; "Song" ("The Sea-Fairies"), 173; "Two Voices," 789; "Ulysses," 787

Terni, Italy, 343

Texas, 475

Thames River, 280

Thayer, Sylvanus, 277

Theanor, 798, 804–5

Thebes, 570, 671, 682, 778

Themistocles, 107, 114, 437

Thénard, Louis-Jacques, 274

Theocritus, 8

Theodosius, 66

Thermopylae, battle of, 133

Thomas à Kempis, 213, 428, 449, 462

Thompson, George, 433–34

Thoreau, Henry David, 576–77, 582, 592, 629, 661–62, 677, 703, 725, 780–81

Thorwaldsen, Bertel, 249, 623

Thucydides, 51, 619

Tiber River, 247, 255, 258

Ticknor, George, 17, 22–23, 164

Timoleon, 230, 263, 453, 630

Tintoretto (Jacopo Robusti), 268

Tischbein, Johann Heinrich, 511–12

Titian (Tiziano Vecelli), 241, 249, 252, 267–68, 374, 389, 391, 396, 473, 689

Tivoli, Italy, 258, 501, 620

Tolman, Albert or Elisha, 674
Tonga, 48–49
Toulouse, France, 511
Transcendental Club, 472–73, 481, 742
Transcendentalism, 144, 481, 594, 688, 699, 754, 765
Treaty of Utrecht, 329
Trieste, Italy, 226
Trinitarians, 29, 142, 390
Trismegistus, Hermes, 366, 766
Trosachs, 282
Troy, 236, 397
Tucker, Abraham (Edward Search), 1
Tucker, Ellen Louisa. See Emerson, Ellen Tucker
Tucker, Margaret, 170, 202–3
Tucker, Paulina, 170, 202
Tuckerman, Jane, 696
Turkey, 510, 652
Turks, 37, 227, 417, 688
Turner, Laban, 551
Turner, Mr., 366
Turner, Sharon: History of the Anglo-Saxons, 64–65
Tuscaloosa, Ala., 551
Tuscany, 237, 265
Tuscany, Grand Duke of, 262–64, 671
Tyrol, 513

Underhill, John, 106
Underwood, Joseph R., 569
Unitarians, 29, 84, 181, 212–13, 279, 312, 334, 373, 385, 389–90, 402, 449, 561, 590, 619
United States Military Academy, 568
Upham, Charles Wentworth, 19
Ursula (saint), 602
Utica, 602

Valhalla, 15
Valletta, Malta, 203–5, 227–28
Van Buren, Martin, 592, 642–43, 716, 750
Vandals, 37
Vane, Henry, 196, 459
Varus, Quintilius, 258
Vasari, Giorgio, 264, 716
Vatican, 248–56, 671, 679, 689
Vaudreuil, Philippe de Rigaud de, 329
Vedas, 458, 476, 587, 724, 755

Venice, Italy, 24, 207–8, 267–69
Venus, 807
Venus (statue), 207, 233, 248, 259–60, 263, 689
Vermont, 173, 184, 510, 643, 677
Veronese, Paolo (Paolo Caliari), 268, 391
Versailles, 773–74, 781
Very, Jones, 593, 650, 653–54, 656–57, 680, 684–85, 706, 794
Vespucci, Amerigo, 758
Vesuvius, Mount, 241, 245–47
Vienna, Austria, 9, 252, 570
Viguier, Paule de, 511
Vikings, 64–65
Villiers, George (Duke of Buckingham), 107
Villiers de L'Isle-Adam, Philippe de, 227
Virgil, 158, 242, 286; Aeneid, 493, 726; Eclogues, 10; Georgics, 15, 92
Virginia, 106, 146–47, 654, 790–91
Visconti, Giovanni Galeazzo, 46
Visconti, Giovanni Maria, 46
Vitruvius, Marcus, 355, 750
Voltaire (François-Marie Arouet), 64, 263–64, 272; Adelaide de Guesclin, 23–24
Vyasa (Krishna Dvaipayana), 366

Wachusett, Mount, 90
Walden Pond, 470, 498, 539, 555, 617, 628, 661–62, 726, 794
Wales, 683
Walker, James, 473
Wall, William Allen, 258, 264, 270
Walpole, Horace, 702–3
Waltham, Mass., 90, 179, 322, 360, 482, 506, 593, 627, 676, 702
War of 1812, 174
Warburton, William, 474
Ward, Anna Barker, 700–1, 753, 763
Ward, Nathaniel: The Simple Cobbler of Aggawam, 120
Ward, Samuel Gray, 623, 688, 713, 717, 733, 763, 785
Warden, David Bailie, 275
Ware, Henry, 321, 794
Ware, Mass., 85
Warren, Abigail, 696

Warren, Charles, 547
Warren, Cyrus, 593, 614
Warren, Deacon, 366
Warren, James Sullivan, 249
Warren, John C., 7
Warren, Mr., 405
Warton, Thomas: *History of English Poetry*, 417, 420
Washburn, Abdiel, 346–47
Washington, D.C., 771, 778
Washington, George, 99, 106, 126, 168, 174, 197, 219, 262–63, 272, 298, 315, 324, 339, 347, 355, 376, 452, 564, 667–68, 707, 766
Waterford, Me., 777
Waterland, Daniel, 389
Watertown, Mass., 322, 540
Watt, James, 101, 452
Watts, Isaac, 337
Webster, Daniel, 4–5, 53, 136, 162, 164, 176, 181, 296, 300, 315, 317, 325, 338, 340, 343, 365, 374, 377, 406–7, 420, 422, 433, 475, 481, 484, 489, 509, 519, 535, 557, 569, 586, 595, 675–76, 722, 749, 788
Weimar, Germany, 284, 515, 540
Weld, Thomas, 250
Wendell, Mass., 89
Wentworth, Mr., 576
West Brookfield, Mass., 85
West Point, military academy at, 568
Western, Mass., 85
Westminster Catechism, 432
Whateley, Mass., 89
Whig Party, 348, 352–53, 569, 750, 762
White, Gilbert, 315
White Mountains, 194–95, 691–92
Whitefield, George, 126–27, 393
Whitney, Reverend, 127
Wieland, Christoph Martin, 511–12
Wight, Mr., 460
Wilberforce, William, 339
Williamson, William D., 584; *History of the State of Maine*, 329–32
Wilson, John, 391
Wilson, John (Christopher North), 727; "On Reading Mr. Clarkson's History of the Abolition of the Slave Trade," 199
Wilson, Orin, 635

Wincklemann, Johann Joachim, 441
Windsor, England, 206
Winthrop, John, 106
Wisner, Benjamin B., 342
Witherspoon, John, 106
Withington, William, 622
Wittenberg, Germany, 357
Wolf, Mr., 272–73
Wolcott, John (Peter Pindar): *Lyric Odes to the Royal Academicians*, 396
Wollaston, William, 101
Wolsey, Mr., 716
Women, 206, 296, 299, 322, 327, 363, 470, 559, 624–25, 681, 725, 759, 802
Wood, Daniel, 607
Wood, Nathaniel, 90
Woodbury, Levi, 750
Worcester, I. F., 547
Worcester, Mass., 83, 90
Wordsworth, William, 136–38, 144, 158, 176, 210, 263, 283–87, 336, 339, 341, 347, 355, 371, 383, 391, 402, 404, 416, 420, 438–39, 458, 506, 521, 535, 545, 577, 584, 599, 602, 727, 795; "Dion," 530; *The Excursion*, 138, 215, 218, 286, 308, 326, 457, 743; "Fidelity," 529; "The Force of Prayer," 530; "The Happy Warrior," 182–83, 530; "Laodamia," 530, 787; "Lines composed a few miles above Tintern Abbey," 203, 286, 529; "Lines on the Death of Fox," 530; "The Oak and the Broom," 487; "Ode: Intimations of Immortality," 501, 530; "Ode to Duty," 203, 530; "Ode to Lycoris," 395, 530; "The Old Cumberland Beggar," 529–30, 785; "Peter Bell," 330; "Poems dedicated to National Independence and Liberty," 347; "September 1802," 530; sonnets, 176, 285–86, 381; "To a Skylark," 286; *The White Doe of Rylstone*, 621; *Yarrow Revisited*, 530
Worms, Germany, 201
Worsley, Thomas, 263
Wotton, Henry, 163, 215, 394
Wotton, William, 8
Wren, Christopher, 452, 493

Wright, Silas, 300
Wulfstan, 65

Xenophanes, 445
Xenophon, 51; *Anabasis*, 490–91, 511
Xerxes, 376, 736

Yale College, 749, 778
York, Me., 522

Young, Edward, 545; *Night Thoughts*, 101, 137, 177, 780
Yverdon, Switzerland, 557

Zeno, 355, 613, 797
Zenobius (saint), 266
Zoroaster, 476, 533, 586, 613, 648, 667, 782

THE LIBRARY OF AMERICA SERIES

The Library of America fosters appreciation and pride in America's literary heritage by publishing, and keeping permanently in print, authoritative editions of America's best and most significant writing. An independent nonprofit organization, it was founded in 1979 with seed money from the National Endowment for the Humanities and the Ford Foundation.

1. Herman Melville, *Typee, Omoo, Mardi* (1982)
2. Nathaniel Hawthorne, *Tales and Sketches* (1982)
3. Walt Whitman, *Poetry and Prose* (1982)
4. Harriet Beecher Stowe, *Three Novels* (1982)
5. Mark Twain, *Mississippi Writings* (1982)
6. Jack London, *Novels and Stories* (1982)
7. Jack London, *Novels and Social Writings* (1982)
8. William Dean Howells, *Novels 1875–1886* (1982)
9. Herman Melville, *Redburn, White-Jacket, Moby-Dick* (1983)
10. Nathaniel Hawthorne, *Collected Novels* (1983)
11. Francis Parkman, *France and England in North America*, vol. I (1983)
12. Francis Parkman, *France and England in North America*, vol. II (1983)
13. Henry James, *Novels 1871–1880* (1983)
14. Henry Adams, *Novels, Mont Saint Michel, The Education* (1983)
15. Ralph Waldo Emerson, *Essays and Lectures* (1983)
16. Washington Irving, *History, Tales and Sketches* (1983)
17. Thomas Jefferson, *Writings* (1984)
18. Stephen Crane, *Prose and Poetry* (1984)
19. Edgar Allan Poe, *Poetry and Tales* (1984)
20. Edgar Allan Poe, *Essays and Reviews* (1984)
21. Mark Twain, *The Innocents Abroad, Roughing It* (1984)
22. Henry James, *Literary Criticism: Essays, American & English Writers* (1984)
23. Henry James, *Literary Criticism: European Writers & The Prefaces* (1984)
24. Herman Melville, *Pierre, Israel Potter, The Confidence-Man, Tales & Billy Budd* (1985)
25. William Faulkner, *Novels 1930–1935* (1985)
26. James Fenimore Cooper, *The Leatherstocking Tales*, vol. I (1985)
27. James Fenimore Cooper, *The Leatherstocking Tales*, vol. II (1985)
28. Henry David Thoreau, *A Week, Walden, The Maine Woods, Cape Cod* (1985)
29. Henry James, *Novels 1881–1886* (1985)
30. Edith Wharton, *Novels* (1986)
31. Henry Adams, *History of the U.S. during the Administrations of Jefferson* (1986)
32. Henry Adams, *History of the U.S. during the Administrations of Madison* (1986)
33. Frank Norris, *Novels and Essays* (1986)
34. W.E.B. Du Bois, *Writings* (1986)
35. Willa Cather, *Early Novels and Stories* (1987)
36. Theodore Dreiser, *Sister Carrie, Jennie Gerhardt, Twelve Men* (1987)
37A. Benjamin Franklin, *Silence Dogood, The Busy-Body, & Early Writings* (1987)
37B. Benjamin Franklin, *Autobiography, Poor Richard, & Later Writings* (1987)
38. William James, *Writings 1902–1910* (1987)
39. Flannery O'Connor, *Collected Works* (1988)
40. Eugene O'Neill, *Complete Plays 1913–1920* (1988)
41. Eugene O'Neill, *Complete Plays 1920–1931* (1988)
42. Eugene O'Neill, *Complete Plays 1932–1943* (1988)
43. Henry James, *Novels 1886–1890* (1989)
44. William Dean Howells, *Novels 1886–1888* (1989)
45. Abraham Lincoln, *Speeches and Writings 1832–1858* (1989)
46. Abraham Lincoln, *Speeches and Writings 1859–1865* (1989)
47. Edith Wharton, *Novellas and Other Writings* (1990)
48. William Faulkner, *Novels 1936–1940* (1990)
49. Willa Cather, *Later Novels* (1990)

50. Ulysses S. Grant, *Memoirs and Selected Letters* (1990)
51. William Tecumseh Sherman, *Memoirs* (1990)
52. Washington Irving, *Bracebridge Hall, Tales of a Traveller, The Alhambra* (1991)
53. Francis Parkman, *The Oregon Trail, The Conspiracy of Pontiac* (1991)
54. James Fenimore Cooper, *Sea Tales: The Pilot, The Red Rover* (1991)
55. Richard Wright, *Early Works* (1991)
56. Richard Wright, *Later Works* (1991)
57. Willa Cather, *Stories, Poems, and Other Writings* (1992)
58. William James, *Writings 1878–1899* (1992)
59. Sinclair Lewis, *Main Street & Babbitt* (1992)
60. Mark Twain, *Collected Tales, Sketches, Speeches, & Essays 1852–1890* (1992)
61. Mark Twain, *Collected Tales, Sketches, Speeches, & Essays 1891–1910* (1992)
62. *The Debate on the Constitution: Part One* (1993)
63. *The Debate on the Constitution: Part Two* (1993)
64. Henry James, *Collected Travel Writings: Great Britain & America* (1993)
65. Henry James, *Collected Travel Writings: The Continent* (1993)
66. *American Poetry: The Nineteenth Century,* Vol. 1 (1993)
67. *American Poetry: The Nineteenth Century,* Vol. 2 (1993)
68. Frederick Douglass, *Autobiographies* (1994)
69. Sarah Orne Jewett, *Novels and Stories* (1994)
70. Ralph Waldo Emerson, *Collected Poems and Translations* (1994)
71. Mark Twain, *Historical Romances* (1994)
72. John Steinbeck, *Novels and Stories 1932–1937* (1994)
73. William Faulkner, *Novels 1942–1954* (1994)
74. Zora Neale Hurston, *Novels and Stories* (1995)
75. Zora Neale Hurston, *Folklore, Memoirs, and Other Writings* (1995)
76. Thomas Paine, *Collected Writings* (1995)
77. *Reporting World War II: American Journalism 1938–1944* (1995)
78. *Reporting World War II: American Journalism 1944–1946* (1995)
79. Raymond Chandler, *Stories and Early Novels* (1995)
80. Raymond Chandler, *Later Novels and Other Writings* (1995)
81. Robert Frost, *Collected Poems, Prose, & Plays* (1995)
82. Henry James, *Complete Stories 1892–1898* (1996)
83. Henry James, *Complete Stories 1898–1910* (1996)
84. William Bartram, *Travels and Other Writings* (1996)
85. John Dos Passos, *U.S.A.* (1996)
86. John Steinbeck, *The Grapes of Wrath and Other Writings 1936–1941* (1996)
87. Vladimir Nabokov, *Novels and Memoirs 1941–1951* (1996)
88. Vladimir Nabokov, *Novels 1955–1962* (1996)
89. Vladimir Nabokov, *Novels 1969–1974* (1996)
90. James Thurber, *Writings and Drawings* (1996)
91. George Washington, *Writings* (1997)
92. John Muir, *Nature Writings* (1997)
93. Nathanael West, *Novels and Other Writings* (1997)
94. *Crime Novels: American Noir of the 1930s and 40s* (1997)
95. *Crime Novels: American Noir of the 1950s* (1997)
96. Wallace Stevens, *Collected Poetry and Prose* (1997)
97. James Baldwin, *Early Novels and Stories* (1998)
98. James Baldwin, *Collected Essays* (1998)
99. Gertrude Stein, *Writings 1903–1932* (1998)
100. Gertrude Stein, *Writings 1932–1946* (1998)
101. Eudora Welty, *Complete Novels* (1998)
102. Eudora Welty, *Stories, Essays, & Memoir* (1998)
103. Charles Brockden Brown, *Three Gothic Novels* (1998)
104. *Reporting Vietnam: American Journalism 1959–1969* (1998)
105. *Reporting Vietnam: American Journalism 1969–1975* (1998)
106. Henry James, *Complete Stories 1874–1884* (1999)

107. Henry James, *Complete Stories 1884–1891* (1999)
108. *American Sermons: The Pilgrims to Martin Luther King Jr.* (1999)
109. James Madison, *Writings* (1999)
110. Dashiell Hammett, *Complete Novels* (1999)
111. Henry James, *Complete Stories 1864–1874* (1999)
112. William Faulkner, *Novels 1957–1962* (1999)
113. John James Audubon, *Writings & Drawings* (1999)
114. *Slave Narratives* (2000)
115. *American Poetry: The Twentieth Century,* Vol. 1 (2000)
116. *American Poetry: The Twentieth Century,* Vol. 2 (2000)
117. F. Scott Fitzgerald, *Novels and Stories 1920–1922* (2000)
118. Henry Wadsworth Longfellow, *Poems and Other Writings* (2000)
119. Tennessee Williams, *Plays 1937–1955* (2000)
120. Tennessee Williams, *Plays 1957–1980* (2000)
121. Edith Wharton, *Collected Stories 1891–1910* (2001)
122. Edith Wharton, *Collected Stories 1911–1937* (2001)
123. *The American Revolution: Writings from the War of Independence* (2001)
124. Henry David Thoreau, *Collected Essays and Poems* (2001)
125. Dashiell Hammett, *Crime Stories and Other Writings* (2001)
126. Dawn Powell, *Novels 1930–1942* (2001)
127. Dawn Powell, *Novels 1944–1962* (2001)
128. Carson McCullers, *Complete Novels* (2001)
129. Alexander Hamilton, *Writings* (2001)
130. Mark Twain, *The Gilded Age and Later Novels* (2002)
131. Charles W. Chesnutt, *Stories, Novels, and Essays* (2002)
132. John Steinbeck, *Novels 1942–1952* (2002)
133. Sinclair Lewis, *Arrowsmith, Elmer Gantry, Dodsworth* (2002)
134. Paul Bowles, *The Sheltering Sky, Let It Come Down, The Spider's House* (2002)
135. Paul Bowles, *Collected Stories & Later Writings* (2002)
136. Kate Chopin, *Complete Novels & Stories* (2002)
137. *Reporting Civil Rights: American Journalism 1941–1963* (2003)
138. *Reporting Civil Rights: American Journalism 1963–1973* (2003)
139. Henry James, *Novels 1896–1899* (2003)
140. Theodore Dreiser, *An American Tragedy* (2003)
141. Saul Bellow, *Novels 1944–1953* (2003)
142. John Dos Passos, *Novels 1920–1925* (2003)
143. John Dos Passos, *Travel Books and Other Writings* (2003)
144. Ezra Pound, *Poems and Translations* (2003)
145. James Weldon Johnson, *Writings* (2004)
146. Washington Irving, *Three Western Narratives* (2004)
147. Alexis de Tocqueville, *Democracy in America* (2004)
148. James T. Farrell, *Studs Lonigan: A Trilogy* (2004)
149. Isaac Bashevis Singer, *Collected Stories I* (2004)
150. Isaac Bashevis Singer, *Collected Stories II* (2004)
151. Isaac Bashevis Singer, *Collected Stories III* (2004)
152. Kaufman & Co., *Broadway Comedies* (2004)
153. Theodore Roosevelt, *The Rough Riders, An Autobiography* (2004)
154. Theodore Roosevelt, *Letters and Speeches* (2004)
155. H. P. Lovecraft, *Tales* (2005)
156. Louisa May Alcott, *Little Women, Little Men, Jo's Boys* (2005)
157. Philip Roth, *Novels & Stories 1959–1962* (2005)
158. Philip Roth, *Novels 1967–1972* (2005)
159. James Agee, *Let Us Now Praise Famous Men, A Death in the Family* (2005)
160. James Agee, *Film Writing & Selected Journalism* (2005)
161. Richard Henry Dana, Jr., *Two Years Before the Mast & Other Voyages* (2005)
162. Henry James, *Novels 1901–1902* (2006)
163. Arthur Miller, *Collected Plays 1944–1961* (2006)

164. William Faulkner, *Novels 1926–1929* (2006)
165. Philip Roth, *Novels 1973–1977* (2006)
166. *American Speeches: Part One* (2006)
167. *American Speeches: Part Two* (2006)
168. Hart Crane, *Complete Poems & Selected Letters* (2006)
169. Saul Bellow, *Novels 1956–1964* (2007)
170. John Steinbeck, *Travels with Charley and Later Novels* (2007)
171. Capt. John Smith, *Writings with Other Narratives* (2007)
172. Thornton Wilder, *Collected Plays & Writings on Theater* (2007)
173. Philip K. Dick, *Four Novels of the 1960s* (2007)
174. Jack Kerouac, *Road Novels 1957–1960* (2007)
175. Philip Roth, *Zuckerman Bound* (2007)
176. Edmund Wilson, *Literary Essays & Reviews of the 1920s & 30s* (2007)
177. Edmund Wilson, *Literary Essays & Reviews of the 1930s & 40s* (2007)
178. *American Poetry: The 17th & 18th Centuries* (2007)
179. William Maxwell, *Early Novels & Stories* (2008)
180. Elizabeth Bishop, *Poems, Prose, & Letters* (2008)
181. A. J. Liebling, *World War II Writings* (2008)
182s. *American Earth: Environmental Writing Since Thoreau* (2008)
183. Philip K. Dick, *Five Novels of the 1960s & 70s* (2008)
184. William Maxwell, *Later Novels & Stories* (2008)
185. Philip Roth, *Novels & Other Narratives 1986–1991* (2008)
186. Katherine Anne Porter, *Collected Stories & Other Writings* (2008)
187. John Ashbery, *Collected Poems 1956–1987* (2008)
188. John Cheever, *Collected Stories & Other Writings* (2009)
189. John Cheever, *Complete Novels* (2009)
190. Lafcadio Hearn, *American Writings* (2009)
191. A. J. Liebling, *The Sweet Science & Other Writngs* (2009)
192s. *The Lincoln Anthology: Great Writers on His Life and Legacy from 1860 to Now* (2009)
193. Philip K. Dick, *VALIS & Later Novels* (2009)
194. Thornton Wilder, *The Bridge of San Luis Rey and Other Novels 1926–1948* (2009)
195. Raymond Carver, *Collected Stories* (2009)
196. *American Fantastic Tales: Terror and the Uncanny from Poe to the Pulps* (2009)
197. *American Fantastic Tales: Terror and the Uncanny from the 1940s to Now* (2009)
198. John Marshall, *Writings* (2010)
199s. *The Mark Twain Anthology: Great Writers on His Life and Works* (2010)
200. Mark Twain, *A Tramp Abroad, Following the Equator, Other Travels* (2010)
201. Ralph Waldo Emerson, *Selected Journals 1820–1842* (2010)
202. Ralph Waldo Emerson, *Selected Journals 1841–1877* (2010)
203. *The American Stage: Writing on Theater from Washington Irving to Tony Kushner* (2010)

To subscribe to the series or to order individual copies,
please visit www.loa.org or call (800) 964.5778.